Comparative Politics

06/07

Twenty-fourth Edition

EDITOR

Christian Søe

California State University, Long Beach

Christian Søe was born in Denmark, studied at the University of British Columbia and the University of Michigan, and received his doctoral degree in political science at the Free University in Berlin. He is professor in political science at California State University in Long Beach, where he teaches courses in comparative politics. His research deals primarily with political developments in contemporary Germany. He visits that country annually to conduct research on parties and elections, as part of an effort to follow continuities and shifts in its politics. His publications include a book he co-edited with Mary N. Hampton, *Between Bonn and Berlin: German Politics Adrift?*, that examines the last years of Helmut Kohl's center-right government and its replacement by a center-left coalition headed by Gerhard Schröder and Joschka Fischer. The milestone election of 1998 is the subject of another book that he co-edited with David Conradt and Gerald R. Kleinfeld, *Power Shift in Germany*. The same team co-edited a recent volume on the 2002 German Bundestag election and its aftermath, *Precarious Victory*. Three other publications include a biographical essay on Hans-Dietrich Genscher, Germany's foreign minister from 1974 to 1992, in *Political Leaders of Contemporary Western Europe*, a chapter on the Free Democratic Party in *Germany's New Politics*, and another chapter on the Danish-German relationship in *The Germans and Their Neighbors*. Dr. Søe is also co-editor of the latter two books. He has been editor of *Annual Editions: Comparative Politics* since the beginning of this series in 1983.

Contemporary Learning Series

2460 Kerper Blvd., Dubuque, IA 52001

Visit us on the Internet
http://www.mhcls.com

Credits

1. **Pluralist Democracies: Country Studies**
   Unit photo—© Corbis/Royalty-Free
2. **Pluralist Democracies: Factors in the Political Process**
   Unit photo—© The McGraw-Hill Companies, Inc./Christopher Kerrigan, photographer
3. **Europe in Transition: West, Center, and East**
   Unit photo—Photograph by Cpl Matthew Roberson, USMC courtesy of USAID
4. **Political Diversity in the Developing World**
   Unit photo—White House photo by Carolyn Drake
5. **Comparative Politics: Some Major Trends, Issues, and Prospects**
   Unit photo—Photograph courtesy of the Audiovisual Library of the European Commission

Copyright

Cataloging in Publication Data
Main entry under title: Annual Editions: Comparative Politics. 2006/2007.
1. Comparative Politics—Periodicals. I. Søe, Christian, *comp*. II. Title: Comparative Politics.
ISBN-13: 978–0–07–351602–8   ISBN-10: 0–07–351602–3   658'.05   ISSN 0741–7233

Twenty-Fourth Edition

Cover image © David C. Johnson/Corbis/Royalty Free
Printed in the United States of America   1234567890QPDQPD9876   Printed on Recycled Paper

Editors/Advisory Board

Members of the Advisory Board are instrumental in the final selection of articles for each edition of ANNUAL EDITIONS. Their review of articles for content, level, currentness, and appropriateness provides critical direction to the editor and staff. We think that you will find their careful consideration well reflected in this volume.

Preface

This collection of readings brings together current articles that will help you understand the politics of foreign countries from a comparative perspective. Such a study opens up a fascinating world beyond our borders. It will also lead to deeper insights into the American political process.

The articles in unit 1 cover Britain or the United Kingdom, France, Germany, Italy, and Japan in a serial manner. In terms of gross domestic product, these countries all belong with the United States among the top six market economies in the world. Each of these modern societies has an individual tradition of politics and governance within a particular institutional framework. Nevertheless, as the readings of unit 2 show, it is possible to point to some comparable patterns of political challenge and response among these and some other representative democracies.

Unit 3 deals with the impact of two major changes that continue to transform the political map of Europe. One of them is the irregular, sometimes halting, but nevertheless impressive growth of the European Union (EU). It began with six member states in 1957, grew incrementally to fifteen, and then in 2004 added ten new countries for a total membership of 25. The other and closely related major change involves the political and economic reconstruction of Central and Eastern Europe, including Russia, after the collapse of the Communist regimes in that region between 1989 and 1991. These developments underscore the continuing political importance of Europe.

Unit 4 looks first at the challenge of globalization and then turns to articles dealing with some of the developing countries and regions, including Mexico and Latin America as a whole, South Africa, Nigeria, India, China, and the Muslim world. The articles will give the careful reader a better understanding of the diversity of social and political conditions in these countries.

Unit 5 considers three major trends in contemporary politics from a comparative perspective. First, the past quarter of a century has seen a remarkable spread of democratic forms of government in the world. This recent "wave of democratization," sometimes described as the "third" of its kind in modern history, seems likely to have a lasting effect on the political process in some countries that previously knew only authoritarian governments. But some recent reversals remind us there is no simple way to construct a stable democracy anywhere—least of all in countries that are divided by deep ethnic, economic, religious and other cleavages.

Second, beginning in the 1980s there has been a major shift in economic policy toward greater reliance on private enterprise and markets, and a corresponding reduction in state ownership and regulation in much of the world, including Communist-ruled China. But there has been a reaction in the advanced industrial societies and in many developing countries against the inequalities, dislocations, and uncertainties associated with the unfettered market economy.

Third, many parts of the world have seen a surge of what has been called "identity politics." This trend has brought group identities more strongly into play when differences are being defined, played out, and resolved in the political arena.

This is an unusually interesting and important time to study comparative politics. The past fifteen years have seen a major restructuring of politics in many countries along with a generational shift in leadership. Even in a time of political transformation, however, there will be significant patterns of continuity as well as change.

This is the twenty-fourth edition of *Annual Editions: Comparative Politics*. Over the years, the successive editions have reflected the developments that eventually brought about the post–cold war world of today. This present volume tries to present information and analyses that are useful in the quest to understand today's political world and the parameters it sets for tomorrow's developments.

A special word of thanks goes to my own past and present students at California State University, Long Beach. They are wonderfully inquisitive and help keep me posted on matters that this anthology must address. Several of my past students have helped me gather material. As always, I am particularly grateful to Susan B. Mason, who received her master's degree in political science over a decade ago. She continues to volunteer as a superb research assistant. Once again I also wish to thank some other past and present students at Cal State, Linda Wohlman, Erika Reinhardt, Erik Ibsen, Jon Nakagawa, Perry Oliver, Mike Petri, Richard Sherman, and Ali Taghavi. Like so many others, these individuals first encountered the anthology in comparative politics courses. It is a great joy to have worked with such fine students. Their enthusiasm for the project has been contagious.

I am very grateful also to members of the advisory board and McGraw-Hill Contemporary Learning Series as well as to the many readers who have made useful comments on past selections and suggested new ones. I ask you all to help improve future editions by keeping me informed of your reactions and suggestions for change.

Please complete and return the article rating form in the back of the book.

Christian Søe

Editor

Contents

UNIT 1
Pluralist Democracies: Country Studies

The concepts in bold italics are developed in the article. For further expansion, please refer to the Topic Guide and the Index.

The concepts in bold italics are developed in the article. For further expansion, please refer to the Topic Guide and the Index.

UNIT 2
Pluralist Democracies: Factors in the Political Process

The concepts in bold italics are developed in the article. For further expansion, please refer to the Topic Guide and the Index.

UNIT 3
Europe in Transition: West, Center, and East

The concepts in bold italics are developed in the article. For further expansion, please refer to the Topic Guide and the Index.

UNIT 4
Political Diversity in the Developing World

The concepts in bold italics are developed in the article. For further expansion, please refer to the Topic Guide and the Index.

The concepts in bold italics are developed in the article. For further expansion, please refer to the Topic Guide and the Index.

UNIT 5
Comparative Politics: Some Major Trends, Issues, and Prospects

The concepts in bold italics are developed in the article. For further expansion, please refer to the Topic Guide and the Index.

The concepts in bold italics are developed in the article. For further expansion, please refer to the Topic Guide and the Index.

Topic Guide

This topic guide suggests how the selections in this book relate to the subjects covered in your course. You may want to use the topics listed on these pages to search the Web more easily.

On the following pages a number of Web sites have been gathered specifically for this book. They are arranged to reflect the units of this *Annual Edition*. You can link to these sites by going to the student online support site at *http://www.mhcls.com/online/*.

ALL THE ARTICLES THAT RELATE TO EACH TOPIC ARE LISTED BELOW THE BOLD-FACED TERM.

Internet References

The following internet sites have been carefully researched and selected to support the articles found in this reader. The easiest way to access these selected sites is to go to our student online support site at *http://www.mhcls.com/online/*.

AE: Comparative Politics 06/07

The following sites were available at the time of publication. Visit our Web site—we update our student online support site regularly to reflect any changes.

General Sources

Central Intelligence Agency
http://www.odci.gov
Use this official home page to get connections to *The CIA Factbook,* which provides extensive statistical and political information about every country in the world.

National Geographic Society
http://www.nationalgeographic.com
This site provides links to National Geographic's archive of maps, articles, and documents. There is a great deal of material related to political cultures around the world.

U.S. Agency for International Development
http://www.info.usaid.gov
This Web site covers such broad and overlapping issues as democracy, population and health, economic growth, and development about different regions and countries.

U.S. Information Agency
http://usinfo.state.gov/
This USIA page provides definitions, related documentation, and discussion of topics on global issues. Many Web links are provided.

World Bank
http://www.worldbank.org
News (press releases, summaries of new projects, speeches) and coverage of numerous topics regarding development, countries, and regions are provided at this site.

World Wide Web Virtual Library: International Affairs Resources
http://www.etown.edu/vl/
Surf this site and its extensive links to learn about specific countries and regions, to research international organizations, and to study such vital topics as international law, development, the international economy, and human rights.

UNIT 1: Pluralist Democracies: Country Studies

France.com
http://www.france.com
The links at this site will lead to extensive information about the French government, politics, history, and culture.

GermNews
http://www.germnews.de/dn/about/
Search this site for German political and economic news covering the years 1995 to the present.

Japan Ministry of Foreign Affairs
http://www.mofa.go.jp
Visit this official site for Japanese foreign policy statements and discussions of regional and global relations.

UNIT 2: Pluralist Democracies: Factors in the Political Process

Carnegie Endowment for International Peace
http://www.ceip.org
This organization's goal is to stimulate discussion and learning among both experts and the public at large on a wide range of international issues. The site provides links to the well-respected journal *Foreign Policy,* to the Moscow Center, to descriptions of various programs, and much more.

Inter-American Dialogue (IAD)
http://www.iadialog.org
This is the Web site for IAD, a premier U.S. center for policy analysis, communication, and exchange in Western Hemisphere affairs. The 100-member organization has helped to shape the agenda of issues and choices in hemispheric relations.

The North American Institute (NAMI)
http://www.northamericaninstitute.org
NAMI, a trinational public-affairs organization concerned with the emerging "regional space" of Canada, the United States, and Mexico, provides links for study of trade, the environment, and institutional developments.

UNIT 3: Europe in Transition: West, Center, and East

Europa: European Union
http://europa.eu.int
This server site of the European Union will lead you to the history of the EU; descriptions of EU policies, institutions, and goals; discussion of monetary union; and documentation of treaties and other materials.

NATO Integrated Data Service (NIDS)
http://www.nato.int/structur/nids/nids.htm
NIDS was created to bring information on security-related matters to the widest possible audience. Check out this Web site to review North Atlantic Treaty Organization documentation of all kinds, to read *NATO Review,* and to explore key issues in the field of European security.

Research and Reference (Library of Congress)
http://lcweb.loc.gov/rr/
This massive research and reference site of the Library of Congress will lead you to invaluable information on the former Soviet Union and other countries attempting the transition to democracy. It provides links to numerous publications, bibliographies, and guides in area studies.

Russian and East European Network Information Center, University of Texas at Austin
http://reenic.utexas.edu/reenic/index.html
This is *the* Web site for information on Russia and the former Soviet Union.

www.mhcls.com/online/

UNIT 4: Political Diversity in the Developing World

Africa News Online
http://allafrica.com/

Open this site for extensive, up-to-date information on all of Africa, with reports from Africa's leading newspapers, magazines, and news agencies. Coverage is country-by-country and regional. Background documents and Internet links are among the resource pages.

ArabNet
http://www.arab.net

This home page of ArabNet, the online resource for the Arab world in the Middle East and North Africa, presents links to 22 Arab countries. Each country Web page classifies information using a standardized system of categories.

Inside China Today
http://www.einnews.com/china/

Part of the European Internet Network, this site leads to information on China, including recent news, government, and related sites pertaining to mainland China, Hong Kong, Macao, and Taiwan.

Organization for Economic Cooperation and Development
http://www.oecd.org/home/

Explore development, governance, and world trade and investment issues on this OECD site. It provides links to many related topics and addresses global economic issues on a country-by-country basis.

Sun SITE Singapore
http://sunsite.nus.edu.sg/noframe.html

These South East Asia Information pages provide information and point to other online resources about the region's 10 countries, including Vietnam, Indonesia, and Brunei.

UNIT 5: Comparative Politics: Some Major Trends, Issues, and Prospects

Commission on Global Governance
http://www.sovereignty.net/p/gov/gganalysis.htm

This site provides access to *The Report of the Commission on Global Governance,* produced by an international group of leaders who want to find ways in which the global community can better manage its affairs.

IISDnet
http://www.iisd.org/default.asp

This site of the International Institute for Sustainable Development, a Canadian organization, presents information through links on business and sustainable development, developing ideas, and Hot Topics. Linkages is its multimedia resource for environment and development policy makers.

ISN International Relations and Security Network
http://www.isn.ethz.ch

This site, maintained by the Center for Security Studies and Conflict Research, is a clearinghouse for extensive information on international relations and security policy. Topics are listed by category (Traditional Dimensions of Security, New Dimensions of Security) and by major world regions.

United Nations Environment Program
http://www.unep.ch/

Consult this home page of UNEP for links to critical topics about global issues, including decertification and the impact of trade on the environment. The site leads to useful databases and global resource information.

We highly recommend that you review our Web site for expanded information and our other product lines. We are continually updating and adding links to our Web site in order to offer you the most usable and useful information that will support and expand the value of your Annual Editions. You can reach us at: *http://www.mhcls.com/annualeditions/.*

World Map

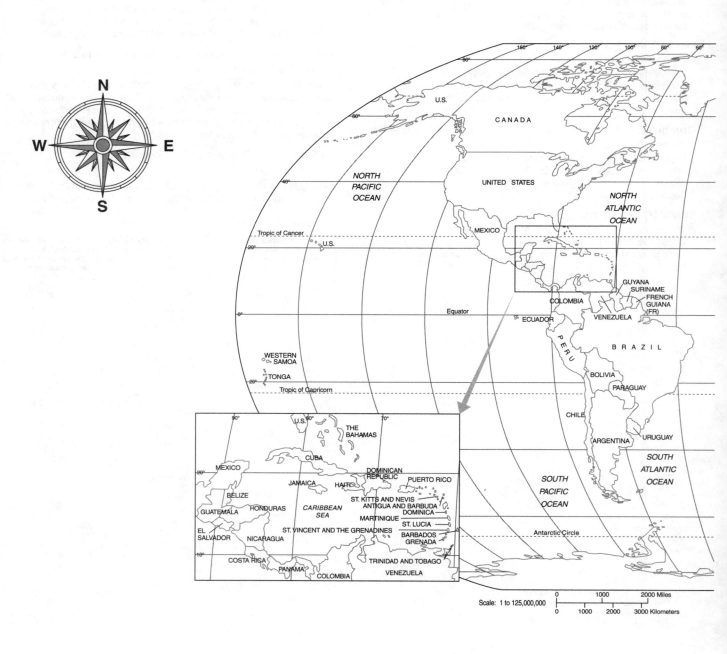

N
W   E
S

CANADA

U.S.

NORTH
PACIFIC
OCEAN

UNITED STATES

NORTH
ATLANTIC
OCEAN

MEXICO

Tropic of Cancer

U.S.

COLOMBIA

GUYANA
SURINAME
FRENCH
GUIANA
(FR)

Equator

ECUADOR

VENEZUELA

PERU

B R A Z I L

WESTERN
SAMOA

BOLIVIA

TONGA

PARAGUAY

Tropic of Capricorn

CHILE

ARGENTINA

URUGUAY

SOUTH
ATLANTIC
OCEAN

SOUTH
PACIFIC
OCEAN

Antarctic Circle

Inset map:

U.S.

THE
BAHAMAS

CUBA

MEXICO

DOMINICAN
REPUBLIC

JAMAICA

HAITI

PUERTO RICO

BELIZE

ST. KITTS AND NEVIS
ANTIGUA AND BARBUDA
DOMINICA

GUATEMALA

HONDURAS

CARIBBEAN
SEA

MARTINIQUE

ST. LUCIA

EL
SALVADOR

NICARAGUA

ST. VINCENT AND THE GRENADINES

BARBADOS
GRENADA

COSTA RICA

PANAMA

COLOMBIA

TRINIDAD AND TOBAGO

VENEZUELA

Scale: 1 to 125,000,000

0   1000   2000 Miles

0   1000   2000   3000 Kilometers

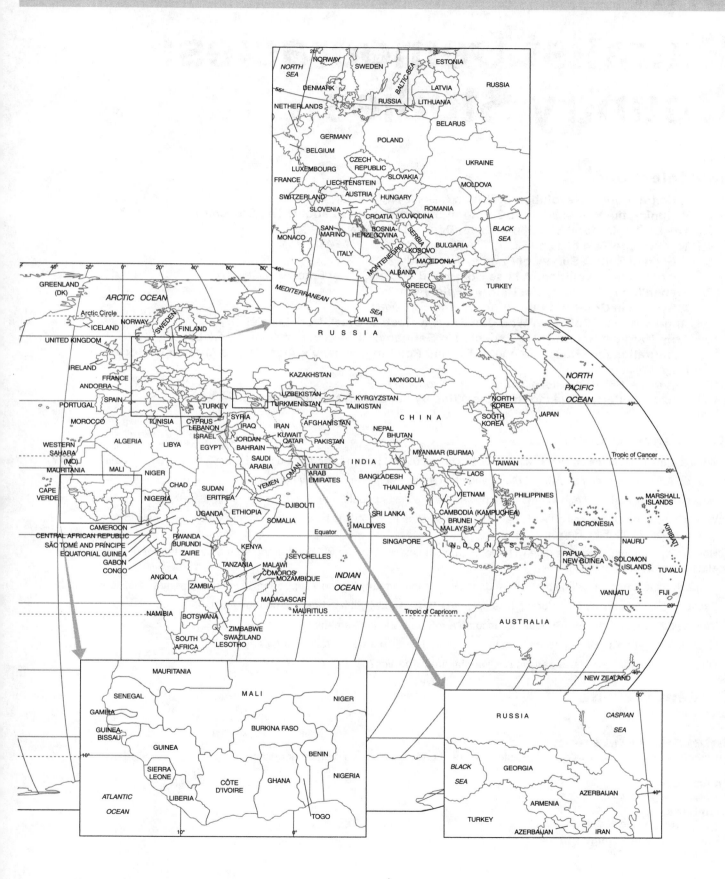

UNIT 1

Pluralist Democracies: Country Studies

Unit Selections

Key Points to Consider

- What are the main items on Prime Minister Blair's constitutional reform agenda, and how far have they become reality by now?

- How do Anthony Giddens and David Marquand differ in their perception of New Labour?

- How does Tony Blair manage to hold on to power despite his unpopular Iraq policy?

- Why did Jacques Chirac call an early parliamentary election in 1997, and how did the outcome produce a new form of "cohabitation" in the Fifth Republic?

- How did the formula, "first time vote with the heart, next time with the head," boomerang for the Left in the French presidential elections of 2002?

- Name three factors that helped the SPD and the Greens in Germany find new supporters in the parliamentary elections of 2002.

- Explain what is meant by the reform packet, *Agenda 2010*, and why it has been so controversial.

- Why has the federal council (Bundesrat) become a reform issue in Germany?

- Explain why Japan's LDP is jokingly said to be "neither liberal, nor democratic, nor a party."

- What has been the role of this party in postwar Japanese politics?

Student Website

www.mhcls.com/online

Internet References

Further information regarding these websites may be found in this book's preface or online.

France.com
http://www.france.com

GermNews
http://www.germnews.de/dn/about/

Japan Ministry of Foreign Affairs
http://www.mofa.go.jp

Britain, France, Germany, and Italy are the most prominent industrial societies in Western Europe. Their modern political histories vary considerably, but all have developed from oligarchic forms of rule into pluralist democracies with representative forms of government. None of them is without democratic shortcomings, but each includes a democratic infrastructure and a robust civil society, with regular elections, active citizens, competing political parties, assertive interest groups, and a free press. It is a well-established tradition that the "rule of law" must prevail, with government officials and civil servants alike bound by legal rules in their public acts.

Japan has developed its own, less overt forms of pluralist expression and competition. It too is a representative democracy and occupies a similar position of political prominence in Eastern Asia.

Each of these countries has developed a distinctive set of political institutions, defined its own public agenda, and found a dynamic balance of political continuity and change. Their peculiarities are an open invitation to individual narrative and country specialization. But a comparativist will look for patterns of similarity as well as difference among political systems—and seek to explain both.

The five countries all belong in the relatively small category of **"older democracies."** This is how political scientist Robert A.Dahl refers to the 22 countries—15 of them located in Western Europe—that have continuously maintained democratic forms of governance since at least 1950. Had Dahl set his starting point just a few years earlier, let us say 1942, the list of "older democracies" would have been much shorter. It is sobering to remember that in our group of five countries, only Britain did not interrupt its democratic development at some point in the twentieth century. Three of them (Italy, Japan, and Germany) abandoned the democratic road in the period between the two world wars, and France did the same after its defeat and partial military occupation by Germany in 1940. After World War II, these four all started out with new democratic constitutions, whereas Britain continued to function—as it had for centuries—within an evolving framework of basic laws, rules, and conventions often referred to as its "unwritten" or uncodified constitution.

The four West European countries in our group show the impact of some major developments that are changing the political, social, and economic map of their continent. This was the birthplace of **the modern nation state,** and it is now the location where that basic political construct is undergoing a partial and ambiguous transformation. In principle and practice, all of the member nations of the **European Union (EU)** have agreed to an unprecedented dilution of their traditional sovereignty. For these countries, the fulcrum of much policy-making has been shifting away from the national arena to the EU, particularly in economic matters. As a result, some familiar aspects of their political identity, like national borders or distinctive national currencies, have been reduced in importance or entirely replaced.

None of this signals the end of the modern nation state or its imminent displacement by a United States of Europe. But no student of comparative politics will want to ignore the European Union as a novel political formation—so novel, that a former

Commission President memorably referred to the EU as an "unidentified political object" (UPO). It began with a core group of six member states in the 1950s and grew incrementally to fifteen by 1996. In May of 2004, however, the EU in one major move almost doubled its membership to 25. The ten newcomers differ greatly from the older membership, and their inclusion would have been unthinkable less than two decades earlier. They are less developed economically, and eight of them spent the Cold War under communist governments, as integral units of the Soviet bloc in Central and Eastern Europe. With about 450 million people since this recent expansion, the EU now overshadows the United States by more than 150 million in population. One of the big questions is how this regional organization will change as a result of its enlargement and diversification. A closely related question is how the European states will respond and adapt. Part three returns to this topic.

Europeans have begun to examine carefully another of their major contributions to contemporary politics, **the modern welfare state.** In practically every country, there are attempts to define a new balance between economic efficiency and social justice, as governments and publics are confronted with the increasing costs of a popular and relatively generous system of welfare and service entitlements. If the funding problem were merely a cyclical one, it would lend itself more easily to solutions within the existing policy framework. But there are structural components that seem to require a thorough revamping or "reinvention" of the welfare state. The problem is exacerbated by the overall aging of the population in these societies, where longer life expectancies and lower birthrates have become the rule. Almost everywhere in Europe, this is causing strains on the social budget and its "pay-as-you-go" formula that in practice involves an intergenerational transfer of wealth.

When compared in economic strength, the five countries have relatively high and fairly similar rankings. They are all members of the **Group of Seven (G 7),** where they rank behind the United States in places two (Japan), three (Germany), four (Britain), five (France), and six (Italy) among the world's biggest market economies. If China's economy were included, that huge and rapidly developing country would probably take third place in terms of gross domestic product (GDP). On the other hand, if national economies were compared in terms of their **GDP per capita,** China would fall far behind. By this measure, our five countries would themselves slip somewhat in ranking, as they were passed and became separated by a few smaller but high-performing economies. Yet even in terms of per capita product, the five remain at the high end of the world's economies and keep approximately the same internal ranking, except that Britain moves ahead of Germany. On the other hand, the economies of four of them—Japan, Germany, France, and Italy—have recorded **low rates of economic growth** and **high unemployment rates** for years, and there is little reason to believe that they will find a politically acceptable way of returning to their strong growth patterns of the early post-World War II period.

The five countries record a high performance when it comes to a standard measure of the **quality of life**. The *Human Development Index (HDI)* places Japan slightly ahead of equidistant Britain and France, closely followed by Germany, with Italy trailing. Once again, the aggregate figures are strikingly similar for the five countries.

All five have arrived at some **"mixed" form of market capitalism,** but their manner and degree of state intervention in the economy show considerable variations. Since the "Thatcher Revolution" of the 1980s, Britain has moved closer to the relatively open market conditions of the United States, while France and Germany have followed a more organized and regulated form of capitalism that Germans often refer to as a social market economy. The highly protected and corporatist Japanese economy is less competitive and sometimes described as neo-mercantilist.

When compared for **disparity in income,** as measured by the *gini index,* the five countries show notable differences. Yet none of them records as big a gap between the highest 10 percent and the lowest 10 percent of the household incomes as the one found in the United States. The income gap is lowest in Japan and highest—and thus closest to the U.S. situation—in Britain. It is noteworthy that some of Europe's smaller countries, like the five Scandinavian nations and the Netherlands, demonstrate that it is possible to build a form of market economy that combines overall prosperity, high taxation of income, and relatively small income discrepancies. Such differences in the pattern of income distribution presumably reflect distinctive national traditions and public policy choices that modify the workings of the market economy and the distribution of its product.

There are some additional developments that underscore the continuing importance of European developments for comparative political science. For example, it is faced with a growing **ethnic and cultural diversity** brought about by the arrival of many economic migrants and political refugees during and after the cold war. Japan remains far more homogeneous, but even this Asian island nation has experienced some ethnic diversification and could one day conclude that it needs an active immigration policy to offset the aging of the Japanese population. In Western Europe it is generally understood that the influx of the newcomers has had some stimulating economic and cultural effects on the host countries, but it has also brought issues of multicultural co-existence and tolerance back onto the political agenda in a new and intensified form. An example is the current controversy in France over an official ban on wearing a piece of clothing that could be regarded as a religious symbol, such as a head scarf or a yarmulke, in public schools or other secular institutions.

Even as West Europeans seek to come to terms with this challenge of greater diversity, their politics have been affected by a growing **ecological awareness**. It shows up in widespread support for national and international initiatives to protect the environment, such as the Kyoto Treaty. They are also trying to adjust to the new information technologies and the many **challenges of the global market** with its opportunities for expansion and its threats of job insecurity and economic instability.

The **events of September 11, 2001,** and its aftermath have added a new element of organized violence and unpredictability to our political world. The terrorist attacks on the World Trade Towers and the Pentagon were directed at the United States, but the clandestine network of supporters and sympathizers appears to have reached deep into the immigrant communities of several European countries, including the ones we have singled out for special discussion here. Similar strikes could affect Europe at anytime. In fact, they have already done so in the case of the train-bombings in Madrid in the spring of 2004 and in London in the summer of 2005. The sharpened awareness of vulnerability has affected the politics of every one of these countries. It helped mobilize their early support for U.S.–led military countermeasures in Afghanistan.

It soon became clear that there is no transatlantic consensus on the most effective strategy for dealing with the new terrorism. One crucial assumption of the traditional policy of containment does not apply to this kind of activity, namely that the desire for self-preservation will restrain potential opponents by making them reluctant to risk severe retaliation. Thus the primary responsibility of the state, to provide security for its citizens in a dangerous world, has acquired a new dimension in light of the willingness of individual terrorists to risk or even seek out self-destruction (understood as noble self-sacrifice). The search for an appropriate and effective response will preoccupy our politics for a long time to come.

The lack of consensus became particularly evident in the controversy about how to deal with Iraq and its ruler, Saddam Hussein. The U.S. government was determined to move decisively to disarm Iraq of the weapons of mass destruction, which President George W. Bush believed the Baghdad government to be developing and accumulating. In addition, the United States spoke openly of seeking a "regime change," leaving no one in doubt about its readiness to conduct what was presented as a preemptive strike to achieve its goals.

Chancellor Gerhard Schröder and President Jacques Chirac, the political leaders of Germany and France, reacted critically to President Bush's position. Their preference for giving more time to the search by UN weapon inspectors for hidden weapons in Iraq ran counter to the official American determination to use military pressure and intervention to force the issue. British Prime Minister Tony Blair played a markedly different role, in the tradition of his country's vaunted **special relationship** to the United States. He was largely supportive of President Bush's strategy, even as he stressed that the *casus belli* had been Iraq's failure to meet UN-backed resolutions on weapons inspection. As a result, a significant number of British troops joined the American ones in the invasion and occupation of Iraq in April 2003. Blair has had to pay a heavy political price for extending political and military support. In Britain, he ran into a barrage of criticism, much of it from within his own party. The widespread political mistrust he engenders is explored in an article in unit one, "The Strange Tale of Tony Blair."

It is hardly surprising that the transatlantic debate has revived the time-honored practice of engaging in public reflections on more **fundamental cultural and political differences** between continental Europe and the United States. One of the most widely discussed contributions has come from the American political writer Robert Kagan. He argues that Europe and America are not just separated on the important issue of Iraq. The "older" continent has been exhausted by two world wars followed by colonial conflicts. As a result, it is far more reluctant than a "younger" and more powerful United States to employ military power as a means of foreign policy. In a widely quoted phrase, Kagan sums up his perception of the difference: **"Americans are from Mars and Europeans are from Venus."** He points out that Europeans are more likely than Americans to favor multilateral approaches and to prefer the resort to "soft" rather than "hard" power in international relations. Indeed, he finds little fundamental agreement between the two sides, and less and less mutual understanding. Moreover, the deep lying causes of their present estrangement are likely to endure past the Iran conflict. Kagan's thesis has touched off a lively debate, much of it critical of the simple dichotomy he sometimes adopts. In his spirited response, found in unit two, Timothy Garton Ash critically discusses "The Great Divide" from a British perspective and explains why he finds Kagan to be only "half right."

The transatlantic values gap is illuminated by the world values survey, an ambitious project led by Ronald Inglehart at the University of Michigan. It studies cross-cultural similarities and differences in 81 societies around the world—including all the countries we have discussed so far. One of its major findings is that while contemporary Americans and West Europeans share some basic values of "self-expression" that are closely associated with political and economic freedoms, Americans are far more traditional, religious, and patriotic in their values than their more "secular-rational" West European contemporaries (with the exception of the Irish). The resulting "values gap" between the United States and Western Europe is evident on the cultural map that accompanies the article "Living With a Superpower," in unit two. This finding corresponds with more anecdotal observations about a greater American tendency to see foreign policy in moral terms. Skeptics may wish to question such sweeping generalizations about "American" and "European" cultural traits. Or they may regret the absence of a demonstrated linkage between such different value clusters and major policy choices.

This is the point at which to embark on a serial discussion of each of our countries. We start with a word of caution: In our concern to include the most recent changes and newest challenges, we must not lose sight of some equally important if less dramatic elements of continuity or even inertia. In the stable democracies of Western Europe and Japan, the political process is usually defined by a relatively mild blend of change and continuity. Here political agendas are normally modified rather than discarded entirely, and shifts in the balance of power do not take the form of revolutionary displacements of a ruling group. Instead, there are occasional changes of government as a result of coalition disagreements or routine elections.

Britain has long been regarded as "the mother" of the parliamentary system of government. In contrast to a presidential system, where the chief executive and legislatures are separately elected by the voters for fixed terms of office, a parliamentary government is often described as based on **the "fusion"** of the executive and legislative powers. Its most distinctive trait is that the prime minister, as head of government, is in some way "chosen" or "approved" by and usually from the popularly elected legislature and remains dependent on its sustained majority support or toleration to stay in office. Should the prime minister lose a sustained majority support in the legislature, he or she will normally be replaced as head of government, perhaps—but not necessarily—after an intervening general election that reshuffles the parliamentary balance of power among the parties.

There are numerous variations in the institutional workings of parliamentary government over time or locale. In Britain, for example there is no formal "election" of the prime minister in the House of Commons. Instead, the person who is the recognized leader of the majority party in the House of Commons will be asked by the monarch to form a government. In Germany, on the other hand, the federal chancellor is formally elected by the Bundestag, normally as the result of the prior formation of a parliamentary majority based on a coalition of two or more political parties. Denmark is one of several countries that have a long tradition of minority governments, which rely on their political networks and ability to build legislative support for their proposals. By contrast, Switzerland has deliberately sought to build governments based on very large, "oversized" four-party coalitions.

In today's British version of parliamentary government, called the **Westminster model**, there is usually one party that wins a majority of the seats in the House of Commons. The result is single-party government and a form of majoritarian politics in which the main opposition party of **"outs"** plays the adversary role of an **institutionalized critic** and rival of the government party of **"ins."** In continental Europe, where elections seldom result in a single party majority in the legislature, the prime minister is normally supported by a **parliamentary coalition of parties** that provide the crucial flow of majority support or toleration required for the political executive to stay in office. Under such power-sharing coalition governments, the political process tends to be **less adversary and more inclusive or consensual** than in the majoritarian Westminster system.

Politically, a British prime minister can stay in power between elections as long as he or she continues to receive majority support from the elected legislature. It is possible to lose the prime ministerial office through a parliamentary vote of no confidence. Such an overthrow is relatively rare in contemporary British politics, because the electoral system—based on single member districts that are won in plurality (**"first past the post" or FPTP**) elections—tends to produce a single party majority that is then kept together by political self-interest and other factors that produce a strong party discipline. A motion of no confidence can only threaten a prime minister whose own parliamentary base of supporters has for some reason—such as attrition or desertion—become too weak to ensure a dependable majority in favor of the government.

A far more likely cause for turnovers in British government is a general election that results in the governing party losing its parliamentary majority. This has happened in seven of the 17 general elections held between 1945 and 2005—compared to our seven party alternations in the White House resulting from 15 U.S. presidential elections in the same time period. The most recent British example took place in 1997, when Labour defeated the Conservatives and replaced them in office.

It is also fairly common for prime ministers to step down at midterm, voluntarily or as the result of political pressure from members of their own party. Since 1945, there have been four such cases of early resignation when a British prime minister has been replaced by a leading member of the same party without an intervening general election. The most recent case is that of Margaret Thatcher, who headed a Conservative government for more than eleven years, beginning in May 1979. In November 1990, she faced a potential revolt by members of her own parliamentary party, as many Conservatives concluded that she had become a political liability. She stepped down reluctantly, making the way free for another leading Tory, John Major, to succeed her as party leader and prime minister. Such an early resignation is rare in the U.S. system, where heads of government are elected for fixed terms of office.

Since 1945 Britain can be said to have had **three major reform governments** that greatly altered some key features of British society and politics. The first of these was **Clement Atlee's Labour Government (1945–51)** that came to power immediately after World War II and replaced the wartime coalition government led by Winston Churchill. In a nation weary of war and depression, Labour had won a sweeping victory over the Conservatives. During its first five years in office, Labour established a comprehensive welfare state in Britain, nationalized some key parts of the economy ("the commanding heights"), and took the first major steps to dismantle the large overseas empire by releasing the huge Indian subcontinent. The result was a sea change that turned Britain toward a more egalitarian form of society. Labour scraped through the general election of 1950 with a tiny parliamentary majority, too weak to continue with major new reforms. A year later, it called an early election in a bid to win another "working" parliamentary majority. The stakes were unusually high in 1951, and the result was a milestone election that recorded one of the biggest voter turnouts in British history. Labour won a narrow plurality of the popular vote, but the Conservatives won a majority of the seats in the House of Commons and therefore formed the next government.

During the first five years in office, Atlee's Labour government had taken full advantage of the British political system's acclaimed capacity for effective, comprehensive yet accountable action. This institutional trait has impressed many reform-minded U.S. political scientists since Woodrow Wilson. The British system's capacity for effective action was much less in evidence during the next quarter of a century. Instead, the British governmental process from 1950 until the late 1970s seemed to be better captured in the phrase "muddling through." Some historians would later refer to these years as an **era of "consensus politics."**

Having come back to power in 1951 by a whisker, the Conservatives refrained from a "roll back" of the welfare state reforms. They did return some parts of the nationalized economy to private hands, but they engaged in no major reform program of their own. Decolonization continued and reduced Britain's international presence. When Labour finally regained government office, between 1964 and 1970, it talked a lot about policy innovation but failed like its Tory predecessor to deal effectively with some mounting economic problems. In the regular confrontation between "ins" and "outs" in the House of Commons, the British tradition of **adversary rhetoric** continued to flourish. In practice, however, the differences between the two major political parties seemed often to have been reduced to relatively minor matters.

Specific foreign policy issues continued to provide the occasion for some severe political disagreements that sometimes ran through as well as between the main political parties. In 1956, Conservative Prime Minister Eden tried in collusion with the leaders of the Fourth French Republic and Israel to wrest control of the nationalized Suez Canal from President Nasser's Egypt. The military intervention led to a deep division in British politics and caused a temporary rift in relations with the United States. Britain's withdrawal from the Suez engagement underscored its **decline as a major power**. Prime Minister Eden's resignation a few months later made possible a resolution of this foreign policy fiasco. He was succeeded by Harold Macmillan, who turned out to be a superb practitioner of consensus politics until he too felt obliged to step down, in his case because of a scandal involving a member of the government.

The relationship to the European Economic Community (originally EEC, then EC, now EU) became the source of another political division. Britain had chosen not to join the original six founding members, who signed the Treaty of Rome at the beginning of 1957. The British government soon came to regret its decision and sought entry in the early 1960s. At this point, however, French President Charles de Gaulle blocked the latecomer who would inevitably have challenged France's political leadership of the Community. After a second rebuff, Britain finally became a member in 1973, under its conservative Prime Minister Edward Heath. The Labour Party was deeply divided over the issue. When it returned to power in the following year, Labour therefore felt obliged to use a **national referendum**—the first and so far only one in British political history—to decide whether Britain should stay a member. The decision was affirmative, but to this day there continue to be elements in both major parties that are, at best, reluctant "Europeans."

By the late 1960s and throughout the 1970s, Britain could no longer be said to live up to its earlier reputation for effective government. Instead, the country became notorious for its chronic governing problems. Even serious observers spoke of Britain as "the sick man of Europe." They referred to the "English disease", or *Englanditis,* as a condition that brought together such problems as economic stagnation, social malaise, and a general incapacity of elected governments to deal effectively with such relative deterioration.

In the years before Margaret Thatcher became Prime Minister, there were several attempts to give a macro-explanation of Britain's problems. Some British political scientists defined their country's condition as one of **"governmental overload."** According to this diagnosis, British governments had become so entangled by socioeconomic entitlements that the country was on the edge of

4

political paralysis or **"ungovernability."** In the United States, the political economist Mancur Olson developed a more general but in some ways similar explanation of **political "sclerosis"** in advanced pluralist democracies like Britain. He explained it in terms of the clotting effects of a highly developed interest group system that made excessive demands on government and thereby reduced its ability to perform its tasks very well.

A second cluster of interpretations explained Britain's relative decline primarily in terms of **structural inertia** that prevented the country from keeping pace with its economically dynamic European neighbors, like Germany. From this perspective, the problems were primarily explained as a hangover effect resulting from Britain's long tradition as a class-divided society and imperial power. Compared to its more modern European neighbors, this view argued, the United Kingdom was hampered by the remnants of an **outmoded and dysfunctional social order**. It needed to promote greater equality of opportunity and a general societal "modernization." Abroad, the U.K. needed to disentangle itself from the unproductive legacy of **over-commitment or "overstretch" in international affairs**. The British-American historian Paul Kennedy later pursued the warning against an imperial overextension in his widely discussed book on the rise and fall of the great powers.

Yet another explanation of Britain's governing crisis focused, ironically enough, on the Westminster model as the culprit—or at least part of the problem. It argued that government by a single majority party, accompanied by the ritualized parliamentary confrontation of two major parties, served to polarize political discourse and leave the moderate center underrepresented. It also led to a disruption of the governmental process whenever there was a transfer of power between the "ins" and the "outs." This interpretation may have idealized the broader power-sharing and consensus-seeking forms of coalition government in continental Europe, but it understandably found credence among centrist Liberals.

By the mid-1970s, this last explanation gained some plausibility, as the mounting British problems weakened the British version of consensus politics by "muddling through." The two main parties diverged and became more polarized in their search for political answers to Britain's economic and social problems. As Labour and Conservatives moved away from their long-held centrist positions, toward a traditionally socialist vision on the Left and an entrepreneurial vision of a dynamic business society on the Right, some voters in the middle turned to the Liberals and thereby helped them revive as a national "third" party. In the early 1980s, British party politics became more complex, when a group of moderates defected from Labour to form a new center-left party. Led by such well-known Labour politicians as Roy Jenkins, David Owen, and Shirley Williams, this Social Democratic Party (SDP) cooperated with the old Liberals in an electoral "Alliance." In this manner, the two "third" parties avoided competing against each other and managed to win about a quarter of the popular vote in 1983 and 1987. Under the plurality election rules of FPTP, however, the two Alliance parties received only about three percent of the seats in the House of Commons.

The Conservatives, led since 1975 by Margaret Thatcher, were the immediate political beneficiaries of the fragmentation of the non-Conservative vote between Labour, the Liberals, and the Social Democrats. James Callaghan, the last Labour prime minister before the Thatcher revolution, seemed helpless during the 1978–79 "winter of discontents," when strikes paralyzed much of the British economy. The Conservatives swept into power in May 1979 with 43 percent of the total vote but over 60 percent of the seats, and they went on to win with similar margins in the general elections of 1983 and 1987. This could hardly have been predicted in the early 1980s, when the new prime minister and her party plummeted in popularity as a result of their first radical measures of economic reform. The situation changed suddenly in 1982, when Argentina's navy invaded the British-held Falkland Islands in the South Atlantic. The challenge elicited a swift and determined military response from Prime Minister Thatcher. Her success in restoring British control of the distant islands had symbolic significance for many British people who had been uncomfortable with their country's "Little England" role.

This **second major reform government** in Britain since World War II (1979 to 1990) saw itself as an overdue corrective to the general political direction taken by Britain since Clement Atlee's earlier reform government and the consensus politics it had spawned. Prime Minister Thatcher prided herself on being a **"conviction politician"** with policies that were based on sound conservative principles. Thatcher was determined to replace what she saw as a sluggish socialist torpor with a dynamic entrepreneurial spirit. Her policies were designed to stimulate the private sector and the interplay of market forces, weaken the obstructing trade unions, and generally reduce the interventionist role of the government. She stayed in office for over eleven years or about twice as long as Atlee's postwar reform government. Moreover, her successor was another Conservative, John Major, whose additional six and a half years in office (1990 to 1997) served to consolidate the Thatcher legacy.

As prime minister, Thatcher dismissed the centrist path taken by Britain's **"consensus politicians,"** as she referred to her immediate Labour and Conservative predecessors. Her radical rhetoric, unaccommodating style and somewhat less drastic policy changes spawned yet another debate about "the Thatcher Effect." The disagreement was not only about how best to achieve economic growth but also about the kind of polity and society Britain should aspire to be. Even among the observers who were impressed by the economic revival of Britain in the mid-1980s, there were many who became disturbed by some social and political trade-offs. In particular, the income gap between households in Britain grew precipitously, as compared to Western Europe. And in the late 1980s critics could also point to the return of **stagflation,** or sluggish economic performance coupled with fairly high inflation.

The British debate had never been restricted to the economy only. The concerns about an alleged "ungovernability" were now joined by questions about the dislocating consequences of the Conservative government's economic and social policies. In addition, some decried what they saw as emerging authoritarian and centralizing tendencies in British government. They cited an array of high-handed moves by the national government—such as its imposition of central direction over education at all levels, introduction of greater cost controls in the popular National Health Service, privatization of electricity and water industries, or drastic inroads upon what had long been considered established rights in such areas as local government powers and civil liberties.

In foreign affairs, Prime Minister Thatcher combined an assertive role for Britain in Europe and close cooperation with the United States under the leadership of Presidents Ronald Reagan and George Bush. As a patriot and staunch defender of both market economics and national sovereignty, Thatcher distrusted the drive toward monetary and greater political union in the European Community. She became known throughout the continent for her unusually sharp public attacks on the "Eurocrats" in Brussels and what she pilloried as their bureaucratic interventions or technocratic socialism. There were critics in her own party who regarded her "eurocritical" position as untenable, also because it isolated Britain and reduced its influence on strategic planning for the EC's future.

For the mass electorate, however, nothing seems to have been as upsetting as Thatcher's introduction of the community charge or "poll tax." This was a tax on each adult resident that would replace the local property tax or "rates" as a means of financing local public services. Although the new tax was extremely unpopular from the start, the veteran prime minister resisted all pressures to abandon the project before its full national implementation in early 1990. Not only did such a poll tax appear inequitable or regressive, as compared to one based on property values, it also turned out to be set much higher by local governments than the national government originally had estimated.

The politically disastrous result was that, as a revenue measure, the poll tax was anything but neutral in its impact. It created an unexpectedly large proportion of immediate losers, that is, people who had to pay considerably more in local taxes than previously. The immediate winners were people who had previously paid high property taxes. Not surprisingly, the national and local governments disagreed about who was responsible for the high poll tax bills, but the voters seemed to have little difficulty in assigning blame to Margaret Thatcher and the Conservative Party as originators of the unpopular reform. Many voters were up in arms, and some observers correctly anticipated that the tax rebellion would undermine Thatcher's position in her own party and become her political Waterloo.

The feisty prime minister had weathered many previous challenges, but by 1990 there was mounting speculation that the Tories might try to replace her with a more attractive leader before the next general election. The issue that finally triggered such a development was Thatcher's stepped-up attacks on closer European integration during 1990. It led her deputy prime minister and party colleague, Sir Geoffrey Howe, to resign on November 1, 1990, with an unusually sharp public rebuke of her attitude toward the EC. There followed a leadership challenge in the Conservative Party that ended with Thatcher's resignation in advance of an expected defeat in the internal vote taken by her own parliamentary party.

The transition in power was remarkably smooth. John Major, who was chosen by his fellow Conservatives in Parliament to be Thatcher's successor as party leader and thus prime minister, had long been regarded as one of her closest cabinet supporters. In economic policy, he basically supported her "tough love" approach, which she had often described as "dry"—in contrast to the "wet" or soft approach of accommodating "consensus" politicians. Although Major seemed to prefer a somewhat more compassionate social policy than Thatcher, he followed her general rejection of the Tory tradition of welfare paternalism. Not surprisingly, he abandoned the hated poll tax. His governing style was far less dramatic or confrontational than that of his predecessor, and some nostalgic critics were quick to call him dull. During the Gulf War of 1991, he continued Thatcher's policy of giving strong British support for firm and ultimately military measures against the government of Iraq, whose troops had invaded and occupied oil-rich Kuwait.

By the time of Thatcher's resignation, Labour appeared to be in a position to capitalize on the growing disenchantment with the Conservative government. Led by Neil Kinnock, the opposition party had begun to move back toward its traditional center-left position, presenting itself as a politically moderate and socially caring agent of reform. But Labour was now troubled by a new version of the centrist alternative that had helped keep Thatcher in power by fragmenting the non-Conservative camp in the elections of 1983 and 1987. After operating as an electoral coalition or "Alliance" in those years, the Liberals and Social Democrats had finally joined together as a single party, the Liberal Democrats.

Under the leadership of Paddy Ashdown and later Charles Kennedy, the Liberal Democrats have sought to overcome the electoral system's bias against third parties by promoting themselves as an attractive alternative to the Conservatives on the right and Labour on the left. Their strategic goal has been to win the balance of power in a "hung" parliament and then, taking on the role of parliamentary majority-makers, enter a government coalition with one of the two big parties, presumably Labour. One of their main demands would then be the adoption of some form of proportional representation (PR). Such an electoral system, which is used widely in Western Europe, would almost surely guarantee the Liberal Democrats a much larger base in the House of Commons. This would in turn give them a pivotal role in the coalition politics that would henceforth replace the single party majorities in the House of Commons.

In the general election called by Prime Minister Major for April 9,1992, the Conservatives surprised many observers by winning an unprecedented fourth consecutive term of office. The Tories garnered almost the same percentage of the popular vote as in 1987 (about 42 percent), while Labour increased its total share slightly, from 31 to 34 percent. Support for the Liberal Democrats declined to 18 percent. In the House of Commons, the electoral system's bias in favor of the front-runners showed up once again. The Conservatives lost 40 seats but ended up with 336 of the 651 members, enough to form another single-party government. Labour increased its number of seats from 229 to 271, and the Liberal Democrats—with half as many voters as Labour—ended up with only 20 seats. As usual, a few remaining seats went to candidates of the small regional parties from Northern Ireland, Scotland, and Wales.

As a result, the Conservatives and Prime Minister Major stayed in office for another five years. But the majority party had lost its drive to continue the Thatcher Revolution. The Conservatives were divided, and their new leader was not a dynamic leader or reformer. Nevertheless, John Major's presence as prime minister for six and a half years made a big difference by essentially consolidating his predecessor's controversial reforms. Thatcher would surely have tried to push them further, while Kinnock's Labour would have wanted a partial roll back.

The extended period in opposition had a profound effect on Labour. In the years after the 1992 election, the party came under the increasingly centrist leadership first of John Smith and then, after the latter's sudden death, of Tony Blair. It was Blair who succeeded in mobilizing party support for removing **Clause Four**, with its demand for socialization, from the program. He promoted the ideas of a "Third Way" as an approach to societal reform that included an acceptance of "a market economy" but not "a market society." Labour became "New Labour," and the hard-Left remnants in the party, who had seemed so dominant a few years earlier, were marginalized.

Labour lost its radical image, and became increasingly acceptable to many moderate voters who a few years earlier might have shied away from it. In the public opinion polls, Labour took a commanding and continuous lead over the Conservatives. John Major had good reason to delay the next election as long as possible, until May 1997.

This election's only surprise was the enormous parliamentary landslide that greeted the victor. With just over 43 percent of the British vote (or almost the same share as the Conservatives had won in their four consecutive victories), the Labour Party won a commanding majority of 418 of 659 seats in the House of Commons. The Liberal Democrats saw their share of the vote drop to 17 percent, but widespread tactical voting in swing districts more than doubled their number of parliamentary seats to 46, their best showing in seven decades. Labour had also benefited from such tactical voting that was aimed at unseating the Conservatives. As a result, the Liberal Democrats failed once again to reach their strategic goal of becoming majority-makers in a governing coalition. Labour had a huge parliamentary majority of its own and formed a single-party government.

Labour's victory brought the U.K. its **third reform government** in Britain since World War II. Unlike Prime Ministers Atlee or Thatcher, however, Tony Blair did not focus primarily on major social and economic policy changes. Since the mid-1990s, the British economy had once again revived well ahead of those on the mainland in Western Europe. A growing number of observers seemed willing to conclude that Thatcher's "neo-liberal" policies had played a key role in stimulating the U.K. economy. It had become more flexible and dynamic, leading to higher growth rates and lower unemployment. But there were serious tradeoffs that Blair's government could have been expected to give more remedial attention—above all Britain's growing income disparities and the neglected and sometimes dilapidated infrastructure of the public service sector, where greater investments were badly needed for maintenance and renewal.

Blair's reform agenda gave prominence to the growing demand for constitutional change in Britain. In the late 1980s, an ad hoc reform coalition had launched **Charter 88,** an interest group that calls for a bill of rights, electoral reform, and a modernization of the basic "rules of the game" in British politics. The chartists chose the tricentennial of Britain's Glorious Revolution of 1688 to launch their effort. It triggered a broad discussion in the country and several different proposals for constitutional reform.

The Liberal Democrats had been in the vanguard of such reform efforts from the beginning. Even some Conservatives entered the fray, primarily to establish citizenship rights against state bureaucracy. Labour's position became crucial after it took office in May 1997. While he was still opposition leader, Tony Blair had identified himself and his party with the institutional modernization of the U.K. But he had expressed reservations about abandoning the plurality electoral system for the House of Commons that underpins the Westminster form of government by creating single-party majorities.

In contrast to France, Britain's evolutionary constitutional development and its piecemeal approach to institutional change have produced a remarkable **pattern of asymmetry** in the country's political structures. The Blair reforms fit well into that pattern. This is illustrated by the way the new government dealt with the recurrent demand for setting up special regional assemblies in Scotland and Wales. Soon after Labour took power, regional referendums resulted in majority approval of

such assemblies—a regional parliament (with very limited powers of taxation) for Scotland and a weaker assembly for Wales. In both cases, the regional assembly was to be elected by a form of proportional representation (PR), even as the United Kingdom continued to elect the House of Commons using the FPTP or "first past the post" system. The Scottish case turned out to be a textbook example of the political impact of an electoral system: PR resulted in a multiparty regional parliament in Edinburgh, where majorities are only possible by way of two or more parties building a coalition. Presumably, similar conditions would prevail in Britain, if PR were adopted for the House of Commons.

In his important article on Britain, Donley Studlar examines each of the institutional reforms and reviews their impact until the end of the year 2005. Can we speak of a constitutional revolution in a country that is usually associated with change by slow mutation? The author leaves no doubt that the series of reforms since 1997 represent important acts of constitutional engineering, even if Blair's product reflects a selective approach to change and lacks the symmetrical qualities of a complete constitutional blueprint. Clearly these matters would have been approached very differently, if at all, under a Conservative government.

Most of these reforms were implemented relatively quickly. That was hardly surprising in view of Labour's huge parliamentary majority and the Westminster model's proven capacity for effective legislative work. There were some delays, as with implementing the devolution policy in Ulster or completing the second stage of the reform of the House of Lords, but no permanent setbacks.

What remains less certain is how the reforms contributed to Labour's electoral triumph in June 2001. The victory was not free of imperfections. The voter turnout, which had consistently been over 70 percent since World War II, sank in 2001 by more than 10 points to only 59.4 percent—the lowest since the electoral reform of 1918. Compared to the election four years earlier, there were only minor changes in the share of the vote received by each of the parties. The Liberal Democrats again failed to become a balancer, but they did win six additional seats for a new high of 52. With close to 41 percent of the popular vote, Labour won 413 of the 659 seats in the House of Commons—another disproportional result that helped Tony Blair overcome critics in his own party who disagreed strongly with his support of U.S. policy in Iraq.

By the time of the next general election, in May 2005, Labour was generally expected to win an unprecedented third consecutive victory, but with a sharply reduced majority. That was indeed how it turned out. Voter turnout was 61 percent, slightly better than in 2001 but still the second lowest on record since 1918. Labour's share of the vote cast was reduced to 35 percent, down from 43 percent. The result was one of the smallest winning vote shares in British political history. Under the FPTP rules, Labour won 55 percent of the parliamentary seats, as Donley Studlar points out in his report— 8 percent less than in 2001, but still a working majority unless there are divisions in the governing party.

Before the election, Tony Blair had announced that he would step down before the government's third term had been completed. Both the Conservatives and the Liberal Democrats began to look for new party leaders soon after the election, but media speculation centered on the succession question in Labour. When at year's end Labour defectors contributed to a defeat for a major bill sponsored Blair supporters, it was widely speculated that Gordon Brown could well become the party's new leader and prime minister before another year had passed.

France had impressive plans to celebrate the bicentennial of its Revolution in 1989, but the anniversary was overshadowed by another great political upheaval. That year, East Germans scaled the Berlin Wall and several Communist regimes in Central and Eastern Europe began to totter before they eventually collapsed. In the end, the curious coincidence stimulated a discussion about the costs and benefits of the revolutionary French model for transforming society, in which one heard echoes of Edmund Burke's contemporary advocacy of an alternative British tradition of societal change by slow and incremental growth. In reality, the British experience has included some periods of accelerated and politically driven reform, offset by times of consolidation or stagnation. Yet modern French political development has been far more discontinuous, recording numerous attempts at a fresh start since 1789: For example, historians count between 13 and 17 French constitutions in the first two centuries that followed the great Revolution.

By now, however, France seems to have found its own form of political stability and continuity. There are radical residues on the far Right and far Left, but moderate center-left and center-right positions have become more prevalent and respectable. The trend toward political moderation has been accompanied by a relative consolidation of the French party system. In the Third Republic (1870 to 1940) and Fourth Republic (1946 to 1958), French politics were notorious for their multiplicity of undisciplined parties and groupings. They provided a weak and unreliable support for prime ministers and their cabinets, resulting in a combination of political paralysis and instability that plagued its many short-lived governments. In the frequent absence of responsible political direction and oversight, a well-trained civil service maintained administrative continuity but it could not resolve major political issues. There developed a risky tradition, known in France as **Bonapartism**, of intermittently calling for strong political saviors who were to lead the country out of its recurrent crises. Ironically, it was such a Bonapartist leader who ended up delivering an institutional solution to the problem.

In 1958 a political emergency caused by the colonial war in Algeria gave Charles de Gaulle the opportunity to become architect of a new political system. He had already played a Bonapartist role in World War II and later as interim leader of postwar France before the adoption—against his strong warnings—of the constitution of the Fourth Republic. Having long viewed the unruly French parties as beyond reform, de Gaulle decided to prune their power base in the legislature and instead concentrate authority in the executive. In the constitution of the Fifth Republic, the prime minister remains responsible to the National Assembly but enjoys far more prerogatives and is far less vulnerable to legislative power plays than previously. Above all, de Gaulle strengthened the government by adding a politically powerful president in what became known as a **dual executive** or **semi-presidential system.** The president is directly elected—until 2002 for a 7-year term, since then for a 5-year term—and has powers that include the appointment and dismissal of the prime minister and the dissolution of the National Assembly. The result is a presidential-prime ministerial system in which the president played the leading role for the first quarter of a century. It has found some imitation in the post-Communist political systems set up in Central and Eastern Europe.

Ironically, the political framework of the Fifth Republic became the setting for the evolution of a more moderate and less fragmented French party system. The Communists (PCF) were once the main party of the Left in France, receiving about 20 percent of the vote in parliamentary elections until the late 1970s. They were relatively late to join their colleagues elsewhere in Western Europe in the painful withdrawal from a common Leninist and Stalinist heritage. By now they have been reduced to less than half their former electoral strength, but they have gained a chance to play a role in coalition politics that was previously denied them. Between 1997 and 2002, they were a small partner in the coalition government dominated by the Socialists, who had overtaken them on the Left in 1978.

On the extreme Right, Le Pen's National Front (FN) seemed to have been weakened by internal splits and rivalries, before it surprised many by capturing nearly 17 percent of the vote in the first round of the presidential election in 2002. The party continues to find some right-wing populist support for its authoritarian and xenophobic rhetoric directed primarily against the country's many residents of Arab origin.

Although it has become increasingly moderate and centrist, French party politics can still be highly volatile. To gain a little perspective, it makes sense to briefly review the electoral politics of the past decade, beginning with the parliamentary contest of 1993. Here the Socialists suffered a major setback after 5 years of serving as the main government party. Together, the loosely organized neo-liberals of the Union for French Democracy (UDF) and the more conservative neo-Gaullists in the Rally for the Republic (RPR) won about 40 percent of the first round vote. Beginning with that plurality, these two coalition parties of the Right ended up with an overwhelming majority of nearly 80 percent of the seats in the 577-member National Assembly.

The parliamentary election of 1993 resulted in one of the largest electoral landslides in French democratic history, and the parties of the Left were clearly the big losers. The Socialists plummeted from their previous share of 274 seats to 61 seats or less than one-quarter of their previous parliamentary strength. The Communists, with only 9 percent of the first-round vote, were able to win 24 seats because much of their electoral support was concentrated in a few urban districts where their candidates ran ahead of all others. With a slightly higher share of the total vote, the ultra-right National Front won no seats at all, having failed to arrive "first past the post" anywhere.

Socialist president François Mitterrand's second 7-year presidential term lasted until May 1995. After the parliamentary rout of the Socialists in March 1993, he was faced—for the second time in his presidency—with the question of whether to resign early from the presidency. Alternatively, he could appoint a conservative prime minister for a period of "cohabitation," as he had after a smaller setback in the parliamentary elections of 1986. Mitterrand opted again for the latter solution, making sure to appoint a moderate Gaullist, Edouard Balladur, to this position.

For a time, the new prime minister enjoyed considerable popularity, and this encouraged him to enter the presidential race in 1995. By declaring his own candidacy, Balladur in effect snubbed Jacques Chirac, the assertive neo-Gaullist leader who had served as prime minister in the first period of cohabitation (1986–1988). In 1995, Chirac had expected to be the only serious Gaullist candidate for the presidency, as he had been 7 years earlier, in 1988, when he lost against the incumbent Mitterrand.

The presidential race in France tends to become highly individualized. Eventually the tough and outspoken Chirac pulled ahead of his more consensual and lackluster party colleague. In the first round of the 1995 presidential election, however, a surprising plurality of the vote went to the main socialist candidate, Lionel Jospin, a former education minister and party leader. In the run-off election, two weeks later, Chirac defeated Jospin and thereby ended 14 years of Socialist control of the presidency. He appointed another Gaullist and close political ally, Alain Juppé, to replace the faithless Balladur as prime minister.

The new conservative dominance lasted only until 1997, when France entered into a new version of "cohabitation" as the result of another electoral upset. No parliamentary elections were necessary in France until the end of the National Assembly's five-year term in 1998, but President Chirac sensed a leftward drift in the country and decided to renew the legislature ten months early while the conservative coalition still appeared to be ahead of the Left. As it turned out, Chirac totally underestimated how far public confidence in Juppé's government had already slipped. The two-stage elections for the National Assembly took place in May and early June of 1997, and the result was a major setback for the neo-Gaullists (RPR) and their increasingly divided neo-liberal allies (mainly the loosely organized UDF). Their combined share of the popular vote dropped to 31 percent, and their parliamentary strength was reduced by 200 seats, to 249. The Socialists quadrupled their strength from 61 to 245 seats, while their non-Communist allies won another 13 seats in the 577-seat National Assembly. In order to form a majority coalition government, they included the small Communist Party, with its 37 seats.

In one respect, the 1997 parliamentary election resembled all the elections to the National Assembly since 1981: Each time, the incumbent majority, whatever its orientation, had been replaced with its opposite—Left with Right, and Right with Left: 1981, 1986, 1988, 1993, and 1997. When the Left won in 1997, President Chirac appointed the Socialist leader, Lionel Jospin, to be prime minister— the very politician he had narrowly defeated in the presidential race barely 2 years earlier. Thus began France's third and so far longest experiment in cohabitation. It lasted a full parliamentary term of 5 years, when Right again replaced Left in the majority position. The novelty was that the third cohabitation had a conservative president and a socialist prime minister.

After three separate periods of cohabitation, between 1986 and 2002, it is possible to conclude that such Left-Right split executives encourage a prime ministerial form of governance that differs from the Gaullist model of a strong presidential leadership. So far, however, the end of cohabitation has always brought a return to the original dual executive of the Fifth Republic with its strong president dominating a clearly subordinate prime minister—as from 1988 to 1993, from 1995 to 1997, and again since 2002.

In some ways, the latest experiment in cohabitation can be seen as a test of how far the moderate Left and Right in France have really overcome their once very deep ideological differences. During the 1997 election campaign, the political distance between them seemed to have grown. The Socialists sharply criticized neo-Gaullist Prime Minister Juppé's austerity measures and neo-liberal deregulation. Instead, they promised a more traditional program to attack unemployment by priming the economy, creating new public service jobs, and reducing the workweek to 35 hours from 39 without lowering pay. Conservative political critics were quick to attack the approach as fiscally irresponsible, but they could not deny that Jospin's government set off to an excellent start in restoring public confidence.

Meanwhile, the French parties of the Right seem to have been weakened by their internal disagreements on policy and strategy as well as their personal rivalries at the leadership level. The UDF, organized by former President Giscard d'Estaing in the 1970s, has always been a loose coalition of disparate political groups and tendencies that differed from the neo-Gaullists by showing a greater support for European integration, civil rights, and free market economics. The more conservative and nationally oriented RPR, founded by Jacques Chirac in the 1970s as well, experienced its own internecine battles. Since 2002, when he successfully ran for another term as president, Chirac and some of his followers have attempted to revitalize and modernize their party as a less traditionalist element of the French center-right. It now forms the core of a more inclusive Union for a Political Majority (UMP).

The first article in this section provides many insights on a country that one author describes as a "divided self." Few who know the country would refer without reservation to "the new France." Instead, contemporary French politics and society combine some traits that reflect a strong sense of continuity with the past and others that suggest a spirit of innovation. One major change is the decline of the previously sharp ideological struggle between the Left and the Right. This seems to have resulted in a sense of loss among some French intellectuals who still prefer the political battle to have apocalyptic implications. They seem to find it hard to accept that the grand struggle between Left and Right has been replaced by a more moderate and seemingly more mundane party politics of competition among groups that tend to cluster fairly close to the center of the political spectrum.

In the end, French intellectuals may discover that what they have long regarded as a tedious political competition between those who promise a "little more" or a "little less" can have considerable practical consequences in terms of "who gets what, when, and how." Moreover, such incremental politics need not be without dramatic conflict, since new issues, events, or leaders often emerge to sharpen the differences and increase the stakes of politics. In the last months of 1995 and again in late 1996, for example, French politics took on a dramatic immediacy when workers and students resorted to massive strikes and street demonstrations against a new austerity program introduced by the then conservative government of Prime Minister Juppé. The proposed cutbacks in social entitlements such as pension rights were perceived by many as unnecessary, drastic, and unfair. They were difficult to explain to the public at large, and many observers saw the political confrontation in France as a major test for the welfare state or "social market economy" that is now being squeezed throughout Western Europe in the name of general affordability as well as international or global "competitiveness."

The loss of the grand ideological alternatives may help account for the mood of political malaise that many observers report about contemporary France. But the French search for political direction and identity in a changing Europe has another major source as well. The sudden emergence of a larger and politically less inhibited Germany next door cannot but have a disquieting effect on France. French elites now face the troubling question of redefining their country's role in a post–cold war world, in which Russia has lost in power and influence while Germany has gained in both. The French resistance to a large American role in Europe adds another source of friction. Together with Germany's Chancellor Schröder, President Chirac went out of his way to emphasize Franco-German friendship and cooperation. Both publicly disagreed with President Bush's approach in the Iraq

Question. Chirac appears to be searching for a distinctive European position on such international problems.

Some observers have even suggested that we may expect a major new cleavage in French politics. It runs between those who favor a reassertion of the traditional French nation-state ideal—a kind of isolationist "neo-Gaullism" that can be found on both the Left and Right—and those who want the country to accept a new European order, in which the sovereignty of both France and Germany would be further diluted or contained by a network of international obligations within the larger European framework.

A persistent question is whether the long-run structural problems of France—similar to those of some of her neighbors—can be handled without a resort to the very market-oriented "therapy" that seems to be alien in spirit to many French voters and political leaders. French capitalism (like its German counterpart) is significantly different from its British and American counterparts. Yet careful observers point out that in his 5 years as prime minister, Jospin engaged in a skillful political sleight of hand by introducing some economic reforms like deregulation and privatization that had the effect of reducing the traditional interventionist role of the French state. Once again, the moderate Left appears to promote a kind of "new centrism" in politics—but it has not embraced the vague rhetoric of "the third way."

The French faced an electoral marathon in 2002, when there were two-stage elections for both the presidency and the National Assembly. It was expected in advance that the focus of the relatively short presidential campaign would be on the two veteran warhorses, Chirac and Jospin. The big surprise came with the elimination of Jospin in the first stage: He ran a close third behind Chirac, who came first, and the far right candidate, Le Pen, who came second. As in 1995, many people on the Left had apparently voted "with their hearts" in the first round. The result was that the Left vote was split among a multiplicity of candidates, none of whom had a chance of making it into the second round. This time, however, the result was the failure of the main candidate of the Left to make it into the second round. In the run-off between Chirac and Le Pen, the incumbent president won an overwhelming victory by attracting moderate votes from both Right and Left. The electoral statistics can be found in the first article on France.

In the two-stage elections of the National Assembly in June of 2002, the parties of the moderate Right, led by Chirac's neo-Gaullist conservatives, won a major victory over the parties of the Left. Voter turnout was unusually low, as it had been in Britain's general election the year before. President Chirac called on the relatively obscure Pierre Raffarin (DL) to form a new, moderately conservative government in place of the defeated left-of-center government that Jospin had headed for the previous 5 years. Three years later, on May 29, 2005, French voters rejected a proposed EU Constitution that Chirac had strongly recommended. Two days later, Prime Minister Raffarin resigned. Chirac promptly replaced him with Dominique de Villepin, who had served as foreign minister.

No matter how resilient Chirac and other established leaders of France may be, there is a generational change coming. Chirac's fellow conservative Nicholas Sarkozy is one of the younger politicians who are now pushing ahead. He has shown himself to be talented and ambitious, and he has experience as former finance minister and present leader of the president's party, the UMP. A likely Gaullist rival has already appeared. He is prime minister Dominique de Villepin.

In the second half of 2005, France was torn by a prolonged series of suburban riots in which young people of North African descent played a major role. Order was eventually restored, but the damage went far beyond the toll of human injuries or the torched cars and buildings. Major politicians seemed to be in a state of shock, and their responses came slowly and unclearly. Sarkozy stood apart by combining an early and unambiguous demand for law and order with suggestions for constructive public policy measures to give more reality to the French promise of integration. As Peter Ford points out in his article, "Next French Revolution," the dramatic events drew attention to flaws in the celebrated French policy of full assimilation of immigrants. It became the occasion for a consideration of different models

Germany was united in 1990, when the eastern German Democratic Republic, or GDR, joined the western Federal Republic of Germany. The two German states had been established in 1949, four years after the total defeat of the German Reich in World War II. During the next 40 years, their rival elites subscribed to the conflicting ideologies and interests of East and West in the cold war. **East Germany** comprised the territory of the former Soviet Occupation Zone of Germany, where the Communists exercised a power monopoly and established an economy based on Soviet-style central planning. In contrast, **West Germany**, comprising the former American, British, and French zones of postwar occupation, developed a pluralist democracy and a flourishing market economy, modified by an extensive social policy.

West Germans generally spoke with approval of their arrangement as a "social market economy." The large and center-right party of Christian Democrats (CDU/CSU), who had headed the government for the first twenty years after 1949, liked to claim this form of modified capitalism as their original idea—but the more market-oriented small party of Free Democrats identified with it as well. So did the other large and center-left party of reformist Social Democrats. In the 1970s, when the Social Democrats were themselves in power with the FDP at the federal level and before structural problems had darkened the economic horizon, the German political class began to refer with growing self-confidence to *Modell Deutschland,* "the German model."

Communist-ruled East Germany lagged far behind, even though it had gained a reputation for being one of the most productive economies within the Soviet bloc. When the two German states were getting ready to celebrate their fortieth anniversaries in 1989, no leading politician was on record as having foreseen that the forced political division was about to come to an end. In fact, a leading American dictionary published in 1988 defined Germany as a "*former* country in Central Europe."

Mass demonstrations in several East German cities and the dramatic westward flight of thousands of defiant citizens brought the GDR government to make an increasing number of concessions in the last months of 1989 and early 1990. The Berlin Wall ceased to be a hermetical seal after November 9, 1989, and East Germans began to stream over into West Berlin. Collectors and entrepreneurs broke pieces from the Wall, before public workers set about to remove the rest of this symbol of the cold war and Germany's division. After choosing a new leadership and a new party name, the ruling Communists of East Germany made a last ditch stand by introducing a form of power-sharing with noncommunist groups and parties. They agreed to seek democratic legitimation by holding a free East German election in March 1990, in the hope of reducing the westward flight of thousands of people with its devastating consequences for the eastern economy.

The popular demonstrations and the willingness of East Germans to "vote with their feet" had been made possible by two major preconditions. First, the Soviet leader, Mikhail Gorbachev, had abandoned the so-called **Brezhnev Doctrine,** under which the Soviets claimed the right of military intervention on behalf of the established communist regimes in Central and Eastern Europe. And second, the imposed communist regimes of these countries turned out to have lost their will—and ability—to hold on to power at any cost.

At first, the East German Communists only modified their control of power and positions in the German Democratic Republic. The results of the March 1990 election, however, made it clear that the pressure for national unification could no longer be stemmed. An eastern alliance of Christian Democrats, largely identified with and supported by Chancellor Helmut Kohl's party in West Germany, recorded a surprisingly decisive victory, by winning about one-half of the votes throughout East Germany. It advocated a short, quick route to unification, beginning with an early monetary union in the summer and a political union by the fall of 1990. Almost immediately a new noncommunist coalition government was installed in East Germany. Headed by Lothar de Maizière (CDU), it followed the shortcut to a merger with the Federal Republic, under Article 23 of the West German Basic Law. The Social Democrats, or SPD, had won only 22 percent of the East German vote. That was widely interpreted as a defeat for their alternative strategy for unification that would have involved the protracted negotiation of a new German constitution, as envisaged in Article 146 of the Federal Republic's Basic Law.

During the summer and fall of 1990, the governments of the two German states and the four former occupying powers completed their so-called two-plus-four negotiations that resulted in a mutual agreement on the German unification process. The **monetary union** in July was quickly followed by a **political merger** in October 1990. In advance of unification, Bonn negotiated an agreement with Moscow in which the latter accepted not only the gradual withdrawal of Soviet troops from eastern Germany but also the membership of the larger, united Germany in NATO, in return for considerable German economic support for the Soviet Union. The result was a major shift in both the domestic and international balance of power.

The moderately conservative Christian Democrats, led by Chancellor Helmut Kohl, received a temporary boost from the unification. In the first Bundestag election to include former East Germany, held in early December 1990, they captured almost 44 percent of the vote. Their main rivals, the Social Democrats (SPD), recorded a long-time low of 33.5 percent. Kohl's small coalition partner of liberal Free Democrats (FDP) did unusually well (11 percent of the vote). The environmentalist Greens, on the other hand, failed to get the required minimum of 5 percent of the vote in western Germany and dropped out of the Bundestag for the next four years. Under a special dispensation for the 1990 election only, the two parts of united Germany were regarded as separate electoral regions as far as the 5 percent threshold was concerned. That made it possible for two small eastern parties to get at least a temporary foothold in the Bundestag. One was a coalition of political dissidents and environmentalists (Alliance 90/Greens); the other was the communist descended Party of Democratic Socialism. The PDS was able to win about 11 percent of the vote in the East by appealing to those who felt displaced and alienated in the new order. Its voters included many former privileged party members but also some rural workers and young people. Ironically, the communist-descended party received only weak support among blue-collar workers.

The election results of December 1990 suggested that national unification could eventually modify the German party system significantly. By the time of the next national election, in October 1994, more evidence had emerged for a new east-west divide in German politics. This time, the far-left PDS was able to almost double its support and attract 20 percent of the vote in the East, where only one-fifth of Germany's total population lives. At the same time, the PDS won only about 1 percent of the vote in the far more populous West. Its total electoral support in Germany thus fell slightly below the famous **"5 percent hurdle"** that had been established in Germany's electoral law as a minimum for a party to win proportional representation in the Bundestag. The PDS was nevertheless able to keep and expand its parliamentary foothold, because it met an almost forgotten alternative seating criterion by winning pluralities in at least three single member districts under Germany's double-ballot electoral system. Thus the political descendants of the former ruling Communists were given proportional representation after all. They won seats in the Bundestag for 30 deputies, who now presented themselves as a democratically sensitive, far-left party of socialists and regionalists.

Despite a widespread unification malaise in Germany, the conservative-liberal coalition government headed by Chancellor Helmut Kohl won reelection in 1994. His Christian Democrats, who benefited from a widely perceived if only temporary improvement in the German economy, won 41.4 percent of the vote. Their Free Democratic ally barely scraped through with 6.9 percent of the vote. Together, the two governing parties had a very slim majority of 10 seats more than the combined total of the three opposition parties, the SPD (36.4 percent), the revived and united Greens (7.3 percent), and the PDS (4.4 percent).

In the federal upper house, or Bundesrat, the SPD held a majority of the seats, based on their control of many state governments. This situation gave the SPD considerable leverage or blocking power in federal legislative politics. The Kohl government charged that the resulting **parliamentary gridlock** stalled its economic reform initiatives. It would be only a few years before the tables were turned.

Between 1949 and 1999, the seat of government for the Federal Republic had been the small Rhineland town of **Bonn.** Reunification made possible the move of the government and parliament several hundred miles eastward to the old political center of **Berlin.** The transfer was controversial in Germany, because of the monetary and symbolic costs involved. Nevertheless, it had already been approved by the Bundestag in 1991, with a narrow parliamentary majority, and was then delayed until 1999. Observers generally agree that the "Berlin Republic" will continue the democratic tradition that was firmly established during the Cold War years of the "Bonn Republic." But they also point to the need for a revamping of the economic and social arrangements that worked so well during much of the Bonn period.

Unlike their British counterparts, German governments are regularly produced by **coalition politics**. In the multiparty system, based on the country's modified form of proportional representation, a single party is unlikely to win a parliamentary majority at the federal level of politics. In some German states, however, single party government has become familiar, as in Bavaria with its powerful CSU (a Bavarian sister party of the CDU). Coalition politics has its own patterns, and it opens up strategic opportunities for small parties. Until 1998, the Free Democratic Party—which regularly received less than one-half of the share of the vote won by the Liberal Democrats in Britain—managed to win a larger percentage of the parliamentary seats and regularly played a pivotal role as majority maker to one of the big parties in federal politics.

It is remarkable that between1949 and 1998 there had never been a complete replacement of a governing coalition in Bonn. Even when there was a change of government, at least one partner of the previous coalition—usually the FDP—had always managed to hang on as majority maker in the next cabinet. This German pattern of incomplete power transfers came to an abrupt end with the clean sweep brought by the Bundestag election of September 1998.

In advance of the contest, it had been widely expected that the outcome once again would be only a partial shift in power. This time, however, it was expected to result in a **"grand coalition"** of the two big parties, the Social Democrats (SPD) and Christian Democrats (CDU/CSU). In such a situation, the chancellorship would go to the leader of the front-running party—most likely the SPD. With the presence of the CDU/CSU in the coalition, the result would have been a considerable element of continuity. As interpreted by rival scenarios, the grand coalition was likely to produce either a pervasive inertia or a newfound vigor, when the big parties came to share the responsibility for dealing with Germany's backlog of social and economic reforms. The one previous government by a "grand coalition" had been between 1966 and 1969. Selective memories of those three years lent support for both scenarios.

As it turned out, the grand coalition was postponed. Instead, the 1998 election made possible a **complete turnover in power**. It brought into office the **first completely Left government** at the federal level since the republic's founding in 1949. (By comparison, the British had their first Left government right after the war, while the French waited until 1981 to elect a Left government). Using the German party color scheme, the new government was a "red-green" coalition. It was composed of the Social Democrats ("red"), who had won 40.9 percent of the popular vote, and the environmentalist Greens, who had won 6.7 percent. This gave them a sufficient margin over the Christian Democrats (35.1 percent) and the FDP (6.2 percent) to form a majority coalition. German voters in effect had decided it was "time for a change" in their country, similar to the political turnabouts that had taken place in Britain and France a year earlier. As in these neighboring countries, the main party of the Left was very careful to present itself as a moderate reform agent that would provide security along with both "continuity and change." The SPD borrowed freely from both British and American political imagery by proclaiming that it represented a non-radical "new middle" (*neue Mitte*). With all its imprecision, it had turned out to be a successful campaign slogan, but it was clearly an inadequate formula for policy directions.

The complete change in governing parties also brought a generational turnover at the top level of German government. In the federal chancellery, Social Democrat Gerhard Schröder, born in 1944, replaced Christian Democrat Helmut Kohl, born in1930. Most of the other leading members of the new government had spent their childhood years in postwar Germany. In many cases they had their initial political experiences in youthful opposition to the societal establishment of the late 1960s. By now the "68ers" were well into middle age, but they had ascended to power as successors to Kohl's generation, whose po-

litically formative years coincided with the founding period of the Federal Republic. The new German leaders had no youthful memories of the Third Reich, World War II, or even, in many cases, the postwar military occupation. They were truly Germany's first postwar generation in power as well as its first left-of-center governing coalition.

The larger political system was affected by the shifts in the power balance among the small political parties and their leaders. On the far left, the post-communist PDS managed for the first time to pass the 5 percent threshold, if only barely, by winning 21.6 percent of the vote in eastern Germany. It had advanced only slightly to 1.2 percent of the vote in the far more populous West, where approximately 80 percent of the German population lives. To improve its chances for a future parliamentary survival, the PDS needed to improve its position in both East and West. It was not yet clear how it could simultaneously advance in both parts of Germany.

The liberal Free Democrats ended up with another close scrape (6.2 percent). In contrast to the PDS, the Liberals now appeared to be a party of the West, where they received 7 percent of the vote as compared to only 3.3 percent in the East. After 29 years as junior government party, their struggle for political survival now had to be conducted in the unfamiliar role of a marginal opposition party.

The third small party, the Greens, had also slipped back (to 6.7 percent), but this was enough to replace the FDP as majority maker in the federal government. Like the other small parties, the Greens bore marks of the east-west divide: They received only 4.1 percent in the East versus 7.3 percent in the West.

Germany was in effect moving toward a slightly more complex party system. It consisted of the two major parties of the moderate center-left (SPD) and the moderate center-right (CDU/CSU) along with three small parties that each had a regional concentration either in the West (Greens and FDP) or almost exclusively in the East (PDS). Some observers referred to a **"two and three-halves"** party system. Each of the three "halves" had an impact on the overall balance of power and what the Germans call the system's "coalition arithmetic," but each was also small enough to be in danger of slipping below the 5 percent mark at any time. Another important result of the 1998 Bundestag election was the continued failure of the parties of the extreme right, with their authoritarian and xenophobic rhetoric, to mobilize a significant support in the German electorate.

For the Greens, the first-time role as junior coalition partner in the national government was not easy. In fact, some close observers spoke of an identity crisis of the German Left that includes parts of the Social Democratic Party. It was fed by controversies linked to domestic economic and environmental issues as well as the German military participation in Kosovo in early 1999 and later in Afghanistan. There followed a remarkable political recovery of the SPD in the latter half of that year. The abrupt resignation of the key Social Democrat Oskar Lafontaine, as both finance minister and party leader in March 1999, gave Schröder a welcome opportunity to take over the SPD leadership. The assumption that this move would give him more authority within both the party and the cabinet did not pan out. Instead, the dual set of responsibilities turned out to be very demanding, and the battle weary chancellor soon became known for his repeated threats to resign from one or both positions.

The federal system, which now had 16 states, turned out to be an obstacle to the new government. As leader of the SPD, Lafontaine had used the Bundesrat to obstruct some of the initiatives taken by Kohl's government, and the Christian Democrats now turned the tables on the red-green government. The staggered elections in the states sometimes seemed to have become a means for shifting the balance of power in Berlin.

In the first year after taking power, the Social Democrats suffered several setbacks in state elections. They were ousted from enough state governments to lose their majority control of the federal upper house or Bundesrat. Beginning in late 1999, however, the Christian Democrats suddenly found themselves in disrepute as the result of sensational revelations of a major party finance scandal that had taken place under the leadership of Helmut Kohl, the veteran chancellor. Basically the problem stemmed from transfers to a slush fund of huge political contributions that were kept secret or not properly reported as required by law.

Dubbed "Kohlgate," the finance scandal resulted in immediate setbacks for the CDU in several state elections. This had the effect of turning some disaffected CDU supporters to the Free Democrats as a familiar center-right alternative. The FDP had spent the 29 years between 1969 and 1998 as a member of the federal government office—a record even in Germany, with its long governing cycles. It had not adjusted well to the new role as junior opposition party, but the sudden boost from disaffected CDU supporters had a tonic effect on the Free Democrats. Under a youthful and flamboyant new leader, it appeared as though the FDP had a chance to regain its familiar position of balancer in German electoral and coalition politics—a role that before 1998 had made it the most successful small party in West European politics. Instead, in a strategic decision that seemed based on sheer chutzpah, the FDP decided to aim at breaking out of their junior position in the German party system. They adopted what became known as a "fun" campaign, replete with staged happenings and a focus on winning 18 percent of the vote. The Free Democrats repeated this number like a mantra, as though they were engaged in a political act of self-hypnosis or self-levitation.

As the election came closer, voters again shifted their attention to the lackluster economic performance of the Schröder government. The poll standings of the CDU improved, and it was widely believed by midsummer that the revived Christian Democrats would return to government office in coalition with the recharged FDP.

The two other small parties also played an important role in the competition for place and influence. The Greens had suffered a long string of electoral setbacks at the state level of politics. They had been damaged by internal quarrels, sometimes touched off by the compromises they made as coalition partner in the federal government. The unconventional party had also lost some of its appeal to younger voters, as the founder generation grew older and became more established.

The PDS had most reason to tremble at its electoral prospects. It had passed the 5 percent hurdle in only one of the three Bundestag elections since unification, and only barely at that (5.1 percent in 1998). Since then, it had lost some of its previous voters and largely failed to win many new ones. It had made little progress in improving its position in the western states. And the alternate route to proportional representation in the Bundestag also looked bleak for the PDS: The boundaries of the single-member districts in Berlin had recently been redrawn in a way that diluted the PDS strength and made it less likely to win pluralities in at least three districts.

In the end, the Bundestag election of 2002 did keep the PDS from sharing in the proportional allocation of parliamentary seats. The post-Communists won two single-member districts in eastern Berlin, enough for only two deputies. Had the PDS won a third district, the 5 percent clause would have been set aside, and its 4.0 percent share of the party vote would then have entitled it to about 24 of the 603 seats in the new Bundestag. Some observers concluded that the PDS was headed for further marginalization and eventual oblivion.

Ironically, in 2002 it was the near shutout of the PDS that enabled the left-wing, red-green government to hold on to power in one of Germany's closest elections ever. Both SPD and CDU/CSU won 38.5 percent of the vote, but a quirk in the two-vote electoral law gave the SPD three more seats than its major rival. The SPD had overcome its poor stand in the polls to come within 2.4 percent of its result in 1998. Most observers explained the SPD's electoral recovery by referring to points earned by Chancellor Schröder through (1) his performance in the televised debates with the chancellor candidate of the CDU/CSU, Edmund Stoiber, (2) his unusually critical disavowal of President Bush's "adventurous" strategy toward Iraq, and (3) his well-timed appearance as a decisive leader in dealing with the great floods that ravaged parts of eastern Germany in the month before the Bundestag election.

The Free Democrats had been losing ground with an increasingly controversial "fun" campaign since midsummer. They fell back to 7.4 percent of the vote—an improvement over their share of 6.2 percent four years earlier, but a far cry from the trumpeted goal of 18 percent. The Greens advanced to 8.6 percent, providing Chancellor Schröder with the majority margin he needed to stay in office. They had benefited from the revival of war fears in connection with Iraq as well as from the popularity of their foreign minister, Joschka Fischer. While they continued to perform poorly in the eastern states, where the SPD picked up many former CDU and PDS voters, the Greens benefited from the renewal of ecological concerns in the wake of the August floods.

After the 2002 election, German politics returned to a discussion of basic structural reform. The two main topics were the country's federal structure and its economic model. Federalism is a crucial element not only in the country's governance but also in its self-understanding, as reflected in its official name, the Federal Republic of Germany. The founders of the West German state regarded a strong federal arrangement as a key safeguard against a dangerous concentration and potential abuse of power in the central government. Since then, federalism has set Germany apart from France, which is still fairly centralized even after Mitterrand's regional reforms. Italy and Britain have carried out some regional devolution, but neither comes anywhere close to having a federal system like the one that was projected into the eastern part of Germany at the time of unification. Today there is a growing conviction that sometimes federal entanglements impede effective governance in Germany. At the same time, there are strong arguments and vested interests for keeping the present arrangement, perhaps with some modifications.

It is also widely agreed that there is a need for a basic socioeconomic reform in Germany, but there is no consensus about the specific reform measures themselves. In some respects, the discussion resembles that of other advanced countries. It proceeds from the insight that Germany's generous social welfare model will be unsustainable in its present form over the long run. But Germany faces the familiar demographic shifts of an aging society as well as the stiff economic competition from abroad. Its problems are compounded by the challenge of postcommunist reconstruction in eastern Germany.

Germans have traditionally favored a more socially contained form of capitalism than the untrammeled version that prevails in Britain or the United States. They are unlikely to accept the kind of shock therapy of massive deregulation that was introduced in the United States and Britain by conservative governments in the 1980s and largely accepted by their left-of-center successors in the following decade. Both the political culture and institutional framework of Germany (and much of mainland Europe) lean far more toward corporatist and communitarian solutions than their British and American counterparts.

At the beginning of 2004, Chancellor Schröder succeeded in mobilizing parliamentary support for a comprehensive structural reform package, *Agenda 2010*. It provoked a public outcry as Germans began to anticipate the painful reforms they were facing. At this point, Schröder decided to concentrate on governing and have a trusted supporter, Franz Müntefering, take over the leadership of the SPD. The party was in need of special attention to quell the protests and stem a massive loss of dues-paying members.

With his reform packet, Chancellor Schröder appeared to bite the bullet, but his demonstrated commitment to a reform of the labor market and social security provisions intensified the electoral problems facing the Social Democrats and their small coalition partner, the Greens. They came to a head when the SPD lost the state election in North Rhine-Westphalia in late May of 2005. This industrial power house is by far the most populous of the sixteen states that comprise the Federal Republic—and its population is greater than that of former East Germany. It had been governed by the SPD without interruption for almost forty years, but now a "black-yellow" coalition of Christian Democrats and Free Democrats replaced the red-green government in Düsseldorf. The symbolic significance of the transfer of power at the state level was reinforced by the power shift in federal politics, where the Christian Democrats had gained enough votes in the federal upper house, the Bundesrat, to have a two-thirds blocking majority.

With this turn of events, Chancellor Schröder faced the highly unattractive prospect of a year-long stalemate or else an arrangement that would make possible an informal co-governing with the opposition party. He decided for a surprising alternative. A few hours after the closing of the polls in North Rhine-Westphalia, he announced that he would seek a political clearance by calling for an early Bundestag election. That is no simple matter in the German political system. As part of its general attempt to stabilize government, the German constitution makes an early dissolution of the legislature considerably more difficult than it would be in Britain or in many other parliamentary systems. It required, first, that the government lose a formal vote of confidence in the Bundestag—and that could only happen if a number of parliamentary deputies from the government's parliamentary majority did not support the vote of confidence. Next, came a month-long scrutiny and eventual approval of the dissolution request by Germany's President, followed by his announcement of September 18, 2005, as election date. Finally, the Federal Constitutional Court dealt with the question of the constitutionality of calling for an early election in a situation where the government had not "really" lost its majority in the Bundestag.

All of these hurdles were passed, and Germany held a Bundestag election a year earlier than planned. The result did not resolve the German political stalemate. At the beginning of the campaign, polls had shown the CDU/CSU leading the SPD by well above 10 percent. It was widely assumed that the red-green coalition would be replaced by a black-yellow one, comprised of the Christian Democrats and their old allies, the Free Democrats. This time, the CDU/CSU chose to campaign with Angela Merkel as chancellor candidate, a move explained by Mark Landler's article in this unit. The SPD, led by Gerhard Schröder, pulled all the stops and ended up closing most of the gap that separated it from the CDU/CSU.

In the end, the Christian Democrats came out ahead, with 35.2 percent of the party vote, while the Social Democrats closed in with 34.2 percent. The three small parties were once again important as balancers. The FDP waged a traditional campaign and did relatively well, with 9.8 percent. The Greens fell behind the FDP for the first time since 1990, but they did better than expected with 8.1 percent. Once again, as in 2002, the third small party on the far Left had an important impact on the parliamentary balance of power and the coalition options available to the more mainstream parties.

This time it had presented itself as the Left Party/PDS and won 8.7 percent of the vote or more than twice as much as the PDS had won four years earlier. As its name indicates, it was not a wholly new factor. It brought together the eastern PDS and left critics of Schröder's reforms who had gathered behind Oskar Lafontaine and were located primarily in the western part of Germany. Time would tell whether this political alliance, standing with a leg in each part of Germany, would provide a sufficiently broad basis for a viable political party to the left of the SPD. Its links to both Lafontaine and the PDS made it an unacceptable coalition partner for the Social Democrats at the federal level.

The coalition possibilities were greatly restricted. The "black-yellow" coalition of Christian and Free Democrats was arithmetically impossible, since the two parties did not have a parliamentary majority. The so-called "traffic light" coalition (red, yellow, green) was arithmetically possible but politically impossible, because it lacked support among the two small rivals, the Greens and the Free Democrats. A replacement of the SPD by the CDU/CSU in a so-called "Jamaica coalition" (named after the colors of the West Indian country's flag: black, yellow and green) was similarly ruled out by small party rivalry. In the end, the two big parties (CDU/CSU and SPD) decided to form a "grand coalition," headed by Angela Merkel. The challenges facing this "black-red" coalition and its remarkable leader are discussed in the readings on German politics in unit one.

Japan has long fascinated comparative social scientists as a country that modernized rapidly without losing its non-Western, Japanese identity. The article, "Japanese Spirit, Western Things," explains how this was possible and why it is important. It begins by recounting the story of Commodore Perry's arrival in Tokyo harbor in the 1850s and his role in forcing the country to "open up." The Japanese rulers decided in effect to learn from the West in order to strengthen Japan and maintain its independence. The special conditions that made the modernization possible have become a staple topic on the social science agenda. About one hundred years later, a few other countries in East and South Asia began taking tentative steps toward what soon became a rapid and self-sustained modernization. Soon known as the "Asian tigers" or "dragons," the New Industrial Countries include South Korea, Taiwan, and Singapore.

Japan's tentative move toward a parliamentary form of government after World War I was blocked by a militarist takeover in the early 1930s. After World War II, a parliamentary form of representative democracy was installed in Japan under American supervision. This political system soon acquired indigenous

Japanese characteristics that set it off from the other major democracies examined here.

For almost four decades following its creation in 1955, the Liberal Democratic Party (LDP) played a hegemonic role in Japanese politics. The many opposition parties were divided and provided little effective competition for the LDP, which according to a popular saying, was really "neither liberal, nor democratic, nor a party." It has essentially been a conservative political machine that loosely unites several rival and delicately balanced factions. The factions in turn consist mostly of the personal followers of political bosses who stake out factional claims to benefits of office.

In 1993, the LDP temporarily lost its parliamentary majority, when a couple of its factions joined the opposition. This set the stage for a vote of no confidence, followed by new elections in which the LDP lost its parliamentary majority. Seven different parties, spanning the spectrum from conservative to socialist, thereupon formed a fragile coalition government. It was incapable of defining or promoting a coherent policy program and stood helpless as the Japanese economy continued on its course of stagnation that began at the outset of the 1990s after a long postwar economic boom.

Two prime ministers and several cabinet reshuffles later, a revived LDP managed by the summer of 1994 to return to the cabinet by way of a coalition with its former rival, the Socialists. The peculiar alliance was possible because the leadership of both these major parties had adopted a pragmatic orientation at this juncture. By December 1995, the LDP had recaptured the prime ministership. There followed a rapid succession of short-lived governments headed by LDP factional leaders. When the post once again became open in April 2001, there were a surprising number of willing candidates.

The unexpected winner of the leadership contest in the LDP and new prime minister of Japan was Junichiro Koizumi. Although he was no beginner in Japanese party politics, he seemed to personify a more unconventional approach than most veteran politicians in Japan. He spoke the language of structural reform, and immediately took some symbolic steps to show that he meant business. His cabinet included five women, including the controversial Makiko Tanaka as head of the foreign ministry. Koizumi soon ran into resistance from conservative elements in the political class, including factional leaders of his own party and members of the high civil service. By January 2002, he dismissed the assertive Tanaka, who had become a favorite target of those who opposed the new political style and possible major policy changes. The move triggered widespread public dissatisfaction. Koizumi countered by appointing another prominent woman, Yoriko Kawaguchi, to head the foreign ministry. By this time, however, his own popularity rating was rapidly falling. It seemed unlikely that his remaining public support provided enough political capital to offset the entrenched foes of a reform of the Japanese economy and fiscal policy. Koizumi now seemed disinclined to try. Some observers argued that the prime minister himself had little realistic understanding of or commitment to the kind of structural change that Japan needed. Thus continuity seemed once again more likely than basic change in Japan.

It is remarkable that Japan's prolonged economic stagnation has not resulted in more political protests and electoral repercussions. But the public has not been oblivious to the country's prolonged economic stagnation. There now seems to be an emerging consensus that fundamental change must be based on an "opening up" of Japanese society to more competition. From this perspective, the entrenched bureaucratic elites and their cozy relationships with business leaders need to become prime targets of reform.

It will probably take more than a flamboyant prime minister to revitalize Japanese politics and society, but reform steps are more likely under Koizumi than any of his handful of recent predecessors. A key question becomes whether the fragmented parliamentary opposition will one day take advantage of the situation and become a more coherent, alternative force for reform. There are no clear answers as yet, but the parliamentary elections of 2003 and 2005 seemed to give some positive indications.

The immediate result of the 2003 election was that Koizumi remained prime minister. His party lost ten seats, but the LDP could claim exactly one-half of the 480 seats in the House of Representatives after three independents joined its ranks. Together with two smaller partners, however, Koizumi's ruling coalition commanded a total of 275 seats.

The main change brought by the election lay in its apparent consolidation of the hitherto fragmented opposition. Here the Democratic Party of Japan (DPJ), formed in 1996, gained 40 seats for a total of 177 in all. The young party seemed to have emerged as a major mainstream challenger to the LDP by mopping up voters from other parties. In its assessment, *The Economist* saw the possible emergence of a two-party system and referred to the DPJ as the clear alternative choice for mainstream voters.

Some observers suggested that the new strength of the DPJ could make it easier for Prime Minister Koizumi to neutralize resistance in his own party and the bureaucracy to the structural reforms that he intermittently advocates. In a sense, he appeared to have been given the proverbial second chance.

Two years later, the optimistic readings of the 2003 election results had not panned out. Prime Minister Koizumi continued to run into opposition from members of his own party. His economic reform program, which involved privatization and other market-oriented policies, ran into the usual political difficulties.

In the summer of 2005 Koizumi decided, like Gerhard Schröder in Germany, to attempt to break the stalemate by calling an early election that would decisively reshuffle the balance of power among and within the political parties. He used the occasion to rejuvenate the LDP with new candidates, many of them loyal to him. The move was not without risks, as the German case proved. In contrast, however, Japan's election resulted in a landslide victory for the prime minister's party. In his detailed report on the election, Norimitsu Onishi explains that the electoral triumph will strengthen the LDP leadership and give the prime minister more authority and room to maneuver in pursuing his reform program. It is a familiar tune, but the alternative would be more of the same. At this point, the Japanese voters appear to be braced for the changes Koizumi has promised to bring.

A Constitutional Revolution In Britain?*

Donley T. Studlar

Since its re-election to a third consecutive term of office under Tony Blair's leadership in 2005, assessments of "New Labor's" long-term effects on the British constitution have become more numerous and more reflective, especially since Blair has pledged to leave the prime ministership by the time of the next election (2009 or 2010). The most distinctive campaign policies of the first New Labor government in 1997 were those on constitutional reform. From its earliest days in power, Labor promoted its constitutional reform agenda: (1) devolution to Scotland and Wales, (2) an elected mayor and council for London and potentially other urban areas, (3) removal of the voting rights of hereditary peers in the House of Lords, (4) incorporation of the European Convention on Human Rights into British law, (5) a Freedom of Information Act, and (6) electoral reform at various levels of government, including a referendum on changing the electoral system for Members of Parliament. These reforms, plus a stable agreement for governing Northern Ireland, the constitutional implications of membership of the European Union, the question of modernization of the monarchy, and the Labor government's recent legislation for a separate Supreme Court, will be considered here. The article analyzes the nature of Labor's constitutional proposals, including their inspiration, implementation, and potential impact.

Traditional British Constitutional Principles

The United Kingdom as a state in international law is made up of four constituent parts—England, Scotland, Wales, and Northern Ireland—all under the authority of the Queen in Parliament in London. The constitution is the structure of fundamental laws and customary practices that define the authority of state institutions and regulate their interrelationships, including those to citizens of the state. Although in principle very flexible, in practice the "unwritten" British constitution (no single document) is difficult to change. The socialization of political elites in a small country leads to a political culture in which custom and convention make participants reluctant to change practices that brought them to power.

Even though Britain is under the rule of law, all constitutional provisions are subject to change through parliamentary sovereignty. Instead of a written constitution with a complicated amending process, a simple voting majority of the House of Commons can change any law, even over the objections of the House of Lords if necessary. Individual rights are protected by ordinary law and custom, not by a constitutionally entrenched Bill of Rights.

Officially Britain remains a unitary state, with all constitutional authority belonging to the central government, rather than a federal state with a formal, even if vague, division of powers between the center and a lower level. Some commentators argue that Britain should be considered a "union-state," since the relationship of the four parts to the central government is not uniform. Although limited devolution has been utilized in the past, especially in Northern Ireland, 1921–1972, central government retains the constitutional authority to intervene in lower-level affairs, including local government. At a parliamentary general election, voters are asked once every four or five years to choose a team of politicians to manage the central authority, based on having majority support in the House of Commons at Westminster. Under the single member district, simple plurality electoral system, the outcome usually has been a single-party government (prime minister and cabinet). This is a fusion of power between the legislative and executive branches. Referendums have been rare and are only advisory; parliament retains final authority on all legislation. The judiciary seldom makes politically important decisions. If a court finds that the executive has exceeded its lawful authority, such a decision can be overridden by having a parliamentary majority pass an appropriate law, even retrospectively. Thus, in the United Kingdom almost any alteration of the interrelationship of political institutions can be considered constitutional in nature.

16

Constitutional issues were one of the subjects of major party debate during the 1997 election campaign. Labor and the third party, the Liberal Democrats, had developed an agreed agenda for constitutional change. The Conservatives upheld traditional British constitutional principles, including the unwritten constitution, no guarantees of civil liberties except through the laws of parliament, maintenance of the unitary state, and a House of Lords composed of hereditary peers and some life peers, the latter appointed by the prime minister.

Other features of the British constitution have also resisted change. British government has been one of the most secretive among Western democracies, with unauthorized communication of information punishable by law, principally the Official Secrets Act. Large cities did not elect their own mayors or even their own metropolitan governing councils. The House of Commons is one of the few remaining democratic legislatures elected by the single member district, simple plurality electoral system, which rewards a disproportionate shares of parliamentary seats to larger parties having geographically concentrated voting strength. Thus the membership and organization of the House of Commons has remained largely two-party despite having a multiparty electorate since 1974.

Even though the elected Labor government proposed to institute reforms of several of these procedures, there was doubt about its commitment. Like the Conservatives, traditionally Labor had embraced the almost untrammeled formal power that the "elective dictatorship" of British parliamentary government provides for a party with a majority in the House of Commons. Although Labor sometimes voiced decentralist and reformist concerns when in opposition, in government it usually proved to be as centralist as the Conservatives.

Labor's Constitutional Promises

The most radical aspect of Labor's 1997 election manifesto was constitutional reform. This program was designed to stimulate the normally passive, relatively deferential British public into becoming more active citizens with a wider range of choices. In addition to parliamentary elections, they would vote in more frequent referendums and for other levels of government with significant authority. In addition, they would have more individual civil rights.

Prior to becoming prime minister, Tony Blair had advocated a more participatory British citizenship. In his book *New Britain*, Blair criticized the traditional Westminster system as too centralized, secretive, and unrepresentaltive. Blair called Labor's constitutional program "democratic renewal." He argued that since World War I there had been an erosion of consent, self-government, and respect for rights under governments of all parties in Britain; a leftist party true to its own instincts should extend political rights as well as pursuing its recognized goals of economic and social equality.

Developing a Program for Constitutional Change

Several events and trends focused Labor's thinking on constitutional reform. Labor had suffered four consecutive general elec-

tion losses (1979, 1983, 1987, 1992) even though the Conservatives never achieved above 43 percent of the popular vote. Eighteen consecutive years out of government made Labor fearful of ever returning as a single-party government. The possibility of permanent opposition made the party more receptive to arguments for weakening central authority.

Groups interested in constitutional reform grew more numerous. The third party in Britain, the Liberal Democrats, long have advocated several of these reforms, including decentralization, increased protection for civil liberties, and changing the electoral system. The latter would allow them to have their voting support more proportionally represented in parliament. Since 1988, a nonpartisan lobby group, Charter 88, has proposed a number of reforms, including even a written constitution and a bill of rights. Other influential thinkers on the moderate left argued that a precondition for social and economic change in an increasingly middle-class Britain was to encourage citizen involvement by limiting central government authority. In Scotland, the broadly-based Scottish Constitutional Convention encouraged devolution of power. The Electoral Reform Society has been an active proponent for a more proportional voting system. Eventually Labor and the Liberal Democrats formed a pre-election commission on constitutional matters, which continued after the election in the form of a special cabinet committee on constitutional reform.

Skeptics have argued that public support for constitutional change is a mile wide and an inch deep. Surveys indicate that the public usually supports constitutional reform proposals in principle without understanding very much about the specifics. Intense minorities, such as Charter 88, fueled the discussion. Although constitutional issues featured prominently in elite discussions of party differences during the 1997 campaign, they did not emerge as a critical voting issue, except perhaps in Scotland.

New Labor had multiple incentives for the development of an agenda for constitutional change. It provided a clear sense of party distinctiveness from the Conservatives, especially important when there were only minimal differences on social and economic policy. It also helped to alleviate threats to Labor by Scottish and Welsh nationalist parties arguing for more autonomy and even independence for their regions. There was also a longer-term prospect of a realignment of the party system through the cooptation of the Liberal Democrats into a more permanent alliance of the center, thereby reducing both the Conservatives and die-hard socialists of the Labor party left wing to permanent minority status. The large single-party majority that Labor surprisingly gained in the House of Commons in the 1997 election did not discourage it from pursuing most of its constitutional reform program.

Constitutional Change under Labor

It is commonly stated in the British press that Labor's constitutional agenda, considered as a whole, represents the most fundamental changes in 400 years. There are now legislatures with devolved powers in Northern Ireland, Scotland, and Wales. All but 92 hereditary peers have been removed from the House of Lords, with the pledge of the eventual elimination of those as well. Although a report from the Independent Commission on the Voting System advocated a change in the electoral system for the House of Commons, no government legislation was proposed. The European Convention on Human Rights has been incorporated into British law through the Human Rights Act and is effective. A Freedom of Information Act was passed and implemented. In 1998, Londoners voted favorably for a referendum proposal for the city to be governed by a directly-elected mayor and assembly; these elections were held in 2000 and 2004. Other cities have now adopted this measure through referendums. The judiciary has been separated to a degree from the other branches of government.

The Labor government immediately set out to implement more decentralized authority, subject to its acceptance through referendums in the affected regions. The Scottish Parliament has more authority, covering nearly all of domestic policy as well as limited taxation powers while the Welsh Assembly is responsible for implementing legislation after the primary bills have passed through the Westminster House of Commons and no taxation powers. Elections in each region in 1999 and 2003 were held under a combination of the traditional single member district, simple plurality electoral system and party list proportional representation; these yielded no clear majority in either legislature. Instead, Labor-Liberal Democrat coalition governments and minority governments have been formed. Both have functioned largely as anticipated. With an organized women's movement taking advantage of the opportunity to choose legislators in a new institution without incumbents, women's representation in both devolved chambers has been high, with the Welsh Assembly becoming the first in the world with a majority of women in 2003. Perhaps surprisingly, no major disagreements on the constitutional allocation of powers have occurred. The Welsh Labor party has advocated greater authority for the Assembly, and the British Labor government promised to consider this in the post-election session of parliament. However, the "West Lothian" question has still not been seriously addressed. This refers to the fact that now MPs from Scotland can still vote on legislation affecting England, Wales, and Northern Ireland even though the devolved Scottish parliament has authority over the same topic there.

Eighty percent of the population of the United Kingdom, however, lives in England, which has been treated as a residual consideration in the plans for devolution. Labor has promised to form devolved governments in "regions with strong identities of their own," as expressed through voting in referendums. However, when the region showing the greatest amount of interest, the Northeast, was offered limited devolution in 2004, it was rejected overwhelmingly. Nevertheless, with encouragement from the regional aid policies of the European Union, the Northeast does have a considerable amount of administrative devolution, even if it lacks legislative devolution.

The Mayor of London is the first modern directly-elected executive in the United Kingdom. The introduction of party primary elections for mayoral candidates led to less central party control over candidates and a more personalized contest. The first mayor, re-elected in 2004, was a dissident leftwing Labor MP and former London official, Ken Livingstone, who has proven to be relatively conciliatory in office.

Northern Ireland is a perennial problem, a hangover of the separation of Ireland from the United Kingdom in 1922. Six counties in the northern part of the island of Ireland, with the majority of the population consisting of Protestants favoring continued union with Great Britain, remained in the United Kingdom. Many Catholics north and south remain convinced that there should be one, united country of Ireland on the island. This fundamental division of opinion over which country should have sovereignty over the territory led to organized violence by proponents of both sides; some 3,600 people have died in sectarian violence since 1968. The provisional Irish Republican Army (IRA) was the main organization using violence in the cause of a united Ireland.

The Good Friday Agreement of 1998, brokered by the U.S. administration of Bill Clinton, was a peace accord that promised a different future through new institutions. In 1999, devolution of power from the Westminster parliament to the Belfast parliament ushered in a period of what the British call "power sharing," or "consensus democracy." This entailed not only joint authority over internal matters by both Protestants (Unionists) and Catholics (Nationalists) through the requirement of super-majorities in the Northern Ireland Assembly and executive, but also regular consultation between the United Kingdom and Ireland. Both countries pledged that Northern Ireland would remain part of the United Kingdom as long as a majority of the population in the province wishes. The latest census showed Protestants to be in the majority, 53 to 44 percent.

Referendums on the Good Friday Agreement passed overwhelmingly in both Northern Ireland and the Irish Republic; the latter also repealed its constitutional claim over the province. As expected, devolved government in Northern Ireland has been rocky. Groups representing formerly armed adversaries, including Sinn Fein, closely linked to the IRA, assumed ministerial positions in the power-sharing executive. Some dissident factions refused to renounce violence. The major issues have been the need for verification of the decommissioning of weapons and renunciation of violence by the IRA, incorporation of Catholics into the overwhelmingly Protestant police service, and divisions among Protestants about how far to cooperate with the new government. In October, 2002, these divisions led to the suspension of the Northern Ireland Assembly and government for the fourth time in three years. Direct rule from the central government in London replaced the power-sharing executive. Elections in November, 2003 resulted in the Democratic Unionist Party (DUP), which had opposed the Good Friday Agreement as a "sell out" to Catholics, becoming the largest Protestant party while Sinn Fein became the largest Catholic party. This further complicated discussions.

In 2005 the IRA finally provided evidence of decommissioning of weapons, a clear commitment to move from violence to politics although there are still concerns about its extensive involvement in criminal activities. Protestant paramilitary groups also disarmed. Nevertheless, re-forming a devolved government has been stalled by the deep cleavages and lack of trust. The British and Irish governments hope to return devolution to the province in early 2006. However, the long-awaited report of the official investigation into the circumstances of "Bloody Sunday" in 1972, in which British troops shot and killed 14 Catholic demonstrators, may further acerbate divisions. Despite progress in making peace, "normal politics" has not emerged in this most abnormal part of the United Kingdom.

Britain signed the European Convention on Human Rights in 1951. Since 1966 it has allowed appeals to the European Court of Human Rights at Strasbourg, where it has lost more cases than any other country. Under New Labor, a law was passed incorporating the European Convention on Human Rights into domestic law. British judges rather than European judges now make the decisions about whether Britain is conforming to the Convention, which enhances the ability of British citizens to raise issues of human rights in domestic courts. Parliamentary sovereignty supposedly is maintained because Westminster retains final authority on whether judicial decisions will be followed. Under the Human Rights Act, foreigners suspected of terrorism have appealed against government detention and extradition to countries where they could face persecution. In response, the government has proposed legislation constraining judges to place a higher value on national security concerns. However, this has raised questions about whether such action would interfere with judicial independence in deciding particular cases. Constitutional scholar Vernon Bogdanor has argued that the Human Rights Act is now "fundamental law," which suggests it might be beyond the ordinary reach of parliament.

The first-term Labor government later addressed other measures of constitutional reform—the electoral system for the House of Commons, freedom of information, and the House of Lords. The Freedom of Information Act eventually enacted does allow public access to more government information, but within considerable limits. Applications for information go to the ministry involved, with an Information Commissioner handling appeals. However, department ministers still can overrule decisions of the Information Commissioner. When the act began implementation in 2005, there were both rumors of departments destroying information beforehand and new revelations of what had transpired in previous governments, usually upon inquiries from media organizations. Nevertheless, British governments can still withhold a large amount of information. Overall, the United Kingdom remains one of the most secretive democracies in the world, under the doctrine of executive prerogatives of ministers of the crown.

Superficially House of Lords reform appears simple since the Parliament Act 1949, allows a government majority in the House of Commons to override any objections from the Lords. However, the capacity of the Lords to delay legislation makes reform difficult to complete, especially when there is no agreement about new arrangements. New Labor pledged to abolish voting by hereditary peers, leaving only life peers appointed by the prime minister remaining. Life peers are often senior political figures who want a more limited political role after a long career in the House of Commons. Critics labeled this a plan to make the second chamber one consisting solely of "Tony's Cronies," an entirely patronage-based body under prime ministerial

influence. In order to accomplish some early reform despite such criticism, Prime Minister Blair accepted a temporary arrangement in 1999 allowing 92 hereditary peers to remain in the 720-member House of Lords while eliminating 667 others.

There followed a plethora of proposals for the second stage of Lords reform from several official sources, including a Royal Commission, the government, a joint cross-party parliamentary committee of MPs and peers, and a cross-party group in the House of Commons. These ranged from a fully elected to a fully appointed second chamber. No consensus emerged, which further delayed the process. Critics have complained that the government's preference for a largely appointed chamber, plus possibly further limits on the power of the Lords to delay legislation, would lead to a weakened second chamber, less able to act as a check on the government. In contrast, a body with at least some elected members would provide greater democratic legitimacy. Both the Conservatives and Liberal Democrats back a partially-elected second chamber. Although still committed to eventual elimination of the remaining hereditary peers, the government has agreed not to demand party unity but to allow a free vote in parliament on the question of the new composition of the Lords. But trying to reach a decision through this process has already failed once.

Although the Prime Minister indicated that he was not "personally convinced" that a change in the electoral system was needed, he appointed an Independent Commission on the Voting System to consider alternatives to the current electoral system for the House of Commons. In 1998, the Commission recommended what is called "Alternative Vote Plus." The single-member district system would be retained, but instead of casting a vote for one person only, the electorate would rank candidates in order of preference, thus assuring a majority rather than a plurality vote for the winner. There would also be a second vote for a "preferred party." These votes would be distributed regionally, with 15-20 percent of the total seats being awarded to parties based on their proportional share, a favorable development for smaller parties.

Even such a relatively mild reform, however, generated substantial political controversy, as expected when the basis by which legislators gain their seats is challenged. The proposed change was criticized not only by the opposition Conservatives, but by also by Labor members because it might make it more difficult for Labor to obtain a single-party parliamentary majority. With Labor winning 55 percent of the seats in the election of 2005 with only 35 percent of the popular vote (and only 22% of the electorate), there were renewed calls for a new voting system.

In 2003 the government decided to move toward greater separation of powers among the executive, legislative, and judicial branches of government. Previously the Lord Chancellor was a member of all three parts—a minister in the cabinet, head of the judiciary (including authority to appoint judges), and also Speaker of the House of Lords. The highest appeals court has been the Appellate Committee of the House of Lords (Law Lords) consisting of the Lord Chancellor, twelve life peers specially appointed for this purpose, and other members of the Lords who have held high judicial office. Acting within his executive prerogative, Prime Minister Blair renamed the Lord Chancellor's position in the cabinet the Secretary for Constitutional Affairs, mainly responsible for legal administration (although this person is still often referred to as the Lord Chancellor). The government introduced legislation to remove the judiciary from the House of Lords and to designate the highest appellate court as the Supreme Court, with a reformed Judicial Appointments Commission to make recommendations for all judgeships. Despite considerable controversy, the government eventually enacted the Constitutional Reform Act 2005, which established the new Supreme Court and is due to take effect by 2008.

Some analysts argue that the most significant constitutional change in United Kingdom has been brought about not by Labor but by three actions of Conservative governments—joining the European Community (now European Union) in 1972, approving the *Single European Act* (1986), and signing the *Maastricht Treaty* (1992). Lord Denning famously observed that the European Union is an incoming tide that cannot be held back. Within the ever-expanding areas of EU competence, EU law supersedes British law, including judicial review by the European Court of Justice. Almost one half of total annual legislation in the United Kingdom now arises from the European Union. In the negotiations over the proposed EU Constitution, Britain was largely successful in maintaining its "red lines" against further centralization of the EU. Although Tony Blair promised that the United Kingdom would hold a referendum on the Constitution, its defeat in referendums in the Netherlands and France in 2005 allowed him to cancel the British referendum, thus avoiding further rancorous debate on this issue.

Britain continues to be a leading member of the "awkward squad" of countries within the EU who want to maintain strong state sovereignty within the organization rather than surrendering more authority to a supranational organization. It remains one of only three long-standing EU members not to join the European Monetary Union and its currency, the euro. If Britain were to join the central bank and adopt the euro, then control over monetary policy would effectively pass into the hands of the European Union. The Chancellor of the Exchequer (Treasury Secretary) periodically announces whether economic conditions meet the "five tests" necessary for him to recommend that Britain should converge with the Eurozone. Tony Blair has indicated that this step would only be taken with public support in a countrywide referendum.

Although not on the Labor party agenda of constitutional change, the role of the monarchy has also come under increased scrutiny in recent years. The Queen's Golden Jubilee Year in 2002, celebrating the first 50 years of her reign, was not a happy one, with two deaths and more scandals in the royal family. A resolution of the Scottish Parliament, supported by some MPs and Lords at Westminster, has petitioned the government to allow the monarch or her spouse to be a Roman Catholic, a practice forbidden by the *Act of Settlement* (1701) at the end of a period of religious wars. The heir to the throne, Prince Charles, has proposed removing the monarch's connection to the Church of England in favor of the title of a more general

"defender of faith" in what is now, despite appearances, a highly secularized country.

More vaguely, the government has suggested moving toward a "people's monarchy"—a simpler, slimmer, and less ritualized institution, perhaps with a gender-neutral inheritance. This would be more congruent with the lower profile "bicycle monarchs" common in other European countries. For the first time since Queen Victoria, there is substantial, if muted, public expression of anti-monarchist (republican) sentiments, largely in elite circles on the Labor left. However, tampering with this traditional institution, still widely revered by the public, requires extremely careful preparation as many are opposed to change.

Conflicting Views on the Effects of Constitutional Change

Labor's program of constitutional renewal already has brought about some changes in Britain. Instead of near-uniform use of the single member district, simple plurality electoral system, there are now five different systems in operation: Single Transferable Vote (a form of proportional representation with candidate choice) in Northern Ireland, party list proportional representation for European Parliament elections, alternative member systems (a combination of single member district and party list proportional) for the devolved legislatures in Scotland and Wales and the London Assembly, and a popularly elected executive through the Supplementary Vote (voting for two candidates in order of preference) for London. Plurality elections remain the norm only for the House of Commons at Westminster and English local government elections.

Until 1997 there had been only four referendums in the entire history of the United Kingdom. In its first year of office, Labor held four additional referendums (in Wales, Scotland, Northern Ireland, and London). Other countrywide ones, however, on the EU constitution, the European single currency, and the Westminster electoral system, have been canceled or postponed. There also have been local referendums on elected mayors and potentially others on regional government. Despite these increased opportunities for participation, voting turnout at all elections has plunged, reaching a low of 59 percent in the Westminster parliamentary elections of 2001 and barely increasing in 2005; turnout for the second devolved elections also decreased.

Broadly, commentators have offered four interpretations of these developments. We might term these the (1) popular social liberalism, (2) lukewarm reform/symbolic politics, (3) radicalism, and (4) constitutional incoherence. These contending explanations exist at least partially because Labor itself has never outlined a comprehensive theory behind its constitutional reforms. Constitutional reform has consisted of a series of *ad hoc* measures rather than a general constitutional convention.

The well-known American analyst of Britain, Samuel H. Beer, has compared Blair's reforms to the popular social liberalism of the early twentieth century Liberal governments, which included restricting the power of the House of Lords and devolving power to Ireland. After the First World War, however, electorally the Conservatives came to dominate Britain, as the

Left divided between an insurgent Labor Party and the remaining Liberals. In the first term of office for New Labor, social and constitutional reform served as a substitute for a more traditional Labor program of increased government spending. This was important for establishing the long-term political dominance of a revitalized center-left by appealing to the "median voter."

Another constitutional scholar, Philip Norton, has argued that New Labor's proposals are radical in concept but moderate in form and effects, e.g., lukewarm reform. Similarly, Anthony Barnett of Charter 88 claims that the government practices *constitutus interruptus*. Another British academic, Patrick Dunleavy, has suggested that constitutional reform for New Labor represents continuous but financially cheap activity at a time when the government is wary of alienating its middle-class supporters by appearing to be another Labor "tax and spend" administration. This amounts to little substantive change, however, until the two critical questions, electoral reform for the House of Commons and Britain's relationship to the EU, are addressed.

Although there has been some grudging acceptance from constitutional conservatives who originally opposed change, they are still fearful of the implications of some reforms. The former editor of *The Times*, William Rees-Mogg, envisions Labor's constitutional changes eroding democracy in the United Kingdom through a semi-permanent Labor-Liberal governing coalition in Westminster, Scotland, and Wales, a House of Lords based on patronage, and a more centralized, bureaucratic European superstate. More sanguinely, *The Economist* foresees a weakening of Westminster's authority through the combined forces of devolution and a more integrated European Union. More recently it has warned that Blair's reform program will be judged a "hypocritical failure" unless it produces a democratically-elected second chamber.

Finally, another prominent British political scientist, Anthony King, has argued that Britain no longer has a coherent set of constitutional principles. Because of the piecemeal constitutional changes over the past quarter century by both Conservative and Labor governments, traditional interpretations of the British constitution no longer adequately describe contemporary practice. But no alternative theory has emerged as a guide. Britain has moved away from its traditional status as a majoritarian democracy (all-powerful single-party governments based on holding a majority of seats in the House of Commons) without becoming a fully-fledged consensus democracy, featuring proportional representation and coalition governments.

Further Consequences Over the Horizon?

The second and third Labor terms have consolidated and extended constitutional reforms despite their lack of emphasis in party election manifestos and discussion during election campaign. Broadly, Labor has endorsed further, if gradual, reform. The Conservatives have opposed measures such as an appointed House of Lords, the Human Rights Act, further devolu-

tion to Wales, and the new Supreme Court, plus, of course, greater integration into Europe. Their major reforms would be a strengthened House of Commons less under government control and an elected House of Lords. The Liberal Democrats have the most radical positions on constitutional reform, advocating a written constitution, a bill of rights, and a more proportional voting system.

Despite Labor's constitutional reforms, commentators refer to what is often called the "Blair paradox." While the Labor government led by Blair has engaged in various constitutional innovations for decentralization and individual rights, it has not disturbed the core of the strongly executive-centered Westminster system. In fact, by dominating the cabinet, the extensive use of politically-appointed advisers throughout the executive, keeping the House of Commons under strong party direction, rarely attending parliamentary debates, and desire to have a completely appointed House of Lords, Blair's style has been claimed, debatably, to be more "presidential" than that of previous prime ministers.

Nevertheless, institutional rearrangements often have unanticipated consequences. Although New Labor legislation on constitutional matters claims not to disturb the principle of parliamentary sovereignty, this constitutional convention has already been compromised. Congruent with the process of decentralization in other European countries, devolution is likely to be entrenched *de facto* if not *de jure*. Some observers have begun calling Britain a "federal" political system. Although specific powers are granted to each devolved government, disputes over which level has authority over certain policies will eventually arise, especially if the governments are led by different parties. Even without a comprehensive Bill of Rights, incorporation of the European Convention on Human Rights may mean a stronger, more politically active judiciary, a form of creeping judicial review. House of Lords reform has become so controversial because it is a struggle over how much the second chamber should be allowed to check the House of Commons and the sitting government. Incorporation of the European Convention on Human Rights, as well as a limited form of joint authority with Ireland over Northern Ireland and possible membership of the European common currency and central bank, suggest that Britain may be moving into new patterns of international shared authority in areas heretofore considered exclusively within the domain of the sovereign state. Regional policies of the European Union even may be helping sustain ethnonationalist demands. If the Scottish National Party, still committed to independence for Scotland, ever wins a majority in the Scottish Parliament, the United Kingdom could be faced with a "Quebec scenario," whereby control of a subordinate level of government enhances secessionist claims. The SNP wants Scotland to join the EU as an independent state.

The "third way" ideas of Anthony Giddens, influential in the New Labor government, propose a restructuring of government to promote "subsidiarity" (the taking of decisions at the lowest level possible) and correcting the "democratic deficit" through constitutional reform, greater transparency, and more local democracy. In such a process, Britain would become a more complex polity institutionally. This would demand cultivating habits of conciliation, cooperation, and consent rather than the usual reliance upon single party government, parliamentary laws, and executive orders. Already this has occurred through the formation of coalition governments in Scotland and Wales as well as in Northern Ireland. Having additional levels of elected government also has created difficulties for central party organizations attempting to exert control over their parties in these jurisdictions.

The electoral system, however, may be the linchpin of the British parliamentary system as it currently exists. Even the relatively modest changes proposed by the Commission on the Voting System could realign the party system. Because of fears this arouses within the Labor party, electoral reform at Westminster is not likely to occur in the near future.

Whatever one's view of the desirability and impact of the changes, New Labor under Tony Blair has largely pursued and fulfilled its 1997 pledges on constitutional reform. Although delays and retreats have occurred on some issues, the implications of these changes will continue to be felt in British politics for some time to come.

Donley T. Studlar *is Eberly Family Distinguished Professor of Political Science at West Virginia University, served as Executive Secretary of the British Politics Group from 1994 to 2005, and wrote* Great Britain: Decline or Renewal? *(Westview Press, 1996). This article originated as the 1998 Taft Lecture, delivered to the undergraduate Honors recognition ceremony of the Political Science Department, University of Cincinnati.*

---

*This article was prepared in December, 2005. It is a revision of an article that first appeared in *Harvard International Review*, Spring 1999.

Weighing the votes
Why the electoral system favours Labour

IN THEORY, elections in Britain are beautifully simple. There are 646 seats, with boundaries set by a scrupulously independent commission. In each seat, whoever gets the most votes wins. The biggest party forms the government.

In practice, the system works like a complicated and very unfair board game. For a start (see chart), you can poll lots of votes and get far fewer seats. The big losers here are the Liberal Democrats, who won only 62 seats—just under a tenth—despite getting 22% of the vote.

Second, some votes count more than others. English constituencies have historically been bigger than those in Scotland and Wales. That hurts the Conservatives, who do better in England than elsewhere, and favours Labour.

Third, it matters hugely whose voters turn out where. Turnout was an average of 65% in Conservative-held seats, compared to around 58% in Labour seats, so a given number of votes delivers more Labour than Tory MPs. In Glasgow Central, for example, Labour won with 13,518 votes, with

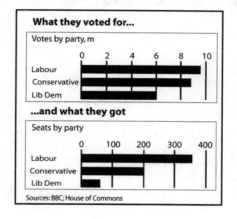

What they voted for...

Votes by party, m

Sources: BBC; House of Commons

44% bothering to vote. For the Tories, though, 21,744 votes piled up to elect their candidate in Louth and Horncastle, where turnout was 62%. Overall, it took Labour only 26,872 votes to elect an MP, the Conservatives 44,531 and the Lib Dems 96,485.

In England, where the Conservatives narrowly outpolled Labour, they still lagged 93 seats behind. That's dismal enough. But the truly awesome difficulty is in improving on it. Even new constituency boundaries based on data from 2001, rather than the current ones based on the 1991 electoral register, will continue to lag behind the big demographic shifts from inner cities to prosperous suburbs. Seats in Wales (where Labour is strong) will continue to be smaller than in the rest of the country, and the population there and in Scotland is likely to continue to shrink. That will continue to help Labour for years to come.

John Curtice of Strathclyde University says that on the new boundaries, assuming a uniform swing, the Tories will need a lead of eight to nine percentage points over Labour to gain a majority. That's a bit better than the mountainous 12 points they needed in this election, but still daunting. Tories resting their hopes on the increasing conservatism of an ageing population face a long wait.

The British General Election of 2005

Donley T. Studlar

A Historic Result

At the end of a one-month-long campaign, the Labour party achieved its third consecutive electoral victory on May 5, 2005, winning 356 seats out of 646 in the House of Commons, 55 percent of the total. The runner-up Conservatives won 197 seats, 31 percent; the Liberal Democrats 62 seats (their largest amount since the 1920s), 10 percent; and other parties, primarily in Northern Ireland, Scotland, and Wales, 30 seats, or 5 percent. Three independents, including anti-Iraq War candidate and former Labour member of Parliament George Galloway, won seats, the most since World War II.

Nevertheless, this was hardly a resounding victory. As Table 1 indicates, the shares of the vote did not correspond to the seat shares. Labour won only 35 percent of the votes cast, or only 22 percent of the total eligible electorate of the United Kingdom. This was a record low for a victorious party in a British election. Turnout was 61 percent, a slight increase on the modern record low at the last general election in 2001. "No excuse" postal voting was allowed for the first time. The Conservatives won 33 percent of the vote and actually outpolled Labour in England, where approximately 80 percent of the British population lives, by 36 percent to 35 percent, although they lost in seats there, 54 percent to 37 percent, with the Liberal Democrats gaining 23 percent of the vote in England but only 9 percent of the seats. Throughout the United Kingdom, the Liberal Democrats won 22 percent, and other parties received 10 percent.

For the ninth consecutive general election since 1974, the United Kingdom showed itself to have a multiparty electorate, even though it continues to have a largely two-party House of Commons. This is due not to gerrymandering but rather to the territorial distribution of party votes, the loss of population in many inner-city constituencies where Labour does well, and the fact that only one member is elected through plurality voting for each district. Constituency boundary revisions are not due until 2007. This result has reignited demands for a change in the single-member-district, simple-plurality electoral system to one reflecting more proportional results. But with the usual single-party majority in the legislature and government, any immediate change is unlikely.

Campaign Styles and Issues

The election campaign was a relatively dull affair until the closing days. The three major parties were not widely separated in ideology or positions on most issues. The major issues were the economy, social policy, and trust in leaders. Labour touted its record of good economic growth along with better health and educational services. The Conservatives complained about Prime Minister Tony Blair's untrustworthiness, especially over Iraq (although they supported the war on principle), and promised to improve health, education, and policing while exercising tighter control on immigration. The Liberal Democrats claimed to be the only alternative to two parties who were both to the right of center. They stood out for their positions against the Iraq War and student tuition fees.

Unlike the United States, there was not extensive debate on issues of moral values. Conservative leader Michael Howard suggested tightening the law on abortion early in the campaign, but then the parties agreed not to discuss it further. Such issues are subject to "free votes," not under party discipline, in the House of Commons.

Despite the presence of some small anti-European Union parties, one important issue that surprisingly did not feature much in the campaign was Britain's relationship to the European Union. Tony Blair's pledge to hold a referendum in 2006 on approval of the proposed EU constitution apparently took the immediate controversy out of this issue. Britain took over the rotating presidency of the European Union for six months in July 2005, gaining the opportunity to set the agenda of discussion.

Trust in the Government

During the latter part of the campaign, the issue of trust in the government focused on the shifting prewar advice that the attorney general had given the prime minister on the legality of the Iraq War. This raised an issue on which Tony Blair has been beleaguered, both within and outside his party, for three years, since a majority of the British public did not favor going to war.

Nevertheless, Labour survived this controversy electorally, although its vote and seats dropped from 2001 (see Table 1). Conservative leader Michael Howard, although able to unite his party better than recent leaders, was unable to overcome the image that the Conservatives would govern little differently from Labour other than that they were less caring about social welfare. After the election, Howard announced that he would step down as Conservative leader as soon as a replacement was chosen. This will be the fifth Conservative party leader since 1997, while Labour has had only one.

But Tony Blair already had pledged that this campaign would be his last as leader of the party. No sooner had the campaign ended than speculation began about how long he would remain. The heir apparent is his longtime chancellor of the exchequer (treasury secretary) Gordon Brown, whom many Labour activists consider to be more left wing than Blair.

With only marginal differences on issues, the campaign focused more on personalities, especially those of the party leaders, than ever before. Furthermore, campaign appeals were influenced by foreign political consultants, from the Australian Liberals (a right-wing party) in the case of the Conservatives and from the U.S. Democrats in the case of Labour. Thanks to Labour support for the Iraq policy of the U.S. administration of George W. Bush, U.S. Republican consultants stayed away from their previous natural allies, the Conservatives.

Regional Variations in Party Results

In Scotland, the number of seats was reduced by 13 to correct for previous central-level overrepresentation, since most domestic issues now are under the authority of the devolved Scottish parliament. Although Labour won 41 of the 59 seats in Scotland on 40 percent of the vote, there is four-party politics in that part of the United Kingdom. Each major party won seats; the Liberal Democrats finished second, with 23 percent of the vote and 11 seats. The party championing Scottish independence, the Scottish National Party (SNP), won six seats. The situation was similar in Wales. Labour won 29 of the 40 seats on 43 percent of the votes. The nationalist party, Plaid Cymru, won three.

In Northern Ireland, the party system is very different from the rest of the country. The two parties representing the less-compromising elements in each community, the Democratic Unionists (DUP) for the Protestants and Sinn Fein for the Catholics, won seats at the expense of the more moderate Protestant party, the Ulster Unionists (UUP). UUP leader and Nobel Peace

Table 1: Party Votes and Seats in Last Two General Elections, United Kingdom

	2001		2005	
	% of Votes	% of Seats	% of Vote	% of Seats
Labour	41	63	35	55
Conservative	32	25	32	31
Liberal Democrats	18	8	22	10
Other	9	5	10	5
	2001		2005	
Voter turnout	59%		61%	

Prize winner David Trimble lost his seat and resigned as party leader.

Despite Labour losing 47 seats, the number of women members of Parliament (MPs) rose slightly, mainly through internal Labour party efforts. Women now constitute 19.8 percent of MPs, up from 17.9 percent. Of the 128 women, 98 are Labour, an increase of three from 2001. Fifteen ethnic minority MPs of black or Asian descent were elected, 13 for Labour, despite Labour's loss of support among Muslims in several seats because of the Iraq War.

As noted, the results were very regional. Labour lost seats to the Liberal Democrats in the north of England and Scotland, while the Conservatives were their major competitors in the southeast around London. Among socioeconomic groups, Labour support held up better among women, the middle-aged, the middle class, and homeowners. Older voters were disproportionately Conservative, while the Liberal Democrats did especially well among women and younger voters. The major issues on people's minds were health care, education, crime, and pensions. While its support eroded in almost every social category, Labour's inroads into the middle class over the past three general elections, plus its remaining base in the working class, make it difficult to beat.

The cabinet Tony Blair appointed from MPs and members of the House of Lords contained many familiar faces, often in the same positions as in the previous Labour government. In opening Parliament the week after the election, the Queen's Speech set forth the new Labour government's agenda for the next year, including 44 bills. This included measures to introduce identity cards, reform disability benefits, restrict immigration and asylum claims, boost school standards, improve hygiene in public hospitals, tighten policing against antisocial behavior in cities, introduce a law against religious hatred, extend maternity leave benefits, restrict smoking indoors, strengthen antiterrorism legislation, and complete reform of the House of Lords. Once a royal commission reports, there will be a draft bill on pension reform. In foreign affairs, the government pledged to take a lead in securing more aid for Africa and in moderating climate change.

In summary, Labour won its third consecutive election for the first time ever, but with a reduced majority in Parliament and an even greater loss of votes. It showed not so much widespread popular support for the government as lack of confidence in the major alternative, the Conservatives, and an increasingly fragmented and apathetic electorate. Once Tony Blair departs as prime minister, the major question will be whether British electoral politics stabilizes under continued dominance of the Labour party or becomes more volatile.

References

BBC: www.bbc.co.uk
The British Politics Group at the University of Cincinnati: www.uc.edu/bpg

Market and Opinion Research International (MORI): www.mori.com

---

Donley T. Studlar is Eberly Family Distinguished Professor of Political Science at West Virginia University, where he teaches courses in comparative politics. For eleven years he served as Executive Secretary of the British Politics Group. A member of the Development Committee for AP Government and Politics for four years and also a Reader for the Comparative Politics exam, he is the author/editor of five books and over 100 articles, including the newly-revised co-authored text, Comparative Politics (4th ed., CQ Press 2006) and the widely-read article, "A Constitutional Revolution in Britain?" in Christopher Soe, ed., Annual Editions: Comparative Politics (Dushkin).

Politics

The strange tale of Tony Blair

**Tony Blair said he would transform British politics, and has done just that.
So why is Britain disappointed with him?**

As THIS article went to press, Tony Blair's Labour Party was preparing to celebrate its third successive election victory. The pollsters, mindful of earlier embarrassments, were emphasising the volatility of pre-election opinion, the unusually large number of undecided voters, and the disproportionate weight of a few dozen closely contested seats, many of them harder than usual to call. Even so, it seemed that the best the Tory opposition could plausibly hope for was to reduce Labour's mighty parliamentary majority. That this should be the limit of their ambitions was surprising, given that Mr Blair's popularity with voters is no longer what it was. If Britain has indeed re-elected Labour—never mind how large the majority—it will have done so with no great enthusiasm. Britain, like *The Economist*, may see no clear alternative to Mr Blair, but it has come to wish there were one.

In 1998 this newspaper called Mr Blair "the strangest Tory ever sold". The years since then have done nothing to render that judgment incorrect. Mr Blair is no Thatcherite: be clear about that. But he is nonetheless a Tory, of the old-fashioned, pre-Thatcher, one-nation sort, superbly repackaged for the modern era. The fact that he presides over an electorally successful and substantially reconstructed Labour Party, a movement that still in its heart despises every species of Tory, is one of

the things that make him such a strange and fascinating politician.

The strangeness does not stop there. Mr Blair's eight years in office have won him extraordinary standing abroad, something which he plainly relishes. In America he is talked of reverently by Democrats and Republicans alike. In a country where politics has become ever more viciously polarised, it often seems that adoration of Mr Blair is the one thing the opposing tribes can agree on. Republicans love him for his unflinching support of America's assertive foreign policy; Democrats because they see a towering figure of the centre-left, a man with the magnetism and the energy of Bill Clinton, if not quite the brains—and, would you believe it, no bimbos. They rightly give Mr Blair the credit for reinventing the Labour Party and transforming its electoral prospects. If only, they tell themselves, we could find a leader like that.

Continental Europe's regard for Mr Blair is mostly cooler, as you would expect, yet there too he is respected and, after a fashion, admired. Paradoxically (because he is uncomfortable with it) he gains a kind of strength from his country's instinctive Euroscepticism. He is viewed as expressing and representing a distinctive view of how the European Union should be run, and of Europe's place in the world, views that have gathered new support as the club has grown. His special friendship with

the United States is acknowledged, albeit grudgingly. In Europe as in America, he is seen as a bridge across the Atlantic. In its own way, Europe is impressed by Mr Blair—and will be all the more now he has won a third election victory. What would Europe's other leaders not give for that kind of longevity in power?

Yet Britain's electorate is no longer so impressed. The politician who could once say, "Trust me", or "I'm a pretty straight kinda guy", and expect an indulgent response would no longer dare: today, the response would be derision. "Lack of trust" in the government has been the motif of this election campaign. According to the polls, most voters believe that Mr Blair lied to them about Iraq. His assurances about many other aspects of government policy have come to be heavily discounted as well. His perceived qualities of firm leadership and personal appeal still register strongly with voters, but when the prime minister says something, he can no longer expect to be believed. The loss is all the greater for a man who began by making honesty and straightforwardness, against the odds, such central elements of his political personality.

A remarkable sign of his diminished standing—and of the fact that Mr Blair and his party recognise it—is that the prime minister, still a comparatively young man, recently promised that this will be his last election. In British politics, this was an unprecedented declaration. Evidently it was judged to be a vote-winner.

How did Mr Blair come to fall so far in Britain's esteem—and why, incidentally, did that fall not guarantee a sweeping victory at this election for the Tories? Iraq is part of the answer to both questions. The war has seriously damaged Mr Blair; yet it gave no clear advantage to the Tories, since on the big decisions about Iraq, as they have said, they would have done the same. On the other hand, you could argue that Iraq was only an instance, though doubtless a very important one, of a larger perceived failure of the Blair project.

Across the board, the government stands accused of elevating presentation over substance and political expediency over principle: that is what the complaint about "lack of trust" really means. Mr Blair is not charged with an occasional lapse in this regard: many voters have come to see this pattern as his basic mode of operation. In some ways the accusation is no doubt unfair, yet it has stuck.

Before Labour came to power in 1997, Mr Blair might have hoped that the term Blairism would come to stand for a distinctive set of policies, as Thatcherism did and still does. Revealingly, the word has never been needed. There is no such thing as Blairism—and if there were, the term would far more likely denote spin and other dark political arts than policy.

Arguably, though, it had to be this way. When Mr Blair seized the leadership of the Labour Party in 1994, in a manoeuvre that left Gordon Brown, the chancellor, and his supporters cursing the new leader's ruthlessness, he set himself the task of making the party electable. This was not a universally popular ambition within the party. It was also a colossal task. Examine what Mr Blair did in the period that followed, and you cannot question the man's vision or courage. Under his leadership, against the wishes of many and perhaps most of its members, the Labour Party was completely reinvented—and in a hurry, too. Mr Blair and his team were not

shy about what they were doing. Just the opposite: they boasted about it.

This was not merely a dusted-down and smartened-up Labour Party, this was New Labour—to all intents and purposes, another party altogether. Shibboleths such as clause four (the party's absurd yet cherished commitment to take the whole economy into public ownership) were ritually torn down. These were fights Mr Blair chose to pick; he won every one. The changes were not superficial. They ripped the party up by its roots, and that was the idea. The trade unions, formerly the party's paymasters and the font of its old ideology, were appalled. Mr Blair loved it that they were appalled: what could be more pleasing to voters at large? His mission was to steal the party from its previous owners, and have it understood that that was what he had done. He succeeded.

Was New Labour really so different? Refresh your memory of the previous version by looking at John Prescott—the pantomime socialist thug conveniently retained by Mr Blair in the meaningless post of deputy prime minister to appease the old guard. Mr Prescott, virtually invisible during this campaign, was the party Mr Blair inherited. Ponder that, look at the party now, and see how far it has come.

But effecting this astounding transformation, and then securing that first electoral victory in 1997 (to which everything else came second), called for two more things. One was a ruthless world-class election-winning machine, capable of steering the press, shredding the Tories every time they opened their mouths and exerting ferocious discipline on the party's hitherto-wayward members and MPs. That fearsome machine was duly built. Britain had seen nothing like it.

The other requirement was a completely new programme for government—new to Labour, that is. This had to strike a very difficult balance. It had to be specific and detailed enough to allay suspicions that a party so long in opposition

might be unprepared for government. It had to stifle concerns that New Labour would be as loose with public money as the old party. It had to recognise, silently, that many of the economic reforms of the Thatcher era had been both necessary and overdue; it had to promise, under its breath, that those reforms would not be reversed. And yet it had to convey to the party's core supporters, who deplored the Thatcher era and all its works, that New Labour was still worth voting for.

The two Faces of Tony Blair

From its very conception, in other words, New Labour had two faces—and had to have. It presented one of them to the new supporters it needed to reach: voters who had elected four consecutive Conservative administrations, who were ready (to put it mildly) for a change, but who did not want to see the policies of those administrations simply reversed. The other face was shown to the party's members and traditional supporters: they might no longer be very clear about their socialist principles, but they knew that if they were anything, they were still anti-Tory. Happily for Mr Blair, many of these, even now, regard adopting soft Tory policies as a small price to pay for kicking the despised Conservatives out of power. At any rate, this was the unsteady coalition on which New Labour based its rule.

In a survey of "Britain's new politics" which appeared in *The Economist* in 1996, we argued that holding this peculiar coalition together, in such a way that neither side became so bitterly disappointed with Mr Blair's Labour Party that they chose to abandon it, would require the leadership of a political genius. The article also acknowledged the possibility that Mr Blair, who by that time had already stamped himself indelibly on British political history, might in fact be a political genius. Sure enough, though his coalition has come under strain from time to time, it has not yet—or so it appears—fallen apart.

Even recognising Mr Blair's talents, it must be noted that the Tories themselves deserve much of the credit. The memory of Britain's humiliating ejection from Europe's exchange-rate mechanism in 1992 is still vivid, neither forgotten nor forgiven: "Black Wednesday" destroyed the Tories' reputation for economic competence in the space of an hour, and more than ten years later the damage has not been repaired. Polls have consistently shown that Labour is regarded as a better steward of the economy. One particularly remarkable sign of this is a recent poll finding (YouGov in the *Daily Telegraph* of April 18th) that Britain believes the Tories would be about as likely to raise taxes after the election, were they to win it, as Labour. The Tories' greater desire to keep taxes low can hardly be in doubt: apparently, their competence on the point is what is questioned.

Labour, with luck on its side (and by 1997 with strongly improving public finances too, courtesy of the Tories), has run the economy pretty well. To that end, its instant granting of control over interest rates to the Bank of England was a masterstroke. The Tories make a sad contrast. Even under the relatively competent leadership of Michael Howard, they have often seemed to be reeling still from the setbacks of more than a decade ago.

Be that as it may, New Labour came to power with an intellectually ambivalent programme, and relying on the support of an unruly and uncomfortable alliance of constituencies. As a result, its preoccupations with spin, with tyrannical centralised party discipline and with the need for a marked flexibility of political principle were not optional extras. New Labour could not have ground the Tories down so effectively without them. The problem for Mr Blair was that as these necessary methods of political control became more obtrusive—not least over Iraq—Britain grew disenchanted with them. The leader could no

longer get away with his always disingenuous pose of "what you see is what you get."

Groucho Marx once famously observed, "The secret of success is sincerity. Once you can fake that, you've got it made." Mr Blair faked it too much, and got found out. But in a way, justice is served: now, even when he really is sincere, he is assumed to be faking it.

There is no evidence that Mr Blair ever "lied" about Iraq. That is true of the controversy over what was known about weapons of mass destruction, and it is also true of the most recent disclosures about the advice given to him about whether an attack on Iraq would conform to international law. In all likelihood Mr Blair believed, along with all the experts advising him, that Iraq did indeed have weapons of mass destruction. And most likely he also believed that Britain's interests and the greater good required him to support George Bush's plan to oust Saddam Hussein—and that a strong case for such action could be made in international law.

Phoney Tony

Yet Mr Blair was not, as he would put it, straight with the people, or with Parliament, or even with much of his own government, in stating these convictions. The real calculations, defensible as they may have been, were done by the prime minister's small circle of trusties and spin-doctors. The flow of information to the cabinet, to the wider civil service and to the public at large was controlled and manipulated not (or not only) according to the demands of national security, but mainly to smooth Mr Blair's political path. (This, remember, was a government that had promised a brave new openness and "transparency".) Thus, for instance, the government evaded and denied the awkward truth that compliance with international law might forbid the course of action that was nonetheless, all things considered, in the country's best interests. Mr Blair, as always,

hoped to have it both ways. And who can blame him? More often than not in the course of his career, he managed to do just that.

At home, the main awkward truth that needed to be brushed over was that New Labour was largely consolidating, albeit softening, the reforms of previous Tory administrations. Again, that policy was not wrong. It was most likely in Britain's best interests, and for New Labour it was anyway politically necessary. But for a man of Mr Blair's ambition and vanity, it was also embarrassing. He wanted to be regarded as a radical in his own right—a transformer of the country, in the mould of Margaret Thatcher, not merely of his own party. This inclined Mr Blair and his circle to a perpetual state of making a great fuss over nothing. What New Labour lacked in substance, it could make up for in public relations. And, to be sure, the team for that was in place.

Remember the "Third Way"? Probably not. That was New Labour's grand unified theory of the new politics—a distinct ideology, neither socialism nor neoliberalism, to explain how kindly 1970s-vintage Tory policies were really a fresh-minted response to the 21st-century challenges of globalisation, post-modern international relations, the end of history and so forth. The policies weren't bad, on the whole. The encompassing new ideology did not even survive the first term.

At the smaller scale, New Labour's hyper-energetic public-relations machine ensured that every fluctuation in policy was elaborately packaged and repackaged, launched and repeatedly relaunched, each time as an entirely new policy more radical than any previously conceived. Initiatives and their supporting documentation poured forth in a torrent. The method soon descended into self-parody. At some point, diminishing returns, so far as the public's perception was concerned, set in. Worse than generating mere boredom, the strategy of permanent policy revolution bred weariness and cynicism. Politically, it became counter-productive: often the government now finds itself getting less credit than it deserves for its innovations, such as they are.

In only one broad area of policy can the government claim to have been genuinely radical, in fact: constitutional reform. The government granted substantial devolution to Scotland, and recast the House of Lords. Unfortunately, the reform of the Lords was a debacle. Overturning the hereditary principle was both popular and right, but the government's consequently increased powers of patronage are a travesty of democratic propriety. In other areas of policy, there is often plenty to like, but rarely much that is really new—most good things (as in health and education) being variations of earlier Tory ideas, either retained, or belatedly rediscovered, or extended; and always, of course, the tiresome threadbare pretence that the policies are wholly New.

The strangest Tory over-sold

To a large extent, therefore, Britain is disappointed with Mr Blair and New Labour simply because it is tired of the party's remorseless, pathological, high-pressure salesmanship. Circumstances surrounding the party's rebirth decreed it had to be that way. And it need not subtract much, if anything, from history's verdict on Mr Blair. If he has succeeded, after all, in consolidating centrist politics within the Labour Party, and hence in the country, that will be something to be proud of. Has he? In all likelihood, yes—though it will take a full term of Labour in power under a different leader to be sure.

A divided self:
A Survey of France

France has an identity problem. It needs to find the courage
to redefine itself, says John Andrews

"I HAVE heard and understood your call: that the republic should live, that the nation should reunite, that politics should change." On a cold evening in early May, Jacques Chirac found the right words for the moment. He had just been re-elected president of the French republic, with 82% of the vote, in a run-off with Jean-Marie Le Pen, the leader of the extreme-right National Front. Two weeks earlier, in the first round of the election, Mr Le Pen had eliminated the Socialist candidate (and incumbent prime minister), Lionel Jospin, from the contest. For left-leaning voters, Mr Chirac was clearly the lesser evil, so in the run-off they joined forces with Mr Chirac's centre-right to humble Mr Le Pen. Hence Mr Chirac's carefully chosen words: his victory may have been sweet, but it was hardly unqualified.

Doubtless that is why as prime minister of his "government of mission", Mr Chirac appointed Jean-Pierre Raffarin, a pudgy and amiable former senator from the Poitou-Charentes region. Mr Raffarin's motto is *la France d'en bas*, grassroots France, which is supposed to mean not only a government closer to the people but a government that comes from the people.

So six months later, is the nation "reunited"; has politics changed; is the republic "alive"? The answers are horribly muddled, mainly because the French themselves are muddled: over France's place in Europe, over the impact of globalisation and, at root, over what it means to be French. In their hearts they want precious little to change; in their heads they suspect change is inevitable.

If it is, their worry is not just what the change will be, but how and when it will come. On June 17th, the day after a parliamentary election in which Mr Chirac's supporters (most of them members of the newly assembled and aptly named Union for the Presidential Majority) won 399 of the National Assembly's 577 seats, the headline of the conservative *Le Figaro* proclaimed: "Five years to change France". Given that there will be no significant elections before the next presidential and parliamentary polls, due in 2007, the opportunity is there. But if change does come, many will not like it: the leftist *Libération*'s headline sarcastically predicted "A five-year sentence".

Whatever the headlines say, for most of France's 59m people not much has changed since the bout of elections in the spring. Around 9% of the workforce is still without a job; the rest troop off to their offices and factories just as before, cosseted by laws that protect them from quick lay-offs, provide them with one of the world's shortest working weeks—just 35 hours—and give them holiday entitlements Americans can only dream of. Meanwhile, their country remains as beautiful and seductive as ever, and the two-hour lunch is alive and well. Add trains that run fast and on time, modern motorways in good repair, and a med-

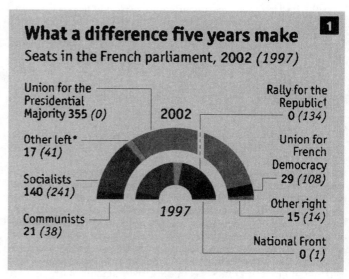

What a difference five years make

Seats in the French parliament, 2002 *(1997)*

Union for the Presidential Majority 355 *(0)* 2002

Other left* 17 *(41)*

Socialists 140 *(241)*

Communists 21 *(38)* *1997*

Rally for the Republic† 0 *(134)*

Union for French Democracy 29 *(108)*

Other right 15 *(14)*

National Front 0 *(1)*

*Includes Radical Party of the Left, 7 (12); Greens, 3 (7)
†In 2002 it was absorbed into the Union for the Presidential Majority
Sources: French interior ministry; *The Economist*

ical system at the top of the World Health Organisation's international rankings. Surely the French have a right to feel pleased with themselves?

Not altogether superior

So why do they feel so insecure? Why do politicians, pundits and philosophers (a breed revered on French television) feel a need to bolster the country's collective morale by pointing out the deficiencies of the "Anglo-Saxon" way, be they fraudulent accountancy practices in America or decrepit private railways in Britain?

One reason is doubtless a dash of *Schadenfreude*. Within the lifetime of its senior citizens, France has been occupied by Germany, rescued by America and Britain, and then divested—bloodily in the case of Algeria and Indochina—of almost all its colonies. Since then English has become the world's common language (so much so that France's own politicians will now

Same bed, different dreams
Better to cohabit than be out in the cold

IS IT sensible for France to have a president from one side of the political divide and a government from the other? Olivier Schrameck, chief of staff to Mr Jospin from 1997 until May this year, devoted much of a recent book, "Matignon Rive Gauche, 1997–2001", to denouncing such "cohabitation" as a waste of energy and a recipe for immobility. Under cohabitation, the government would run the country, but the president, who retains traditional authority over defence and foreign policy (the constitutional authority is rather vague), would be tempted to snipe from the sidelines.

Yet French voters have forced such liaisons on their country three times since the birth of the Fifth Republic in 1958. The first time was when the left was defeated in the parliamentary elections of 1986. The Socialist François Mitterrand, who had been elected president in 1981, had to put up with a centre-right government led by Jacques Chirac as prime minister. In 1988 Mitterrand was re-elected president and dissolved parliament. In the ensuing elections the Socialists returned to power. In 1993, however, the left-wing government was voted out and Mitterrand had to cohabit with the centre-right once again, this time with Edouard Balladur as prime minister. Two years later this cohabitation ended with the election of Mr Chirac as president. But in 1997 Mr

Chirac provoked the third cohabitation—much tenser than the first two—by calling early parliamentary elections that the left, led by Mr Jospin, won handsomely.

Such cohabitations could happen because the presidential term was for seven years and that of the lower house of parliament, the National Assembly, for five. But in future there will be less opportunity for these oddball relationships. In September 2000, after an arcane debate between constitutional experts and self-interested politicians, a bemused electorate decided in a referendum (in which only 30% cast a vote) that, beginning with the elections of 2002, the president would have the same five-year term as the parliament.

Since a president might die in office, or might dissolve parliament early, there could still be cohabitations in the future. But as long as President Chirac remains in the post, he is unlikely to call early elections again. For the record, he used to be a fierce opponent of reducing the seven-year presidential term, but changed his mind. His critics say he feared that voters in 2002 might think him too old for another seven-year term but young enough for five years (he will be 70 later this month). He himself claims he supported the change in order to modernise France.

---

speak it in public), America has turned into the world's only superpower and Hollywood has come to dominate the world's entertainment industry. For France, a country which believes that its revolution, just as much as America's, bears a universal message, these changes have not been easy to accept. Seeing someone else having a hard time provides some light relief.

But there are also more troubling reasons for this lack of confidence. One is the feeling, especially among industrialists and businessmen, that France's economic formula, involving higher taxes and social charges than in most of the countries its firms compete with, will not work forever. Indeed, it is already fraying at the edges. At the start of the 1990s, France ranked eighth in the world in terms of economic output per person, but by the end of the decade it had slipped to 18th.

The most important reason, however, is a lurking suspicion that French society itself is not working. Go back to the first round of the presidential election on April 21st, with its 16 candidates, and ask a few simple questions. Why did Mr Jospin, arguably France's most effective prime minister in the 44 years of the Fifth Republic, get only 16.2% of the vote? Why, in that round, did Mr Chirac get only 19.9%, the lowest ever for an incumbent president? Why did 13 no-hoper candidates gather up 47% of the vote between them? And why did a record 28.4% of the electorate abstain? Most bothersome of all, why did Mr Le Pen, ostracised throughout his 40-odd years in politics, win 16.9% of the vote and so pass through to the second round?

There are plenty of superficial answers: Mr Jospin lacked charm; Mr Chirac was stained by alleged corruption; the electorate felt free to indulge its whims because it assumed that a runoff between Messrs Jospin and Chirac was pre-ordained; and Mr Le Pen is a brilliant orator. But there is a more fundamental explanation. As one French journalist, Philippe Manière, puts it in a recent book, the first-round result was "the vengeance of the people".

A question of colour, a matter of faith
France must face up to its immigrant problems

JEAN-MARIE LE PEN, at ease in his drawing room, waves an arm as if to state the obvious: "The greatest challenge is demographic. The countries of the north—the world of the white man, or let's say the non-black world—have an ageing population. They are rich, and they are facing a third world of 5 billion people, maybe more tomorrow, who are very young and dynamic. This dynamism will be translated into immigration."

Outside the room, the guard-dogs are asleep. In the urban plain below the Le Pen mansion (inherited from a political admirer) in Saint-Cloud, the Paris evening rush-hour is under way. The National Front leader goes on: "The rise of Islam is more the result of its youth and dynamism than its religious values. It's a demographic problem which will lead to immigration, whose consequences could lead, if nothing is done, to the submersion of our country, our people, our civilisation... No government, whether by ideology or by blindness, has realised the danger."

France's far-right bogeyman gained second place in the presidential election by saying what few other politicians would either want to or dare to: that the French republic has too many immigrants, who in turn have too many children. But that is putting it politely. What the National Front and the National Republican Movement, its rival on the extreme right, really mean is that France has too many inhabitants who are black, brown and Muslim. And lots of them are not immigrants at all, but were born in France and are French citizens.

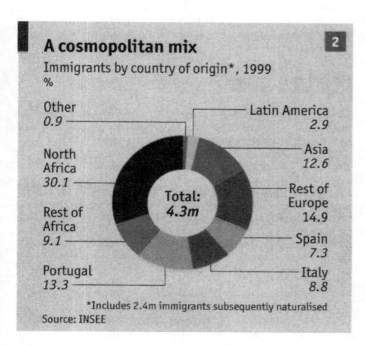

A cosmopolitan mix
Immigrants by country of origin*, 1999
%

Other 0.9

North Africa 30.1

Rest of Africa 9.1

Portugal 13.3

Latin America 2.9

Asia 12.6

Rest of Europe 14.9

Spain 7.3

Italy 8.8

Total: 4.3m

*Includes 2.4m immigrants subsequently naturalised
Source: INSEE

There are plenty of other politicians who have dabbled in the politics of race. Governments of the right have over the years enacted increasingly strong laws to restrict immigration, and governments of the left have for the most part accepted them. Mr Chirac, definitely not a racist himself, found it useful in the 1988 presidential election campaign to refer to the "odours" of immigrant cooking.

What makes Mr Le Pen different is that he has consistently preached the same xenophobic message ever since he entered politics. He became France's youngest member of parliament in 1956, at the age of 27, and first stood for the presidency in 1974. France's ills, he has said all along, are the fault of foreigners, including fellow members of the European Union. The remedy is to keep out foreigners, produce more French children, build more prisons, cut taxes and leave the EU.

The question is why that message suddenly found more resonance with the voters in last spring's presidential election than ever before in Mr Le Pen's political career. Mr Le Pen's previous best score was 14.4% in the first round in 1988, and the only time his party has ever gained more than one seat in the National Assembly was in 1986, when the elections, exceptionally, were held by proportional representation.

The answer is surely not that nearly a fifth of the voters suddenly decided that Mr Le Pen's programme made practical sense, nor that all those who cast their ballot for him are anti-Semitic fascists (Mr Le Pen has described the gas chambers as a "detail" of the second world war, and thinks that Maurice Pa-

pon, the Vichy official who in the late 1990s was eventually convicted for crimes against humanity, was innocent). More likely, the voters wanted to jog the governing elite into action. As a former Socialist prime minister, Laurent Fabius, once said, "Le Pen poses good questions and offers bad solutions."

So what might a good solution look like? A useful start would be, literally, to enumerate France's problems. Malek Boutih, the French-born son of Algerian immigrants and now the president of SOS-Racisme, an anti-racism organisation, argued in a recent book that "France is wrong not to publish, as other countries like America do, statistics of criminality by social category, age, place, type of city development and so on. It is even more wrong not to establish a public debate on the question, as though the French are so irrational that they cannot calmly consider the reality of their problems."

Crime matters

But should that mean a debate on crime as well? Polls before the election showed that the subject topped the list of their concerns, ahead of the state of the economy or pensions or even unemployment. Whether crime in France is worse than in other countries is a moot point: criminal statistics are hard to compare, and although one study showed that France in 2000 had proportionately more crimes than America, other studies suggest that it did a little better than, say, Germany or Belgium. However, what matters to French people is what happens in France.

Or more precisely, what they think is happening. Nicolas Sarkozy, the interior minister, has won plaudits for not only identifying crime as a serious problem but being seen to be doing something about it. Barely a week goes by without him being photographed with a smiling collection of police or gendarmes. Mr Sarkozy has secured the money to add another 6,500 police to the 146,000 he took over from his predecessor. And Mr Raffarin has appointed a junior minister in the justice ministry specifically to supervise a building programme that will add 11,000 prison places to the 47,000 already occupied.

In terms of public perception, such measures will help. One poll in September found that the proportion of those questioned who felt they were "often" at risk of crime was 49%—shockingly high in absolute terms but actually slightly less than in the autumn of last year. Mr Sarkozy has been able to trumpet a reduction in reported crime, by 4.5% in August compared with a year earlier, the first such fall for five years. In Paris, where the tourist industry has long complained about the plague of pickpockets, the fall was 11%.

Whether the momentum can be sustained is another matter. In the country that produced the Declaration of Human Rights (in 1789, a satisfying two years before America's Bill of Rights), the new enthusiasm for "zero tolerance" becomes hard to swallow when it means giving the authorities greater powers of arrest and punishment.

According to critics, many of them well placed in the judiciary and the media, the government is eroding the presumption of innocence (never particularly robust in France, which has no Anglo-Saxon protection of *habeas corpus*); it casually treats many young offenders as though they were adults; and it is callously cracking down on France's most marginal residents, from Romanian beggars to African prostitutes. In other words, the critics allege that the Raffarin government—and Mr Sarkozy in particular—is doing the work of Mr Le Pen for him.

Press Mr Boutih on whether criminal statistics should include a breakdown by race or religion, and he immediately says no: "I remain convinced that ethnic origin is less relevant than the level of education and social status." He has a point: a well-educated Arab or black Frenchman with a decent job is unlikely to turn to petty drug-dealing or car-stealing. The trouble, according to Tahar Ben Jelloun, a Moroccan who is one of France's finest writers, is that only 4% of the children of immigrants get to university, compared with 25% of their native contemporaries.

Our ancestors the Gauls

But the main reason for Mr Boutih's resistance is that to collect information by race or religion would offend the very French concept of "republican values", because it would discriminate between citizens rather than treat them as equal. France makes no allowance for cultural differences: "our ancestors the Gauls" applies to schoolchildren of every hue. In this secular republic, the idea of collecting racial and religious statistics is a virtual taboo across the whole of the political spectrum. Such statistics, it is feared, will lead France along the Anglo-Saxon road of "communautarisme" (in which the idea of separate communities within the country as a whole is acceptable). In the words of the constitution, the French republic is indivisible, and having separate communities is seen as automatically leading to divisions.

Yet the sad reality is that France's race relations are no better than anyone else's. Arab and black minorities are as much as ever excluded from the mainstream. In opinion polls in the late 1990s, two-fifths of the respondents admitted to being at least "a little bit" racist (more than in any other European Union country except Belgium), and just over half thought there were "too many Arabs" in France.

The lack of solid figures leads to the sort of guesswork that plays into the far-right's hands. The state statistics office, INSEE, reckons that in 1999 (the year of the most recent census) the total number of foreign-born residents in metropolitan France, including 2.4m who have acquired French nationality, was 4.3m, or 7.4% of the metropolitan population of 58.5m. Of these, 1.3m had come from Algeria, Morocco and Tunisia. But the official figures end with that breakdown by country of origin.

The best estimate for the religious breakdown that INSEE is not allowed to publish comes from a scholarly report presented to the prime minister two years ago by the High Council for Integration, a committee of academics and experts. The report reckoned that France is home to 4m–5m Muslims—defined by culture rather than religious observance—of whom up to half have French nationality. Of the Muslim total, almost 3m are of North African origin or ancestry, with 1.5m from Algeria, 1m from Morocco and the rest from Tunisia. Of the other Muslims, Turks probably number 350,000, sub-Saharan Africans about 250,000, and assorted Middle Easterners (Iranians and Kurds, as well as Arabs) the remainder. So France's Muslims make up at most one in 12 of the population—and its Arabs one in 20.

Yet the media keep repeating that there are at least 6m Arabs in France, and quite possibly as many as 8m, who are regularly accused of crime, vandalism, the abuse of social services and other wrongdoings. It is easy for the elite and the comfortable middle classes to dismiss Mr Le Pen's view of the world, but less so for those—especially les petits blancs (poor whites)—who live in crime-ridden working-class neighbourhoods. According to the analysts, in the first round of the presidential election Mr Le Pen won the support of only 8% of those with a college education, but 30% of blue-collar voters and 38% of the unemployed.

Chronic or curable?

Pessimists argue that the situation will get worse before it gets better. France's high rate of unemployment is not about to tumble overnight. Nor are the high-rise public housing blocks built from the 1950s to the 1970s in the banlieue, or suburbs, of most French towns. At the time, they were intended to provide affordable housing to the influx of workers from the countryside

and from the colonies or ex-colonies. Now they have all too often become virtual ghettoes, each storey dotted with satellite dishes pointed towards the television stations of the Maghreb. But the problem extends far beyond the banlieue. The same combination of poverty, race and social exclusion can be found in the medieval villages of Provence, or in some down-at-heel parts of Paris such as the 10th or 19th arrondissements.

The passage of time, say the pessimists, is not healing cultural rifts but making them worse. The generation of immigrants from the Maghreb were often illiterate peasants, keen to work hard in a country whose language they could barely understand. By contrast, their children, and now their children's children, are French-born and French-educated, and have lost respect for their immigrant parents or grandparents. That has caused a loss of parental authority, and often a multitude of behavioural problems in the disciplined world of French schools.

How French can you get?

Moreover, being French-born and French-educated does not mean that an Abdel-Karim or a Samira will be treated the same as a Jean-Pierre or a Marianne. To be white and born in France of French parents and grandparents means you are a Français de souche—of "French stock". But to be born in France of Arab ancestry makes you a beur, a word which for most Arab Frenchmen has no pejorative undertone (there is, for example, the Beur-FM radio station). The word is a kind of inversion of the word Arabe, part of an argot of inversion called verlan (l'envers, or back-to-front), which turns français into cefran and café into féca. This is undoubtedly of linguistic interest, but the language is also a sign of exclusion, sometimes self-imposed. Beur is now so universal that the new word among the beurs is rebeu, a verlan of a verlan.

How to end that exclusion? In America the answer might be affirmative action or positive discrimination, but in France such notions are seen as a threat to a republic which presumes its citizens to be free, equal and brotherly to begin with. When Sciences-Po, an elite university, last year began a special entry programme for a handful of bright students from the "zones of priority education" in the banlieue around the cities of Paris and Nancy, current and former students reacted with horror: their beloved meritocratic institution was slipping down the Anglo-Saxon slope.

Mr Boutih understands the gap between republican theory and everyday practice all too well: "The republican model is not a natural one. It exists through political will. Communautarisme is the natural model." So why not adopt the natural one instead? "Because society will explode from within. Each community will define itself against another, as in the United States."

Arguably, that process is already under way. In October last year, at a soccer match in Paris between France and Algeria, young beurs greeted the French national anthem with a storm of whistles and later invaded the pitch, brandishing Algerian flags. Young beurs are increasingly turning to Islam, not so much as a faith but as a symbol of identity: they fast during the month of Ramadan, insist on religiously correct food in their school canteens and stay at home to mark religious holidays.

A small minority go a lot further, falling under the influence of extremist imams from the Gulf or North Africa. In their fight to dismantle al-Qaeda, Europe's and America's intelligence services have uncovered a disturbing number of French suspects, not least Zacarias Moussaoui, currently on trial in America for his alleged role in the September 11th attacks on America last year. And a number of young beur layabouts have used the excuse of the Arab-Israeli conflict to indulge in anti-Jewish violence and vandalism (at over 600,000, France's Jewish minority is Europe's largest).

The *Français de souche* are accomplices in this process, not just in the April 21st vote for Mr Le Pen or in their reluctance to offer Arabs (and blacks) the same job prospects as whites, but also in the open antagonism some of them display towards the Arabs in their midst. To justify their stance, they quote the inferior status of Muslim women, or the dreadful gang-rapes of "easy" Muslim girls that some Muslim boys regard as a rite of passage. It is no accident that Oriana Fallaci's book "The Rage and the Pride", an extremist tirade against Muslims in general and Arabs in particular, spent so many weeks on this year's French bestseller list.

Could the pessimists be wrong? Back in 1998, France rejoiced in the World Cup victory of a French soccer team starring plenty of blacks and *beurs* (including the incomparable Zinedine Zidane, born of Algerian parents in the Marseilles *banlieue*). Sami Naïr, an Algerian-born member of the European Parlia-

ment and formerly an adviser on immigration to the Jospin government, points out that in an earlier wave of immigration into France, in the early part of the 20th century, Roman Catholics from Italy and Poland were accused of "trying to impose religion on our secular state". Yet in the end, he says, the discrimination fades and the newcomers' descendants end up as *Français de souche*: "I think it will be solved in a generation."

Yet there is an obvious difference between the present wave of migrants and previous waves: the *beurs* and their parents are the first minority that can be physically distinguished from the *Français de souche*. Their assimilation cannot be achieved by fading into the background. Instead, Mr Naïr proposes a pact: the government must live up to the values of the republic when dealing with its Arabs—and the *beurs* must accept the duties that go with them, including equality of the sexes. That might be easier if the economy could deliver more jobs.

A new kind of solidarity

France needs more jobs and less state. The two are not unconnected

NOW is not a good time to be prime minister of France, and Jean-Pierre Raffarin knows it only too well. The world economy is in the doldrums, and the French economy is becalmed with it; investor confidence is low; and the trade unions are restive. Last month, for example, thousands of public-sector workers (80,000 according to the unions; 40,000 according to the police) marched through the centre of Paris to defend their privileges as public servants or agents of the state, and to denounce modest plans for privatisation. On the same day, INSEE, the government statistical office, announced that economic growth for this year was now likely to be only 1%, compared with its forecast in June of 1.4% (and the previous government's self-serving prediction of 2.5% before the elections).

If INSEE is right, then the budget for next year presented in October by the finance minister, Francis Mer, becomes an exercise in fiction. It assumes growth of 1.2% this year and 2.5% next, and a budget deficit of 2.6% of GDP. Instead, the deficit could well break through the 3% limit set by the European Union in its collective quest for economic stability. In other words, crisis looms: the EU will want French belts to be tightened, whereas the voters, worried about their jobs and mortgages, want them loosened.

Engraved in the country's political consciousness is the memory of 1995, the last time a centre-right president was elected with a centre-right majority in parliament. The prime minister of the day was the intellectually brilliant but aloof Alain Juppé; he was determined that France should qualify for membership of the euro zone, which meant keeping the franc closely in line with the D-mark while simultaneously cutting the budget deficit (then running at 5% of GDP). This he hoped to do by reforming the public sector, which would restrain public spending. Instead, he saw hundreds of thousands of public-sector workers taking to the streets in a wave of protests and strikes, with the sympathy of most of the population. Two years later, when President Chirac rashly called an early general election to obtain a popular mandate for the EU's single currency, the right was swept from power.

Not surprisingly, Mr Raffarin and his colleagues are keen to prevent history repeating itself. Their strategy is to tread softly, even to speak softly. In opposition, the right accused Lionel Jospin of "immobility". Now the bosses' association, Medef (Mouvement des Entreprises de France), lays the same charge

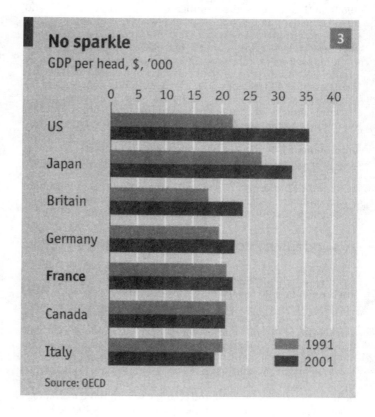

No sparkle
GDP per head, $, '000

Source: OECD

against Mr Raffarin: it accuses him of being too timid in dealing with the consequences of the 35-hour working week, introduced by Mr Jospin (who cut it from 39 hours with no loss of pay), or with the previous government's "Law on Social Modernisation" (which makes it harder than ever for employers to fire people, thus discouraging them from hiring in the first place). The bosses fear that if Mr Raffarin shows the same timidity in other areas, notably slimming down the civil service and reforming pensions, the country will continue its slide down the international scale of GDP per person.

Just as this is a bad time for Mr Raffarin to be prime minister, the previous period was a good time for Mr Jospin. The world economy, powered by America and its dotcom infatuation, was growing strongly, and France, the world's fifth-biggest exporter, reaped the benefits. A series of partial privatisations (or "openings of capital", in the words of Mr Jospin, an ex-Trotskyist well aware of the need to placate the Communists in his coalition) helped to keep the country's finances in excellent shape. Inflation, the public debt and the budget deficit were all low, and economic growth in 1998–2000 averaged 3.3% a year. Successive finance ministers basked in the plaudits of the International Monetary Fund and the OECD.

Growing jobs

All this may have encouraged Mr Jospin to believe that full employment had become a realistic target for France. Certainly a report in December 2000 by Jean Pisani-Ferry, of the Council of Economic Analysis, a body of experts set up by Mr Jospin to give him independent advice, seemed to be suggesting as much. The report noted that in the four years from the start of 1997 France had created 1.6m jobs, "twice as many as during the 1960s and ten times the number created between 1974 and 1996". The drop in the jobless, it said, was "unprecedented".

The government was keen to take the credit. In the run-up to this year's elections, it claimed that the 35-hour week, which came into effect in February 2000 for firms with more than 20 employees (it has yet to be fully applied to small firms), had already created 400,000 jobs. The idea was that to compensate for the shorter week, bosses would have to take on more employees, and could be encouraged to do so through temporary relief on their payroll taxes. The government noted, too, that 320,000 young people had found work since 1997 through the youth employment scheme, under which young people were given five-year contracts in the public sector, for example as school playground assistants or as guards at railway stations and other public buildings. At the beginning of 2001 the government had also taken steps to lessen the poverty trap, in which recipients of state benefits lose out if they take a low-paid job.

A success of sorts

But how much of the credit for all these extra jobs did the Jospin government really deserve? On closer scrutiny, the Pisani-Ferry report reads less like a congratulatory pat on the government's back and more like a warning that things must change. For a start, much of the job creation was simply the result of economic growth. Further, full employment was defined as a jobless rate of 5% or less of the workforce, a rate that in happier days for the world economy would have been considered fairly disastrous in, say, Japan or Singapore. The report also argued that to achieve this target by 2010, the country would have to create at least 300,000 new jobs a year, perhaps as many as 400,000.

That, however, would require large-scale liberalisation, of the sort introduced by Margaret Thatcher, Britain's radical prime minister of the 1980s—and French vested interests are most unlikely to allow that to happen. Besides, there is little sign of a French Lady Thatcher emerging. Only Alain Madelin, of the Liberal Democrats, currently speaks a Thatcherite language of free markets and a minimalist state, and he won a mere 3.9% of the vote on April 21st.

All this puts a different perspective on the labour-market "success" of the Jospin term. True, unemployment fell from the 12.2% of the workforce inherited from the right in 1997, but only

to 9%, getting on for twice as much as in Britain or America—at a time when the economy was booming and employers had jobs they could not fill. The economists concluded that 9%, or a smidgen less, was—and is—France's "structural" rate of unemployment, which can be reduced only by changing the make-up of the economy.

Go to the lovely Place du Capitole in Toulouse, or ride the subway system in Lyons, or watch a game of street-soccer in a Marseilles housing estate, and the economic jargon translates into bored young men whiling away their days doing nothing in particular: no wonder many of them trade drugs to supplement their meagre state benefits. People over 25 receive the RMI (*revenu minimum d'insertion*), created in 1988 to provide a "minimum income for inclusion in society". For a single man with no dependants, this amounts to €406 ($405) a month. In a land of plenty, some 1m of France's 24m households rely on the income of the country's 2.2m *eremistes*.

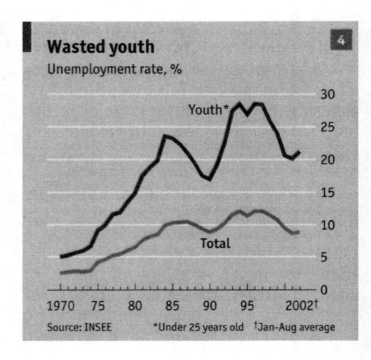

Wasted youth
Unemployment rate, %

Youth*

Total

1970　75　80　85　90　95　2002†

Source: INSEE　*Under 25 years old　†Jan-Aug average

That is a waste of young energy and talent; but a similar waste goes on at the other end of the age range too. In Antibes, a town on the Côte d'Azur sandwiched between Cannes and Nice, men in their 50s and 60s go down to the seafront each afternoon to play *boules*, as do thousands of other perfectly healthy contemporaries throughout the country (albeit perhaps in less pleasant surroundings). In most other industrialised countries, they would still be toiling at the office desk or on the factory floor; in France, they are enjoying a comfortable retirement.

In other words, France's unemployment rate, already bad enough by international standards, is even worse than it looks. In Switzerland, more than 70% of the 55–64 age group are in the labour market; in Japan two-thirds; and in Britain just over half. The average for the OECD group of rich countries is 51%. But in France the share is a mere 37%.

So what, you might say with a Gallic shrug. One of France's many attractive features is that its people work to live, not the other way round (which is what critics say is wrong with the Anglo-Saxon model). Patrick Artus, the chief economist of the Caisse de Dépôts et Consignations, a venerable state-owned bank, makes a joke of it: "No one wants to increase the [labour-market] participation rate except economists over the age of 55.

As the Pisani-Ferry report notes: "Inactivity was viewed in France for many years as an alternative to unemployment." In other words, the government encouraged mothers to stay at home and workers over 50 to retire. This was particularly true for the Mitterrand era of the 1980s and early 90s: legislation to protect workers' rights and the proliferation of payroll charges created an exceptionally illiquid labour market. As a result, *les trentes glorieuses* (the 30 years from 1945 to 1975 when the economy boomed and jobs were there for the taking) were followed by a quarter-century in which high unemployment, especially among the young, became part of the economic landscape.

Embracing business

Could the Raffarin government begin to turn things round? Not in the short term, but at least Mr Raffarin and his team have understood a vital precondition: it is business that must create the jobs of the future, not government. The daily *Le Figaro* went to the trouble of analysing the words used by Mr Raffarin in a recent television programme about his future plans, and found that the second most frequent subject on his lips was "*entreprise*" (business)—surpassed only by the word "France". Compared with Mr Jospin, who spent little time with business bosses during his five-year tenure, Mr Raffarin's interest in *entreprise* seems promising. On the other hand, words are not the same as deeds. For all its alleged antipathy to business, the Jospin government privatised far more of French industry than its centre-right predecessors had done. Mr Raffarin will have to show that he can do better than Mr Jospin.

In part, this will involve more privatisation. Amazingly, there are still around 1,500 companies—compared with 3,500 in 1986—in which the state has a controlling share. In theory, most of the icons of French industry are up for grabs—France Telecom, Air France and even the hitherto sacrosanct Electricité de France (EDF) and Gaz de France (GDF). But at least three things could get in the way.

One is a disinclination on the part of the government to let key industries such as electricity escape from its control, which means that in practice only minority stakes will be sold; a second is union opposition to any loss of pension and other privileges if control goes to the private sector; and the third is the abysmal state of the stockmarket. Air France, 54% owned by the state, may—when market conditions eventually suit the government—be a safe enough bet to fly further into private ownership; France Telecom, 55.5% owned by the state, risks a flop thanks to its debt of around €70 billion.

But the main challenge for Mr Raffarin goes far beyond selling the family silver: it involves lightening the government's hold on the economy in general and the private sector in particular. Government spending accounts for over 53% of GDP, way above the OECD average of 38%. A steeply progressive system of income tax, for example, can claim as much as 60% of an individual's pay-packet, and even the moderately rich have to pay a wealth tax. Virtually every French citizen gripes about taxes or social charges. Admittedly, because of various exemptions, only half of all wage-earners have to pay income tax; the trouble is that the non-paying half are still subject to a variety of payroll charges that make no allowances for income differentials. Value-added tax, levied at 19.6%, also has to be paid by rich and poor alike.

Taxes on business were reduced by the Jospin government, but employers complain that heavy payroll charges still make it hard for them to compete internationally. Medef has calculated that the Jospin government's measures, if they had been fully implemented by their 2003 deadline (in fact some changes will be made), would still have left France bottom out of 14 EU countries. For example, for every €100 an employee takes home, a French employer would still have had to shell out €288, compared with €227 for a German boss and €166 for a British one. Only a Belgian employer would pay more.

Individual taxpayers who are rich and mobile enough vote with their feet. For instance, Laetitia Casta, a model whose face now graces the country's stamps as the national figurehead, Marianne, lives for the most part outside the country; so do virtually all of the French soccer team who won the World Cup for France in 1998 (and lost it so ingloriously in 2002). It is said that up to 300,000 French people now live in south-east England, where the taxes are lower. There is clear evidence that fewer foreigners want to set up business in France, and more French people want to shift their investment abroad.

The government seems to have accepted the need to act. During his election campaign, President Chirac promised to cut income tax by 5% this year and by 30% over his five-year term; to reduce bureaucracy; and to create a million new businesses. Last month Mr Raffarin and his minister for small and medium-sized businesses, Renaud Dutreil, announced that from next autumn the charge for setting up a limited-liability company will be cut from €7,500 to just €1; the company will be able to operate from the entrepreneur's home for up to five years, instead of two (which still raises the question why this kind of restriction should be imposed at all); the tax-exemption limit for capital gains will rise by a third or more; and payment of the first year's social charges can be spread over five years.

French entrepreneurs will be grateful for any lightening of their load. Two years ago the OECD found that France had more business red tape than any other member, and more barriers to entrepreneurs than all but Italy. For example, simply to register a company could take four months.

Let 1m flowers bloom

Will Mr Dutreil's measures meet Mr Chirac's target for 1m new businesses by the next election? At present more than 170,000 companies are created each year, so another 30,000 a year does not look out of the question. It is not as though the country lacked talent and initiative: the Côte d'Azur science park of Sophia-Antipolis is full of high-technology start-ups and foreign investment.

The question is whether France wants that business badly enough. Back in 1925, an American president, Calvin Coolidge, famously declared: "The chief business of the American people is business." It is hard to imagine a French politician ever embracing that sentiment on behalf of his countrymen. In an opinion poll last year, 56% of the respondents said their idea of France was "a country of solidarity and social justice".

They are deluding themselves. According to Timothy Smith, a Canadian historian who specialises in French social policy, "a truly solidaristic society is one which pays the price for its solidarity in the here and now, instead of leaving the bill for future generations, instead of taking raises and an extra month of paid vacation (which is the consequence of the shift from the 39-hour to the 35-hour week) or an expensive pension at 55 years of age, on the backs of 2m-3m unemployed people—most of them under the age of 40." But in France that sort of solidarity still seems a long way off.

The French exception

From agriculture to Europe, France gets away with doing its own thing

THE vineyards bake in the sun of Provence; vast cornfields stretch golden across the plains of Picardy; in Brittany the cattle slowly munch their way from one deep green field to another; in the Dordogne the geese are having their livers fattened for the world's best foie gras. All this is *la France profonde*, that entrancing country of picturesque villages and revered cuisine. No wonder France is by far the world's most popular tourist destination for foreigners. And no wonder the French themselves, not least President Chirac, are determined to preserve it.

Yet the pastoral idyll is in part a myth. The country towns are surrounded by hypermarkets and car-lots; the villages have garish kiosks dispensing videos; and, all too often, the fields and rivers are polluted with pesticides. Meanwhile, the true *paysans* (the word translates better as "country folk" rather than "peasants") are dwindling in number: down to 627,000 in the 1999 census, a drop of 38% on ten years earlier. Their place has been taken by the modern barons of industrialised agriculture (the average farm now is half as large again as in 1988); or the workers who commute to the nearest town; or the Parisians and foreigners who have bought second homes in the country.

Rus in urbe

So why is the myth so important? The answer is a mix of nostalgia, culture and economic self-interest. Only two generations ago, agriculture accounted for one-third of the nation's workforce, which explains why even the most confirmed city types usually still have some rural connection. Mr Chirac once said: "The farmers are the gardeners of our country and the guardians of our memory." But there is rather more to it than gardening: helped by an EU Common Agricultural Policy designed with French farmers in mind, France has become the world's fourth-biggest producer of cereals and meat and pockets a quarter of the CAP's funds.

That does not please José Bové, the pipe-smoking, moustachioed leader of the Confédération Paysanne. Mr Bové, a former student activist turned occasional goat-cheese maker, is demanding a more literal interpretation of the myth. He has become a popular hero by attacking globalisation and the CAP for industrialising agriculture at the expense of the small farmer. Two years ago, when he appeared in court for trashing the site for a new McDonalds restaurant, 30,000 demonstrators gathered in his support. He was briefly imprisoned earlier this year.

By contrast, the politicians think the myth is best served by holding on to the status quo. When the European Commission earlier this year proposed replacing production subsidies for farmers with direct payments geared to their care for the environment, Hervé Gaymard, France's agriculture minister, led the counter-attack. Gathering the signatures of six other EU agriculture ministers, Mr Gaymard sent a letter to several European newspapers, noting: "For us, agricultural products are more than marketable goods; they are the fruit of a love of an occupation and of the land, which has been developed over many generations... For us, farmers must not become the 'variable adjustment' of a dehumanised and standardised world."

Cri de coeur or hypocritical power politics? Perhaps a bit of both. Mr Gaymard's argument is that the CAP has served Europe well, and that its reform should not be rushed, but should involve a debate going back to first principles. Then again, the letter was published on September 24th, to coincide with a meeting of agriculture ministers in Brussels. Moreover, it guaranteed a French victory: the signatories represented a minority big enough to defeat not just the commission's plans but also the wish of several northern countries, particularly Britain, to renegotiate the CAP before the present agreement on the EU's finances expires at the end of 2006.

What kind of Europe?

All this, say the critics, is proof that France, a founder member of the EU, sees it only as a vehicle for its own national interests. But that hardly seems a damning verdict. After all, why join a club if it does not serve your interests? For France, the European club has always served two purposes: to ensure peace with Germany after three wars within a century; and to provide a counterweight to America's power.

Still, the French seem to have a way of bending the club rules to their advantage. For example, back in 1965, when the France of President De Gaulle boycotted Europe's institutions for six months, its "empty chair" policy successfully checked Europe's supranational course, guaranteeing each nation the right to a veto if its vital interests were at stake. And in the early 1990s France held the Uruguay Round of trade negotiations hostage until it won the right to a "cultural exception", allowing it, in effect, to subsidise French films and discriminate against American ones.

In the same vein, Mr Raffarin's finance minister, Francis Mer, blithely told his EU colleagues last June that their "Stability and Growth Pact", a 1997 accord under which all countries had pledged to balance their public-sector budgets by 2004, was "not set in stone." The commission and the other EU members agreed, giving France until 2006 to meet the deadline. But the medium-term budget plans which Mr Mer announced in September show that France will still have a 1% deficit in 2006, prompting open criticism by the commission. Mr Mer seemed unfazed. After a meeting with his EU counterparts last month, he declared: "We decided there were other priorities for France—for instance, increased military spending. Other countries have not taken this kind of decision, but we are still in a Europe where budgetary policy and political decisions are under national control."

It sounds rather like a Europe in which France remains an independent nation-state, choosing for itself when and how to cooperate with the rest of the club. That is one reason why the tie with Gerhard Schröder's federalist-minded Germany has come under strain. However, the tie still holds: last month in Brussels, Mr Chirac, outmanoeuvring—and enraging—Britain's prime minister, Tony Blair, persuaded Mr Schröder that the CAP should remain unchanged until 2006.

Back home, François Bayrou, leader of the Union for French Democracy and a member of the European Parliament, is one of very few French politicians to share the Belgian, Italian or German vision of a powerfully supranational EU. Other visions for the future of the EU, from a confederation of nation-states to a "hard core" of "the willing and the able", all have one thing in common: in essence, France will retain its freedom of action and Europe will serve France's purpose. How else could De Gaulle and his political descendants, including Mr Chirac, have accepted the notion of a communal Europe? Nor are such attitudes confined to Gaullists: the Socialists' François Mitterrand may

High and mighty

France's elite is too clever by half

ALL nations—even those who once believed in Marx—have their elites, so why should France be any different? Philippe Méchet, a well-known opinion pollster, jokes: "We're a very royalist country, and we killed the king. So now we've monarchised the republic."

You can see his point. The American president lives in the White House, but the French president lives in the Elysée Palace, a choice of noun that conjures up a whole retinue of courtiers and uniformed flunkies. Indeed, when the Socialist François Mitterrand inhabited the Elysée, he lavished so much public money on grand schemes for the capital and its monuments that he was often compared to Louis XIV, the "Sun King".

Take the analogy a touch further and you have a modern nobility, products of the *grandes écoles*, a handful of universities—such as Sciences-Po in Paris or the Polytechnique just south of the capital—that are acknowledged to be centres of excellence. In particular, you have the *énarques*, graduates of the Ecole Nationale d'administration (ENA), a postgraduate school established by De Gaulle in 1945 to train a civil service untarnished by the Vichy regime's collaboration with the Nazis.

It has long been fashionable, even among *énarques*, to criticise ENA as being too elitist for the national good. Recruiting through fiercely competitive written and oral exams, the school has an intake of just 120 students a year for its 27-month-long curriculum. Multiply that by the number of years since ENA was established, allow for some natural wastage, and you get a total figure for living *énarques* of perhaps 5,000.

Monarchs of all they survey

That elite, minuscule compared with the massed alumni of Britain's Oxbridge or America's Ivy League, commands most of what matters in France. Mr Chirac is an *énarque*, as is Mr Jospin (but not Mr Raffarin); so too the head of the employers' association, Ernest-Antoine Seillière, and many of the bosses of leading banks and businesses, from Jean Peyrelevade of Crédit Lyonnais to Jean-Cyril Spinetta of Air France.

Is this a good or a bad thing? It depends how you look at it. As one *énarque* at the finance ministry says scathingly, "*Énarques* are pretty smart individually, and pretty dumb collectively." ENA's graduates can hardly help being clever: the meritocratic recruitment process is designed to draw bright children from humble backgrounds into the elite (one example is Hervé Geymard, the agricultural minister). They are also competant: having been groomed for the task of administering the state, by and large they make a good job of it.

The reason that they can be "collectively dumb" is that they all come from the same educational mould, which makes their responses somewhat predictable. Their civil-service instinct is to mistrust the private sector and private initiative. Given their predominance in so many key posts, they have been criticised for holding back France's energy and creativity. But perhaps the dumbest thing they do is to ignore the views of lesser mortals, and assume that they always know best.

---

have talked of "the European project" and "the European construction", but in his alliance with Germany's Chancellor Kohl he preserved France's role as the architect.

Quite contrary

The same streak of Gaullist independence is evident in the way France so often disagrees in public with the United States, in particular over the Middle East. The most obvious example is the squabbling over what kind of UN resolution to use against Iraq, but there are plenty of others. When President Bush linked Iraq, Iran and North Korea in an "axis of evil", the Socialist foreign minister of the day described the American approach as "simplistic"—the same adjective Mr Raffarin now uses for America's policy.

All this is fine for France's *classe politique*, trained to deal with the intellectual contortions of being an insider in the rich world's councils yet an outside critic at the same time. Earlier this year, for example, both the Jospin government and the opposition sent representatives to the World Economic Forum in New York—but also sent twice as many to the rival, anti-globalisation summit in Porto Alegre, Brazil.

But what of those lesser mortals who make up the electorate? For them it smacks of double-talk. No wonder so many, either by abstaining or by casting a protest vote, took their revenge in the presidential election last spring. They felt lost, and the elite had not bothered to show them the way.

A magic moment

President Chirac has five years in which to reform France

THE French body politic has had quite a momentous year, but the sense of shock is now fading. The new obsession of the chattering classes is Iraq and American foreign policy (which has catapulted two thoughtful books on French anti-Americanism into the bestseller list). For the political right, the obsession is unity: let the rival parties that coalesced into the Union for the Presidential Majority become a single vehicle to elect the next president in 2007 (Mr Juppé, or Mr Sarkozy, or—some now whisper—Mr Chirac again?). For the opposition, so much in retreat that the Communist Party, once the largest party of the left, is now struggling to survive with just 21 supporters in the National Assembly, the task is not so much to bind its wounds, but to fight it out until the would-be modernisers of the Socialist Party, such as Dominique Strauss-Kahn and Laurent Fabius, either win or lose.

The government, for its part, talks of "decentralisation". Patrick Devedjian, the "minister of local freedoms", argues that it is time to give power to local officials and to get away from the Napoleonic military logic of a "chain of command" that always leads to Paris. In that way, perhaps a solution could at last be found for Corsica, whose bomb-planting extremists are bent on secession.

But does any of this indicate that the country is facing up to its problems? Sadly, not enough. The *fracture sociale*—a campaign slogan of Jacques Chirac's in his first bid for the presidency, in 1995—still divides the nation; the elites still pontificate at an arrogant distance from *la France d'en bas*; necessary economic reforms still remain a matter of talk rather than achievement; and policy is all to often a consequence of confrontation rather than negotiation. Worst of all, perhaps, is the temptation to seek refuge in a false comfort zone: France as an independent nuclear power, as a permanent member of the UN Security Council, as a member of the G8 club of economic powers—and, of course, as a country that takes culture seriously. France may not match the Anglo-Saxons for Nobel laureates in economics, but in literature it comes top.

Yet there is no need for such a comfort zone. France's engineers are among the best in the world—witness not just high-technology triumphs such as the Ariane rocket programme or the TGV railway system, but also lower-technology successes such as Michelin tyres or the cars of Citroën and Renault (a good enough company to take over Japan's Nissan and return it to profit). The same is true of some of its bankers, insurers and retailers, who successfully compete on the world stage. AXA, for example, will insure your life in America; Carrefour will sell you groceries whether you live in China or Chile.

The disappointment is that such assets are undervalued in the public mind, especially since the fall from grace of Jean-Marie Messier (a graduate both of ENA and the Polytechnique), with his improbable dream of turning a sewage and water company into the Vivendi Universal media giant. Denis Ranque, the boss of Thalès, a French defence and electronics group operating in more than 30 countries, has an explanation: "Popular knowledge of the economy is weak in France. We have important industries, but the French don't like them. They associate them with pollution, not jobs."

Elie Cohen, the economist at Sciences-Po, argues that France has been an ordinary market economy since the mid-1980s, when the folly of Mitterrand's nationalisation programme of 1981–82 became obvious even to the president, but: "The spirit of Gallo-capitalism remains. Each time there's a problem, you appeal to the state." Yet surely an "ordinary" market economy would not go to the lengths France does to resist the liberalising demands of the EU, in particular in the energy market, where EDF is protected at home even as it creates an empire abroad.

Face up to reality

No matter, you might say: France has prospered regardless. Indeed, there is a certain pragmatism behind the rhetoric: criticise globalisation but profit from it too; criticise America but support it at the same time. The problem is that sooner or later this form of self-deception could turn into self-destruction. In 1995, it prevented France's government from getting the popular backing to carry out reforms that have now become all the more necessary.

During his first presidential term, Jacques Chirac's critics had a common taunt: he was a man who knew how to win power, but now how to wield it. But there was a reason: from 1995 he was locked by the voters into cohabitation with his political opponents. For the next five years, he has no such excuse: having promised to reform France, he now has the power to do so. May he use it wisely.

Next French revolution:
a less colorblind society

Proudly held French ideals of citizenship have been shaken by the riots.

Peter Ford

Now comes the hard part. As the nationwide violence that has racked France for two weeks begins to abate, the country's leaders and citizens find themselves facing tough questions about the fundamental values that define the French dream: liberty, equality, and fraternity.

In the face of dramatic evidence that so many of France's ethnic minority citizens and recent immigrants feel that their society has betrayed its promises, one of the pillars supporting France's vision of itself is shaking.

"The events mark a failure and perhaps the decline of the French model of integration [of its immigrants]," says Michel Wieviorka, director of studies at the School for Higher Social Science Studies in Paris. "It is not working any more, and needs at least reform, if not replacement."

This will take a revolution in French thinking about integration, but there are signs that the recent violence has begun to persuade some policymakers that they'll have to overhaul their color-blind ideals of citizenship and face up to the existence of ethnic minorities.

That is likely to be a long and difficult job. France is proud of its ideals and the way it thought it was offering them to newcomers. French politicians may not find it easy to acknowledge how far the country has fallen short of its goals, some immigration experts predict, though Prime Minister Dominique de Villepin acknowledged last week to parliament that, "the effectiveness of our integration model is in question."

Paris remained relatively quiet over the weekend, with authorities implementing a state-of-emergency ban on meetings. Lyon and other cities were ensconced in the ongoing rioting widely seen to be protesting inequalities suffered by France's immigrant population. Nationwide, fewer than 400 vehicles burned, down from highs of more than 1,000 last week.

"When the flames are out, we will have to rebuild not just schools but trust and fraternity," says Marc Cheb Sun, an Egyptian-Italian journalist who edits "Respect," a magazine aimed mainly at young ethnic minorities.

Even before the recent trouble erupted in the country's poorest and most heavily immigrant suburbs, business leaders, government advisory boards, and the intellectuals who dominate the policy debate in France had been inching toward new ways of thinking about immigrant integration. Their moves could provide the foundations for future reform, optimists say.

For example, 40 of France's top companies—including Total, Peugot-Citroën, and Airbus—last year signed a Diversity Charter that commits them, among other things, to "seek to reflect the diversity of French society" in their hiring policies. And one of France's most prominent business leaders, Claude Bébéar, is leading a campaign in favor of anonymous résumés, so that job applicants are not rejected because their names are not French.

France's policy is to treat all its people as citizens, with no consideration of their color, creed, or race that could undermine national unity. The republic does not recognize ethnic differences; there is no room in the official view for "Arab-Frenchmen," in the way a "Mexican-American" is seen as such in the United States. No official statistics are compiled to count the number of people descended from immigrants, or to pinpoint the number of Muslims in France.

Acknowledging ethnic differences and measuring them, runs the official view, would lead to ethnic separatism and weaken the unitary state.

"The French approach is that if you don't attach too much importance [to ethnic and racial divisions in society] and don't talk about them, they will shrink and disappear," explains Patrick Simon, a social demographer, who says that the riots have created a general awareness—similar to that experienced by Americans in the 1960s—that the inequalities faced by ethnic minorities go beyond individual cases of discrimination.

"The system is theoretically defensible but ineffective in practice," continues Professor Simon. "Instead of having the positive effects that were hoped for, it has the opposite effect."

That supposedly color-blind treatment has not led to equal outcomes is clear from the suburbs where violence exploded two weeks ago: The poorest districts of French cities are overwhelmingly inhabited by North African and black African immigrants and their descendants who complain bitterly about discrimination.

"Your name says everything in France," says a young black man in the Paris suburb of Grigny, who gave his name as Billy Fabrice. "If you are called Diallo or Amir, that's all they want to know. If you are called Jean-Pierre, you show up for a job and they take you."

"It's as if we were here just as extras," agrees Mr. Fabrice's friend Amadi Boda, whose parents came to France from Senegal.

Forbidden by their mind-set from targeting social programs at ethnic groups, the French authorities have instead directed their money and their efforts geographically, targeting the most deprived districts. Since that is where a lot of North African and black African families live, they say, those are the people who will benefit.

Though this approach has not worked as well as it was intended to, French politicians have stuck to their conceptual guns.

At a ceremony last June that launched the "High Authority Against Discrimination and For Equality" (HALDE), President Jacques Chirac was blunt. "There is a limit that we should not cross because that would touch what, in my eyes, is our very identity," he warned. "It would consist of choosing a conception in which some Frenchmen should define themselves according to their origins in order to pursue their rights. That would lead to juridically enshrining inequality and open the way to ethnic separatism."

'The effectiveness of our integration model is in question.'
—Dominique de Villepin

Some critics say the problem is not cultural integration but straightforward discrimination in a society that has not allowed the arrival of millions of immigrants from different countries to change its view of itself.

"In spirit and behavior I am French, but my skin color is black," says Abdelouaye Juye, a retired woodworker who left Senegal 31 years ago. "How can I be asked to integrate into my own country?

"What do they mean by integration?" he asks, hitching up his gray *jellabah*, a dress-like garment. "Putting on a jacket and tie? Conforming with everything my neighbor expects? Do all citizens have to be 100 percent conformist?"

"A lot of young people see 'integration' as an insult," adds Alec Hargreaves, an expert in French immigration policy at Florida State University. "They say, 'we've integrated culturally into your norms, but you don't let us participate in your society,'" he explains.

Policy planners are unable, though, to measure the extent to which immigrants' descendants are excluded from jobs, housing, or educational opportunities, and thus are unable to do much about it, because they cannot measure ethnic disparities.

"The last great taboo the French need to face … the one absolutely critical part of the jigsaw that is still missing," is ethnic monitoring, says Professor Hargreaves. That would allow businesses and government agencies to measure their workforce, or their provision of services, by ethnic category, and thus identify discrimination.

There are signs that this will happen. Equal Opportunities Minister Azouz Begag told FranceInter radio last week that after 25 years of "blah-blahing about integration, without giving ourselves any goals to meet" the government intends to "give ourselves the means, commit money, and evaluate the results."

An advisory board led by former Education Minister Luc Ferry, in a September report to the government, recommended ethnic monitoring, as carried out in Britain and the United States, on a voluntary basis.

In addition to the Diversity Charter of Frances' top companies, other moves are afoot, including the nomination of Mr. Begag, a sociologist born in a Lyon slum to illiterate Algerian parents, to a cabinet job that had never existed before. Still, no members of parliament are of immigrant descent.

One of France's most prestigious elite institutions, the "Sciences Politiques" college, two years ago instituted a special admissions program for young people from the most disadvantaged neighborhoods. The state-owned television channels have committed themselves to "positive action" that has put two black women in anchors' chairs for the first time, and the government last June created the independent HALDE, to which citizens can report cases of discrimination. The organization can demand inquiries on the practices of a particular agency and bring court cases on behalf of citizens.

Another sign of a new approach came last week in the influential daily "Le Monde," where the country's best known sociologist, Alain Touraine, urged a rethink. "Rejection of ethnic separatism must be matched by a recognition of differences," he argued. "France as a society could become a threat to itself unless it manages to combine integration with differences and universalism with individual cultural rights."

French inch toward social reform

*A majority say France's safety nets are broken, but they're
divided on a solution.*

Peter Ford

Slumped on a bench outside the unemployment office, folding and unfolding a slip of official paper that testifies to another fruitless visit, Fremo is bitter.

He won't give his full name; a young out-of-work man of Arab origin, he prefers his anonymity. But he is blunt. "They do nothing to help," he complains, jerking a thumb toward the job center. "They ring me every six months to check that I'm looking for work, and that's it.

"I'd love them to find me a job," he adds. "But there are three million people like me in France who'd love them to find them a job. We've been sacrificed."

After more than two decades of jobless rates hovering stubbornly around 10 percent, France's chronic unemployment crisis "is the one big problem with the French social model," says John Martin, a senior official with the Organization for Economic Cooperation and Development. "If a social model should deliver a satisfactory labor market," says Mr. Martin, as European leaders gather outside London for talks about how to adjust their economies and social benefits, "this one has failed dismally for the best part of three decades."

Indeed, 68 percent of the French public said last month that their social safety net was broken. But they are divided over what to do about it.

Many are angry at what they see as hectoring from European Union leaders who have been urging big European nations such as France and Germany to apply free-market remedies (also known as the Anglo-Saxon model) to their flagging economies. And the French rejection last May of a putative European constitution—seen as paving the way for a more competitive, less comfortable Europe—was due in part to a reluctance to relax protective regulations and trim the welfare state.

But in executive suites and even on factory floors around the country, others recognize that global competition is already forcing change upon France. And they're not waiting for the government to refurbish the social model.

Working harder to make more pillows

Christian Dumas, for example, sees a new competitive attitude that's boosting productivity in his own business. It may be the only thing keeping his small firm, and thousands of French firms like it, alive.

Mr. Dumas runs the family-owned firm making quilts and pillows that his grandfather founded outside Tonnerre, in northern Burgundy, more than 50 years ago. The business has grown, allowing Dumas and his 45 employees to prosper, but in recent months they have been feeling the heat of international competition.

First, eight low-wage eastern European countries entered the European Union last year; then the EU ended quotas on imports of Chinese textiles used in making quilts and pillows.

"We are up against terrible competition," says Dumas. "I told my people that either we give up, and the company goes under in two or three years, or we face the challenge, which means every single employee increases his productivity, and we all improve the quality of our goods. They were absolutely with me."

Dumas says he has "seen a change in mentality." "People realize that jobs are leaving France, and they are ready now to question themselves and the way that they work." Dumas says his workers are willing to find new, more efficient ways to do their jobs, allowing the business to prosper—without benefit or wage cuts.

But observers here question whether the country's leaders—or the public as a whole—are similarly willing to adjust.

President Jacques Chirac, adept at feeling the national pulse, lashed out earlier this year at US-style unregulated capitalism as "the communism of our new century."

Stalled by lack of consensus

"The French won't change just because they are told that change is inevitable," says Marjorie Jouen, an analyst with the Paris based pro-European think tank Notre Europe. "Recognizing that there is a crisis does not put people in the mood for reform unless someone offers a project to motivate us."

"We are in a crisis today because the practical consensus between the left and the right, linking economic efficiency with social protection, has broken down," says French philosopher and writer André Glucksmann.

"A significant part of the left argues that liberalism and social policy are antagonistic, that we have to choose one or the other."

That attitude, which dominates the current debate over France's future path, dismays EU leaders who are anxious to encourage the sort of economic growth

43

that will help fund welfare programs for aging populations.

"In a number of member states, particularly some older ones, there is a fear that economic reform will undermine social protection," Irish European Commissioner Charlie McCreevy said in a recent speech. "Such fear is not only misplaced but counterproductive."

Often caricatured as the economic "sick man of Europe," France has already made some adjustments to make it more competitive: Worker productivity per hour is the third highest in the industrial world; financial markets are more open; the number of French shareholders has quadrupled in the last 20 years; and top French companies in sectors such as energy and pharmaceuticals are global leaders.

The government has extended the length of time one must work to receive a pension, it has rolled back the previous Socialist government's 35-hour limit on the work week, and it has introduced a new labor contract making it easier for the smallest firms to hire and fire.

But most economists consider these to be relatively minor reforms. And they've been introduced in the teeth of opposition from powerful public sector trade unions, whom some blame for hindering deeper reforms that would make the job market more flexible.

"France has chosen unemployment," charges Michel Debarnady, head of the national unemployment agency for the Seine-et-Marne region south of Paris.

"We have chosen to give precedence to those who have work, to keep their jobs alive as long as possible, with all the social advantages they have acquired, at the cost of those who don't have jobs, who are outside the system and who find it harder and harder to get in," such as women, immigrants, young people, and less skilled workers, he argues.

Want to fire someone? Wait six months.

Some critics blame rigid French labor laws for discouraging employers from taking on new hands, since it is complicated and expensive to sack workers employed on indefinite contracts.

In fact, says Dumas, "we have all the flexibility we need when there is a lot of work—we hire temporary workers. It's when there is not enough work, and you need to let people go in order to restructure, that you have problems."

It takes at least six months to fire an employee for economic reasons, following strictly defined procedures that are "expensive, risky, and administratively long," complains Dumas, who went through the lengthy process with two of his employees last year.

International experts also say the French authorities should do more to encourage the unemployed to take a job, both helping them more actively, and getting tougher on those who stay on generous benefits for a long time without trying to find work.

Fremo, out of work for 18 months, says he is fed up with either being ignored by his unemployment office, or being sent on IT training courses that he says are much too complicated for a young man who left school at 16 and has done nothing but unskilled construction work since.

"It would be more useful if they really gave me some follow-up, and sent me on courses that I could use," he says.

France's 'gentler' approach

Where other European countries such as Britain and Denmark have introduced strict "welfare-to-work" programs that cut the benefits of claimants who don't take advantage of highly personalized job-seeking advice, the French prefer a gentler approach.

In the new town of Sénart, which has sprung up 30 miles south of Paris, for example, the authorities are setting up a planning commission that puts local employers, town councils, national and regional employment agencies, and job-seekers in touch with each other.

The goal is to provide a personalized service that "matches the needs of local enterprises with the public's needs," says Françoise Herbreteau, who is in charge of the project.

Such case-by-case care, though labor-intensive, works, according to an EU report released last week. It found that this approach, including personal career coaching, training, and carefully targeted higher spending have helped lower unemploy-

ment in countries such as Denmark and the Netherlands.

Unless France makes some adjustments, the country faces major financial problems, warns the OECD's Mr. Martin, who heads the international organization's Employment and Social Affairs department.

"A fragile equilibrium has emerged under which 85 percent of the population is OK and 15 percent get benefit support," Martin explains.

"But in the long run an aging population is going to knock real holes in that." Already the government is having difficulty financing the growing gap between the social security system's revenues and its expenditures, leading to arguments over how to proceed.

Politicians and the 'pensions bomb'

Prime Minister Dominique de Villepin insists that cautious reform, such as the new labor contract he introduced this summer, will modernize France's social model sufficiently to keep it afloat. His leading challenger for the ruling party's presidential candidate's slot at the 2007 elections, Nicolas Sarkozy, advocates a "rupture" with the past.

"We must break with the unstable reforms and the hypocritical prudence which have led us up blind alleys for the last 30 or 40 years" he told a meeting of businessmen earlier this month. "The only social model worth the name is one that gives everybody a job, which ours does not," alluding to Britain's relatively successful "Anglo-social" model.

Mr. Sarkozy has not said how far he would break with tradition, and how broadly he would deregulate the economy. But his willingness to speak bluntly about the country's problems has won him growing support on both the right and the left.

"Most politicians will not risk saying that things cannot go on like this," says Mr. Glucksmann.

"But the French are smarter than their politicians believe: they know there is a pensions bomb, they know 10 percent unemployment is serious, so it is not impossible for a political leader to break the conspiracy of silence.

"The ones who talk about it are in a minority still," Glucksmann adds. "But they are beginning to talk."

A system in crisis, a country adrift

Post-election paralysis has dashed the hope that Germany could build quickly on its economic recovery and embrace reform

The Economist

YOU'VE heard of the perfect storm; now meet the perfect stalemate. After its parliamentary election on Sunday September 18th, Germany seems stuck in the worst logjam of its post-war history. None of the coalitions that might form a parliamentary majority looks possible. Worse, Gerhard Schröder, the chancellor, and Angela Merkel, the opposition leader, both claim to have won. If no player in this poker game backs down, you can expect a showdown not seen since the Weimar Republic. New elections may be the only way to break the deadlock.

That concern may prove overdone. But even if a stable government does emerge in the days and weeks to come, one thing is already clear: Germany is unlikely any time soon to become the model of a big, rich country that can muster the political courage to reform itself. And the fledgling recovery of Europe's biggest economy could then peter out.

This has been a rude shock for many Germans, especially businessmen. While the margin had been shrinking, most polls forecast victory for the combined opposition of Christian Democrats (CDU) and Free Democrats (FDP). Even days before last Sunday's vote, pollsters said the CDU would top 40%—and that Angela Merkel, the party's boss, would at least be unchallenged to head a big left-right coalition.

Yet when the exit polls began circulating on Sunday afternoon, pundits were amazed. And the final tally confirmed the upset: the CDU and its Bavarian sister party, the Christian Social Union (CSU), came in at only 35.2% of votes, not even a full point ahead of Mr Schröder's Social Democrats

(SPD) at 34.3%. The best news for the opposition was the FDP's good showing, just shy of 10%. The Greens and the Left Party, a new amalgam of ex-communists from the east and western lefties, got 8.1% and 8.7% respectively.

Drilling deeper, the results look even worse for the CDU and Ms Merkel. The SPD led the field in 12 of Germany's 16 states, many of which had seen big CDU wins in recent state elections. Most notably, the SPD again overtook the CDU in North Rhine-Westphalia (with 40%, compared with 34.4% for the CDU). It was the SPD's crushing defeat there in the spring that led Mr Schröder to seek early national elections. Yet these gains for the SPD were not enough to compensate for new losses to the Left Party. As a result, neither the governing coalition nor the opposition managed to win the absolute majority of seats needed to elect a new chancellor. This implies one of two outcomes: either the CDU will have to form a grand coalition with the SPD, or each big group must find at least one small party with which to form an alliance. Yet neither the Greens nor the FDP (nobody will talk to the Left Party) appear keen to co-operate.

One big-small combination, called the "traffic light coalition", would include the SPD (party colour: red), the FDP (yellow) and the Greens. The other would unite CDU, FDP and Greens in a "Jamaica coalition", so-called because the parties' colours (black, yellow and green) match that island's flag.

What is to blame for this stalemate? For one, a complex election law, giving two votes to each citizen. With their first, they elect half their legislators directly. But it is

the second ballot that shapes the composition of parliament, giving Germany a partly proportional form of representation. This was fine as long as there were only two big parties (the CDU and SPD) and one kingmaker, the FDP. Now that both titans have shrunk (their combined result has dropped below 70%) and the Greens as well as the Left Party have crossed the 5% threshold for parliamentary representation, building a coalition with a majority has become very hard. In Britain, with its first-past-the-post system, Ms Merkel would now be forming her government, and grooming herself as a German version of Margaret Thatcher.

A nation splits

Yet the messy result and the growing number of parties also reveal splits in German society, especially over economic change. About half of voters want to press ahead (as Ms Merkel wanted), while the other half would prefer to continue muddling through (Mr Schröder's proposal), according to polls taken after the election. This also explains why voters had such a "trembling hand", says Richard Hilmer of Infratest Dimap, a polling firm. Many clearly changed their minds in the final days, or moments, before the vote.

Perhaps more importantly, the two main camps are also split within, according to Franz Walter, a political scientist at Göttingen University. Many of those who can't cope with an accelerating, globalising, knowledge-based society (or fear they can't), he argues, cast their ballot for the Left Party. At the other extreme, the winners in the globalisation game, the "busy burghers", who are losing patience with slow state bureaucracies, opted for the FDP. This, perhaps even more than the fear of a do-nothing grand coalition, prompted many CDU voters to give their second vote to the liberal, pro-reform party.

Yet the main culprits are probably the two candidates for chancellor themselves—for deepening these rifts rather than trying to bridge them. Ms Merkel now appears to have been the wrong candidate to sell unpalatable reforms. Many see her as disciplined and hard working, but not likeable or dynamic. The remarried Protestant from eastern Germany may also have scared away voters in the more Catholic, conservative south. In Bavaria, the CSU dropped below 50%—a political revolution in that hitherto one-party state.

The CDU candidate also ran a lacklustre campaign, making many small, unforced errors and one big mistake: the nomination of Paul Kirchhof, a judge-turned-professor who favours a flat tax, as her prospective finance minister. This not only confused Ms Merkel's message (her programme included a different kind of tax reform), but also gave the SPD a badly needed boost since it allowed Mr Schröder to switch from a tired defence of his own reforms to an assault on Ms Merkel.

A stiff-necked pair

But it is above all the stubbornness of both the chancellor and his challenger that has led to the current deadlock: both refuse to concede defeat—one with a good argument, the other with a less compelling one. Ms Merkel insists that she ought to lead the next government: the governing coalition has lost and the CDU and CSU now form the biggest parliamentary group. Mr Schröder says he should remain in office: people should see the CDU and the CSU as separate parties—making the SPD the strongest party in parliament.

Even some SPD leaders admit that this argument is questionable (although the CSU has always insisted on its independence when it comes to getting state money). Indeed, Mr Schröder's real train of thought is very different. Although most of the media had already written him off, he has single-handedly achieved the near-impossible with personal popularity and campaign magic: a respectable result for the SPD. To him, it seems, he has won a virtual presidential election.

This is at least how Mr Schröder behaved on election night. He first gave a speech worthy of Caesar to supporters at SPD party headquarters in Berlin. "I'm proud of the people of our country who didn't give in to media manipulation and power," he said, to loud cheers. Later, in a televised debate, he appeared so punch-drunk that observers were left amazed by the intoxicating effects of victory. He refused to shut up, challenged his journalist interlocutors and seemed to question the whole electoral process: "You can't just demand power for formalistic reasons!"

Yet his behaviour may be more rational than it seems. By confronting the CDU head on, Mr Schröder hopes he can make that party start bickering again and even bring down Ms Merkel. In the hope of encouraging Ms Merkel's rivals to unseat her, he has reportedly offered the CDU a deal like the one made by Israel's main parties in the 1980s: he would remain chancellor for two years, then let a CDU leader have the job.

If this is Mr Schröder's strategy, it doesn't seem to be working so far. In a show of solidarity, the CDU's parliamentary group re-elected Ms Merkel as their chairwoman with a whopping 98%. Meanwhile, she and the SPD's boss, Franz Müntefering, are both trying to build a Jamaica and a traffic-light coalition respectively. But such efforts are unlikely to succeed: the FDP won't form a coalition with the SPD and Greens because it ruled that out during the campaign—a vow that impressed voters. And the cultural gap between the CDU and the Greens is vast. In the words of Joschka Fischer, about to step down as parliamentary leader of the Greens, it's hard to imagine bonding with Christian Democrats over joints and reggae.

Unsurprisingly, there is now feverish speculation about the next move. There is unlikely to be a big shift until October 2nd, when voters in a district of Dresden will cast their ballots. (Voting had to be postponed for two weeks there after the sudden death of a parliamentary candidate.) Contrary to what had been expected, the vote will not deprive the CDU of its place as the strongest party in parliament even if all the district's citizens vote SPD (the CDU may, however, lose a seat if it gets more than 41,226 second votes—another oddity of German election law). Forming a coalition before the Dresden vote, in any event, could cause legal problems that would void the entire election.

What comes next is anyone's guess. Forces of reason hope that Mr Schröder will get off his Gaullist high horse and let Ms Merkel lead a grand coalition. It is also possible that both will step down, letting others take the reins, most likely Roland Koch, the CDU premier of the state of Hesse, and Peer Steinbrück, the former SPD premier of North Rhine-Westphalia. Such a solution has been dubbed the "Glienicke Bridge"—the place in Berlin where spies were swapped in the cold war.

More likely, Mr Schröder will continue to gamble, forcing a parliamentary showdown. For this, the constitution lays down a clear script. The new parliament has to be constituted at least 30 days after the election, on October 18th at the latest, when it will also vote on a candidate for chancellor proposed by the federal president, Horst Köhler. If this proposal doesn't win an absolute majority, the current chancellor stays in power while parliament has another two weeks to elect the same candidate or another one, with an absolute majority. If this fails, a simple majority of votes cast suffices—but Mr Köhler must then decide whether to accept the vote or dissolve parliament and call a new poll.

Everybody expects Mr Köhler to propose Ms Merkel, if she hasn't been dethroned by her own camp. Since she is unlikely to win an absolute majority either on October 18th, or in the two weeks after this first vote, high noon will be in early November: parliament will have to decide whether it wants to keep Mr Schröder or elect Ms Merkel. The incumbent could get votes from the Left Party, while the challenger could win some from the Greens. If this fails to produce an absolute majority, Mr Köhler may well call for new elections, either later this year or early in 2006.

Mr Schröder may yet win the biggest gamble of his career. He might, in effect, transform Germany from a parliamentary democracy into a presidential one—recalling what Charles de Gaulle did to France, more formally, when he created the Fifth Republic. That may win the chancellor a place in history, but will it solve Germany's economic problems? In the campaign, he never said what he would really do if re-elected. In any case, he is unlikely to achieve the goal he proclaimed when calling early elections: a stable majority for reform. Last week, it seemed that Mr Schröder might have realised his time at the top was up. But reports of his political death turned out to be exaggerated.

Angela Merkel

Politician Who Can Show a Flash of Steel

MARK LANDLER

*O*n Nov. 9, 1989, the day the Berlin Wall fell, Angela Merkel made her weekly visit to a sauna. Hours later, she caught up with thousands of East Germans, who were streaming jubilantly into the West. It was not the last time her rendezvous with German history was delayed.

On Monday, three weeks after a deadlocked election that she had once been expected to win handily Mrs. Merkel finally emerged as the designated leader of Germany's next government.

To get the job, she had to make major concessions to the departing chancellor, Gerhard Schröeder, and his party. And her ascension must still be ratified in a vote in the Parliament, to be held next month.

Still, these provisos should not obscure Mrs. Merkel's achievement: At 51, she is poised to become the first woman to serve as chancellor of Germany and the first eastern German to lead the reunified country.

Mrs. Merkel's journey from Protestant minister's daughter in East Germany to the pinnacle of German politics—as the boss of a male-dominated, Catholic-leaning conservative party—is so improbable that it has left political analysts here grasping for what she might do as chancellor.

"With that kind of background, she obviously has extraordinary gifts," said Ulrich von Alemann, a professor of politics at the University of Düesseldorf. "But her career has also been marked by chance and good fortune. It's very difficult to predict what kind of role she will play."

Mrs. Merkel, he said, is a genuinely new figure in German politics, someone who could potentially bridge the two halves of Germany, which have drifted apart in recent years, as the financial burden of reunification and a stagnant eastern economy have bred mutual resentment.

And yet the attenuated circumstances of her victory underscore the reservations Germans have about her. She was chosen not with a rousing popular mandate, but after protracted backroom negotiations between her party, the Christian Democratic Union, and the Social Democrats of Mr. Schröder.

Despite her political odyssey, much remains of the regimented young woman who kept her date at the sauna that day. Dogged, earnest, almost willfully bland, Mrs. Merkel is an unlikely historic figure.

"She has a cool personality," said Gerd Langguth, who has written a biography of Mrs. Merkel. "She does not easily express her emotions. That may explain why people have difficulty identifying with her."

Even her politics defy easy categorization. Mrs. Merkel's firsthand experience of Communism has left her with a fervent conviction in the power of free markets, according to analysts. But she is unlikely to become a German Margaret Thatcher—Maggie Merkel, as some here hopefully put it—especially now that she must share power with the Social Democrats.

Others see in her background a champion of democracy, a leader more naturally inclined to support the policies of President Bush, as she did on Iraq, than was Schröeder. Yet her most notable foreign-policy position has been to oppose Turkey's entry into the European Union.

The deliberately bland manner may hide some surprises.

Until recently, when she spruced up her wardrobe and began wearing her hair in a stylish layered cut, Mrs. Merkel looked as if she would still be at home in the drab confines of East Germany. While campaigning, she projected a stern image, offering few glimpses of her personal side.

Mrs. Merkel, who has no children, is married to a chemistry professor, Joachim Sauer. He steers clear of her political career. She is said to like cooking for friends, and has a soft spot for the actor Dustin Hoffman.

Even in victory, though, she remains less popular personally than the avuncular Schröeder. In part, that has to do with her stubborn refusal to turn herself into a symbol—either of East Germany and its reunification with the West, or of women and their changing role in German society.

Eastern Germans yearning for an advocate have been disappointed by how little she focuses on their plight. Women did not turn out to vote in droves to show solidarity with her precedent-setting career.

"She is a stranger to most Germans," Langguth said, explaining why she faded in the election. "Many East Germans think of her as a West German, while West Germans think she is an East German."

In truth, she is both.

Born in Hamburg on July 17, 1954, to a Protestant minister, Horst Kasner, and his wife, Herlind, Angela Dorothea Kasner was 3 months old when her father was asked to take over a country church in Brandenburg.

Growing up in an intellectual household, Angela excelled in school and hoped to become a teacher and translator. But because of her father's pastoral work, she found those careers closed to her. So in 1973, she decided to study physics at Leipzig University.

As an 8-year-old, Angela could rattle off the names of the ministers in the West German government. Yet as a young adult, she showed little interest in politics. Instead, she worked toward a Ph.D. in physics and married a fellow student, Ulrich Mrs. Merkel; they divorced in 1982.

Mrs. Merkel was settling in to a career at the Academy of Sciences in East Berlin in 1989, when the wall fell. A month later, she joined a coalition of pro-democracy parties. "It was clear they were going to need people," she said in a typically circumspect interview in the Frankfurter Allgemeine Zeitung.

That coalition was absorbed into the Christian Democrats, and Mrs. Merkel found her party. Mr. Langguth suggested that she was reacting in part to her father, with whom she has had a fraught relationship.

Mrs. Merkel became the spokeswoman for Lothar de Maizère, a lawyer chosen to wind down the affairs of the East German state. In the first post-reunification election, she won a seat in Parliament, and later a Cabinet post in the government of Helmut Kohl.

He famously referred to Mrs. Merkel as "the girl," but rewarded her with a series of powerful posts. She proved herself to be a skillful political player, unafraid to eviscerate rivals. In 1999, after Mr. Kohl had been implicated in a financial scandal, Mrs. Merkel cut loose her old mentor.

"The party must learn to walk," she said at the time. "It must trust itself to fight its political opponents without its old battle horses."

It was a brazen act of rebellion. But within months, Mrs. Merkel was elected party leader. "The episode symbolized that she is capable of making unexpected decisions in difficult situations," Mr. Langguth said.

Only Marginal Reforms Are Expected in Germany

Coalition and Tradition Seen as Restraints

RICHARD BERNSTEIN and MARK LANDLER

Udo Pfeiffer, the head of a small machinery maker in the Rhineland, is a disappointed man. He was hopeful that Angela Merkel, Germany's presumptive new chancellor, would sweep to power with a mandate to eliminate the cumbersome regulations that make doing business here difficult.

But when Mrs. Merkel faltered and was forced into a coalition with her political rivals, the Social Democrats, Mr. Pfeiffer and many others like him felt that an opportunity of historic dimensions had been missed.

They had hoped that, like Margaret Thatcher almost a generation ago, Mrs. Merkel would breeze to victory and take on the country's powerful unions, loosening job-protection laws and lowering non-wage labor costs, which are among the world's highest—actions that they believe would go a long way toward restoring Germany's competitive position in the global economy.

"Merkel needs to speak honestly to the German people," Mr. Pfeiffer said. "She needs to tell them, 'Either we have to work longer hours for the same pay, or if we stick to a 35-hour week, we have to lower wages.'"

But many people here, including what seem to be a majority of commentators and political analysts, now believe that marginal reforms are probably the most that can be expected of the coalition government that, presumably, will be formed in the next several weeks.

The reasons for that go well beyond the constricting factor of operating within a coalition of political rivals with competing policies and constituencies. They have to do as well with the very nature of Germany's traditions and the powerful public attachment to the idea of big government as the guarantor of personal security, an attachment that goes beyond Germany to many other countries in Europe, from France to Scandinavia to Austria.

"In my opinion, this is the main cleavage in the West," Claus Leggewie, a professor of political science at Giessen University, said in an interview, speaking about the gap between the British-American faith in free markets and the Continental European reliance on the state.

"There is always this ongoing yearning for security and the belief that security cannot be given by the market economy," Mr. Leggewie continued. "It can only be given by the state."

In declining to give a majority to Mrs. Merkel and, in a sense, forcing her into a coalition with the Social Democrats, Germany's voters acted pretty much in accordance with tradition. They gave their approval, perhaps, to a modest increase in the reforms, known as Agenda 2010, that were put into place by Chancellor Gerhard Schröder, but nothing more radical than that.

"Mrs. Merkel will be a Christian Democratic chancellor in a Social Democratic government," Mr. Leggewie said.

The problem for many economists is that even after Mr. Schröder's reforms—which were so angrily opposed and bitterly resented that they led to defections in his own Social Democratic Party—Germany still has a social welfare system of, to Americans, astonishing generosity.

The most controversial aspect of Agenda 2010, which became effective at the beginning of this year, involved new restrictions on the length of time a worker who lost a job could receive unemployment benefits, after which that person is put on the regular welfare rolls, which are less generous, indefinitely.

According to the new measure, called Hartz IV, unemployed people who have gone on welfare still have their rent paid for by the state, 100 percent of it, including heat and electricity. They are provided with health insurance, nursing insurance and pension insurance. They are reimbursed for the purchase of major appliances like stoves and refrigerators.

In addition, each welfare recipient gets a stipend of nearly $420 a month plus $240 a month for each child under 14 for additional living expenses. In other words, a family of four people with two children, assuming both parents are unemployed, would receive free rent and utilities plus $1,350 per month, with no time limit on the benefits. Even after Hartz IV, in other words, Germany has one of the most generous social welfare systems in Europe.

A public attachment to big government as the guarantor of personal security.

Another reform central to Mrs. Merkel's free market philosophy, and the one that most concerns Mr. Pfeiffer, is giving greater flexibility to the strict rules that govern wage agreements.

Mr. Pfeiffer's 280 workers are covered by an industry-wide labor contract negotiated by the powerful metalworkers union, IG Metall. Mr. Pfeiffer would like a more flexible deal that, he said, might be acceptable to at least some of the worker representatives in his company, who recognize that it could help protect their jobs.

But the union opposes such exceptions, and its authority is not likely to be challenged, because Mrs. Merkel's proposal during the campaign to weaken collective-bargaining agreements will probably be shelved.

"Germany does not need abstract economic ideas; it needs labor market reforms," said Holger Schmieding, an economist at Bank of America.

But in a sense, such labor market reforms would reverse trends in Germany that go all the way back to the country's first chancellor, Otto von Bismarck, and that certainly formed the basis for the kind of buffered capitalism, often called Rhine capitalism, that has formed Germany's economy in just about the entire post-World War II era. It is a capitalism, as Mr. Leggewie put it, that is "more egalitarian, more distributive, a capitalism where the state always plays a role as moderator between labor and capital."

Moreover, the system has worked well historically, making Germany one of the world's richest and most productive countries, without the bitter and even bloody labor strife that has afflicted the British-American world.

Today, despite its zero growth and high unemployment, Germany remains the world's biggest exporter, even in this age of globalization and cheap manufactured goods from China.

That is one reason many people here believe that small reforms are all that is needed, and that Germany can end its stagnation with small reforms and cooperation between capital and labor of the sort that have already led to some important reductions in labor costs.

But many other people, including many economists, are convinced that the country, living on borrowed capital, will decline unless major reforms are undertaken.

"We have to change the widespread idea that the economic miracle, the good times, are coming back," Wolfgang Nowak, a former adviser to Mr. Schröder who is now an official at Deutsche Bank, said in an interview shortly before the coalition government was announced. "The German dream is over. Other countries are making cars as wonderful as German cars. We aren't better than the others anymore, and we're more expensive."

Immigration law hailed as a vital turning point in Germany's attitude to a multiracial society

After three painful years of negotiations, minister says: 'We are now a modern country'.

Hugh Williamson

A wide-ranging new immigration law expected to pass its final legislative hurdle today represents a "clear paradigm shift for Germany", Otto Schily, interior minister, said yesterday.

"It was a painful process to reach agreement on this law," he said, referring to three years of often bitter negotiations, both with the conservative opposition and within the ruling coalition of Social Democratic and Green parties.

The resulting legislation will make it easier for skilled workers to enter Germany but at the same time will tighten measures against suspected terrorists and allow the authorities to expel foreigners accused of "preaching hatred".

The new law will be adopted today on a cross-party basis in parliament's upper house. Mr Schily told the Financial Times approval would mean Germany had "recognised that immigration is a reality, that it is positive, and that it needs to be managed".

That is a bold statement about a country that for decades has embodied contradictory views on immigration: while Germany has many multicultural neighbourhoods and the largest proportion of foreigners of any European nation (9 per cent of the population), it has also tradi-

tionally refused to see itself as a place where migrants settle.

That is now likely to change, though slowly. In the short term, only highly skilled specialists such as professors and engineers will find it easier to get work permits to join the 7.3m foreigners in Germany. Companies complain that lawmakers have missed a chance to create mechanisms to attract the larger numbers of migrants that may be needed after 2010, when the population is projected to begin declining.

Looking beyond the law's fine-print, however, experts agree it has symbolic importance both for Germany and for other European countries.

Kay Hailbronner, a Constance university law professor and adviser to Mr Schily on immigration, said the rules "mark a turning point for Germans in that they are accepting that they live in a multicultural society".

Gervais Appave, policy director at the International Organisation for Migration, the Geneva-based intergovernmental agency, said the law is "very significant because Germany has recognised, at least to a degree, that we live in a mobile world, and that migration is a social, economic and demographic feature of that world".

The millions of "guest workers" from Turkey and elsewhere who flocked to Germany in the 1950s and 1960s to do manual jobs were treated in a second-class way, unable to gain citizenship and expected to return home, although many did not.

More recently, the increased support for far-right political parties has stirred racial tensions and further sensitized debates on immigration.

With the new law, however, "we've abandoned the myth that we're not a country of immigration, and the myth that so-called guest workers only stay for a short time, outside our society then go home", says Mr Schily.

He notes that Germany regularly receives net immigration of 200,000–300,000 a year. In future, more of these will be economic migrants, with fewer asylum seekers and family members of those already settled in Germany, he predicted.

Mr Appave said the law's broad sweep, combining measures on labour migration, asylum, residency and integration of foreigners, and security, was also "impressive".

Most European countries had a jumble of separate laws that often only allowed in migrants under obscure exception clauses, he said.

But Mr Schily acknowledges the legislation is also a compromise, a much watered-down version of proposals made by a government-appointed commission that in 2001 called for radical steps including annual quotas of non-EU migrants and an elaborate points system to assess applicants.

Neither suggestion made it into the new law, largely because the opposition, which repeatedly used its majority in the upper house to block earlier drafts, argued that Germany needed few migrants when unemployment was more than 4m.

The opposition also demanded the inclusion of the security measures ultimately incorporated into the law. These measures were resisted initially by the Greens.

Due to ageing and a low birth rate, Germany's labour force is expected to fall from the current 42m to about 30m by 2050.

Immigration could help counter this fall, "but only in a modest way", Mr Hailbronner said. Mr Schily agreed: "Immigration can reduce the impact of demographic trends but it can't compensate for them entirely—such an idea is an illusion."

He preferred to focus on the new law's underlying message: "We are now a modern country, with open doors and windows, but one that does not allow in immigrants on an arbitrary basis."

Japanese spirit, western things

When America's black ships forced open Japan, nobody could have predicted that the two nations would become the world's great economic powers

OPEN up. With that simple demand, Commodore Matthew Perry steamed into Japan's Edo (now Tokyo) Bay with his "black ships of evil mien" 150 years ago this week. Before the black ships arrived on July 8th 1853, the Tokugawa shoguns had run Japan for 250 years as a reclusive feudal state. Carrying a letter from America's president, Millard Fillmore, and punctuating his message with cannon fire, Commodore Perry ordered Japan's rulers to drop their barriers and open the country to trade. Over the next century and a half, Japan emerged as one of history's great economic success stories. It is now the largest creditor to the world that it previously shunned. Attempts to dissect this economic "miracle" often focus intently on the aftermath of the second world war. Japan's occupation by the Americans, who set out to rebuild the country as a pacifist liberal democracy, helped to set the stage for four decades of jaw-dropping growth. Yet the origins of the miracle—and of the continual tensions it has created inside Japan and out—stretch further back. When General Douglas MacArthur accepted Japan's surrender in 1945 aboard the battleship Missouri, the Americans made sure to hang Commodore Perry's flag from 1853 over the ship's rear turret. They had not only ended a brutal war and avenged the attack on Pearl Harbour—they had also, they thought, won an argument with Japan that was by then nearly a century old.

America's enduring frustration—in the decades after 1853, in 1945, and even today—has not been so much that Japan is closed, but that it long ago mastered the art of opening up on its own terms. Before and after those black ships steamed into Edo Bay, after all, plenty of other countries were opened to trade by western cannon. What set Japan apart—perhaps aided by America's lack of colonial ambition—was its ability to decide for itself how to make the process of opening suit its own aims.

One consequence of this is that Japan's trading partners, especially America, have never tired of complaining about its economic practices. Japan-bashing reached its most recent peak in the 1980s, when American politicians and businessmen blamed "unfair" competition for Japan's large trade surpluses. But similar complaints could be heard within a few decades of Commodore Perry's mission. The attitude was summed up by "Mr Dooley", a character created by Peter Finley Dunne, an American satirist, at the close of the 19th century: "Th' trouble is whin the gallant Commodore kicked opn th' door, we didn't go in. They come out."

Nowadays, although poor countries still want Japan (along with America and the European Union) to free up trade in farm goods, most rich-country complaints about Japan are aimed at its approach to macroeconomics and finance, rather than its trade policies. Japan's insistence on protecting bad banks and worthless companies, say its many critics, and its reluctance to let foreign investors help fix the economy, have prevented Japanese demand from recovering for far too long. Once again, the refrain goes, Japan is unfairly taking what it can get from the world economy—exports and overseas profits have been its only source of comfort for years—without giving anything back.

While these complaints have always had some merit, they have all too often been made in a way that misses a crucial point: Japan's economic miracle, though at times paired with policies ranging from protectionist to xenophobic, has nevertheless proved a huge blessing to the rest of the world as well. The "structural impediments" that shut out imports in the 1980s did indeed keep Japanese consumers and foreign exporters from enjoying some of the fruits of that miracle; but its export prowess allowed western consumers to enjoy better and cheaper cars and electronics even as Japanese households grew richer. Similarly, Japan's resistance to inward investment is indefensible, not least because it allows salvageable Japanese companies to wither; but its outward investment has helped to transform much of East Asia into a thriving economic region, putting a huge dent in global poverty. Indeed, one of the most impressive aspects of Japan's economic miracle is that, even while reaping only half the potential gains from free trade and investment, it has still managed to do the world so much good over the past half-century.

Setting an example

Arguably, however, Japan's other big effect on the world has been even more important. It has shown clearly that you do not have to embrace "western" culture in order to modernise your economy and prosper. From the very beginning, Japan set out to have one without the other, an approach encapsulated by the saying "Japanese spirit, western things". How did Japan pull it off? In part, because the historical combination of having once been wide open, and then rapidly slamming shut, taught Japan how to control the aperture through which new ideas and practices streamed in. After eagerly absorbing Chinese culture, philosophy, writing and technology for roughly a millennium, Japan followed this with 250 years of near-total isolation. Christianity was outlawed, and overseas travel was punishable by death. Although some Japanese scholars were aware of developments in Europe—which went under the broad heading of "Dutch studies"—the shoguns strictly limited their ability to put any of that knowledge to use. They confined all economic and other exchanges with Europeans to a tiny man-made island in the south-western port of Nagasaki. When the Americans arrived in 1853, the Japanese told them to go to Nagasaki and obey the rules. Commodore Perry refused, and Japan concluded that the only way to "expel the barbarians" in future would be to embrace their technology and grow stronger.

But once the door was ajar, the Japanese appetite for "western things" grew unbounded. A modern guidebook entry on the port city of Yokohama, near Tokyo, notes that within two decades of the black ships' arrival it boasted the country's first bakery (1860), photo shop (1862), telephone (1869), beer brewery (1869), cinema (1870), daily newspaper (1870), and public lavatory (1871). Yet, at the same time, Japan's rulers also managed to frustrate many of the westerners' wishes. The constant tension between Japan's desire to measure up to the West—economically, diplomatically, socially and, until 1945, militarily—and its resistance to cultural change has played out in countless ways, good and bad, to this day. Much of it has reflected a healthy wish to hang on to local traditions. This is far more than just a matter of bowing and sleeping on futons and tatami, or of old women continuing to wear kimonos. The Japanese have also clung to distinct ways of speaking, interacting in the workplace, and showing each other respect, all of which have helped people to maintain harmony in many aspects of everyday life. Unfortunately, however, ever since they first opened to the West, anti-liberal Japanese leaders have preferred another interpretation of "Japanese spirit, western things". Instead of simply trying to preserve small cultural traditions, Japan's power-brokers tried to absorb western technology in a way that would shield them from political competition and protect their interests. Imitators still abound in Japan and elsewhere. In East Asia alone, Malaysia's Mahathir Mohamad, Thailand's Thaksin Shinawatra, and even the Chinese Communist Party all see Japan as proof that there is a way to join the rich-country club without making national leaders or their friends accountable. These disciples of Japan's brand of modernisation often use talk of local culture to resist economic and political threats to their power. But they are careful to find ways to do this without undermining all trade and investment, since growth is the only thing propping them up.

Japan's first attempt to pursue this strategy, it must never be forgotten, grew increasingly horrific as its inconsistencies mounted. In 1868, while western writers were admiring those bakeries and cinemas, Japan's nationalist leaders were "restoring" the emperor's significance to that of an imaginary golden age. The trouble, as Ian Buruma describes in his new book, "Inventing Japan" (see article), is that the "Japanese spirit" they valued was a concoction that mixed in several bad western ideas: German theories on racial purity, European excuses for colonialism, and the observation from Christianity that a single overarching deity (in Japan's case the newly restored emperor) could motivate soldiers better than a loose contingent of Shinto gods. This combination would eventually whip countless young Japanese into a murderous xenophobic frenzy and foster rapacious colonial aggression.

It also led Japan into a head-on collision with the United States, since colonialism directly contradicted America's reasons for sending Commodore Perry. In "The Clash", a 1998 book on the history of American-Japanese relations, Walter LaFeber argues that America's main goal in opening Japan was not so much to trade bilaterally, as to enlist Japan's support in creating a global marketplace including, in particular, China. At first, the United States opened Japan because it was on the way to China and had coal for American steamships. Later, as Japan gained industrial and military might, America sought to use it as a counterweight to European colonial powers that wanted to divide China among their empires. America grew steadily more furious, therefore, as Japan turned to colonialism and tried to carve up China on its own. The irony for America was that at its very moment of triumph, after nearly a century of struggling with European powers and then Japan to keep China united and open, it ended up losing it to communism.

A half-century later, however, and with a great deal of help from Japan, America has achieved almost exactly what it set out to do as a brash young power in the 1850s, when it had barely tamed its own continent and was less than a decade away from civil war. Mainland China is whole. It has joined the World Trade Organisation and is rapidly integrating itself into the global economy. It is part of a vast East Asian trade network that nevertheless carries out more than half of its trade outside the region. And this is all backed up by an array of American security guarantees in the Pacific. The resemblance to what America set out to do in 1853 is striking.

For both Japan and America, therefore, the difficult 150-year relationship has brought impressive results. They are now the world's two biggest economies, and have driven most of the world's technological advances over the past half-century. America has helped Japan by opening it up, destroying its militarists and rebuilding the country afterwards, and, for the last 50 years, providing security and market access while Japan became an advanced export dynamo. Japan has helped America by improving on many of its technologies, teaching it new manufacturing techniques, spurring on American firms with its competition, and venturing into East Asia to trade and invest.

And now?

What, then, will the continuing tension between Japanese spirit and western things bring in the decades ahead? For America, though it will no doubt keep complaining, Japan's resistance to change is not the real worry. Instead, the same two Asian challenges that America has taken on ever since Commodore Perry sailed in will remain the most worrying risks: potential rivalries, and the desire by some leaders to form exclusive regional economic blocks. America still needs Japan, its chief Asian ally, to combat these dangers. Japan's failure to reform, however, could slowly sap its usefulness.

For Japan, the challenges are far more daunting. Many of them stem from the increasing toll that Japan's old ways are taking on the economy. Chief among these is Japan's hostility towards competition in many aspects of economic life. Although competitive private firms have driven much of its innovation and growth, especially in export-intensive industries, Japan's political system continues to hobble competition and private enterprise in many domestic sectors.

In farming, health care and education, for example, recent efforts to allow private companies a role have been swatted down by co-operatives, workers, politicians and civil servants. In other inefficient sectors, such as construction and distribution, would-be losers continue to be propped up by government policy. Now that Japan is no longer growing rapidly, it is harder for competitive forces to function without allowing some of those losers to fail.

Japan's foreign critics are correct, moreover, that its macroeconomic and financial policies are a disgrace. The central bank, the finance ministry, the bank regulators, the prime minister and the ruling-party politicians all blame each other for failing to deal with the problems. All the while, Japan continues to limp along, growing far below its potential as its liabilities mount. Its public-sector debt, for instance, is a terrifying 140% of GDP.

Lately, there has been much talk about employing more western things to help lift Japan out of its mess. The prime minister, Junichiro Koizumi, talks about deregulatory measures that have been tried in North America, Europe and elsewhere. Western auditing and corporate governance techniques—applied in a Japanese way, of course—are also lauded as potential fixes. Even inward foreign direct investment is held out by Mr Koizumi as part of the solution: he has pledged to double it over the next five years. The trouble with all of these ideas, however, is that nobody in Japan is accountable for implementing them. Moreover, most of the politicians and bureaucrats who prevent competitive pressures from driving change are themselves protected from political competition. It is undeniable that real change in Japan would bring unwelcome pain for many workers and small-business owners. Still, Japan's leaders continue to use these cultural excuses, as they have for 150 years, to mask their own efforts to cling to power and prestige. The ugly, undemocratic and illiberal aspects of Japanese traditionalism continue to lurk behind its admirable elements. One reason they can do so is because Japan's nationalists have succeeded completely in one of their original goals: financial independence. The desire to avoid relying on foreign capital has underlain Japan's economic policies from the time it opened up to trade. Those policies have worked. More than 90% of government bonds are in the hands of domestic investors, and savings accounts run by the postal service play a huge role in propping up the system.

Paradoxically, financial self-reliance has thus become Japan's curse. There are worse curses to have, of course: compare Japan with the countless countries that have wrecked their economies by overexposing themselves to volatile international capital markets. Nevertheless, Japan's financial insularity further protects its politicians, who do not have to compete with other countries to get funding.

Theories abound as to how all of this might change. Its history ought to remind anyone that, however long it takes, Japan usually moves rapidly once a consensus takes shape. Potential pressures for change could come from the reversal of its trade surpluses, an erosion of support from all those placid postal savers, or the unwinding of ties that allow bad banks and bad companies to protect each other from investors. The current political stalemate could also give way to a coherent plan, either because one political or bureaucratic faction defeats the others or because a strong leader emerges who can force them to co-operate. The past 150 years suggest, however, that one important question is impossible to answer in advance: will it be liberalism or its enemies who turn such changes to their advantage? Too often, Japan's conservative and nationalist leaders have managed to spot the forces of change more quickly than their liberal domestic counterparts, and have used those changes to seize the advantage and preserve their power. Just as in the past, East Asia's fortunes still greatly depend on the outcome of the struggle between these perennial Japanese contenders.

Koizumi's Party, Backing Reforms, Wins by Landslide

NORIMITSU ONISHI

Prime Minister Junichiro Koizumi's Liberal Democratic Party won by a wider than expected landslide in Japan's general election on Sunday, earning a popular mandate to push through market reforms in the world's second largest economy.

The magnitude of the victory reversed the decade-long decline of the Liberal Democratic Party, which has ruled Japan nearly continuously for 50 years but had depended increasingly on its junior coalition partner, the New Komeito Party, to govern effectively. The results were a devastating setback for the Democratic Party, the main opposition, whose gains in recent elections had raised expectations that Japanese democracy was maturing into an era of two-party rule.

The results, reinforced by a high voter turnout, also amounted to a huge personal victory for Mr. Koizumi, who called an early election last month after rebellious members of his own party had rejected his bill to privatize Japan's postal service, the world's largest financial institution with $3 trillion in assets and an important part of the Japanese postwar political and economic structure.

In an election that Mr. Koizumi had successfully framed as a referendum on restructuring the postal services and making other economic reforms, his triumph suggested that voters agreed with his vision of invigorating Japan's economy, which has only started recovering from years of stagnation.

The Liberal Democratic Party won 296 seats in the 480-seat lower house of Parliament, up from 249 when the election was called. The Democratic Party's share of seats dropped to 113 from 175.

Along with the 31 seats held by the New Komeito Party, the Liberal Democratic Party will have more than the two-thirds of the lower house's seats to overrule decisions by the upper house, which voted down the postal bill.

"I thought it would be O.K. for the L.D.P. to get a simple majority, but people gave us even better results than we had expected," Mr. Koizumi said of his party. "I'm overwhelmed with gratitude.

"I think the people handed down a verdict that postal reform is right," he said from the party's headquarters.

The victory by Mr. Koizumi, who has been one of the strongest backers of the American-led war in Iraq and enjoys a personal relationship with President Bush, will be welcomed in Washington. But it is likely to be greeted with caution in Asia, especially in China and South Korea, which view with trepidation the rightward tilt and rising nationalism in Japan on Mr. Koizumi's watch.

Mr. Koizumi's repeated visits to Yasukuni Shrine, the memorial where war criminals are deified, have harmed relations with China, whose booming economy has lifted Japan's. After his victory on Sunday, Mr. Koizumi, who has pledged to visit the shrine every year, said he had not changed his position.

During the 12-day campaign, Mr. Koizumi succeeded in narrowing the electorate's focus to postal reform and domestic issues. The main opposition Democratic Party—which opposed the Yasukuni visits, pledged to withdraw Japanese troops from Iraq and repair relations with China and South Korea—failed to widen the focus to issues that could have hurt Mr. Koizumi at the ballot.

"I firmly believe our stance to focus on our policies was not wrong," said the Democratic Party leader, Katsuya Okada. "Our message didn't reach the people."

Mr. Okada announced that he would step down as party leader because of the loss. Analysts have said that a big loss could lead to the breakup of the Democratic Party, which was formed in 1998 by former Liberal Democrats, Socialists and other members.

Other parties vying in the election opposed postal privatization but, in an appeal to the deep-rooted popular feeling that Japan needs to transform itself to move forward, said they supported political and economic reforms. But by making postal privatization—an arcane issue little understood by most voters—a litmus test for reform, Mr. Koizumi was able to paint its opponents, including the Democratic Party, as reactionaries.

"This election shows how Koizumi is in a league of his own in his political skills and media savvy," said Gerald Curtis, an expert on Japanese politics at Columbia University who is visiting Tokyo. "He did the impossible. He managed to convince the electorate that his party, which was opposed to his own reforms, was for change, and that the Democratic Party, which was a party founded for reform, was against change."

Mr. Koizumi wants to break up and privatize Japan Post, which in addition to delivering mail holds $3 trillion in savings and life insurance deposits that politicians have dipped into for decades to finance public works and reward their backers. He has said that it is the prerequisite for further, if vaguely defined, reforms in the Japanese economy, the world's second largest behind that of the United States.

In his four years in office, Mr. Koizumi's economic policies, including reductions in public spending and the cleaning of bad loans from the banking sector, have been faulted by some economists for not going far enough. But there is also a sense in Japan, which has always had ambivalent feelings toward American-style capitalism at home, that the policies have hurt the Japanese and helped create a society of economic losers and winners.

Opponents of postal reform said Japan's peculiar postal system, for all its faults, also helped create an egalitarian society by spreading wealth from urban to rural areas.

"If things keep going like this, this will be the end of Japan," Shizuka Kamei, a postal rebel who was expelled from the Liberal Democratic Party by Mr. Koizumi but was reelected as a member of a new party, said Sunday night on Japanese television.

By replacing postal opponents with younger, mostly female candidates, Mr. Koizumi succeeded in changing the image of the Liberal Democratic Party, long asso-ciated with old men in dark suits. The strong results suggested that Mr. Koizumi had made his party more attractive to the same younger and urban voters who had handed the opposition Democratic Party victories in cities in previous elections.

"We've destroyed the old L.D.P.," Mr. Koizumi said.

UNIT 2
Pluralist Democracies: Factors in the Political Process

Unit Selections

Key Points to Consider

- What is meant by the term *social capital* as used by Robert Putnam?
- How do you explain the apparent shifts toward the political center made by parties of the moderate Left and moderate Right?
- Why are women so poorly represented in Parliament and other positions of political leadership? Where and why?
- Would you agree with the inventory of democratic essentials as discussed by Philippe Schmitter and Terry Lynn Karl?
- What are some of the major arguments made in favor of the parliamentary system of government?
- Why do you think Christopher S. Allen includes a multiparty system in his discussion of institutional transplantation?
- Why did de Gaulle include a national referendum in the constitution of the Fifth Republic?
- Do you agree with Robert Kagan, that "Americans are from Mars, Europeans are from Venus"? Why or why not?

Student Website
www.mhcls.com/online

Internet References
Further information regarding these websites may be found in this book's preface or online.

Carnegie Endowment for International Peace
   http://www.ceip.org
Inter-American Dialogue (IAD)
   http://www.iadialog.org
The North American Institute (NAMI)
   http://www.northamericaninstitute.org

Observers of contemporary Western societies frequently refer to the emergence of a new politics in these countries. They are not always very clear or in agreement about what is supposedly novel in the political process or why it is significant. Although no one would dispute that there have been major changes in these societies during the last three decades or more, affecting both political attitudes and behavior, it is very difficult to establish comparable patterns of transformation or to gauge their impact and endurance. Yet making sense of continuities and changes in political values and behavior must be one of the central tasks of a comparative study of government.

In two important lines of inquiry, political comparativists have examined the rise and spread of a new set of "postmaterial" values and, more recently, the growing signs of political disaffection in both "older" and "newer" democracies. The articles in this reader also explore some other trends with major impacts on contemporary politics. Very high on the list is the recent wave of democratization—that is, the uneven, incomplete, and unstable but nevertheless remarkable spread of democratic forms of governance to many countries during the last three decades. An important place must also go to the controversial "paradigm shift" toward a greater reliance on some kind of market economics in much of the world. This move, which has created its own problems and conflicts, also comes in different forms that span the gamut from partial measures of deregulation and privatization in some countries to the practical abandonment of central planning in others. Finally, political scientists recognize the important rise or revival of various forms of "identity politics." This shift has intensified the political role of ethnicity, race, gender, religion, language, and other elements of group identification that go beyond more traditional social, economic, and ideological lines of political division.

Since the early 1970s, political scientists have followed Ronald Inglehart and other careful observers who first noted a marked increase in what they called postmaterial values, especially among younger and more highly educated people in the skilled service and administrative occupations in Western Europe. Such voters showed less interest in the traditional material values of economic well-being and security, and instead stressed participatory and environmental concerns in politics as a way of improving democracy and the general "quality of life." Studies of postmaterialism form a very important addition to our ongoing attempt to interpret and explain not only the so-called youth revolt but also some more lasting shifts in lifestyles and political priorities. It makes intuitive sense that such changes appear to be especially marked among those who grew up in the relative prosperity of Western Europe, after the austere period of reconstruction that followed World War II.

The shift in the postmaterial direction has not been complete, nor is it necessarily permanent. It is possible to find countervailing trends such as the apparent revival of material concerns among some younger people, as economic prosperity and security seem to have become less certain. There are also some indications that political reform activities evoke considerably less interest and commitment than they did in the 1970s.

None of this should be mistaken for a return to the political patterns of the past. Instead, we may be witnessing the emergence of a still somewhat incongruent new mix of material and postmaterial orientations, along with "old" and "new" forms of political self-expression by the citizenry. Established political parties appear to be in somewhat of a quandary in redefining their positions, at a time when the traditional bonding of many voters to one or another party seems to have become weaker, a phenomenon also known as dealignment. Some observers perceive a condition of political malaise in advanced industrial countries, suggesting that the decline of confidence in public officials and government show up not only in opinion polls but also in voting behavior.

The readings in this unit begin with three political briefs that present a comparative perspective on public disillusionment and the decline in voter turnout, the partial weakening of the political parties, and the apparent growth of special interest lobbying. These briefs contain a rich assortment of comparative data and interpretation.

Without suggesting a simple cause-effect relationship, the British observer Martin Jacques has pointed to possible connections between electoral "dealignment" and the vague rhetoric offered by many political activists and opinion leaders. He believes that the end of the cold war and the collapse of communism in Europe have created a situation that demands a reformulation of political and ideological alternatives. In light of the sharpened differences between much of Europe and the United States over how to approach the Middle East and some other topics such as the Kyoto Accords, some observers wonder whether the end of the cold war will also mean the permanent weakening of the familiar transatlantic relationship. At this point, the situation is still in flux.

Most established parties seem to have developed an ability to adjust to change, even as the balance of power within each party system shifts over time and occasional newcomers are admitted to the club—or excluded from it. Each country's party system remains uniquely shaped by its political history, but it is possible to delineate some very general patterns of development. One frequently observed trend is toward a narrowing of the ideological distance between the **moderate Left and Right** in many European countries. Because of this partial political convergence, it now often makes more sense to speak of the **Center-Left and Center-Right** respectively.

Even where such a convergence is observable, there are still some important ideological and practical differences between the two orientations. Thus **the Right** is usually far more ready to accept as "inevitable" the existence of social or economic inequalities along with the social hierarchies they reflect and reinforce. The Right normally favors lower taxes and the promotion of market forces—with some very important exceptions intended to protect the nation as a whole (national defense and internal security) as well as certain favorite interest groups (clienteles) and values within it. In general, the Right sees the state as an instrument that should provide security, order, and protection for an established way of life. **The Left,** by contrast, traditionally emphasizes that government has an important task in opening greater opportunities or life chances for everyone, delivering affordable public services, and generally reducing social inequalities. On issues such as higher and more progressive taxation, or

their respective concern for high rates of unemployment and inflation, there continue to be considerable differences between moderates of the Left and Right.

Even as the ideological distance between Left and Right narrows but remains important, there are also signs of some political differentiation within each camp. On the center-right side of the party spectrum in European politics, **economic neoliberals** (who often seem to speak for high riding and self-confident elements in the business sector) must be clearly distinguished from the social conservatives (who are more likely to advocate traditional values and authority). **European liberalism** has its roots in a tradition that favors civil liberties and tolerance but that also emphasizes the importance of individual achievement and laissez-faire economics. In both European and Latin American politics one encounters neoliberals. For them, the state has an important but limited role to play in providing an institutional framework within which individuals and social groups pursue their interests without much government intervention—or, as they might say, "interference."

Traditional social conservatives, by contrast, emphasize the importance of societal stability and continuity, and point to the social danger of disruptive change. They often value the strong state as an instrument of order, but many of them also show a paternalist appreciation for welfare state programs that will help keep "the social fabric" from tearing apart. For them, there is a conservative case for a limited welfare state that is not rooted in social liberal or socialist convictions. Instead, it is supported by traditional sentiments of *noblesse oblige* (roughly translated as "privilege has its obligations") and a practical concern for maintaining social harmony.

In British politics, Margaret Thatcher promoted elements from each of these traditions in what could be called her own mix of **"business conservatism."** The result was a peculiar tension between **"drys"** and **"wets"** within her Conservative Party, even after she ceased to be its leader. In France, on the other hand, the division between neoliberals and conservatives until recently ran more clearly between the two major center-right parties, the very loosely united Giscardist UDF (Union for French Democracy), and the more stable neo-Gaullist RPR (Rally for the Republic). They have been coalition partners in several governments and also form electoral alliances at the second, run-off stage in French elections. In Germany, the Free Democrats

(FDP) most clearly represent the traditional liberal position, including its compromises on behalf of special clienteles (the pharmaceutical industry, for example), while traditional conservative elements can be found alongside business conservatives among the country's Christian Democrats (CDU/CSU).

On the Left, democratic socialists and ecologists stress that the sorry political, economic, and environmental record of communist-ruled states in no way diminishes the validity of their own commitment to social justice and environmental protection in modern industrial society. For them, capitalism will continue to produce its own social problems and dissatisfactions. No matter how efficient capitalism may be, they argue, it will continue to result in inequities and alienation that require politically directed redress. Today, many on the Left show a pragmatic acceptance of the modified market economy as an arena within which to promote their goals of redistribution. Social Democrats in Scandinavia and Germany have long been known for taking such positions. In recent years their colleagues in Britain and, to a lesser degree, France have followed suit by abandoning some traditional symbols and goals, such as major programs of nationalization. The moderate Socialists in Spain, who governed that new democracy after 1982, also adopted business-friendly policies before they lost office in early 1996. They were returned to government in a stunning electoral upset in March 2004 that appears to have been a protest against the support of the invasion of Iraq by the conservative incumbents. The socialists had trailed the conservatives until a few days before the election, when terrorist train bombings in Madrid killed about 200 people and injured many hundreds more. The new socialist Prime Minister, José Luis Rodriguez Zapatero, quickly carried out his promise to withdraw Spanish troops from Iraq.

Some other West European parties, further to the left, have also moved in the centrist direction in recent years. Two striking examples of this shift can be found among the Greens in Germany and in what used to be the Communist Party of Italy. The **German Greens** are by no means an establishment party, but they have served as a pragmatic coalition partner with the Social Democrats in several state governments and have gained respect for their mixture of practical competence and idealism. Members of what has been dubbed their "realo" or realist faction appear to have outmaneuvered their more radical or "fundamentalist" rivals (the so-called Fundis). The Greens were finally able to enter government at the national level in 1998. In Gerhard Schröder's government of Social Democrats and Greens, the leading "realo" Joschka Fischer became foreign minister and two other cabinet posts were held by fellow environmentalists. Many German Greens identified with the pacifist tradition and had a difficult time accepting their country's military involvement in the Kosovo conflict in 1999 and, more recently, in Afghanistan. There were additional policy compromises by the new government that were difficult to square with the idealist origins of the Greens and their supporters, but Germany's public disagreement with the United States on the invasion of Iraq helped them recover after a string of electoral setbacks. They now appear to have become a firmly established small party with a distinctive program and a solid record in coalition politics.

The **Italian Communists** have come an even longer way in reaching their present center-left position. In 1991, they renamed themselves the Democratic Party of the Left (PDS), now Left Democrats (DS). Already years before, they had begun to abandon the Leninist revolutionary tradition and adopt reformist goals and strategies that were similar to those identified with social democratic parties elsewhere in Western Europe. The Italian Communists were long kept out of national coalition politics, but they gained credibility through their pragmatic and often competent performance in local and regional politics. Not every Italian Communist went along with the party's deradicalization, and a fundamentalist core broke away to set up a new far left party of Refounded Communists. In 1998, however, the post-Communists fully joined the establishment they had once fought, when their leader, Massimo D'Alema became Italy's new prime minister, who for more than a year headed a broad center-left coalition of parties.

Both center-left and center-right moderates in Europe face a challenge from the populist tendency on the **Far Right** that usually seeks to curtail or halt immigration. There is sometimes a separate neo-fascist or fascist-descended challenge as well. In Italy, for example, the populist Northern League and the fascist descended National Alliance represent positions that seem to be polar opposites on such key issues as government devolution (favored by the former, opposed by the latter). Sometimes a charismatic leader can speak to both orientations, by appealing to their shared fears and resentments. That seems to be the case of Jörg Haider, whose Freedom Party managed to attract over one-quarter of the vote in Austria in the late 1990s. The electoral revival of the far-right parties can be linked in considerable part to anxieties and tensions that affect some socially and economically insecure groups in the lower middle class and some sectors of the working class.

Ultra-right nationalist politicians and their parties typically eschew a complex explanation of the structural and cyclical problems that beset the European economies. Instead, their simple answer is to blame external scapegoats, namely the many immigrants and refugees from Eastern Europe as well as developing countries in Africa and Asia. These far-right parties can be found in many countries, including some that have earned a reputation for tolerance like the Netherlands and Denmark. Nowhere are these parties in control of a national government, but they represent a potential threat to the established parties, which have responded by making concessions on immigration and refugee policy.

Women in politics are the concern of the second section in this unit. There continues to be a strong pattern of underrepresentation of women in positions of political and economic leadership practically everywhere. Yet there are some notable differences from country to country, as well as from party to party. Generally speaking, the parties of the Left have been far more ready to place women in positions of authority. There are some remarkable exceptions, as the center-right cases of Margaret Thatcher in Britain, Angela Merkel in Germany, and Simone Weil in France illustrate. Far-right parties tend to draw markedly less support from female voters, but at least one of them is led by a woman: Pia Kjaersgaard founded and still heads the People's Party of Denmark.

On the whole, the system of proportional representation gives parties both a tool and an added incentive to place female candidates in positions where they will be elected. But here too, there can be exceptions, as in the case of France in 1986 when women did not benefit from the one-time use of proportional representation in the parliamentary elections. Clearly it is not enough to have a relatively simple means, such as proportional representation, for promoting a hitherto underrepresented group. There must also be an organized will and a strategy among decision makers to use the available tool for the purpose of such a clearly defined reform.

This is where affirmative action can become a decisive strategic element for promoting change. The Scandinavian countries illustrate better than any other example how the breakthrough may occur. There is a markedly higher representation of women in the parliaments of Denmark, Finland, Iceland, Norway, and Sweden, where the political center of gravity is somewhat to the Left and where proportional representation makes it possible to set up party lists that are more representative of the population as a whole than a FPTP system would be. It is of some interest that Iceland has for years had a special women's party with parliamentary representation and that Sweden is now following suit with such a party as well. Far more important is the fact that women are found in leading positions within most of the parties of this and the other Scandinavian countries. It usually does not take long for the more centrist or moderately conservative parties to adopt the new concern of gender equality, and these may even move toward the forefront. Thus women have in recent years held the leadership of three of the main parties in Norway (the Social Democrats, the Center Party, and the Conservatives), which together normally receive roughly two-thirds of the total popular vote. It is no longer newsworthy, when a Swedish government of Social Democrats has an equal number of women and men in the cabinet.

In another widely reported sign of change, the relatively conservative Republic of Ireland several years ago chose Mary Robinson as its first female president. It is a largely ceremonial post, but it has a symbolic potential that Mary Robinson, an outspoken advocate of liberal reform in her country, was willing to use on behalf of social change. In 1998, a second woman president was elected in Ireland, while Ms Robinson went on to a leading position in the United Nations. Perhaps most remarkable of all, the advancement of women into high political ranks has now also touched Switzerland, where they did not get the right to vote until 1971. It is equally noteworthy that Prime Minister Koizumi of Japan appointed five women to his cabinet when he assumed office in 2001, an absolute first in that male-dominated society.

Altogether, there is a growing awareness of the pattern of gender discrimination in most Western countries, along with a greater will to do something to rectify the situation. It seems likely that there will be a significant improvement over the course of the next decade if the pressure for reform is maintained. Several countries have now passed the 30 percent level in their national parliaments, regarded by some observers like Mary Hampton as a "critical mass." In France, it was lack of political will that derailed one of the most remarkable recent attempts at reform, at least on the first try. It took the form of a statute, promoted by the socialist-led government of France, which required the country's political parties to field an equal number of male and female candidates for office in most elections. The first major test of this new party measure came in the French parliamentary elections of 2002, where it was widely flouted.

Changes that erode gender inequality have already occurred in other areas, where there used to be significant political differences between men and women. At one time, for example, there used to be a considerably lower voter turnout among women, but this gender gap has been practically eliminated in recent decades. Similarly a tendency for women to be more conservative than men in their party and candidate preferences has given way to a more liberal disposition among younger women in their foreign and social policy preferences. These are aggregate differences, of course, and it is important to remember that women, like men, do not present a monolithic bloc in political attitudes and behavior but are divided by a variety of interests and priorities. One generalization seems to hold: namely, that there is much less inclination among women to support parties or candidates that have a decidedly "radical" image. Thus there is considerably more support among men for extreme right-wing parties in contemporary Europe.

In any case, there are some very important policy questions that affect women more directly than men. Any careful statistical study of women in the paid labor force of Europe would still be likely to support three widely shared impressions: (1) In recent decades there has been a considerable increase in the absolute number and relative proportion of women who take up paid jobs; (2) these jobs are more often unskilled and/or part-time than in the case of men's employment; and (3) women generally receive less pay and less social protection than men in similar positions. Such a study would also show that there are considerable differences among Western European countries in the relative position of their female workers. The findings would also be likely to support the argument that political intervention in the form of appropriate legislation can lead to an improvement in the employment status of women. Without political action, it seems doubtful that much would be accomplished.

The socioeconomic status of women in other parts of the world is often far worse. According to reports of the UN Development Program, there have been some rapid advances for women in the field of education and health opportunities, but the doors to economic opportunities are barely ajar. In the field of political leadership, the picture is more varied, as the UN reports indicate, but women generally hold few positions of importance in national politics. Rwanda is an exception. Here genocide has left women, who now make up nearly two-thirds of the country's population, in positions of leadership.

The institutional framework of representative government is the subject of the third section of this unit. Here the authors examine and compare a number of institutional arrangements: (1) essential characteristics and elements of a pluralist democracy, (2) two major forms of representative government, (3) varieties of judicial review, and (4) the use of national and regional referendums as well as other forms of direct democracy. The topic of pluralist democracy is a complex one and needs to be discussed from different perspectives. Robert Dahl draws on a lifelong commitment to present what he regards as the basic institutional infrastructure of a representative form of government. Philippe Schmitter and Terry Lynn Karl present a superb discussion of what a democracy "is and "isn't." The next two political briefs examine the remarkable growth and variety of forms taken by judicial review in recent years as well as the arguments for and against the use of the referendum as a way of increasing the electoral involvement with policy-making.

American Politics in Comparative Perspective. The last articles in this unit show some ways in which American politics can be usefully included in our comparative studies. Timothy Garton Ash critically reviews Robert Kagan's argument about the "Great Divide" between the United States and Western Europe in the prevailing approach to international relations. He does not dismiss the alleged differences. Instead he modifies them by pointing to some shared values and interests that continue to link the two. In its discussion of American beliefs and values, *The Economist* also sees areas of similarity and dissimilarity. It singles out the high incidence of traditional beliefs in the United States that contrasts with the more secular orientation prevailing in Europe. Americans, for example, are far more likely to express patriotic sentiments and religious beliefs than their West European contemporaries.

Finally, Christopher S. Allen brings U.S. political institutions into our comparative framework. His article can be seen as part of a long tradition of American interest in the parliamentary form of government and, to a lesser degree, in a multiparty system. Allen organizes his argument as a mental experiment in institutional transplantation, in order to explore how a multiparty parliamentary system would be likely to change the American political process. His intriguing rearrangement of our familiar political setting serves as a reminder that institutions are not neutral but have important consequences for the political process.

Public Opinion: Is there a crisis?

After the collapse of communism, the world saw a surge in the number of new democracies. But why are the citizens of the mature democracies meanwhile losing confidence in their political institutions? This is the first in a series of articles on democracy in transition.

Everyone remembers that Winston Churchill once called democracy the worst form of government—except for all the others. The end of the cold war seemed to prove him right. All but a handful of countries now claim to embrace democratic ide-

als. Insofar as there is a debate about democracy, much of it now centers on how to help the "emerging" democracies of Asia, Africa, Latin America and Eastern Europe catch up with the established democratic countries of the West and Japan.

The new democracies are used to having well-meaning observers from the mature democracies descend on them at election time to ensure that the voting is free and fair. But is political life in these mature democracies as healthy as it should be?

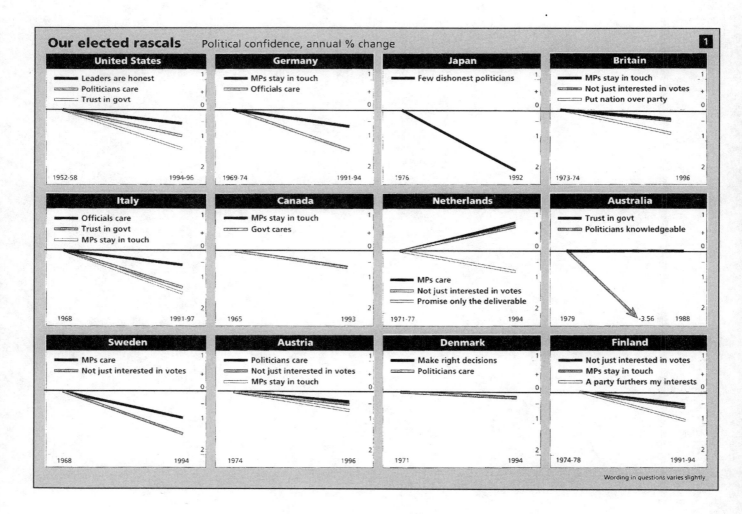

Our elected rascals Political confidence, annual % change

United States
— Leaders are honest
— Politicians care
— Trust in govt
1952-58 — 1994-96

Germany
— MPs stay in touch
— Officials care
1969-74 — 1991-94

Japan
— Few dishonest politicians
1976 — 1992

Britain
— MPs stay in touch
— Not just interested in votes
— Put nation over party
1973-74 — 1996

Italy
— Officials care
— Trust in govt
— MPs stay in touch
1968 — 1991-97

Canada
— MPs stay in touch
— Govt cares
1965 — 1993

Netherlands
— MPs care
— Not just interested in votes
— Promise only the deliverable
1971-77 — 1994

Australia
— Trust in govt
— Politicians knowledgeable
1979 — -3.56 — 1988

Sweden
— MPs care
— Not just interested in votes
1968 — 1994

Austria
— Politicians care
— Not just interested in votes
— MPs stay in touch
1974 — 1996

Denmark
— Make right decisions
— Politicians care
1971 — 1994

Finland
— Not just interested in votes
— MPs stay in touch
— A party furthers my interests
1974-78 — 1991-94

Wording in questions varies slightly

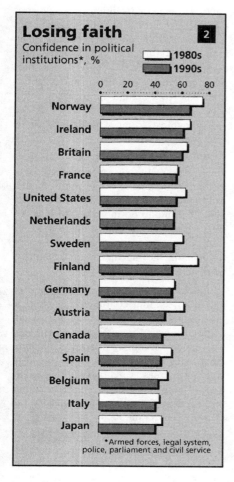

Losing faith

Confidence in political institutions*, %

☐ 1980s
■ 1990s

Norway
Ireland
Britain
France
United States
Netherlands
Sweden
Finland
Germany
Austria
Canada
Spain
Belgium
Italy
Japan

*Armed forces, legal system, police, parliament and civil service

Sources: R. Dalton; World Values Surveys

If opinion research is any guide, the mature democracies have troubles of their own. In the United States in particular, the high opinion which people had of their government has declined steadily over the past four decades. Regular opinion surveys carried out as part of a series of national election studies in America show that the slump set in during the 1960s. The civil-rights conflict and the Vietnam war made this an especially turbulent decade for the United States. But public confidence in politicians and government continued to decline over the next quarter-century. Nor (remember the student unrest in Paris and elsewhere in 1968) was this confined to the United States.

It is hard to compare attitudes toward democracy over time, and across many different countries. Most opinion surveys are carried out nation-by-nation: they are conducted at different times and researchers often ask different sorts of questions. But some generalizations can be made. In their introduction to a forthcoming book "What is Troubling the Trilateral Democracies?", Princeton University Press, 2000) three ac-

ademics—Robert Putnam, Susan Pharr, and Russell Dalton—have done their best to analyze the results of surveys conducted in most of the rich countries.

Chart 1 summarises some of these findings. The downward slopes show how public confidence in politicians seems to be falling, measured by changes in the answers voters give to questions such as "Do you think that politicians are trustworthy?"; "Do members of parliament (MPS) care about voters like you?"; and "How much do you trust governments of any party to place the needs of the nation above their own political party?" In most of the mature democracies, the results show a pattern of disillusionment with politicians. Only in the Netherlands is there clear evidence of rising confidence.

Nor is it only politicians who are losing the public's trust. Surveys suggest that confidence in political institutions is in decline as well. In 11 out of 14 countries, for example, confidence in parliament has declined, with especially sharp falls in Canada, Germany, Britain, Sweden and the United States. World-wide polls conducted in 1981 and 1990 measured confidence in five institutions: parliament, the armed services, the judiciary, the police and the civil service. Some institutions gained public trust, but on average confidence in them decreased by 6% over the decade (see chart 2). The only countries to score small increases in confidence were Iceland and Denmark.

Other findings summarised by Mr Putnam and his colleagues make uncomfortable reading:

• In the late 1950s and early 1960s **Americans** had a touching faith in government. When asked "How many times can you trust the government in Washington to do what is right?", three out of four answered "most of the time" or "just about always". By 1998, fewer than four out of ten trusted the government to do what was right. In 1964 only 29% of the American electorate agreed that "the government is pretty much run by a few big interests looking after themselves". By 1984, that figure had risen to 55%, and by 1998 to 63%. In the 1960s, two-thirds of Americans rejected the statement "most elected officials don't care what people like me think". In 1998, nearly two-thirds agreed with it. The proportion of Americans who expressed "a great deal of" confidence in the executive branch fell from 42% in 1966 to 12% in 1997; and trust in Congress fell from 42% to 11%.

• **Canadians** have also been losing faith in their politicians. The proportion of Canadians who felt that "the government doesn't care what people like me think" rose from 45% in 1968 to 67% in 1993. The proportion expressing "a great deal of" confidence in political parties fell from 30% in 1979 to 11% in 1999. Confidence in the House of Commons fell from 49% in 1974 to 21% in 1996. By 1992 only 34% of Canadians were satisfied with their system of government, down from 51% in 1986.

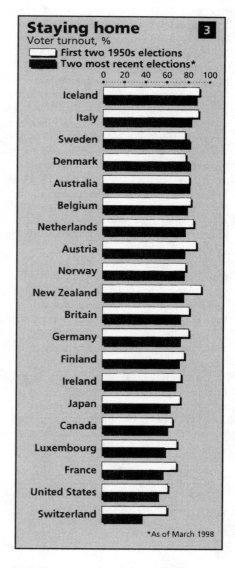

Staying home

Voter turnout, %

☐ First two 1950s elections
■ Two most recent elections*

Iceland
Italy
Sweden
Denmark
Australia
Belgium
Netherlands
Austria
Norway
New Zealand
Britain
Germany
Finland
Ireland
Japan
Canada
Luxembourg
France
United States
Switzerland

*As of March 1998

Source: Martin P. Wattenberg, University of California, Irvine

• Less information is available about attitudes in **Japan**. But the findings of the few surveys that have been carried out there match the global pattern. Confidence in political institutions rose in the decades following the smashing of the country's old politics in the second world war. Happily for democracy, the proportion of Japanese voters who agree that "in order to make Japan better, it is best to rely on talented politicians, rather than to let the citizens argue among themselves" has been falling for 40 years. However, the proportion who feel that they exert at least "some influence" on national politics through elections or demonstrations also fell steadily between 1973 and 1993.

• Although it is harder to generalize about **Western Europe**, confidence in political institutions is in decline in most countries. In 1985 48% of Britons expressed quite a lot of confidence in the House of Commons. This number had halved by 1995. The proportion of Swedes disagreeing with the statement that "parties are only interested in people's votes, not in their opinions" slumped from 51% in 1968 to 28% in 1994. In 1985 51% expressed confidence in the Rikstad (parliament); by 1996 only 19% did. In Germany, the percentage of people who said they trusted their Bundestag deputy to represent their interests rose from 25% in 1951 to 55% in 1978, but had fallen again to 34% by 1992. The percentage of Italians who say that politicians "don't care what people like me think" increased from 68% in 1968 to 84% in 1997.

Such findings are alarming if you take them at face value. But they should be interpreted with care. Democracy may just be a victim of its own success. It could just be that people nowadays expect more from governments, impose new demands on the state, and are therefore more likely to be disappointed. After all, the idea that governments ought to do such things as protect or improve the environment, maintain high employment, arbitrate between moral issues, or ensure the equal treatment of women or minorities, is a relatively modern and still controversial one. Or perhaps

the disillusionment is a healthy product of rising educational standards and the scepticism that goes with it. Or maybe it is caused by the media's search-light highlighting failures of government that were previously kept in the dark. Whatever the causes, the popularity of governments or politicians ought not to be the only test of democracy's health.

Moreover, there is encouraging evidence to put beside the discouraging findings. However much confidence in government may be declining, this does not seem to have diminished popular support for democratic principles. On average, surveys show, more than three out of four people in rich countries believe that democracy is the best form of government. Even in countries where the performance of particular governments has been so disappointing as to break up the party system itself (such as Japan and Italy in 1993–95), this has brought no serious threat to fundamental democratic principle. It may seem paradoxical for people to express strong support for democracy even while their confidence in politicians and political institutions crumbles. But it hardly amounts to the "crisis of democracy" which political scientists tend to proclaim from time to time.

Nor, though, is it a ringing endorsement, especially given that the evidence of opinion surveys is reinforced by other trends. These include a decline both in the membership of political parties and in the proportion of people who turn out to vote. Numbers compiled by Martin Wattenberg, also at the University of California, show that in 18 out of 20 of the rich established democracies the proportion of the electorate voting has been lower than it was in the early 1950s (see chart 3), with the median change being a decline of 10%. More controversially, some political scientists see the growth of protest movements since the

1960s as a sign of declining faith in the traditional institutions of representative democracy, and an attempt to bypass them. Others reckon that the most serious threat comes from the increasingly professional pressure groups and lobbying organisations that work behind the scenes to influence government policy and defend special interests, often at the expense of the electorate as a whole.

What is to be done? Those who believe that government has over-reached itself call on governments to become smaller and to promise less. Thus, it is hoped, people will come to do more for themselves. But whatever the appropriate size and reach of governments, there is also scope for making the machinery of democracy work better.

Indeed, some commentators see the public's declining confidence in political institutions as an opportunity for democratic renewal. Pippa Norris, at Harvard University's Kennedy School of Government, hails the advent of a new breed of "critical citizens" (in a book of that name, Oxford University Press, 1999) who see that existing channels of participation fall short of democratic ideals and want to reform them.

There are some signs of this. Countries as different as Italy, Japan, Britain and New Zealand have lately considered or introduced changes in their electoral systems. Countries around the world are making growing use of referendums and other forms of direct democracy. Many are reducing the power of parliaments by giving judges new powers to review the decisions that elected politicians make. And governments everywhere are introducing new rules on the financing of politicians and political parties. The rest of the articles in this series will look at some of these changes and the forces shaping them.

Political Parties: Empty vessels?

Alexis de Tocqueville called political parties an evil inherent in free governments. The second of our briefs on the mature democracies in transition asks whether parties are in decline

WHAT would democracy look like if there were no political parties? It is almost impossible to imagine. In every democracy worth the name, the contest to win the allegiance of the electorate and form a government takes place through political parties. Without them, voters would be hard put to work out what individual candidates stood for or intended to do once elected. If parties did not "aggregate" people's interests, politics might degenerate into a fight between tiny factions, each promoting its narrow self-interest. But for the past 30 years, political scientists have been asking whether parties are "in decline". Are they? And if so, does it matter?

Generalising about political parties is difficult. Their shape depends on a country's history, constitution and much else. For example, America's federal structure and separation of powers make Republicans and Democrats amorphous groupings whose main purpose is to put their man in the White House. British parties behave quite differently because members of Parliament must toe the party line to keep their man in Downing Street. An American president is safe once elected, so congressmen behave like local representatives rather than members of a national organisation bearing collective responsibility for government. Countries which, unlike Britain and America, hold elections under proportional representation are different again: they tend to produce multi-party systems and coalition governments.

Despite these differences, some trends common to almost all advanced democracies appear to be changing the nature of parties and, on one view, making them less

influential. Those who buy this thesis of decline point to the following changes:

People's behaviour is becoming more **private**. Why join a political party when you can go fly fishing or surf the web? Back in the 1950s, clubs affiliated to the Labour Party were places for Britain's working people to meet, play and study. The Conservative Party was, among other things, a marriage bureau for the better-off. Today, belonging to a British political party is more like being a supporter of some charity: you may pay a membership fee, but will not necessarily attend meetings or help to turn out the vote at election time.

Running out of ideas

Politics is becoming more **secular**. Before the 1960s, political struggles had an almost religious intensity: in much of Western Europe this took the form of communists versus Catholics, or workers versus bosses. But ideological differences were narrowing by the 1960s and became smaller still after the collapse of Soviet communism. Nowadays, politics seems to be more often about policies than values, about the competence of leaders rather than the beliefs of the led. As education grows and class distinctions blur, voters discard old loyalties. In America in 1960, two out of five voters saw themselves as "strong" Democrats or "strong" Republicans. By 1996 less than one in three saw themselves that way. The proportion of British voters expressing a "very strong" affinity with one party slumped from 44% to 16% between 1964 and 1997. This process of **"partisan de-**

alignment" has been witnessed in most mature democracies.

The erosion of loyalty is said to have pushed parties towards the **ideological centre**. The political extremes have not gone away. But mainstream parties which used to offer a straight choice between socialists and conservatives are no longer so easy to label. In the late 1950s Germany's Social Democrats (SPD) snipped off their Marxist roots in order to recast themselves is a *Volkspartei* appealing to all the people. "New" Labour no longer portrays itself as the political arm of the British working class or trade-union movement. Bill Clinton, before he became president, helped to shift the Democratic Party towards an appreciation of business and free trade. Neat ideological labels have become harder to pin on parties since they have had to contend with the emergence of what some commentators call **post-material issues** (such as the environment, personal morality and consumer rights) which do not slot elegantly into the old left-right framework

The **mass media** have taken over many of the information functions that parties once performed for themselves. "Just as radio and television have largely killed off the door-to-door salesman," says Anthony King, of Britain's Essex University, "so they have largely killed off the old-fashioned party worker." In 1878 the German SPD had nearly 50 of its own newspapers. Today the mass media enable politicians to communicate directly with voters without owning printing presses or needing party workers to knock on doors. In many other ways, the business of winning elections has become more capital-intensive and less labour-intensive, making political donors matter more and political activists less.

Another apparent threat to the parties is the growth of **interest and pressure groups**. Why should voters care about the broad sweep of policy promoted during elections by a party when other organisations will lobby all year round for their special interest, whether this is protection of the environment, opposition to abortion, or the defence of some subsidy? Some academics also claim that parties are playing a smaller role, and **think tanks** a bigger one, in making policy. Although parties continue to draw up election manifestos, they are wary of being too specific. Some hate leaving policymaking to party activists, who may be more extreme than voters at large and so put them off. Better to keep the message vague. Or why not let the tough choices be taken by **referendums**, as so often in Switzerland?

Academics have found these trends easier to describe than to evaluate. Most agree that the age of the "mass party" has passed and that its place is being taken by the "electoral-professional" or "catch-all" party. Although still staffed by politicians holding genuine beliefs and values, these modern parties are inclined to see their main objective as winning elections rather than forming large membership organisations or social movements, as was once the case.

Is this a bad thing? Perhaps, if it reduces participation in politics. One of the traditional roles of political parties has been to get out the vote, and in 18 out of 20 rich countries, recent turnout figures have been lower than they were in the 1950s. Although it is hard to pin down the reasons, Martin Wattenberg, of the University of California at Irvine, points out that turnout has fallen most sharply in countries where parties are weak: Switzerland (thanks to those referendums), America and France (where presidential elections have become increasingly candidate- rather than party-centred), and Japan (where political loyalties revolve around ties to internal factions rather than the party itself). In Scandinavia, by contrast, where class-based parties are still relatively strong, turnout has held up much better since the 1950s.

Running out of members

It is not only voters who are turned off. Party membership is falling too, and even the most strenuous attempts to reverse the decline have faltered. Germany is a case in point. The Social Democrats there increased membership rapidly in the 1960s

and 1970s, and the Christian Democrats responded by doubling their own membership numbers. But since the end of the 1980s membership has been falling, especially among the young. In 1964 Britain's Labour Party had about 830,000 members and the Conservatives about 2m. By 1997 they had 420,000 and 400,000 respectively. The fall is sharper in some countries than others, but research by Susan Scarrow of the University of Houston suggests that the trend is common to most democracies (see chart). With their membership falling, ideological differences blurring, and fewer people turning out to vote, the decline thesis looks hard to refute.

Or does it? The case for party decline has some big holes in it. For a start, some academics question whether political parties ever really enjoyed the golden age which other academics hark back to. Essex University's Mr King points out that a lot of the evidence for decline is drawn from a handful of parties—Britain's two main ones, the German SPD, the French and Italian Communists—which did indeed once promote clear ideologies, enjoy mass memberships, and organise local branches and social activities. But neither of America's parties, nor Canada's, nor many of the bourgeois parties of Western Europe, were ever mass parties of that sort. Moreover, in spite of their supposed decline, parties continue to keep an iron grip on many aspects of politics.

In most places, for example, parties still control **nomination for public office**. In almost all of the mature democracies, it is rare for independent candidates to be elected to federal or state legislatures, and even in local government the proportion of independents has declined sharply since the early 1970s. When state and local parties select candidates, they usually favour people who have worked hard within the party. German parties, for example, are often conduits to jobs in the public sector, with a say over appointments to top jobs in the civil service and to the boards of publicly owned utilities or media organisations. Even in America, where independent candidates are more common in local elections, the parties still run city, county and state "machines" in which most politicians start their careers.

Naturally, there are some exceptions. In 1994 Silvio Berlusconi, a media tycoon, was able to make himself prime minister at the head of Forza Italia, a right-wing movement drawing heavily on his personal fortune and the resources of his television empire. Ross Perot, a wealthy third-party

candidate, won a respectable 19% vote in his 1992 bid for the American presidency. The party declinists claim these examples as evidence for their case. But it is notable that in the end Mr Perot could not compete against the two formidable campaigning and money-raising machines ranged against him.

This suggests that a decline in the membership of parties need not make them weaker in **money and organisation**. In fact, many have enriched themselves simply by passing laws that give them public money. In Germany, campaign subsidies to the federal parties more than trebled between 1970 and 1990, and parties now receive between 20% and 40% of their income from public funds. In America, the paid professionals who have taken over from party activists tend to do their job more efficiently. Moreover, other kinds of political activity—such as donating money to a party or interest group, or attending meetings and rallies—have become more common in America. Groups campaigning for particular causes or candidates (the pro-Republican Christian Coalition, say, or the pro-Democrat National Education Association) may not be formally affiliated with the major party organisations, but are frequently allied with them.

The role of the mass media deserves a closer look as well. It is true that they have weakened the parties' traditional methods of communicating with members. But parties have invested heavily in managing relations with journalists, and making use of new media to reach both members and wider audiences. In Britain, the dwindling of local activists has gone hand-in-hand with a more professional approach to communications. Margaret Thatcher caused a stir by using an advertising firm, Saatchi & Saatchi, to push the Tory cause in the 1979 election. By the time of Britain's 1997 election, the New Labour media operation run from Millbank Tower in London was even slicker.

Another way to gauge the influence of parties is by their **reach**—that is, their power, once in office, to take control of the governmental apparatus. This is a power they have retained. Most governments tend to be unambiguously under the control of people who represent a party, and who would not be in government if they did not belong to such organisations. The French presidential system may appear ideal for independent candidates, but except—arguably—for Charles de Gaulle, who claimed to rise above party, none has ever been elected without party support.

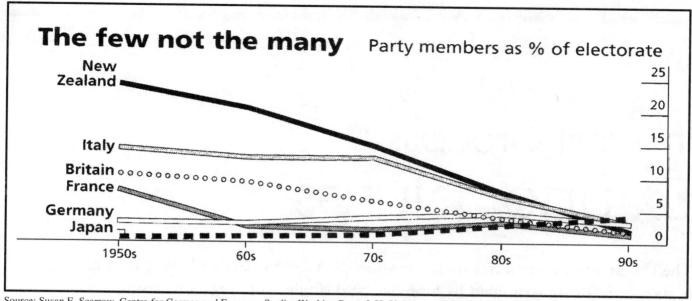

Source: Susan E. Scarrow, Centre for German and European Studies Working Paper 2.59, University of California, Berkeley

The fire next time

Given the cautions that must be applied to other parts of the case for party decline, what can be said about one of the declinists' key exhibits, the erosion of ideological differences? At first sight, this is borne out by the recent movement to the centre of left-leaning parties such as America's Democrats, New Labour in Britain, and the SPD under Gerhard Schröder. In America, Newt Gingrich stoked up some fire amongst Republicans in 1994, but it has flickered out. The most popular Republican presidential hopefuls, and especially George W. Bush, the front-runner, are once again stressing the gentler side of their conservatism.

Still, the claim of ideological convergence can be exaggerated. It is not much more than a decade since Ronald Reagan and Mrs Thatcher ran successful parties with strong ideologies. And the anecdotal assumption that parties are growing less distinct is challenged by longer-term academic studies. A look at the experience of ten western democracies since 1945 ("Parties, Policies and Democracy", Westview Press, 1994) concluded that the leading left and right parties continued to keep their distance and maintain their identity, rather

than clustering around the median voter in the centre. Paul Webb of Britain's Brunel University concludes in a forthcoming book ("Political Parties in Advanced Industrial Democracies", Oxford University Press) that although partisan sentiment is weaker than it was, and voters more cynical, parties have in general adapted well to changing circumstances.

Besides, even if party differences are narrowing at present, why expect that trend to continue? In Western Europe, the ending of the cold war has snuffed out one source of ideological conflict, but new sparks might catch fire. Battered right-wing parties may try to revive their fortunes by pushing the nationalist cause against the encroachments of the European Union. In some places where ideas are dividing parties less, geography is dividing them more. Politics in Germany and Britain has acquired an increasingly regional flavour: Labour and the Social Democrats respectively dominate the north, Conservatives and Christian Democrats the south. Disaffected *Ossis* are flocking to the Party of Democratic Socialism in eastern Germany. Britain, Italy, Canada and Spain have strong separatist parties.

So there is life in the party system yet. But the declinists are on to something. The

Germans have a word for it. One reason given for the rise of Germany's Greens in the 1980s and America's Mr Perot in 1992 was *Parteienverdrossenheit*—disillusionment with mainstream parties that seemed to have abandoned their core beliefs and no longer offered meaningful choices. A "new politics" of citizens' protests appeared to be displacing conventional politics.

In the end, far from undermining the domination of the parties, the German Greens ended up by turning themselves into one and joining the government in an uneasy coalition with the SPD. The balance of evidence from around the world is that despite all the things that are changing them, parties continue to dominate democratic politics.

Indeed, there are grounds for wondering whether their continuing survival is more of a worry than their supposed decline. Is it so very comforting that parties can lose members, worry less about ideas, become detached from broader social movements, attract fewer voters and still retain an iron grip on politics? If they are so unanchored, will they not fall prey to special-interest groups? If they rely on state funding instead of member contributions, will they not turn into creatures of the state? The role of money in politics will be the subject of another brief.

Interest Groups:
Ex uno, plures

The last article in our series on the mature democracies asks whether they are in danger of being strangled by lobbyists and single-issue pressure groups

PREVIOUS briefs in this series have looked at the imperfections in democracy as it is currently practised in the rich countries, and at some of the efforts that different countries are making to overcome them. Evidence that all is not well includes declining public confidence in politicians, falling membership of political parties and smaller turnouts for elections. Ideas for improvement range from making greater use of referendums and other forms of direct democracy, to giving more power to courts to check the power of politicians. This article asks a different question: far from being too powerful, are elected politicians in modern democracies too weak?

When Alexis de Tocqueville visited the United States in the 19th century, he was impressed by the enthusiasm of Americans for joining associations. This, he felt, spread power away from the centre and fostered the emergence of democratic habits and a civil society. Until quite recently, most political scientists shared De Tocqueville's view. Lately, however, and especially in America, doubts have set in. At a certain point, say the doubters, the cumulative power of pressure groups, each promoting its own special interests, can grow so strong that it prevents elected politicians from adopting policies that are in the interest of the electorate as a whole.

A hitch-hiker's guide

A key text for such critics was a short book published in 1965 by Mancur Olson, an American economist. Called "The Logic of Collective Action", this took issue with the traditional idea that the health of democracy was served by vigorous competition between pressure groups, with governments acting as a sort of referee, able to choose the best policy once the debate between the contending groups was over. The traditional view, Olson argued, wrongly assumed that pressure groups were more or less equal. In fact, for a reason known to economists as the free-rider problem, they weren't.

Why? Take the example of five car firms, which form a lobbying group in the hope of raising the price of cars. If they succeed, each stands to reap a fifth of the gains. This makes forming the group and working for its success well worth each firm's investment of time and money. If the car makers succeed, of course, motorists will suffer. But organising millions of individual motorists to fight their corner is a great deal harder because it involves co-ordinating millions of people and because the potential gain for each motorist will be relatively small. Individual motorists will be tempted to reason that, with millions of other people involved, they do not need to do anything themselves, but can instead hitch a "free ride" on the efforts of everyone else.

This simple insight has powerful implications. Indeed, in a later book Olson went on to argue that his theory helped to explain why some nations flourish and others decline. As pressure groups multiply over time, they tend to choke a nation's vitality by impairing the government's ability to act in the wider interest. That, he argued, is why countries such as Germany and Japan—whose interest groups had been cleared away by a traumatic defeat—had fared better after the second world war than Britain, whose institutions had survived intact. With its long record of stability, said Olson, "British society has acquired so many strong organisations and collusions that it suffers from an institutional sclerosis that slows its adaptation to changing circumstances and changing technologies."

Olson's ideas have not gone unchallenged. But they have had a big impact on contemporary thinking about what ails American democracy. In "Demosclerosis" (Times Books, 1994), Jonathan Rauch, a populariser of Olson's work, says that America is afflicted by "hyperpluralism". With at least seven out of ten Americans belonging to at least one such association, the whole society, not just "special" parts of it, is now involved in influence peddling.

The result is that elected politicians find it almost impossible to act solely in the wider public interest. Bill Clinton wants to reform the health system? The health-insurance industry blocks him. China's membership in the World Trade Organisation would benefit America's consumers? America's producers of textiles and steel stand in the way. Jimmy Carter complained when he left the presidency that

Americans were increasingly drawn to single-issue groups to ensure that, whatever else happened, their own private interest would be protected. The trouble is, "the national interest is not always the sum of all our single or special interests".

Pressure groups are especially visible in the United States. As Oxford University's Jeremy Richardson puts it ("Pressure Groups", Oxford University Press, 1993), "pressure groups take account of (and exploit) the multiplicity of access points which is so characteristic of the American system of government—the presidency, the bureaucracy, both houses of Congress, the powerful congressional committees, the judiciary and state and local government."

Nevertheless pressure groups often wield just as much influence in other countries. In those where parliaments exercise tighter control of the executive—Canada, Britain or Germany, say—the government controls the parliamentary timetable and the powers of committees are much weaker. This means that pressure groups adopt different tactics. They have more chance of influencing policy behind closed doors, by bargaining with the executive branch and its civil servants before legislation comes before parliament. In this way pressure groups can sometimes exert more influence than their counterparts in America.

Political tribes

Many European countries have also buttressed the influence of pressure groups by giving them a semi-official status. In Germany, for example, the executive branch is obliged by law to consult the various big "interest organisations" before drafting legislation. In some German states, leading interest groups (along with political parties) have seats on the supervisory boards of broadcasting firms.

French pressure groups are also powerful, despite the conventional image of a strong French state dominating a relatively weak civil society. It is true that a lot of France's interest groups depend on the state for both money and membership of a network of formal consultative bodies. But a tradition of direct protest compensates for some of this institutional weakness. In France, mass demonstrations, strikes, the blocking of roads and the disruption of public services are seen as a part of normal democratic politics.

In Japan, powerful pressure groups such as the Zenchu (Central Union of Agricultural Co-operatives) have turned large

areas of public policy into virtual no-go areas. With more than 9m members (and an electoral system that gives farming communities up to three times the voting weight of urban voters), farmers can usually obstruct any policy that damages their interests. The teachers' union has similarly blocked all attempts at education reform. And almost every sector of Japanese society has its *zoku giin* (political tribes), consisting of Diet members who have made themselves knowledgeable about one industry or another, which pays for their secretaries and provides campaign funds. A Diet member belonging to the transport tribe will work hand-in-glove with senior bureaucrats in the transport ministry and the trucking industry to form what the Japanese call an "iron triangle" consisting of politicians, bureaucrats and big business.

Pressure groups are also increasingly active at a transnational level. Like any bureaucracy, the European Union has spawned a rich network of interest groups. In 1992 the European Commission reckoned that at least 3,000 special-interest groups in Brussels employing some 10,000 people acted as lobbyists. These range from big operations, such as the EU committee of the American Chamber of Commerce, to small firms and individual lobbyists-for-hire. Businesses were the first to spot the advantages of influencing the EU's law making. But trade unions swiftly followed, often achieving in Brussels breakthroughs (such as regulations on working conditions) that they could not achieve at home.

The case for the defense

So pressure groups are ubiquitous. But are they so bad? Although it has been influential, the Olson thesis has not swept all before it. Many political scientists argue that the traditional view that pressure groups create a healthy democratic pluralism is nearer the mark than Olson's thesis.

The case in favour of pressure groups begins with some of the flaws of representative democracy. Elections are infrequent and, as a previous brief in this series noted, political parties can be vague about their governing intentions. Pressure groups help people to take part in politics between elections, and to influence a government's policy in areas that they care and know about. Pressure groups also check excessive central power and give governments expert advice. Although some groups may flourish at the expense of the common weal, this danger can be guarded against if there are

many groups and if all have the same freedom to organise and to put their case to government

Critics of Olson's ideas also point out that, contrary to his prediction, many broad-based groups have in fact managed to flourish in circumstances where individual members stand to make little personal gain and should therefore fall foul of his "free-rider" problem. Clearly, some people join pressure groups for apparently altruistic reasons—perhaps simply to express their values or to be part of an organisation in which they meet like-minded people. Some consumer and environmental movements have flourished in rich countries, even though Olson's theory suggests that firms and polluters should have a strong organisational advantage over consumers and inhalers of dirty air.

Moreover, despite "demosclerosis", well-organised pressure groups can sometimes ease the task of government, not just throw sand into its wheels. The common European practice of giving pressure groups a formal status, and often a legal right to be consulted, minimises conflict by ensuring that powerful groups put their case to governments before laws are introduced. Mr Richardson argues in a forthcoming book ("Developments in the European Union", Macmillan, 1999) that even the pressure groups clustering around the institutions of the EU perform a valuable function. The European Commission, concerned with the detail of regulation, is an eager consumer of their specialist knowledge. As the powers of the European Parliament have grown, it too has attracted a growing band of lobbyists. The parliament has created scores of "intergroups" whose members gain expertise in specific sectors, such as pharmaceuticals, from industry and consumer lobbies.

Governments can learn from pressure groups, and can work through them to gain consent for their policies. At some point, however, the relationship becomes excessively cosy. If pressure groups grow too strong, they can deter governments from pursuing policies which are in the wider public interest. The temptation of governments to support protectionist trade policies at the behest of producer lobbies and at the expense of consumers is a classic example supporting Olson's theories. But problems also arise when it is governments that are relatively strong, and so able to confer special status on some pressure groups and withhold it from others. This puts less-favoured groups at a disadvantage, which they often seek to redress by finding new and sometimes less democratic ways of making their voices heard.

In Germany, for example, disenchantment with what had come to be seen as an excessively cosy system of bargaining between elite groups helped to spark an explosion of protest movements in the 1980s. In many other countries, too, there is a sense that politics has mutated since the 1960s from an activity organised largely around parties to one organised around specialised interest groups on the one hand (such as America's gun lobby) and broader protest and social movements on the other (such as the women's movement, environmentalism and consumerism). One reason for the change is clearly the growth in the size and scope of government. Now that it touches virtually every aspect of people's lives, a bewildering array of groups has sprung up around it.

Many of Olson's disciples blame pressure groups for making government grow. As each special group wins new favours from the state, it makes the state bigger and clumsier, undermining the authority of elected parties, loading excessive demands on government in general, and preventing any particular government from acting in the interest of the relatively disorganised majority of people. By encouraging governments to do too much, say critics on the right, pressure groups prevent governments from doing anything well. Their solution is for governments to do less. Critics on the left are more inclined to complain that pressure groups exaggerate inequalities by giving those better-organised (ie, the rich and powerful) an influence out of all proportion to their actual numbers.

So what is to be done? A lot could be, but little is likely to be. There is precious little evidence from recent elections to suggest that the citizens of the rich countries want to see a radical cut in the size or scope of the state. As for political inequality, even this has its defenders. John Mueller, of America's University of Rochester, argues that democracy has had a good, if imperfect, record of dealing with minority issues, particularly when compared with other forms of government But he claims that this is less because democratic majorities are tolerant of minorities and more because democracy gives minorities the opportunity

to increase their effective political weight—to become more equal, more important, than their arithmetical size would imply—on issues that concern them. This holds even for groups held in contempt by the majority, like homosexuals. Moreover, the fact that most people most of the time pay little attention to politics—the phenomenon of political apathy—helps interested minorities to protect their rights and to assert their interests.

Adaptability

This series of briefs has highlighted some of the defects in the practice of democracy, and some of the changes that the mature democracies are making in order to improve matters. But the defects need to be kept in perspective.

One famous critic of democracy claimed that for most people it did nothing more than allow them "once every few years, to decide which particular representatives of the oppressing class should be in parliament to represent and oppress them". When Marx wrote those words in the 19th century, they contained an element of truth. Tragically, Lenin treated this view as an eternal verity, with calamitous results for millions of people. What they both ignored was democracy's ability to evolve, which is perhaps its key virtue. Every mature democracy continues to evolve today. As a result, violent revolution in those countries where democracy has taken deepest root looks less attractive, and more remote, than ever.

ADVANCED DEMOCRACIES AND THE NEW POLITICS

Russell J. Dalton, Susan E. Scarrow, and Bruce E. Cain

Over the past quarter-century in advanced industrial democracies, citizens, public interest groups, and political elites have shown decreasing confidence in the institutions and processes of representative government. In most of these nations, electoral turnout and party membership have declined, and citizens are increasingly skeptical of politicians and political institutions.[1]

Along with these trends often go louder demands to expand citizen and interest-group access to politics, and to restructure democratic decision-making processes. Fewer people may be voting, but more are signing petitions, joining lobby groups, and engaging in unconventional forms of political action.[2] Referenda and ballot initiatives are growing in popularity; there is growing interest in processes of deliberative or consultative democracy;[3] and there are regular calls for more reliance on citizen advisory committees for policy formation and administration—especially at the local level, where direct involvement is most feasible. Contemporary democracies are facing popular pressures to grant more access, increase the transparency of governance, and make government more accountable.

Amplifying these trends, a chorus of political experts has been calling for democracies to reform and adapt. Mark Warren writes, "Democracy, once again in favor, is in need of conceptual renewal. While the traditional concerns of democratic theory with state-centered institutions remain importantly crucial and ethically central, they are increasingly subject to the limitations we should expect when nineteenth-century concepts meet twenty-first century realities."[4] U.S. political analyst Dick Morris similarly observes, "The fundamental paradigm that dominates our politics is the shift from representative to direct democracy. Voters want to run the show directly and are impatient with all forms of intermediaries between their opinions and public policy."[5] As Ralf Dahrendorf recently summarized the mood of the times, "Representative government is no longer as compelling a proposition as it once was. Instead, a search for new institutional forms to express conflicts of interest has begun."[6]

Many government officials have echoed these sentiments, and the OECD has examined how its member states could reform their governments to create new connections to their publics.[7] Its report testifies:

> New forms of representation and public participation are emerging in all of our countries. These developments have expanded the avenues for citizens to participate more fully in public policy making, within the overall framework of representative democracy in which parliaments continue to play a central role. Citizens are increasingly demanding more transparency and accountability from their governments, and want greater public participation in shaping policies that affect their lives. Educated and well-informed citizens expect governments to take their views and knowledge into account when making decisions on their behalf. Engaging citizens in policy making allows governments to respond to these expectations and, at the same time, design better policies and improve their implementation.[8]

If the pressures for political reform are having real effects, these should show up in changes to the institutional structures of democratic politics. The most avid proponents of such reforms conclude that we may be experiencing the most fundamental democratic transformation since the beginnings of mass democracy in the early twentieth century. Yet cycles of reform are a recurring theme in democratic history, and pressures for change in one direction often wane as new problems and possibilities come to the fore. What is the general track record for democratic institutional reforms in the advanced industrial democracies over the latter half of the twentieth century? And what are the implications of this record for the future of democracy?

Three Modes of Democracy

In a sense, there is nothing new about the call to inject "more democracy" into the institutions of representative government. The history of modern democracies is punctuated by repeated waves of debate about the nature of the democratic process, some of which have produced major institutional reforms. In the early twentieth century, for example, the populist movement in the United States prompted extensive electoral and governing-process reforms, as well as the introduction of new forms of direct democracy.[9] Parallel institutional changes occurred in Europe. By the end of this democratic-reform period in the late 1920s, most Western democracies had become much more "democratic" in the sense of providing citizens with access to the political process and making governments more accountable.

A new wave of democratic rhetoric and debate emerged in the last third of the twentieth century. The stimulus for this first appeared mainly among university students and young professionals contesting the boundaries of conventional representative democracy. Although their dramatic protests subsequently waned, they stimulated new challenges that affect advanced industrial democracies to this day. Citizen interest groups and other public lobbying organizations, which have proliferated since the 1960s, press for more access to government; expanding mass media delve more deeply into the workings of government; and people demand more from government while trusting it less.

The institutional impact of the reform wave of the late twentieth century can be understood in terms of three different modes of democratic politics. One aims at improving the process of *representative democracy* in which citizens elect elites. Much like the populism of the early twentieth century, reforms of this mode seek to improve electoral processes. Second, there are calls for new types of *direct democracy* that bypass (or complement) the processes of representative democracy. A third mode seeks to expand the means of political participation through a new style of *advocacy democracy,* in which citizens participate in policy deliberation and formation—either directly or through surrogates, such as public interest groups—although the final decisions are still made by elites.

1) *Representative democracy.* A major example of reform in representative democracy can be seen in changes to processes of electing the U.S. president. In a 30-year span, these elections underwent a dramatic transformation, in which citizen influence grew via the spread of state-level primary elections as a means of nominating candidates. In 1968, the Democratic Party had just 17 presidential primaries while the Republicans had only 16; in 2000 there were Democratic primaries in 40 states and Republican primaries in 43. As well, both parties-first the Democrats, then the Republicans—instituted reforms intended to ensure that convention delegates are more representative of the public at large, such as rules on the representation of women. Meanwhile, legislators introduced and expanded public funding for presidential elections in an effort to limit the influence of money and so promote citizen equality. If the 1948 Republican and Democratic candidates, Thomas E. Dewey and Harry S. Truman, were brought back to observe the modern presidential election process, they would hardly recognize the system as the same that nominated them. More recently, reformers have championed such causes as term limits and campaign-finance reform as remedies for restricting the influence of special interests. In Europe, populist electoral reform has been relatively restrained by institutionalized systems of party government, but even so, there are parallels to what has occurred in the United States in many European countries. On a limited basis, for example, some European political parties have experimented with, or even adopted, closed primaries to select parliamentary candidates.[10]

> In recent decades, changes in both attitudes and formal rules have brought about a greater general reliance on mechanisms of direct democracy within the advanced industrial democracies.

Generally, the mechanisms of representative democracy have maintained, and in places slightly increased, citizen access and influence. It is true that, compared with four decades ago, electoral turnout is generally down by about 10 percent in the established democracies.[11] This partially signifies a decrease in political access (or in citizens' use of elections as a means of political access). But at the same time, the "amount of electing" is up to an equal or greater extent. There has been a pattern of reform increasing the number of electoral choices available to voters by changing appointed positions into elected ones.[12] In Europe, citizens now elect members of Parliament for the European Union; regionalization has increased the number of elected subnational governments; directly elected mayors and directly elected local officials are becoming more common; and suffrage now includes younger voters, aged 18 to 20. Moreover, the number of political parties has increased, while parties have largely become more accountable—and the decisions of party elites more transparent—to their supporters. With the general expansion in electoral choices, citizens are traveling to the polls more often and making more electoral decisions.

2) *Direct democracy.* Initiatives and referenda are the most common means of direct democracy. These allow citizens to decide government policy without relying on the mediating influence of representation. Ballot initiatives in particular allow nongovernmental actors to control the framing of issues and even the timing of policy debates, further empowering the citizens and groups that take up this mode of action. In recent decades, changes in both attitudes and formal rules have brought about a greater general reliance on mechanisms of direct democracy within the advanced industrial democracies. The Initiative and Referendum Institute calculates, for example, that there were 118 statewide referenda in the United States during the 1950s but 378 such referenda during the 1990s. And a number of other nations have amended laws and constitutions to provide greater opportunities for direct democracy at the national and local levels.[13] Britain had its first national referendum in 1975; Sweden introduced the referendum in a constitutional reform of 1980; and Finland adopted the referendum in 1987. In these and other cases, the referendum won new legitimacy as a basis for national decision making, a norm that runs strongly counter to the ethos of representative democracy. There has also been mounting interest in expanding direct democracy through the innovation of new institutional forms, such as methods of deliberative democracy and citizen juries to advise policy makers.[14]

How fundamental are these changes? On the one hand, the political impact of a given referendum is limited, since only a single policy is being decided, so the channels of direct democracy normally provide less access than do the traditional channels of representative democracy. On the other hand, the increasing use of referenda has influenced political discourse—and the principles of political legitimacy in particular—beyond the policy at stake in any single referendum. With Britain's first referendum on European Community membership in 1975, for instance, parliamentary sovereignty was now no longer absolute, and the concept of popular sovereignty was concomitantly legitimized. Accordingly, the legitimacy of subsequent decisions on devolution required additional referenda, and today contentious issues, such as acceptance of the euro, are pervasively considered as matters that "the public should decide." So even though recourse to direct democracy remains relatively limited in Britain, the expansion of this mode of access represents a significant institutional change—and one that we see occurring across most advanced industrial democracies.

3) Advocacy democracy. In this third mode, citizens or public interest groups interact directly with governments and even participate directly in the policy-formation process, although actual decisions remain in the official hands. One might consider this as a form of traditional lobbying, but it is not. Advocacy democracy involves neither traditional interest groups nor standard channels of informal interest-group persuasion. Rather, it empowers individual citizens, citizen groups, or nongovernmental organizations to participate in advisory hearings; attend open government meetings ("government in the sunshine"); consult ombudsmen to redress grievances; demand information from government agencies; and challenge government actions through the courts.

Evidence for the growth of advocacy democracy is less direct and more difficult to quantify than is evidence for other kinds of institutional change. But the overall expansion of advocacy democracy is undeniable. Administrative reforms, decentralization, the growing political influence of courts, and other factors have created new opportunities for access and influence. During the latter 1960s in the United States, "maximum feasible participation" became a watchword for the social-service reforms of President Lyndon Johnson's "Great Society" programs. Following this model, citizen consultations and public hearings have since been embedded in an extensive range of legislation, giving citizens new points of access to policy formation and administration. Congressional hearings and state-government meetings have become public events, and legislation such as the 1972 Federal Advisory Committee Act even extended open-meeting requirements to advisory committees. While only a handful of nations had freedom-of-information laws in 1970, such laws are now almost universal in OECD countries. And there has been a general diffusion of the ombudsman model across advanced industrial democracies.[15] "Sunshine" provisions reflect a fundamental shift in understanding as to the role that elected representatives should play-one which would make Edmund Burke turn in his grave, and which we might characterize as a move away from the *trustee* toward the *delegate* model.

Reforms in this category also include new legal rights augmenting the influence of individuals and citizen groups. A pattern of judicialization in the policy process throughout most Western democracies, for instance, has enabled citizen groups to launch class-action suits on behalf of the environment, women's rights, or other public interests.[16] Now virtually every public interest can be translated into a rights-based appeal, which provides new avenues for action through the courts. Moreover, especially in European democracies, where direct citizen action was initially quite rare, the expansion of public interest groups, *Bürgerinitiativen,* and other kinds of citizen groups has substantially enlarged the public's repertoire for political action. It is worth noting that "unconventional" forms of political action, such as protests and demonstrations, have also grown substantially over this time span.

Citizens and the Democratic State

If the institutional structure of democracy is changing, how does this affect the democratic process? The answer is far from simple and not always positive, for democratic gains in some areas can be offset by losses in others, as when increased access produces new problems of democratic governability. In the following pages, we limit our attention to how these institutional changes affect the relationship between citizens and the state.

Robert A. Dahl's writings are a touchstone in this matter.[17] Like many democratic theorists, Dahl tends to equate democracy with the institutions and processes of representative democracy, paying much less attention to other forms of citizen participation that may actually represent more important means of citizen influence over political elites. Thus, while we draw from Dahl's *On Democracy* to define the essential criteria for a democratic process, we broaden the framework to include not only representative democracy but direct democracy and advocacy democracy also. Dahl suggests five criteria for a genuinely democratic system:[18]

1. **Inclusion:** With minimal exceptions, all permanent adult residents must have full rights of citizenship.
2. **Political equality:** When decisions about policy are made, every citizen must have an equal and effective opportunity to participate.
3. **Enlightened understanding:** Within reasonable limits, citizens must have equal and effective opportunities to learn about relevant policy alternatives and their likely consequences.
4. **Control of the agenda:** Citizens must have the opportunity to decide which matters are placed on the public agenda, and how.
5. **Effective participation:** Before a policy is adopted, all the citizens must have equal and effective opportunities for making their views known to other citizens.

The first column of the Table lists Dahl's five democratic criteria. The second column summarizes the prevailing view on how well representative democracy fulfills these criteria. For example, advanced industrial democracies have met the *inclusion* criterion by expanding the franchise to all adult citizens (by way of a long and at times painful series of reforms). General success in this regard is illustrated by the bold highlighting of "universal suffrage" in the first cell of this column.

Nearly all advanced industrial democracies now meet the *political equality* criterion by having enacted the principle of "one person, one vote" for elections, which we have highlighted in the second cell. In most nations today, a majority of citizens participate in voting, while labor unions, political parties, and other organizations mobilize participation to achieve high levels of engagement. Indeed, that noted democrat, the late Mayor Richard Daley of Chicago, used to say that electoral politics was the only instrument through which a working-class citizen could ever exercise equal influence with the socially advantaged. At the same time, certain problems of equality remain, as contemporary debates about campaign financing and voter registration illustrate, and full equality in political practice is probably unattainable. We note these problems in the shaded area of the second cell. Nevertheless, overall the principle of equality is now a consensual value for the electoral processes of representative democracy.

At first glance, it may seem that expanding the number of elections amounts to extending these principles. But increasing the number of times that voters go to the polls and the number of items on ballots actually tends to depress

Table Robert A. Dahl's Democratic Criteria

DEMOCRATIC CRITERIA	REPRESENTATIVE DEMOCRACY	DIRECT DEMOCRACY	ADVOCACY DEMOCRACY
Inclusion	**Universal suffrage provides inclusion**	**Universal suffrage provides inclusion**	Equal citizen acces
			(Problems of access to nonelectoral arenas)
Political Equality	**One person, one vote with high turnout maximizes equality**	**On person, one vote with high turnout maximizes equality.**	Equal opportunity
	(Problems of low turnout, inequality due to campaign finance issues, etc.)	*(Problems of equality with low turnout)*	*(Problems of very unequal use)*
Enlightened Understanding	*(Problems of information access, voter decision processes)*	*(Problems of greater information and higher decision-making costs)*	**Increased public access to information**
			(Problems of even greater information and decision-making demands on citizens)
Control of the Agenda		**Citizen initiation provides control of agenda**	**Citizens and groups control the locus and focus of activity**
	(Problems of control of campaign debate, selecting candidates, etc.)	*(Problems of influence by interest groups)*	
Effective Participation	**Control through responsible parties**	**Direct policy impact ensures effective participation**	**Direct access avoids mediated participation**
	(Principal-agent problems: fair elections, responsible party government, etc.)		

Note: Criteria that are well addressed are presented in **bold,** criteria that are at issue are presented in *italics* in the shaded cells.

turnout. And when voter turnout is less than 50 percent, as it tends to be in, say, EU parliamentary elections-or less than 25 percent, as it tends to be in local mayoral or school-board elections in the United States-then one must question whether the gap between "equality of access" and "equality of usage" has become so wide that it undermines the basic principle of *political equality*. Moreover, second-order elections tend to mobilize a smaller and more ideological electorate than the public at large, and so more second-order elections tend to mean more distortions in the representativeness of the electoral process.

The tension between Dahl's democratic criteria and democratic practice becomes even more obvious when we turn to the criterion of *enlightened understanding*. Although we are fairly sanguine about voters' abilities to make informed choices when it comes to high-visibility (for instance, presidential or parliamentary) elections, we are less so when it comes to lower-visibility elections. How does a typical resident of Houston, Texas, make enlightened choices regarding the dozens of judgeship candidates whose names appeared on the November 2002 ballot, to say nothing of other local office seekers and referenda? In such second- and third-order elections, the means of information that voters can use in first-order elections may be insufficient or even altogether lacking. So the expansion of the electoral marketplace may empower the public in a sense, but in another sense may make it hard for voters to exercise meaningful political judgment.

Another criterion is citizen *control of the political agenda*. Recent reforms in representative democracy have gone some way toward broadening access to the political agenda. Increasing the number of elected offices gives citizens more input and presumably more avenues for raising issues, while reforming political finance to equalize campaign access and party support has made for greater openness in political deliberations. More problematic, though, is performance on the *effectiveness of participation* criterion. Do citizens get what they vote for? Often, this principal-agent problem is solved through the mechanism of party government: Voters select a party, and the party ensures the compliance of individual members of parliament and the translation of electoral mandates into policy outcomes.[19] But the impact of recent reforms on the *effectiveness of participation* is complex. On the one hand, more openness and choice in elections should enable people to express their political preferences more extensively and in more policy areas. On the other hand, as the number of office-holders proliferates, it may become more difficult for voters to assign responsibility for policy outcomes. Fragmented decision making, divided government, and the sheer profusion of elected officials may diminish the political responsiveness of each actor.

How much better do the mechanisms of direct democracy fare when measured against Dahl's five criteria (see column 3 of the Table)? Because referenda and initiatives are effectively mass elections, they seek to ensure inclusion and political equality in much the same way as representa-

tive elections do. Most referenda and initiatives use universal suffrage to ensure inclusion and the "one person, one vote" rule to ensure political equality. However, whereas turnout in direct-democracy elections is often lower than in comparable elections for public officials, the question of democratic inclusion becomes more complicated than a simple assessment of equal access. For instance, when Proposition 98—which favored altering the California state constitution to mandate that a specific part of the state budget be directed to primary and secondary education—appeared on the 1996 general election ballot, barely half of all voting-age Californians turned out, and only 51 percent voted for the proposition. But as a consequence, the state's constitution was altered, reshaping state spending and public financing in California. Such votes raise questions about the fairness of elections in which a minority of registered voters can make crucial decisions affecting the public welfare. Equality of opportunity clearly does not mean equality of participation.

Moreover, referenda and initiatives place even greater demands for information and understanding on voters. Many of the heuristics that they can use in party elections or candidate elections are less effective in referenda, and the issues themselves are often more complex than what citizens are typically called upon to consider in electing office-holders. For instance, did the average voter have enough information to make enlightened choices in Italy's multi-referendum ballot of 1997? This ballot asked voters to make choices concerning television-ownership rules, television-broadcasting policy, the hours during which stores could remain open, the commercial activities which municipalities could pursue, labor-union reform proposals, regulations for administrative elections, and residency rules for mafia members. In referenda, voters can still rely on group heuristics and other cues that they use in electing public officials,[20] but obviously the proliferation of policy choices and especially the introduction of less-salient local issues raise questions about the overall effectiveness of such cue-taking.

The real strengths of direct democracy are highlighted by Dahl's fourth and fifth criteria. Referenda and initiatives shift the focus of agenda-setting from elites toward the public, or at least toward public interest groups. Indeed, processes of direct democracy can bring into the political arena issues that elites tend not to want to address: for example, tax reform or term limits in the United States, abortion-law reform in Italy, or the terms of EU membership in Europe generally. Even when referenda fail to reach the ballot or fail to win a majority, they can nevertheless prompt elites to be more sensitive to public interests. By definition, moreover, direct democracy should solve the problem of effective participation that exists with all methods of representative democracy. Direct democracy is unmediated, and so it ensures that participation is effective. Voters make policy choices with their ballot-to enact a new law, to repeal an existing law, or to reform a constitution. Even in instances where the mechanisms of direct democracy require an elite response in passing a law or a revoting in a later election, the link to policy action is more direct than is the case with the channels of representative democracy. Accordingly, direct democracy seems to fulfill Dahl's democratic criteria of agenda control and effective participation.

But direct democracy raises questions in these areas as well. Interest groups may find it easier to manipulate processes of direct democracy than those of representative democracy.[21] The discretion to place a policy initiative on the ballot can be appealing to interest groups, which then have unmediated access to voters during the subsequent referendum campaign. In addition, decisions made by way of direct democracy are less susceptible to bargaining or the checks and balances that occur within the normal legislative process. Some recent referenda in California may illustrate this style of direct democracy: Wealthy backers pay a consulting firm to collect signatures so as to get a proposal on the ballot, and then bankroll a campaign to support their desired legislation. This is not grassroots democracy at work; it is the representation of wealthy interests by other means.

The expansion of direct democracy has the potential to complement traditional forms of representative democracy. It can expand the democratic process by allowing citizens and public interest groups new access to politics, and new control over political agendas and policy outcomes. But direct democracy also raises new questions about equality of actual influence, if not formal access, and the ability of the public to make fair and reasoned judgments about issues. Perhaps the most important question about direct democracy is not whether it is expanding, but *how* it is expanding: Are there ways to increase access and influence without sacrificing inclusion and equality? We return to this question below.

Formal Access and Actual Use

The final column in our Table considers how new forms of advocacy democracy fulfil Dahl's democratic criteria. These new forms of action provide citizens with significant access to politics, but it is also clear that this access is very unevenly used. Nearly everyone can vote, and most do. But very few citizens file lawsuits, file papers under a freedom-of-information act, attend environmental-impact review hearings, or attend local planning meetings. There is no clear equivalent to "one person, one vote" for advocacy democracy. Accordingly, it raises the question of how to address Dahl's criteria of inclusion, political equality, and enlightened understanding.

"Equality of access" is not adequate if "equality of usage" is grossly uneven. For instance, when Europeans were asked in the 1989 European Election Survey whether they voted in the election immediately preceding the survey, differences in participation according to levels of education were very slight (see the Figure, Social-Staus Inequality in Participations). A full 73 percent of those in the "low education" category said they had voted in the previous EU parliamentary election (even though it is a second-order

election), and an identical percentage of those in the "high education" category claimed to have voted. Differences in campaign activity according to educational levels are somewhat greater, but still modest in overall terms.

A distinctly larger inequality gap emerges when it comes to participation through forms of direct or advocacy democracy. For instance, only 13 percent of those in the "low education" category had participated in a citizen action group, while nearly three times the percentage of those in the "high education" category had participated. Similarly, there are large inequalities when it comes to such activities as signing a petition or participating in a lawful demonstration.

With respect to the criterion of *enlightened understanding,* advocacy democracy has mixed results. On the one hand, it can enhance citizen understanding and make for greater inclusion. Citizens and public interest groups can increase the amount of information that they have about government activities, especially by taking advantage of freedom-of-information laws, attending administrative hearings, and participating in government policy making. And with the assistance of the press in disseminating this information, citizens and public interest groups can better influence political outcomes. By ensuring that the public receives information in a timely fashion, advocacy democracy allows citizens to make informed judgments and hold governments more accountable. And by eliminating the filtering that governments would otherwise apply, advocacy democracy can help citizens to get more accurate pictures of the influences affecting policy decisions, with fewer cover-ups and self-serving distortions. On the other hand, advocacy democracy makes greater cognitive and resource demands on citizens, and thus may generate some of the same inequalities in participation noted above. It requires much more of the citizen to participate in a public hearing or to petition an official than it does simply to cast a vote. The most insightful evidence on this point comes from Jane Mansbridge's study of collective decision making in New England town meetings.[22] She finds that many participants were unprepared or overwhelmed by the deliberative decision-making processes.

Advocacy democracy fares better when it comes to the remaining two criteria. It gives citizens greater control of the political agenda, in part by increasing their opportunity to press their interests outside of the institutionalized time and format constraints of fixed election cycles. By means of advocacy democracy, citizens can often choose when and where to challenge a government directive or pressure policy makers. Similarly, even though advocacy democracy typically leaves final political decisions in the hands of elites, it nevertheless provides direct access to government. Property owners can participate in a local planning hearing; a public interest group can petition government for information on past policies; and dissatisfied citizens can attend a school board session. Such unmediated participation brings citizens into the decision-making process-which ultimately might not be as effective as the efforts of a skilled representative, but greater direct involvement in the demo-

Figure-Social-Status Inequality in Participation

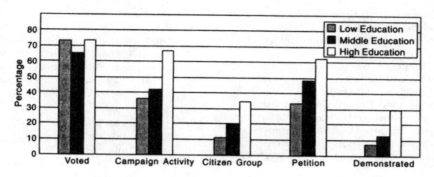

Source: Eurobarometers 31 and 31A conducted in connection with the 1989 European Parliament election. Results combine the 12 nations weighted to represent the total EU population.

cratic process should improve its accountability and transparency (see the bold entries in these last two cells of the Table).

All in all, advocacy democracy increases the potential for citizen access in important ways. It can give citizens and public interest groups new influence over the agenda-setting process, and it can give them unmediated involvement in the policy-formation process. These are significant extensions of democratic participation. At the same time, advocacy democracy may exacerbate political inequality on account of inequalities in usage. New access points created through advisory panels, consultative hearings, and other institutional reforms empower some citizens to become more involved. But other citizens, relatively lacking in the skills or resources to compete in these new domains, may be left behind. In other words, advocacy democracy may in some ways respond to the strength of the claimants, rather than to the strength of their claims. It can even alter the locus of political expertise. While advocacy democracy values know-how and expertise in the citizenry, it devalues those same characteristics among policy makers.

Environmental policy provides a good illustration of this problem. Here, citizens and public interest groups have gained new rights and new access to the policy process. But these are disproportionately used by relatively affluent and skilled citizens, who are already participating in conventional forms of representative democracy, while the poor, the unskilled, and the otherwise disadvantaged tend to get left behind. So while environmentalism is an example of citizen empowerment, it is also a source of increasing inequality.

No form of democratic action is ideal, each having its advantages and limitations. As democratic practice shifts from a predominant reliance on representation toward a mixed repertoire—including greater use of direct and advocacy democracy—a new balance must be struck among democratic goals. It is possible that new institutional arrangements will maximize the benefits of these new modes while limiting their disadvantages—as, for example, the in-

stitutions of representative democracy depend on parties and interest groups. But thus far, the advanced industrialized democracies have not fully recognized the problems generated by the new mixed repertoire of democratic action, and so have yet to find institutional or structural means of addressing them. Democratic reforms create opportunities, but they also create challenges. Our goal should be to ensure that progress on some democratic criteria is not unduly sacrificed for progress on others.

Notes

1. Martin P. Wattenberg, *Where Have All the Voters Gone?* (Cambridge: Harvard University Press, 2002); Susan E. Scarrow, "From Social Integration to Electoral Contestation," in Russell J. Dalton and Martin P. Wattenberg, eds., *Parties Without Partisans: Political Change in Advanced Industrial Democracies* (New York: Oxford University Press, 2000); Russell J. Dalton, *Democratic Challenges, Democratic Choices: The Decline in Political Support in Advanced Industrial Democracies* (Oxford: Oxford University Press, 2004); Susan J. Pharr and Robert D. Putnam, eds., *Disaffected Democracies: What's Troubling the Trilateral Countries?* (Princeton: Princeton University Press, 2000).

2. Russell J. Dalton, *Citizen Politics: Public Opinion and Political Parties in Advanced Industrial Democracies* (New York: Chatham House, 2002), ch. 4; Ronald Inglehart, *Modernization and Postmodernization: Cultural, Economic, and Political Change in 43 Societies* (Princeton: Princeton University Press, 1997); Sidney Verba, Kay Schlozman, and Henry Brady, *Voice and Equality: Civic Volunteerism in American Politics* (Cambridge: Harvard University Press, 1995), 72.

3. James S. Fishkin, *The Voice of the People: Public Opinion and Democracy* (New Haven: Yale University Press, 1995); John Elster, *Deliberative Democracy* (New York: Cambridge University Press, 1998).

4. Mark Warren, *Democracy and Association* (Princeton: Princeton University Press, 2001), 226.

5. Dick Morris, *The New Prince: Machiavelli Updated for the Twenty-First Century* (New York: Renaissance Books, 2000).

6. Ralf Dahrendorf, "Afterword," in Susan J. Pharr and Robert D. Putnam, eds., *Disaffected Democracies: What's Troubling the Trilateral Countries?* 311.

7. OECD, *Government of the Future: Getting from Here to There* (Paris: Organization for Economic Co-operation and Development, 2000).

8. OECD, *Citizens as Partners: OECD Handbook on Information, Consultation and Public Participation in Policy-Making* (Paris: Organization of Economic Cooperation and Development, 2001), 9.

9. Lawrence Goodwyn, *Democratic Promise; The Populist Movement in America* (New York: Oxford University Press, 1976).

10. Susan E. Scarrow, Paul Webb, and David M. Farrell, "From Social Integration to Electoral Contestation," in Russell J. Dalton and Martin P. Wattenberg, eds., *Parties without Partisans: Political Change in Advanced Industrial Democracies;* Jonathan Hopkin, "Bringing the Members Back in: Democratizing Candidate Selection in Britain and Spain," *Party Politics* 7 (May 2001): 343–61.

11. Martin P. Wattenberg, *Where Have All the Voters Gone?*

12. Russell J. Dalton and Mark Gray, "Expanding the Electoral Marketplace," in Bruce E. Cain, Russell J. Dalton, and Susan E. Scarrow, eds., *Democracy Transformed? Expanding Political Opportunities in Advanced Industrial Democracies* (Oxford: Oxford University Press, 2003).

13. Susan E. Scarrow, "Direct Democracy and Institutional Design: A Comparative Investigation," in *Comparative Political Studies* 34 (August 2001): 651–65; also see David Butler and Austin Ranney, eds., *Referenda Around the World* (Washington, D.C.: American Enterprise Institute, 1994); Michael Gallagher and Pier Vincenzo Uleri, eds., *The Referendum Experience in Europe* (Basingstoke: Macmillan, 1996).

14. James S. Fishkin, *The Voice of the People: Public Opinion and Democracy;* Forest David Matthews, *Politics for People: Finding a Responsive Voice,* 2nd ed. (Urbana: University of Illinois Press, 1999).

15. Roy Gregory and Philip Giddings, eds., *Righting Wrongs: The Ombudsman in Six Continents* (Amsterdam: IOS Press, 2000); see also Christopher Ansell and Jane Gingrich, "Reforming the Administrative State," in Bruce E. Cain, Russell J. Dalton, and Susan E. Scarrow, eds., *Democracy Transformed? Expanding Political Opportunities in Advanced Industrial Democracies.*

16. Alec Stone Sweet, *Governing with Judges: Constitutional Politics in Europe* (New York: Oxford University Press, 2000).

17. Robert A Dahl, *Polyarchy: Participation and Opposition* (New Haven: Yale University Press, 1971); *Democracy and Its Critics* (New Haven: Yale University Press, 1991); *On Democracy* (New Haven: Yale University Press, 1998).

18. Robert A. Dahl, *On Democracy,* 37–38.

19. 1Hans-Dieter Klingemann et al., *Parties, Policies, and Democracy* (Boulder: Westview, 1994).

20. Arthur Lupia, "Shortcuts versus Encyclopedias," *American Political Science Review* 88 (March 1994): 63–76.

21. Elisabeth Gerber, *The Populist Paradox: Interest Group Influence and the Promise of Direct Legislation* (Princeton: Princeton University Press, 1999); see also David S. Broder, *Democracy Derailed: Initiative Campaigns and the Power of Money*

22. Jane Mansbridge, *Beyond Adversary Democracy* (New York: Basic Books, 1980).

Russell J. Dalton is director of the Center for the Study of Democracy at the University of California, Irvine. **Susan E. Scarrow** is associate professor of political science at the University of Houston. **Bruce E. Cain** is Robson Professor of Political Science at the University of California, Berkeley, and director of the Institute of Governmental Studies. This essay is adapted from their edited volume, Democracy Transformed? Expanding Political Opportunities in Advanced Industrial Democracies (*2003*).

From *Journal of Democracy* 15:1 (2004), 124-138. Copyright © 2004 National Endowment for Democracy and The Johns Hopkins University Press. Reprinted with permission of The Johns Hopkins University Press.

Women
in National Parliaments

The data in the table below has been compiled by the Inter-Parliamentary Union on the basis of information provided by National Parliaments by 30 November 2005. **187 country** are classified by **descending order of the percentage of women in the lower or single House**. Comparative data on the world and regional averages as well as data concerning the two regional parliamentary assemblies elected by direct suffrage can be found on separate pages. You can use the PARLINE database to view detailed results of parliamentary elections by country.

New: you can now consult an archive of statistical data on women in National Parliaments.

		| WORLD CLASSIFICATION							
Rank	**Country**	**Lower or single House**				**Upper House or Senate**			
		Elections	**Seats***	**Women**	**% W**	**Elections**	**Seats***	**Women**	**% W**
1	Rwanda	09 2003	80	39	48.8	09 2003	26	9	34.6
2	Sweden	09 2002	349	158	45.3	---	---	---	---
3	Norway	09 2005	169	64	37.9	---	---	---	---
4	Finland	03 2003	200	75	37.5	---	---	---	---
5	Denmark	02 2005	179	66	36.9	---	---	---	---
6	Netherlands	01 2003	150	55	36.7	06 2003	75	22	29.3
7	Cuba	01 2003	609	219	36.0	---	---	---	---
"	Spain	03 2004	350	126	36.0	03 2004	259	60	23.2
8	Costa Rica	02 2002	57	20	35.1	---	---	---	---
9	Mozambique	12 2004	250	87	34.8	---	---	---	---
10	Belgium	05 2003	150	52	34.7	05 2003	71	27	38.0
11	Austria	11 2002	183	62	33.9	N.A.	62	17	27.4
12	Iceland	05 2003	63	21	33.3	---	---	---	---
13	South Africa [1]	04 2004	400	131	32.8	04 2004	54	18	33.3
14	New Zealand	09 2005	121	39	32.2	---	---	---	---
15	Germany	09 2005	614	195	31.8	N.A.	69	13	18.8

Rank	Country	Lower or single House				Upper House or Senate			
		Elections	Seats*	Women	% W	Elections	Seats*	Women	% W
16	Iraq	01 2005	273	86	31.5	---	---	---	---
17	Guyana	03 2001	65	20	30.8	---	---	---	---
18	Burundi	07 2005	118	36	30.5	07 2005	52	17	32.7
19	Seychelles	12 2002	34	10	29.4	---	---	---	---
20	Belarus	10 2004	110	32	29.1	11 2004	58	18	31.0
21	Andorra	04 2005	28	8	28.6	---	---	---	---
22	Afghanistan	09 2005	249	68	27.3	09 2005	102	?	?
"	Viet Nam	05 2002	498	136	27.3	---	---	---	---
23	Namibia	11 2004	78	21	26.9	11 2004	26	7	26.9
24	Grenada	11 2003	15	4	26.7	11 2003	13	5	38.5
25	Timor-Leste [2]	08 2001	87	22	25.3	---	---	---	---
26	Switzerland	10 2003	200	50	25.0	10 2003	46	11	23.9
27	Australia	10 2004	150	37	24.7	10 2004	76	27	35.5
28	Mexico	07 2003	500	121	24.2	07 2000	128	28	21.9
29	Liechtenstein	03 2005	25	6	24.0	---	---	---	---
30	Uganda	06 2001	305	73	23.9	---	---	---	---
31	Luxembourg	06 2004	60	14	23.3	---	---	---	---
32	Lao People's Democratic Rep.	02 2002	109	25	22.9	---	---	---	---
33	Tunisia	10 2004	189	43	22.8	07 2005	112	15	13.4
34	Saint Vincent & the Grenadines	03 2001	22	5	22.7	---	---	---	---
35	Bulgaria	06 2005	240	53	22.1	---	---	---	---
36	Eritrea	02 1994	150	33	22.0	---	---	---	---
"	Lithuania	10 2004	141	31	22.0	---	---	---	---
37	Republic of Moldova	03 2005	101	22	21.8	---	---	---	---
38	Croatia	11 2003	152	33	21.7	---	---	---	---
39	United Rep. of Tanzania	10 2000	295	63	21.4	---	---	---	---
40	Pakistan	10 2002	342	73	21.3	03 2003	100	18	18.0
"	Portugal	02 2005	230	49	21.3	---	---	---	---
41	Ethiopia	05 2005	546	116	21.2	10 2005	120	?	?
42	Canada	06 2004	308	65	21.1	N.A.	89	33	37.1
43	Lativa	10 2002	100	21	21.0	---	---	---	---
44	Monaco	02 2003	24	5	20.8	---	---	---	---
45	Nicaragua	11 2001	92	19	20.7	---	---	---	---
46	Poland	09 2005	460	94	20.4	09 2005	100	13	13.0
47	China	02 2003	2980	604	20.3	---	---	---	---
48	Dem. People's Rep. of Korea	08 2003	687	138	20.1	---	---	---	---
49	Bahamas	05 2002	40	8	20.0	05 2002	16	7	43.8

Rank	Country	Lower or single House				Upper House or Senate			
		Elections	Seats*	Women	% W	Elections	Seats*	Women	% W
50	United Kingdom	05 2005	646	127	19.7	N.A.	707	126	17.8
51	Suriname	05 2005	51	10	19.6	---	---	---	---
52	Trinidad and Tobago	10 2002	36	7	19.4	10 2002	31	10	32.3
53	Guinea	06 2002	114	22	19.3	---	---	---	---
54	Bolivia	06 2002	130	25	19.2	06 2002	27	3	11.1
"	Senegal	04 2001	120	23	19.2	---	---	---	---
"	The F.Y.R. of Macedonia	09 2002	120	23	19.2	---	---	---	---
55	Estonia	03 2003	101	19	18.8	---	---	---	---
56	Peru	04 2001	120	22	18.3	---	---	---	---
57	Equatorial Guinea	04 2004	100	18	18.0	---	---	---	---
58	Tajikistan	02 2005	63	11	17.5	03 2005	34	8	23.5
"	Uzbekistan	12 2004	120	21	17.5	01 2005	100	15	15.0
59	Dominican Republic	05 2002	150	26	17.3	05 2002	32	2	6.3
60	Mauritius	07 2005	70	12	17.1	---	---	---	---
61	Czech Republic	06 2002	200	34	17.0	10 2004	81	10	12.3
62	Bosnia and Herzegovina	10 2002	42	7	16.7	10 2002	15	0	0.0
"	Panama	05 2004	78	13	16.7	---	---	---	---
"	San Marino	06 2001	60	10	16.7	---	---	---	---
"	Slovakia	09 2002	150	25	16.7	---	---	---	---
"	Zimbabwe	03 2005	150	25	16.7	11 2005	66	21	31.8
63	Cyprus	05 2001	56	9	16.1	---	---	---	---
64	Ecuador	10 2002	100	16	16.0	---	---	---	---
"	Singapore	11 2001	94	15	16.0	---	---	---	---
"	Turkmenistan	12 2004	50	8	16.0	---	---	---	---
65	Philippines	05 2004	236	36	15.3	05 2004	24	4	16.7
66	United States of America	11 2004	435	66	15.2	11 2004	100	14	14.0
67	Angola	09 1992	220	33	15.0	---	---	---	---
"	Israel	01 2003	120	18	15.0	---	---	---	---
68	Bangladesh [3]	10 2001	345	51	14.8	---	---	---	---
69	Sudan	08 2005	450	66	14.7	08 2005	50	2	4.0
70	Sierra Leone	05 2002	124	18	14.5	---	---	---	---
71	Guinea-Bissau	03 2004	100	14	14.0	---	---	---	---
72	Malawi	04 2004	191	26	13.6	---	---	---	---
73	Republic of Korea	04 2004	299	40	13.4	---	---	---	---
74	Barbados	05 2003	30	4	13.3	05 2003	21	5	23.8
"	Ireland	05 2002	166	22	13.3	07 2002	60	10	16.7
75	Gambia	01 2002	53	7	13.2	---	---	---	---

Rank	Country	Lower or single House				Upper House or Senate			
		Elections	Seats*	Women	% W	Elections	Seats*	Women	% W
76	Greece	03 2004	300	39	13.0	---	---	---	---
77	Dominica	05 2005	31	4	12.9	---	---	---	---
78	Zambia	12 2001	158	20	12.7	---	---	---	---
79	Chile	12 2001	120	15	12.5	12 2001	48	2	4.2
"	Liberia	10 2005	64	8	12.5	10 2005	30	5	16.7
80	Niger	11 2004	113	14	12.4	---	---	---	---
81	France	06 2002	574	70	12.2	09 2004	331	56	16.9
"	Slovenia	10 2004	90	11	12.2	12 2002	40	3	7.5
82	Colombia	03 2002	165	20	12.1	03 2002	102	9	8.8
83	Dem. Republic of the Congo	08 2003	500	60	12.0	08 2003	120	3	2.5
"	Maldives	01 2005	50	6	12.0	---	---	---	---
"	Syrian Arab Republic	03 2003	250	30	12.0	---	---	---	---
84	Burkina Faso	05 2002	111	13	11.7	---	---	---	---
"	Jamaica	10 2002	60	7	11.7	10 2002	21	4	19.0
"	Lesotho	05 2002	120	14	11.7	N.A.	33	12	36.4
85	Italy	05 2001	616	71	11.5	05 2001	321	26	8.1
86	Indonesia	04 2004	550	62	11.3	---	---	---	---
87	Romania	11 2004	331	37	11.2	11 2004	137	13	9.5
88	Botswana	10 2004	63	7	11.1	---	---	---	---
"	Cape Verde	01 2001	72	8	11.1	---	---	---	---
"	Saint Lucia	12 2001	18	2	11.1	12 2001	11	4	36.4
"	Uruguay	10 2004	99	11	11.1	10 2004	31	3	9.7
89	Ghana	12 2004	230	25	10.9	---	---	---	---
90	Djibouti	01 2003	65	7	10.8	---	---	---	---
"	Morocco	09 2002	325	35	10.8	10 2003	270	3	1.1
"	Swaziland	10 2003	65	7	10.8	10 2003	30	9	30.0
91	El Salvador	03 2003	84	9	10.7	---	---	---	---
92	Thailand	02 2005	500	53	10.6	03 2000	200	21	10.5
93	Antigua and Barbuda	03 2004	19	2	10.5	03 2004	17	3	17.6
94	Kazakhstan	09 2004	77	8	10.4	09 2004	39	3	7.7
95	Mali	07 2002	147	15	10.2	---	---	---	---
96	Paraguay	04 2003	80	8	10.0	04 2003	45	4	8.9
97	Cambodia	07 2003	123	12	9.8	03 1999	61	8	13.1
"	Russian Federation	12 2003	447	44	9.8	N.A.	178	6	3.4
98	Venezuela	07 2000	165	16	9.7	---	---	---	---
99	Georgia	03 2004	235	22	9.4	---	---	---	---
100	Gabon	12 2001	119	11	9.2	02 2003	91	14	15.4

Rank	Country	Lower or single House				Upper House or Senate			
		Elections	Seats*	Women	% W	Elections	Seats*	Women	% W
"	Malta	04 2003	65	6	9.2	---	---	---	---
101	Hungary	04 2002	385	35	9.1	---	---	---	---
"	Malaysia	03 2004	219	20	9.1	03 2004	70	18	25.7
"	Sao Tome and Principe	03 2002	55	5	9.1	---	---	---	---
102	Japan	09 2005	480	43	9.0	07 2004	242	34	14.0
103	Cameroon	06 2002	180	16	8.9	---	---	---	---
104	Bhutan	N.A.	150	13	8.7	---	---	---	---
105	Brazil	10 2002	513	44	8.6	10 2002	81	10	12.3
106	Congo	05 2002	129	11	8.5	10 2002	60	8	13.3
"	Cote d'Ivoire	12 2000	223	19	8.5	---	---	---	---
"	Fiji	08 2001	71	6	8.5	08 2001	32	4	12.5
107	India	04 2004	543	45	8.3	06 2004	242	28	11.6
108	Guatemala	11 2003	158	13	8.2	---	---	---	---
109	Somalia	03 2004	275	22	8.0	---	---	---	---
110	Serbia and Montenegro [4]	02 2003	126	10	7.9	---	---	---	---
111	Togo	10 2002	81	6	7.4	---	---	---	---
112	Benin	03 2003	83	6	7.2	---	---	---	---
113	Albania	07 2005	140	10	7.1	---	---	---	---
"	Kenya	12 2002	224	16	7.1	---	---	---	---
114	Madagascar	12 2002	160	11	6.9	03 2001	90	10	11.1
115	Belize	03 2003	30	2	6.7	03 2003	12	3	25.0
"	Mongolia	06 2004	75	5	6.7	---	---	---	---
116	Chad	04 2002	155	10	6.5	---	---	---	---
117	Nigeria	04 2003	360	23	6.4	04 2003	109	4	3.7
118	Algeria	05 2002	389	24	6.2	12 2003	144	4	2.8
119	Samoa	03 2001	49	3	6.1	---	---	---	---
120	Nepal	05 1999	205	12	5.9	06 2001	60	5	8.3
121	Jordan	06 2003	110	6	5.5	11 2003	55	7	12.7
122	Armenia	05 2003	131	7	5.3	---	---	---	---
"	Ukraine	03 2002	450	24	5.3	---	---	---	---
123	Sri Lanka	04 2004	225	11	4.9	---	---	---	---
124	Kiribati	05 2003	42	2	4.8	---	---	---	---
125	Lebanon	05 2005	128	6	4.7	---	---	---	---
"	Libyan Arab Jamahiriya	03 1997	760	36	4.7	---	---	---	---
126	Turkey	11 2002	550	24	4.4	---	---	---	---
127	Iran (Islamic Rep. of)	02 2004	290	12	4.1	---	---	---	---
128	Vanuatu	07 2004	52	2	3.8	---	---	---	---

Rank	Country	Lower or single House				Upper House or Senate			
		Elections	Seats*	Women	% W	Elections	Seats*	Women	% W
129	Haiti	05 2000	83	3	3.6	05 2000	27	7	25.9
130	Tonga	03 2005	29	1	3.4	---	---	---	---
131	Kyrgyzstan	02 2005	63	2	3.2	---	---	---	---
132	Comoros	04 2004	33	1	3.0	---	---	---	---
"	Marshall Islands	11 2003	33	1	3.0	---	---	---	---
133	Egypt	11 2000	454	13	2.9	05 2004	264	18	6.8
134	Oman	10 2003	83	2	2.4	N.A.	58	9	15.5
135	Kuwait	07 2003	65	1	1.5	---	---	---	---
136	Papua New Guinea	06 2002	109	1	0.9	---	---	---	---
137	Yemen	04 2003	301	1	0.3	---	---	---	---
138	Bahrain	10 2002	40	0	0.0	11 2002	40	6	15.0
"	Micronesia (Fed. States of)	03 2005	14	0	0.0	---	---	---	---
"	Nauru	10 2004	18	0	0.0	---	---	---	---
"	Palau	11 2004	16	0	0.0	11 2004	9	0	0.0
"	Saint Kitts and Nevis	10 2004	15	0	0.0	---	---	---	---
"	Saudi Arabia	04 2005	150	0	0.0	---	---	---	---
"	Solomon Islands	12 2001	50	0	0.0	---	---	---	---
"	Tuvalu	07 2002	15	0	0.0	---	---	---	---
"	United Arab Emirates	02 2003	40	0	0.0	---	---	---	---
?	Argentina	10 2005	257	?	?	10 2005	72	?	?
?	Azerbaijan	11 2005	124	?	?	---	---	---	---
?	Central African Republic	05 2005	105	?	?	---	---	---	0.0
?	Honduras	11 2005	128	?	?	---	---	---	---

* Figures correspond to the number of seats currently filled in Parliament

(1) South Africa: The figures on the distribution of seats do not include the 36 special rotating delegates appointed on an ad hoc basis, and the percentages given are therefore calculated on the basis of the 54 permanent seats

(2) Timor-Leste: The purpose of elections held on 30 August 2001 was to elect members of the Constituent Assembly of Timor-Leste. This body became the National Parliament on 20 May 2002, the date on which the country became independent, without any new elections

(3) Bangladesh: In 2004, the number of seats in parliament was raised from 300 to 345, with the addition of 45 reserved seats for women. These reserved seats were filled in September and October 2005, being allocated to political parties in proportion to their share of the national vote received in the 2001 election.

(4) Serbia and Montenegro: For the first time since Yugoslavia ceased to exist and the new State, Servia and Montenegro, was created, indirect elections were held in the two assemblies of the two member states.

From *Inter-Parliamentary Union*, November 30, 2004. Copyright © 2004 by Interparliamentary Union (IPU). Reprinted by permission.
http://www.ipu.org

The True Clash of Civilizations

Samuel Huntington was only half right. The cultural fault line that divides the West and the Muslim world is not about democracy but sex. According to a new survey, Muslims and their Western counterparts want democracy, yet they are worlds apart when it comes to attitudes toward divorce, abortion, gender equality, and gay rights—which may not bode well for democracy's future in the Middle East.

By Ronald Inglehart and Pippa Norris

Democracy promotion in Islamic countries is now one of the Bush administration's most popular talking points. "We reject the condescending notion that freedom will not grow in the Middle East," Secretary of State Colin Powell declared last December as he unveiled the White House's new Middle East Partnership Initiative to encourage political and economic reform in Arab countries. Likewise, Condoleezza Rice, President George W. Bush's national security advisor, promised last September that the United States is committed to "the march of freedom in the Muslim world."

Republican Rep. Christopher Shays of Connecticut: "Why doesn't democracy grab hold in the Middle East? What is there about the culture and the people and so on where democracy just doesn't seem to be something they strive for and work for?"

But does the Muslim world march to the beat of a different drummer? Despite Bush's optimistic pronouncement that there is "no clash of civilizations" when it comes to "the common rights and needs of men and women," others are not so sure. Samuel Huntington's controversial 1993 thesis—that the cultural division between "Western Christianity" and "Orthodox Christianity and Islam" is the new fault line for conflict—resonates more loudly than ever since September 11. Echoing Huntington, columnist Polly Toynbee argued in the British *Guardian* last November, "What binds together a globalized force of some extremists from many continents is a united hatred of Western values that seems to them to spring from Judeo-Christianity." Meanwhile, on the other side of the Atlantic, Republican Rep. Christopher Shays of Connecticut, after sitting through hours of testimony on U.S.-Islamic relations on Capitol Hill last October, testily blurted, "Why doesn't democracy grab hold in the Middle East? What is there about the culture and the people and so on where democracy just doesn't seem to be something they strive for and work for?"

Huntington's response would be that the Muslim world lacks the core political values that gave birth to representative democracy in Western civilization: separation of religious and secular

The Cultural Divide

Approval of Political and Social Values in Western and Muslim Societies

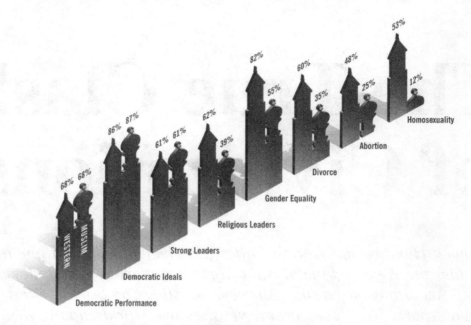

SOURCE: WORLD VALUES SERVEY, POOLED SAMPLE 1995-2001; CHARTS (3) BY JARED SCHNEIDMAN FOR FP

The chart above draws on responses to various political and social issues in the World Values Survey. The percentages indicate the extent to which respondents agree/disagree with or approved/disapproved of the following statements and questions:

DEMOCRATIC PERFORMANCE
- Democracies are indecisive and have too much quibbling. (Strongly disagree.)
- Democracies aren't good at maintaining order. (Strongly disagree.)

DEMOCRATIC IDEALS
- Democracy may have problems, but it's better than any other form of government. (Strongly agree.)
- Approve of having a democratic political system. (Strongly agree.)

STRONG LEADERS
- Approve of having experts, not government, make decisions according to what they think is best for the country. (Strongly disagree.)
- Approve of having a strong leader who does not have to bother with parliament and elections. (Strongly disagree.)

RELIGIOUS LEADERS
- Politicians who do not believe in God are unfit for public office. (Strongly disagree.)
- It would be better for [this country] if more people with strong religious beliefs held public office. (Strongly disagree.)

GENDER EQUALITY
- On the whole, men make better political leaders than women do. (Strongly disagree.)
- When jobs are scarce, men should have more right to a job than women. (Strongly disagree.)
- A university education is more important for a boy than for a girl. (Strongly disagree.)
- A woman has to have children in order to be fulfilled. (Strongly disagree.)
- If a woman wants to have a child as a single parent but she doesn't want to have a stable relationship with a man, do you approve or disapprove? (Strongly approve.)

DIVORCE
- Divorce can always be justified, never be justified, or something in between. (High level of tolerance for divorce.)

ABORTION
- Abortion can always be justified, never be justified, or something in between. (High level of tolerance for abortion.)

HOMOSEXUALITY
- Homosexuality can always be justified, never be justified, or something in between. (High level of tolerance for homosexuality.)

authority, rule of law and social pluralism, parliamentary institutions of representative government, and protection of individual rights and civil liberties as the buffer between citizens and the power of the state. This claim seems all too plausible given the failure of electoral democracy to take root throughout the Middle East and North Africa. According to the latest Freedom House rankings, almost two thirds of the 192 countries around the world are now electoral democracies. But among the 47 countries with a Muslim majority, only one fourth are electoral democracies—and none of the core Arabic-speaking societies falls into this category.

> ... the real fault line between the West and Islam... concerns gender equality and sexual liberation... the values separating the two cultures have much more to do with eros than demos.

Yet this circumstantial evidence does little to prove Huntington correct, since it reveals nothing about the underlying beliefs of Muslim publics. Indeed, there has been scant empirical evidence whether Western and Muslim societies exhibit deeply divergent values—that is, until now. The cumulative results of the two most recent waves of the World Values Survey (wvs), conducted in 1995–96 and 2000–2002, provide an extensive body of relevant evidence. Based on questionnaires that explore values and beliefs in more than 70 countries, the wvs is an investigation of sociocultural and political change that encompasses over 80 percent of the world's population.

A comparison of the data yielded by these surveys in Muslim and non-Muslim societies around the globe confirms the first claim in Huntington's thesis: Culture does matter—indeed, it matters a lot. Historical religious traditions have left an enduring imprint on contemporary values. However, Huntington is mistaken in assuming that the core clash between the West and Islam is over political values. At this point in history, societies throughout the world (Muslim and Judeo-Christian alike) see democracy as the best form of government. Instead, the real fault line between the West and Islam, which Huntington's theory completely overlooks, concerns gender equality and sexual liberalization. In other words, the values separating the two cultures have much more to do with eros than demos. As younger generations in the West have gradually become more liberal on these issues, Muslim nations have remained the most traditional societies in the world.

This gap in values mirrors the widening economic divide between the West and the Muslim world. Commenting on the disenfranchisement of women throughout the Middle East, the United Nations Development Programme observed last summer that "no society can achieve the desired state of well-being and human development, or compete in a globalizing world, if half its people remain marginalized and disempowered." But this "sexual clash of civilizations" taps into far deeper issues than

how Muslim countries treat women. A society's commitment to gender equality and sexual liberalization proves time and again to be the most reliable indicator of how strongly that society supports principles of tolerance and egalitarianism. Thus, the people of the Muslim world overwhelmingly want democracy, but democracy may not be sustainable in their societies.

TESTING HUNTINGTON

Huntington argues that "ideas of individualism, liberalism, constitutionalism, human rights, equality, liberty, the rule of law, democracy, free markets, [and] the separation of church and state" often have little resonance outside the West. Moreover, he holds that Western efforts to promote these ideas provoke a violent backlash against "human rights imperialism." To test these propositions, we categorized the countries included in the wvs according to the nine major contemporary civilizations, based largely on the historical religious legacy of each society. The survey includes 22 countries representing Western Christianity (a West European culture that also encompasses North America, Australia, and New Zealand), 10 Central European nations (sharing a Western Christian heritage, but which also lived under Communist rule), 11 societies with a Muslim majority (Albania, Algeria, Azerbaijan, Bangladesh, Egypt, Indonesia, Iran, Jordan, Morocco, Pakistan, and Turkey), 12 traditionally Orthodox societies (such as Russia and Greece), 11 predominately Catholic Latin American countries, 4 East Asian societies shaped by Sino-Confucian values, 5 sub-Saharan Africa countries, plus Japan and India.

Despite Huntington's claim of a clash of civilizations between the West and the rest, the wvs reveals that, at this point in history, democracy has an overwhelmingly positive image throughout the world. In country after country, a clear majority of the population describes "having a democratic political system" as either "good" or "very good." These results represent a dramatic change from the 1930s and 1940s, when fascist regimes won overwhelming mass approval in many societies; and for many decades, Communist regimes had widespread support. But in the last decade, democracy became virtually the only political model with global appeal, no matter what the culture. With the exception of Pakistan, most of the Muslim countries surveyed think highly of democracy: In Albania, Egypt, Bangladesh, Azerbaijan, Indonesia, Morocco, and Turkey, 92 to 99 percent of the public endorsed democratic institutions—a higher proportion than in the United States (89 percent).

Yet, as heartening as these results may be, paying lip service to democracy does not necessarily prove that people genuinely support basic democratic norms—or that their leaders will allow them to have democratic institutions. Although constitutions of authoritarian states such as China profess to embrace democratic ideals such as freedom of religion, the rulers deny it in practice. In Iran's 2000 elections, reformist candidates captured nearly three quarters of the seats in parliament, but a theocratic elite still holds the reins of power. Certainly, it's a step in the right direction if most people in a country endorse the idea of democracy. But this sentiment needs to be complemented by

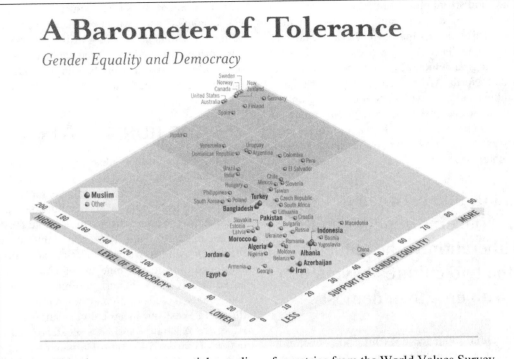

A Barometer of Tolerance

Gender Equality and Democracy

Note: This chart represents a partial sampling of countries from the World Values Survey.
*Sum of Freedom House ratings, 1981–1998
†Percentage disagreeing with statement: "Men make better political leaders than women."

Sources: World Values Survey, pooled sample 1995–2001; *Freedom in the World: The Annual Survey of Political Rights and Civil Liberties* (New York: Freedom House, 1981–1998).

deeper underlying attitudes such as interpersonal trust and tolerance of unpopular groups—and these values must ultimately be accepted by those who control the army and secret police.

The wvs reveals that, even after taking into account differences in economic and political development, support for democratic institutions is just as strong among those living in Muslim societies as in Western (or other) societies [see chart, The Cultural Divide]. For instance, a solid majority of people living in Western and Muslim countries gives democracy high marks as the most efficient form of government, with 68 percent disagreeing with assertions that "democracies are indecisive" and "democracies aren't good at maintaining order." (All other cultural regions and countries, except East Asia and Japan, are far more critical.) And an equal number of respondents on both sides of the civilizational divide (61 percent) firmly reject authoritarian governance, expressing disapproval of "strong leaders" who do not "bother with parliament and elections." Muslim societies display greater support for religious authorities playing an active societal role than do Western societies. Yet this preference for religious authorities is less a cultural division between the West and Islam than it is a gap between the West and many other less secular societies around the globe, especially in sub-Saharan Africa and Latin America. For instance, citizens in some Muslim societies agree overwhelmingly with the statement that "politicians who do not believe in God are unfit for public office" (88 percent in Egypt, 83 percent in Iran, and 71 percent in Bangladesh), but this statement also garners

strong support in the Philippines (71 percent), Uganda (60 percent), and Venezuela (52 percent). Even in the United States, about two fifths of the public believes that atheists are unfit for public office.

Today, relatively few people express overt hostility toward other classes, races, or religions, but rejection of homosexuals is widespread. About half of the world's populations say that homosexuality is "never" justifiable.

However, when it comes to attitudes toward gender equality and sexual liberalization, the cultural gap between Islam and the West widens into a chasm. On the matter of equal rights and opportunities for women—measured by such questions as whether men make better political leaders than women or whether university education is more important for boys than for girls—Western and Muslim countries score 82 percent and 55 percent, respectively. Muslim societies are also distinctively less permissive toward homosexuality, abortion, and divorce.

These issues are part of a broader syndrome of tolerance, trust, political activism, and emphasis on individual autonomy

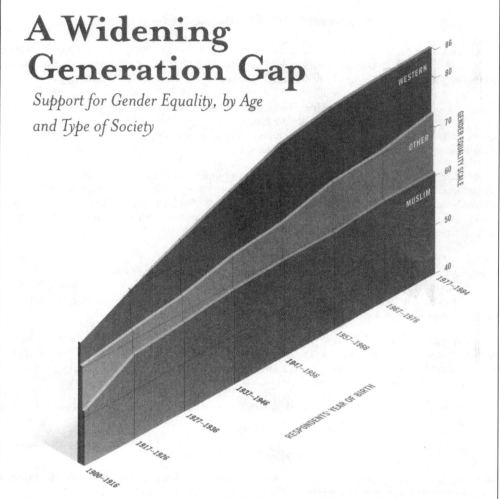

A Widening Generation Gap

Support for Gender Equality, by Age and Type of Society

* The 100-point Gender Equality Scale is based on responses to the following five statements and questions: "If a woman wants to have a child as a single parent but she doesn't want to have a stable relationship with a man, do you approve or disapprove?"; "When jobs are scarce, men should have more right to a job than women"; "A university education is more important for a boy than a girl"; "Do you think that a woman has to have children in order to be fulfilled or is this not necessary?"; and "On the whole, men make better political leaders than women do." The scale was constructed so that if all respondents show high scores on all five items (representing strong support for gender equality), it produces a score of 100, while low scores on all five items produce a score of 0.

Source: World Values Surveys, pooled 1995–2001

that constitutes "self-expression values." The extent to which a society emphasizes these self-expression values has a surprisingly strong bearing on the emergence and survival of democratic institutions. Among all the countries included in the wvs, support for gender equality—a key indicator of tolerance and personal freedom—is closely linked with a society's level of democracy [see chart, A Barometer of Tolerance].

In every stable democracy, a majority of the public disagrees with the statement that "men make better political leaders than women." None of the societies in which less than 30 percent of the public rejects this statement (such as Jordan, Nigeria, and Belarus) is a true democracy. In China, one of the world's least democratic countries, a majority of the public agrees that men make better political leaders than women, despite a party

line that has long emphasized gender equality (Mao Zedong once declared, "women hold up half the sky"). In practice, Chinese women occupy few positions of real power and face widespread discrimination in the workplace. India is a borderline case. The country is a long-standing parliamentary democracy with an independent judiciary and civilian control of the armed forces, yet it is also marred by a weak rule of law, arbitrary arrests, and extra-judicial killings. The status of Indian women reflects this duality. Women's rights are guaranteed in the constitution, and Indira Gandhi led the nation for 15 years. Yet domestic violence and forced prostitution remain prevalent throughout the country, and, according to the wvs, almost 50 percent of the Indian populace believes only men should run the government.

Want to Know More?

Samuel Huntington expanded his controversial 1993 article into a book, *The Clash of Civilizations and the Remaking of World Order* (New York: Simon and Schuster, 1996). Among the authors who have disputed Huntington's claim that Islam is incompatible with democratic values are Edward Said, who decries the clash of civilizations thesis as an attempt to revive the "good vs. evil" world dichotomy prevalent during the Cold War ("**A Clash of Ignorance,**" *The Nation*, October 22, 2001); John Voll and John Esposito, who argue that "The Muslim heritage… contains concepts that provide a foundation for contemporary Muslims to develop authentically Muslim programs of democracy" ("**Islam's Democratic Essence,**" *Middle East Quarterly*, September 1994); and Ray Takeyh, who recounts the efforts of contemporary Muslim scholars to legitimize democratic concepts through the reinterpretation of Muslim texts and traditions ("**Faith-Based Initiatives,**" FOREIGN POLICY, November/December 2001).

An overview of the Bush administration's **Middle East Partnership Initiative**, including the complete transcript of Secretary of State Colin Powell's speech on political and economic reform in the Arab world, can be found on the Web site of the U.S. Department of State. Marina Ottaway, Thomas Carothers, Amy Hawthorne, and Daniel Brumberg offer a stinging critique of those who believe that toppling the Iraqi regime could unleash a democratic tsunami in the Arab world in "**Democratic Mirage in the Middle East**" (Washington: Carnegie Endowment for International Peace, 2002).

In a poll of nearly 4,000 Arabs, James Zogby found that the issue of "civil and personal rights" earned the overall highest score when people were asked to rank their personal priorities (***What Arabs Think: Values, Beliefs and Concerns***, Washington: Zogby International, 2002). A poll available on the Web site of the Pew Research Center for the People and the Press ("**Among Wealthy Nations …U.S. Stands Alone in Its Embrace of Religion,**" December 19, 2002) reveals that Americans' views on religion and faith are closer to those living in developing nations than in developed countries.

The Web site of the **World Values Survey** (WVS) provides considerable information on the survey, including background on methodology, key findings, and the text of the questionnaires. The second iteration of the A.T. Kearney/FOREIGN POLICY Magazine Globalization Index ("**Globalization's Last Hurrah?**" FOREIGN POLICY, January/February 2002) found a strong correlation between the wvs measure of "subjective well-being" and a society's level of global integration.

For links to relevant Web sites, access to the FP Archive, and a comprehensive index of related FOREIGN POLICY articles, go to **www.foreignpolicy.com.**

> Muslim societies are neither uniquely nor monolithically low on tolerance toward sexual orientation and gender equality…. However, on the whole, Muslim countries not only lag behind the West but behind all other societies as well.

The way a society views homosexuality constitutes another good litmus test of its commitment to equality. Tolerance of well-liked groups is never a problem. But if someone wants to gauge how tolerant a nation really is, find out which group is the most disliked, and then ask whether members of that group should be allowed to hold public meetings, teach in schools, and work in government. Today, relatively few people express overt hostility toward other classes, races, or religions, but rejection of homosexuals is widespread. In response to a wvs question about whether homosexuality is justifiable, about half of the world's population say "never." But, as is the case with gender equality, this attitude is directly proportional to a country's level of democracy. Among authoritarian and quasi-democratic states, rejection of homosexuality is deeply entrenched: 99 per-

cent in both Egypt and Bangladesh, 94 percent in Iran, 92 percent in China, and 71 percent in India. By contrast, these figures are much lower among respondents in stable democracies: 32 percent in the United States, 26 percent in Canada, 25 percent in Britain, and 19 percent in Germany.

Muslim societies are neither uniquely nor monolithically low on tolerance toward sexual orientation and gender equality. Many of the Soviet successor states rank as low as most Muslim societies. However, on the whole, Muslim countries not only lag behind the West but behind all other societies as well [see chart, A Widening Generation Gap]. Perhaps more significant, the figures reveal the gap between the West and Islam is even wider among younger age groups. This pattern suggests that the younger generations in Western societies have become progressively more egalitarian than their elders, but the younger generations in Muslim societies have remained almost as traditional as their parents and grandparents, producing an expanding cultural gap.

CLASH OF CONCLUSIONS

"The peoples of the Islamic nations want and deserve the same freedoms and opportunities as people in every nation," President Bush declared in a commencement speech at West Point last summer. He's right. Any claim of a "clash of civilizations" based on fundamentally different political goals held by

Western and Muslim societies represents an oversimplification of the evidence. Support for the goal of democracy is surprisingly widespread among Muslim publics, even among those living in authoritarian societies. Yet Huntington is correct when he argues that cultural differences have taken on a new importance, forming the fault lines for future conflict. Although nearly the entire world pays lip service to democracy, there is still no global consensus on the self-expression values—such as social tolerance, gender equality, freedom of speech, and interpersonal trust—that are crucial to democracy. Today, these divergent values constitute the real clash between Muslim societies and the West.

But economic development generates changed attitudes in virtually any society. In particular, modernization compels systematic, predictable changes in gender roles: Industrialization brings women into the paid work force and dramatically reduces fertility rates. Women become literate and begin to participate in representative government but still have far less power than men. Then, the postindustrial phase brings a shift toward greater gender equality as women move into higher-status economic roles in management and gain political influence within elected and appointed bodies. Thus, relatively in-dustrialized Muslim societies such as Turkey share the same views on gender equality and sexual liberalization as other new democracies.

Even in established democracies, changes in cultural attitudes—and eventually, attitudes toward democracy—seem to be closely linked with modernization. Women did not attain the right to vote in most historically Protestant societies until about 1920, and in much of Roman Catholic Europe until after World War II. In 1945, only 3 percent of the members of parliaments around the world were women. In 1965, the figure rose to 8 percent, in 1985 to 12 percent, and in 2002 to 15 percent.

The United States cannot expect to foster democracy in the Muslim world simply by getting countries to adopt the trappings of democratic governance, such as holding elections and having a parliament. Nor is it realistic to expect that nascent democracies in the Middle East will inspire a wave of reforms reminiscent of the velvet revolutions that swept Eastern Europe in the final days of the Cold War. A real commitment to democratic reform will be measured by the willingness to commit the resources necessary to foster human development in the Muslim world. Culture has a lasting impact on how societies evolve. But culture does not have to be destiny.

EUROPE CRAWLS AHEAD...

By Megan Rowling

As Speaker of the Riksdagen, the Swedish parliament, Birgitta Dahl holds Sweden's second-highest political office. But when she was first elected back in 1969, as a 30-year-old single mother, she was regarded as "very odd."

"To be accepted and respected, you had to act like a bad copy of a man," Dahl recalls of her early years in politics. "But we tried to change that, and we never gave up our identity. Now women have competence in Parliament, and they have changed its performance and priorities."

Back then, women of her generation were eager for change. From the beginning, they based their demands on the right of the individual—whether male or female—to have equal access to education, work and social security. And as politicians, they fought hard to build a legal framework for good childcare and parental leave, for fathers as well as mothers. "We got this kind of legislation through," Dahl says, "even though it took 15 years of serious conflict, debate and struggle."

And their efforts paid off. Sweden now has the highest proportion of women parliamentarians in the world, at 42.7 percent—up from just 12 percent in 1969. Two of its three deputy speakers are also women. Other Nordic countries too have high levels of female representation: In rankings compiled by the Inter-Parliamentary Union (IPU), Denmark takes second place behind Sweden, with women accounting for 38 percent of parliament members, followed by Finland and Norway with around 36.5 percent. (Finland also has one of the world's 11 women heads of state.) These nations' Social Democratic and far-left governing coalitions have made impressive progress toward equality in all areas of society in the past 40 years. But the nature of their electoral systems is also very important.

Julie Ballington, gender project officer at the Stockholm-based International Institute for Democracy and Electoral Assistance (IDEA), points out that the top 10 countries in the IPU ranking all use some form of proportional representation. This kind of voting system, in which parties are allocated seats in multi-member districts according to the percentage of votes they win, Ballington says, "offers a way to address gender imbalance in parliaments." With single-member districts, parties are often under pressure to choose a male candidate. But where they can contest and win more than one seat per constituency, they tend to be more willing to field female candidates. And by improving the gender balance on their slates, they widen their appeal among women voters.

Most European countries now use proportional representation or a combination of proportional representation and majoritarian voting, the system in use in the United States and the United Kingdom. In Europe, the widespread use of proportional representation has boosted the number of women politicians—particularly in the past three decades. And in the Nordic countries, where left-wing parties have enjoyed long periods in power and feminism has received strong support, the combination of these factors has led to significant progress toward gender parity in politics.

But even within Europe, some countries continue to lag behind. In Britain, which uses a single-member district plurality system, women members of parliament make up just 17.9 percent of the House of Commons. In the general elections of 2001, the ruling Labour Party stipulated that half those on its candidate shortlists be women. But research conducted by the Fawcett Society, a British organization that campaigns for gender equity, showed that some female hopefuls experienced overt discrimination and even sexual harassment when interviewed by local party members during the selection process.

"You are told things like 'your children are better off with you at home'... 'you are the best candidate but we are not ready for a woman.' They would select the donkey rather than the woman," said one candidate. Another complained: "They are absolutely adamant they will not consider a woman.... It was said to me... 'we do enjoy watching you speak—we always imagine what your knickers are like.' It is that basic." In light of such attitudes, it is not surprising that women candidates were selected for only four out of 38 vacant seats.

Thanks to new governmental legislation, however, the party is set to reintroduce the controversial method of all-women shortlists it used in the general election of 1997. The use of these shortlists saw the number of British women MPs double to 120 in that election, which swept

Labour to power with a landslide victory. The technique was later ruled illegal because it was judged to discriminate against men. But in early 2002, the government returned to the idea, passing a bill that will allow political parties to take measures in favor of women when choosing parliamentary candidates—what's often referred to as "positive discrimination."

"Critical mass," or the level of representation above which women make a real difference to the political agenda, is widely judged to be around 30 percent.

Judith Squires, a political researcher at Bristol University, believes that the new legislation got such an easy ride partly because it does not stipulate that parties must take action: "We had expected it to be a hard battle. But there has been a change of mood in the Conservative Party, and the fact that it is permissive, and there is a sunset clause [the legislation expires in 2015], all helped to push it through."

In France, where until the recent election women accounted for only 10.9 percent of National Assembly members, the government opted for a more extreme method: a law aimed at securing political parity between men and women. Now half of all contesting parties' candidates in National Assembly elections and most local ballots must be women. In National Assembly elections, which do not use proportional representation, parties that deviate from the 50 percent target by more than two percent are fined a proportion of their public financing.

The law's first test in the municipal elections of March 2001 saw the percentage of elected women councilors in towns of more than 3,500 almost double, to 47.5 percent. But in June's National Assembly elections, the proportion of women deputies increased by less than 1.5 points, to just 12.3 percent—way below expectations. The main factor behind this disappointing result was the success of right-wing parties that ignored the new law, says Mariette Sineau, research director at the Center for the Study of French Political Life. "The big parties decided it was better to incur the financial penalty than to sacrifice their 'favored sons.' And this was particularly so with parties on the right."

Another problem with the law, Sineau explains, is that it does not apply to regional assemblies, "which is a shame, because most National Assembly deputies are recruited there." And the recent victory of the right suggests that France's ruling—and predominantly male—elite are in no hurry to change the system that has allowed them to hold on to power up until now, law or no law. As Chantal Cauquil, a French deputy at the European Parliament and member of the Workers' Struggle Party, argues, other aspects of French society must change before real

parity can be achieved. "There's no doubt that economic and social conditions—which weigh on women earning the lowest salaries, in the most precarious situations, and with the biggest problems caused by a notable lack of childcare infrastructure—have a negative impact on women's political participation," she says. Moreover, governing parties of both the right and left are influenced by social prejudices and are not inclined to regard women as full citizens. It requires real political will to go against such prejudices and allow women to take on the same responsibilities as men."

Such deep-rooted but hidden obstacles, faced by women everywhere, are precisely why proponents of the use of gender quotas on lists for both party and national elections believe positive discrimination is essential. "Everybody hates quotas, and everyone wishes they weren't necessary," says Drude Dahlerup, professor of politics at the University of Stockholm. "But we have to start from the point that there are structural barriers. Then quotas can be seen as compensation." Currently, political parties in some 40 countries appear to agree, with quota systems in operation from Argentina and India to Uganda.

The use of quotas in Europe varies significantly from country to country and from party to party, but where a quota system is applied, it tends to lead to a rise in women's representation. In 1988, for example, Germany's Social Democrats adopted a system of flexible quotas, under which at least one-third of all candidates for internal party election must be female—and between 1987 and 1990, the number of Social Democratic women in the German parliament, the Bundestag, doubled. In Sweden, parties didn't introduce quotas until the '90s, but the principle of "Varannan Damernas" ("Every Other Seat A Woman's Seat") has been widespread since the '80s. Dahl, the Swedish speaker, argues that "it is not only legislation that changes the world, but convincing people that change is necessary."

Yet, as Dahlerup notes, women in some Scandinavian countries have worked to improve gender equality since the end of World War I, and "other countries are not going to wait that long—they are showing impatience." "Critical mass," or the level of representation above which women make a real difference to the political agenda, is widely judged to be around 30 percent. And in countries such as France and the United Kingdom, where that is still a long way off, measures such as parity laws and all-women shortlists are a way to speed up progress.

Even in countries that are close to achieving political parity, however, women are quick to warn against complacency. Dahlerup emphasizes the case of Denmark, where quotas have been abandoned. "Young women say they don't want and don't need quotas. The discourse is that equality has already been achieved. But I think Denmark could go backward again, and that is dangerous."

Squires of Bristol University also talks about a backlash in Britain's Liberal Democratic Party against what younger women regard as "old-fashioned feminist policies." At the party conference last year, she says, many women in their twenties and early thirties lobbied against any form of positive discrimination, wearing pink T-shirts emblazoned with the words "I'm not a token woman." But Squires suggests that this attitude is somewhat misguided: "All parties [in the United Kingdom] have set criteria that discriminate against women. It is not a supply-side problem, it is a demand-side problem."

"People are waking up and saying that it's not right that there are so few women in politics."

In an attempt to address this "demand-side problem," activists are targeting not only national political institutions, but also those of the European Union. The number of women members of the European Parliament increased from 25.7 percent in 1994 to 29.9 percent in the 1999 elections—not very impressive considering that some countries introduced proportional representation voting, and some parties alternated women and men on their lists to boost women's chances. More worrying perhaps is the gender imbalance in the convention on the Future of Europe, a body charged with the important task of drafting a new treaty for the European Union. Its presidium includes only two women among its 12 members, and the convention itself only 19 out of 118 members.

"The establishment of the convention is a response to the need for transparency and democracy. How can we explain the fact that women are not included?" asks Denise Fuchs, president of the European Women's Lobby. "It is simply not coherent." The EWL has launched a campaign to rectify the problem and is lobbying to achieve parity democracy across all other European institutions as well.

Yvonne Galligan, director of the Belfast-based Center for Advancement of Women in Politics, points out that "there has been a groundswell of support for women in political life across Western Europe, but this has not yet translated into numbers in the United Kingdom, Ireland and the European Union." In May's elections in the Irish Republic, for example, women parliamentarians in Ireland's Dail gained just one seat, and are now at 12.7 percent, according to the IPU.

Galligan is now working with political parties to set targets for Ireland's local elections in a couple of years' time—a tough job, because most parties oppose any form of positive discrimination. Parity in Ireland isn't likely to happen for a long while yet, but Galligan believes the social backdrop is improving. She cites a controversial referendum in March, in which the Irish electorate narrowly voted against a proposal to tighten the country's strict abortion laws even further. "That raised the status of women," she explains. "The underlying question was, how do we perceive the role of women? Now that is carrying over into elections. People are waking up and saying that it's not right that there are so few women in politics."

But where a sea-change in attitudes has not already occurred, it is almost certainly emerging. Naturally, there are fears that the apparent resurgence of the right in Europe could reverse the trend. But most of those interviewed for this article say women have already progressed far enough to prevent a significant decline in representation.

As Linda McAvan, deputy leader of Britain's Labour MEPs, argues: "If we look at how things were 20 years ago, they have changed enormously. Young women are different now. They see what has been done by women politicians before them, and they want to do it too."

What Political Institutions Does Large-Scale Democracy Require?

ROBERT A. DAHL

What does it mean to say that a country is governed democratically? Here, we will focus on the political institutions of *democracy on a large scale*, that is, the political institutions necessary for a *democratic country*. We are not concerned here, then, with what democracy in a very small group might require, as in a committee. We also need to keep in mind that every actual democracy has always fallen short of democratic criteria. Finally, we should be aware that in ordinary language, we use the word *democracy* to refer both to a goal or ideal and to an actuality that is only a partial attainment of the goal. For the time being, therefore, I'll count on the reader to make the necessary distinctions when I use the words *democracy, democratically, democratic government, democratic country*, and so on.[1]

How Can We Know?

How can we reasonably determine what political institutions are necessary for large-scale democracy? We might examine the history of countries that have changed their political institutions in response, at least in part, to demands for broader popular inclusion and effective participation in government and political life. Although in earlier times those who sought to gain inclusion and participation were not necessarily inspired by democratic ideas, from about the eighteenth century onward they tended to justify their demands by appealing to democratic and republican ideas. What political institutions did they seek, and what were actually adopted in these countries?

Alternatively, we could examine countries where the government is generally referred to as democratic by most of the people in that country, by many persons in other countries, and by scholars, journalists, and the like. In other words, in ordinary speech and scholarly discussion the country is called a democracy.

FIGURE 1
What Political Institutions Does Large-Scale Democracy Require?

Large-scale democracy requires:
1. Elected officials
2. Free, fair, and frequent elections
3. Freedom of expression
4. Alternative sources of information
5. Associational autonomy
6. Inclusive citizenship

Third, we could reflect on a specific country or group of countries, or perhaps even a hypothetical country, in order to imagine, as realistically as possible, what political institutions would be required in order to achieve democratic goals to a substantial degree. We would undertake a mental experiment, so to speak, in which we would reflect carefully on human experiences, tendencies, possibilities, and limitations and design a set of political institutions that would be necessary for large-scale democracy to exist and yet feasible and attainable within the limits of human capacities.

Fortunately, all three methods converge on the same set of democratic political institutions. These, then, are minimal requirements for a democratic country (Figure 1).

The Political Institutions of Modern Representative Democracy

Briefly, the political institutions of modern representative democratic government are

- *Elected officials*. Control over government decisions about policy is constitutionally vested in officials elected by citizens. Thus modern, large-scale democratic governments are *representative*.

- *Free, fair and frequent elections*. Elected officials are chosen in frequent and fairly conducted elections in which coercion is comparatively uncommon.
- *Freedom of expression*. Citizens have a right to express themselves without danger of severe punishment on political matters broadly defined, including criticism of officials, the government, the regime, the socioeconomic order, and the prevailing ideology.
- *Access to alternative sources of information*. Citizens have a right to seek out alternative and independent sources of information from other citizens, experts, newspapers, magazines, books, telecommunications, and the like. Moreover, alternative sources of information actually exist that are not under the control of the government or any other single political group attempting to influence public political beliefs and attitudes, and these alternative sources are effectively protected by law.
- *Associational autonomy*. To achieve their various rights, including those required for the effective operation of democratic political institutions, citizens also have a right to form relatively independent associations or organizations, including independent political parties and interest groups.
- *Inclusive citizenship*. No adult permanently residing in the country and subject to its laws can be denied the rights that are available to others and are necessary to the five political institutions just listed. These include the right to vote in the election of officials in free and fair elections; to run for elective office; to free expression; to form and participate in independent political organizations; to have access to independent sources of information; and rights to other liberties and opportunities that may be necessary to the effective operation of the political institutions of large-scale democracy.

THE POLITICAL INSTITUTIONS IN PERSPECTIVE

Ordinarily these institutions do not arrive in a country all at once; the last two are distinctly latecomers. Until the twentieth century, universal suffrage was denied in both the theory and practice of democratic and republican government. More than any other single feature, universal suffrage distinguishes modern representative democracy from earlier forms of democracy.

The time of arrival and the sequence in which the institutions have been introduced have varied tremendously. In countries where the full set of democratic institutions arrived earliest and have endured to the present day, the "older" democracies, elements of a common pattern emerge. Elections to a legislature arrived early on—in Britain as early as the thirteenth century, in the United States during its colonial period in the seventeenth and eighteenth centuries. The practice of electing higher lawmaking officials was followed by a gradual expansion of the rights of citizens to express themselves on political

matters and to seek out and exchange information. The right to form associations with explicit political goals tended to follow still later. Political "factions" and partisan organization were generally viewed as dangerous, divisive, subversive of political order and stability, and injurious to the public good. Yet because political associations could not be suppressed without a degree of coercion that an increasingly large and influential number of citizens regarded as intolerable, they were often able to exist as more or less clandestine associations until they emerged from the shadows into the full light of day. In the legislative bodies, what once were "factions" became political parties. The "ins" who served in the government of the day were opposed by the "outs," or what in Britain came to be officially styled His (or Her) Majesty's Loyal Opposition. In eighteenth-century Britain, the faction supporting the monarch and the opposing faction supported by much of the gentry in the "country" were gradually transformed into Tories and Whigs. During that same century in Sweden, partisan adversaries in Parliament somewhat facetiously called themselves the Hats and the Caps.[2]

During the final years of the eighteenth century in the newly formed republic of the United States, Thomas Jefferson, the vice president, and James Madison, leader of the House of Representatives, organized their followers in Congress to oppose the policies of the Federalist president, John Adams, and his secretary of the treasury, Alexander Hamilton. To succeed in their opposition, they soon realized that they would have to do more than oppose the Federalists in the Congress and the cabinet: they would need to remove their opponents from office. To do that, they had to win national elections, and to win national elections they had to organize their followers throughout the country. In less than a decade, Jefferson, Madison, and others sympathetic with their views created a political party that was organized all the way down to the smallest voting precincts, districts, and municipalities, an organization that would reinforce the loyalty of their followers between and during election campaigns and make sure they came to the polls. Their Republican Party (soon renamed Democratic Republican and, a generation later, Democratic) became the first popularly based *electoral* party in the world. As a result, one of the most fundamental and distinctive political institutions of modern democracy, the political party, had burst beyond its confines in parliaments and legislatures in order to organize the citizens themselves and mobilize party supporters in national elections.

By the time the young French aristocrat Alexis de Tocqueville visited the United States in the 1830s, the first five democratic political institutions described above had already arrived in America. The institutions seemed to him so deeply planted and pervasive that he had no hesitation in referring to the United States as a democracy. In that country, he said, the people were sovereign, "society governs itself for itself," and the power of the majority was unlimited.[3] He was astounded by the multiplicity of associations into which Americans organized themselves, for every purpose, it seemed. And towering among these associations were the two major political parties. In the United States, it appeared to Tocqueville, democracy was about as complete as one could imagine it ever becoming.

During the century that followed, all five of the basic democratic institutions Tocqueville observed during his visit to America were consolidated in more than a dozen other countries. Many observers in Europe and the United States concluded that any country that aspired to be civilized and progressive would necessarily have to adopt a democratic form of government.

Yet everywhere, the sixth fundamental institution— inclusive citizenship—was missing. Although Tocqueville affirmed that "the state of Maryland, which had been founded by men of rank, was the first to proclaim universal suffrage," like almost all other men (and many women) of his time he tacitly assumed that "universal" did not include women.[4] Nor, indeed, some men. Maryland's "universal suffrage," it so happened, also excluded most African Americans. Elsewhere, in countries that were otherwise more or less democratic, as in America, a full half of all adults were completely excluded from national political life simply because they were women; in addition, large numbers of men were denied suffrage because they could not meet literacy or property requirements, an exclusion supported by many people who considered themselves advocates of democratic or republican government. Although New Zealand extended suffrage to women in national elections in 1893 and Australia in 1902, in countries otherwise democratic, women did not gain suffrage in national elections until about 1920; in Belgium, France, and Switzerland, countries that most people would have called highly democratic, women could not vote until after World War II.

Because it is difficult for many today to grasp what "democracy" meant to our predecessors, let me reemphasize the difference: in all democracies and republics throughout twenty-five centuries, the rights to engage fully in political life were restricted to a minority of adults. "Democratic" government was government by males only—and not all of them. It was not until the twentieth century that in both theory and practice democracy came to require that the rights to engage fully in political life must be extended, with very few if any exceptions, to the entire population of adults permanently residing in a country.

Taken in their entirety, then, these six political institutions constitute not only a new type of political system but a new kind of popular government, a type of "democracy" that had never existed throughout the twenty-five centuries of experience since the inauguration of "democracy" in Athens and a "republic" in Rome. Because the institutions of modern representative democratic government, taken in their entirety, are historically unique, it is convenient to give them their own name. This modern type of large-scale democratic government is sometimes called *polyarchal* democracy.

Although other factors were often at work, the six political institutions of polyarchal democracy came about, in part at least, in response to demands for inclusion and participation in political life. In countries that are widely referred to as democracies today, all six exist. Yet you might well ask: Are some of these institutions no more than past products of historical struggles? Are they no longer necessary for democratic government? And if they are still necessary today, why?[5]

THE FACTOR OF SIZE

Before answering these questions, I need to call attention to an important qualification. We are considering institutions necessary for the government of a democratic country. Why "country"? *Because all the institutions necessary for a democratic country would not always be required for a unit much smaller than a country.*

Consider a democratically governed committee, or a club, or a very small town. Although equality in voting would seem to be necessary, small units like these might manage without many elected officials: perhaps a moderator to preside over meetings, a secretary-treasurer to keep minutes and accounts. The participants themselves could decide just about everything directly during their meetings, leaving details to the secretary-treasurer. Governments of small organizations would not have to be full-fledged *representative* governments in which citizens elect representatives charged with enacting laws and policies. Yet these governments could be democratic, perhaps highly democratic. So, too, even though they lacked political parties or other independent political associations, they might be highly democratic. In fact, we might concur with the classical democratic and republican view that in small associations, organized "factions" are not only unnecessary but downright harmful. Instead of conflicts exacerbated by factionalism, caucuses, political parties, and so on, we might prefer unity, consensus, agreement achieved by discussion and mutual respect.

The political institutions strictly required for democratic government depend, then, on the size of the unit. The six institutions listed above developed because they are necessary for governing *countries*, not smaller units. Polyarchal democracy is democratic government on the large scale of the nation-state or country.

To return to our questions: Are the political institutions of polyarchal democracy actually necessary for democracy on the large scale of a country? If so, why? To answer these twin questions, let us recall what a democratic process requires (Figure 2).

FIGURE 2

Why the Institutions Are Necessary

In a unit as large as a country, these political institutions of polyarchal democracy …	are necessary to satisfy the following democratic criteria:
1. Elected representatives…	Effective participation Control of the agenda
2. Free, fair and frequent elections…	Voting equality Control of the agenda
3. Freedom of expression…	Effective participation Enlightened understanding Control of the agenda
4. Alternative information…	Effective participation Enlightened understanding Control of the agenda
5. Associational autonomy…	Effective participation Enlightened understanding Control of the agenda
6. Inclusive citizenship…	Full inclusion

WHY (AND WHEN) DOES DEMOCRACY REQUIRE ELECTED REPRESENTATIVES?

As the focus of democratic government shifted to large-scale units like nations or countries, the question arose: How can citizens *participate effectively* when the number of citizens becomes too numerous or too widely dispersed geographically (or both, as in the case of a country) for them to participate conveniently in making laws by assembling in one place? And how can they make sure that matters with which they are most concerned are adequately considered by officials—that is, how can citizens *control the agenda of* government decisions?

How best to meet these democratic requirements in a political unit as large as a country is, of course, enormously difficult, indeed to some extent unachievable. Yet just as with the other highly demanding democratic criteria, this, too, can serve as a standard for evaluating alternative possibilities and solutions. Clearly the requirements could not be met if the top officials of the government could set the agenda and adopt policies independently of the wishes of citizens. The only feasible solution, though it is highly imperfect, is for citizens to elect their top officials and hold them more or less accountable through elections by dismissing them, so to speak, in subsequent elections.

To us that solution seems obvious. But what may appear self-evident to us was not at all obvious to our predecessors.

Until fairly recently the possibility that citizens could, by means of elections, choose and reject representatives with the authority to make laws remained largely foreign to both the theory and practice of democracy. The election of representatives mainly developed during the Middle Ages, when monarchs realized that in order to impose taxes, raise armies, and make laws, they needed to win the consent of the nobility, the higher clergy, and a few not-so-common commoners in the larger towns and cities.

Until the eighteenth century, then, the standard view was that democratic or republican government meant rule by the people, and if the people were to rule, they had to assemble in one place and vote on decrees, laws, or policies. Democracy would have to be town meeting democracy; representative democracy was a contradiction in terms. By implication, whether explicit or implicit, a republic or a democracy could actually exist only in a small unit, like a town or city. Writers who held this view, such as Montesquieu and Jean-Jacques Rousseau, were perfectly aware of the disadvantages of a small state, particularly when it confronted the military superiority of a much larger state, and were therefore extremely pessimistic about the future prospects for genuine democracy.

Yet the standard view was swiftly overpowered and swept aside by the onrushing force of the national state. Rousseau himself clearly understood that for a government of a country as large as Poland (for which he proposed a constitution), representation would be necessary. And shortly thereafter, the standard view was driven off the stage of history by the arrival of democracy in America.

As late as 1787, when the Constitutional Convention met in Philadelphia to design a constitution appropriate for a large country with an ever-increasing population, the delegates were acutely aware of the historical tradition. Could a republic possibly exist on the huge scale the United States had already attained, not to mention the even grander scale the delegates foresaw?[6] Yet no one questioned that if a republic were to exist in America, it would have to take the form of a *representative* republic. Because of the lengthy experience with representation in colonial and state legislatures and in the Continental Congress, the feasibility of representative government was practically beyond debate.

By the middle of the nineteenth century, the traditional view was ignored, forgotten, or, if remembered at all, treated as irrelevant. "It is evident," John Stuart Mill wrote in 1861

that the only government which can fully satisfy all the exigencies of the social state is one in which the whole people participate; that any participation, even in the smallest public function, is useful; that the participation should everywhere be as great as the general degree of improvement of the community will allow; and that nothing less can be ultimately desirable than the admission of all to share in the sovereign power of the state. But since all cannot, in a community exceeding a single small town, participate personally in any but some very minor portions of the public business, it follows that the ideal type of a perfect government must be representative.[7]

WHY DOES DEMOCRACY REQUIRE FREE, FAIR, AND FREQUENT ELECTIONS?

As we have seen, if we accept the desirability of political equality, then every citizen must have an *equal and effective opportunity to vote, and all votes must be counted as equal*. If equality in voting is to be implemented, then clearly, elections must be free and fair. To be free means that citizens can go to the polls without fear of reprisal; and if they are to be fair, then all votes must be counted as equal. Yet free and fair elections are not enough. Imagine electing representatives for a term of, say, twenty years! If citizens are to retain *final control over the agenda*, then elections must also be frequent.

How best to implement free and fair elections is not obvious. In the late nineteenth century, the secret ballot began to replace a public show of hands. Although open voting still has a few defenders, secrecy has become the general standard; a country in which it is widely violated would be judged as lacking free and fair elections. But debate continues as to the kind of voting system that best meets standards of fairness. Is a system of proportional representation (PR), like that employed in most democratic countries, fairer than the first-past-the-post system used in Great Britain and the United States? Reasonable arguments can be made for both. In discussions about different voting systems, however, the need for a fair system is assumed; how best to achieve fairness and other reasonable objectives is simply a technical question.

How frequent should elections be? Judging from twentieth-century practices in democratic countries, a rough answer might be that annual elections for legislative representatives would be a bit too frequent and anything more than five years would be too long. Obviously, however, democrats can reasonably disagree about the specific interval and how it might vary with different offices and different traditional practices. The point is that without frequent elections, citizens would lose a substantial degree of control over their elected officials.

WHY DOES DEMOCRACY REQUIRE FREE EXPRESSION?

To begin with, freedom of expression is required in order for citizens to *participate* effectively in political life. How can citizens make their views known and persuade their fellow citizens and representatives to adopt them unless they can express themselves freely about all matters bearing on the conduct of the government? And if they are to take the views of others into account, they must be able to hear what others have to say. Free expression means not just that you have a right to be heard. It also means that you have a right to hear what others have to say.

To acquire an *enlightened understanding* of possible government actions and policies also requires freedom of expression. To acquire civic competence, citizens need opportunities to express their own views; learn from one another; engage in discussion and deliberation; read, hear, and question experts, political candidates, and persons whose judgments they trust; and learn in other ways that depend on freedom of expression.

Finally, without freedom of expression, citizens would soon lose their capacity to influence *the agenda* of government decisions. Silent citizens may be perfect subjects for an authoritarian ruler; they would be a disaster for a democracy.

WHY DOES DEMOCRACY REQUIRE THE AVAILABILITY OF ALTERNATIVE AND INDEPENDENT SOURCES OF INFORMATION?

Like freedom of expression, the availability of alternative and relatively independent sources of information is required by several of the basic democratic criteria. Consider the need for *enlightened understanding*. How can citizens acquire the information they need in order to understand the issue if the government controls all the important sources of information? Or, for that matter, if any single group enjoys a monopoly in providing information? Citizens must have access, then, to alternative sources of information that are not under the control of the government or dominated by any other group or point of view.

Or think about *effective participation* and influencing the *public agenda*. How could citizens participate effectively in political life if all the information they could acquire were provided by a single source, say the government, or, for that matter, a single party, faction, or interest?

WHY DOES DEMOCRACY REQUIRE INDEPENDENT ASSOCIATIONS?

It took a radical turnabout in ways of thinking to accept the need for political associations—interest groups, lobbying organizations, political parties. Yet if a large republic requires that representatives be elected, then how are elections to be contested? Forming an organization, such as a political party, gives a group an obvious electoral advantage. And if one group seeks to gain that advantage, will not others who disagree with their policies? And why should political activity cease between elections? Legislators can be influenced; causes can be advanced, policies promoted, appointments sought. So, unlike a small city or town, the large scale of democracy in a country makes political associations both necessary and desirable. In any case, how can they be prevented without impairing the fundamental right of citizens to participate effectively in governing? In a large republic, then, they are not only necessary and desirable but inevitable. Independent associations are also a source of *civic education and enlightenment*. They provide citizens not only with information but also with opportunities for discussion, deliberation, and the acquisition of political skills.

WHY DOES DEMOCRACY REQUIRE INCLUSIVE CITIZENSHIP?

We can view the political institutions summarized in Figure 1 in several ways. For a country that lacks one or more of the institutions, and is to that extent not yet sufficiently democratized, knowledge of the basic political institutions can help us to design a strategy for making a full *transition* to modern representative democracy. For a country that has only recently made the transition, that knowledge can help inform us about the crucial institutions that need to be *strengthened, deepened, and consolidated*. Because they are all necessary for modern representative democracy (polyarchal democracy), we can also view them as establishing a *minimum level for democratization*.

Those of us who live in the older democracies, where the transition to democracy occurred some generations ago and the political institutions listed in Figure 1 are by now solidly established, face a different and equally difficult challenge. For even if the institutions are necessary to democratization, they are definitely not *sufficient* for achieving fully the democratic criteria listed in Figure 1. Are we not then at liberty, and indeed obligated, to appraise our democratic institutions against these criteria? It seems obvious to me, as to many others, that judged against democratic criteria, our existing political institutions display many shortcomings.

Consequently, just as we need strategies for bringing about a transition to democracy in nondemocratic countries and for consolidating democratic institutions in newly democratized countries, so in the older democratic countries, we need to consider whether and how to move beyond our existing level of democracy.

Let me put it this way. In many countries, the task is to achieve democratization up to the level of polyarchal democracy. But the challenge to citizens in the older democracies is to discover how they might achieve a level of democratization *beyond* polyarchal democracy.

NOTES

1. Political *arrangements* sound as if they might be rather provisional, which they could well be in a country that has just moved away from nondemocratic rule. We tend to think of *practices* as more habitual and therefore more durable. We usually think of *institutions* as having settled in for the long haul, passed on from one generation to the next. As a country moves from a nondemocratic to a democratic government, the early democratic *arrangements* gradually become *practices*, which in due time turn into settled *institutions*. Helpful though these distinction may be, however, for our purposes it will be more convenient if we put them aside and settle for *institutions*.

2. "The Hats assumed their name for being like the dashing fellows in the tricorne of the day.... The Caps were nicknamed because of the charge that they were like timid old ladies in nightcaps." Franklin D. Scott, *Sweden: The Nation's History* (Minneapolis: University of Minnesota Press, 1977), 243.

3. Alexis de Tocqueville, *Democracy in America*, vol. 1 (New York: Schocken Books, 1961), 51.

4. Tocqueville, *Democracy in America*, 50.

5. Polyarchy is derived from Greek words meaning "many" and "rule," thus "rule by the many," as distinguished from rule by the one, or monarchy, and rule by the few, oligarchy or aristocracy. Although the term had been rarely used, a colleague and I introduced it in 1953 as a handy way of referring to a modern representative democracy with universal suffrage. Hereafter I shall use it in that sense. More precisely, a polyarchal democracy is a political system with the six democratic institutions listed above. Polyarchal democracy, then, is different from representative democracy with restricted suffrage, as in the nineteenth century. It is also different from older democracies and republics that not only had a restricted suffrage but lacked many of the other crucial characteristics of polyarchal democracy, such as political parties, rights to form political organizations to influence or oppose the existing government, organized interest groups, and so on. It is different, too, from the democratic practices in units so small that members can assemble directly and make (or recommend) policies or laws.

6. A few delegates daringly forecast that the United States might ultimately have as many as one hundred million inhabitants. This number was reached in 1915.

7. John Stuart Mill, *Considerations on Representative Government* [1861] (New York: Liberal Arts Press, 1958), 55.

ROBERT A. DAHL is Sterling Professor Emeritus of Political Science, Yale University. He has published many books on democratic theory and practice, including A Preface to Democratic Theory *(1956) and* Democracy and Its Critics *(1989). This article was adapted from his recent book,* On Democracy, *Yale University Press.*

WHAT DEMOCRACY IS... AND IS NOT

Philippe C. Schmitter & Terry Lynn Karl

For some time, the word democracy has been circulating as a debased currency in the political marketplace. Politicians with a wide range of convictions and practices strove to appropriate the label and attach it to their actions. Scholars, conversely, hesitated to use it—without adding qualifying adjectives—because of the ambiguity that surrounds it. The distinguished American political theorist Robert Dahl even tried to introduce a new term, "polyarchy," in its stead in the (vain) hope of gaining a greater measure of conceptual precision. But for better or worse, we are "stuck" with democracy as the catchword of contemporary political discourse. It is the word that resonates in people's minds and springs from their lips as they struggle for freedom and a better way of life; it is the word whose meaning we must discern if it is to be of any use in guiding political analysis and practice.

The wave of transitions away from autocratic rule that began with Portugal's "Revolution of the Carnations" in 1974 and seems to have crested with the collapse of communist regimes across Eastern Europe in 1989 has produced a welcome convergence toward [a] common definition of democracy.[1] Everywhere there has been a silent abandonment of dubious adjectives like "popular," "guided," "bourgeois," and "formal" to modify "democracy." At the same time, a remarkable consensus has emerged concerning the minimal conditions that polities must meet in order to merit the prestigious appellation of "democratic." Moreover, a number of international organizations now monitor how well these standards are met; indeed, some countries even consider them when formulating foreign policy.[2]

WHAT DEMOCRACY IS

Let us begin by broadly defining democracy and the generic *concepts* that distinguish it as a unique system for organizing relations between rulers and the ruled. We will then briefly review *procedures*, the rules and arrangements that are needed if democracy is to endure. Finally, we will discuss two operative *principles* that make democracy work. They are not expressly included among the generic concepts or formal procedures, but the prospect for democracy is grim if their underlying conditioning effects are not present.

One of the major themes of this essay is that democracy does not consist of a single unique set of institutions. There are many types of democracy, and their diverse practices produce a similarly varied set of effects. The specific form democracy takes is contingent upon a country's socioeconomic conditions as well as its entrenched state structures and policy practices.

Modern political democracy is a system of governance in which rulers are held accountable for their actions in the public realm by citizens, acting indirectly through the competition and cooperation of their elected representatives.[3]

A *regime or system of governance* is an ensemble of patterns that determines the methods of access to the principal public offices; the characteristics of the actors admitted to or excluded from such access; the strategies that actors may use to gain access; and the rules that are followed in the making of publicly binding decisions. To work properly, the ensemble must be institutionalized—that is to say, the various patterns must be habitually known, practiced, and accepted by most, if not all, actors. Increasingly, the preferred mechanism of institutionalization is a written body of laws undergirded by a written constitution, though many enduring political norms can have an informal, prudential, or traditional basis.[4]

For the sake of economy and comparison, these forms, characteristics, and rules are usually bundled together and given a generic label. Democratic is one; others are autocratic, authoritarian, despotic, dictatorial, tyrannical, totalitarian, absolutist, traditional, monarchic, obligarchic, plutocratic, aristocratic, and sultanistic.[5] Each of these regime forms may in turn be broken down into subtypes.

Like all regimes, democracies depend upon the presence of *rulers*, persons who occupy specialized authority roles and can give legitimate commands to others. What distinguishes democratic rulers from nondemocratic ones are the norms that condition how the former come to power and the practices that hold them accountable for their actions.

"However central to democracy, elections occur intermittently and only allow citizens to choose between the highly aggregated alternatives offered by political parties..."

The *public realm* encompasses the making of collective norms and choices that are binding on the society and backed by state coercion. Its content can vary a great deal across democracies, depending upon preexisting distinctions between the public and the private, state and society, legitimate coercion and voluntary exchange, and collective needs and individual preferences. The liberal conception of democracy advocates circumscribing the public realm as narrowly as possible, while the socialist or social-democratic approach would extend that realm through regulation, subsidization, and, in some cases, collective ownership of property. Neither is intrinsically more democratic than the other—just *differently* democratic. This implies that measures aimed at "developing the private sector" are no more democratic than those aimed at "developing the public sector." Both, if carried to extremes, could undermine the practice of democracy, the former by destroying the basis for satisfying collective needs and exercising legitimate authority; the latter by destroying the basis for satisfying individual preferences and controlling illegitimate government actions. Differences of opinion over the optimal mix of the two provide much of the substantive content of political conflict within established democracies.

Citizens are the most distinctive element in democracies. All regimes have rulers and a public realm, but only to the extent that they are democratic do they have citizens. Historically, severe restrictions on citizenship were imposed in most emerging or partial democracies according to criteria of age, gender, class, race, literacy, property ownership, tax-paying status, and so on. Only a small part of the total population was eligible to vote or run for office. Only restricted social categories were allowed to form, join, or support political associations. After protracted struggle—in some cases involving violent domestic upheaval or international war—most of these restrictions were lifted. Today, the criteria for inclusion are fairly standard. All native-born adults are eligible, although somewhat higher age limits may still be imposed upon candidates for certain offices. Unlike the early American and European democracies of the nineteenth century, none of the recent democracies in southern Europe, Latin America, Asia, or Eastern Europe has even attempted to impose formal restrictions on the franchise or

eligibility to office. When it comes to informal restrictions on the effective exercise of citizenship rights, however, the story can be quite different. This explains the central importance (discussed below) of procedures.

Competition has not always been considered an essential defining condition of democracy. "Classic" democracies presumed decision making based on direct participation leading to consensus. The assembled citizenry was expected to agree on a common course of action after listening to the alternatives and weighing their respective merits and demerits. A tradition of hostility to "faction," and "particular interests" persists in democratic thought, but at least since *The Federalist Papers* it has become widely accepted that competition among factions is a necessary evil in democracies that operate on a more-than-local scale. Since, as James Madison argued, "the latent causes of faction are sown into the nature of man," and the possible remedies for "the mischief of faction" are worse than the disease, the best course is to recognize them and to attempt to control their effects.[6] Yet while democrats may agree on the inevitability of factions, they tend to disagree about the best forms and rules for governing factional competition. Indeed, differences over the preferred modes and boundaries of competition contribute most to distinguishing one subtype of democracy from another.

The most popular definition of democracy equates it with regular *elections*, fairly conducted and honestly counted. Some even consider the mere fact of elections—even ones from which specific parties or candidates are excluded, or in which substantial portions of the population cannot freely participate—as a sufficient condition for the existence of democracy. This fallacy has been called "electoralism" or "the faith that merely holding elections will channel political action into peaceful contests among elites and accord public legitimacy to the winners"—no matter how they are conducted or what else constrains those who win them.[7] However central to democracy, elections occur intermittently and only allow citizens to choose between the highly aggregated alternatives offered by political parties, which can, especially in the early stages of a democratic transition, proliferate in a bewildering variety. During the intervals between elections, citizens can seek to influence public policy through a wide variety of other intermediaries: interest associations, social movements, locality groupings, clientelistic arrangements, and so forth. *Modern democracy, in other words, offers a variety of competitive processes and channels for the expression of interests and values—associational as well as partisan, functional as well as territorial, collective as well as individual. All are integral to its practice.*

Another commonly accepted image of democracy identifies it with *majority rule*. Any governing body that makes decisions by combining the votes of more than half of those eligible and present is said to be democratic, whether that majority emerges within an electorate, a parliament, a committee, a city council, or a party caucus.

For exceptional purposes (e.g., amending the constitution or expelling a member), "qualified majorities" of more than 50 percent may be required, but few would deny that democracy must involve some means of aggregating the equal preferences of individuals.

A problem arises, however, when *numbers* meet *intensities*. What happens when a properly assembled majority (especially a stable, self-perpetuating one) regularly makes decisions that harm some minority (especially a threatened cultural or ethnic group)? In these circumstances, successful democracies tend to qualify the central principle of majority rule in order to protect minority rights. Such qualifications can take the form of constitutional provisions that place certain matters beyond the reach of majorities (bills of rights); requirements for concurrent majorities in several different constituencies (confederalism); guarantees securing the autonomy of local or regional governments against the demands of the central authority (federalism); grand coalition governments that incorporate all parties (consociationalism); or the negotiation of social pacts between major social groups like business and labor (neocorporatism). The most common and effective way of protecting minorities, however, lies in the everyday operation of interest associations and social movements. These reflect (some would say, amplify) the different intensities of preference that exist in the population and bring them to bear on democratically elected decision makers. Another way of putting this intrinsic tension between numbers and intensities would be to say that "in modern democracies, votes may be counted, but influences alone are weighted."

Cooperation has always been a central feature of democracy. Actors must voluntarily make collective decisions binding on the polity as a whole. They must cooperate in order to compete. They must be capable of acting collectively through parties, associations, and movements in order to select candidates, articulate preferences, petition authorities, and influence policies.

But democracy's freedoms should also encourage citizens to deliberate among themselves, to discover their common needs, and to resolve their differences without relying on some supreme central authority. Classical democracy emphasized these qualities, and they are by no means extinct, despite repeated efforts by contemporary theorists to stress the analogy with behavior in the economic marketplace and to reduce all of democracy's operations to competitive interest maximization. Alexis de Tocqueville best described the importance of independent groups for democracy in his *Democracy in America*, a work which remains a major source of inspiration for all those who persist in viewing democracy as something more than a struggle for election and re-election among competing candidates.[8]

In contemporary political discourse, this phenomenon of cooperation and deliberation via autonomous group activity goes under the rubric of "civil society." The diverse units of social identity and interest, by remaining independent of the state (and perhaps even of parties), not only can restrain the arbitrary actions of rulers, but can also contribute to forming better citizens who are more aware of the preferences of others, more self-confident in their actions, and more civic-minded in their willingness to sacrifice for the common good. At its best, civil society provides an intermediate layer of governance between the individual and the state that is capable of resolving conflicts and controlling the behavior of members without public coercion. Rather than overloading decision makers with increased demands and making the system ungovernable,[9] a viable civil society can mitigate conflicts and improve the quality of citizenship—without relying exclusively on the privatism of the marketplace.

Representatives—whether directly or indirectly elected—do most of the real work in modern democracies. Most are professional politicians who orient their careers around the desire to fill key offices. It is doubtful that any democracy could survive without such people. The central question, therefore, is not whether or not there will be a political elite or even a professional political class, but how these representatives are chosen and then held accountable for their actions.

As noted above, there are many channels of representation in modern democracy. The electoral one, based on territorial constituencies, is the most visible and public. It culminates in a parliament or a presidency that is periodically accountable to the citizenry as a whole. Yet the sheer growth of government (in large part as a byproduct of popular demand) has increased the number, variety, and power of agencies charged with making public decisions and not subject to elections. Around these agencies there has developed a vast apparatus of specialized representation based largely on functional interests, not territorial constituencies. These interest associations, and not political parties, have become the primary expression of civil society in most stable democracies, supplemented by the more sporadic interventions of social movements.

The new and fragile democracies that have sprung up since 1974 must live in "compressed time." They will not resemble the European democracies of the nineteenth and early twentieth centuries, and they cannot expect to acquire the multiple channels of representation in gradual historical progression as did most of their predecessors. A bewildering array of parties, interests, and movements will all simultaneously seek political influence in them, creating challenges to the polity that did not exist in earlier processes of democratization.

PROCEDURES THAT MAKE DEMOCRACY POSSIBLE

The defining components of democracy are necessarily abstract, and may give rise to a considerable variety of institutions and subtypes of democracy. For democracy to thrive, however, specific procedural norms must be followed and civic rights must be respected. Any polity that fails to impose such restrictions upon itself, that fails to follow the "rule of law" with regard to its own procedures, should not be considered democratic. These procedures alone do not define democracy, but their presence is indispensable to its persistence. In essence, they are necessary but not sufficient conditions for its existence.

Robert Dahl has offered the most generally accepted listing of what he terms the "procedural minimal" conditions that must be present for modern political democracy (or as he puts it, "polyarchy") to exist:

1. Control over government decisions about policy is constitutionally vested in elected officials.
2. Elected officials are chosen in frequent and fairly conducted elections in which coercion is comparatively uncommon.
3. Practically all adults have the right to vote in the election of officials.
4. Practically all adults have the right to run for elective offices
5. Citizens have a right to express themselves without the danger of severe punishment on political matters broadly defined....
6. Citizens have a right to seek out alternative sources of information. Moreover, alternative sources of information exist and are protected by law.
7. ... Citizens also have the right to form relatively independent associations or organizations, including independent political parties and interest groups.[10]

These seven conditions seem to capture the essence of procedural democracy for many theorists, but we propose to add two others. The first might be thought of as a further refinement of item (1), while the second might be called an implicit prior condition to all seven of the above.

1. Popularly elected officials must be able to exercise their constitutional powers without being subjected to overriding (albeit informal) opposition from unelected officials. Democracy is in jeopardy if military officers, entrenched civil servants, or state managers retain the capacity to act independently of elected civilians or even veto decisions made by the people's representatives. Without this additional caveat, the militarized polities of contemporary Central America, where civilian control over the military does not exist, might be classified by many scholars as democracies, just as they have been (with the exception of Sandinista Nicaragua) by U.S. policy makers. The caveat thus guards against what we earlier called "electoralism"—the tendency to focus on the holding of elections while ignoring other political realities.
2. The polity must be self-governing; it must be able to act independently of constraints imposed by some other overarching political system. Dahl and other contemporary democratic theorists probably took

this condition for granted since they referred to formally sovereign nation-states. However, with the development of blocs, alliances, spheres of influence, and a variety of "neocolonial" arrangements, the question of autonomy has been a salient one. Is a system really democratic if its elected officials are unable to make binding decisions without the approval of actors outside their territorial domain? This is significant even if the outsiders are relatively free to alter or even end the encompassing arrangement (as in Puerto Rico), but it becomes especially critical if neither condition obtains (as in the Baltic states).

PRINCIPLES THAT MAKE DEMOCRACY FEASIBLE

Lists of component processes and procedural norms help us to specify what democracy is, but they do not tell us much about how it actually functions. The simplest answer is "by the consent of the people"; the more complex one is "by the contingent consent of politicians acting under conditions of bounded uncertainty."

In a democracy, representatives must at least informally agree that those who win greater electoral support or influence over policy will not use their temporary superiority to bar the losers from taking office or exerting influence in the future, and that in exchange for this opportunity to keep competing for power and place, momentary losers will respect the winners' right to make binding decisions. Citizens are expected to obey the decisions ensuing from such a process of competition, provided its outcome remains contingent upon their collective preferences as expressed through fair and regular elections or open and repeated negotiations.

The challenge is not so much to find a set of goals that command widespread consensus as to find a set of rules that embody contingent consent. The precise shape of this "democratic bargain," to use Dahl's expression,[11] can vary a good deal from society to society. It depends on social cleavages and such subjective factors as mutual trust, the standard of fairness, and the willingness to compromise. It may even be compatible with a great deal of dissensus on substantive policy issues.

All democracies involve a degree of uncertainty about who will be elected and what policies they will pursue. Even in those polities where one party persists in winning elections or one policy is consistently implemented, the possibility of change through independent collective action still exists, as in Italy, Japan, and the Scandinavian social democracies. If it does not, the system is not democratic, as in Mexico, Senegal, or Indonesia.

But the uncertainty embedded in the core of all democracies is bounded. Not just any actor can get into the competition and raise any issue he or she pleases—there are previously established rules that must be respected. Not just any policy can be adopted—there are conditions that must be met. Democracy institutionalizes "normal," limited political uncertainty. These boundaries vary from country to country. Constitutional guarantees of property, privacy, expression, and other rights are a part of this, but the most effective boundaries are generated by competition among interest groups and cooperation within civil society. Whatever the rhetoric (and some polities appear to offer their citizens more dramatic alternatives than others), once the rules of contingent consent have been agreed upon, the actual variation is likely to stay within a predictable and generally accepted range.

This emphasis on operative guidelines contrasts with a highly persistent, but misleading theme in recent literature on democracy—namely, the emphasis upon "civic culture." The principles we have suggested here rest on rules of prudence, not on deeply ingrained habits of tolerance, moderation, mutual respect, fair play, readiness to compromise, or trust in public authorities. Waiting for such habits to sink deep and lasting roots implies a very slow process of regime consolidation—one that takes generations—and it would probably condemn most contemporary experiences *ex hypothesi* to failure. Our assertion is that contingent consent and bounded uncertainty can emerge from the interaction between antagonistic and mutually suspicious actors and that the far more benevolent and ingrained norms of a civic culture are better thought of as a *product* and not a producer of democracy.

HOW DEMOCRACIES DIFFER

Several concepts have been deliberately excluded from our generic definition of democracy, despite the fact that they have been frequently associated with it in both everyday practice and scholarly work. They are, nevertheless, especially important when it comes to distinguishing subtypes of democracy. Since no single set of actual institutions, practices, or values embodies democracy, polities moving away from authoritarian rule can mix different components to produce different democracies. It is important to recognize that these do not define points along a single continuum of improving performance, but a matrix of potential combinations that are *differently* democratic.

1. *Consensus*: All citizens may not agree on the substantive goals of political action or on the role of the state (although if they did, it would certainly make governing democracies much easier).
2. *Participation*: All citizens may not take an active and equal part in politics, although it must be legally possible for them to do so.
3. *Access*: Rulers may not weigh equally the preferences of all who come before them, although citizenship implies that individuals and groups should have an equal opportunity to express their preferences if they choose to do so.

4. *Responsiveness*: Rulers may not always follow the course of action preferred by the citizenry. But when they deviate from such a policy, say on grounds of "reason of state" or "overriding national interest," they must ultimately be held accountable for their actions through regular and fair processes.
5. *Majority rule*: Positions may not be allocated or rules may not be decided solely on the basis of assembling the most votes, although deviations from this principle usually must be explicitly defended and previously approved.
6. *Parliamentary sovereignty*: The legislature may not be the only body that can make rules or even the one with final authority in deciding which laws are binding, although where executive, judicial, or other public bodies make that ultimate choice, they too must be accountable for their actions.
7. *Party government*: Rulers may not be nominated, promoted, and disciplined in their activities by well-organized and programmatically coherent political parties, although where they are not, it may prove more difficult to form an effective government.
8. *Pluralism*: The political process may not be based on a multiplicity of overlapping, voluntaristic, and autonomous private groups. However, where there are monopolies of representation, hierarchies of association, and obligatory memberships, it is likely that the interests involved will be more closely linked to the state and the separation between the public and private spheres of action will be much less distinct.
9. *Federalism*: The territorial division of authority may not involve multiple levels and local autonomies, least of all ones enshrined in a constitutional document, although some dispersal of power across territorial and/or functional units is characteristic of all democracies.
10. *Presidentialism*: The chief executive officer may not be a single person and he or she may not be directly elected by the citizenry as a whole, although some concentration of authority is present in all democracies, even if it is exercised collectively and only held indirectly accountable to the electorate.
11. *Checks and Balances*: It is not necessary that the different branches of government be systematically pitted against one another, although governments by assembly, by executive concentrations, by judicial command, or even by dictatorial fiat (as in time of war) must be ultimately accountable to the citizenry as a whole.

While each of the above has been named as an essential component of democracy, they should instead be seen either as indicators of this or that type of democracy, or else as useful standards for evaluating the performance of particular regimes. To include them as part of the generic definition of democracy itself would be to mistake the American polity for the universal model of democratic governance. Indeed, the parliamentary, consociational, unitary, corporatist, and concentrated arrangements of continental Europe may have some unique virtues for guiding polities through the uncertain transition from autocratic to democratic rule.[12]

WHAT DEMOCRACY IS NOT

We have attempted to convey the general meaning of modern democracy without identifying it with some particular set of rules and institutions or restricting it to some specific culture or level of development. We have also argued that it cannot be reduced to the regular holding of elections or equated with a particular notion of the role of the state, but we have not said much more about what democracy is not or about what democracy may not be capable of producing.

There is an understandable temptation to load too many expectations on this concept and to imagine that by attaining democracy, a society will have resolved all of its political, social, economic, administrative, and cultural problems. Unfortunately, "all good things do not necessarily go together."

First, democracies are not necessarily more efficient economically than other forms of government. Their rates of aggregate growth, savings, and investment may be no better than those of nondemocracies. This is especially likely during the transition, when propertied groups and administrative elites may respond to real or imagined threats to the "rights" they enjoyed under authoritarian rule by initiating capital flight, disinvestment, or sabotage. In time, depending upon the type of democracy, benevolent long-term effects upon income distribution, aggregate demand, education, productivity, and creativity may eventually combine to improve economic and social performance, but it is certainly too much to expect that these improvements will occur immediately—much less that they will be defining characteristics of democratization.

Second, democracies are not necessarily more efficient administratively. Their capacity to make decisions may even be slower than that of the regimes they replace, if only because more actors must be consulted. The costs of getting things done may be higher, if only because "payoffs" have to be made to a wider and more resourceful set of clients (although one should never underestimate the degree of corruption to be found within autocracies). Popular satisfaction with the new democratic government's performance may not even seem greater, if only because necessary compromises often please no one completely, and because the losers are free to complain.

Third, democracies are not likely to appear more orderly, consensual, stable, or governable than the autocracies they replace. This is partly a byproduct of democratic freedom of expression, but it is also a reflection of the like-lihood of continuing disagreement over new rules and institutions. These products of imposition or compromise are often initially quite ambiguous in nature and uncertain in effect until actors have learned how to use them. What is more, they come in the aftermath of serious struggles motivated by high ideals. Groups and individuals with recently acquired autonomy will test certain rules, protest against the actions of certain institutions, and insist on renegotiating their part of the bargain. Thus the presence of antisystem parties should be neither surprising nor seen as a failure of democratic consolidation. What counts is whether such parties are willing, however reluctantly, to play by the general rules of bounded uncertainty and contingent consent.

Governability is a challenge for all regimes, not just democratic ones. Given the political exhaustion and loss of legitimacy that have befallen autocracies from sultanistic Paraguay to totalitarian Albania, it may seem that only democracies can now be expected to govern effectively and legitimately. Experience has shown, however, that democracies too can lose the ability to govern. Mass publics can become disenchanted with their performance. Even more threatening is the temptation for leaders to fiddle with procedures and ultimately undermine the principles of contingent consent and bounded uncertainty. Perhaps the most critical moment comes once the politicians begin to settle into the more predictable roles and relations of a consolidated democracy. Many will find their expectations frustrated; some will discover that the new rules of competition put them at a disadvantage; a few may even feel that their vital interests are threatened by popular majorities.

Finally, democracies will have more open societies and polities than the autocracies they replace, but not necessarily more open economies. Many of today's most successful and well-established democracies have historically resorted to protectionism and closed borders, and have relied extensively upon public institutions to promote economic development. While the long-term compatibility between democracy and capitalism does not seem to be in doubt, despite their continuous tension, it is not clear whether the promotion of such liberal economic goals as the right of individuals to own property and retain profits, the clearing function of markets, the private settlement of disputes, the freedom to produce without government regulation, or the privatization of state-owned enterprises necessarily furthers the consolidation of democracy. After all, democracies do need to levy taxes and regulate certain transactions, especially where private monopolies and oligopolies exist. Citizens or their representatives may decide that it is desirable to protect the rights of collectivities from encroachment by individuals, especially propertied ones, and they may choose to set aside certain forms of property for public or cooperative ownership. In short, notions of economic liberty that are currently put forward in neoliberal economic models are not synonymous with political freedom—and may even impede it.

Democratization will not necessarily bring in its wake economic growth, social peace, administrative efficiency, political harmony, free markets, or "the end of ideology." Least of all will it bring about "the end of history." No doubt some of these qualities could make the consolidation of democracy easier, but they are neither prerequisites for it nor immediate products of it. Instead, what we should be hoping for is the emergence of political institutions that can peacefully compete to form governments and influence public policy, that can channel social and economic conflicts through regular procedures, and that have sufficient linkages to civil society to represent their constituencies and commit them to collective courses of action. Some types of democracies, especially in developing countries, have been unable to fulfill this promise, perhaps due to the circumstances of their transition from authoritarian rule.[13] The democratic wager is that such a regime, once established, will not only persist by reproducing itself within its initial confining conditions, but will eventually expand beyond them.[14] Unlike authoritarian regimes, democracies have the capacity to modify their rules and institutions consensually in response to changing circumstances. They may not immediately produce all the goods mentioned above, but they stand a better chance of eventually doing so than do autocracies.

Notes

1. For a comparative analysis of the recent regime changes in southern Europe and Latin America, see Guillermo O'Donnell, Philippe C. Schmitter, and Laurence Whitehead, eds., *Transitions from Authoritarian Rule*, 4 vols. (Baltimore: Johns Hopkins University Press, 1986). For another compilation that adopts a more structural approach see Larry Diamond, Juan Linz, and Seymour Martin Lipset, eds., *Democracy in Developing Countries*, vols. 2, 3, and 4 (Boulder, Colo.: Lynne Rienner, 1989).
2. Numerous attempts have been made to codify and quantify the existence of democracy across political systems. The best known is probably Freedom House's *Freedom in the World: Political Rights and Civil Liberties*, published since 1973 by Greenwood Press and since 1988 by University Press of America. Also see Charles Humana, *World Human Rights Guide* (New York: Facts on File, 1986).
3. The definition most commonly used by American social scientists is that of Joseph Schumpeter: "that institutional arrangement for arriving at political decisions in which individuals acquire the power to decide by means of a competitive struggle for the people's vote." *Capitalism, Socialism, and Democracy* (London: George Allen and Unwin, 1943), 269. We accept certain aspects of the classical procedural approach to modern democracy, but differ prima-rily in our emphasis on the accountability of rulers to citizens and the relevance of mechanisms of competition other than elections.
4. Not only do some countries practice a stable form of democracy without a formal constitution (e.g., Great Britain and Israel), but even more countries have constitutions and legal codes that offer no guarantee of reliable practice. On paper, Stalin's 1936 constitution for the USSR was a virtual model of democratic rights and entitlements.
5. For the most valiant attempt to make some sense out of this thicket of distinctions, see Juan Linz, "Totalitarian and Authoritarian Regimes" in *Handbook of Political Science*, eds. Fred I. Greenstein and Nelson W. Polsby (Reading Mass.: Addison Wesley, 1975), 175–411.
6. "Publius" (Alexander Hamilton, John Jay, and James Madison), *The Federalist Papers* (New York: Anchor Books, 1961). The quote is from Number 10.
7. See Terry Karl, "Imposing Consent? Electoralism versus Democratization in El Salvador," in *Elections and Democratization in Latin America, 1980–1985*, eds. Paul Drake and Eduardo Silva (San Diego: Center for Iberian and Latin American Studies, Center for US/Mexican Studies, University of California, San Diego, 1986), 9–36.
8. Alexis de Tocqueville, *Democracy in America*, 2 vols. (New York: Vintage Books, 1945).
9. This fear of overloaded government and the imminent collapse of democracy is well reflected in the work of Samuel P. Huntington during the 1970s. See especially Michel Crozier, Samuel P. Huntington, and Joji Watanuki, *The Crisis of Democracy* (New York: New York University Press, 1975). For Huntington's (revised) thoughts about the prospects for democracy, see his "Will More Countries Become Democratic?," *Political Science Quarterly* 99 (Summer 1984): 193–218.
10. Robert Dahl, *Dilemmas of Pluralist Democracy* (New Haven: Yale University Press, 1982), 11.
11. Robert Dahl, *After the Revolution: Authority in a Good Society* (New Haven: Yale University Press, 1970).
12. See Juan Linz, "The Perils of Presidentialism," *Journal of Democracy* 1 (Winter 1990): 51–69, and the ensuing discussion by Donald Horowitz, Seymour Martin Lipset, and Juan Linz in *Journal of Democracy* 1 (Fall 1990): 73–91.
13. Terry Lynn Karl, "Dilemmas of Democratization in Latin America" *Comparative Politics* 23 (October 1990): 1–23.
14. Otto Kirchheimer, "Confining Conditions and Revolutionary Breakthroughs," *American Political Science Review* 59 (1965): 964–974.

Philippe C. Schmitter *is professor of political science and director of the Center for European Studies at Stanford University.* **Terry Lynn Karl** *is associate professor of political science and director of the Center for Latin American Studies at the same institution. The original, longer version of this essay was written at the request of the United States Agency for International Development, which is not responsible for its content.*

From *Journal of Democracy*, Summer 1991, p. 19. © 1991 by the National Endowment for Democracy and the Johns Hopkins University Press. Reprinted by permission.

Judicial Review:
The gavel and the robe

Established and emerging democracies display a puzzling taste in common: both have handed increasing amounts of power to unelected judges. Th[is] article examines the remarkable growth and many different forms of judicial review.

To SOME they are unaccountable elitists, old men (and the rare women) in robes who meddle in politics where they do not belong, thwarting the will of the people. To others they are bulwarks of liberty, champions of the individual against abuses of power by scheming politicians, arrogant bureaucrats and the emotional excesses of transient majorities.

Judges who sit on supreme courts must get used to the vilification as well as the praise. They often deal with the most contentious cases, involving issues which divide the electorate or concern the very rules by which their countries are governed. With so much at stake, losers are bound to question not only judges' particular decisions, but their right to decide at all. This is especially true when judges knock down as unconstitutional a law passed by a democratically elected legislature. How dare they?

Despite continued attacks on the legitimacy of judicial review, it has flourished in the past 50 years. All established democracies now have it in some form, and the standing of constitutional courts has grown almost everywhere. In an age when all political authority is supposed to derive from voters, and every passing mood of the electorate is measured by pollsters, the growing power of judges is a startling development.

The trend in western democracies has been followed by the new democracies of Eastern Europe with enthusiasm. Hungary's constitutional court may be the most active and powerful in the world. There have been failures. After a promising start, Russia's constitutional court was crushed in the conflict between Boris Yeltsin and his parliament. But in some countries where governments have long been riven by ideological divisions or crippled by corruption, such as Israel and India, constitutional courts have filled a political vacuum, coming to embody the legitimacy of the state.

In western democracies the growing role of constitutional review, in which judges rule on the constitutionality of laws and regulations, has been accompanied by a similar growth in what is known as administrative review, in which judges rule on the legality of government actions, usually those of the executive branch. This second type of review has also dragged judges into the political arena, frequently pitting them against elected politicians in controversial cases. But it is less problematic for democratic theorists than constitutional review for a number of reasons.

Democracy's referees

The expansion of the modern state has seemed to make administrative review inevitable. The reach of government, for good or ill, now extends into every nook and cranny of life. As a result, individuals, groups and businesses all have more reason than ever before to challenge the legality of government decisions or the interpretation of laws. Such challenges naturally end up before the courts.

In France, Germany, Italy and most other European countries, special administrative tribunals, with their own hierarchies of appeal courts, have been established to handle such cases. In the United States, Britain, Canada and Australia, the ordinary courts, which handle criminal cases and private lawsuits, also deal with administrative law cases.

The growth of administrative review can be explained as a reaction to the growth of state power. But the parallel expansion of constitutional review is all the more remarkable in a democratic age because it was resisted for so long in the very name of democracy.

The idea was pioneered by the United States, the first modern democracy with a written constitution. In fact, the American constitution nowhere explicitly gives the Supreme Court the power to rule laws invalid because of their unconstitutionality. The court's right to do this was first asserted in *Marbury v Madison*, an 1803 case, and then quickly became accepted as proper. One reason for such ready acceptance may have been that a Supreme Court veto fitted so well with the whole design and spirit of the constitution itself, whose purpose was as much to control the excesses of popular majorities as to give the people a voice in government decision-making.

In Europe this was the reason why the American precedent was not followed. As the voting franchise was expanded, the will of the voting majority became ever more sacrosanct, at least in theory. Parliamentary sovereignty reigned supreme. European democrats viewed the American experiment with constitutionalism as an unwarranted restraint on the popular will.

Even in the United States, judicial review was of little importance until the late 19th century, when the Supreme Court became more active, first nullifying laws passed after the civil war to give former slaves equal rights and then overturning laws regulating economic activity in the name of contractual and property rights.

After a showdown with Franklin Roosevelt over the New Deal, which the court lost, it abandoned its defence of laissez-faire economics. In the 1950s under Chief Justice Earl Warren it embarked on the active protection and expansion of civil rights. Controversially, this plunged the court into the mainstream of American politics, a position it retains today despite a retreat from Warren-style activism over the past two decades.

Attitudes towards judicial review also changed in Europe. The rise of fascism in the 1920s and 1930s, and then the destruction wrought by the second world war, made many European democrats reconsider the usefulness of judges. Elections alone no longer seemed a reliable obstacle to the rise of dangerously authoritarian governments. Fascist dictators had seized power by manipulating representative institutions.

The violence and oppression of the pre-war and war years also convinced many that individual rights and civil liberties needed special protection. The tyranny of the executive branch of government, acting in the name of the majority, became a real concern. (Britain remained an exception to this trend, sticking exclusively to the doctrine of parliamentary sovereignty. It is only now taking its first tentative steps towards establishing a constitutional court.)

While the goals of constitutional judicial review are similar almost everywhere, its form varies from country to country, reflecting national traditions. Some of the key differences:

• **Appointments.** The most famous method of appointment is that of the United States, largely because of a handful of televised and acrimonious confir-

mation hearings. The president appoints a Supreme Court judge, subject to Senate approval, whenever one of the court's nine seats falls vacant. Political horse-trading, and conflict, are part of the system. Judges are appointed for life, though very few cling to office to the end.

Other countries may appoint their constitutional judges with more decorum, but politics always plays some part in the process. France is the most explicitly political. The directly elected president and the heads of the Senate and the National Assembly each appoint three of the judges of the Constitutional Council, who serve non-renewable nine-year terms, one-third of them retiring every three years. Former presidents are awarded life membership on the council, although none has yet chosen to take his seat.

Half of the 16 members of Germany's Federal Constitutional Tribunal are chosen by the Bundestag, the lower house of parliament, and half by the Bundesrat, the upper house. Appointments are usually brokered between the two major parties. The procedure is similar in Italy, where one-third of the 15-strong Constitutional Court is chosen by the head of state, one-third by the two houses of parliament and one-third by the professional judiciary.

Senior politicians—both before and after serving in other government posts—have sat on all three constitutional courts, sometimes with unhappy results. In March Roland Dumas, the president of France's Constitutional Council, was forced to step down temporarily because of allegations of corruption during his earlier tenure as foreign minister. The trend in all three countries is towards the appointment of professional judges and legal scholars rather than politicians.

• **Powers.** Most constitutional courts have the power to nullify laws as unconstitutional, but how they do this, and receive cases, varies. Once again, the most anomalous is France's Constitutional Council which rules on the constitutionality of laws only before they go into effect and not, like all other courts, after.

The 1958 constitution of France's Fifth Republic allowed only four authorities to refer cases to the council: the president, the prime minister, and the heads of the two houses of parliament. In 1974, a constitutional amendment authorised 60 deputies or senators to lodge appeals with the council as well. Since then, the council has become more active, and most appeals now come from

groups of legislators. Individuals have no right to appeal to the council.

French jurists argue that judicial review before a law goes into effect is simpler and faster than review after a law's promulgation. But it is also more explicitly political, and leaves no room for making a judgment in the light of a law's sometimes unanticipated effect.

No other major country has adopted prior review exclusively, but it is an option in Germany and Italy as well, usually at the request of the national or one of the regional governments. However, most of the work of the constitutional courts in both countries comes from genuine legal disputes, which are referred to them by other courts when a constitutional question is raised.

The Supreme Courts of the United States, Canada and Australia, by contrast, are the final courts of appeal for all cases, not just those dealing with constitutional issues. The United States Supreme Court does not give advisory or abstract opinions about the constitutionality of laws, but only deals with cases involving specific disputes. Moreover, lower courts in the United States can also rule on constitutional issues, although most important cases are appealed eventually to the Supreme Court.

Canada's Supreme Court can be barred from ruling a law unconstitutional if either the national or a provincial legislature has passed it with a special clause declaring that it should survive judicial review "notwithstanding" any breach of the country's Charter of Rights. If passed in this way, the law must be renewed every five years. In practice, this device has rarely been used.

• **Judgments.** The French and Italian constitutional courts deliver their judgments unanimously, without dissents. Germany abandoned this method in 1971, adopting the more transparent approach of the common-law supreme courts, which allow a tally of votes cast and dissenting opinions to be published alongside the court's judgment. Advocates of unanimity argue that it reinforces the court's authority and gives finality to the law. Opponents deride it as artificial, and claim that publishing dissents improves the technical quality of judgments, keeps the public better informed, and makes it easier for the law to evolve in the light of changing circumstances.

Also noteworthy is the growth in Europe of supra-national judicial review. The European Court of Justice in Luxembourg is the ultimate legal authority for the European Union. The court's primary task is to interpret the treaties upon which the EU is founded. Because EU law now takes precedence over national law in the 15 member states, the court's influence has grown considerably in recent years. The European Court of Human Rights in Strasbourg, the judicial arm of the 41-member Council of Europe, has, in effect, become the final court of appeal on human-rights issues for most of Europe. The judgments of both European courts carry great weight and have forced many countries to change their laws.

Despite the rapid growth of judicial review in recent decades, it still has plenty of critics. Like all institutions, supreme courts make mistakes, and their decisions are a proper topic of political debate. But some criticisms aimed at them are misconceived.

Unelected legislators?

To criticise constitutional courts as political meddlers is to misunderstand their role, which is both judicial and political. If constitutions are to play any part in limiting government, then someone must decide when they have been breached and how they should be applied, especially when the relative powers of various branches or levels of government—a frequent issue in federal systems—are in question. When a court interprets a constitution, its decisions are political by definition—though they should not be party political.

Supreme courts also are not unaccountable, as some of their critics claim. Judges can be overruled by constitutional amendment, although this is rare. They must also justify their rulings to the public in written opinions. These are pored over by the media, lawyers, legal scholars and other judges. If unpersuasive, judgments are sometimes evaded by lower courts or legislatures, and the issue eventually returns to the constitutional court to be considered again.

Moreover, the appointment of judges is a political process, and the complexions of courts change as their membership changes, although appointees are sometimes unpredictable once on the bench. Nevertheless, new appointments can result in the reversal of earlier decisions which failed to win public support.

Constitutional courts have no direct power of their own. This is why Alexander Hamilton, who helped write America's constitution, called the judiciary "the least dangerous branch of government." Courts have no vast bureaucracy, revenue-raising ability, army or police force at their command—no way, in fact, to enforce their rulings. If other branches of government ignore them, they can do nothing. Their power and legitimacy, especially when they oppose the executive or legislature, depend largely on their moral authority and credibility.

Senior judges are acutely aware of their courts' limitations. Most tread warily, preferring to mould the law through interpretation of statutes rather than employing the crude instrument of complete nullification. Even the American Supreme Court, among the world's most activist, has ruled only sections of some 135 federal laws unconstitutional in 210 years, although it has struck down many more state laws.

Finally, it is worth remembering that judges are not the only public officials who exercise large amounts of power but do not answer directly to voters. Full-time officials and appointees actually perform most government business, and many of them have enormous discretion about how they do this. Even elected legislators and prime ministers are not perfect transmitters of the popular will, but enjoy great latitude when making decisions on any particular issue. Constitutional courts exist to ensure that everyone stays within the rules. Judges have the delicate, sometimes impossible, task of checking others' power without seeming to claim too much for themselves.

Referendums: The people's voice

Is the growing use of referendums a threat to democracy or its salvation? The fifth article in our series on changes in mature democracies examines the experience so far, and the arguments for and against letting voters decide political questions directly.

WHEN Winston Churchill proposed a referendum to Clement Attlee in 1945 on whether Britain's wartime coalition should be extended, Attlee growled that the idea was an "instrument of Nazism and fascism". The use by Hitler and Mussolini of bogus referendums to consolidate their power had confirmed the worst fears of sceptics. The most democratic of devices seemed also to be the most dangerous to democracy itself.

Dictators of all stripes have continued to use phony referendums to justify their hold on power. And yet this fact has not stopped a steady growth in the use of genuine referendums, held under free and fair conditions, by both established and aspiring democracies. Referendums have been instrumental in the dismantling of communism and the transition to democracy in countries throughout the former soviet empire. They have also successfully eased democratic transitions in Spain, Greece, South Africa, Brazil and Chile, among other countries.

In most established democracies, direct appeals to voters are now part of the machinery for constitutional change. Their use to resolve the most intractable or divisive public issues has also grown. In the 17 major democracies of Western Europe, only three—Belgium, the Netherlands and Norway—make no provision for referendums in their constitution. Only six major democracies—the Netherlands, the United States, Japan, India, Israel and the Federal Republic of Germany—have never held a nationwide referendum.

The volatile voter

Frustrated voters in Italy and New Zealand have in recent years used referendums to force radical changes to voting systems and other political institutions on a reluctant political elite. Referendums have also been used regularly in Australia, where voters go to the polls this November to decide whether to cut their country's formal link with the British crown. In Switzerland and several American states, referendums are a central feature of the political system, rivalling legislatures in significance.

Outside the United States and Switzerland, referendums are most often called by governments only when they are certain of victory, and to win endorsement of a policy they intend to implement in any case. This is how they are currently being used in Britain by Tony Blair's government.

But voters do not always behave as predicted, and they have delivered some notable rebuffs. Charles de Gaulle skil-fully used referendums to establish the legitimacy of France's Fifth Republic and to expand his own powers as president, but then felt compelled to resign in 1969 after an unexpected referendum defeat.

Francois Mitterrand's decision to call a referendum on the Maastricht treaty in 1992 brought the European Union to the brink of breakdown when only 51% of those voting backed the treaty. Denmark's voters rejected the same treaty, despite the fact that it was supported by four out of five members of the Danish parliament. The Danish government was able to sign the treaty only after renegotiating its terms and narrowly winning a second referendum. That same year, Canada's government was not so lucky. Canadian voters unexpectedly rejected a painstakingly negotiated constitutional accord designed to placate Quebec.

Referendums come in many different forms. **Advisory referendums** test public opinion on an important issue. Governments or legislators then translate their results into new laws or policies as they see fit. Although advisory referendums can carry great weight in the right circumstances, they are sometimes ignored by politicians. In a 1955 Swedish referendum, 85% of those voting said they wanted to continue driving on the left side of the road. Only 12 years later the government went ahead and made the switch to driving on the right without a second referendum, or much protest.

By contrast, **mandatory referendums** are part of a law-making process or, more commonly, one of the procedures for constitutional amendment.

Both advisory and mandatory referendums can usually be called only by those in office—sometimes by the president, sometimes by parliamentarians, most often by the government of the day. But in a few countries, petitions by voters themselves can put a referendum on the ballot. These are known as **initiatives**. Sometimes these can only repeal an already existing law—so-called "abrogative" initiatives such as those in Italy. Elsewhere, initiatives can also be used to propose and pass new legislation, as in Switzerland and many American states. In this form they can be powerful and unpredictable political tools.

The rules for conducting and winning referendums also vary greatly from country to country. Regulations on the drafting of ballot papers and the financing of Yes and No campaigns are different everywhere, and these exert a great influence over how referendums are used, and how often.

The hurdle required for victory can be a critical feature. A simple majority of those voting is the usual rule. But a low turnout can make such victories seem illegitimate. So a percentage of eligible voters, as well as a majority of those voting, is sometimes required to approve a proposal.

Such hurdles, of course, also make failure more likely. In 1978 Britain's government was forced to abandon plans to set up a Scottish parliament when a referendum victory in Scotland failed to clear a 40% hurdle of eligible voters. Referendums have also failed in Denmark and Italy (most recently in April) because of similar voter-turnout requirements. To ensure a wide geographic consensus, Switzerland and Australia require a "double majority", of individual voters and of cantons or states, for constitutional amendments.

The use of referendums reflects the history and traditions of individual countries. Thus generalising about them is difficult. In some countries referendums have played a central, though peripatetic, role. In others they have been marginal or even irrelevant, despite provisions for their use.

Hot potatoes

Although referendums (outside Switzerland and the United States) have been most often used to legitimise constitutional change or the redrawing of boundaries, elected politicians have also found them useful for referring to voters those issues they find too hot to handle or which cut across party lines. Often these concern moral or lifestyle choices, such as alcohol prohibition, divorce or abortion. The outcome on such emotive topics can be difficult to predict. In divorce and abortion referendums, for example, Italians have shown themselves more liberal, and the Irish more conservative, than expected.

One of the best single books on referendums—"Referendums Around the World" edited by David Butler and Austin Ranney, published by Macmillan—argues that many assumptions about them are mistaken. They are not usually habit-forming, as those opposed to them claim. Many countries have used them to settle a specific issue, or even engaged in a series of them, and then turned away from referendums for long periods. But this is mostly because politicians decide whether referendums will be held. Where groups of voters can also put initiatives on the ballot, as in Switzerland and the United States, they have become addictive and their use has grown in recent years.

Messrs Butler and Ranney also point out that referendums are not usually vehicles for radical change, as is widely believed. Although they were used in this way in Italy and New Zealand, referendums have more often been used to support the status quo or to endorse changes already agreed by political parties. Most referendums, even those initiated by voters, fail. In Australia, 34 of 42 proposals to amend the constitution have been rejected by voters. According to an analysis by David Magleby, a professor at Brigham Young University in Utah, 62% of the 1,732 initiatives which reached the ballot in American states between 1898 and 1992 were rejected.

Arguments for and against referendums go to the heart of what is meant by democracy. Proponents of referendums maintain that consulting citizens directly is the only truly democratic way to determine policy. If popular sovereignty is really to mean anything, voters must have the right to set the agenda, discuss the issues and then themselves directly make the final decisions. Delegating these tasks to elected politicians, who have interests of their own, inevitably distorts the wishes of voters.

Referendums, their advocates say, can discipline representatives, and put the stamp of legitimacy on the most important political questions of the day. They also encourage participation by citizens in the governing of their own societies, and political participation is the source of most other civic virtues.

The case against

Those sceptical of referendums agree that popular sovereignty, majority rule and consulting voters are the basic building blocks of democracy, but believe that representative democracy achieves these goals much better than referendums. Genuine direct democracy, they say, is feasible only for political groups so small that all citizens can meet face-to-face—a small town perhaps. In large, modern societies, the full participation of every citizen is impossible.

Referendum opponents maintain that representatives, as full-time decision-makers, can weigh conflicting priorities, negotiate compromises among different groups and make well-informed decisions. Citizens voting in single-issue referendums have difficulty in doing any of these things. And as the bluntest of majoritarian devices, referendums encourage voters to brush aside the concerns of minority groups. Finally, the frequent use of referendums can actually undermine democracy by encouraging elected legislators to sidestep difficult issues, thus damaging the prestige and authority of representative institutions, which must continue to perform most of the business of government even if referendums are used frequently.

Testing any of these claims or counter-claims is difficult. Most countries do not, in fact, use referendums regularly enough to bear out either the hopes of proponents or the fears of opponents. The two exceptions are Switzerland and some American states, where citizen initiatives are frequent enough to draw tentative conclusions on some of these points, although both examples fall far short of full-fledged direct democracy.

Voters in both countries seem to believe that referendums do, in fact, lend legitimacy to important decisions. The Swiss are unlikely now to make a big national decision without a referendum.

Swiss voters have rejected both UN membership and links with the EU in referendums, against the advice of their political leaders. Similarly, American polls show healthy majorities favouring referendums and believing that they are more likely to produce policies that most people want. Polls also show support for the introduction of referendums on the national level.

The claim that referendums increase citizen participation is more problematic. Some referendum campaigns ignite enormous public interest and media attention. Initiatives also give political outsiders a way to influence the public agenda. But in the United States, much of the activity involved in getting initiatives on the ballot, such as collecting signatures, has been taken over by professional firms, and many referendum campaigns have become slick, expensive affairs far removed from the grassroots (so far, this is much less true in Switzerland). Even more surprising, voter participation in American referendums is well below that of candidate elections, even when these are held at the same time. The average turnout for Swiss referendums has fallen by a third in the past 50 years to about 40%. On big issues, however, turnout can still soar.

Many of the fears of those opposed to referendums have not been realised in either country. Initiatives have not usually been used to oppress minorities. A proposal to limit the number of foreigners allowed to live in Switzerland was rejected by two-thirds of voters in 1988. In 1992 Colorado's voters did approve an initiative overturning local ordinances protecting gays from discrimination, but more extreme anti-gay initiatives in Colorado and California have been defeated

by large majorities. Since 1990 voters have consistently upheld certain abortion rights in initiative ballots. Minorities and immigrants have been the targets of initiatives in some states, but voters have generally rejected extreme measures and have often proven themselves no more illiberal than legislators. Most initiatives are, in fact, about tax and economic questions, not civil liberties or social issues, although the latter often gain more attention.

While the frequent use of initiatives has not destroyed representative government, as some feared, it has changed it. Party loyalty among Swiss voters is strong at general elections, but evaporates when it comes to referendum voting. Initiatives, and the threat of mounting one, have become an integral part of the legislative process in Switzerland, as they have in California, Oregon and the other American states where they are most used. Referendums now often set the political agenda in both countries. In the United States they are frequently seen, rightly or wrongly, as a barometer of the national mood. And they can occasionally spark a political revolution. California's Proposition 13, for example, a 1978 initiative lowering local property taxes, set off a tax revolt across America. Elected officials themselves are often active in launching initiatives, and relatively successful in getting their proposals approved, which hardly indicates that voters have lost all faith in their politicians. Initiatives have made legislating more complicated, but also more responsive to the public's concerns.

There is some evidence that American voters, at least, are sometimes overwhelmed by the volume of information coming their way, and cast their vote in

ignorance, as critics contend. Mr Magleby cites studies showing that on several ballots, 10–20% of the electorate mistakenly cast their vote the wrong way. Ballot material dropping through the letterboxes of residents in California is now often more than 200 pages long. According to one poll, only one in five Californians believes that the average voter understands most of the propositions put before him. Quite rationally, this has also bred caution. Californians approve only one-third of initiatives.

Hybrid democracy?

The Swiss and American experience suggests that in the future there is unlikely to be a headlong rush away from representative to direct democracy anywhere, but that, even so, the use of referendums is likely to grow. The Internet and other technological advances have not yet had much impact on referendums, but they should eventually make it easier to hold them, and to inform voters of the issues they are being asked to decide upon.

Representative institutions are likely to survive because of the sheer volume of legislation in modern societies, and the need for full-time officials to run the extensive machinery of government. Nevertheless in an age of mass communication and information, confining the powers of citizens to voting in elections every few years seems a crude approach, a throwback to an earlier era. In a political system based on popular sovereignty, it will become increasingly difficult to justify a failure to consult the voters directly on a wider range of issues.

Reprinted with permission from *The Economist*, August 14, 1999, pp. 45-46. © 1999 by The Economist, Ltd. Distributed by The New York Times Special Features.

The great divide

BY TIMOTHY GARTON ASH

*Robert Kagan's celebrated analysis of the widening Atlantic—in which he claims
that Europe favours peace and negotiation simply out of weakness—is half right.
But, as the split over Iraq shows, Europe is a diverse place and wields power
in other ways. Vulgar Kaganism is exacerbating division*

"ANTI-AMERICANISM HAS reached a fevered intensity," Robert Kagan reported from Europe recently in the *Washington Post.* "In London . . . one finds Britain's finest minds propounding, in sophisticated language and melodious Oxbridge accents, the conspiracy theories of Pat Buchanan concerning the 'neoconservative' (read: Jewish) hijacking of US foreign policy. Britain's most gifted scholars sift through American writings about Europe searching for signs of derogatory 'sexual imagery.'"

The last sentence must be a reference to a recent essay I wrote in the *New York Review Books.* Well, thanks for the compliment but no thanks for the implication. If I'm anti-American, then Robert Kagan is a Belgian. Since he and I have never met or conversed in accents melodious or otherwise, I take it that the earlier sentence cannot refer to me; but whoever it does refer to, its innuendo is even more disturbing. That two-word parenthesis "'neoconservative' (read: Jewish)" can only be taken to imply that this criticism of "neoconservative" views has, at the least, antisemitic overtones. That is a serious charge, which should be substantiated or withdrawn. It illustrates once again how American reports of European anti-Americanism get mixed up with claims, impossible to prove or refute, of antisemitic motivation. I am disturbed to find a writer as sophisticated and knowledgeable as Robert Kagan using such innuendo.

So far as "sexual imagery" is concerned, Kagan seems to have taken offence at a passage in which, discussing the mutual stereotypes of America vs Europe (bullying cowboys vs limp-wristed pansies) I refer to his now famous sentence "Americans are from Mars and Europeans are from Venus," as in "*men* are from Mars and *women* are from Venus." Or perhaps he was irked to find his work discussed under the headline "Anti-Europeanism in America."

So let us start with a necessary clarification: Robert Kagan is no more anti-European than I am anti-American. In his brilliant *Policy Review* article (reprinted in last Au-

gust's *Prospect*), now expanded into a small book, *Paradise and Power* (Atlantic Books), he gives one of the most penetrating and influential accounts of European-American relations in recent years. It is not yet quite in the Fukuyama *End of History* and Huntington *Clash of Civilisations* class for impact—both of them journal articles later turned into books—but it is heading that way. One reason it has had such an impact is his talent for bold generalisation and provocative overstatement.

"It is time to stop pretending," both article and book begin, "that Europeans and Americans share a common view of the world, or *even that they occupy the same world*" (my italics). He goes on to draw what he admits is a "dual caricature" of Europeans—Venusian, believing in a Kantian "self-contained world of laws and rules and transnational negotiation and cooperation"—and Americans—Martian and martial, knowing that decisive national use of military power is needed in the Hobbesian world beyond Europe's cute little US-protected postmodern paradise. "The reasons for the transatlantic divide," he writes, "are deep, long in development, and likely to endure." The current transatlantic controversy over Iraq, to which more reference is now made in the book, is seen to be representative, even archetypical.

Kagan gives three reasons for this divergence. The main one, to which he returns repeatedly, is European weakness and American power. (The original article was called "Power and Weakness.") By this he means military weakness and military power. Pointing to the growing gulf between US and European military spending and capacity, he argues that when you are weak you tend to favour law, peace, negotiation, and not to see the need for the use of force: "when you don't have a hammer, you don't want anything to look like a nail." Not even Saddam's Iraq. In a vivid simile, he writes that a man walking through a forest armed just with a knife will have a different response to a prowling bear than a man armed with a rifle.

His second reason is that history has led Europeans to a different ideology. Humbled and shocked by our bloody past, we place a higher premium on peace as a value in itself. We aspire, with Immanuel Kant, to a world of perpetual peace. We would like others to imitate our European model of integration. We would rather not hear the growls from the jungle outside. There is a certain tension between these two explanations: do Europeans dislike war because they do not have enough guns, or do they not have enough guns because they dislike war? Kagan favours the former, philosophically materialist view: being determines consciousness. But he also allows for an influence the other way round. Finally, he attributes some of these differences to the fact that, since the end of the cold war, Europeans have sought to define "Europe" as something apart from America, rather than seeking a common definition of "the west."

This is a clever, knowledgeable argument, and there is quite a lot in it. Kagan is right to pour scorn on European pretensions to be a world power, without the military clout or—he might have emphasised this more—the foreign policy unity to deliver. He quotes the Belgian foreign minister saying in December 2001 that the ED military force "should declare itself operational without such a declaration being based on any true capability." I would like to know where this quotation came from—unlike most of the direct quotations in the book version, it is not sourced—but if true, it is classic. We have not advanced very far in the ten years since the Luxembourger Jacques Poos pronounced, over disintegrating Bosnia, his equally ridiculous "the hour of Europe has come."

Kagan is also right to remind us how far the "European miracle" that began with Franco-German reconciliation actually depended on the external American pacifier. Even today, he suggests, the US is "manning the walls of Europe's postmodern order." So Europeans are, in Kipling's famous phrase, making mock of uniforms that guard us while we sleep.

His remedy, so far as he has one, is twofold. First, Europe should stop being a "military pygmy"—in the phrase of George Robertson, Nato secretary-general. This means all of us, and Germany in particular, spending more on defence and getting our militaries together. Second, we should follow Robert Cooper's advice and recognise that, beyond our postmodern world of the EU, there is a modern and a pre-modern world outside. We may be Kantian in our village, but we must be Hobbesian in the jungle around. Saddam Hussein lives by the law of the jungle, so we must threaten him with spears. The two parts of the remedy are connected. Like the man in the forest, once you have a rifle you may start hunting the bear—and if you want to hunt the bear, you will go get a rifle.

There are, however, major problems with the Kagan thesis. One is this: if Europe does not exist as a single, foreign policy actor, then how can you generalise about it? Belgium and Luxembourg are certainly not Martian or martial in Kagan's terms, but Britain and France are. As he acknowledges in two slightly embarrassed asides, it was Blair's Britain that pushed, against the resistance of Clinton's America, for ground troops in Kosovo. This at a time when the martial Americans were still bombing from 15,000 feet in case one of their warrior pilots got his little finger burnt. For three decades, from the end of the Vietnam war to 11th September, Britain and France were more ready to take military casualties abroad than the US was.

Moreover, the controversy over the Iraq war has shown that there is no simple divide between "Europe" and "America." American public opinion is torn and Europeans are divided. Kagan's commentary in the *Washington Post* was occasioned by the publication of an article by a European "gang of eight" reaffirming transatlantic solidarity against Saddam, as a rebuke to the Franco-German axis. The "gang of eight" included the prime ministers of Britain, Spain, Italy and Poland—that is, Europe's four most important countries after France and Germany—as well as Václav Havel, then still president of the Czech Republic and one of Europe's greatest moral authorities, and the leaders of Portugal, Denmark and Hungary. (Slovakia subsequently joined, to make it nine.) In his commentary, Kagan welcomed the "political and moral courage" of these leaders of what Donald Rumsfeld called "new Europe" as they paid tribute to "American bravery and farsightedness," against the fevered trend of European anti-Americanism. But he might also have written: "whoops, how does this fit my thesis? If Europe's so thoroughly Venusian, as I argue, how come so much of it is cheering for Mars?"

If I wished to be polemical, I would say: where has Kagan been living all these years? The answer, as I understand it, is Brussels—or between Brussels and Washington. And that may be part of the problem. Sitting in Brussels, listening to so much lofty Eurorhetoric matched by so few effective military or diplomatic deeds, one could easily feel as he does. But in the larger EU of 25 member states from 2004—an enlargement that scarcely features in his account the balance of attitudes will be different. Yes, there is a lot of anti-Americanism about, especially in France, Germany, Luxembourg, Belgium. There is also a lot of reasonable, measured scepticism about Bush's policy on Iraq. And then there is a large constituency of the Americanised and the Atlanticist, especially in the new democracies of central and eastern Europe.

In short, Europe's true hallmark is not weakness but *diversity*. It is the sheer diversity of states, nations and views, as much as the popular reluctance to spend on defence, and more than any programmatic Kantianism, that is the main reason for Europe's feebleness in foreign and security policy. If we could just pool and redirect what we what we already spend on defence, we'd have a formidable European expeditionary force to send to Iraq, or wherever. But we won't, because the French will be French, the British will be British and Belgians will be Belgian.

Kagan stresses military power where Europe is weak and ignores economic and cultural power where it is strong

Another problem with Kagan's book is his emphasis on military power, to the neglect of the two other main dimensions of power: economic and cultural social ("soft power"). He is right to remind Europeans that old-fashioned military power still counts—the postmodern continent is not living in a postmodern world. But he discounts Europe's other forms of power. On a recent trip to the US, I found that what most people are most worried about is not the war on Iraq—it is the state of the US economy. To be sure, there is a two-way interdependence here—Europe cannot be economically strong while America is economically weak, and vice versa—while in the military dimension there is a one-way dependence of Europe on the US. And yes, welfarist complacency, national differences, over-regulation, corporatism, ageing populations and our moral incompetence over immigration are all potential sources of European economic weakness. But the advent of the "Slavonic tigers" will give Europe a shot in the arm. The European economy is already roughly the same size as that of the US. Europe is also growing in a way that America cannot. Its "soft power" is demonstrated by the fact that not only millions of individuals but also whole states want to enter it. Turkey, for example.

Mention of Turkey raises a further difficulty with the Kagan argument: where does the Kantian world end and the Hobbesian begin? Turkey shares a border with Iraq. The frontier runs through the lands of the Kurds, the would-be Kurdistan. Turkey and Iraq have both been hammering their Kurds, on and off, for some time. But the US is urging the EU to take in Turkey, to encourage its adherence to the west by the European process of "conditionality leading finally to accession," while at the same time urging us to join in a war against Saddam. We are being asked to be Kantian-European-postmodern here, but HobbesianAmerican-pre-modern just a hundred yards across the border. In truth, we need to be both—especially if the democratic reconstruction of postwar Iraq is to succeed. In a now familiar quip: America does the cooking, Europe does the washing-up.

Kagan himself concludes in conciliatory fashion. Unlike his compatriot, Charles A Kupchan, he insists that there is no "clash of civilisations" between Europe and America. Europe should beef up its military and use it a bit more roughly in the jungle, and America, he avers on his last page, should manifest a bit more of what the founding fathers called "a decent respect for the opinion decent respect for the opinion of mankind." America needs Europe, Europe needs America, we both share common western values. I agree. His book is a challenge to make it so, to Europeans especially. But this is not what he said on his first page, which is that Europeans and Americans do not *even occupy the same world*. And that, not his conciliatory conclusion, is what he is being so much quoted for. That, in wider circulation, is "the Kagan thesis."

Of course this is what tends to happen with these "big issue" think pieces turned into books. As once upon a time we had vulgar Marxism, so we now have vulgar Fukuyamaism, vulgar Huntingtonism, and will soon have vulgar Kaganism. Francis Fukuyama can go on insisting until he is purple in the face that what he meant was History not history; people will still snort "well, the end of history, my foot!" Yet usually the author is to some degree complicit, abetted by editors and publishers, in making a bold overstatement to grab attention for his thesis—and to sell. The Hobbesian law of the intellectual jungle leads you, perhaps against your better judgement, to become one of what Jacob Burckhardt called the *terribles simplificateurs*.

The real danger now is that vulgar Kaganism will become popular on both sides of the Atlantic because people either believe Kagan's "dual caricature" or—and I think this is happening—are looking for ways to *emphasis* the gulf. In short, Kagan could have the opposite effect to the one he intends. His conclusion will only be proved right if Americans and Europeans agree that his starting point is wrong.

Timothy Garton Ash is director of the European Studies Centre at St Antony's College, Oxford and a senior fellow at the Hoover Institution, Stanford

Living With a Superpower

Some values are held in common by America and its allies. As three studies show, many others are not

"WE SHARE common values—the common values of freedom, human rights and democracy." Thus George Bush in the Czech Republic on November 21st; but it could have been him, his national security adviser or his secretary of state at almost any time.

Now consider this: "It is time to stop pretending that Europeans and Americans share a common view of the world… Americans are from Mars and Europeans are from Venus." Thus the Carnegie Endowment's Robert Kagan; but it could have been any number of transatlantic pessimists at any point in the past two years.

The question of "values" is one of the more contentious and frustrating parts of the foreign-policy debate. Obviously, values matter in themselves and in their influence on the conduct of a nation's affairs. Equally obviously, Europeans and Americans both share and dispute "basic" values. But a concept that can support flatly contradictory views of the world and transatlantic relations evidently stands in need of refinement.

Three new reports attempt to do that job. One cannot say they resolve the question of whether shared values are more important than contested ones. But at least they provide a way of thinking about and judging the so-called "values debate".

Last month, the Pew Research Centre published the broadest single opinion poll so far taken of national attitudes in 44 countries. In general, the findings bear out the president's view, rather than Mr Kagan's: more seems to unite America and its allies than divide them.

In 2002, 61% of Germans, 63% of the French and 75% of Britons said they had a favourable view of the United States. Majorities of the populations liked America in 35 of the 42 countries where this question was asked (it was banned in China).

It is true that America's image has slipped a bit. The pro-American share of the population has fallen since 2000 by between four and 17 points in every west European country bar one (France, where opinion was least favourable to begin with). All the same, the reservoir of goodwill remains fairly deep and reports of sharply rising anti-Americanism in Europe seem to be exaggerated.

This finding is at odds with the reams of editorialising about growing hostility between America and the rest of the world. But it is consistent with another recent survey by the German Marshall Fund and the Chicago Council on Foreign Relations. Asked to rate other countries on a scale of one to 100, the six European countries rated America at 64 (more than France), while Americans gave Europeans between 55 (for France) and 75 (for Britain). Feelings towards Israel diverge sharply: it is rated at only 38 in Europe, against 55 in America. But despite that divide, and whatever the elites may say, the ordinary folk on either side of the Atlantic continue to like one another.

The two sides also share a number of more specific similarities. The Pew study found that between two-thirds and three-quarters of Europeans support "the US-led war on terror". Between two-thirds and four-fifths called Iraq a serious threat. Everyone admires American science, technology and popular culture.

In both the Marshall Fund and Pew studies, there were surprisingly few significant differences in public attitudes towards the armed forces (around three-quarters think their role in their countries is positive), nor was there much difference in public readiness to use force abroad. The Marshall study found that support for multilateral institutions like the United Nations or NATO is every bit as strong in America as Europe. In the Pew study, majorities in nearly every country said the world would be less safe if there were a rival superpower. This was true even in Russia.

Strikingly, over 80% of Americans say they want strong international leadership from the European Union, while over 60% of Europeans say they want the same thing from America. And when asked whether differences between their countries and America were the result of conflicting values or conflicting policies, most respondents in west European, Latin American and Muslim countries chose policies.

Divisions of the ways

All this sounds like music to the ears of the Bush administration. It argues that the way to win hearts and minds is to emphasise universal values: explain your policies, of course, but stress that America strives for values which everyone shares. Unfortunately, there is also much in the Pew study which casts doubt on that idea.

For one thing, the reservoir of goodwill seems to run dry in the Muslim world. The Pew study found that large majorities in four of America's main Muslim allies—Egypt, Pakistan, Jordan and Turkey—dislike America. There are obviously difficulties in measuring opinion in some of these places, but the results are still striking: in Egypt, 6% were favourable, 69% unfavourable; in Jordan, 25% and 75%.

Even where opinion overall is more flattering, as in Europe, there are signs of cultural clashes. If policies were the main problem, rather than values, you would expect people to have a higher opinion of Americans than of America. But the distinction is fading. West Europeans have a slightly more positive view of the people than the country, but they are exceptions: only 14 of 43 countries expressed more positive views about Americans than of America. And even though most Europeans say they like America, between half (in Britain) and three-quarters (in France) also say the spread of American ideas and customs is bad. As many Europeans say they dislike American ideas about democracy as like them. And this is from the part of the world that knows and claims to like America best.

In other words, people outside Muslim countries like America but not some of the most important things it stands for. What is one to make of that conflicting evidence? The short answer is that Europeans and Americans dispute some values and share others. But one can do better than that. Consider the third recent report, the world values survey run by the University of Michigan.

Unlike the other two polls, this survey goes back a long way. The university has been sending out hundreds of questions for the past 25 years (it now covers 78 countries with 85% of the world's population). Its distinctive feature is the way it organises the replies. It arranges them in two broad categories. The first it calls traditional values; the second, values of self-expression.

The survey defines "traditional values" as those of religion, family and country. Traditionalists say religion is important in their lives. They have a strong sense of national pride, think children should be taught to obey and that the first duty of a child is to make his or her parents proud. They say abortion, euthanasia, divorce and suicide are never justifiable. At the other end of this spectrum are "secular-rational" values: they emphasise the opposite qualities.

The other category looks at "quality of life" attributes. At one end of this spectrum are the values people hold when the struggle for survival is uppermost: they say that economic and physical security are more important than self-expression. People who cannot take food or safety for granted tend to dislike foreigners, homosexuals and people

with AIDS. They are wary of any form of political activity, even signing a petition. And they think men make better political leaders than women. "Self-expression" values are the opposite.

Obviously, these ideas overlap. The difference between the two is actually rooted in an academic theory of development (not that it matters). The notion is that industrialisation turns traditional societies into secular-rational ones, while post-industrial development brings about a shift towards values of self-expression.

The usefulness of dividing the broad subject of "values" in this way can be seen by plotting countries on a chart whose axes are the two spectrums. The chart alongside (click to enlarge it) shows how the countries group: as you would expect, poor countries, with low self-expression and high levels of traditionalism, are at the bottom left, richer Europeans to the top right.

But America's position is odd. On the quality-of-life axis, it is like Europe: a little more "self-expressive" than Catholic countries, such as France and Italy, a little less so than Protestant ones such as Holland or Sweden. This is more than a matter of individual preference. The "quality of life" axis is the one most closely associated with political and economic freedoms. So Mr Bush is right when he claims that Americans and European share common values of democracy and freedom and that these have broad implications because, at root, alliances are built on such common interests.

But now look at America's position on the traditional-secular axis. It is far more traditional than any west European country except Ireland. It is more traditional than any place at all in central or Eastern Europe. America is near the bottom-right corner of the chart, a strange mix of tradition and self-expression.

Americans are the most patriotic people in the survey: 72% say they are very proud of their country (and this bit of the poll was taken before September 2001). That puts America in the same category as India and Turkey. The survey reckons religious attitudes are the single most important component of traditionalism. On that score, Americans are closer to Nigerians and Turks than Germans or Swedes.

Of course, America is hardly monolithic. It is strikingly traditional on average. But, to generalise wildly, that average is made up of two Americas: one that is almost as secular as Europe (and tends to vote Democratic), and one that is more traditionalist than the average (and tends to vote Republican).

But even this makes America more distinctive. Partly because America is divided in this way, its domestic political debate revolves around values to a much greater extent than in Europe. Political affiliation there is based less on income than on church-going, attitudes to abortion and attitudes to race. In America, even technical matters become moral questions. It is almost impossible to have a debate about gun registration without it becoming an argument about the right to self-defence. In Europe, even moral questions are sometimes treated as technical ones, as happened with stem-cell research.

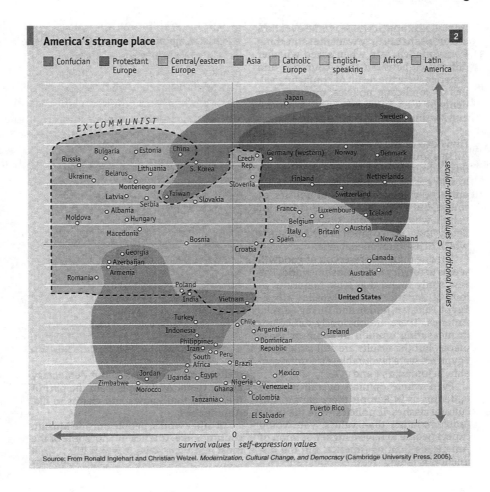

America's strange place

☐ Confucian ☐ Protestant Europe ☐ Central/eastern Europe ☐ Asia ☐ Catholic Europe ☐ English-speaking ☐ Africa ☐ Latin America

Source: From Ronald Inglehart and Christian Welzel. *Modernization, Cultural Change, and Democracy* (Cambridge University Press, 2005).

The difference between the two appears to be widening. Since the first world values survey in 1981, every western country has shifted markedly along the spectrum towards greater self-expression. America is no exception. But on the other spectrum America seems to have become more traditional, rather than less. The change is only a half-step. And Italy, Spain and France have taken the same half-step. But if you look at Europe as a whole, the small movement back towards old-fashioned virtues in big Catholic countries is far outweighed by the stride the other way in post-Protestant countries such as Germany and Sweden. On average, then, the values gap between America and European countries seems to be widening.

Where evil is real

What is the significance of this? If "quality-of-life" values have political implications, helping to underpin democracy, might traditional values help explain differing attitudes to, say, the projection of power?

In principle, two things suggest they might. Patriotism is one of the core traditional values and there is an obvious link between it, military might and popular willingness to sustain large defence budgets. There may also be a link be-

tween America's religiosity and its tendency to see foreign policy in moral terms. To Americans, evil exists and can be fought in their lives and in the world. Compared with Europe, this is a different world-view in both senses: different prevailing attitudes, different ways of looking at the world.

If you go back to the Pew and Marshall Fund studies, you can see hard evidence for this difference—and it goes beyond immediate policy concerns. In the Pew study, three-quarters of west Europeans and an even higher share of east Europeans support the American-led war on terrorism—but more than half in both places say America does not take other countries into account (whereas three-quarters of Americans think their government does).

In both studies, Americans and Europeans put the same issues at the top of their concerns—religious and ethnic hatred, international terrorism and the spread of nuclear weapons. In that respect, America and Europe have more in common with each other than with African, Asian and Latin American countries, for whom the spread of AIDS and the gap between rich and poor are at least as important.

But both studies show differences in the balance of European and American anxieties. In the Pew poll, 59% of Americans think the spread of nuclear weapons is the greatest danger to the world. Between 60% and 70% of Europeans put religious and ethnic hatred first. In the Marshall

Fund study, around 90% of Americans say international terrorism and Iraq's development of weapons of mass destruction are "critical". The comparable figures for Europe are around 60%. In short, even if Americans and Europeans see one another in similar terms, they see the world differently.

One might object that such values-based judgments are still not everything. The two sides of the Atlantic have long lived with a related problem: the cultural split between "vigorous, naive" America and "refined, unprincipled" Europe. They have successfully managed that, just as they have coped with the political awkwardness that America's centre of gravity is further to the right than Europe's.

What is different now? Two things. The first is that the values gap may be widening a little, and starting to affect perceptions of foreign-policy interest on which the transatlantic alliance is based. The second is that, in the past, cultural differences have been suppressed by the shared values of American and European elites—and elite opinion is now even more sharply divided than popular opinion. It is the combination of factors that makes the current transatlantic divisions disturbing. And it is little consolation that, in the face of some mutual hostility, the Bush administration is insisting it is all just a matter of politics, and not of something deeper.

The Case for a Multi-Party U.S. Parliament? American Politics in Comparative Perspective

Abstract

This is a "mental experiment" that illuminates the role of institutions in shaping the political process. It is best viewed as part of the long history of American fascination with the parliamentary system and even multiparty politics. The larger hope is to initiate serious dialogue on the respective strengths and weaknesses of majoritarian and consensus systems with scholars of American politics and include American politics in an explicitly comparative perspective.

CHRISTOPHER S. ALLEN

Introduction

Americans revere the constitution but at the same time also sharply and frequently criticize the government. (Dionne, 1991) Yet since the constitution is responsible for the current form of the American government, why not change the constitution to produce better government? After all, the founders of the United States did create the amendment process and we have seen 27 of them in over 200 years.

Several recent events prompt a critical look at this reverence for the constitution: unusual presidential developments, including the Clinton impeachment spectacle of 1998–1999; the historic and bizarre 2000 Presidential election; and the apparent mandate for fundamental change that President Bush inferred from this exceedingly narrow election. In the early 21st century, American politics confronted at least three other seemingly intractable problems: a significant erosion in political accountability; out of control costs of running for public office; and shamefully low voter turnout. More seriously, none of these four problems is of recent origin, as all four have eroded the functioning of the American government for a period of between 25 and 50 years! The core features of these four problems are:

- Confusion of the roles of head of state and head of government, of which the impeachment issue—from Watergate through Clinton's impeachment—is merely symptomatic of a much larger problem.
- Eroding political accountabilty, taking the form of either long periods of divided government, dating back to the "do nothing" 80th congress elected in 1946, to the recent "gerrymandering industry" producing a dearth of competitive elections. The result is millions

of "wasted votes" and an inability for voters to assign credit or blame for legislative action.
- Costly and perennial campaigns for all offices producing "the best politicians that money can buy." This problem that had its origins with the breakdown of the party caucus system and the growth of primary elections in the 1960s; and
- The world's lowest voter turnout among all of the leading OECD countries, a phenomenon that began in the 1960s and has steadily intensified.

When various American scholars acknowledge these shortcomings, however, there is the occasional, offhand comparison to parliamentary systems which have avoided some of these pathologies. The unstated message is that we don't—or perhaps should never, ever want to—have that here.

Why not? What exactly is the problem with a parliamentary system? Durable trust in government, sense of efficacy, and approval ratings for branches in government have all declined in recent decades. Such phenomena contribute to declining voter turnout and highlight what is arguably a more significant trend toward a crisis in confidence among Americans concerning their governing institutions. So why is institutional redesign off the table?

This article examines these 4 institutional blockages of the American majoritarian/Presidential system and suggests certain features of parliamentary or consensus systems might overcome these persistent shortcomings of American politics.

Less normatively, the article is framed by three concepts central to understanding and shaping public policy in advanced industrialized states with democratic constitutional structures.

First, is the issue of comparability and 'American Exceptionalism'. (Lipset, 1996). The article's goal is to initiate a long-delayed dialogue on comparative constitutional structures with scholars of American politics. Second, the article hopes to participate in the active discussion among comparativists on the respective strengths and weaknesses of majoritarian and consensus systems. (Birchfield and Crepaz, 1998) Third, scandals surrounding money and politics in a number of democratic states (Barker, 1994) should prompt a comparison of parties and party systems and the context within which they function.

This article does not underestimate the quite significant problems associated with "institutional transplantation" (Jacoby, 2000) from one country to another. The more modest and realistic goal is to engage American and Comparative scholars in a fruitful debate about political institutions and constitutional design that (finally) includes American politics in a Comparative orbit.

This article is organized in 5 sections that address: 1) the cumbersome tool of impeachment; 2) eroding political accountability due to divided government and safe seats; 3) the costly, never-ending campaign process; 4) the continued deterioration of voter turnout, and finally, pragmatically; 5) offers a critical analysis of the quite formidable obstacles that initiating a parliamentary remedy to these problems would clearly face.

1. Impeachment: Head of State vs Head of Government

The tool of impeachment is merely a symptom of a larger problem. Its more fundamental flaw is that it highlights the constitutional confusion between the two functions of the US presidency: head of state and head of government.

Americanists have delved deeply into the minutiae of the impeachment process during the past thirty years but comparativists would ask a different question. How would other democracies handle similar crises affecting their political leaders? More than two years transpired from the Watergate break-in to Nixon's resignation (1972–74), the Iran-Contra scandal (1986–87) produced no impeachment hearings; and an entire year (1998–99) transpired from the onset of the Clinton-Lewinsky saga to the completion of the impeachment process. Comparativists and citizens of other democratic polities find this astounding, since in a parliamentary system a fundamental challenge to the executive would take the form of a vote of no confidence, (Lijphart, 1994) and the issue would be politically resolved within weeks. The executive would either survive and continue or resign.

The portrayal of the Clinton impeachment and trial is characterized as historic. For only the second time in American politics, an American president has been impeached in the House and put on trial in the Senate. Yet, the idea of using impeachment has been much less rare, having been raised three times in the past thirty years. Yet impeachment hasn't "worked" at all. It is either not brought to fruition (Watergate), not used when it should have been (Iran-Con-

tra), or completely trivialized (Clinton-Lewinsky) when another path was clearly needed. But impeachment itself isn't the real problem; a larger constitutional design flaw is.

The United States has a constitutional structure based on a separation of powers, while most parliamentary systems have a "fusion" of powers in that the Prime Minister is also the leader of the major party in parliament. However, within the American executive itself, there is a "fusion" of functions, which is the exact opposite of Parliamentary regimes.

The US is the only developed democracy where head of state and head of government are fused in one person. The President is the Head of State and, effectively, the Head of Government. In Parliamentary systems these two functions are performed by two different people. (Linz, 1993) Thus impeachment of one person removes two functions in one and likely explained the dichotomy of popular desire for Clinton's retention on the one hand, but also for some form of political censure on the other.

Beyond the impeachment issue, when American presidents undertake some action as head of government for which they are criticized, they then become invariably more remote and inaccessible. For example, Presidents Johnson (Vietnam), Nixon (Watergate), Reagan(Iran/Contra), Clinton (the Lewinsky Affair) and G.W. Bush (Iraq) all reduced their appearances at press conferences as criticism of their policies mounted. In short, when criticized for actions taken in their head of government capacity, they all retreated to the Rose Garden and sometimes created the impression that criticizing the President—now wearing the head of state hat (or perhaps, crown)—was somehow unpatriotic. This was especially the case with George .W. Bush, who in the post 9/11 and Iraq war periods, has tried to emphasize the commander in chief aspect of the presidency rather than his role as steward of the economy and domestic politics.

Toward a Politically Accountable Prime Minister and a Ceremonial President

A parliamentary system with a separate head of state and head of government would produce two "executive" offices instead of just one. It's odd that the US is so fearful of centralized power yet allows the executive to perform functions that no other leader of an OECD country (France excepted) performs alone. The US Vice President serves many of the functions of heads of state in other countries. But the United States has a comparatively odd way of dividing executive constitutional functions. One office, the Presidency, does everything while the other, the Vice Presidency, does virtually nothing and simply waits until the president can no longer serve. An American parliamentary system would redefine these 2 offices so that one person (the head of state) would serve as a national symbol and preside over ceremonial functions. The second person (the head of government) would function much like a prime minister does in a parliamentary system, namely as the head of government who could be criticized, censured and

124

held accountable for specific political actions without creating a constitutional crisis.

Thus were it necessary to censure or otherwise take action against the head of government (i.e. prime minister), the solution would be a relatively quick vote of no confidence that would solve the problem and move on and let the country address its political business. (Huber, 1996) And unlike impeachment which is the political equivalent of the death penalty, a vote of no confidence does not preclude a politician's making a comeback and returning to lead a party or coalition. Impeachment and removal from office, on the other hand, is much more final.

Prime Ministers, unlike US presidents, are seen much more as active politicians not remote inaccessible figures. In a parliament, the prime minister as the head of government is required to engage—and be criticized—in the rough-and-tumble world of daily politics. In short, the head of government must be accountable. The British prime minister, for example, is required to participate in a weekly "question time" in which often blunt and direct interrogatories are pressed by the opposition. (Rundquist, 1991) There is no equivalent forum for the American president to be formally questioned as a normal part of the political process.

But could such a power might be used in a cavalier fashion, perhaps removing the head of government easily after a debilitating scandal? This is unlikely in a well-designed parliamentary system because such cynicism would likely produce a backlash that would constrain partisanship. In fact, the Germans have institutionalized such constraints in the "constructive vote of no confidence" requiring any removal of the head of government to be a simultaneous election of a new one. The context of such a parliamentary system lowers the incentives to engage in the politics of destruction. The political impact of destroying any particular individual in a collective body such as a cabinet or governing party or coalition is much less significant than removing a directly elected president.

A parliamentary head of state is above the kind of criticism generated in no confidence votes and simply serves as an apolitical symbol of national pride. In nation states that have disposed of their monarchies, ceremonial presidents perform many of the same roles as constitutional monarchs such as Queen Elizabeth do, but much more inexpensively. In fact, many of these ceremonial roles are performed by the American vice president (attending state dinners/funerals, cutting ribbons, presiding over the Senate, etc.) The problem is that the Vice President is often a political afterthought, chosen more for ticket-balancing functions and/or for inoffensive characteristics than for any expected major political contributions. On the other hand, the type of individual usually chosen as a ceremonial president in a parliamentary system is a retired politician from the moderate wing of one of the major parties who has a high degree of stature and can serve as a figure of national unity. In effect, the office of ceremonial president is often a reward or honor for decades of distinguished national service, hardly the characteristics of an American vice president.

In retrospect, one might say that President Clinton was impeached not for abusing head of government functions, but for undermining the decorum and respect associated with heads of state. The separation of head of state and head of government would have a salutary effect on this specific point. Scandals destroying heads of state would have little real political significance since the head of state would not wield real political power. Similarly, scandals destroying heads of government would have significantly less impact than the current American system. The head of government role, once separated from the head of state role, would no longer attract monolithic press and public attention or be subject to extraordinarily unrealistic behavioral expectations.

2. Political Accountabilty: Divided Government & "Safe Seats"

From the "do nothing" 80th Congress elected in 1946 to the 108th elected in 2004, a total of thirty congresses, the United States has experienced divided government for more than two-thirds of this period. In only ten of those thirty Congresses has the president's party enjoyed majorities in both houses of Congress. (Fiorina, 1992) Some might observe this divided government phenomenon and praise the bipartisan nature of the American system. (Mayhew, 1991) But to justify such a conclusion, defenders of bipartisanship would have to demonstrate high public approval of governmental performance, particularly when government was divided. Based on over four decades of declining trust in government, such an argument is increasingly hard to justify.

One explanation for the American preference for divided government is the fear of concentrated political power. (Jacobson, 1990) Yet in a search for passivity, the result often turns out to be simply inefficiency.

While the fear of concentrated government power is understandable for historical and ideological reasons, many of the same people who praise divided government also express concern regarding government efficiency. (Thurber, 1991) Yet divided government quite likely contributes to the very inefficiencies that voters rightfully lament. Under divided government, when all is well, each of the two parties claims responsibility for the outcome; when economic or political policies turn sour, however, each party blames the other. This condition leads to a fundamental lack of political accountability and the self-fulfilling prophesy that government is inherently inefficient.

Rather than being an accidental occurrence, divided government is much more likely to result due to the American constitutional design. For it is constitutional provisions that are at the heart of divided government; 2 year terms for Congress, 4 year terms for the Presidency, and 6 year terms for the Senate invariably produce divided government.

Were it only for these "accidental" outcomes of divided government, political accountability might be less deleterious. Exacerbating the problem, however, is the decline of parties as institutions. This has caused individuals to have

Table 1
Trust in the Federal Government 1964-2002

	None of the Time	Some of the Time	Most of the Time	Just about Always	Don't Know
1964	0	22	62	14	1
1966	2	28	48	17	4
1968	0	36	54	7	2
1970	0	44	47	6	2
1972	1	44	48	5	2
1974	1	61	34	2	2
1976	1	62	30	13	3
1978	4	64	27	2	3
1980	4	69	23	2	2
1982	3	62	31	2	3
1984	1	53	40	4	2
1986	2	57	35	3	2
1988	2	56	36	4	1
1990	2	69	25	3	1
1992	2	68	26	3	1
1994	1	74	19	2	1
1996	1	66	30	3	0
1998	1	58	36	4	1
2000	1	55	40	4	1
2002	0	44	51	5	0

PERCENTAGE WITHIN STUDY YEAR
Source: The National Election Studies

QUESTION TEXT:
"How much of the time do you think you can trust the government in Washington to do what is right—just about always, most of the time or only some of the time?"
Source: The National Election Studies, University of Michigan, 2003

Table 2
The Persistence of Divided Government

Year	President	House	Senate	Divided/Unified Government
1946	D Truman	Rep	Rep	D
1948	D Truman	Dem	Rep	D
1950	D Truman	Rep	Rep	D
1952	R Eisenhower	Rep	Rep	U
1954	R Eisenhower	Dem	Dem	D
1956	R Eisenhower	Dem	Dem	D
1958	R Eisenhower	Dem	Dem	D
1960	D Kennedy	Dem	Dem	U
1962	D Kennedy	Dem	Dem	U
1964	D Johnson	Dem	Dem	U
1966	D Johnson	Dem	Dem	U
1968	R Nixon	Dem	Dem	D
1970	R Nixon	Dem	Dem	D
1972	R Nixon	Dem	Dem	D
1974	R Ford	Dem	Dem	D
1976	D Carter	Dem	Dem	U
1978	D Carter	Dem	Dem	U
1980	R Reagan	Dem	Rep	D
1982	R Reagan	Dem	Rep	D
1984	R Reagan	Dem	Rep	D
1986	R Reagan	Dem	Dem	D
1988	R Bush	Dem	Dem	D
1990	R Bush	Dem	Dem	D
1992	D Clinton	Dem	Dem	U
1994	D Clinton	Rep	Rep	D
1996	D Clinton	Rep	Rep	D
1998	D Clinton	Rep	Rep	D
2000	R Bush	Rep	Dem*	D
2002	R Bush	Rep	Rep	U
2004	R Bush	Rep	Rep	U

* After a 50-50 split (with Vice President Cheney as the tiebreaker), Senator Jeffords (I-VT) switched from the Republican party shortly after the 2000 election, thereby swinging the Senate to the Democrats.

weaker partisan attachments—despite the increased partisan rhetoric of many elected officials since the the 1980s—and has thereby intensified the fragmentation of government. (Franklin and Hirczy de Mino, 1998) Clearly, divided government is more problematic when partisan conflict between the two parties is greater as the sharper ideological conflict and the increased party line congressional voting since the 1990s would suggest. Under these circumstances, divided government seems to be more problematic, since two highly partisan parties within the American political system seems potentially dangerous. Persistent divided government over time will likely produce a fundamental change in the relationship between Presidents and the Congress. Presidents are unable to bargain effectively with a hostile congress—witness the 1995 government shutdown—leading the former to make appeals over the heads of Congress directly and, hence undermine the legitimacy of the legislative branch. (Kernell, 1997) This argument parallels the one made in recent comparative scholarship (Linz, 1993) regarding the serious problem of dual legitimacy in presidential systems.

A second component of the political accountability problem is the increasing uncompetiveness of American elections. Accounts of the 2000 Presidential election stressed its historic closeness, settled by only 540,000 popular votes (notwithstanding the electoral college anomaly). And the narrow Republican majorities in the House and Senate apparently indicated that every congressional or senate seat could be up for grabs each election. The reality is something different. (Center for Voting, 2003) Out of 435 House seats, only 10% or fewer are competitive, the outcome of most Senate races is known well in advance, and the Presidential race was only competitive in 15 of 50 states. In the remaining 35, the state winners (Gore or Bush) were confident enough of the outcome to forgo television advertising in many of them. In essence, voters for candidates who did not win these hundreds of "safe seats" were effectively disenfranchised and unable to hold their representatives politically accountable. Similar uncompetitiveness plagued the 2004 Presidential and Congressional elections.

For those who lament the irresponsibility—or perhaps irrelevance—of the two major parties, an institutional design that would force responsibility should be praised. Quite simply, those who praise divided government because it "limits the damage" or see nothing amiss when there are hundreds of safe seats are faced with a dilemma. They can not simultaneously complain about the resulting governmental inefficiency and political cynicism that ultimately follows when accountability is regularly clouded.

Political Accountability and the Fusion of Government
A number of scholars have addressed the deficiencies of divided government, but they suggest that the problem is that the electoral cycle, with its "off year" elections, intensifies the likelihood of divided government in non-presidential election years. Such advocates propose as a solution the alteration of the electoral cycle so that all congressional elections are on four year terms, concurrent with presidential terms, likely producing a clear majority. (Cutler, 1989) Yet this contains a fatal flaw. Because there is no guarantee that this proposal would alleviate the residual tension between competing branches of government, it merely sidesteps the accountability factor strongly discouraging party unity across the executive and legislative branches of government.

This suggestion could also produce the opposite effect from divided government, namely exaggerated majorities common to parliamentary regimes with majoritarian electoral systems such as the UK. The "safe seats" phenomenon would be the culprit just as in the UK. The most familiar examples of this phenomenon were the "stop-go" policies of post-World War II British governments, as each succeeding government tried to overturn the previous election. While creating governing majorities is important for political accountability, the absence of proportional representation creates a different set of problems.

Under a fusion of power system, in which the current presidency would be redefined, the resulting parliamentary system would make the head of the legislative branch the executive, thus eliminating the current separation of powers. Yet if a government should lose its majority between scheduled elections due to defection of its party members or coalition partners, the head of state then would ask the opposition to form a new government and, failing that, call for new elections. This avoids the constitutional crises that the clamor for impeachment seem to engender in the American system.

But what if coalition members try to spread the blame for poor performance to their partners? In theory, the greater the flexibility available to in shifting from one governing coalition to another (with a different composition), the greater potential for this kind of musical cabinet chairs. The potential for such an outcome is far less than in the American system, however. A century of experience in other parliamentary regimes (Laver and Shepsle, 1995) shows that members of such a party capriciously playing games with governing are usually brought to heel at the subsequent election.

In other words, the major advantage to such a parliamentary system is that it heightens the capacity for voters and citizens to evaluate government performance. Of course, many individuals might object to the resulting concentration of power. However, if voters are to judge the accomplishments of elected officials, the latter need time to succeed or fail, and then the voters can make a judgment on their tenure. The most likely outcome would be a governing party or coalition of parties that would have to stay together

Table 3
Comparative Coalitions

American	Parliamentary
Opaque	Transparent
Issue-by-Issue	Programmatic
Back Room	Open Discussion
Unaccountable	Election Ratifies
Unstable	Generally Stable

to accomplish anything, thereby increasing party salience. (Richter, 2002) Phrased differently, such an arrangement would likely lead to an increase in responsible government.

Many Americans might react unfavorably at the mention of the word coalition due to its supposed instability. Here we need to make the distinction between transparent and opaque coalitions. Some argue that coalition government in parliamentary systems have the reputation of increased instability. That, or course, depends on the substance of the coalition agreement and the willingness of parties to produce a stable majority. (Strom, Budge, and Laver 1994) But in most parliamentary systems, these party coalitions are formed transparently before an election so the voters can evaluate and then pass judgment on the possible coalition prior to election day. It's not as if there are no coalitions in the US Congress. There they take the opaque form of ad-hoc groups of individual members of Congress on an issue-by-issue basis. The high information costs to American voters in understanding the substance of such layered bargains hardly is an example of political transparency.

Finally, for those concerned that the "fusion" of the executive and legislative branches—on the British majoritarian model—would upset the concept of checks and balances, a multiparty consensus parliamentary system produces them slightly differently. (Lijphart, 1984) Majoritarianism concentrates power and makes "checking" difficult, while consensus democracies institutionalize the process in a different, and more accountable form. A multiparty parliamentary system would also provide greater minority representation and protection by reducing majoritarianism's excessive concentration of power. A consensus parliamentary system would also address the "tyranny of the majority" problem and allow checking and balancing by the voters in the ballot box since the multiple parties would not likely allow a single party to dominate. Consensus systems thus represent a compromise between the current U.S. system and the sharp concentration of British Westminster systems. Americans who simultaneously favor checks and balances but decry inefficient government need to clarify what they actually want their government to do.

3. Permanent and Expensive Campaigns

The cost to run for political office in the United States dwarfs that spent in any other advanced industrialized democracy. The twin problems are time and money; more specifically a never-ending campaign "season" and the structure of political advertising that depends so heavily on TV money. (Gans, 1993) In listening to the debates about "reforming" the American campaign finance system, students of other democratic electoral systems find these discussions bizarre. More than $2 billion was raised and spent (Corrado 1997) by parties, candidates and interest groups in the 1996 campaign, and for 2000 it went up to $3 billion. And the Center for Responsive Politics estimated the total cost for 2004 Presidential and congressional elections was $3.9 billion. (Weiss 2004)

The two year congressional cycle forces members of the House of Representatives to literally campaign permanently. The amount of money required to run for a Congressional seat has quadrupled since 1990. Presidential campaigns are several orders of magnitude beyond the House of Representatives or the Senate. By themselves they are more than two years long, frequently longer. Unless a presidential candidate is independently wealthy or willing and able to raise upfront $30–$50 million it is simply impossible to run seriously for this office.

Many of the problems stem from the post-Watergate "reforms" that tried to limit the amount of spending on campaigns which then produced a backlash in the form of a 1976 Supreme Court decision (Buckley vs Valeo) that undermined this reform attempt. In essence, Buckley vs Valeo held that "paid speech" (i.e. campaign spending) has an equivalent legal status as "free speech". (Grant, 1998) Consequently, since then all "reform" efforts have been tepid measures that have not been able to get at the root of the problem. As long as "paid speech" retains its protected status, any changes are dead in the water.

At its essence this issue is a fissure between "citizens" and "consumers". What Buckley vs Valeo has done is to equate the citizenship function (campaigning, voting, civic education) with a market-based consumer function (buying and selling consumer goods as commodities). (Brubaker, 1998) Unlike the United States, most other OECD democracies consider citizenship a public good and provide funding for parties, candidates and the electoral process as a matter of course. The Buckley vs Valeo decision conflates the concepts of citizen and consumer, the logical extension of which is there are weak limits on campaign funding and no limits on the use of a candidate's own money. We are all equal citizens, yet we are not all equal consumers. Bringing consumer metaphors into the electoral process debases the very concept of citizenship and guarantees that the American political system produces the best politicians money can buy.

Free Television Time and the Return of Political Party Dues

Any broadcaster wishing to transmit to the public is required to obtain a broadcast license because the airways have the legal status of public property. To have access to such property, the government licenses these networks, cable channels, and stations to serve the public interest. In return, broadcasters are able to sell airtime to sponsors of

Table 4
Voter Turnout and Type of Electoral System
Major Developed Democracies—1945–2000

Country	% Voter Turnout	Type of Electoral System
Italy	91.9	PR
Belgium	84.9	PR
Netherlands	84.8	PR
Australia	84.4	Mixed Member
Denmark	83.6	PR
Sweden	83.3	PR
Germany	80.0	Mixed-PR
Israel	80.0	PR
Norway	79.2	PR
Finland	79.0	PR
Spain	76.4	PR
Ireland	74.9	SMD
UK	73.0	SMD
Japan	68.3	SMD/Mixed
France	67.3	SMD + runoff
Canada	66.9	SMD
USA – Presidential	55.1	SMD
USA – Congress (Midterm)	40.7	SMD

Source: Voter Turnout: A Global Survey (Stockholm: International IDEA, 2005)

various programs. Unfortunately for campaign costs, candidates for public office fall into the same category as consumer goods in the eyes of the broadcasters. (Weinberg, 1993) What has always seemed odd to observers of other democratic states is that there is no Quid Pro Quo requiring the provision of free public airtime for candidates when running for election.

Any serious reform of campaign finance would require a concession from all broadcasters to provide free time for all representative candidates and parties as a cost of using the public airways. Since the largest share of campaign money is TV money, this reform would solve the problem at its source. Restricting the "window" when these free debates would take place to the last two months before a general election would thus address the time dimension as well. Such practices are standard procedure in all developed parliamentary systems. Very simply, as long as "reform" efforts try to regulate the supply of campaign finance, it will fail. A much more achievable target would be the regulation of demand.

The United States could solve another money problem by borrowing a page from parliamentary systems: changing the political party contribution structure from individual voluntary contributions (almost always from the upper middle class and the wealthy) to a more broad-based dues structure common to parties other developed democracies. This more egalitarian party dues structure would perform the additional salutary task of rebuilding parties as functioning institutions. (Allen, 1999) Rather than continuing in their current status as empty shells for independently wealthy candidates, American political parties could become the kind of dynamic membership organizations they were at the turn of the 20th century when they did have a dues structure.

4. Low Voter Turnout?

The leading OECD countries have voter turnout ranging from 70% to 90% of their adult population while the US lags woefully behind. Among the most commonly raised explanations for the US deficiency are: registration requirements, the role of television, voter discouragement, and voter contentment (although the latter two are clearly mutually exclusive). None are particularly convincing nor do they offer concrete suggestions as to how it might be overcome.

The two party system and the electoral method that produces it: the single member district, first past the post, or winner take all system with its attendant "safe seats" often escapes criticism. The rise of such new organizations as the Reform, Libertarian, and Green parties potentially could threaten the hegemony of the Democrats and Republicans. Yet the problem of a third (or fourth) party gaining a sufficient number of votes to actually win seats and challenge the two party system is formidable. The electoral arithmetic would require any third party to win some 25% of the vote on a nationwide basis—or develop a highly-concentrated regional presence—before it would actually gain more than a token number of seats. And failing to actually win seats produces a "wasted vote" syndrome among party supporters which is devastating for such a party. (Rosenstone, Behr, and Lazarus 1996) Most voters who become disillusioned with the electoral process refer to the "lesser of two evils" choices they face. In such a circumstance, declining voter turnout is not surprising.

The US is a diverse country with many regional, religious, racial, and class divisions. So why should we expect that two "catch all" parties will do a particularly good job in appealing to the interests of diverse constituencies? The solution to lower voter turnout is a greater number of choices for voters and a different electoral system.

Proportional Representation

Under electoral systems using proportional representation, The percentage of a party's vote is equivalent to the percentage of seats allocated to the party in parliament. Comparative analysis shows that those countries with proportional representation—and the multiple parties that PR systems produce—invariably have higher voter turnout. (Grofman and Lijphart, 1986) In other words, PR voting systems provide a wider variety of political choices and a wider variety of political representation.

Eliminating majoritarian single member districts (SMDs) in favor of PR voting would have several immediate effects. First, it would increase the range of choices for voters, since parties would have to develop ideological and programmatic distinctions to make themselves attractive to voters. As examples in other countries have shown, it would lead to formation of several new parties representing long underserved interests.

Such a change would force rebuilding of parties as institutions, since candidates would have to run as members of parties and not as independent entrepreneurs. The so-called

Table 5
The Advantages of Proportional Representation

Higher Voter Turnout
No "Wasted" Votes
Few Safe, Uncontested Seats
More Parties
Greater Minority Representation
Greater Gender Diversity in Congress
Greater Ideological Clarity
Parties Rebuilt as Institutions
6% Threshold Assumed
No More Gerrymandered Redistricting

Progressive "reforms" at the turn of the 20th century and the 1960s introduction of primaries—plus TV advertising—plus the widespread use of referenda have all had powerful effects in undermining parties as coherent political organizations. (Dwyre, 1994) In trying to force market-based individual "consumer choice" in the form of high-priced candidates, the collective institutions that are political parties have been hollowed out and undermined.

There are, of course, a wide range of standard objections to PR voting systems by those favoring retention of majoritarian SMD systems.

The first of these, coalitional instability, was addressed briefly above, but it needs to be restated here. The US has unstable coalitions in the Congress right now, namely issue-by-issue ones, usually formed in the House cloakroom with the "assistance" of lobbyists. Few average voters know with certainty how "their" member of Congress will vote on a given issue. (Gibson, 1995) With ideologically coherent parties, they would.

An American parliament with several parties could produce self-discipline very effectively. Clearly there would have to be a coalition government since it is unlikely that any one party would capture 50% of the seats. The practice in almost all other coalition governments in parliamentary systems is that voters prefer a predictable set of political outcomes. Such an arrangement forces parties to both define their programs clearly and transparently, once entering into a coalition, and to do everything possible to keep the coalition together during the course of the legislative term.

The second standard objection to PR is the "too many parties"issue. PR voting has been practiced in parliaments for almost 100 years in many different democratic regimes. There is a long history of practices that work well and practices that don't. (Norris, 1997) Two countries are invariably chosen as bad examples of PR, namely Israel and Italy. There is an easy solution to this problem of an unwieldy number of parties, namely an electoral threshold requiring any party to receive a certain minimal percentage to gain seats in the parliament. The significant question is what should this minimal threshold be? The Swedes have a 4% threshold and have 6 parties in their parliament, the Germans have a 5% threshold and have 5 parties represented in the Bundestag.

The third standard objection to PR voting is "who's my representative?"In a society so attuned to individualism, most Americans want a representative from their district. This argument presumes that all Americans have a member of Congress that represents their views. However, a liberal democrat who lived in House Speaker Tom Delay's district in Taxas might genuinely wonder in what way he represented that liberal's interests. By the same token, conservative Republicans living in Vermont have the independent socialist, Bernard Sanders as the state's lone member of Congress representing "their" interests.

Yet if Americans reformers are still insistent on having individual representatives (Guinier, 1994) the phenomenon of "Instant Runoff Voting (Hill, 2003) where voters rank order their preferences could produce proportionality among parties yet retain individual single member districts. It also could be used in Presidential elections and avoid accusations of "spoiler" candidates such as Ralph Nader in 2000.

If there were PR voting in an American parliament, what would the threshold be? The US threshold should be at least 6% and possibly as high as 7%. The goal is to devise a figure that represents all significant interests yet does not produce instability. The "shake out" of parties would likely produce some strategic "mergers" of weak parties which, as single parties, might not attain the threshold. For example, a separate Latino party and an African-American party might insure always attaining an 6% threshold by forming a so-called "rainbow" party. Similarly the Reform Party and the Libertarian Party might find it safer electorally to merge into one free market party.

There are four primary arguments in favor of PR. The first is simplicity; the percentage of the votes equals the percentage of the seats. To accomplish this, the individualistic US could borrow the German hybrid system of "personalized" proportional representation. This system requires citizens to cast two votes on each ballot: the first for an individual candidate; and the second for a list of national/regional candidates grouped by party affiliation. (Allen, 2001) This system has the effect of personalizing list voting because voters have their own representative but also can choose among several parties. Yet allocation of seats by party in the Bundestag corresponds strongly with the party's percentage of the popular vote.

The second advantage to PR is diversity. The experience of PR voting in other countries is that it changes the makeup of the legislature by increasing both gender and racial diversity. Obviously, parties representing minority interests who find it difficult to win representation in 2 person races, will more easily be able to win seats under PR. (Rule and Zimmerman, 1992) Since candidates would not have to run as individuals—or raise millions of dollars—the parties would be more easily able to include individuals on the party's list of candidates who more accurately represent the demographics of average Americans. What a multi-party list system would do would provide a greater range of interests being represented and broaden the concept of "representation" to go beyond narrow geography to include representation of such things as ideas and positions on pol-

icy issues that would be understandable to voters. Moreover, as for geographic representation on a list system, it would be in the self interest of the parties to insure that there was not only gender balance—if this is what the party wanted—on their list, but also other forms of balance including geography, ideology, and ethnicity, among others.

The third advantage is government representativeness. Not only is a consensus-based parliamentary system based on proportional representation more representative of the voting public, it also produces more representative governments. (Birchfield and Crepaz, 1998) This study finds that consensus-based, PR systems also produce a high degree of "popular cabinet support," namely the percentage of voters supporting the majority party or coalition.

The fourth advantage to a PR system in the US is that it would eliminate the redistricting circus. Until recently, the decennial census occasioned the excruciating task of micro-managing the drawing of congressional districts. Yet, since the 2002 elections, Republicans in Texas and Georgia have redistricted a second time, creating even "safer" seats by manipulating district lines to their advantage. (Veith, Veith, and Fuery 2003) Under PR however, districts would be eliminated. Candidate lists would be organized statewide, in highly populated states, or regionally in the case of smaller states like New England. To insure geographical representation, all parties would find it in their own self-interest that the candidate list included geographical diversity starting at the top of the list.

Getting from Here to There: From Academic Debates to Constitutional Reform?

Clearly, none of these four structural reforms will take place soon. But if they were, what would be the initial steps? Of the four proposals, two of them could be accomplished by simple statute: campaign reform and the voting system. The other two would require constitutional change: head of state/government and divided government. Given the above caveats, it would be easiest to effect campaign reform (the Supreme Court willing) and to alter the voting system.

The largest obstacles to such a radical change in the American constitutional system are cultural and structural. Culturally, the ethos of American individualism would have difficulty giving up features such as a single all-powerful executive and one's own individual member of congress, no matter how powerful the arguments raised in support of alternatives. Ideology and cultural practice change very slowly. A more serious obstacle would be the existing interests privileged by the current system. All would fight tenaciously to oppose this suggested change.

Finally, specialists in American politics may dismiss this argument as the farfetched "poaching" of a comparativist on a terrain that only Americanists can write about with knowledge and expertise. However, the durability of all four of the above-mentioned problems, stretching back anywhere from 25 to 50 years, suggests that Americanists have no monopoly of wisdom on overcoming these pathologies. More seriously, what this comparativist perceives is a fundamental failure of imagination based largely on the "N of 1" problem that all comparativists struggle to avoid. If a single observed phenomenon—in this case, the American political system—is not examined comparatively, one never knows whether prevailing practice is optimal or suboptimal. In essence, those who do not look at these issues comparatively suffer a failure of imagination because they are unable to examine the full range of electoral and constitutional options.

References

Allen, Christopher S. 1999. *Transformation of the German Political Party System: Institutional Crisis or Democratic Renewal?, Policies and institution; v. 2.* New York: Berghahn Books.

Allen, Christopher S. 2001. Proportional Representation. In *Oxford Companion to Politics of the World*, edited by J. Krieger. Oxford: Oxford University Press.

Barker, A. 1994. The Upturned Stone: Political Scandals and their Investigation Processes in 20 Democracies. *Crime Law and Social Change* 24 (1):337–373.

Birchfield, Vicki, and Markus M. L. Crepaz. 1998. The Impact of Constitutional Structures and Collective and Competitive Veto Points on Income Inequality in Industrialized Democracies. *European Journal of Political Research* 34 (2):175–200.

Brubaker, Stanley C. 1998. The Limits of Campaign Spending Limits. *Public Interest* 133:33–54.

Center for Voting and Democracy. *Overview: Dubious Democracy 2003–2004* June 2003 [cited. Available from http://www.fairvote.org/dubdem/overview.htm.

Corrado, Anthony. 1997. *Campaign Finance Reform: A Sourcebook.* Washington, D.C.: Brookings Institution.

Cutler, Lloyd. 1989. Some Reflections About Divided Government. *Presidential Studies Quarterly* 17:485–492.

Dionne, E. J., Jr. 1991. *Why Americans Hate Politics.* New York: Simon and Schuster.

Dwyre, D., M. O'Gorman, and J. Stonecash. 1994. Disorganized Politics and the Have-Nots: Politics and Taxes in New York and California. *Polity* 27 (1):25–47.

Fiorina, Morris. 1992. *Divided Government.* New York: Macmillan.

Franklin, Mark N., and Wolfgang P. Hirczy de Mino. 1998. Separated Powers, Divided Government, and Turnout in U.S. Presidential Elections. *American Journal of Political Science* 42 (1):316–326.

Gans, Curtis. 1993. Television: Political Participation's Enemy #1. *Spectrum: the Journal of State Government* 66 (2):26–31.

Gibson, Martha L. 1995. Issues, Coalitions, and Divided Government. *Congress & the Presidency* 22 (2):155–166.

Grant, Alan. 1998. The Politics of American Campaign Finance. *Parliamentary Affairs* 51 (2):223–240.

Grofman, Bernard, and Arend Lijphart. 1986. *Electoral Laws and Their Consequences.* New York: Agathon Press.

Guinier, Lani. 1994. *The Tyranny of the Majority: Fundamental Fairness in Representative Democracy.* New York: The Free Press.

Hill, Steven. 2003. *Fixing Elections: The Failure of America's Winner Take All Politics.* New York: Routledge.

Huber, John D. 1996. The Vote of Confidence in Parliamentary Democracies. *American Political Science Review* 90 (2):269–282.

Jacobson, Gary C. 1990. *The Electoral Origins of Divided Government: Competition in U.S. House Elections, 1946–1988.* Boulder, CO: Westview.

Jacoby, Wade. 2000. *Imitation and Politics: Redesigning Germany.* Ithaca: Cornell University Press.

Kernell, Samuel. 1997. *Going Public: New Strategies of Presidential Leadership.* Washington, D.C.: CQ Press.

Laver, Michael, and Kenneth A. Shepsle. 1995. *Making and Breaking Governments: Cabinets and Legislatures in Parliamentary Democracies.* New York: Cambridge University Press.

Lijphart, Arend. 1984. *Democracies: Patterns of Majoritarian and Consensus Government in Twenty-One Countries.* New Haven: Yale University Press.

Lijphart, Arend. 1994. Democracies: Forms, Performance, and Constitutional Engineering. *European Journal of Political Research* 25:1–17.

Linz, Juan. 1993. The Perils of Presidentialism. In *The Global Resurgence of Democracy*, edited by L. Diamond and M. Plattner. Baltimore: Johns Hopkins University Press.

Lipset, Seymour Martin. 1996. *American Exceptionalism: A Double-Edged Sword.* New York: Norton.

Mayhew, David. 1991. *Divided We Govern: Party Control, Lawmaking, and Investigations, 1946–1990.* New Haven: Yale University Press.

Norris, Pippa. 1997. Choosing Electoral Systems: Proportional, Majoritarian and Mixed Systems. *International Political Science Review*, 18 (3):297–312.

Richter, Michaela. 2002. Continuity or Politikwechsel? The First Federal Red-Green Coalition. *German Politics & Society* 20 (1):1–48.

Rosenstone, Steven J., Roy L. Behr, and Edward H. Lazarus. 1996. *Third Parties in America: Citizen Response to Major Party Failure.* Princeton: Princeton University Press.

Rule, Wilma, and Joseph F. Zimmerman, eds. 1992. *United States Electoral Systems: Their Impact on Women and Minorities.* New York: Praeger.

Rundquist, Paul S. 1991. *The House of Representatives and the House of Commons: A Brief Comparison of American and British Parliamentary Practice.* Washington, DC: Congressional Research Service, Library of Congress.

Strom, Kaare, Ian Budge, and Michael J. Laver. 1994. Constraints on Cabinet Formation in Parliamentary Democracies. *American Journal of Political Science* 38 (2):303–335.

Thurber, James A. 1991. Representation, Accountability, and Efficiency in Divided Party Control of Government. *PS* 24:653–657.

Veith, Richard, Norma Jean Veith, and Susan Fuery. 2003. Oral Argument. In *U.S. Supreme Court.* Washington, DC.

Weinberg, Jonathan. 1993. Broadcasting and Speech. *California Law Review* 81 (5):1101–1206.

Weiss, Stephen. 2004. '04 Eections Expected to Cost Nearly $4 Billion. In *opensecrets.org – Center for Responsive Politics:* http://www.opensecrets.org/pressreleases/2004/04spending.asp.

UNIT 3

Europe in Transition: West, Center, and East

Unit Selections

Key Points to Consider

- What are the major obstacles to the emergence of a more unified Europe? Will the new constitution necessarily make matters easier?

- Why does one of the articles suggest that the enlarged EU may become a Europe *à la carte?*

- Why is the voter turnout in the elections for the European Parliament so low?

- What is the evidence that the economic problems of Western Europe could be not just cyclical but also structural in origin?

- How would you compare the plight of immigrants to Europe with immigrants to the United States?

- How do you assess Yeltsin's legacy, and how well is Putin equipped to lead his country to a better future?

- How has President Putin gone about building a strong political base for himself? What seems to be the major items on his political agenda?

Student Website

www.mhcls.com/online

Internet References

Further information regarding these websites may be found in this book's preface or online.

Europa: European Union
http://europa.eu.int

NATO Integrated Data Service (NIDS)
http://www.nato.int/structur/nids/nids.htm

Research and Reference (Library of Congress)
http://lcweb.loc.gov/rr/

Russian and East European Network Information Center, University of Texas at Austin
http://reenic.utexas.edu/reenic/index.html

The articles in this unit deal with two major developments that have greatly altered the political map of contemporary Europe. One is the growth of the supranational project now known as the European Union (EU) and its impact on the European countries, both member and non-member states, and their citizens. The other development consists of the continuing challenges and responses that have resulted from decades of Communist rule in Central and Eastern Europe, followed by its sudden collapse.

These two developments were symbolically linked in 2004, when the EU for the first time admitted to membership eight former Communist-ruled countries in the central and eastern part of the continent. While NATO had moved slightly ahead of the European Union in its own eastward expansion, the EU has very different goals and entry requirements than the defense alliance. They include a set of minimum democratic and economic criteria that each new member must meet before being admitted. The prospect of gaining membership has thus become a kind of reward for good political and economic behavior in Europe. In recent years the EU has used this form of **"soft power"** to encourage several post-authoritarian systems not to backslide on the difficult road to pluralist democracy and a more open economy.

The present time can be seen as an important turning point for the EU—and also as a crucial test of its viability. Its institutional origins go back to 1951, when France, West Germany, Italy, and the

three Benelux countries integrated their coal and steel industries. By 1957 the same six nations already had a running start, when they founded the European Economic Community (EEC) that later became the European Union. Britain "missed the bus" when it declined to join the founders and proceeded to organize a European Free Trade Area (EFTA) instead. The European Community quickly turned out to be a supranational framework that served to stimulate the economies of the member states. Already by the early 1960s, Britain sought to join, but President de Gaulle of France's Fifth Republic opposed Britain's entry. The EU did not add new members until 1973, when Britain finally entered along with two of her closest trading partners in Europe, Ireland and Denmark. Thereafter the European Community continued to expand incrementally in sets of three newcomers per decade. The three former dictatorships, Greece, Portugal, and Spain, entered during the 1980s, after having established their credentials as well functioning new democracies and market economies. In 1995, soon after the end of the Cold War, three neutral countries—Austria, Finland, and Sweden—joined the EU and increased its total membership to fifteen.

In 2004 the EU abandoned this pattern of incremental accretion in favor of what has been called a great leap forward. In one swoop, the EU expanded its membership by two thirds, from fifteen to twenty-five countries. This greatly increased the EU's economic, cultural, and political diversity, even as its population rose from 375 million to some 450 million people.

Eight of the ten newcomers lie in central or eastern Europe: Poland, Hungary, the Czech Republic, Slovakia, Slovenia, and the three Baltic states, Lithuania, Latvia, and Estonia. They differ from most of the first fifteen members in two major respects. First, they all have had a relatively short experience with pluralist democracy, although former Czechoslovakia can look back upon two decades as a liberal democratic republic between the two world wars. Second, their economies are far less productive than those of the older EU members for reasons that include not only the many years of economic mismanagement under imposed Communist rule. Already before World War II, most of these countries lagged behind the more developed parts of Western Europe—again with the notable exception of Czechoslovakia and pockets of modernity elsewhere. The remaining two new entrants are the small Mediterranean island nations of Malta and Cyprus.

Several additional states are applicants, waiting for admission to the EU. They include Romania and Bulgaria, whose entry is planned for 2007, and several other Balkan states. The case of **Turkey** is special. It is a relatively poor and non-modernized country, with some notable urban exceptions. Turkey has a tainted record on human rights and democracy, in part as a result of the escalation of violence associated with a prolonged ethnic minority struggle. Culturally, Turkey differs fundamentally from all EU members. Although the state is officially secular, the Turkish population is overwhelmingly Muslim. There has been a strong opposition in the EU to a Turkish membership, not only from Greece and Cyprus. The reservations are often culturally based, but opponents also fix their sights on the size of Turkey's population. It is now 70 million and growing. Presumably it will outnumber Germany's 80 million within a decade. Opponents of Turkey's admission portray it as a potential economic dead weight and as a political, cultural, and demographic threat by some opponents. Yet, as supporters of Turkey's entry argue, the real hope for a workable model of modernization and democratization in the Middle East may lie in Turkey.

The enlargement of the EU, with or without Turkey, will in any case bring changes and challenges. These are examined in a special report by *The Economist*. It cannot be ruled out that the larger and more diverse EU will begin (or has already begun) to depart from the founders' idealistic vision of **"an ever closer union among the peoples of Europe."** This evocative phrase is contained in the preamble to the Treaty of Rome, the EU's founding document. Although it echoes the goal of a "more perfect union" announced in the preamble to the U.S. Constitution, the EU does not appear to be moving toward a kind of loose-knit United States of Europe. Observers like Robert Cottrell think that it is less likely to become one as it expands and diversifies.

In June 2005, a little more than a year after the latest and greatest expansion of the EU membership, Dutch and French voters rejected a proposed EU constitution. In an earlier version of the document, it had already been pulled back twice for revision, before it began the ratification route that required approval in all 25 member countries. The German approval had come early, by way of a parliamentary vote. Britain had planned to make ratification dependent on the outcome of a national referendum—the second in its history—but it was called off after the French vote. The completion of the process had been planned for November 2006, but that was no longer feasible. One of the most balanced interpretations of Europe's "no" came from Andrew Moravchik.

As it now stands, without a constitution, the EU is an impressive political construct that has no close parallel anywhere. It has largely dismantled national barriers to the free movement of people, goods, services, and capital among the member nations. Above all, the EU has acquired an institutional presence and authority that goes far beyond anything envisaged by NAFTA or other regional free trade arrangements. All member nations have diverted some of their traditional sovereignty to the EU. The appointed **Commission** uses its supranational executive authority to initiate common policy decisions and oversee their implementation. The independent **European Court of Justice** makes binding decisions in its adjudication of EU-related disputes. The **European Parliament** has seen its authority grow over the years, even though it is not a full-blown legislature in the traditional sense. In the 2004 elections of a new European Parliament, the voter turnout averaged 45 percent—at least ten percent lower than the U.S. turnout in the presidential election of the same year. The powerful **Council of Ministers** remains an intergovernmental body, where the national government of every member nation is represented. Until now each nation has had a weighted vote related to the size of its population. *The Economist* explains some of the intricacies of the weighted votes and the qualified and double majorities that are going to replace them under the new EU constitution. They can be compared to the far simpler contrivance of the Connecticut Compromise as a way of giving representation to all members while also recognizing their considerable differences in size of population. In the case of the supranational EU, the smallest member, Malta, has a population of 400,000, while the largest member, Germany, tops 82 million, a ratio of less than 1:200.

The political process continues unabated in the individual nation-states of Western Europe, as they seek to define and implement their own public agendas. Their relative prosperity rests on a base that was built up during the very long postwar economic boom of the 1950s and 1960s. By political choice, a considerable portion of their wealth was channeled toward the public sector and used to develop an array of public goods, social services, and social insurance. Since the early 1970s, however, many West European countries have been beset by economic disruptions or slowdowns offset by periods of cyclical economic upturns. There are also structural reasons why they no longer can take increasing affluence for granted in today's more competitive global economy.

The economic shock that first interrupted the prolonged postwar boom came in the wake of sharp rises in the cost of energy. They were linked to successive hikes in the price of oil imposed by the Organization of Petroleum Exporting Countries (OPEC) after 1973. In the 1980s, OPEC lost its organizational bite, as some of its members began to break the rules by raising production and lowering prices rather than abiding by the opposite practices in the manner of a well-functioning cartel agreement. The exploitation of new oil and gas fields in the North Sea and elsewhere also helped alleviate the energy situation, at least for a time. The resulting improvement for the consumers of oil and gas helped the Western European economies recover, but as a whole they did not rebound to their earlier and much higher growth rates. The short Gulf War in 1991 did not seriously hamper the flow of Middle East oil, but it once again underscored the vulnerability of Europe to external interruptions in its energy supply. Since the beginning of the new century and millennium, there have again been unmistakable signs of a petroleum shortage. Markets have responded quickly, and what first appeared as sharp price hikes, and brought citizen protests in several West European countries, have already become the new norm.

Because of their heavy dependence on international trade, Western European economies are vulnerable to global cyclical tendencies. Another important challenge lies in the stiff competition they face from China and the smaller new industrial countries (NICs) of East and South Asia, where labor costs remain much lower. The emerging Asian factor probably contributed to the increased tempo of the European drive for economic integration in the late 1980s. Some observers have warned of a protectionist reaction, in which major trading blocs in Europe, North America, and Eastern Asia could replace the relatively free system of international trade established in recent decades.

Central Europe still feels the aftershocks from the sudden collapse of Communist rule at the end of the 1980s. Here states, nations, and nationalities broke away from an imposed system of central control, by asserting their independence from the previous ruling group and its ideology. In their attempt to construct a new order for themselves, the postcommunist countries have encountered enormous difficulties. Their transition to pluralist democracy and a rudimentary market-based economy turned out to be much rockier than most had anticipated.

The prospect of membership in the EU became a major incentive to continue with the reforms. Even now that the Central and East European countries have gained entry to the club, it will be a long time before they can hope to catch up economically. Robert Cottrell reports from a study by *The Economist* Intelligence Unit that it will take the new entrants on average more than fifty years to draw level with the old members in average income per person. The forecast is based on the simple and rather optimistic assumption of growth rates averaging 4 percent for the new EU entrants, or double the assumed average rate of 2 percent for the older members from Western Europe.

In some areas of the former Soviet bloc, one encounters some nostalgia for the basic material security and "orderliness" provided by the communist welfare states of the past. This should not be understood as a wish to turn back the wheel of history. Instead, it seems to represent a desire to build buffers and safety nets into the new market-oriented systems. Communist descended parties have responded by abandoning most or all of their Leninist baggage. They now engage in the competitive bidding for votes with promises of social fairness and security. In Poland and elsewhere, such parties have gained political leverage.

Those who attempt the big move to the "Golden West" resemble in many ways the immigrants who have been attracted to the United States in the past and present. But many Western Europeans are unwilling to accept what they regard as a flood of unwanted strangers. The newcomers are widely portrayed as outsiders whose presence will further drain the generous welfare systems and threaten the economic security and established way of life.

Such anxieties are the stuff of sociocultural mistrust, tensions, and conflicts. One serious political consequence has been the emergence of a populist politics on the Far Right that is directed against immigrants. The governments in several countries have tightened their laws on citizenship, asylum, and immigration for fear of otherwise losing voters to ultra-right populist parties. This kind of accommodation has taken place even in countries, such as Denmark or the Netherlands, that until recently had very good records in recognizing and protecting human rights. There can be little doubt that these issues will continue to preoccupy West European politics in coming years.

It is important to remember that there are also individuals and groups who resist the emerging **political nativism** in their own societies. Some enlightened political leaders and commentators seek to promote the reasonable perspective that migrants could turn out to be an important asset rather than a liability. This argument may concede that the foreign influx also involves some social costs in the short run, at least during recessionary periods, but it emphasizes that the newcomers can be a very important human resource who will contribute to mid- and long-term economic prosperity. Quite apart from any such utilitarian considerations, the migrants and asylum-seekers have become an important test of liberal democratic tolerance on the continent.

The Central and East European countries continue to face the challenge of political and economic reconstruction. When they began their post-Communist journey, there were no ready-made strategies of reform. Much theoretical ink had been spilled on the transition from a market economy to state socialism, but there was little theory or practice to guide the countries that tried to make a paradigm shift in the opposite direction. Some economists familiar with Eastern Europe argued that a quick transition to a market economy was a preferable course, indeed the most responsible one, even though such an approach could be very disruptive and painful in the short run. They argued that such a **"shock therapy"** would release human energies and bring economic growth more quickly and efficiently. At the same time, these supporters of a "tough love" strategy warned that compassionate halfway measures could end up worsening the economic plight of these countries. Yet, as David Ost has reported from Poland, these policies create their own problems and are likely to meet with rejection, especially when there is little evidence that neoliberal measures will deliver the promised goods.

Other strategists came out in favor of a more gradual approach to economic reconstruction. They warned that the neoclassical economists, who would introduce a full-scale market economy by fiat, not only ignored the market system's cultural and historic preconditions but also underestimated the turmoil that was likely to accompany the great transition. As a more prudent course of action, these gradualists recommended the adoption of pragmatic strategies of incremental change, accompanied by rhetoric of lower expectations.

Experience and the passage of a few more years would probably have given us better insights into the relative merits of each argument. But a pluralist society rarely permits itself to become a social laboratory for controlled experiments of this kind. Moreover, decision makers must often learn on the job. They cannot afford to become inflexible and dogmatic in these matters, where the human stakes are so high. Instead, competitive politics has produced a "mix" of the two approaches as the most acceptable and practical policy outcome.

A similar debate has been carried out in the former Soviet Union. It could be argued that Mikhail Gorbachev, the last Soviet head of government (1985 to 1991), failed to opt clearly for one or the other approach to economic reform. He seems to have lacked clear ideas about both means and ends of his **perestroika,** or restructuring, of the centrally planned economy. In the eyes of some born-again Soviet marketers, he remained far too socialist. But Communist hard-liners never forgave him for dismantling a system in which they had enjoyed security and privilege.

Gorbachev appears to have regarded his own policies of **glasnost,** or openness, and democratization as essential accompaniments of perestroika in what he perceived as a kind of modernization program. He seems to have understood (or become convinced) that a highly developed economy needs a freer flow of information along with a more decentralized system of decision making if its component parts are to be efficient, flexible, and capable of learning and self-correction. In that sense, a market economy has some integral feedback traits that make it incompatible with the traditional Soviet model of a centrally directed "command economy."

Glasnost and democratization were incompatible with a repressive political system of one-party rule as well. They served Gorbachev as instruments to weaken the grip of the Communist hard-liners and at the same time to rally behind him some reform groups, including many intellectuals and journalists. Within a remarkably short time after he came to power in 1985, a vigorous new press emerged in the Soviet Union headed by journalists who were eager to ferret out misdeeds and report on political reality as they observed it. A similar development took place in the history profession, where scholars used the new spirit of openness to report in grim detail about past Communist atrocities that had previously been covered up or dismissed as bourgeois propaganda. There was an inevitable irony to the new truthfulness. Even as it served to discredit much of the past along with any reactionary attempts to restore "the good old days," it also brought into question the foundations of the Soviet system under the leadership of the Communist Party. Yet Gorbachev had clearly set out to modernize the Soviet system, not to bring it down.

One of the greatest vulnerabilities of the Soviet Union turned out to be its multiethnic character. Gorbachev was not alone in having underestimated the potential centrifugal tendencies of a Union of Soviet Socialist Republics (USSR) erected on the territory of the old, overland Empire that the Russian tsars had conquered and governed before 1917. Many of the non-Russian minorities retained a territorial identification with their homelands, where they often lived as ethnic majorities. This made it easier for them to demand greater autonomy or national independence, when the Soviet regime became weakened. The first national assertions came from the Baltic peoples in Estonia, Latvia, and Lithuania, who had been forced under Soviet rule in 1940, after only two decades of national independence. Very soon other nationalities, including the Georgians and Armenians, expressed similar demands through the political channels that had been opened to them. The death knell for the Soviet Union sounded in 1991, when the Ukrainians, who constituted the second largest national group in the Soviet Union after the Russians, made similar demands for independence.

Gorbachev's political reforms ended up as a mortal threat not only to the continued leadership role by the Communist Party but also to the continued existence of the Soviet Union itself. Gorbachev seems to have understood neither of these ultimately fatal consequences of his reform attempts until late in the day. This explains why he could set in motion forces that would ultimately destroy what he had hoped to make more attractive and productive. In August 1991, Communist hard-liners attempted a coup against the reformer and his reforms, but they acted far too late and were too poorly organized to succeed. The coup was defeated by a popular resistance, led by Russian President Boris Yeltsin, who had broken with Communism earlier and, as it seemed, more decisively.

After his formal restoration to power following the abortive coup, Gorbachev became politically dependent on Yeltsin and was increasingly seen as a transitional figure. His days as Soviet president were numbered, when the Soviet Union ceased to exist a week before the end of 1991. The dissolution of the Soviet state took place quickly and essentially without armed conflict. It was formally replaced by the Commonwealth of Independent States (CIS), a very loose union that lacked both a sufficient institutional framework and enough political will to keep it together. Almost from the outset, the CIS seemed destined to be little more than a loosely structured transitional device.

There is an undeniable gloom or hangover atmosphere in many of the accounts of post-Communist and post–Soviet Russia. A turn to some form of authoritarian nationalist populism cannot be ruled out. Recent parliamentary and presidential elections give a picture of electoral volatility, growing voter apathy or disgruntlement, and widespread authoritarian leanings in a politically exhausted society. They also illustrate how governmental leaders can favor, manipulate, or even help create "loyal" political parties.

Duma Elections 1993. The first elections of a new Russian Duma after the end of the Soviet Union did not provide a propitious start for post-Communist politics. They came in December 1993 and were preceded by a complete breakdown of relations between President Yeltsin and the parliamentary majority. The Duma had originally supported Yeltsin, but opposition had grown over some sweeping economic reforms pushed by his government. The ensuing political conflict ran the gamut from a presidential dissolution of the legislature, through an impeachment vote by the Duma, to street demonstrations. It ended with Russian soldiers entering the parliament to force out deputies who had refused to leave. Yeltsin used the opportunity to have some political parties and publications outlawed. The powers of the president in the dual executive were constitutionally strengthened.

The electoral result was something of a political boomerang for Yeltsin. It resulted in a fragmented Duma, in which nationalists and Communists occupied key positions. The forces that backed market reforms, above all Yabloko, suffered setbacks. Henceforth Yeltsin seemed to play a more subdued role, and the new government pursued far more cautious reform policies. In 1994, Russia's military intervention in Chechnya, a breakaway Caucasian republic located within the Russian Federation, failed to give Yeltsin a quick and easy victory that might have reversed his slide into political unpopularity among Russians.

Duma Elections 1995. The regular parliamentary elections in December 1995 provided a further setback for the democratic and economic reformers in Russia. However, it was far less their rivals' strength than their own disunity and rivalry both before and after the election that weakened the parliamentary position of the liberal reformers. Together, they received close to a quarter of the vote. That was slightly more than the Communists, led as before by Gennady Zyuganov, and it was twice as much as the far-right nationalists in Vladimir Zhirinovsky's misnamed Liberal Democratic Party.

Presidential Election 1996. Yeltsin still knew how to win elections as he showed in the presidential contest of 1996, albeit in a run-off against the Communist leader, Zyuganov. By this time, ill health and heavy drinking had reportedly exacerbated his governing problems. His frequent and seemingly erratic replacements of prime ministers did not improve the situation.

Duma Elections 1999. Always good for a political surprise, Yeltsin saved two for his last hurrah. In the latter half of 1999, he selected a stronger figure for what turned out to be his last prime minister. Vladimir V. Putin, then 47 years old, quickly turned his attention to a tough new military intervention in Chechnya. Within Russia, his strong determination to suppress the breakaway Muslim province generated widespread support, based on its presentation and perception as a counterterrorist move. In the Duma elections of December 1999, the new prime minister's aura of tough leadership probably helped reduce the Communist result to 113 seats, or a quarter of the Duma.

Presidential Election 2000. Without warning but with impeccable timing, President Yeltsin announced his resignation on December 31, 1999, just as the century and millennium came to an end. Putin became the new acting president and easily won the presidential election a few months later. Largely due to a favorable oil market for Soviet exports, the new president inherited a much better fiscal balance than Yeltsin or, especially Gorbachev before him.

In his first term as President of Russia, Putin aroused popular support with tough measures against organized crime and political terrorism. This was also true for the judicial action taken against some of the super-rich "oligarchs," who had made huge fortunes when state owned enterprises were privatized. Their ostentatious wealth, gathered quickly in an otherwise poor country, is highly resented by many Russians. The arrest of Mikhail B. Khodorkovsky, reputedly Russia's richest man, in the fall of 2003 met with far more critical reaction abroad than in Russia. During the previous two years, the billionaire had poured money into schemes for building a civil society in Russia. His new interest in political matters had led him to support some of Putin's critics and rivals. It seemed at least politically convenient to have Khodorkovsky out of the way during the parliamentary election of December 2003.

Duma Election 2003. The election was memorable in several ways. The voter turnout was low (56 percent), at least by Eu-

ropean standards. The democratic middle class parties fared poorly, once again. The Communists received only one-half of their vote share in the previous election (dropping from 24 to 12.7 percent of the vote). And a recently created party, called United Russia, performed better than any party since the end of one-party elections in Russia. Outside observers found evidence of fraud in the election and cited media favors to United Russia. On the other hand, it seems likely that this party, which the press described as largely defined by its loyalty to President Putin, would have done well in any case.

Presidential Election 2004. Putin seemed a sure bet to win the presidential election in March 2004. In advance of the contest, he asserted his authority within the dual executive by dismissing the prime minister and appointing a new one. With the dependable backing of a parliamentary majority, supplied by United Russia and a few independents, the institutional and political basis for a strong presidency until 2008 seemed to have been secured. Some Russians wonder whether Putin will at that time step aside for someone else, seek to determine his successor (as Yeltsin did), or seek a third term (a move that would require a change in the Russian Constitution).

In conclusion, pluralist democracy and the open market economy have once again been discredited for many Russians after being tried out under highly imperfect circumstances. Steven Lee Myers shows how Putin's reactions fit into an established pattern of authoritarian responses. Finally, Peter Lavelle examines what he calls Putin's long-term reform agenda of "managed democracy" and "managed capitalism."

Now that we are all bundled inside, let's shut the door

A year after the new boys entered the European Union, the mood is a mite surly, and definitely unwelcoming

BRATISLAVA, BUDAPEST, PRAGUE AND RIGA

GALEN, that great second-century physician, observed "*Triste est omne animal post coitum*". He might have been reflecting on the mood of the European Union a year after it embraced ten new members, eight of them from central Europe. Most of the newcomers affect a ho-hum indifference to membership now that they have it—even though they worked furiously to get it. The older members ponder, with varying degrees of anxiety, the low tax rates and the even lower wages which most of the new countries have brought with them into the single market.

The new members' singular lack of jubilation might suggest that this latest enlargement, the biggest by far in the Union's history, has been something of a let-down. "We have accepted the dictatorship of Tesco," grumbles Vladimir Zelezny, a Eurosceptic Czech member of the European Parliament.

Only the Slovaks still seem truly excited, perhaps because they came nearest to failing the course. After overthrowing communism, they had to beat back the neo-authoritarian government of Vladimir Meciar, which ran the country in the mid-1990s. "We would not have got rid of Meciar, were it not for the vision of the EU," says Pavol Demes, director of the Bratislava office of the German Marshall Fund of the United States.

In fact, last year's enlargement has gone remarkably well, both for the newcomers and for the Union, and all the more so when measured against the fears that preceded it. The institutions in Brussels have gone on working normally, despite predictions of gridlock. The economies of the new members have gone on growing at a healthy clip, roughly two to four times as fast as the euro-zone average, despite worries that their industry would be choked by regulations and their agriculture ruined by the opening of markets. More often, the opposite has happened, notably in Poland. Manufacturers have done unexpectedly well out of open borders and easier exporting. Farmers have gained from subsidies and new demand.

One problem is that the central Europeans feel themselves, in some respects, to be second-class members of the Union. This spoils their pleasure. They are stuck outside the Schengen zone of passport-free travel for at least another two years. They are denied the freedom to work in most EU countries for perhaps another six years: only Britain, Ireland and Sweden have opened their labour markets right away. The newcomers must meet further tests before they can join the single currency. Their farmers get smaller direct subsidies from EU funds, starting at one-quarter of the payments made to farmers in the 15 "old" members, a money-saving measure meant to speed farm restructuring.

Most painfully, after the ravages of communism and the post-communist transition, it will take the central Europeans decades before they can raise their average wages to western European levels. For most ordinary people, accession last year brought "euphoria on the eve of May 1st, a great historical moment—and then, the next day, nothing had changed," says Robert Braun, former chief strategy adviser to the Hungarian prime minister.

Still, given a few quiet years to bed down, this Union of 25 countries, due to be 27 with the entry of Romania and Bulgaria in 2007, could probably emerge little changed in its habits and workings from the Union of 15. Meetings in Brussels would be longer and wordier, relations with Russia would acquire a new salience, Britain would have a few more allies in its fight against tax harmonisation, and that would be pretty well all. Unfortunately, the quiet years needed for that bedding-down are not in prospect.

Instead, because European governments overestimated both the difficulties of enlargement and the strength of popular support for the EU, they committed themselves last year to the politically exhausting business of ratifying a new constitution. This document need not change much in the way the EU operates, save in some formal respects, but it does require each country to re-examine and re-confirm some fairly open-ended membership commitments in minute detail. No country is enjoying this process, least of all France, which holds its ratification referendum on May 29th, and has emerged as the unforeseen doubter. Opinion polls say the constitution is likely to be rejected there.

What happens if it's no?

The new members are looking on anxiously. If France votes no, its instinct might be to try forming a new small group of the EU's six original members, weakening and perhaps undermining the wider Union. If, on the other hand, France votes yes and then Britain votes no (as Britain probably will), that would be just as worrying, if it

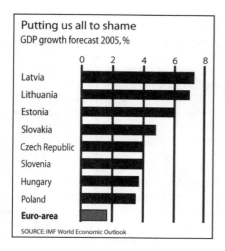

Putting us all to shame
GDP growth forecast 2005, %

SOURCE: IMF World Economic Outlook

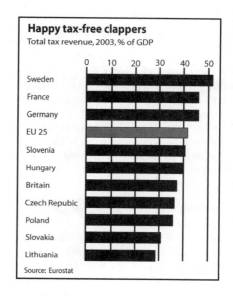

Happy tax-free clappers
Total tax revenue, 2003, % of GDP

Source: Eurostat

pushes Britain to the margins of the EU or out of it entirely.

The Union would become a much less friendly place for the new members, which tend to share Britain's taste for market liberalisation, tax competition, subsidiarity and Atlanticism, and look to it as a guarantor of those things. There is a faint possibility, too, that one of the new members, perhaps the Czech Republic or Poland, might fail to ratify the referendum, putting its own future in doubt. The Czech president, Vaclav Klaus, is the only EU head of state to oppose the constitution, while the Poles fume that the constitution will reduce their country's voting power within the Union.

French angst about Europe owes much to enlargement, and much also to worries about immigration and globalisation. Whereas France felt confident of its leading role in an EU of 15 countries, in an EU of 25 or more it is starting to feel unhappily overwhelmed. The idea that Turkey might one day join the Union weighs heavily on public opinion in France, as it does in Germany and Austria.

France fears not merely that it is losing its historic leadership of the Union, but also that enlargement is bringing in more low-wage, low-tax countries which will further undermine, through competition, the French model of big government and high taxes. It may well be right. Lithuania's tax burden in 2003 was 28.7% of GDP, 17 percentage points less than the French equivalent. Slovakia's 19% flat rate for all main taxes—personal, corporate and VAT—has become the envy of the region. But in the French view all this amounts to "fiscal dumping" by the new members—using low tax rates to lure jobs and investment away from western Europe, then balancing the

state budget with EU cash from French and German pockets. The charge is wrong, but try telling France that.

The new members also tend to be much more Atlanticist in their foreign relations. In the run-up to the Iraq war in 2003 they mostly supported America, leading France's president, Jacques Chirac, to say that they had missed a good opportunity to shut up. The phrase still rankles.

"Now they know we are not going to keep quiet," says Eduard Kukan, Slovakia's foreign minister, pointing to the part the new members have started to play in EU policymaking. Poland and Lithuania saved Europe's face by giving strong early support to Ukraine's orange revolution last year. Slovakia and Hungary have joined Austria to lobby, so far unsuccessfully, for accession talks with Croatia. The Czech Republic has been steering EU policy in relations with Cuba.

Romania looks set to outdo everyone in its pro-Americanism, if and when it joins the Union in two or three years' time. Its new president, Traian Basescu, elected in December, has said that his priority is to work closely with Washington and London, a formula which pointedly omits Paris and Brussels. Last week he said that Romania favoured "a state with minimal involvement in the economy", a rebuke to France's *dirigiste* model. He added for good measure that he resented what Mr Chirac had said in 2003. "Romania is a country which has respect for itself," he said, "we do not like these kinds of declarations."

Mr Basescu may be living dangerously. His country has yet to join the EU, and France could still block its entry. Romania, and its neighbour, Bulgaria, began their negotiations alongside the central Europeans but were deemed unready to join last year. This week they signed accession treaties which will bring them in at the start of 2007, unless the EU sees signs of late disarray, in which case it can set back entry for another year.

But these accession treaties have to be ratified by all member states, including France. If relations deteriorate much further, the French parliament might decide that Romania is still unfit to join, and refuse the treaty. Germany's Christian Democrats are also talking about blocking Romania, and their support is needed for a constitutional majority in the Bundestag.

Keeping Turkey out

The question mark over Romania's accession is a small one. A much bigger one

hangs over any further EU enlargements. Turkey has been accepted as a candidate, but few EU countries can easily conceive of it as a member, even ten years from now. The fear in some quarters of bringing an Islamic country into Europe is at least as great as the desire, in other quarters, to show it can be done. Turkey's size and relative poverty exacerbate the problem. The result is that the EU risks opening negotiations with Turkey later this year with no serious intention of completing them.

The countries of the western Balkans—Albania, Bosnia, Croatia, Macedonia, and Serbia and Montenegro—have all been promised in principle that they can join the Union once they are ready. But that promise, given in 2003, has no timetable attached to it, and most of the countries are still a mess. Indeed, until the final status of Kosovo is decided in talks due to start this year, and until the relationship between Serbia and Montenegro is decided by a referendum next year, it is not even clear how many countries the region will comprise.

Only Croatia is anywhere near ready to start entry negotiations, but its hopes of doing so last month faltered when the EU decided that it was not co-operating with the Hague war-crimes tribunal, a precondition for talks. The Europeans mainly want Croatia to surrender, or to inform on, Ante Gotovina, a fugitive Croat army chief who has been charged with ethnic cleansing during Croatia's war with the Serbs.

Ukraine is not recognised as a candidate for Union membership, but if its new pro-western government forges on with bold political and economic reforms, breaking with Russian and post-Soviet models, accession talks will be hard to resist. But there is a chicken-and-egg problem. Ukraine may be able to hold the course of reform only if it has a clear prospect of EU entry already in front of it, as was the case in Slovakia. Poland and most other central European countries think it is crystal clear that Ukraine should be offered a prospect of membership in order to stiffen its resolve. They want Moldova to follow, and some day even Belarus, if it can ditch its dictator of the past ten years, Alexander Lukashenka.

Losing the will to enlarge

But other EU countries disagree. They do not want to anger Russia, which sees these former Soviet lands as its sphere of influence. France nurtures Russia as a diplomatic ally. Germany relies on it for gas. Both want the Union to be nicer to Russia—unlike the new members, especially the Baltic states, who tend to view Russia as a nuisance if not an outright danger.

It is something of an irony, in sum, that while enlargement has become the most popular and successful instrument of regime change in Europe's history, the European Union is losing the will to enlarge any more. It does not really want any more members, save perhaps for Croatia, and only then because Croatia has such a beautiful coastline.

Of course, if truth were told, there was precious little popular support for last year's enlargement either. Like many other Union policies it was negotiated between governments and then implemented against a background of public indifference. A Eurobarometer opinion poll taken in 2002, just as EU governments were concluding terms for the 2004 enlargement, found that 41% of EU citizens did not want to know any more about the candidate countries, 76% did not wish to live or work in them, and 91% felt "no tie of any kind" with them.

History will surely judge the EU governments to have acted wisely, nonetheless, in pursuing the 2004 enlargement, and with it the rehabilitation of central Europe after half a century of communism. But some of those governments now find that they have frightened themselves, and many of their citizens, with the prospect of a wider and woollier Europe. Public opinion has been aroused. It worries about the shifting of factories and jobs to the low-wage economies of central Europe—*délocalisation,* as the French say.

In fact, the central European countries compete more often for projects against distant low-wage rivals such as China and Brazil, and all Europe benefits from central Europe's success. But still, some industrial capacity is shifting directly from the old to the new members. And some workers from central Europe are indeed entering western labour markets, often illicitly, since most EU governments have bowed to public opinion by closing their job markets to the newcomers. Such migration usually helps local economies, but it still upsets local interests.

Public opinion in western Europe also senses, accurately, that enlargement points the Union down a road which, if followed to its apparent conclusion, would mean open borders with the Balkans, wages in parts of Europe at Chinese levels, and Turkey as *primus inter pares* at EU summits. There may be much good to be said for each of these things, but public and even official opinion in many other EU countries is not yet ready to hear it. Anxieties about cultural integrity and national security are too strong.

Having been conceived as a way of exporting Europe's stability to neighbouring countries, enlargement is coming to be seen more as a way of importing instability. The emphasis throughout the West on national security since September 11th 2001 means that it is no longer clear even when the countries which joined the EU

last year will be admitted to the Schengen zone of passport-free travel, if ever. They can join Schengen only with the unanimous approval of existing members, and that will not come if some interior ministers get their way, says one top EU official.

Whatever the outcome of the French referendum on the EU constitution, therefore, future enlargement is going to be much more difficult. Romania and Bulgaria should count themselves lucky if they get in under the wire, Croatia too. If the Union hangs together in its present form—by no means a certainty if France votes no next month—it may have to look for other ways to spread stability and prosperity to the mostly rackety countries round about. Already it offers nearby countries cash and technical aid, plus market access, in exchange for economic and political reforms based on European norms. But these exchanges are unlikely to produce the deep transformations which countries must attempt when they want to join the Union. They are regarded rather snootily by the recipient countries, which see themselves as being at once excluded and appeased.

One answer might be a two-tier Europe in which new countries would be invited to join the Union, but only on the basis that they would be denied Schengen membership, free movement of labour, farm subsidies, and the right to vote on constitutional issues for a long transitional period or even permanently. This would answer the main public worries in western Europe. It would anger the countries waiting to join, just as the piecemeal postponement of some rights and privileges has angered the countries which joined last year. Even so, would-be members may have to swallow some such deal, if the alternative is no more enlargement.

"Far from demonstrating that the European Union is in decline or disarray, the constitutional crisis demonstrates its essential stability and legitimacy."

A Too Perfect Union?
Why Europe Said "No"

Andrew Moravcsik

The people of France and the Netherlands have spoken. As a result of their referendums this spring, the European Union constitution is dead, as is Turkish membership in the EU, and progress in areas from services deregulation to Balkan enlargement will now be much more difficult. Yet for the chattering classes the outcome was an opportunity to repolish long-held positions. In the face of implacable opposition to Turkish membership, *The Economist* blithely interpreted the rejection of a proposed EU constitution as evidence that Europe has gone too far, too fast—except, of course, on enlargement. Oxford's Timothy Garton Ash, a perennial optimist about the reconciliation of Britain's transatlantic and European vocations, espied another promising moment for Blairite diplomacy. The court philosopher of continental social democracy, Jürgen Habermas, called on European leaders (read: his former student, German Foreign Minister Joschka Fischer) to recapture the "idealism of 1968" by leading a leftist movement against neoliberal US hegemony. With quintessentially French misanthropy, Serge July of *Libération* accused French politicians of opportunism and French voters of racism. Across the Atlantic, *Weekly Standard* editor Bill Kristol, undeterred by the massive protest vote against European economic reform, called for rejection of the welfare state, open borders to immigration, and an embrace of America.

It is time to view Europe as it really is. Far from demonstrating that the European Union is in decline or disarray, the constitutional crisis demonstrates its essential stability and legitimacy. The central error of the European constitutional framers was one of style and symbolism rather than substance. The constitution contained a set of modest reforms, very much in line with European popular preferences. Yet European leaders upset the emerging pragmatic settlement by dressing up the reforms as a grand scheme for constitutional revision and popular democratization of the EU.

Looking back in 50 years, historians will not see this year's referendums as the end of the EU—or as the beginning of the end. The union remains the most successful experiment in political institution building since World War II. Historians will see instead the last gasp of idealistic European federalism born in the mid-1940s, symbolized by the phrase "ever closer union" and aimed at establishing a United States of Europe. It is time to recognize that the EU can neither aspire to replace nation states nor seek democratic legitimacy in the same way nations do. The current EU constitutional settlement, which has defined a stable balance between Brussels and national capitals and democratic legitimacy through indirect accountability and extensive checks and balances, is here to stay. To see why this is so, we must understand the nature of the current constitutional compromise, the reasons European leaders called it into question, and the deeper lessons this teaches us about the limits of European integration.

JUST SAY NO

Voting patterns in the referendums were a reflection of three related motivations that have dominated every EU election in history. First is ideological extremism. The center supported Europe while the extreme right and left, which now account for almost one-third of the French and Dutch electorates, voted "no." Second is protest voting against unpopular governments. Third, and most important, is a reaction against the insecurity felt by poorer Europeans. Whereas business, the educated elite, and wealthier Europeans favored the constitution, those fearful of unemployment, labor market reform, globalization, privatization, and the consolidation of the welfare state opposed it. Today these concerns dovetail with the perceived economic and cultural threat posed by Muslim immigration.

This type of disaffection is the primary political problem for European governments today, since it is directed both against poor economic performance and against reform measures designed to improve it. As *Newsweek*'s Fareed Zakaria has observed, the tragedy is that "Europe needs more of what's producing populist paranoia: economic reform to survive in an era of economic competition, young immigrants to sustain its social market, and a more strategic relationship with the Muslim world, which would be dramatically enhanced by Turkish membership in the EU."

Forgotten in the electoral chaos this spring was the document itself. The constitution is, after all, a conservative text containing incremental improvements that consolidate EU developments of the past 20 years. The "no" campaigns conceded the desirability of the modest reforms from the start—including appointment of a foreign minister, formulation of a stronger anti-crime policy, and streamlining of voting procedures. Such changes are popular, not least in France, which proposed most of them. One is forced to conclude that the constitution became controversial not because its content was objectionable, but because the content was so innocuous that citizens saw a chance to cast an inexpensive protest vote.

What were they protesting against? Here, too, the referendums cannot be viewed as plebiscites directed at the EU's policies. Although the EU is associated, through its advisory "Lisbon process," with labor market and welfare reform, these matters remain firmly within the competence of the member states. The EU's activities as a whole, while they include oversight of state subsidies and trade policy, may just as reasonably be seen as part of a European effort to manage globalization rather than promote it. Opponents made occasional mention of EU policies not contained in the constitution, such as the recent enlargement to 25 members, the introduction of the euro, the deregulation of electricity, and Turkish accession. Yet only the last of these seems to have swayed many voters, and they seem to have been unaware that free migration has been ruled out even before negotiations begin.

So what lesson should the EU take away? The relative lack of direct criticism of the constitution, the lack of fundamental objections to EU policies, and, above all, the stunning lack of positive proposals for reform are striking evidence of the underlying stability of the EU system. The 16 years since the fall of the Berlin Wall have been, after all, the most successful period in EU history. The single market, the euro, and a nascent European foreign and defense policy came into being. EU enlargement was carried out with surprisingly little disruption in existing member states, and proved the most cost-effective Western instrument for advancing global democracy and security. In sum, notwithstanding the rejection of the proposed charter, the EU appears to have quietly reached a stable constitutional settlement.

FIXING THE UNBROKEN

What is this settlement? The EU is now preeminent in trade, agriculture, fishing, eurozone monetary policy, and some business regulation, and helps to coordinate cooperation in foreign policy. Contrary to statistics one often reads, this amounts to only about 20 percent of European regulation and legislation. Most areas of greatest public concern—taxes, health, pensions, education, crime, infrastructure, defense, and immigration—remain firmly national. With a tax base one-fiftieth the size of the member states', an administration smaller than that of a small city, no police force or army, and a narrow legal mandate, the EU will never encompass these fiscally and administratively demanding tasks.

There is no new *grand projet*, akin to the single market of the 1980s or the single currency of the 1990s, to justify change. In 18 months of deliberation, the constitutional convention devoted only two days to the expansion of EU competencies. European health, pension, fiscal, and education policies have little support, while a US-style military buildup exceeds Europe's means and insults its "civilian power" ideals. There was always less to the constitution than both its proponents and its detractors proclaimed.

Many believe that a European defense independent of the United States poses an imminent threat to US interests. Of course, it is true that if the United States were again to attempt an operation on the scale of Iraq with so little substantive justification or multilateral legitimation, European nations would be uniformly opposed. (Even the British government has already declared that it does not see any useful military options for regime change in Iran.) But another Iraq is an unlikely possibility, given the evident costs of that imbroglio; the United States is militarily incapable of repeating this adventure at the current time. More important is the fact that the United States and the EU have agreed on every other major use of force since the 1989 Gulf War. More than 100,000 European troops are currently stationed out of their home countries, most involved in operations that involve the United States.

The ambition to form a European Union military or diplomatic superpower with a principal mission of opposing American "hyperpower" is little more than—and always was little more than—idle talk. Only the combination of ignorance and bias regarding the EU that is so uniquely concentrated among self-reinforcing groups of US neoconservatives and British Euroskeptics could construe the EU as a military or geopolitical threat. As recently as a year ago, many conservatives pleaded with the Bush administration to oppose the EU constitution, encourage British withdrawal, and insist on the unconditional predominance of NATO. With the recent European trips by Secretary of State Condoleezza Rice and President George W. Bush, these demands for an aggressive policy toward Europe have been definitively rebuffed.

Consider also European social policy, of which we heard so much in the referendum campaigns. What concrete EU policies should this imply? Blocking sensible efforts to reform the welfare state for long-term sustainability is shortsighted. While many studies show that a division of labor between the new and old members of the EU will generate growth, there is little evidence of a regulatory or fiscal "race to the bottom" driven by the EU, and plenty of room remains for social policy at the national level. The neoliberal "Anglo-Saxon" threat is a myth. Britain is building up its welfare state faster than any of its partners, based partly on a Scandinavian model. Indeed, with continental liberalization and British social democratization, Europe's social systems are converging—through the pressure of national politics, not as the result of some EU social policy pipe dream.

A similar constitutional compromise has emerged with regard to institutions. Although Anglo-American Euroskeptics have sought to resurrect the bogeyman of a Brussels superstate headed by the European Commission, treaty changes since 1970 have consistently moved Europe in the opposite direction. They have increased the power of the council of ministers (favored by France and Britain, particularly for matters outside the economic core) and the directly elected European parliament (favored by Germany) at the expense of the technocratic commission.

The proposed constitution sought to marginally improve the EU's efficiency and transparency while retaining its basic structure. All of this is the sensible stuff policy wonks love and publics generally support. The constitution called for expanding the role of the directly elected European parliament in EU legislation (termed "co-decision" in Brussels-speak), giving national parliaments an advisory and gate-keeping role, abolishing the rotating presidency, adjusting voting weights to represent large countries more fairly, and centralizing foreign policy coordination in a foreign minister. The proposal was a multinational constitutional compromise that attended to the interests of large and small countries, left and right parties, and Europhile and Euroskeptic tendencies.

> *It is time to recognize that the EU can neither aspire to replace nation states nor seek democratic legitimacy in the same way nations do.*

The reforms enjoyed broad support among member states, and none met a serious challenge in the referendum debates. The biggest change—creation of a European foreign minister empowered to recommend, though not impose, a more coordinated foreign policy—enjoys 70 percent approval across Europe. And recognizing the EU as it is, the constitution struck the classic idealist phrase "ever closer union" from the Treaty of Rome, and substituted the more balanced "unity in diversity."

UNDONE BY IDEALISM

So it was not the substance of the emerging constitutional settlement that triggered opposition. The objectionable aspect was its form: an idealistic constitution. Since the 1970s, lawyers have regarded the 1957 Treaty of Rome as a de facto constitution. The new document was an unnecessary public relations exercise based on the seemingly intuitive, but in fact peculiar, notion that democratization and the European ideal could legitimate the EU. In the wake of the Nice and Amsterdam treaties, which consolidated the union, Euro-enthusiast scholars, politicians, and commentators have argued that the EU is unpopular primarily because it is secretive, complex, unaccountable, and distant from the public— in sum, because it suffers from a "democratic deficit." Fischer, the German foreign minister, gave the idea of constitutional legitimation a big push with his celebrated lecture on the ultimate goal of integration at Humboldt University in 2000. But like the other European leaders who jumped on his bandwagon, Fischer, while ostensibly transcending a narrow, national discourse, was in fact framing the argument in a familiar domestic manner: in his case 1968-style German anti-nationalism.

The idea was to legitimate the EU not through trade, economic growth, and useful regulation, as had been the case for 50 years, but by politicizing and democratizing it. This was to be done through a constitutional convention. Enthused by the prospect of a reenactment of Philadelphia 1787, millions of web-savvy Europeans were supposed to deliberate the meaning of Europe. More pragmatic voices hoped to combat cynicism by simplifying the treaty and delineating EU prerogatives. To justify the need for change, reformers also seized on the perception that the EU would require a radical overhaul to avoid gridlock with 25 rather than 15 members—a fear that now seems unjustified, both because the new states are proving constructive and because the EU is not moving as far or fast as it once did.

Of course, the constitutional deliberation did not mobilize Europeans. Few citizens were even aware of the 200 *conventionnels'* deliberations. When testimony from civil society was requested, professors turned up. When a youth conference was called, would-be Eurocrats attended. When those who did attend came to consider democracy, they found that the arrangement Europe currently has is appropriate to a diverse polity in which member states insist on checks and balances at every level. There was little popular or elite support for democratic reform beyond the modest increases in scrutiny by national and European parliaments the constitution contains.

This is as it should be, for there is no "democratic deficit" in the EU—or not much of one. Once we set aside ideal notions of democracy and look to real-world standards, we see that the EU is as transparent, responsive, accountable, and honest as its member states. The relative lack of centralized financial or administrative discretion all but eliminates corruption. The EU's areas of autonomous authority—trade policy, constitutional adjudication, and central banking—are the same as those in most democracies, where these functions are politically insulated for sound reasons.

The notion of imposing democratic control through multiple checks and balances, rather than through elections to a single sovereign parliament, is more American than European—but it is no less legitimate for that. Everyone gets a say in a system in which a European directive needs approval from a technocratic commission, a supermajority of democratic national governments, and a directly elected parliament, and must then be implemented by national regulators. Studies show that EU legislation is both consensual and relatively responsive to shifts in partisan and popular opinion.

Enthusiasts for democracy fail to grasp its limits. Engaging European citizens will not necessarily create rational (let alone supportive) debate, because those with intense preferences about the EU tend to be its opponents. Average citizens and political parties keep but a few issues—usually those involving heavy taxing and spending—in mind at any one time, and thus respond only to highly salient ideals and issues. The pull of Europe remains weak, while the bread and butter policies citizens care about most, including the welfare and identity issues that dominated the referendum debates, remain almost exclusively in national hands. The failure of European elections to generate high turnouts or focus on EU issues over the years suggests that citizens fail to participate in EU politics not because they are blocked from doing so, but because they have insufficient incentive.

Some democratic enthusiasts propose jump-starting EU democracy by incorporating hot-button issues like social policy and immigration, despite the lack of popular support for doing so. This is, in essence, Habermas's vision. Yet anyone except a philosopher like Habermas can see that this is the sort of extreme cure that will kill the patient. There is little that could lead the European public to decisively reject an institution as deeply embedded as the EU, but transferring controversial issues like social policy to it without justification might just do it.

The constitution became controversial not because its content was objectionable, but because the content was so innocuous that citizens saw a chance to cast an inexpensive protest vote.

More sober voices propose to empower national parliaments, which the constitution sought to do in a modest way. Yet this reveals a final fallacy of the democratizers. There is little reason to believe that turning policy over to a legislature makes it more legitimate. In Western democracies, popularity is inversely correlated with direct electoral accountability. The most popular institutions are the courts, the police, and the military. Parliaments are generally disliked. Whatever the source of Europe's declining popularity—a general decline in political trust, unfamiliarity with institutions, xenophobia, discontent with economic performance—it has little to do with Europe's democratic mandate.

Forcing an unstructured debate about an institution that handles matters like telecommunications standardization, the composition of the Bosnia stabilization force, and the privatization of electricity production inexorably drove debate to the lowest common denominator. When pro-European political elites found themselves defending a constitution with modest content, they felt they had no alternative but to oversell it using inflated notions of what the EU does and rhetoric drawn from 1950s European idealism. Small wonder they were outgunned by grumpy populists with stronger symbols rooted in class, nation, and race (and even more inflated views of what the EU does). Publics became confused and alarmed by the scare tactics of both sides. The referendums came to inhabit a strange twilight zone of symbolic politics, in which claims about the EU bore little relationship to reality, and support and opposition for a status quo constitution became a potent symbol for the myriad hopes and fears of modern electorates.

A UNION THAT WORKS

In the wake of this debacle, European politicians must find a constructive path forward. They should start with a collective mea culpa. The document itself must be renounced. Then, over the next few years, the EU should return to its successful tradition of quiet and pragmatic reform. Europeans consistently support incremental advances in the union's foreign, internal security, and economic policies along the lines set forth in the constitution.

Turkish membership is off the agenda, as it probably would have been even without the referendums, which revealed a considerable degree of popular concern and some virulent opposition to Turkish membership. To quell it, France committed itself to another referendum, should the question arise—a procedure also required by some other EU national constitutions. It is clear that a high-profile move toward Turkey at this point would bolster popular fear of and opposition to the EU—which are otherwise likely to wither

away. Negotiations with Turkey should and will be pursued, so as to maintain the momentum of reform in that country. It should be obvious, however, that no further movement on accession is likely for some time. The best outcome would be for talks to continue quietly for a decade or two while Europeans attend to more pressing and practical plans for Balkan enlargement. Politicians need to concede this, and concede it loud and clear, not least in order to preserve continued EU enlargement in the Balkans.

A halfway arrangement acceptable to both EU and Turkish publics remains a realistic goal over the next 20 years, and may be better for Turkey than the limited type of EU membership that is currently on offer. This arrangement might provide for even freer trade, substantial regulatory convergence, and close cooperation on foreign and internal security policies, perhaps culminating in a privileged associate status. No other European policy could contribute as much to global peace and security.

Above all, European politicians need to acknowledge explicitly the existence of a stable European constitutional settlement. The unique genius of the EU is that it locks in policy coordination while respecting the powerful rhetoric and symbols that still attach to national identity. Publics will be reassured if it is portrayed as stable and successful. There is no shameful compromise with grand principles here. On the contrary, it is a highly appealing constitutional order that preserves national democratic politics for the issues most salient to citizens while delegating to more indirect democratic forms those issues that are of less concern—or on which there is an administrative, technical, or legal consensus.

The EU's distinctive system of multilevel governance is the only new form of state organization to emerge and prosper since the rise of the welfare state at the turn of the twentieth century. Now it is a mature constitutional order, one that no longer needs to move forward to legitimate its past and present successes. Left behind must be the European centralizers and democratizers for whom "ever closer union" remains an end in itself. They will insist that the answer to failed democracy is more democracy and the answer to a failed constitution is another constitution. But Europe has moved beyond them. Disowning this well-meaning, even admirable, band of idealists may seem harsh, but it is both necessary and just. On this basis, Europeans can develop a new discourse of national interest, pragmatic cooperation, and constitutional stability—a discourse that sees Europe as it is. The constitution is dead, long live the constitution!

ANDREW MORAVCSIK is a professor of politics at Princeton University, where he directs the European Union program. He is the editor of Europe without Illusions *(Lanham, Md.: University Press of America, 2005).*

After the votes: Europe's leaders confront the consequences of 'the wrong answer'

Attachment to the European ideal has waned and French and Dutch citizens found few compelling reasons to support the constitutional treaty. It could be years before consensus emerges on what the EU must do.

George Parker

Over the last heady weeks in the European Union, a kind of revolution has been under way: a movement of dissent that found its voice in the votes against the EU constitution in France and the Netherlands and is still fomenting across the continent. French and Dutch voters have almost certainly killed the constitutional treaty but stark images from the campaign tell a more profound story of how the European project and its elite became fatally disconnected from its citizens.

One image is of a desperate Jacques Chirac, French president, thrashing around for ways to convince a television audience of young people why they should love the EU. Pollsters watching the 72-year-old's performance noted how the audience was unmoved as Mr Chirac recalled the union's founding purpose: to remove the threat of war from the continent. He simply failed to connect.

A second image is of a weary Jean-Claude Juncker, the Luxembourg prime minister, insisting on the night of the Dutch No that the constitution was still alive. He wants both countries to vote again so they can give "the right answer".

But the postwar certainty of Europe's elite has been shattered over the last few days, after France voted by a ratio of 55-45 against the proposed new EU constitution and the Dutch by a bigger margin of 62-38.

The new image of Europe is one of No voters in the streets of Toulouse and Amsterdam—some of them waving the EU's version of the star-spangled banner—partying into the night and demanding a new approach.

There has been little attempt to minimise the significance of the French and Dutch No votes. Mr Chirac claimed France would "cease to exist politically"; Mr Juncker warned of a "catastrophe"; Gerrit Zalm, Dutch finance minister, said the "lights would go out". Their predictions are based not so much on the likely demise of the constitution but on the political fall-out from a fundamental rejection of the EU by two of its founding members.

The constitution itself is less than it sounds: "We should never have called it a constitution," admits Denis MacShane, Britain's former Europe minister. "That was our big mistake." In fact it is a dry 324-page international treaty that aims to improve the operation of the enlarged EU of 25, including the creation of a foreign minister, a full-time president and a new voting system to stop the club grinding to a halt.

Some of these may yet be salvaged as the constitution's carcase is picked over. There are proposals to make the union a bit more democratic—a bigger role for national parliaments and for the European parliament—and a modest increase in "federal" powers in areas such as asylum and immigration. But the bulk of the constitution is simply a pulling together of old treaties within one cover. So when French and Dutch voters kicked out the constitution, they were not simply opposing what the European Union might become: they were rejecting what it already is.

"We have a serious problem," admitted José Manuel Barroso, European Commission president. The constitution was supposed to connect Europe to its citizens, not sever the ties. The big question hanging over Europe's elite is: how do we get out of it? The EU has a serious existentialist question when its citizens cannot remember why it was created, they do not appear to like what it has become and they are frightened of what it will be in the future.

It used to be simple. German diplomats recall how, when Hans-Dietrich Genscher was foreign minister, they would pass potentially difficult policy papers to him with a crucial final line: "This will be good for integration." His signature was immediately forthcoming. The European political and economic integration process launched with the Treaty of Rome in 1957 was barely questioned, as it created the prosperity and trust needed to raise western Europe from the rubble of the second world war.

But the EU has become a victim of its own success. War has receded into the distant memory—in western Europe at least—and means little to two generations. Meanwhile, the economic prosperity and comfortable lifestyles of Europe's social model, underpinned by the EU's single market, have already been banked by Europe's citizens. As the union's original emotional power over its citizens—its ability to deliver postwar security and prosperity—has waned, they have started to see the EU more as a bureaucratic machine. "We don't dream of Europe any more," lamented Mr Juncker, the current holder of the EU presidency.

On to this faceless machine have been projected many of the fears and suspicions of the Dutch and French electorates, who found dozens of reasons to vote against Europe and few compelling reasons to vote for it.

From the French, there was opposition to the "Anglo-Saxon" economic model supposedly in the ascendant in Brussels, a distrust of an enlarged Europe and a rejection of future Turkish membership of the EU. Turkophobia was shared by the Dutch No camp but its gripes also included the poor performance of the euro, the domination of Europe by big countries and a loss of national sovereignty to Brussels. It was a mixed message, bound up intrinsically with national political debate, but it sends out a strong warning to Europe's leaders that in future they should not take public opinion for granted.

The first casualty of the French and Dutch No votes is likely to be Europe's future enlargement programme, which has helped to bring stability and prosperity to the former dictatorships of Spain, Portugal, Greece and most recently in eastern Europe. "Enlargement is not guilty of Europe's problems," pleaded Olli Rehn, the Finnish enlargement commissioner, yesterday, arguing that a lack of economic reform in "old" member states was the root cause of their high unemployment. But already Europe's shutters can perhaps be heard coming down; Turkey, Ukraine, the western Balkans and even Romania and Bulgaria could be left outside.

Then there is the risk to Europe's liberal economic reform agenda, promoted by the Barroso Commission, which Mr Chirac denounces as "Anglo-Saxon". Mr Barroso and the British presidency of the EU, which starts on July 1, will attempt to promote reforms including deregulation, a crackdown on state aid and a revival of the controversial plan to open up Europe's services market, which amounts to as much as 70 per cent of EU gross domestic product. While Mr Chirac may try to obstruct liberal economic reforms, Britain and its liberal allies (including many eastern European countries) will act to frustrate any attempts by France to export its creaking social model. Yesterday, Britain assembled a coalition including Germany, Poland and Slovakia to block an attempt—championed by France—to limit working hours in the UK.

The social and liberal camps have fought themselves to a standstill. If the death of the constitution stops Europe moving ahead, some fear the political tension unleashed by the double No votes could lead to the EU's starting to unwind, leaving at risk its most ambitious project: the euro.

The markets have forced the currency sharply lower in recent days against the dollar, with some banks, even speculating on the euro's eventual demise—a view [described] as "utter nonsense" by Nout Wellink, the Dutch central bank governor who is a member of the European Central Bank's governing council. Nevertheless, the euro is part of an intensely political project—an economic and monetary union—that demands from its members a high level of European solidarity, including a willingness to accept the constraints of a one-size-fits-all interest rate and common fiscal rules.

Dutch No voters signalled their suspicion that solidarity is already breaking down, a point illustrated this week when Jean-Louis Debré, a close ally of Mr Chirac, said the French government would increase social spending regardless of whether it broke the EU's deficit rules. "Today that's no longer the problem," he said.

If one includes in the EU's woes the ongoing dispute between rich and poor countries over the financing of the next seven-year EU budget round, the constitutional debacle can be seen as a climactic expression of a general breakdown in European co-operation and confidence in the future.

Where does the European Union go from here? Initially there will be a period of bitter introspection, to the despair of those in Washington and elsewhere who want to see Europe take a more active role in the world. Peter Mandelson, Britain's EU trade commissioner, has called for Europe to "hit the pause button" and stop things spiralling out of control. "The priorities must be survival and revival," he told colleagues this week.

Mr Mandelson believes the EU must set out its vision and sell it; but it could be years before a political consensus emerges to convince a sceptical public of the merits of free trade, deregulated labour markets and a Europe that extends to the steppes and the Black Sea.

But above all Europe needs leadership, at a time when most of its national leaders are clinging to power, buffeted by globalisation and resorting to "Brussels-bashing" as a way of shifting the blame. Traditionally, this would be a time for the Franco-German motor to whir into action—and there is speculation in Brussels that the old couple would try to revive the idea of a "core Europe" to breathe life into the project. "But what would we do?" asks a diplomat from one of affected countries. "Where are the areas of agreement, and who would follow Chirac now?"

Even Germany and France would struggle to come up with policy areas around which a core could be built. "There are no big new projects," admits an aide to Mr Barroso. Others in Brussels argue that Europe will move ahead again only after a wholesale change of the guard in the national capitals, particularly in Berlin, Paris and London. Angela Merkel, Germany's opposition conservative leader, and Nicolas Sarkozy, the populist, liberal rival to Mr Chirac, would bring a dose of free-market enthusiasm to complement that already embraced in London. Since both leaders are also instinctively pro-American, that could ease the geopolitical divide that has gripped Europe since Mr Chirac and Gerhard Schröder, the German chancellor, led opposition to the war in Iraq.

In what one EU official calls "the optimist scenario", Tony Blair would be replaced by Gordon Brown, his chancellor of the exchequer, who has a more continental approach to strong public service provision. "He's seen as less of a threat than Blair," the official says.

Ms Merkel, Mr Sarkozy and Mr Brown might offer a fresh start for Europe, but they are no euro-dreamers; any enthusiasm for Brussels they might have is based on what it can deliver in terms of jobs, growth and international clout. But hard-headed realism and results may well be what the young people on the streets of France and the Netherlands were asking for when they voted Non or Nee, not Europe's lofty founding vision of "ever closer union".

Article 30. After the votes: Europe's leaders confront the consequences of 'the wrong answer'

Mr Sarkozy struck a chord—a rarity in the French Yes campaign—when he told students that Europe had given them cheap mobile phones and budget airlines. It lacks the emotional appeal of the likes of Francois Mitterrand and Helmut Kohl, the former leaders of France and Germany, whose vision of Europe was inspired by the horrors of their countries' 1916 battle of Verdun. But it may be a European message for our times.

Putin Gambles on Raw Power

By STEVEN LEE MYERS

MOSCOW

Countries react differently to terror. After the Sept. 11 attacks, Americans rallied behind their government of their own free will. After the Madrid train bombings last March, Spaniards ousted theirs. President Vladimir V. Putin took steps last week that seem to ensure that Russians will do neither.

After modern Russia's worst terrorist act—the horrifying seizure of a school that ended with more than 300 hostages dead—Mr. Putin ordered an overhaul of the political system, stripping Russians of their right to elect their governors and district representatives in Parliament. Mr. Putin's response seemed like a non sequitur, since how the country conducts its elections on the regional level has little, if anything, to do with fighting the terrorism that war in Chechnya has spawned. But there was a logic to it, at least for Mr. Putin and his supporters, and it was one that dashed—perhaps decisively—hopes here and abroad that Russia had left behind its long, tortured history of authoritarianism when the Soviet Union collapsed.

The Kremlin has tried the iron hand before. In the end, it fails.

Democracy, Mr. Putin suggested in remarks after the school siege, does not result in stability, but rather instability. It does not unify, but rather divides. The principal threat posed by democracy in Russia today, he made clear on separate occasions in the last two weeks, lies in simmering ethnic and religious tensions along the rim of Russia where ethnically non-Russian people live. That division, he suggested, can only be controlled with an iron hand from above.

The attack on the school in Beslan was a watershed in a country that has had its share of them in history. And to Mr. Putin's critics, it confirmed their fears that, instinctively, he puts his faith in the Kremlin's unquestioned authority as the force to hold Russia together.

In the tragic arc of Russian history, it has always been so—even if, in the end, the rigid power of the center has always failed.

A theme of those who accepted Mr. Putin's prescription was distrust of the unruliness of electoral will in a country with deep ethnic, social, class and religious divisions.

It was those divisions that the fighters who seized the school—terrorists loyal to the Chechen separatist commander Shamil Basayev—seemed eager to stoke when they struck in multiethnic North Ossetia.

They seemed well aware that what Russia has failed to do in more than 13 years of post-Soviet politics is develop a sense of national identity that might overcome those divisions. Indeed, in the southern and Asian areas where Russia's Muslim groups live, an ardent religious identification is threatening to take its place.

"We live in conditions of aggravated internal conflicts and interethnic conflicts that before were harshly suppressed by the governing ideology," Mr. Putin said the night after the siege in Beslan ended on Sept. 3. In his speech, he lamented the demise of "a huge, great country," the Soviet Union, and rued the forces of disorder that its dissolution unleashed in Russia.

He returned to the theme four days later when he met with a group of American and European academics and analysts. Media accounts afterward focused on his pointed rebuff of calls to negotiate with Chechnya's separatists, whom he equated with Al Qaeda and Osama bin Laden. More telling about his plans to come was his reference to an obscure electoral dispute in Karachayevo-Cherkessia, one of the troubled republics of the North Caucasus.

In 1999, a disputed presidential election split the republic's two main ethnic groups, the Karachai and the Cherkess. As Mr. Putin recounted it, only his intervention—as prime minister, at the time—averted a civil war.

Clifford Kupchan, vice president of the Nixon Center in Washington, attended the meeting with Mr. Putin, and summarized Mr. Putin's dark view of democracy as "one man, one vote, one war."

"Given that Russia is not a melting pot, but rather a fragmented pot," Mr. Kupchan said in an interview, "he does not believe that democracy is the solution."

As he has before, Mr. Putin insisted last week that Russia remained on a democratic course, but he did so more reservedly than ever. When he announced his political overhaul on Monday, he said, "we must also, of course, react adequately to everything happening within the country."

In the turbulent years since the Soviet Union collapsed in 1991, Russia's embrace of democracy—and Mr. Putin's—has always been awkward.

The country's Constitution, written in 1993 after President Boris N. Yeltsin ordered the shelling of Parliament to roust defiant legislators, codifies basic democratic freedoms. In practice, though, democracy has been treated as little more than a license for a well-positioned few to steal and loot the old Soviet assets and to exploit Russians' baser instincts, especially when it comes to ethnic minorities.

Grigory A. Yavlinsky, one of the country's most prominent liberals, said the public's concept of democracy had been tainted by financial scandals and crises, by the consolidation of wealth in the hands of a few well-connected billionaires, by a decade of war in Chechnya, and lately by a wave of terrorist attacks, staged not in symbols of grandeur like skyscrapers and government buildings, but in places chillingly familiar to virtually every Russian: trains, subways, airplanes, a theater and, worst, a school.

On the southern rim, religion has begun to challenge the nation as a source of identity.

"All this period of time was called democracy," Mr. Yavlinsky said in an interview. "The people looked at it and said, 'If that is democracy, then, thank you very much.'" But he added, angrily: "All these things had nothing in common with democracy. It was Potemkin democracy."

During his presidency, Mr. Putin has shown little enthusiasm for the democratic experience. He has smothered political opponents, wrested control of independent television and manipulated the outcome of regional elections, none more so than the two presidential elections in Chechnya, where loyalists were elected by Soviet-like margins last October and again last month, after credible challengers were struck from the ballots.

Still, until Monday, Mr. Putin had never before reversed the fundamental democratic right of representation through the ballot—a right enshrined in the Constitution's letter and spirit, according to his critics. Under his proposal, which the Parliament will almost certainly adopt since it is dominated by parties loyal to him, Mr. Putin will appoint governors, presidents or other leaders who are now elected in each of country's 89 regions. Mr. Putin's proposals also would eliminate the district elections that choose half of the 450 seats in Parliament; instead, they will be selected based on national party lists drafted in Moscow in close consultation with Mr. Putin's Kremlin.

What was striking last week was how many Russian elected officials heartily endorsed Mr. Putin's plan.

"Elections are often dirty, with money from the shadow economy and criminal groups trying to influence the results," Valentina I. Matviyenko, the governor of St. Petersburg, told Itar-Tass on Wednesday as she fell into line behind a proposal that would deny her much of her electoral legitimacy and political authority. (She was elected last fall and, apparently, knew whereof she spoke.) "All this causes concern and alarm."

Her counterpart, Murat M. Zyazikov, president of the semi-autonomous republic of Ingushetia, who was elected with the Kremlin's help, echoed her fears. In a telephone interview, he said that elections had turned into "competitions between people with more money, which resulted in tensions in society."

"Western and human values are very close to us, but we have our own way of development," he said. "I think this was done in order to consolidate society."

In other words, it would seem, "the people have spoken" remains a phrase that strikes fear in Russia's ruling elite, which presumes to know better what is better for the country.

"It is soft Stalinism," Mr. Yavlinsky said.

He and others have spoken out against Mr. Putin's reordering, but they have done so from the margins. A rally organized by Mr. Yavlinsky's Yabloko party—with posters of Mr. Putin as Hitler—drew a handful of protesters. A few of the 15 independent members of Parliament voiced objections and then admitted there was little they could do to stop Mr. Putin.

The most prominent criticism came from the two men who, arguably, did much to create the system Russia has today, for better or worse. In twinned essays that appeared on Friday in the newsweekly Moskovskiye Novosti, Mr. Yeltsin and Mikhail S. Gorbachev wrote that Russia should preserve the democratic gains of the last 13 years.

"Strangling freedoms and curtailing democratic rights," Mr. Yeltsin wrote, "marks, among other things, the victory of terrorists."

What Does Putin Want?

"It is not hard to see Putin as an authoritarian. In most ways he is, based on Western standards. But, given Russia's current development trajectory, he probably has to be.... Either the Kremlin continues its very hard-handed approach to restructuring the economy or Russia risks becoming in effect a Burkina Faso with nuclear weapons."

PETER LAVELLE

With Russia seemingly returning to its opaque Soviet-like state, many Western journalists and analysts have also returned to their favorite Russia-watching pastime: asking the question, "Who is Putin?" Attempts at answers have rendered limited results, and they mostly overlook what is happening in Vladimir Putin's Russia. More times than not, perceptions of Russia remain at sharp variance with reality. Asking a better question—"What does Putin want?"—may tell us something about the Russia he intends to create.

President Putin's agenda is, if anything, straightforward. What may seem a lurch back to the Soviet past or a lunge forward to a new form of authoritarianism is in fact Russia overcoming the chaos of the first decade of postcommunism. Putin wants to develop a modern economy, end economic oligarchy, and assure that Russia's energy resources serve the national interest. He is willing to strengthen the state at the expense of democratic institutions if necessary. He wants to protect property rights, attract foreign investment, and restore an image of strength in the world. His pragmatism is evident for anyone who wishes to see it.

THE ECONOMIC REFORM AGENDA

Recently, much of the mainstream media and a number of academics have cast doubt on Putin's commitment to the development of a modern market economy in Russia. When Putin entered office, his support for liberalizing economic reform was clear to anyone who had taken care to note his past as a key aide to St. Petersburg Mayor Anatoly Sobchak, as well as his statements in his early days as acting president. Putin saw market reforms then as Russia's only credible future. A reasonable assessment of his economic agenda suggests he still does today—albeit to further the political goal of more broadly dispersed prosperity.

The economic reality presented to Putin when he assumed office in 2000 essentially consisted of competing claims made by the oil sector and the much weaker industrial lobby. The top five oil producers early on announced

a plan to significantly expand capacity, aggressively pushing for almost uninterrupted growth in oil production and exports. Market observers and analysts assessed the oil lobby's strategy as the "easy money" option. An eager and prepared market for oil and gas exports awaited in the United States, as well as in Russia's European and Asian neighbors, all seeking another source of energy besides the volatile Middle East.

The counterpoised agenda came from the weak but resurgent industrial lobby, which has been campaigning hard to have the Russian government diversify away from a dangerously high reliance on the oil and gas sector. This lobby petitions for government special preferences and investment incentives for Russia's other traditional industries, including aerospace, aviation, defense, and steel fabrication. Advocates argue that Russia still has a chance to develop global leadership in these areas, and they also push for building a domestic financial services industry.

Both lobbying groups have been forceful in the media in conveying their respective agendas to determine Russia's economic future. During Putin's first term the oil lobby appeared ascendant, and it has remained so to the present. But this ascendance may prove temporary.

Another plan for Russia's longer-term economic future has been aired, and repeatedly supported by none other than President Putin, yet analysts often neglect it. Announced at the start of 2000, this budgetary and economic policy calls for exploiting high inflows of cash from oil and gas exports to aggressively push broad-based growth across all economic sectors. Putin's objective, clearly and consistently stated over the past four years, is to eventually achieve a more diversified and balanced economy—an economy, that is, along lines seen in most European Union countries—with the intent of creating a greater and more egalitarian dispersion of wealth across the entire population.

A June 2004 study by the World Bank confirms Putin's political instincts. The report concludes, insofar as international comparisons are possible, that Russia has one of the most concentrated economies in the world, if not the most concentrated. A group of billionaires called the "oligarchs" largely controls the economy. Furthermore, ownership concentration is highly sector-specific: major owners dominate large industrial and raw materials sectors. Clearly, with these sectors constituting the Russian economy's main pillar (and primary source of exports), their owners can dominate the economy and, ultimately, politics and economic strategy. The World Bank analysis notes that, because of the immature market for ownership rights, "ownership in Russia's economy has not yet gone through the sort of 'remixing' which would have eliminated the most obvious traces of the transition from state to private ownership."

One key to creating a modern market economy in Russia is to reform, and in many cases gut, outdated and economically dysfunctional Soviet social services. To achieve this goal, Putin has risked his stellar public opinion ratings. He also has embarked on these structural changes while trying to break up economic and political oligarchy. This is no coincidence.

At the center of attempts to purge the Russian economy of residual Soviet elements is the monetization of the country's social benefits. Although Russia's economy was largely monetized between 1991 and 1992, it is often overlooked that the system of social benefits remained virtually unchanged from the Soviet era. The government continued to mandate discounts on pharmaceuticals, transportation, communications, and housing for retirees, military personnel, the disabled, and other dependent groups. As in the Soviet system, programs of in-kind benefits remained rife with corruption.

Putin's response has been to dismantle and remove the Soviet social programs, even though the political costs in doing so may rise as new benefit programs are put into place between now and 2006 and as the transition costs pile up. Thus far the reform project has been highly unpopular among recipients of outdated Soviet benefits, with Putin's popularity taking a strong hit for the first time during his presidency.

CUTTING DOWN THE OLIGARCHS

This is where the Yukos affair comes in. It would have been politically irresponsible, even dangerous, for Putin to impose additional sacrifices on ordinary Russians as part of structural reforms effected over the next few years without the recent demonstration of state power against the oligarchs. The prosecution of Mikhail Khodorkovsky, the head of Yukos Oil and Russia's richest man, has added to Putin's public support. The oligarchs, after all, are the personification of what went wrong during the 1990s, when a group of super-wealthy individuals essentially ruled Russia, and economic and political power was intensely concentrated as it had been during the Soviet era.

While trying to reduce the state's role in mandating costly entitlements, Putin has sought to increase the state's ability to govern by taking in more tax revenue that the growing economy generates. Only with effective tax collection can Moscow deal with the country's pervasive poverty and gross income differentials. And this, too, is related to the Yukos affair. The Kremlin has put on display an enormous legal arsenal in going after billions of dollars in taxes

allegedly owed by Yukos. Other major tax offenders are unlikely to challenge the Kremlin again.

The effect is not lost on the public. Public opinion has long regarded the oligarchs as gross tax avoiders. Putin is attempting to completely reorder Russia's tax payment and collection system as part of his plans to modernize the economy. To convince ordinary Russians to honor their tax obligations, a public example had to be made of the oligarchs—with Yukos, Russia's largest privately held company, the signature demonstration. In this respect, Moscow is employing a strategy similar to one used by governments to prosecute organized crime. Since the state's resources are limited, it pursues the offender with the highest profile, hoping that others, along with ordinary Russians, will get the message and act accordingly.

The message appears to be working. Russian oil companies such as Tyumen Oil-British Petroleum, Sibneft, and Slavneft have announced that they will increase effective tax rates. In addition, as with most governments in oil-exporting nations, higher effective tax rates are expected during a time of extraordinarily high international petroleum prices. Overall, Russia's tax revenues during the first half of 2004 rose by 23 percent. Increased tax collection in the oil sector has allowed the government to lower tax obligations elsewhere.

With Yukos and its core shareholders serving as a test case, Russia's oligarchs will find themselves either cut down to size or allowed the kind of role that big business plays in other modernized economies. This outcome should not be regarded as regressive. Almost by definition, oligarchy represents a manner of fusing economic and political power within one person that institutions in the West have precluded since the 1920s.

In Russia, the concentration of both economic and political power in the hands of a few natural-resource oligarchs has been a brake on economic growth and diversification. Through their political influence, and in the face of weak state oversight and a weak industrial sector lobby, the oligarchs were generally able to divert public economic resources toward their own core business concerns and away from other parts of the investment-starved economy. The outcome of this arrangement has been all too obvious: cash generation, in the form of largely untaxed profits, was transferred abroad to avoid the tax authorities and the Russian public, should the state ever start questioning the legitimacy of the gains.

The Yukos affair represents a strong effort to alter the correlation of power between the regime and the oligarchs, designed to turn them into allies and servants rather than competitors and opponents of the state. Putin's thinking on the subject was revealed in a remarkable statement in 2003. "We have a category of people who have become rich and billionaires ... overnight," he said. "The state has appointed them billionaires, simply by giving away its assets practically free."

While more cases similar to the Yukos affair may occur, a comprehensive annihilation of the oligarchs appears unlikely. Putin wants a partial "nationalization" of the oligarch class, not the complete renationalization of their assets. Moving forward, the Kremlin will in effect appoint or dismiss or tolerate oligarchs-cum-big-businessmen based on their performance and their compatibility with national economic goals.

ENDING BIG OIL'S SELF-SERVICE

Seen in this light, the Kremlin's assault on Yukos is hardly an impulsive act of political and economic terrorism against property rights in the oil industry. Compared internationally, Russia is the only major oil exporter (and the only major oil-producing country with the two exceptions of the United States and United Kingdom) where the state is not the major operator drilling and lifting crude for production and export. The Kremlin is reordering the oil sector to roughly match international norms.

Putin is also looking to the future. Since 1999, Russia's petroleum production has increased 48 percent, primarily because of new wells. Turning out 9 million barrels of oil a day, Russia competes with Saudi Arabia as the world's largest exporter. Now Putin has called on his oil ministers to finalize plans for adding export pipelines to boost output to 11 million barrels per day by 2009. Russia's expected export increase, in conjunction with other world suppliers, could lower the cost of crude oil as early as 2006.

Because of almost unprecedented global demand and equally unprecedented high oil prices, the Kremlin's coffers receive an additional $1.5 billion per month over budget projections. A number of experts claim high petroleum prices last year accounted for almost half of Russia's 7.3 percent growth in gross domestic product. But who benefits from this? Putin has stated that "The government must base its decisions on the interests of the state as a whole and not on those of individual companies." And these are not just words; Russia's oil giants Lukoil and Sibneft are acutely aware that Putin means business.

Lukoil, Russia's second-largest petroleum firm, already has expressed its willingness to pay more taxes and work as a loyal foreign policy conduit on energy matters for the Kremlin. Sibneft, the third-ranked oil producer owned by oligarch and English football enthusiast Roman Abramovich, has also caught the Kremlin's attention. With investigations of Sibneft and Abramovich mushrooming, it appears only a matter of time before Sibneft will be under the Kremlin's heel as well.

The fate of Yukos's assets if it is forced into bankruptcy is open to speculation. The government-owned Rosneft Oil Company is rumored to be the Kremlin's favorite—some of Putin's key aides sit on Rosneft's board of directors. The natural gas monopoly Gazprom, government-owned as well, is also thought to be in the running. In the end it does not really matter. Yukos's transformation will essentially create what has been the Kremlin's goal from the advent of this affair: the creation of what could be called "KremPEC," the Kremlin Petroleum Export Corporation. This outcome would increase revenues and restore a large chunk of the economy under the state's purview for market reforms.

In addition to benefiting ordinary Russians, Putin wants the energy sector to serve the country's international political and economic interests. Russia has never had a meaningful relationship with the Organization of Petroleum Exporting Countries because independent domestic producers have been able to make petroleum policy without Kremlin consent. The impending breakup of Yukos and changes in ownership of the company's assets will allow the Kremlin to speak with a single voice when making international strategic petroleum alliances.

The international environment would appear to support KremPEC's ambitious goals. Terrorism threatens oil export giant Saudi Arabia, the cost of oil hovers around $45 a barrel, a gallon of gasoline costs up to $2.50 in the United States and far more in Europe, and continuing turmoil in Iraq limits the prospect of Iraqi oil significantly affecting international oil markets any time soon. Meanwhile, energy-hungry China and India are eager to find new and secure energy export markets to support their rapid economic growth.

The Kremlin has carefully thought out what the future might hold if Saudi Arabia, OPEC's powerbroker, becomes a target of larger and increased terrorist attacks. As the largest producer in the world, Russia might rethink its position concerning membership in the international petroleum cartel if Saudi exports were to face long-term risk.

In any event, the Yukos affair will quickly become part of history, its lessons absorbed. When that happens, Russia's oil patch will become more secure, attracting international petroleum investment, as well as providing Russia with needed cash flow to continue the reform of its economy. The difference is that energy negotiations and strategizing will take place behind Kremlin walls, instead of with oil oligarchs. For an energy-hungry world, doing business with KremPEC will become almost risk-free and eventually will make OPEC's current hold over world petroleum markets irrelevant. OPEC is about to be dethroned, with Putin's KremPEC its successor.

PROTECTING PROPERTY RIGHTS

The high-profile legal assault against Yukos has encouraged the perception that Putin is indifferent to property rights in Russia. But, beyond the state bureaucracy's sometimes aggressive, inefficient, or selective application of property rights law, the legal protection of private property is in fact being strengthened.

On June 10, 2004, Russia's parliament, the State Duma, adopted in the first of three readings 27 new bills introducing changes to the existing housing code, confirming the principle of private property by emphasizing the centrality of the state registry of property titles and by easing the property registry process and making it more transparent and affordable. The Kremlin designed all of these bills for the legislature. When the Western media comment that Putin is forcing legislation through without debate, these are the kinds of laws that are being passed.

Many observers claim that the Kremlin is most interested in asserting the "property rights" of the state, but this focus is overplayed. Putin is trying to redress the claims of property of the average Russian, which ultimately will create more confidence in property rights generally. Indeed, in Russia the government's treatment of Yukos is perceived as a reassertion of property-rights principles that were violated during the free-for-all privatization of public property in the 1990s.

Protecting property rights is one way Putin hopes to draw more foreign investment to his country. During five straight years of robust economic growth, Russia became an attractive investment target. Today, according to Western media, the Yukos affair has caused enormous concern that Putin is indifferent to minority shareholders in Russian companies. But the reality paints a different picture. Even though Russia is again experiencing net capital outflows (primarily from Russian nationals' expatriating funds), foreign investment has not stopped or reversed, and foreign companies continue to funnel money into Russia.

Final resolution of the Yukos affair could invite renewed interest in Russia as an investment target. If in fact smallish Kremlin-owned Rosneft becomes the flagship of Russia's oil sector, absorbing most of Yukos's lucrative assets, there is every reason to believe a company such as ExxonMobil would be interested in partnering with it or creating a joint venture. Such an arrangement would carry little if any political risk. Most analysts fail to understand that in Russia, just as with other emerging markets, the most solid and profitable business partner is the state. A number of Western oil giants have recognized this and are knocking on the Kremlin's door.

RUSSIA'S IMAGE IN THE WORLD

Since becoming president, Putin has demonstrated flexibility on a number of foreign policy issues that past Russian or Soviet leaders would have deemed unthinkable. Arms agreements can be concluded with a handshake. Expensive bases around the world are closed. Understanding and patience are shown when America establishes bases in parts of the former Soviet Union. Putin's foreign policy has emphasized constructively joining international institutions.

Yet the Kremlin's image in the world continues to suffer from charges of authoritarianism and revisionist imperialism. As mainstream analysts see it, the former KGB official has lived up to their expectations that he would clamp down on the "exuberance" of the 1990s; having established his "controlled democracy," Putin proceeds to choke Russia's nascent freedom to death.

A fairer assessment is that Putin will not be deterred from his domestic reform agenda, which includes a liberalized economy. The Russian leader has consistently adhered to the belief that his country can enjoy a good and strong image in the world only when it is economically competitive at home and abroad. Putin's regime is sending unambiguous signals that it is prepared to go to any length—including undermining its international reputation in the short term—to pursue its objective of rearranging the oligarchic economy inherited from the 1990s.

Putin also wants Russia to have strong neighbors and meaningful trading partners. What many call "Kremlin meddling" in the "near abroad" more often than not reflects efforts to promote political and economic stability on Russia's borders. It is often overlooked that millions of ethnic Russians live beyond the country's borders. Destabilized regimes and distressed economies in the countries that make up most of the Commonwealth of Independent States often negatively affect Russia's diaspora.

It is also often overlooked, and strangely so in light of the imperialist tendencies of czarist and Soviet forebears, that Putin is far more interested in promoting Russia's economic interests with neighboring countries than in pursuing heavy-handed military ambitions. Putin's Kremlin has learned well the cost of empire and is trying to avoid it.

THE NECESSARY AUTHORITARIAN?

All too often Russia watchers focus their analysis on what is called Russia's "managed democracy." Commentators are not wrong to worry about the present state of the country's political parties and weakened opposition, the Duma's tendency to rubberstamp Kremlin initiatives, the lack of checks and balances in government, and the electronic media's insufficient independence. Putin's decisions in September to abolish direct popular election of regional governors and to introduce legislation clearly designed to create Kremlin super majorities in the federal parliament have nothing to do with democracy in a Western sense. However, for democracy to have any meaning in Russia, the Kremlin must first create conditions in which the majority of Russians feel they have a stake in the country's destiny. This can come about with the kind of "managed capitalism" Putin is promoting. "Managed capitalism" is not state capitalism. The state does not want complete control of the economy. But Putin's government does want to help the economy find a more equitable and competitive balance.

Putin's crackdown on electronic media makes clear that the Kremlin will forgo public discussion of its policies as it reorders the country's economic priorities. Indeed, it is not hard to see Putin as an authoritarian. In most ways he is, based on Western standards. But, given Russia's current development trajectory, he probably has to be. Russia is at an extremely important juncture. Either the Kremlin continues its very hard-handed approach to restructuring the economy or Russia risks becoming in effect a Burkina Faso with nuclear weapons. It is very clear which future Putin wants.

Time is not on Russia's side. During Putin's presidency the country has experienced a remarkable economic recovery, but its infrastructure remains in a perilous state of disrepair, its demographic trends portend enormous difficulties, and domestic terror—the September hostage crisis in Beslan being the most horrific example—appears on the rise. This is why Putin is pushing the clock as hard as he can without engendering the kind of chaos that Russia experienced during the first failed decade of reform away from communism. The historical question—"Who is Putin?"—ultimately will find an answer. In the meantime, the Kremlin's economic-reform juggernaut continues its course, right on schedule.

PETER LAVELLE *is a Moscow-based senior analyst for United Press International and author of an electronic newsletter on Russia, "Untimely Thoughts" <untimely-thoughts.com>.*

Reprinted with permission from *Current History* Magazine (October 2004, pp. 314–318). © 2004 by Current History, Inc.

UNIT 4

Political Diversity in the Developing World

Unit Selections

Key Points to Consider

- What do developing countries have in common, and how are they diverse?

- How did the PRI maintain its dominance in Mexican politics for so long?

- What has caused the apparent impasse in Mexico's politics?

- How has multiracial democracy functioned in South Africa? What are some of the country's major political, economic, and social problems?

- How has Nigeria landed in its fourth republic since independence?

- How do you explain China's relative success in turning toward market reforms, as compared to the Soviet Union?

- How do you explain the apparent resilience of Indian democracy?

- What are some of the most common obstacles to the installation of a democracy in a country like Iraq or Afghanistan?

- Why is there so much attention paid to Turkey in the discussion of both the European Union and the development of the Middle East?

Student Website

www.mhcls.com/online

Internet References

Further information regarding these websites may be found in this book's preface or online.

Africa News Online
http://allafrica.com/

ArabNet
http://www.arab.net

Inside China Today
http://www.einnews.com/china/

Organization for Economic Cooperation and Development
http://www.oecd.org/home/

Sun SITE Singapore
http://sunsite.nus.edu.sg/noframe.html

The Third World was a widely used umbrella term for a disparate group of states that are now more frequently called the developing countries. Their most important shared characteristic may well be that these countries have not become relatively modern industrial societies. Most of these developing nations also share the problems of poverty and, though now less frequently, rapid population growth. In many other ways, the developing countries vary tremendously in their sociocultural and political characteristics. Some of them have representative systems of government, and a few of these, such as India, even have an impressive record of political stability. Many of them have been governed by authoritarian regimes that normally claim to represent the best interests of the people. Closer examination will often reveal that the avowed determination of self-appointed leaders to improve their societies is frequently less significant than their determination to maintain and expand their own power and privilege.

In recent years, market-oriented development has gained in favor in many countries that previously subscribed to some version of heavy state regulation or socialist planning of the economy. Their renewed interest in markets resembles the strategic policy shift that has also occurred in former Communist-ruled nations as well as the more advanced industrial countries. It usually represents a pragmatic acceptance of a "mixed economy" rather than a doctrinaire espousal of laissez-faire capitalism. In other words, targeted state intervention continues to play a role in economic development, but it is no longer as pervasive, rigid, or heavy-handed as often in the past.

In studying the attempts by developing countries to create institutions and policies that will promote their socioeconomic development, it is important not to leave out the international context. In the recent past, the political and intellectual leaders of these countries have often drawn upon some version of what is called dependency theory to explain their plight, sometimes combining it with demands for special treatment or compensation from the industrial world. In some of its forms, dependency theory is itself an outgrowth of the Marxist or Leninist theory of imperialism, according to which advanced capitalist countries have established exploitative relationships with the weaker economic systems of the less developed world. Such theories have often focused on external factors to explain a country's failure to generate self-sustained growth. They differ strikingly from explanations that give greater emphasis to a country's internal obstacles to development (whether sociocultural, political, environmental, or a combination of these). Such theoretical disagreements are not merely of academic interest. The theories themselves are likely to provide the intellectual basis for strikingly different policy conclusions and development strategies. In other words, ideas and theory can have important consequences.

The debate has had some tangible consequences in recent years. It now appears that dependency theory, at least in its simplest and most direct form, has lost intellectual and political support. Instead of serving as an explanatory paradigm, it is now more frequently encountered as part of more pluralist explanations of lagging development that recognize the tangled complexity of both internal and external factors likely to affect economic

growth and change. There is much to be said for middle-range theory that pays greater attention to the contextual or situational aspects of each case of development. On the whole, multivariable explanations seem preferable to monocausal ones. That is also true for policy responses: Strategies of development that may work in one setting may come to naught in a different environment. One size rarely fits all.

Sometimes called the Group of 77, but eventually consisting of some 120 countries, the developing states used to link themselves together in the United Nations to promote whatever interests they may have had in common. They focused on promoting changes designed to improve their relative commercial position vis-à-vis the affluent industrialized nations of the North. Their common front, however, turned out to be more rhetorical than real, when interest divergences became apparent. It would be a mistake to assume that there must be a necessary identity of interest among these countries or that they pursue complementary foreign policies.

Outside the United Nations, some of these same countries have occasionally tried to increase and control the price of industrially important primary exports through the building of cartel agreements among themselves. Sometimes the result has been detrimental to other developing nations. The most successful of these cartels, the Organization of Petroleum Exporting Countries (OPEC), was established in 1973 and held sway for almost a decade. Its cohesion eventually eroded, resulting in drastic reductions in oil prices. While this latter development was welcomed in the oil-importing industrial world as well as in many developing countries, it left some oil-producing nations, such as Mexico, in economic disarray for a while. Moreover, the need to find outlets for the huge amounts of petrodollars, which had been deposited by some oil producers in Western banks during the period of cartel-induced high prices, led some financial institutions to make huge and often ill-considered loans to many developing nations. The frantic and often unsuccessful efforts to repay on schedule created new economic, social, and political dislocations, which hit particularly hard in Latin America during the 1980s.

Some of the poorer oil-producing nations recaptured a degree of economic leverage at the turn of the new century. In a reduced form, the situation resembled a déjà vu, as global energy consumption increased and the OPEC countries proved willing and able, at least for a while, to return to a coordinated policy of limiting the production and hence the supply of petroleum. As a result, energy prices rose rapidly, and the advanced industrial nations were once again made aware of their economic vulnerability, stemming from a dependence on a regular flow of relatively low-priced oil.

The problems of poverty, hunger, and malnutrition in much of the developing world are socially and politically explosive. In their fear of revolution and their opposition to meaningful reform, the privileged classes have often resorted to brutal repression as a means of preserving a status quo favorable to themselves. In Latin America, this led to politicization during the 1970s of many lay persons and clergy of the Roman Catholic Church, who demanded social reform in the name of what was called liberation theology. For them, this variant of dependency theory filled a very practical ideological function by providing a relatively simple analytical and moral explanation of a complex reality. It also gave some strategic guidance for political activists who were determined to change this state of affairs. Their views on the inevitability of class struggle, and the need to take an active part in it, often clashed with the Vatican's far more conservative outlook. Like dependency theory, liberation theology today appears to have been effectively absorbed into more pluralist outlooks and pragmatic strategies for socioeconomic development.

The collapse of Communist rule in Europe has had a profound impact on the ideological explanation of the developing world's poverty and on the resulting strategies to overcome it. The Soviet model of modernization now appears to offer very little of practical value. And, the Communists who remain in power in China have been eager to experiment widely with market reforms, including the private profit motive, adding to the general discredit of the centrally planned economy. Perhaps even more important, there seemed for a while to be a positive demonstration effect in some countries in Africa and Latin America that pursued more market-oriented strategies of development. On the whole, they appeared, at least until recently, to perform much better than some of their more statist neighbors tied to highly regulated and protected economies. This realization may help explain the intellectual journey of someone like the now-deceased Michael Manley, the former prime minister of Jamaica, who broke away from the combination of dependency theory and socialist strategies that he had once defended vigorously. During the 1980s, Manley made an intellectual U-turn as he gained a new respect for market-oriented economic approaches, without abandoning his interest in using reform politics to promote the interests of the poor. A similar political shift

was taken by Fernando Henrique Cardoso, who came to embrace market economics before he became president of Brazil until 2002. In his youth, Cardoso had been exiled by the then-ruling military junta for having written a book on dependency and underdevelopment that became a primer of left-wing analysis in Latin America. More recently, the political scientist and activist Jorge G. Castañeda called upon the Left in Latin America to abandon utopian goals and seek social reforms within "mixed" market economies. Until his resignation in 2003, he served as foreign minister of Mexico in President Fox's relatively market-friendly government.

But the story does not end there. In today's Latin America, there is an unmistakable leftward turn. It can be explained by disillusionment with the so-called **Washington Consensus**, with its free-market approach that replaced such nationalist nostrums as **import-substitution and protectionism.** This should not be misunderstood as a call for turning back the clock, but it reflects a recognition that neo-liberal policies have not worked as promised by their promoters.

Latin America illustrates the difficulty of establishing stable pluralist democracies in many parts of the developing world. Some authors have argued that its dominant political tradition is basically authoritarian and corporatist rather than competitively pluralist. They see the region's long tradition of centralized oligarchic governments, usually of the Right, as the result of an authoritarian "unitary" bias in the political culture. From this perspective, there would seem to be little hope for a lasting pluralist development, and the current trend toward democratization in much of Latin America would also appear unlikely to last. There are indeed signs pointing in that direction. On the other hand, there are other countries with corporatist traditions where democracy has taken roots. Also, it is no mean accomplishment that one after the other dictatorship in Latin America has been replaced by an elected government. The demonstration effect of democratic governments in Spain and Portugal may well have played a role for the Latin American countries. Finally, the negative social, economic, and political experience with authoritarian rulers is one of the strongest cards held by their democratic successors.

In order to survive and develop, each of the new democracies must meet the pragmatic test ("does it work?"), by providing evidence of social and economic progress. Many of them may yet turn out to have been short interludes between authoritarian regimes. Strife-torn Venezuela is a case in point. The even grimmer case of Argentina, which was one of the world's most prosperous countries at the beginning of the twentieth century, serves as a warning that both authoritarian-populist and neoliberal policy directions can end in social and political disaster. Even the president of Brazil, who started out with sterling left-wing credentials, has lost much of his initial support as a result of charges of corruption against his government.

In much of Latin America there seems to be a new questioning of the turn toward a greater emphasis on market economics that replaced the traditional commitment to strategies of statist interventions. It is too simple to explain this phenomenon as a product of impatience alone. A basic problem is that the benefits of economic growth do not "trickle down" as freely in practice as they do in economic theory. Instead, there are many instant losers in the economic dislocations that usually attend free market reforms.

There can be other serious problems as well, as shown in the attempt by former president Carlos Salinas of **Mexico** to move his country toward a more competitive form of market enterprise. His modernization strategy included Mexico's entry into the North American Free Trade Agreement (NAFTA) with the United States and Canada. In a time of enormous socioeconomic dislocations, however, Salinas showed considerable reluctance to move from an economic to a thorough political reform. Such a shift would have undermined the longtime hegemony of his own Institutional Revolutionary Party (PRI) and given new outlets for protest by self-perceived losers in the process. On the other hand, some observers criticized the market-oriented approach as too one-sidedly economic in its implicit assumption that modernization could be accomplished without a basic change of the political system. During his last year in office, Salinas was confronted by an armed peasant rebellion in the southern province of Chiapas, which gave voice to the demand for land reform and economic redistribution. Mexican criticism of Salinas intensified after he left office in December 1994 and 3 months later sought political exile abroad. Soon after, some top Mexican officials and their associates were accused of having links to major drug traffickers with a sordid record of corruption and political assassination.

The successor to Salinas was elected in August 1994, in a competitive contest that was reported as not seriously distorted by fraud. The ruling party won with 51 percent of the vote. The PRI's first presidential candidate, Luis Donaldo Colosio, had been assassinated in the early part of the campaign. His place was taken by Ernesto Zedillo, an economist and former banker who fit the technocratic mold of recent Mexican leaders. As president, he continued the basic economic policies of Salinas, but Zedillo appeared far more willing to listen to demands for meaningful political reform as well. In other ways too, his governmental performance was remarkable. Shortly after he took office at the beginning of December 1994, the Mexican peso collapsed and brought the economy into disarray. A major factor was the country's huge trade deficit and the resultant loss of confidence in the peso. This setback could have paralyzed the new president. Instead, he dealt energetically and skillfully with the problem. By early 1997, the Mexican government was able to announce that it had paid back a huge relief loan provided by the United States. The overall economic prospect for the struggling country appeared to improve considerably.

The Mexican elections of July 1997 represented something of a political milestone in the country's recent history. In retrospect, they were an omen of things to come. The basic result was a considerable setback for the Institutional Revolutionary Party—an outcome that would have been unthinkable in earlier years. In the lower house of Congress, the two main opposition parties deprived the ruling PRI of its habitual controlling majority. They began to transform what had been regarded as a rubber stamp chamber into a political check on the president.

Some months before the new presidential elections were held in the summer of 2000, the PRI appeared to have recovered electoral support. Many observers thought it could once again win the country's highest political office, which the party had occupied for 72 years. This time, however, the election process appeared to be more democratic than in the past, beginning with a much-touted, first-ever selection of the PRI candidate in a contested "primary" race that differed from the traditional "handpicking" used in the past. Looked at more closely, the political reality was not so very different, for the party apparatus was geared to promote Francisco Labastida, who eventually won the nomination.

In the end, the PRI lost its grip on power when Labastida was defeated decisively by the charismatic businessman, Vicente Fox. The latter's center-right National Action Party (PAN) also became the leading force in both houses of Congress. As a result, Mexico has now experienced a major political turnover as the result of a general election. It is necessary to add that the great experiment with political and economic liberty in Mexico has coincided with political gridlock and economic setbacks. Here, as in much of the rest of Latin America, the high expectations that accompanied long-awaited political changes have been followed by disappointments.

South Africa faces the monumental task of making democracy work in a multiracial society where the ruling white minority had never shared political or economic power with black Africans or Asian immigrants. A new transitional constitution was adopted in late 1993, followed by the first multiracial national elections in April 1994. Former president F. W. de Klerk may go into history as a late reformer, but his political work was bound to displease many members of South African society. If the reforms were judged to have gone much too far and too fast by many members of the privileged white minority, they clearly did not go far enough or come quickly enough for many more people who demanded measures that went beyond formal racial equality.

Nelson Mandela, who succeeded de Klerk in the presidency, faced an even more difficult historical task. On the other hand, he possessed some strong political cards in addition to his undisputed leadership qualities. He represented the aspirations of a long-repressed majority, yet he was able to retain the respect of a large number of the white minority. It will be important that his successor continues to bridge the racial cleavages that otherwise threaten to ravage South African society. In an early interim constitution for post-apartheid South Africa, the reformers had sought political accommodation through an institutional form of power sharing. A new constitution, adopted in 1996, lays the foundation for creating simple majority-based governments that are bound to be dominated for now by the African National Congress (ANC), Mandela's political party. The new charter contains many guarantees of individual and group rights, but political prudence would seem to recommend some form of meaningful interracial coalition-building in South Africa's policy-making process. The continued task of finding workable forms of power sharing is only one of many problems. In order for the democratic changes to have much meaning for the long-suppressed majority, it will be necessary to find policies that reduce the social and economic chasm separating the races. The politics of redistribution will be no simple or short-term task, and one may expect many conflicts in the future. There is a host of other social problems confronting the leaders of this multiracial democracy. Nevertheless, for the first time since the beginning of colonization, South Africa now offers some hope for an improvement in interracial relations.

In December 1997, Mandela stepped down from the leadership of the ANC as a first step in his eventual retirement from politics. His place was taken by Thabo Mbeki, the country's deputy president, who became president in June 1999, soon after the parliamentary elections in which the ANC won 266 of the 400 seats, or one short of a two-thirds majority. The new leaders appear to have done their best to provide for political continuity instead of a divisive power struggle after Mandela's departure. Mbeki (and everyone else) lacks Mandela's great moral authority. He is widely described as "businesslike" and competent, but Mbeki's dismissive and poorly informed views on the country's serious AIDS problem have caused international alarm. Recently Mandela has stepped back into the public limelight by announcing his intention to play a leading role in promoting policies that will seriously identify and confront this issue.

Nigeria covers a large area and has more than 100 million inhabitants, making it the most populous country in Africa. The former British colony has returned to electoral politics after 15 years of oppressive military rule that brought economic havoc to the potentially rich nation. The path towards stable and effective democratic governance in this culturally diverse country will be long and difficult. Ethnic and religious conflicts threaten the emergence of both a well-functioning civil society and a stable form of representative government. Nigeria bears close watching by students of comparative politics.

China is the homeland of nearly 1.3 billion people, or about one-fifth of the world's population. Here the reform Communists, who took power after Mao Zedong's death in 1976, began much earlier than their Soviet counterparts to steer the country toward a relatively decontrolled market economy. They also introduced some political relaxation, by ending Mao's recurrent ideological campaigns to mobilize the masses. In their place came a domestic tranquility such as China had not known for over half a century. But the regime encountered a basic dilemma: it wished to maintain tight controls over politics and society while freeing the economy. When a new openness began to emerge in Chinese society, comparable in some ways to the pluralism encouraged more actively by Gorbachev's glasnost policy of openness in the Soviet Union, it ran into determined opposition among hard-line Communist leaders. The aging reform leader, Deng Xiaoping, presided over a bloody crackdown on student demonstrations in Beijing's Tiananmen Square in May 1989. The regime has refused to let up on its tight political controls of society, but it continues to loosen the economic controls in the areas or zones designated for such reforms. In recent years, China has experienced a remarkable economic surge with growth rates unmatched elsewhere in the world. A still unanswered question is whether the emerging market-oriented society can long coexist with a tightly controlled political system. In February 1997 Beijing announced the death of Deng Xiaoping.

Jiang Zemin, chosen by Deng as his successor in 1989, had been the country's president since 1993. As government and party leader, he appeared determined to continue the relatively pragmatic course adopted by Deng. It needs to be added that the regime has revived a hard line in dealing with real, imagined, or potential political dissidence, which includes some forms of religious expression. Moreover, there are familiar signs of social tension, as China's mixed economy leaves both "winners" and "losers" in its wake. Despite the country's undeniable problems and shortcomings, China's leaders have steered clear of the chaos that has plagued post-Soviet Russia. They seem determined to continue with their tight political controls, even as their economy becomes freer and more market-oriented. Some observers believe that the basic economic and political norms will eventually begin to converge, but that remains to be seen. A test case is the movement known as Falun Gong, which the ruling Communists see as a threat because of its effective organization and solidarity—qualities that no longer characterize the Communist Party to the same degree as earlier.

It remains to be seen whether Hu Jintao, who was named party leader in the latter half of 2002, will turn out to move the country further in a technocratic direction, as many observers expect. What seems certain is that Hu Jintao has moved quietly to further concentrate power in his own hands. In September 2004 he replaced Jiang Zemin as the country's military chief—a major political change.

India is often referred to as a subcontinent. With more than one billion people, this country ranks second only to China in population and ahead of the continents of Latin America and Africa combined. India is deeply divided by ethnic, religious, and regional differences. It is a secular state, but tense relations between politicized Hindu extremists and members of the large Muslim minority occasionally erupt in violence. For the vast majority of the huge population, a life of material deprivation has long seemed inescapable. That may be changing. There is now a possibility of meaningful relief if the country's struggling economy could be freed from heavy-handed state interference. The turn in that direction can be traced back to the early 1990s, when the market revolution cautiously touched India.

The economic changes have taken place in a context that carries the potential for political chaos. In 1992 the national elections were marred by the assassination of Rajiv Gandhi, a former prime minister. When his Congress party won the election, one of its veteran politicians, P.V. Narasimha Rao, headed the new government. He followed in the steps of other reformers in the developing world by loosening economic planning and controls on international trade and investment. These market-oriented policies brought substantial economic gains but were accompanied by a flurry of corruption scandals that tainted several members of Rao's cabinet. His Congress party was badly defeated in the general election of May 1996. There followed some short-lived multiparty coalition governments.

In the spring of 1998, parliamentary elections produced a result that seemed to promise even more instability for the world's largest democracy. The Bharatiya Janta Party (BJP), dominated by Hindu nationalists, won the most seats, but it was only able to govern in alliance with several smaller parties. The coalition provided a weak parliamentary majority, but it was able to survive just over a year, partly because the BJP leader, Prime Minister Atal Behari Vajpayee, was able to tame the rhetoric of his own party's more militant Hindu-nationalist members. As long expected, the government collapsed in April 1999, when a small coalition member defected.

Some 300 million Indian voters took part in the new elections that followed. The result was a clear victory for the incumbent governing coalition, now numbering 24 parties. It was the first time in 27 years that an incumbent prime minister won re-election in India. Once the dominant Congress party, which had hoped to revive and return to power, instead suffered its worst defeat since independence. In the elections of 2004, however, it recuperated and returned to power as key member of the United Progressive Alliance. The BJP returned to the opposition.

In the near future, at least, the dramatic political change seems likely to be accompanied by continuity of economic strategy, for the new Prime Minister, Mr. Singh, is also identified with market-friendly policies. Ironically, this deregulating and increasingly dynamic economy may be the source of "real change" in India, but the cumbersome political institutions provide the framework that holds the country together, as Rajan Menon observes. Some India watchers warn that the country's market reforms have caused social and economic dislocations that could spark new political turmoil and ethnic strife. As always, this huge multiethnic democracy bears watching.

Fox's Mexico: Democracy Paralyzed

"Mexico appears to be speaking the vocabulary of disenchantment. The words 'failure,' 'disillusion,' 'lack of leadership' have become a daily part of national conversation. The consensus seems to be that [Vicente] Fox's presidency is over, that he is no longer a lame duck but a dead duck."

DENISE DRESSER

In Mexico today, people laugh at the country's politicians. Laughter has become a national antidote to what would instead bring tears. This explains why Mexico's most popular political analyst, until he resigned several months ago, was a red-nosed, green-haired clown named Brozo. As the host of a morning news show on Mexican television, Brozo poked fun at the country's politicians, exposed their corrupt activities, and acted as a public watchdog.

Mexico provided him with endless grist for his morning mill: the governor of the state of Oaxaca who stages an assassination attempt on himself to bolster his party's political fortunes in a local race; a senator from the Green Party who is videotaped negotiating a bribe from a businessman who wants to build a hotel on an ecological preserve; a city government official caught on tape as he receives a bribe from a powerful contractor; the director of Mexico City's finances gambling with public money at a Las Vegas casino.

Democratic Mexico has not eliminated corruption: the country is producing a reality show with it. Democracy has inaugurated a political system that is freer but not necessarily cleaner. Mexico continues to be a country of crimes without punishment, of people who are identified as guilty on-screen but cannot be proved so in court, of politicians who enrich themselves because they still can.

This has become the greatest problem that the government of President Vicente Fox faces. Day after day, Mexican newspapers portray a paralyzed country. Mexicans do not talk about what has been accomplished, but about what could have been. Mexico appears to be speaking the

vocabulary of disenchantment. The words "failure," "disillusion," "lack of leadership" have become a daily part of national conversation. The consensus seems to be that Fox's presidency is over, that he is no longer a lame duck but a dead duck.

BETWEEN BAD AND WORSE

Mexican politics has turned into a blood sport. Political battles are not fought between Congress and the president over pending structural reforms; they are being waged among the three political parties and their presidential hopefuls over who will occupy the presidential chair in 2006. Precisely because Fox is perceived as increasingly irrelevant as a decision maker, the presidential race has begun in earnest—and succession politics determine what every politician says and what party positions are taken. Because Fox's presidency seems to have evaporated into thin air, both the Institutional Revolutionary Party (PRI) and the left-leaning Party of the Democratic Revolution (PRD) believe that they can win the presidency and are using every weapon at their disposal. Hardball politics, mudslinging, character assassination, and the use of the Mexican judiciary as a political tool to undermine opponents have all become a permanent fixture of Mexico's political landscape.

Over the next two years, Mexican politics will unfold in a context in which the PRI wields growing power, Mexico City Mayor Andrés Manuel López Obrador fights for his political life in increasingly hostile circumstances, and very little is accomplished in legislative terms because Fox's presidency, for all practical purposes, is over. The focus now and until 2006 is on the presidential race and its pre-electoral dramas. The video scandals that have ensnared government officials in Mexico City over the past six months seem to have one purpose: to remove López Obrador, the left-wing mayor of the city, from his position as frontrunner in the presidential race. The concerted attacks on the Mexican left—coupled with Fox's failures—open a dangerous door in Mexican politics, one that could lead to the return of the PRI and the ascendance of its current party chairman and presidential contender, Roberto Madrazo.

Madrazo's PRI is a party run by corrupt mafias that are itching to act freely, and will dismantle the country's few democratic institutions to do so.

Whether the PRI—which ruled Mexico for 71 uninterrupted years until Fox won the presidency in 2000—returns to power in 2006 will depend to a large extent on the positions that both Fox and his National Action Party (PAN) adopt between now and the election. Most likely, the contest will feature a two-man race, between López Obrador and Madrazo, with a PAN candidate (probably Interior Minister Santiago Creel) running in third place. So the issue for the PAN becomes whom it blocks and whom it helps. Does the PAN allow the PRI to return by undermining the left—which it hates—and López Obrador at every turn? Or does it do everything in its power to prevent the return of the PRI, knowing that if that happens, it will mean a setback for democratic consolidation in Mexico? This is the devilish dilemma that the PAN currently faces: a choice between bad and worse.

THE BESIEGED FRONTRUNNER

Day in and day out, come rain or shine, Mayor Andrés Manuel López Obrador—AMLO, as he is often referred to—gives a public press conference in his office at 6 AM in an effort to show that he is a man of the people and working for them. He is widely perceived as one, and therein lies his appeal. Despite a spate of scandals involving several of his close collaborators, the mayor remains a political force to contend with, given his high approval ratings in Mexico City and, to a lesser extent, nationwide. That support has been gradually eroding but still places him 10 points ahead of his rivals in the presidential race.

Buttressed by the combination of a massive public works program, populist policies, and savvy political positioning, López Obrador is the most popular politician in Mexico. That is what makes him so dangerous to so many vested interests, which in turn explains why he has many powerful enemies obsessed with bringing him down and bribing—and videotaping—those who could do so. As a result of the Fox government's deliberate attempts to sabotage him through the use of the justice system, AMLO faces a legal battle in Congress that could strip him of his immunity from prosecution, making it impossible for him to run in 2006.

López Obrador's political strategy since the beginning of the video scandals has been to argue that he is being set up, that it is all a plot hatched by the Fox government, former President Carlos Salinas, and a vast array of vested interests in the system, designed to bring him down. He has tried to focus public attention on the alleged conspiracy and shift it away from undeniable corruption in his government. That strategy has worked with broad swaths of his political base in Mexico City—the poor, the less educated—for whom corruption is a relative issue: what López Obrador's collaborators have done pales in comparison with the pillaging the PRI and Salinas undertook.

There seems to be some truth to López Obrador's claim about a plot. Evidence points to a series of behind-the-scenes plans carried out by Carlos Ahumada (a contractor now in jail), prominent members of the PAN, and employees of Mexico's attorney general's office to videotape city officials stuffing briefcases with money and then release those tapes on national television. Whether or not Fox knew about these plans and allowed them to be carried out remains an open question.

What is clear is Fox's approval of the politicization of the attorney general's office and the judiciary against the mayor. López Obrador is currently caught in a legal battle wherein the attorney general's office has accused him of ignoring a restraint order issued by the courts by allowing the construction of a public road (providing access to a hospital) on a piece of land whose ownership has been contested. So Mexico's presidential race may be determined by a small plot of land, known as "El Encino."

The attacks on López Obrador have led to his increasing radicalization. Two years ago, he was viewed as a potential "Lula" (after Luiz Inácio "Lula" Da Silva, the left-wing president of Brazil who has governed in a pragmatic and moderate fashion). Now he's feared as a possible Hugo Chávez (the populist and divisive president of Venezuela). Two years ago, businesspeople applauded his moderation; now they condemn his stridency. Before the video scandals he appeared the inevitable leader of a modern left; today he seems the desperate leader of a recalcitrant left. For many members of Mexico's middle class, López Obrador is not a politician to support but a proto-populist to fear. This wariness stems from the mayor's public denunciations of Mexico's legal system and the politicization of its judicial system. In Mexico, although the rule of law is, in many areas, nonexistent, citizens expect politicians to obey it. López Obrador questions its very existence and pays a political price. As a result, he has been losing political ground and supporters.

In many ways, his enemies have achieved their objective. López Obrador spends more time dodging political blows than governing the city. His public outbursts against the judiciary have diminished his credibility, and led to the gradual weakening of the heterogeneous, multi-class coalition he attempted to build. The mayor seems to govern with an angel on one shoulder and a devil on the other. The angel whispers that he should govern for all Mexicans; the devil tells him that only the poor deserve his help. The angel says he will need to build support among all social groups; the devil answers that the dispossessed are enough. The angel urges him to be conciliatory while the devil pushes him to be divisive.

López Obrador's latter tack may allow him to mount a good defense but it could hamper his electoral prospects, given that he needs to construct a broad-based coalition to win. Although the left governs Mexico City, the PRD performs badly at the national level and has lost more than half the congressional seats it was able to win in the late 1990s. The PRD is gambling on AMLO's personal attractiveness as a guiding political force. The question is whether a single politician's popularity will be enough to assemble a winning electoral coalition on the back of a fractured party. Can he bring political moderates back into the fold? Will he even be allowed to compete? Today the PRD is a collection of warring factions, united around the embattled presidential bid of a man who argues that his enemies tout "the rule of law" in Mexico as if it existed.

THE RESILIENT PRI

Many Mexicans who voted for Fox are bewildered. Four years into his term, the man who promised to kick the PRI out of power forever seems to have been kidding. Politics cannot tolerate vacuums and the PRI is filling the one created by Fox's failures. The PRI is coming back, winning state election after state election, and Mexico's first democratically elected president appears unperturbed. If the former ruling party returns to office in the 2006 presidential election, the country's experiment with democracy will have been short-lived. If the PRI is re-elected, it will come back to stay.

Four years ago millions of Mexicans voted for change. They heard Fox's promises and believed them. They elected a candidate who would kill the dinosaurs and tame the dragons. But he could not, or did not want to. Instead of wielding his sword, he tripped and fell on it. Rather than confront those who had despoiled Mexico, he ended curled up next to them. Instead of weakening the PRI when he could, he tried to collaborate with it in Congress and refused to take on the vested interests in the unions that the former ruling party had created. By attempting to co-govern with the PRI, Fox has breathed new life into it. Unwittingly, the president has become the PRI's secret weapon. The results of this mistaken accommodation are there for all to see: an emboldened PRI and a weakened government, a cornered president and more of the same old politics.

While Fox offers carrots instead of sticks, the PRI has been organizing itself at the state and local level, retaking ground in the periphery as a way of regaining control of the center. And as recent results in the states of Oaxaca and Veracruz underscore, the party will resort to fear and loathing on the campaign trail if it has to. The PRI is pulling out old tricks—intimidation, vote buying, patronage—and weak electoral institutions combined with low voter turnout mean they still work.

Work they did for the new mayor of Tijuana, Jorge Hank Rhon, elected despite rumors of drug trafficking, an arrest for smuggling, and the fact that two of his bodyguards are in jail for the assassination of a prominent journalist. Hank's victory last year sent a clear message: in order to win, the PRI does not have to modernize itself, does not have to change. It can remain the same and still orchestrate a comeback. It can nominate political dinosaurs and still win in Mexico's new, fragile democracy.

Today the PRI's presidential hopeful, Roberto Madrazo, is positioning himself as the candidate of those who are disappointed with democracy. He is the candidate of those who believe that power sharing has been a road to nowhere, who prefer the efficient corruption of the PRI to the chronic ineptitude of Fox's National Action Party. A vintage dinosaur with numerous accusations of electoral fraud hidden under his tail, Madrazo represents the old system at its worst and is pushing for its revival. The PRI is poised to take full advantage of the government's paralysis, not because of what the party offers but because of the vacuum it fills. The PRI is coming back because there is nothing to stop it.

Madrazo is gambling on those who miss the old system of clear rules and predictable complicities. And he has found a constituency among Mexicans who prefer a perfect dictatorship to a paralyzed democracy. In the absence of presidential leadership, the PRI is building a coalition of the disaffected. It sells itself as the party that can get things done, even if that means doing them in the old way. Some argue that this may not necessarily be a bad outcome: in Mexico's new circumstances, they suggest, the PRI will be reined in and Madrazo will be constrained by institutions that now act as counterweights to the president.

What is so troubling about the current situation is that many members of Fox's own party believe this. PAN leaders also think that if they join hands with the PRI in Congress to strip López Obrador of his immunity—and preempt the advance of the Mexican left—they will clear the way for their own presidential hopeful, Santiago Creel. The PAN, however, is probably mistaken. Without a charismatic candidate like Fox, the PAN will return to its traditional vote levels. The issue is not whether the PAN can retain control of the presidency, but to which party it will hand it over. Will the PAN offer the presidency on a silver platter to the PRI by keeping the popular mayor of Mexico City out of the race, or will it run the risk of empowering the left by allowing López Obrador to run?

THE INEFFECTUAL PRESIDENT

President Fox does not seem to realize what is at stake. He proclaims that he is happy all the time. He argues that the country is marching forward, despite what his critics say. He continues to spout numbers and data that confirm his optimistic views, however politically irrelevant they may be. He obsesses about his approval in the polls, even though they reveal that he is perceived as popular but ineffectual.

Fox may go down in history as both the man who led the democratic transition and the president who squandered it.

The prevailing view of Fox is that he knows how to be a good cheerleader, but does not know how to make decisions. He knows how to sell ideas, but does not know how to put them into practice. He knows how to charm the media, but does not know how to horse trade with Congress to get his legislative agenda approved. The public, however, knows this and forgives him for it, because he is perceived as a good, well-intentioned man.

The reasons behind Fox's failures are complex and varied: the appointment of a cabinet of strangers, the misuse of his political capital during his first year in office, the lack of clear priorities and concrete strategies, the decision to negotiate with the PRI instead of dividing it after the 2000 election, the use of the bully pulpit in a country with no congressional or presidential reelection, the persistence of institutions created for dominant party rule, the intermittent sabotage of Fox by members of his own party, the uncontrollable activism and presidential ambitions of his wife, Marta Sahagun. Fox painted himself into a corner but also allowed others to help.

Yet he remains popular because, in the minds of many Mexican voters, Fox is one thing and his party is another. Electoral results have shown that citizens can love Fox and hate the PAN. In the 2003 midterm election, Fox supporters stayed home, a move that benefited the PRI, which became the majority party in Congress. This paradox will continue throughout the remaining two years of his term. Fox will continue to soar in the polls as the PAN crashes everywhere else.

The PAN today is a party with its head in its hands. Its inability to deliver better government has paved the way for a PRI comeback; its constant bickering with Fox over the past four years has made it possible for the electorate to punish the party at the polls while sparing the president. Without the benefit of the multiplier effect that Fox had on the party in the 2000 presidential race, the PAN is shrinking back to its normal size of about 25 percent of the electorate. This is bad news for Creel, its potential presidential contender and current minister of the interior. Instead of combating the PRI's record of corruption he has ignored it for the sake of congressional votes that never materialized.

As a result, policy paralysis in Mexico will prevail and the PRI is poised to take full advantage of it. Madrazo will now use his party's recent victories to unite disparate factions in favor of a common cause: tripping up Fox and sabotaging the PAN. The PRI has no incentive to collaborate in Congress, because the party is not blamed for the stalemate there. The PRI will continue to be intransigent about pending economic reforms because it has nothing to lose and much to gain. Fox promised change and the PRI capitalized on the legislative paralysis that prevented him from pushing it through.

Seventy-five percent of Mexicans tell pollsters they have little or no confidence in political parties, 60 percent of the electorate did not show up at the polls in the 2003 midterm election, and 54 percent of those who voted for Fox in 2000 declare themselves dissatisfied with democracy. Given these sentiments, Fox may go down in history as both the man who led the democratic transition and the president who squandered it.

THE LAST LAUGH

What will we see between now and the presidential election in 2006? An empowered PRI, a cornered PAN, a weakened but still popular López Obrador, and the persistence of hardball politics. The PRI will dictate the policy agenda in Congress, and try to present itself as something of a modernizing force in order to woo the business class. But the PRI will not push for economic modernization policies, such as privatization of electric utilities, that could alienate the hard-core base that just empowered it in Oaxaca, Veracruz, and Baja California Norte. Major reforms to the electricity sector will not take place, although some minor tinkering with the labor code might occur. Madrazo may unveil a public safety package this coming session— crime is a huge issue in Mexico— and that should protect his right-wing flank. Madrazo's rivals are all walking wounded, but López Obrador should survive as a finalist, with steady erosion of his support among independents. For Fox, the key political question seems to be just how distant a third place the PAN is slouching toward.

In the absence of effective presidential leadership, the scenario for Mexico appears to be PRI driven marginal reform, designed to bolster the party's electoral fortunes and build a coalition of those that have become disaffected with the inefficacy of PAN rule. The PRI will try to position itself, in contrast to Fox and the PAN, as the party that can propel Mexico out of its current paralysis, even if it has to rely on traditional methods to do so.

But Madrazo's way is not only the old way. It is the worst way. The PRI he has reassembled is not the modernizing, technocratic party that pushed forward Mexico's much-needed economic restructuring in the 1990s. Madrazo's PRI is a group of *caudillos* who view the country as their personal fiefdom and intend to govern it as such. Madrazo's PRI is a party run by corrupt mafias that are itching to act freely, and will dismantle the country's few democratic institutions to do so.

Ultimately, what is at stake for Mexico with the PRI's return is the viability, the longevity, the survival of Mexican democracy beyond 2006. Because, if the PRI returns to the presidency, Mexico will slide back from an imperfect democracy to the government it lived with for 71 years—only worse. And the one barrier against this outcome is a proto-populist politician who wants to govern Mexico by polarizing it. Perhaps Brozo the clown knew this when he resigned from his television show a few months ago. He said that he just could not be a clown anymore. His wife had died and he no longer felt like laughing. Many Mexicans, anticipating the choice for 2006 as a contest between bad and worse, feel the same way.

DENISE DRESSER *is a professor of political science at the Autonomous Technological Institute of Mexico.*

Latin America Looks Leftward Again

JUAN FORERO

At first glance, there's nothing cutting edge about this isolated highland town of mud-brick homes and cold mountain streams. The way of life is remarkably unchanged from what it was centuries ago. The Aymara Indian villagers have no hot water or telephones, and each day they slog into the fields to shear wool and grow potatoes.

But Tacamara and dozens of similar communities across the scrub grass of the Bolivian highlands are at the forefront of a new leftward tide now rising in Latin American politics. Tired of poverty and indifferent governments, villagers here are being urged by some of their more radical leaders to forget the promises of capitalism and install instead a community-based socialism in which products would be bartered. Some leaders even talk of forming an independent Indian state.

"What we really need is to transform this country," said Rufo Yanarico, 45, a community leader. "We have to do away with the capitalist system."

In the burgeoning cities of China, India and Southeast Asia, that might sound like a hopelessly outdated dream because global capitalism seems to be delivering on its promise to transform those poor societies into richer ones. But here, the appeal of rural socialism is a powerful reminder that much of South America has become disenchanted with the poor track record of similar promises made to Latin America.

So the region has begun turning leftward again.

That trend figures heavily in a presidential election being held today in Bolivia, in which the frontrunner is Evo Morales, a charismatic Aymara Indian and former coca farmer who promises to decriminalize coca production and roll back market reforms if he wins. Though he leads, he is unlikely to gain a clear majority; if he does not, Bolivia's Congress would decide the race.

Still, he is the most fascinating candidate, because he is anything but alone in Latin America. He considers himself a disciple of the region's self-appointed standard-bearer for the left, President Hugo Chávez of Venezuela, a populist who has injected the state into the economy, showered the nation's oil profits on government projects aimed at the poor, and antagonized the Bush administration with constant invective.

"In recent years, social movements and leftist parties in Latin America have reappeared with a force that has no parallel in the recent history in the region," says a new book on the trend, "The New Left in Latin America," written by a diverse group of academic social scientists from across the Americas.

Peru also has a new and growing populist movement, led by a cashiered army officer, Ollanta Humala, who is ideologically close to Mr. Chávez. Argentina's president, Nestor Kirchner, who won office in 2003, announced last week that Argentina would sever all ties with the International Monetary Fund, which he blames for much of the country's long economic decline, by swiftly paying back its $9.9 billion debt to the fund.

The leftist movement that has taken hold in Latin America over the last seven years is diverse. Mr. Chávez is its most extreme example. Brazil's president, Luiz Inácio Lula da Silva, by contrast, is a former labor leader who emphasizes poverty reduction but also practices fiscal austerity and gets along with Wall Street. Uruguay has been pragmatic on economic matters, but has had increasingly warm relations with Venezuela. In Mexico, the leftist who is thought to have a good chance to be the next president, Andrés Manuel López Obrador, has distanced himself from Mr. Chávez.

What these leaders share is a strong emphasis on social egalitarianism and a determination to rely less on the approach known as the Washington Consensus, which emphasizes privatization, open markets, fiscal discipline and a follow-the-dollar impulse, and is favored by the I.M.F. and United States officials.

"You cannot throw them all in the same bag, but this is understood as a left with much more sensitivity toward the social," said Augusto Ramírez Ocampo, a former Colombian government minister who last year helped write a United Nations report on the state of Latin American democracy. "The people believe these movements can resolve problems, since Latin American countries have seen that the Washington Consensus has not been able to deal with poverty."

With poverty up, old promises from capitalists don't look so good. New promises from populists do.

The Washington Consensus became a force in the 1980's, after a long period in which Latin American governments, many autocratic, experimented with nationalistic economic nostrums like import-substitution and protectionism. These could not deliver sustained growth. The region was left on the edge of economic implosion.

With the new policies of the 1980's came a surge toward democracy, a rise of technocrats as leaders and, in the last 20 years, a general acceptance of stringent austerity measures prescribed by the I.M.F. and the World Bank. Country after country was told to make far-reaching changes, from selling off utilities to cutting pension costs. In return, loans and other aid were offered. Growth would be steady, economists in Washington promised, and poverty would decline.

But the results were dismal. Poverty rose, rather than fell; inequality remained a curse. Real per capita growth in Latin America since 1980 has barely reached 10 percent, according to an analysis of I.M.F. data by the Washington-based Center for Economic and Policy Research. Meanwhile, many Latin Americans lost faith in traditional political parties that were seen as corrupt vehicles for special interests. That led to uprisings that toppled presidents like Bolivia's Gonzalo Sánchez de Lozada and Ecuador's Lucio Gutiérrez; it also spawned demagogues who blame free-market policies for everything without offering detailed alternatives.

The new populism is perhaps most undefined here in the poorest and most remote corner of South America. Mr. Morales promises to exert greater state control over foreign energy firms and focus on helping micro-businesses and cooperatives. "The state needs to be the central actor," he said in a recent interview. But he is short on details, and that worries some economists.

Jeffrey Sachs, a Columbia University development economist and former economic adviser here, says he empathizes with Bolivia's poor and agrees that energy companies should pay higher taxes. But he says Bolivia cannot close itself off to the world. "Protectionism isn't really a viable strategy for a small country," he said.

If Mr. Morales does become president, he might well find that the slogans that rang in the streets are not much help in running a poor, troubled country.

Mr. da Silva, the Brazilian president, acknowledged as much in comments he made Wednesday in Colombia: The challenge, he said, is "to show if we are capable as politicians to carry out what we, as union leaders, demanded of government."

Return to Lundazi

John Grimond, former foreign editor,
revisits the corner of Zambia where he taught in 1965

GOD must have been working to a budget when He came to make Zambia for, after the spectacular creation of the Victoria Falls and a few lesser bursts of exuberance, it was nearly all monotonous bush for the rest of the country, and by the time He got to Lundazi the cash was clearly at an end. Lundazi is an unremarkable place, way out east on the Malawi border, and on the road to nowhere much. The only town—township, technically—in an area the size of Ohio, it has just one building of note, a hotel built in imitation of a small Norman castle by a district commissioner in the late 1940s, when the country was run by the British. The Castle is a charming curiosity, but from its battlements the horizons hold none of the views for which Africa is famous. For the most part, Lundazi is quiet, mildly decrepit and, in the dry season at least, always dusty. Yet, for all that, it is unpretentiously welcoming, and its people are delightful.

So it certainly seemed in 1965, when I went there first, as a British 18-year-old filling the gap between school and university, and so it seemed again when I revisited it a few months ago for the first time in 40 years. In 1965 Zambia, hitherto called Northern Rhodesia, was enjoying its first year of independence from Britain. The hated federation with Southern Rhodesia and Nyasaland had been dissolved at the end of 1963, and Ian Smith's Southern Rhodesia had not yet made its unilateral declaration of independence, which, when it came (in November 1965), was to bring turmoil to the entire region. Zambia, with huge reserves of copper, was potentially rich. It was led by a man of some decency, Kenneth Kaunda, and, all in all, there was a sense of hope. I shared it.

The next decades, though, were not good for Africa. Political instability, economic stagnation, corruption and civil breakdown overtook many of its countries, and Zambia had its share of setbacks. Yet it suffered no military coup (overlooking a little incident in 1997), no civil war and certainly no genocide. To people outside its borders, its travails were portrayed more in the statistics of international reports than in images on the evening news. So how had things changed in out-of-the-way Lundazi?

Not much, to judge by the state of the road I was again travelling, 40 years on. The road is important to Lundazi. There is only one of significance, which runs the 186km (116 miles) from Chipata, which was called Fort Jameson—or, more familiarly, Fort Jim—until 1969. Chipata is the capital of the Eastern province, and pretty much the endpoint of the Great East Road from the capital, Lusaka, so virtually everyone going to or from Lundazi uses the road from Chipata. In 1965 it was an unpaved artery, alternately hard and corrugated, then soft and sandy, always dusty and often, when unmarked bends or unseen chasms suddenly appeared, rather dangerous. That was in the dry season. In the rainy season it could be so muddy as to be impassable. Wet or dry, there would be monkeys in the trees, nightjars in the headlights and silent figures walking, running or mounted—often two at a time—on unlit bicycles. Sometimes, too, there would be huge trucks, throwing up clouds of dust and threatening to send any would-be overtaker hurtling into the bush.

The road has since been tarred, and a 4X4 can now bowl along the first 130km of the approach to Lundazi at some speed. But then, at Kazonde, the tar stops and thereafter, despite the patching and grading in progress, all vehicles must slow to little more than walking pace to navigate the slopes, trenches and pot-holes of the remaining 50km. Repairs had been started before but the contractors stopped work when they were not paid, and in 2004 locals removed many of the new metal culverts in order to fashion tools from them. The people here are so poor that all road signs—there are not many—are deliberately perforated, for otherwise they would soon be removed and turned into pots and pans.

Many sights along the road are unchanged after 40 years: the women carrying huge baskets on their heads, or bundles of logs, or drums of water; the broken-down lorries, one whose driver is asleep beneath the back axle, another whose sackclothed cargo has tumbled off and burst on the ground; the ox-carts, the bicycles, the wayside hawkers selling bananas, charcoal and sugarcane. But there are changes, too. For the first 60km going north, schools, brick houses and tin roofs suggest greater prosperity. The source of this seems to be a new diversification of crops. In the past, farming was almost entirely a subsistence affair with little grown except for maize, and the granaries visible from the road show that this remains the staple food. Now, though, there is evidence of cash crops: the tobacco sheds just outside Chipata and a store 115km beyond; two lorries laden with cotton; people selling sweet potatoes; patches of cassava under cultivation. And minds are evidently fed too. A sign at Lumezi points to a secondary school that was not there in 1965. More sinisterly, after 87km, an orphanage now stands by the road. This turns out to be a portent of one of the biggest changes since the 1960s.

Courage, Brother

Education had never been a priority for the authorities in Northern Rhodesia. The country had only three secondary schools for Africans in the mid-1950s, and two of those were run by churches. An expansion began in 1960, with talk of a secondary school for the capital of each of the seven rural provinces, but it was not until independence that one was opened in Lundazi. It was a simple affair: two classes to start with, all boys, four teachers (I was the fourth), few books and not much else. The dearth of equipment extended to hymn books, important as they were in a part of Africa which still showed the influence of David Livingstone and his Presbyterian beliefs. One or two hymns, however, had been cyclostyled, taught to the boys and committed to memory. "Courage, Brother, do not stumble" was particularly popular. Each day, morning assembly would start with the words, "We will now sing our hymn." A pause followed, just long enough to allow the possibility of suspense as to what the choice would be. Then, almost invariably, came, "Let us sing 'Courage, brother'," and the air swelled with a lowing of deep male voices.

The headmaster was Arthur Lewanika, a scion of the Lozi royal family whose kingdom, Barotseland, lay in western Zambia. He and his deputy, Roger Zulu, had been the only teaching staff until I and another recruit, Alfred Zaranyika, a Southern Rhodesian, arrived. Neither Alfred nor I had had any training as teachers, and I at least had no books for the lessons in French, maths and physics that I was supposed to give. It is difficult to believe that I taught anyone anything. Still, I had heard in Lusaka before returning to Lundazi that about ten of my former pupils had eventually graduated from university and some had become engineers (Alex Barton Manda), accountants (Major Mkandawire) or lawyers (Masuzu Zimba). At independence in 1964, the country had had fewer than 100 graduates.

The students, who came from far and wide within the surrounding area, were boarders, and so the school was always busy. But life in Lundazi, a town of perhaps 2,000-3,000 in those days, was quiet. In the evenings, the only noises apart from human voices were the hiss of the Tilley lamps that provided our light—no electricity then—and the calls of the hyenas that sometimes ate the Lewanikas' chickens and often came right up to the house that Alfred and I shared. The main amusements were provided by the trials of daily life: Alfred's mile-long sprint pursued by a swarm of bees; my old car catching alight as I drove past the market one day; Alfred's attempt to extend the life of his car battery by warming it up in the oven, an experiment that caused Arthur huge amusement when "over-baking" led to muffled explosions and quantities of boiling acid that seeped on to our kitchen floor.

It was almost impossible to get a car mended in Lundazi, or even to replace a battery. The shops were basic. Food could be bought in the market and sometimes people would come to the door offering a (live) chicken or some oranges. But Alfred was always scornful about the lack of choice: people were so much more enterprising, he said, in Southern Rhodesia (that was, of course, before Robert Mugabe had done his best to wreck the country). Anything even slightly sophisticated—oil lamps, blankets, cloth for *chitenges*, the nearly universal garment for women in those days—was available only from the shops owned by "Asians", notably Mulla Stores, founded by old Mr Mulla, who had made his way to Lundazi from Gujarat via Mozambique in the 1930s.

For a drink or a meal out, the place to go was the Castle, which was presided over by Lyn Jonquière, the only other "European", as whites were then called, in Lundazi. The Castle was where visiting politicians, contractors and civil servants would stay. It was kept spick and span by Mrs Jonquière. Of an evening, she could be found behind the bar, genially dispensing cold Castles (the hotel shared a name with a popular beer) or Portuguese wine brought in from Mozambique, Zambia's neighbour to the east, while Jim Reeves played on the gramophone. Thanks to its generator, the Castle had electricity.

You do not need a generator today in Lundazi: electricity is (usually) available from the Malawian national grid across the border, and the Castle now has television. It does not, however, have running water—except through the roof in the rainy season. The building is in a sad state, though its new leaseholder, Chifumu Banda, promises improvements.

Mr Banda, a native of Lundazi who is now a prominent lawyer in Lusaka, had warned me that I would see that Lundazi was now "worse off". The school, though, is vastly improved. The four teachers and 70 or so students have become 43 teachers and 864 students, and they occupy a bigger site. Though no one remembers any of the original staff, Arthur's name is memorialised in the name of one of the four boarding houses. As for the students' names, neither their first nor their surnames seem to have changed much: there are Ndhlovus, Phiris, Nyirendas and Bandas galore, preceded perhaps by Best, Gift, Major,

Mercy or Memory, even if, on this occasion, I meet no Time, Meat or Section Eight.

The school has its own water (pumped from three boreholes), a fish pond, four plump pigs and several sheep and goats. It grows its own vegetables. But only rarely do the students eat meat, and the relentless diet of *nshima*—maize porridge—has apparently provoked protests in the not-too-distant past. Little money has been available for maintenance, but broken windows are being replaced, prefects now have "executive neckties", the library contains a modest variety of books and there are ten computers, though not, as yet, an internet connection. (High telecoms charges and an overburdened relay station still keep most of Lundazi offline, though mobile phones have just arrived.) Another sign of change is that, in place of the "Procrastination is the thief of time" written on the blackboard by Alfred in 1965, a notice on a door now reads, "Don't trust corrupt politicians."

The new plague

Basic tuition is provided free, but the fees for boarding and any extra lessons come to nearly $200 a year, and uniform costs almost another $40. For most families, that is a fortune: about 70% of Zambians live on less than $1 a day. But in the past a family that could muster enough to start sending a child to school would usually be able to see the endeavour through. Today that is often untrue, simply because so many families are falling apart. In the list of students, the letter S (for a "single" orphan, i.e., a child who has lost one parent) or D (for a "double" orphan) occurs ever more often against the names as the classes grow older: 14 in Grade Nine, 60 in Grade Ten. The cause is AIDS. In total, over 120 of the 864 students have lost one or both parents to this latter-day plague.

Lundazi is far from insouciant about AIDS. The district has an AIDS co-ordinator, Christa Nyirenda, who struggles to carry out her work in the face of a constant lack of money. The churches also do their best. The Rev Frighted Mwanza's Presbyterian church, for example, is helping to look after several orphans and 55 others who are HIV-positive, some of them chronically ill. And along the road from the Castle, the Thandizani (meaning "Let's help one another") centre also offers advice, support and HIV testing. Set up in 1999 in a former cocktail bar, whose name is still clearly legible outside, it is considered a model non-governmental organisation, but it does not offer treatment.

That is done at Lundazi district hospital, or rather it is meant to be done there. The difficulty is that the hospital is old (1950s vintage), has only two doctors (for all the 290,000 people in the district) and has to charge for the anti-retroviral drugs that can arrest the ravages of AIDS in infected people. The very poor, about 20% of those who receive these drugs, get them free; the others must pay about $10 a month. The result is that only 114 people are getting treatment out of more than 500 who are known to need it. In reality, hundreds, if not thousands, should be receiving drugs. That is evident both from the number of orphans in the school and from a sign not far from the hospital: "Coffin Workshop".

Fortunately, coffins are not the only source of new jobs in Lundazi. The second-hand clothes market that has sprung up is another. On a dusty patch of ground now stands rack upon rack of western clothes, made perhaps in China or other parts of Asia but already worn in Europe or America and then given away to charities to be sold, for very little, all over Africa, even in places like Lundazi. This phenomenon, known as *salaula*, explains why so few of the women along the road now wear *chitenges*, and also why a man on a bicycle too poor to have shoes may be wearing a formal dress shirt. The trade provides T-shirts and skirts and trousers for many who could not afford them in the past, and jobs for those who sell the clothes. But it has made it difficult for Zambian textile producers to compete; this is dumping in the true sense of the word.

More hopeful for Lundazi is the slow, belated improvement in agriculture. On the outskirts of town are some new tobacco sheds, built by Stancom, an American multinational. It provides loans to small farmers, trains them in agronomy and sells them seeds and fertiliser, as well as the saplings they must plant if they cut other trees down for fuel to flue-cure their crop. A Malawian company, Limbe Leaf, has also come to Lundazi, as have several cotton companies—Dunavant, an American firm, Clark Cotton, from South Africa, and Chipata Cotton, a Chinese joint-venture. Lundazi now accounts for about 12% of Zambia's cotton production, and there is talk of Dunavant building a ginnery.

For all these welcome developments, agriculture around Lundazi is woefully undeveloped. Many people have gone hungry in the past few months thanks to a poor harvest: instead of falling evenly through the 2004-05 growing season, the rains came all at once, mostly early on. Yet the land is good. It could provide much more food and cash crops too, perhaps two harvests a year, with proper irrigation. But only now are some of the dams of the colonial era being restored to use, after years of neglect and silting up.

Hope on hold

It is time to leave Lundazi. Outside Mulla Stores, which seems to have had not even a lick of paint in 40 years, a few people are chatting. One or two others are bicycling from the direction of the *boma*, the administrative centre. Here again not much has changed. The impression is reinforced on the journey back along the pot-holed road to Chipata, even after a brief stop to greet Father Morrison and the other Catholic Fathers at Lumezi mission. But then there are the signs, really quite a lot of them, to the schools: primary schools, "basic" schools (which give a couple of years of secondary education) and Lumezi's secondary school. That is encouraging. So is the farming. But every so often are reminders of a darker side of the new reality: branches, laid down on the road to indicate a funeral. Bicyclists are expected to dismount, and trucks and cars to slow down, out of respect. I assume, perhaps wrongly, that AIDS has claimed another vicitm.

I had been prepared for most of what I found in Lundazi: I knew that half a century ago Zambia and South Korea had had roughly the same income per person, and now Korea's was 32 times greater. So I was expecting the accumulated evidence of 40 years of needless poverty, misgovernment and dashed hopes. Many of those dashed hopes I shared. But my main regret was that, back in 1965, I had not been able, instead of French and physics, to teach Korean studies, even if I had had no books. Perhaps it is not too late for someone else.

"The ruling party is the state, the regime, and the government melded into a seamless whole, sustained by violence and deploying violence to eviscerate all obstacles to its endless trips to the oil wells."

Nigeria: Chronicle of a Dying State

IKE OKONTA

To understand Nigeria today it may help to return to a bloody event that took place in early July 2002 in the country's oil-rich Niger Delta. Primary elections for the country's ruling People's Democratic Party were held in the town of Nembe that month. Two PDP factions, led by local politicians with substantial youth followings, supported separate candidates whom they hoped to see nominated local council chairman in the primary. The stakes were high. Whoever emerged victorious would most certainly move easily to victory when the main interparty elections were conducted in a year's time, given the PDP's near-total grip on power and strategic resources in Nigeria's various states and the country's capital. The new leader would in turn oversee the five oil fields in the area surrounding Nembe, from which Shell Petroleum Development Company, the Nigerian subsidiary of Royal Dutch/Shell, produces an estimated 200,000 barrels of oil per day.

By the evening of July 6, when primary elections came to an end in Nembe and the seven other local councils in Bayelsa State, 40 people had been killed in election-related violence, most of them in Nembe and Brass, a satellite community where the local subsidiary of Agip of Italy operates an oil terminal. The two factional leaders and their storm troopers were at the heart of the political violence that engulfed Nembe and forced many of its residents to flee.

Lionel Jonathan, one of the factional leaders, was head of Isongufuro, a cultural organization formed in 1992 that had metamorphosed into one of the most feared youth vigilante groups in Nembe. Jonathan, a former Bayelsa state commissioner for the environment, and his band of vigilantes were the state governor's political enforcers in Nembe. (He would later act as campaign manager for the governor's bid for reelection in April 2003.) Pitted against Jonathan and Isongufuro was Nimi Barigha-Amange, a former oil executive who nursed the ambition of displacing the governor and saw the local council primary election

as his opening move. Barigha-Amange was leader of Isenasawo, a rival vigilante group that emerged in 1998 to counter Isongufuro's excesses in Nembe. Although Isongufuro had the state government's backing and the machinery of "legitimate" violence at its disposal, Isenasawo was the dominant political force in Nembe at the time of the elections.

HOW TO RIG AN ELECTION

The primary elections were a farce, in which men of violence played the starring role. The governor, anxious to ensure that candidates of his choice emerged victorious, had dispatched teams of heavily armed anti-riot police on the evening of July 4 to Nembe, Brass, and other areas where he feared a free and open vote would go against him. Groups like Isongufuro were to provide local backup.

When party members in the region came out to vote on the morning of July 5, they found that voters' cards and other electoral materials had been diverted to the homes of local politicos loyal to the governor and his henchmen. In Nembe, Isongufuro dispersed voters, murdered several people who attempted to put up a fight, and confiscated election materials. In Brass, supporters of the governor, aided by a full complement of anti-riot police, launched a violent attack on politicians and their youth followers, beating them and setting their homes on fire. Officials dispatched by the PDP from the national capital to ensure an impartial vote were kidnapped when they proved "uncooperative."

Officials of Shell and Agip were on hand to lend support to the governor. Ordinarily, nonpartisan party officials would have taken election materials directly to voting centers, since the governor was also a PDP member and had a compelling interest in shaping the vote's outcome. Instead, Creek House, the governor's office and official residence in the state capital of Yenogoa, became a clearinghouse and storage center for voter cards. It was from here that helicopters provided by Shell airlifted the materials to Nembe, where Jonathan and Isongufuro then took over proceedings. Agip also airlifted voting material directly to its own terminal in Brass instead of to Twon, the local council headquarters designated by the party's national executive as the voting center. Votes were then allocated to candidates favored by the governor by aides sent from the capital for the purpose. A violent clash ensued between protesting locals and the anti-riot police and local toughs in the pay of the governor.

When the results of the party primaries were announced a week later, all the governor's candidates in the eight local councils, including Nembe and Brass, either were returned unopposed or "won" outright. The governor expressed satisfaction with the outcome and declared that the elections had been conducted in an atmosphere of "peace and tranquility." The state police chief dismissed as "unfounded" press reports that the primary election had been marked by murder, brigandage, and vote rigging. Local nongovernment organizations and journalists who had monitored the elections called for their cancellation and the removal of the head of police. No one paid attention to their pleas. Ordinary Nigerians picked up their disrupted lives and continued to plod on.

BORN AND RAISED IN VIOLENCE

Clearly, the political order in Nembe is founded on and sustained by violence. The British colonial project inaugurated this order in 1895 with unprecedented violence. Local Nigerian political elites reproduced and institutionalized it following formal independence in 1960. Yet, today, this malformed political order is in its last throes—with Nembe and the Niger Delta's other oil-bearing communities at the epicenter of a death dance.

Central to the order is a regime of rapine despotism and the poverty and powerlessness that are born of this condition. Producing political repression and material scarcity instead of the freedom and prosperity that are the legitimate goals of citizens globally, this order has not been able to find legitimacy in the eyes of the local people whom it has reduced to subjects these past 100 years. Thus, it is unable to find fertile soil in which to root and flourish. This malformed political order is dying because new social forces, forged in a cauldron of violence and the unremitting serfdom and scarcity that are its legacy, are now pressing against the barricades.

The prominent symptoms of the order's precariousness can be seen in the political and social crisis in which Nembe, the wider Niger Delta, and Nigeria are currently engulfed. The three components of this crisis are an accelerating loss of state sovereignty and concomitant decay of state institutions, locally and nationally; the government's failure to promote economic development, including for the people of Nigeria's oil communities; and worsening communal violence and youth anomie that are reshaping social relations into malignant forms in a region already awash in weapons and riven by ethnic conflict. Tensions that increasingly cut across local (Nembe), national (Nigeria), and global (Shell in Nembe oil fields) arenas suggest

that the current regime of institutionalized despotism is collapsing under the weight of past violence and present inequities.

WHEN POLITICS FAILS

Rory Carrol, the Africa correspondent of the *Guardian* of London, has written about a central feature of Nigerian economic life today. "What Nigerians call bunkering and oil executives call rustling has hit the big time," he wrote. "Criminal gangs are siphoning so much crude oil from pipelines in the Niger Delta that they have started using tankers to spirit it away.... Siphoning off such quantities amid a landscape of jungle and marsh, with thousands of creeks, requires sophisticated equipment and organization. To the dismay of the government and oil companies, the thieves have proved that they have this in abundance."

Nigeria is the world's seventh-largest exporter of oil, and Africa's largest. The country's daily output of 2.2 million barrels accounts for 80 percent of state revenues and 90 percent of foreign exchange earnings. (The government owns all oil rights in Nigeria and has a majority interest in every oil company operating there, including the joint venture with Royal Dutch/Shell Group.) Oil, clearly, is a strategic resource, at least viewed from the perspective of the country's governing elites.

Yet government power and the administrative structures vital to securing the all-important oil fields are dramatically shrinking in the Niger Delta and elsewhere in the country. What the *Guardian* neglected to point out was why the oil "bunkerers" are able to so flagrantly ply their illegal trade with impunity: the thieves too are members of the governing elite—invariably senior political figures and military officers deployed to the delta to police the oil fields and ensure that production is not disrupted by "restless" youth protesting the oil industry's adverse effects on their farmlands and water sources.

As social and economic conditions worsen in Nigeria, politics is no longer the instrument through which contending interests are conciliated in a structured framework. Politics is itself a struggle for control of the country's oil largesse, which, once secured in the form of loot, is used to further and consolidate political ends. In this struggle, the state and the means of violence at its disposal are the ultimate spoils. For whoever dominates the state necessarily controls the means to displace rival contenders for a disproportionate share of the oil bonanza. The adept, the unscrupulous, and sometimes the lucky emerge triumphant in this bruising contest. The losers, smarting from defeat and humiliation, turn their sights to lesser prizes. Some steal oil from pipelines.

An estimated 200,000 barrels are piped out of Nembe daily and the inhabitants receive neither rent nor royalties.

Terry Lynn Karl argues in *The Paradox of Plenty: Oil Booms and Petro-States* that "the revenues a state collects, how it collects them, and the uses to which it puts them define its nature."

Oil revenues and the array of political and economic arrangements thrown up to perpetuate this predatory enclave economy powerfully shape the nature of the Nigerian state, preoccupied as it is with a vicious, bare-knuckled struggle between dominant and rising elites to control this revenue.

The state as a result cannot act as the impartial arbiter of last resort between competing interests, embedded in social, economic, and political society but sitting above them. As a political instrument hijacked by the temporarily successful faction in the struggle for the oil prize, the Nigerian state is resented by unsuccessful rival factions. It may still be able to project power, but it is power lacking in real authority because its motives are suspect. It is also power without legitimacy, because rival factions and ordinary people on whom it is exercised see only commandments backed up by the threat of violence. And the commandments appear designed to make them part with their property on the pain of death.

ENTER THE MILITARY

Those able to challenge this illegitimate power, such as the oil rustlers, do. Ordinary citizens, such as the people of Nembe and the other oil-bearing communities in the Niger Delta, resort to civil disobedience, angry that their traditional sources of livelihood—their farmlands and fishing waters—have been devastated by half a century of uncontrolled oil exploitation. In the case of youth, this involves direct confrontation with Nigerian troops and riot police—the immediate, direct face of the oil rentiers who have visited so much grief and ruin on their communities.

The victorious faction responds by dispatching to the "volatile" region special forces equipped with rocket-propelled grenades, machine guns, tear gas, stun grenades, attack helicopters, fast-attack naval patrol boats, and the other paraphernalia of modern warfare, including experts in psychological terror. Entire hamlets and villages are razed and some of the inhabitants murdered or mutilated.

Even peaceful demonstrations provoke harsh reaction. On November 20, 2004, seven men were killed and many more injured when they attempted to mount a demonstration at an oil rig operated by Shell. More than 100 protesters had gathered on a barge near the rig and sent leaders to demand a meeting with oil officials to discuss languishing development projects. Instead, army troops appeared in boats and opened fire on the barge.

When faced with well-organized and determined opposition with popular grassroots support—as they have been with the 500,000 Ogoni people in the eastern Niger Delta fringes—government forces may decide to "sanitize" troublesome sites and root out the "subversive elements" disturbing the "public peace." An entire area may be secured in a lightning military maneuver. Death squads are sent in. When a squad suffers fatalities, as happened in Odi, a central Niger Delta town, in December 1999, remaining squad members may shoot everything in sight—including goats, chickens, and an 85-year-old woman too frail to leave her hut. The houses are torched and the experts in psychological warfare scrawl graffiti on the charred walls insulting the dead town and its gods.

It is all very impressive, all very military. This must be a powerful state, with its arm reaching out to smite its enemies even in the furthest uncharted parts of the empire! In fact, all this display of disproportionate violence, obscene in its extravagance, this spectacle—it is all a show.

The rentiers and the men of violence in their employ may be deadly serious in their determination to maintain their grip on the oil fields; this is demonstrated clearly enough by the shootings of unarmed youths and the raping of young girls. The piling of corpses and the young innocents traumatized for life testify to their earnestness. But the soldiers have no heart in the fight. They pile back into their trucks and beat a hasty retreat as soon as the latest round of killing is done. They do not hold conquered territory. There are no proconsuls to discipline and punish the new subjects. A few soldiers are left to guard the oil wells and the oil company workers, and the rest scamper off. The survivors crawl out of the bush, bury their dead, and resume their calls for justice.

THE HOLLOW STATE

In the capital, spokesmen for the rentiers deny that massacres are taking place in the delta oil fields. They speak only of rival ethnic militias hacking each other to death with blunt machetes. They are killing each other because … well, they hate each other. It is a "tribal" thing; ancient, not at all amenable to rational political solutions. They speak also of the bunkerers, loudly, threatening them with the full weight of the law.

The oil companies join the charade. Indeed, they amplify it by flying in obliging journalists from London and Paris and Houston to witness "firsthand" what these tribesmen are doing to each other. "This has nothing to do with us," they note. "We don't understand the thinking of these people. They are not like 'us.' Frankly, we don't know why they are fighting and killing each other." Then they bring up the subject of oil bunkerers. "They are ruining our business! We don't know what to do about them. And the guns. Where did they get such sophisticated weapons? The government must step in. We need more security or else this place will go up in flames!"

> *Government power and the administrative structures vital to securing the all-important oil fields are dramatically shrinking in the Niger Delta and elsewhere.*

It all rings hollow. Everybody, the rentiers and oil executives included, knows who the oil bunkerers are. They cannot move against them because they are all partners in the same dirty crime: plunder. They also all know the source of the guns that have flooded the delta: poorly paid soldiers selling their weapons to anyone, including "enemy" youth, for hard cash; the oil companies, stocking up their private caches and arming company police who subsequently pass them on to third parties; youth vigilantes recruited by the oil companies to protect their facilities and who use the money so obtained to buy rifles and machine guns to secure yet more "protection" work.

These are guns for hire, as in the American West during the gold rush. Only here crude oil is the new gold. The government's presence is only felt in the form of machine guns and jackboots. But that presence has an eerie evanescent quality: here now and gone the next instant, leaving bullet-perforated bodies to bear mute witness.

The decay of state institutions continues apace. The April 2003 presidential and governorship elections were openly and blatantly rigged by the PDP, in some areas returning more votes than there were actual people in the electoral register. The US-based Carter Center, which had sent a team to monitor the exercise, declared it a fraud.

The inspector general of police, the nation's chief law enforcement officer, was accused of soliciting and accepting financial rewards from state governors in return for "cooperation" during election time—that is, turning a blind eye when thugs hijacked ballot boxes from polling stations to enable them to inflate the vote in the governors' favor. A former deputy governor, under investigation for aiding and abetting the murder of the country's minister of justice, was released from detention and elected a senator on the ruling party's platform. High court judges assigned the case dropped it when they began receiving threatening phone calls in the night.

Elsewhere in that election year, in one of Nigeria's eastern states, a political contractor whose only claim to fame was that his brother was President Olusegun Obasanjo's chief of staff, organized the abduction of the governor whose election he had bankrolled only the previous month, sequestered him in a hotel room, and obtained his resignation at gun point. But not before readying a more pliable candidate to take over. In so doing he offered clear proof, if indeed any more were needed, that the ruling party is the state, the regime, and the government melded into a seamless whole, sustained by violence and deploying violence to eviscerate all obstacles to its endless trips to the oil wells.

THE LION WITHOUT CLAWS

The Maxim machine gun brooked no opposition in colonial times when Her Majesty's proconsuls embarked on the hazardous but very profitable project of taking the fat of the land, and in the process reduced its owners from citizens to subjects. A hundred years later their local clones continue dutifully on this path. The state sits on society; it does not emanate from it the better to secure it and make it more prosperous. Lacking a raison d'être, the Nigerian state looks more and more like a beached whale thrashing on the sand before its inevitable demise.

Meanwhile, the violent unrest spreads. In September 2004, Moujahid Dokubo-Asari, the head of a militia group called the Niger Delta People's Volunteer Force, declared war on the region's oil companies, interrupting production for several days and sending world oil prices above $50 a barrel. He succeeded in drawing senior government officials into negotiations, which resulted in a tentative peace deal. But Dokubo-Asari, who says he is fighting on behalf of more than 8 million Ijaws—the dom-

inant ethnic group in the southern delta region—warns he could shut off oil flows at any time. In the past he has called for secession of the Niger Delta as the only means for residents to gain control of its oil wealth. Violent conflict between his militia and a rival group, Niger Delta Vigilante, has resulted in numerous deaths of innocents.

The US government has sent warships to President Obasanjo under a security cooperation program ostensibly to check unrest and crude oil theft in the delta. But the youth insurgents there are not impressed. Poverty, state violence, and the bald fact of a dying ecosystem have combined to drive them to stand firm. The soldiers do not like what they hear. Entire swathes of the delta are now virtually no-go for them. Nor are they particularly unhappy about this. It is not really their fight. The petrodollars, after all, are shared in the presidential fortress in the capital.

Slowly, relentlessly, the sharp edge of the all-important instrument of violence is being blunted. It may not be immediately apparent, but the Nigerian state is dying. A lion without his claws may as well be dead.

BREAKDOWN IN NEMBE

How do these symptoms of a dying political order play out in Nembe? The signs of morbidity apparent in the wider Nigerian system are very much evident in the present political, economic, and social life of Nembe. The political order has broken down. The two rival militias are locked in a deadly duel for power. The traditional king of Nembe lives in Port Harcourt, some 100 nautical miles away, and rarely visits his people. He steers clear of the political turbulence generated by the militias. The majority of his council of chiefs also live in Port Harcourt, and the handful in Nembe do not participate in public affairs. Youth and vigilantes alike hold king and council partly responsible for the social and economic crisis that has taken over their lives.

The little semblance of authority that does exist is the armed anti-riot police dispatched by federal authorities. An uneasy truce holds between the police and the warring factions. Each watches the other carefully. All are armed and patrol the streets ostentatiously, brandishing machine guns. The vigilantes say the police are partisan—they support their rivals and also give protection to oil company officials whose activities have laid waste to their farmlands and fishing waters. The police say the two vigilante groups are criminal elements that have been terrorizing the city and extorting money from law-abiding oil workers. The ordinary people distrust all three groups, but keep their heads down in the face of the guns. Violence, not public virtue, is the basis of authority in Nembe.

The economic life of the people once turned on fishing. This was before the incessant oil spills, some of them caused by sabotage and theft, began to take their toll on fish life in Nembe creek and the surrounding lakes, ponds, and rivers. Now Nembe fishermen and women spend hours in the open sea and sometimes go home with no catch at all. The gas flaring in the vicinity of the oil fields has also substantially damaged plant life. Tidal waves spread spilled oil through the mangroves and onto farmlands, rendering them infertile. There is no manufacturing;

indeed, there is little economic life in Nembe. The bulk of the city's food is brought from Port Harcourt. The oil fields are all that is left, yet an estimated 200,000 barrels are piped out of Nembe daily and the inhabitants receive neither rent nor royalties. The anti-riot police are there to ensure that the arrangement remains in place.

Nembe is a city under permanent curfew. The streets are deserted. Social capital is a scarce commodity. All are at war with each other: king against his council; youth vigilantes against both and against themselves. The youths accuse the king and his council of "eating" the oil money and giving none to the ordinary people. Youth accuse youth of accepting money from Shell and refusing to share it. The quarrel usually ends in violence. Elders and women have been elbowed out of the public arena; they raise their voices on the pain of death and physical punishment, administered with relish by the vigilantes.

The factions of Nembe fight each other intermittently. They quarrel about whose leaders are supreme and which have the right to represent the city at the state level. Fierce arguments erupt over where local council buildings and other social facilities should be placed. Gunshots are exchanged. Young men die. Clashes with Okrika, a neighboring community, also are frequent, chalking up more bodies. Ownership of oil-bearing land is the perennial source of conflict. Neither thoughtful government policies nor mediating civil society agencies exist to deliver permanent peace.

TWILIGHT OF A MALFORMED ORDER

The political order in Nembe, based on rapine despotism, has not embedded itself in local society because its project runs against the deep desire of ordinary Nigerians for democracy and its material fruits. Power, social theorists have told us, is the ability to make someone do what you desire of them. During the colonial period violence, not capital, was used to extract wealth from the colonized. The state did not deliver development; it was the very repository of the violence necessary to reduce the inhabitants into subjects and coerce them to give up their wealth, in labor and raw material.

This predatory framework, since taken over by indigenous Nigerian elites, could not be permanently institutionalized. It has encountered sustained and determined resistance since the early years of the twentieth century from those to whom it has given only poverty and arbitrary rule. To maintain this illegitimate regime, constantly at risk of collapse, violence has to be applied and re-applied.

But herein lies the paradox of violence as the structuring basis of a political order. The more violence is deployed to prop up and sustain unjust economic and social arrangements, the more it undermines the very goal it seeks to achieve: a degree of social order within which the dominant elite can continue its business of seizing loot. People forcefully deprived of the right to represent their own interests in the crucial arenas of political and economic life are by definition discontented and impoverished subjects.

The discontented represent a real threat to the existing order, and that order is also deprived of vital contributions to the project of creating prosperity for the commonweal. Scarcity is the soil in which revolt is nurtured. Political violence deployed to maintain control over the dollars generated by oil wealth may work in the short term, but ultimately it defeats its own purpose. This process is clearly evident in Nembe and throughout Nigeria today. And that is why the malformed political order is dying.

IKE OKONTA is a visiting fellow at the University of California at Berkeley and coauthor, with Oronto Douglas, of Where Vultures Feast: Shell, Human Rights, and Oil *(London: Verso, 2003).*

China
The Quiet Revolution
The Emergence of Capitalism

Doug Guthrie

When Deng Xiaoping unveiled his vision of economic reform to the Third Plenum of the 11th Central Committee of the Chinese Communist Party in December 1978, the Chinese economy was faltering. Reeling from a decade of stagnation during the Cultural Revolution and already falling short of the projections set forth in the 1976 10-year plan, China needed more than a new plan and the Soviet-style economic vision of Deng's political rival, Hua Guofeng, to improve the economy. Deng's plan was to lead the country down a road of gradual and incremental economic reform, leaving the state apparatus intact, while slowly unleashing market forces. Since that time, the most common image of China, promulgated by members of the US Congress and media, is of an unbending authoritarian regime that has grown economically but seen little substantive change.

There is often a sense that China remains an entrenched and decaying authoritarian government run by corrupt Party officials; extreme accounts depict it as an economy on the verge of collapse. However, this vision simply does not square with reality. While it is true that China remains an authoritarian one-party system, it is also the most successful case of economic reform among communist planned economy in the 20th century. Today, it is fast emerging as one of the most dynamic market economies and has grown to be the world's sixth largest. Understanding how this change has come about requires an examination of three broad changes that have come together to shape China's transition to capitalism: the state's gradual recession from control over the economy, which caused a shift in economic control without privatization; the steady growth of foreign investment; and the gradual emergence of a legal-rational system to support these economic changes.

Reform Without Privatization

During the 1980s and 1990s, economists and institutional advisors from the West advocated a rapid transition to market insti-

tutions as the necessary medicine for transforming communist societies. Scholars argued that private property provides the institutional foundation of a market economy and that, therefore, communist societies making the transition to a market economy must privatize industry and other public goods. The radical members of this school argued that rapid privatization—the so-called "shock therapy" or "big bang" approach to economic reforms—was the only way to avoid costly abuses in these transitional systems.

The Chinese path has been very different. While countries like Russia have followed Western advice, such as rapidly constructing market institutions, immediately removing the state from control over the economy, and hastily privatizing property, China has taken its time in implementing institutional change. The state has gradually receded from control over the economy, cautiously experimenting with new institutions and implementing them incrementally within existing institutional arrangements. Through this gradual process of reform, China has achieved in 20 years what many developing states have taken over 50 to accomplish.

The success of gradual reform in China can be attributed to two factors. First, the gradual reforms allowed the government to retain its role as a stabilizing force in the midst of the turbulence accompanying the transition from a planned to a market economy. Institutions such as the "dual-track" system kept large state-owned enterprises partially on the plan and gave them incentives to generate extra income by selling what they could produce above the plan in China's nascent markets. Over time, as market economic practices became more successful, the "plan" part of an enterprise's portfolio was reduced and the "market" part grew. Enterprises were thus given the stability of a continued but gradually diminishing planned economy system as well as the time to learn to set prices, compete for contracts, and produce efficiently. Second, the government has gradually promoted ownership-like control down the government administrative hierarchy to the localities. As a result, the central government was able to give economic control to local administrators without privatization. But with economic control came accountability, and local administrators became very invested in the successful economic reform of the villages, townships, and municipalities under their jurisdictions. In a sense, as Professor Andrew Walder of Stanford University has argued, pushing economic responsibilities onto local administrators created an incentive structure much like those experienced by managers of large industrial firms.

Change From Above

Even as economic reform has proceeded gradually, the cumulative changes over two decades have been nothing short of radical. These reforms have proceeded on four levels: institutional changes instigated by the highest levels of government; firm-level institutions that reflect the legal-rational system emerging at the state level; a budding legal system that allows workers institutional backing outside of the factory and is heavily influenced by relationships with foreign investors; and the emergence of new labor markets, which allow workers the freedom and mobility to find new employment when necessary. The result of these changes has been the emergence of a legal-rational regime of labor, where the economy increasingly rests upon an infrastructure of ordered laws that workers can invoke when necessary.

Under Deng Xiaoping, Zhao Ziyang brought about radical change in China by pushing the country toward constitutionality and the rule of law to create rational economic processes. These changes, set forth ideologically as a package of reforms necessary for economic development, fundamentally altered the role of politics and the Communist Party in Chinese society. The early years of reform not only gave a great deal of autonomy to enterprise managers and small-scale entrepreneurs, but also emphasized the legal reforms that would undergird this process of change. However, by creating a body of civil and economic law, such as the 1994 Labor Law and Company Law and the 1995 National Compensation Law upon which the transforming economy would be based, the Party elites held themselves to the standards of these legal changes. Thus the rationalization of the economy led to a decline in the Party's ability to rule over the working population.

In recent years, this process has been continued by global integration and the tendency to adopt the norms of the international community. While championing global integration and the Rule of Law, Zhu Rongji also brought about broader political and social change, just as Zhao Ziyang did in China's first decade of economic reform. Zhu's strategy has been to ignore questions of political reform and concentrate instead on the need to adopt economic and legal systems that will allow the country to integrate smoothly into the international community. From rhetoric on "linking up with the international community" to laws such as the 2000 Patent Law to institutions such as the State Intellectual Property Office and the Chinese International Economic Trade and Arbitration Commission, this phase of reform has been oriented toward enforcing the standards and norms of the international investment community. Thus, Zhu's

objective is to deepen all of the reforms that have been discussed above, while holding these changes to the standards of the international community.

After two decades of transition, the architects of the reforms have established about 700 new national laws and more than 2,000 new local laws. These legal changes, added regulations, and experiments with new economic institutions have driven the reform process. A number of laws and policies in the 1980s laid the groundwork for a new set of policies that would redefine labor relations in fundamental ways. For example, the policies that set in motion the emergence of labor contracts in China were first introduced in an experimental way in 1983, further codified in 1986, and eventually institutionalized with the Labor Law in 1994. While there are economic incentives behind Chinese firms' willingness to embrace labor contracts, including the end of lifetime employment, these institutional changes have gradually rationalized the labor relationship, eventually providing a guarantee of due process in the event of unfair treatment and placing workers' rights at the center of the labor relationship. Incremental changes such as these have been crucial to the evolution of individual rights in China.

The obvious and most common response to these changes is that they are symbolic rather than substantive, that a changing legal and policy framework has little meaning when an authoritarian government still sits at the helm. Yet the scholarship that has looked extensively at the impact of these legal changes largely belies this view. Workers and managers take the new institutions seriously and recognize that the institutions have had a dramatic impact on the structure of authority relations and on the conception of rights within the workplace.

Other research shows that legal and policy changes that emphasize individual civil liberties are also significant. In the most systematic and exhaustive study to date of the prison system, research shows that changes in the treatment of prisoners have indeed resulted in the wake of the Prison Reform Law. And although no scholarship has been completed on the National Compensation Law, it is noteworthy that 97,569 suits were filed under this law against the government in 1999, a proportional increase of over 12,000 percent since the beginning of the economic reforms. These institutions guarantee that, for the first time in the history of the People's Republic of China, individuals can have their day in court, even at the government's expense.

The 1994 Labor Law and the Labor Arbitration Commission (LAC), which has branches in every urban district, work hand-in-hand to guarantee workers their individual rights as laborers. Chapter 10 of the Labor Law, entitled "Labor Disputes," is specifically devoted to articulating due process, which laborers are legally guaranteed, should a dispute arise in the workplace. The law explicitly explains the rights of the worker to take disputes to outside arbitration (the district's LAC) should the resolution in the workplace be unsatisfactory to the worker. Further, many state-owned enterprises have placed all of their workers on fixed-term labor contracts, which significantly rationalize the labor relationships beyond the personalized labor relations of the past. This

An Age of Jurisprudence

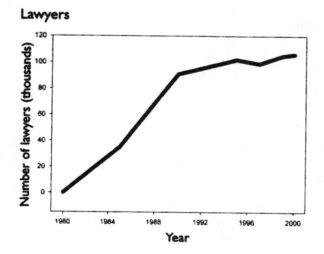

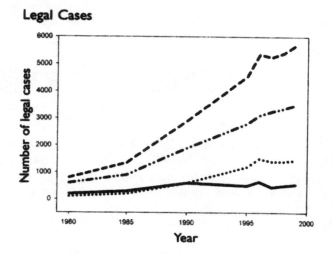

The above graphs depict two recent trends in China: a growing body of lawyers and an increasing number of legal cases. As the graph at left indicates, the number of lawyers in China has increased dramatically in the past 20 years, rising from fewer than 10,000 in 1980 to over 100,000 in 2000. The graph at right shows the growth in various types of legal cases over the same period. In particular, there have been significant increases in civil, economic, and first-trial cases.

2002 Statistical Yearbook of China

bundle of changes has fundamentally altered the nature of the labor relationship and the mechanisms through which authority can be challenged. For more than a decade, it has been possible for workers to file grievances against superiors and have those grievances heard at the LACs. In 1999, 52 percent of the 120,191 labor disputes settled by arbitration or mediation were decided wholly in favor of the workers filing the suits. These are official statistics from the Chinese government, and therefore should be viewed skeptically. However, even if the magnitude is incorrect, these numbers illuminate an important trend toward legal activity regarding workers' rights.

Many of these changes in labor practices were not originally adopted with workers' rights in mind, but the unintended consequence of the changes has been the construction of a regime of labor relations that emphasizes the rights of workers. For instance, extending the example of labor contracts that were being experimented with as early as 1983, these were originally intended as a form of economic protection for ailing enterprises, allowing a formal method of ending lifetime employment. However, workers began using the terms of employment codified in the contracts as the vehicle for filing grievances when contractual agreements were not honored. With the emergence of the LACs in the late 1980s and the further codification of these institutions in the Labor Law, the changes that were in progress became formalized in a set of institutions that ultimately benefited workers in the realm of rights. In a similar way, workers' representative committees were formed in the

state's interest, but became an institution workers claimed as their own. These institutions, which many managers refer to as "our own little democracy," were adopted early in the reforms to co-opt the agitation for independent labor unions. These committees do not have the same power or status as independent labor unions in the West, but workers have made them much more significant in factories today than they were originally intended to be.

Foreign Investment's Impact

At the firm level, there is a process of rationalization in which firms are adopting a number of rational bureaucratic systems, such as grievance filing procedures, mediation committees, and formal organizational processes, that are more often found in Western organizations. In my own work on these issues, I have found that joint venture relationships encourage foreign joint ventures to push their partner organizations to adopt stable legal-rational structures and systems in their organizations. These stable, legal-rational systems are adopted to attract foreign investors, but have radical implications for the structure of authority relations and the lives of individual Chinese citizens. Chinese factories that have formal relationships with foreign, and particularly Western, firms are significantly more likely to have institutionalized formal organizational rules, 20 times more likely to have formal grievance filing procedures, five times more likely to have worker representative committee meetings, and about two times more likely to have institutionalized formal hiring procedures. They also pay about 50 percent higher wages than other factories and are more likely to adopt China's new Company Law, which binds them to abide by the norms of the international community and to respect international legal institutions such as the Chinese International Economic Arbitration and Trade Commission. Many managers openly acknowledge that the changes they have set in place have little to do with their own ideas of efficient business practices and much more to do with pressure brought on them by their foreign partners. Thus, there is strong evidence that foreign investment matters for on-the-ground change in China.

> Foreign investors and Chinese firms are not interested in human rights per se, but the negotiations in the marketplace lead to transformed workplaces, which affect millions of Chinese citizens on a daily basis.

Given the common image of multinational corporations seeking weak institutional environments to capitalize on cheap labor, why would joint venture relationships with Western multinationals have a more positive impact in the Chinese case? The answer has to do with the complex reasons for foreign investment there. Corporations are rarely the leading advocates of civil liberties and labor reform, but many foreign investors in China are more interested in long-term investments that position them to capture market share than they are in cheap labor. They generally seek Chinese partners that are predictable, stable, and knowledgeable about Western-style business practices and negotiations. Chinese factories desperately want to land these partnerships and position themselves as suitable investment partners by adopting a number of the practices that Western partners will recognize as stable and reform-minded. Among the basic reforms they adopt to show their fitness for "linking up" with the international community are labor reforms. Thus, the signaling of a commitment to stable Western-style business practices through commitments to labor reform has led to fundamental changes in Chinese workplace labor relations. Foreign investors and Chinese firms are not interested in human rights per se, but the negotiations in the marketplace lead to transformed workplaces, which affect millions of Chinese citizens on a daily basis.

However, changes at the firm level are not meaningful if they lack the legal infrastructure upon which a legal-rational system of labor is built. The construction of a legal system is a process that takes time; it requires the training of lawyers and judges, and the emergence of a culture in which individuals who are part of the legal system come to process claims. This process of change is difficult to assess because it relies on soft variables about the reform process, such as, for example, how judges think about suits and whether a legal-rational culture is emerging. But we can look at some aspects of fundamental shifts in society. All of these changes, in turn, rest upon a legal-rational system that is slowly but surely emerging in China.

Finally, beyond the legal and institutional changes that have begun to transform Chinese society fundamentally, workers are no longer tied to workplaces in the way that they once were. In the pre-reform system, there was very little mobility of labor, because workers were generally bound to their "work units" for life. The system created a great deal of stability for workers, but it also became one of the primary means through which citizens were controlled. Individuals were members of their work units, which they were dependent on for a variety of fundamental goods and services.

This manufactured dependence was one of the basic ways that the Party exercised control over the population. Writing about the social uprisings that occurred in 1989, Walder points out that the erosion of this system is what allowed citizens to protest with impunity on a scale never before observed in communist China: "[W]hat changed in these regimes in the last decade was not their economic difficulties, widespread cynicism or corruption, but that the institutional mechanisms that served to promote order in the past—despite these long-standing problems—lost their capacity to do so." It is precisely because labor markets have opened up that workers are no longer absolutely dependent upon the government for job placements; they now have much more leverage to assert the importance of their own rights in the workplace. And while the private sector was nonexistent when the economic reforms began, the country has seen this sector, which includes both private enterprises and household businesses, grow to more than 30 million individuals. With the growth of the private sector, there is much greater movement and autonomy among laborers in the economy. This change has afforded workers alternative paths to status attainment, paths that were once solely controlled by the government.

Quiet Revolution

Much like the advocates of rapid economic reform, those demanding immediate political and social reform often take for granted the learning that must occur in the face of new institutions. The assumption most often seems that, given certain institutional arrangements, individuals will naturally know how to carry out the practices of capitalism. Yet these assumptions reflect a neoclassical view of human nature in which rational man will thrive in his natural environment—free markets. Completely absent from this view are the roles of history, culture, and pre-existing institutions; it is a vision that is far too simplistic to comprehend the challenge of making rational economic and legal systems work in the absence of stable institutions and a history to which they can be linked. The transition from a command economy to a market economy can be a wrenching experience, not only at the institutional level but also at the level of individual practice. Individuals must learn the rules of the market and new institutions must be in place long enough to gain stability and legitimacy.

The PRC government's methodical experimentation with different institutional forms and the Party's gradual relinquishing of control over the economy has brought about a "quiet revolution." It is impossible to create a history of a legal-rational economic system in a dramatic moment of institutional change. The architects of China's transition to capitalism have had success in reforming the economy because they have recognized that the transition to a radically different type of economic system must occur gradually, allowing for the maximum possible institutional stability as economic actors slowly learn the rules of capitalism. Capitalism has indeed arrived in China, and it has done so via gradual institutional reform under the communist mantle.

DOUG GUTHRIE is Associate Professor of Sociology at New York University.

China's Leader, Ex-Rival at Side, Solidifies Power

JOSEPH KAHN

Three years after becoming China's top leader, Hu Jintao has solidified his grip on power and intimidated critics inside and outside the Communist Party with the help of the man once seen as his most potent rival.

Mr. Hu, China's president and Communist Party chief, and Zeng Qinghong, vice president and the man in charge of the party's organizational affairs, have tackled the most delicate domestic and foreign policy issues as a team, governing as hardliners with a deft political touch, former Chinese officials and scholars with leadership connections said.

Their bond is a surprise because Mr. Zeng was the longtime right-hand man of the previous No. 1 leader, Jiang Zemin. A skillful backroom political operator considered to have strong military ties, Mr. Zeng was long viewed as the only person capable of challenging Mr. Hu for power.

Instead, Mr. Zeng and Mr. Hu joined forces last year to push Mr. Jiang to retire and to give up his position as leader of China's military, party insiders said. That cleared the way for Mr. Hu to become military chief and weakened the formidable political network Mr. Jiang had constructed in his 13 years at the helm.

Their alliance has shored up the Communist Party as it faces enormous stresses, including simmering social unrest and an uphill struggle to curtail corruption. They have quieted talk of serious factional splits and paved the way for Mr. Hu to impose his orthodox, repressive stamp on Chinese politics.

Mr. Hu and Mr. Zeng made back-to-back addresses at a secretive party conclave in May to promote a "smokeless war" against "liberal elements" in society that they contended were supported by the United States, said people who said they had been told about the speeches. They have also clamped down on nongovernmental organizations, tightened media controls and forced all of the 70 million Communist Party members to submit self-criticisms as an act of ritualistic submission to their authority.

Strong leaders unite to shore up a Communist Party facing social unrest and corruption.

At the same time, Mr. Hu and Mr. Zeng have taken bold and unexpected steps. They courted opposition political parties in rival Taiwan, plunged deeply into Hong Kong's political affairs and agreed to commemorate a late Communist Party leader popular among some liberals.

Cooperation between the men may be temporary, some knowledgeable about the party said, but the consensus among those who follow leadership affairs is that the two have decided they have more to gain by working together than by pursuing rival agendas.

"With Hu and Zeng working together, the leadership is very strong and hard-line," said one person with high-level connections. "I think China can maintain stability as long as they are together." Like others interviewed for this article, this person asked not to be identified because the authorities often punish people who speak publicly about high-level politics.

On paper, Mr. Hu, 62, has enormous authority on his own. He was anointed the future leader by Deng Xiaoping in 1992 at the relatively young age of 49. He then had a decade to cultivate allies before his formal accession in 2002.

Even so, he was never a part of Mr. Jiang's Shanghai-linked faction that held sway over the country since the mid-1990's. He now presides over the Politburo Standing Committee, the country's top governing body, that was expanded to include nine men, at least five of whom owed their promotions mainly to Mr. Jiang.

Mr. Hu also lacks deep ties in the military and the government bureaucracy, having risen through the party ranks in China's western region. He had virtually no public persona before assuming the top titles, and since then has presented a cardboard, dogmatic face to the world, generating little enthusiasm among the Chinese people.

He has emphasized collective decision making, submitting his proposed speeches, travels and major meetings to a formal vote of the Politburo. Mr. Zeng's influence may have increased more than that of any of the other top leaders.

Mr. Zeng, 66, has a very different political résumé. He owes his rise mainly to Mr. Jiang. The elder leader valued Mr. Zeng's military ties—Mr. Zeng's father was a revolutionary army commander and his brother is a senior military officer—and the skill Mr. Zeng displayed during the political battles Mr. Jiang faced until late in his reign. Party officials credit Mr. Zeng with helping to eclipse several of Mr. Jiang's political and military rivals.

Mr. Zeng also appears to have some clout among Westernized party officials, and China's class of wealthy entrepreneurs and the children of the party elite. He has taken a greater interest in China's ties with the United States than Mr. Hu has. He even plays tennis with Clark T. Randt Jr., the United States ambassador to China.

Mr. Zeng assumed control of the party's day-to-day organizational affairs in 1999 and was later made vice president and a member of the Politburo Standing Committee. That prompted speculation that Mr. Zeng might someday make a bid for the top leadership posts himself and that he would seek to keep Mr. Hu in check in the meantime.

The pressure, however, fell more on Mr. Jiang, now fully retired at age 79.

In the summer of 2004, Mr. Jiang, who had retained control over China's military after handing off his other titles to Mr. Hu, was viewed as competing with Mr. Hu for influence and creating a potentially dangerous rift in the power structure.

In one version of what followed, Mr. Zeng suggested to Mr. Jiang that he offer to resign ahead of the party's annual planning session that September. He implied that the resignation offer, which he suggested would be rejected by Mr. Jiang's loyalists on the Politburo, could clear the air and give Mr. Jiang a fresh mandate to retain his control over the military.

Mr. Jiang did something similar two years earlier, before an important party congress, and the tactic worked.

This time it did not. Mr. Hu, acting as vice chairman of the military commission, circulated Mr. Jiang's resignation among the military brass instead of the Politburo. Many military officers wanted to see the leadership transition completed and rallied around Mr. Hu as their new civilian leader. Mr. Jiang's resignation was then presented to the Politburo as a fait accompli.

Mr. Jiang, sidelined at his retreat in the Fragrant Hills outside Beijing, was described as furious and tearful when he realized he had been outmaneuvered.

Whether or not Mr. Jiang's departure resulted from a plot, the relationship between Mr. Hu and Mr. Zeng grew closer, party insiders said.

"I think they both have an special ability to wage political battles," said one person who has studied the events leading to Mr. Jiang's retirement. "They may have seen how much they could get done by working together."

Mr. Hu now relies on Mr. Zeng to manage crises, much as Mr. Jiang once did.

It was Mr. Zeng who oversaw the arrangements for the funeral of Zhao Ziyang, the party chief who became a hero to many government critics for opposing the leadership's decision to forcibly suppress the Beijing democracy protests in 1989. Mr. Zhao was purged and spent 15 years under house arrest before he died in January.

Mr. Zhao was given a public funeral and was buried in the elite Babaoshan cemetery in Beijing. But Mr. Zeng mobilized a huge police force and kept dissidents under house arrest during the event to prevent protests.

Just one month later, he and Mr. Hu sought to soften the repressive atmosphere that surrounded the funeral by agreeing to commemorate another fallen party chief, Hu Yaobang. The former party chief, who is not related to Mr. Hu, the president, lost power in 1987 and was remembered as a proponent of faster political change.

In February, President Hu visited Li Zhao, the widow of the former party chief, and told her that the party planned to commemorate her husband's achievements, said several people who said they had been told about the visit. They said it showed how President Hu and Mr. Zeng wanted to guard against accusations that they had ignored the contributions of their elders.

"It was a delicate balancing act to ensure stability," one person said.

Perhaps the biggest area of cooperation between Mr. Hu and Mr. Zeng has been rolling back what they argued had been a dangerous trend toward liberalization in the media and civil society.

In May, Mr. Hu and Mr. Zeng convened top officials to warn that just as governments in Ukraine, Georgia and Kyrgyzstan had been toppled, the government in China could be, too. They argued that the United States had fostered social unrest in those places and had similar designs on China, said people who said they had been told about the speeches.

They have since forced nongovernment organizations that focus on the environment, legal aid, health and education to find government sponsors or shut down. Many groups are also under pressure to stop accepting money from the United States and other foreign countries.

The leadership has also fired editors at publications that defied orders from the party's Propaganda Department, including, most recently, the bosses of the elite Workers' Daily newspaper and its associated publishing house, party insiders said. They have also tight-ened rules on foreign investment in China's television industry.

Although campaigns against China's increasingly diverse media happen periodically without lasting effect, several observers said the latest crackdown had been waged with an intensity that suggested that top leaders were paying more attention to the issue than they had in the past decade.

Chris Buckley contributed reporting for this article.

Sonia: and yet so far

Formed in a shambles, India's new government can only get better

THE comparisons that have been drawn with the Buddha and Mohandas Gandhi seem a bit overblown. But India reveres re-nunciation, and the decision by Sonia Gandhi (no relation to the Mahatma) to forgo the chance to become India's prime minister has mightily enhanced her stature. It has probably also been good for her party, Congress, and the prospects of the govern-ment it will lead under Manmohan Singh, her anointee, who was due to be sworn in on May 22nd.

The party itself found this hard to accept. Its members of par-liament seemed to think they had wandered into a production of "King Lear", a less happy tale of renunciation. In an emotional—nay, hysterical—meeting on May 18th they hectored, cajoled and begged Mrs Gandhi to change her mind and take the job. The un-bridled sycophancy was a reminder of the party's feudal attach-ment to the Nehru-Gandhi dynasty, and fear that, without her as a neutral figurehead, its kingdom will fall apart.

Mrs Gandhi was swayed neither by them nor by the several hundred equally high-pitched party activists gathered outside her front gate, some of whom felt genuinely cheated. They had worked hard to help her achieve the election result announced on May 13th, bringing a Congress-led coalition back to power against all expectations. They had rooted for her right to be prime minister despite being born in Italy. Some argued, incred-ibly, that if she was unwilling to serve, then her son Rahul, a 33-year-old first-time MP, should step in. Others complained she was yielding to a xenophobic campaign that should have been confronted.

That may indeed have been one factor in Mrs Gandhi's deci-sion. The Bharatiya Janata Party (BJP), the former ruling party, and its coalition partners had said they would boycott her swearing-in, though the BJP's leader and former prime min-ister, Atal Behari Vajpayee, would attend. One former BJP gov-ernment minister, Sushma Swaraj, and her husband were to resign their seats in the upper house of parliament in protest at the "national shame" of installing an Italian-born prime min-ister. Similarly, another senior BJP leader, Uma Bharti, had re-signed as chief minister of the state of Madhya Pradesh. After Mrs Gandhi's sacrifice though, Miss Bharti, a *sanyasin,* or reli-gious renunciate, looked rather silly.

Other groups linked to the Rashtriya Swayamsevak Sangh (RSS), the Hindu-nationalist mass organisation that spawned the BJP, had already taken this campaign to the streets. Ram Madhav, an RSS spokesman, blamed the BJP's electoral defeat in part on its failure to find "any real national-level emotive or ideological issue". There was a risk that Mrs Gandhi's Italian origins might fill that void and prove the dominant theme of the new government's early days. Rahul Gandhi and his sister Priy-anka were also said to oppose their mother's taking office, fearing for her life, though Rahul denied this. Their father, Mrs Gandhi's husband Rajiv, and grandmother, Indira, both former prime ministers, were each assassinated.

Mr Madhav claims that even some Congress voters were un-easy about being ruled by a native Italian, and he probably has a point. She speaks Hindi, wears sarees and says she prefers *naan* to pasta. But her foreign birth would always have been a stick to beat her with. Her party's mandate in the election was hardly a clear-cut endorsement either of its policies or its leader. Congress gained just under 27% of the national vote, about 1.5 percentage points less than in the last election in 1999. Its coa-lition won almost exactly the same share of the votes, about 36%, as the BJP's.

Mrs Gandhi herself had always been careful not to promote herself as a prime-ministerial candidate. During the campaign, this was seen as a shrewd tactic to stop the BJP turning it into a presidential-style contest between an untested, foreign-born novice and the popular, statesmanlike Mr Vajpayee. It now seems that Mrs Gandhi all along saw her duty as limited to res-cuing her late husband's party from its recent slump and, in her words, to providing India with "a secular government that is strong and stable"; but not leading it.

Outside the Congress hot-house, some were relieved at that. The political drama in Delhi was played out against the distant thud of a crashing stockmarket. The Mumbai exchange suffered its worst-ever day on May 17th, at one point having fallen by more than 17%. The next day, news that Mrs Gandhi was thinking of stepping aside helped spur a recovery.

One reason for the market's cheer was the assumed identity of Mrs Gandhi's replacement. Having attributed to her the

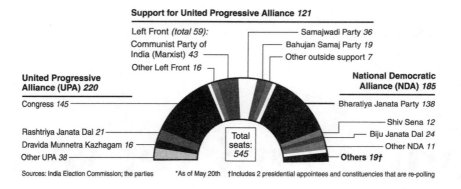

Support for United Progressive Alliance *121*

Left Front *(total 59)*:
Communist Party of India (Marxist) *43*
Other Left Front *16*

Samajwadi Party *36*
Bahujan Samaj Party *19*
Other outside support *7*

United Progressive Alliance (UPA) *220*

Congress *145*

Rashtriya Janata Dal *21*
Dravida Munnetra Kazhagam *16*
Other UPA *38*

Total seats: *545*

National Democratic Alliance (NDA) *185*

Bharatiya Janata Party *138*

Shiv Sena *12*
Biju Janata Dal *24*
Other NDA *11*

Others *19†*

Sources: India Election Commission; the parties   *As of May 20th   †Includes 2 presidential appointees and constituencies that are re-polling

wisdom of the Buddha it was inevitable that Mrs Gandhi's parliamentary colleagues would ask her to nominate one. Her choice, Manmohan Singh, is popular with investors as the author of India's economic liberalisation. An academic economist, he was Congress's finance minister in 1991, when, in response to a balance-of-payments crisis, the government launched a package of reforms, beginning the dismantling of the "licence raj" of state planning, import controls and excessive regulation that was Nehru's legacy.

So his presence is heartening for investors who have two worries about the new government: first, that it will be hostile to business and reluctant to continue or accelerate the liberalisation Mr Singh began; second, that it will be unstable and short-lived. The fears stem partly from its status as a minority government. Not only will Congress rely on a coalition—to be known as the United Progressive Alliance (UPA)—but the UPA will itself be a minority (see chart), relying on the "outside support" of other parties, of which much the biggest is a "Left Front" dominated by the Communist Party of India (Marxist), or CPI (M).

Playing the red card

The CPI (M) has been in power in the state of West Bengal since 1977, and like ruling communist parties elsewhere, has become pragmatic in office. Once notorious for red tape and strikes, the state has recently been hard-selling its attractions as a destination for inward investment in information technology and services such as call-centres. The Communist chief minister, Buddhadeb Bhattacharjee, boasts of its success in promoting enterprise: exporting roses to the Netherlands, and housing potato-processing facilities for PepsiCo. It has even, with the help of British government aid, been closing down some of its loss-making state enterprises.

But during the election, Mr Bhattacharjee said that the CPI (M) could never join a Congress-led coalition, because of differences on economic policy. Mr Singh, whom the Communists are now happy to accept as a prime minister, was "the first torch-bearer for the IMF". One cause of the stockmarket crash was a suggestion by a Communist spokesman that the disinvestment ministry, which oversees India's privatisation programme, should be abolished (not a bad idea in itself, but he appeared to want to abolish privatisation as well).

The possibility of an end to the "disinvestment" of state enterprises, which in recent months helped fuel a surging stockmarket, is a specific fear of investors. A broader concern is that all economic policy will likewise be hostage to the populist demands of Congress's coalition partners. A number of the reforms that economists argue are most needed will probably not make much headway. Labour laws, for example, which make it hard to shed staff without state-government permission, are unlikely to be tackled.

The same is true of the reform that Arun Shourie, the outgoing BJP disinvestment minister, believed the most important of all, to the system by which funds are allocated to government departments and states. He argued that these reward poor performance—"the bigger the deficit, the bigger the grant". But tampering with this system may not appeal to state leaders whose support Congress needs, such as Laloo Prasad Yadav of Bihar, a state notorious for economic underperformance.

However, fears that reforms are about to be shelved, and the markets' reaction, seem excessive. The reform process has always involved more stops than starts, and Congress may be no worse placed to pursue it than was the BJP. Surjit Bhalla, of Oxus Fund Management, a hedge fund in Delhi, says that, since 1991, every government that has taken power in India has accelerated the reforms, and he expects this one to be no different. The Left, he says, is to Congress as the RSS was to the BJP, minus the RSS's communal tendencies. Just as the BJP had to resist the protectionist "self-reliant" economic tendency within the RSS, so Congress will be fending off leftist conservatism.

The markets are now awaiting the "common minimum programme" Congress and its partners are drafting. To the extent that this mirrors Congress's own manifesto, it will differ little from the BJP's approach, though privatisation is to be "more selective", and not pursued, in Mr Singh's phrase, "as an ideology".

The national vote was too evenly split, and too driven by local factors, to be interpreted as a clear mandate; much less, despite some attempts to do so, could it be seen as a national indictment of the reforms. But it has been taken as a slap in the face for the BJP from the mass of Indians who live in poverty in the countryside. Every new government pays them lip-service. This one, relishing the shock of victory, knows better than most how much it needs to concentrate on agriculture and rural infrastructure. That, however, is itself an argument for accelerated reform.

Stability pacts

The other fear about the new government is that it will prove shaky. Because it tends to be a competitor for power at the state level with its potential partners, Congress has in the past found it hard to forge national coalitions. Many UPA members have a price: one wants a new state carved out of Andhra Pradesh; another demands the ditching of harsh anti-terrorist legislation. Others, notably the Left parties and the Samajwadi ("Socialist") Party, which won 36 seats in India's largest state, Uttar Pradesh, are not actually joining the coalition: a form of power without accountability. Not having the responsibility that goes with cabinet seats, they could blackmail the government on issue after issue, and risk turning policymaking into a saga of serial brinksmanship.

Power in Indian politics is a great adhesive. Having touched it, the Left will be loth to let it slip. But managing such a complex and potentially fissile arrangement will demand great political skill. Mr Singh is, in this respect, untried. He is much admired as a kind, courteous and clever man. As a Sikh, he is India's first non-Hindu prime minister and living testimony to its secular traditions. But he sits in the upper house of parliament and has never won a direct election, though he will now have to do so in the next six months.

His first challenge will be to form a government that satisfies his coalition partners without sacrificing his policy goals. He is fortunate in being able to fill most jobs from Congress ranks. Besides the economic portfolios, much interest focuses on the foreign ministry and the post of national security adviser.

The next stage in the peace process with Pakistan—talks on measures to build confidence about the two countries' nuclear arsenals—is due next week. In August, foreign ministers are to meet, and by then the two sides should have begun to discuss the hardest issue, the status of Kashmir. Congress has supported the peace initiative Mr Vajpayee launched last year.

But it may find it harder to negotiate on Kashmir than would the BJP, whose Hindu-nationalist background makes it less vulnerable to attack from chauvinists. The peace process was to be Mr Vajpayee's claim to a place in history. It would be good if, in opposition, he ensured that it enjoys bipartisan support. But his party's willingness to stoke racist antipathy to Mrs Gandhi, and his own silence as it did so, do not bode well for restraint.

India's Democracy Provides Lessons

The struggling nation has integrated its diversity in a way that could be an example to Iraq.

Rajan Menon

NORTH SUTTON, N.H.—India's failures are legion and impossible to ignore. Poverty and desperation abound. Infant mortality is unacceptably high. Schools and healthcare are substandard—if available at all.

Roads and other infrastructure are primitive or in poor repair. The Indian government seems unable to adequately protect the country's Muslim minority (about 12% of the population) from periodic pogroms, and violence against lower castes erupts regularly.

Conflicts with Pakistan over Kashmir continue, made more alarming by the fact that both countries now possess nuclear weapons.

But despite these very real problems, most of what we read about India misses what is most remarkable about the country: its sheer survival.

As the United States attempts to shape a new government in Iraq, the lessons of India are perhaps worth considering, not least because the challenge Iraq faces—keeping a multiethnic country whole without sliding into dictatorship—is one that India, despite all its difficulties, has faced and overcome against considerable odds.

When India gained independence in 1947, it seemed too big and too diverse to hold together. Though a majority of the country's 400 million people were Hindus, there were Muslims, Christians (Protestants and Catholics), Jews, Jains, Buddhists and Zoroastrians. An array of languages (18 now have official status), thousands of dialects and a labyrinthine system of castes and sub-castes added to this bewildering complexity. Few outside

India believed that such an unwieldy behemoth could remain a single country.

But the system has held together, and it has done so despite some fearsome shocks, starting with the assassination of Mahatma Gandhi soon after Indian independence and continuing with the slaying of two prime ministers, three wars and numerous crises with neighboring Pakistan, the emasculation of democracy during the "emergency" proclaimed from 1975 to 1977 by then-Prime Minister Indira Gandhi, widespread and devastating riots sparked by plans to declare Hindi the national language, and separatist movements of Muslims in Kashmir, Sikhs in the Punjab and Nagas and Mizos in India's remote northeast.

Not only has Indian polity proved sturdy enough to weather these shocks, it has done so without abandoning democracy. With the exception of Indira Gandhi's "emergency," there has not been an interruption in—or even a real threat to—democratic institutions. Political power in the country has been passed from party to party frequently in federal and local elections, and voter turnout is high. The military has remained thoroughly under civilian control. Furthermore, India has consistently allowed a free press—in English and the many Indian languages. And a staggering array of civic groups promotes the interests of women, castes and language groups, professions and the environment. Labor unions engage in collective bargaining and strike regularly. Political demonstrations are a daily occurrence.

If the survival of India as a unified country is remarkable, the survival of its democracy is astonishing. When India became independent, it lacked any tradition of modern democracy. It had an abysmally low per capita income and a minuscule middle class, and most of its people were illiterate. Democracy, so social scientists tell us, cannot survive under such circumstances.

The standard explanation for how India has managed to reconcile diversity and unity while also fostering democracy invokes the country's colonial legacy. The British, so the explanation goes, transplanted their hallowed traditions, ideas and institutions of civil liberties and the rule of law.

Yet this account doesn't hold up on closer inspection. Let's leave aside for the moment the fact that most expansions of democratic rights in colonial India were not the products of benevolent tutelage but necessary and shrewd responses to the gathering momentum of an Indian nationalist movement. The main problem with crediting the British with India's success at democracy is that there is no shortage of former British colonies that, upon becoming independent, turned thoroughly undemocratic, with the military seizing power and ruling through naked force. Consider, for example, the post-colonial histories of Egypt, Iraq, Ghana, Nigeria, Kenya and Burma. Consider, in particular, India's neighbor and cultural cousin Pakistan, which has been ruled by the military for most of its existence.

There is no simple explanation for why India has not only survived but also maintained a fairly robust democracy. But what is clear is that the first could not have been attained without the other. A democratic order has been critical in preventing India's fragmentation.

Elections, a free press and civil society have provided multiple mechanisms for political participation—for power to be pursued, for grievances to be aired and for resources and remedies to be sought. India's democratic institutions work as a series of safety valves that prevent conflict from becoming the prevalent mechanism for deciding the most basic societal questions: who gets what, and when and how.

Moreover, India's federal system of 28 states, which were created to represent major linguistic and cultural groups, provides for substantial decentralization and autonomy, both of which have increased as local parties representing the interests of particular peoples have grown in number. The design is at times unwieldy and untidy, but it has served to prevent contentious issues from being automatically projected onto the national stage.

This arrangement, along with India's heterogeneity, has helped prevent crises in one region of the country from rattling the entire political system; instead, disturbances remain localized. In distant Kerala (both spatially and culturally removed), Kashmir's violence is viewed with a degree of detachment. Likewise, the bloodshed that accompanied Sikh separatism in the northern state of Punjab did not inflame passions in the southern state of Tamil Nadu.

The paradox, then, is that India's diversity and its seemingly cumbersome political system have enabled unity and democracy to combine. Seeming weaknesses have proved to be assets.

Now that economic reform, which was initiated in 1991, is well underway, India's growth rates have picked up, averaging 6% since 1992, compared with 3.5% in the 1970s and early 1980s. Foreign investment is increasing as barriers to entry are being dismantled. And a wealth of English-speaking scientists and engineers is enabling India to exploit the opportunities provided by globalization.

India's democratic politics rule out any Chinese-style economic reform by fiat. Nor will there be any counterpart to Deng Xiaoping, the all-powerful moving force behind the Chinese economic miracle. Democracy, which requires compromise, will ensure that India's pace of change is slow and that there are plenty of setbacks.

But the gradualism necessitated by participation and the reconciliation of differences will give the reforms that emerge greater legitimacy. And if, in its lumbering fashion, India does get its economic act together, it will combine unity, democracy and prosperity. It will then have performed a miracle of its own. Whether Iraq, like India, can defy the odds remains to be seen, but Iraq's leaders could certainly look east for some useful lessons.

Rajan Menon is Monroe J. Rathbone professor of international relations at Lehigh University and a fellow at the New America Foundation.

MIDDLE EAST DEMOCRACY

People in the Middle East want political freedom, and their governments acknowledge the need for reform. Yet the region appears to repel democracy. Arab regimes only concede women's rights and elections to appease their critics at home and abroad. If democracy arrives in the Middle East, it won't be due to the efforts of liberal activists or their Western supporters but to the very same Islamist parties that many now see as the chief obstacle to change.

By Marina Ottaway and Thomas Carothers

"The Middle East Is the Last Holdout Against the Global Democratic Trend"

No. The Middle East is on the wrong side of the global democratic divide, but unfortunately it does not lack company. As Russia slides into authoritarianism, the former Soviet Union is becoming a democratic wasteland with only a few shaky pockets of pluralism, such as Georgia, Ukraine, and Moldova. Central Asia is no better off than the Arab world in terms of democracy. A depressingly large swath of East and Southeast Asia from North Korea and China down through Vietnam, Laos, and Burma to Malaysia and Singapore—is a democracy-free zone that shows few signs of change.

Nor was the Middle East immune to the "Third Wave," the decisive expansion of democracy that started in southern Europe and Latin America 30 years ago and subsequently spread to other parts of the world. During the 1980s, several Arab countries, including Egypt, Tunisia, and Jordan, initiated political reforms to permit multiparty competition. These reforms lost momentum or were undone in the 1990s, however, as Arab leaders proved unwilling to risk their own power through genuine processes of democratization. Tunisia, for example, moved back to rigid authoritarian rule.

Today, political reform is percolating again in the region, amid growing public frustration over chronic corruption, poor socio-economic performance, and a pervasive sense of stagnation. The Sept. 11, 2001, terrorist attacks also created pressure for reform—from both the United States and some Arabs who began to question why their societies were so widely viewed as dangerous political cesspools. Talk about political reform and democracy is rife even in the Gulf monarchies where such issues had been taboo. The steps taken thus far in most countries, however, are modest. Although the Arab world is not impervious to political change, it has yet to truly begin the process of democratization.

"Democracy in the Middle East Is Impossible Until the Arab-Israeli Conflict Is Resolved"

Wrong. Arab governments curb political participation, manipulate elections, and limit freedom of expression because they do not want their power challenged, not because tension with Israel requires draconian social controls. When the government of Kuwait refuses to give women the right to vote, it does so out of deference to the most conservative elements of its population, not out of fear that voting women will undermine the country's security. Fear of competition, not of a Zionist plot, leads the Egyptian ruling party to oppose competitive presidential elections. When it comes to democratic reform, the Zionist threat is merely a convenient excuse.

Yet failure to resolve the Arab-Israeli conflict prevents the United States from gaining credibility as an advocate of democracy in the Middle East. Liberal Arabs perceive claims by the United States that it wants democracy in the Middle East as hypocritical, pointing to what they see as American indifference to the rights of the Palestinians and unconditional support for Israel. For their part, many Arab governments do not take U.S. pressure to democratize their region seriously, believing that the need for oil and fear of upsetting regimes that recognize Israel will trump Washington's desire for democratic change. U.S. credibility in the Middle East will not be restored—and the unprecedented level of anti-American resentment will not abate-until the United States makes a serious, balanced effort to tackle the conflict. Without such credibility, Washington's effort to stimulate democratization in the region will be severely constrained.

"The United States Wants Democracy in the Middle East"

Up to a point. The democratic transformation of the Middle East emerged as a central objective of U.S. foreign policy during the Bush administration. This new policy is a sharp reversal of several decades of steadfast support for many autocratic regimes in the region, such as those in Egypt, Saudi Arabia, and Jordan. It reflects the new post-9/11 conventional wisdom that Middle East democracy is the best antidote to Islamist terrorism.

Although this desire for democracy may be heartfelt, the United States has a lengthy laundry list of other priorities in the region: access to oil, cooperation and assistance on counterterrorism, fostering peace between Israel and its neighbors, stemming the proliferation of weapons of mass destruction, and preventing Islamist radicals from seizing power.

The newfound U.S. enthusiasm for democracy competes for a place in this mix. Fighting Islamist militants and safeguarding oil still compels the United States to cooperate with authoritarian regimes. People in the region watched as the United States took a tough line against Iran and Syria while failing to push Saudi Arabia, Egypt, Tunisia, or other friendly tyrants very hard. The Bush administration launched new diplomatic endeavors and aid programs to support positive change, such as the Broader Middle East and North Africa Initiative and the Middle East Partnership Initiative. But they consist of mild, gradual measures designed to promote democratic change without unduly challenging the authority of incumbent governments.

Moreover, despite the president's conviction that democratic change in the Middle East is necessary, a great deal of ambivalence remains within the U.S. policy bureaucracy about the prospect of any rapid political openings in the region. This sentiment is particularly true of the State Department and the intelligence community. Some experts worry that, given the political mood of most Arab citizens—who are angry at the United States and sympathetic to political Islam—free and open elections could result in some distinctly unfriendly regimes.

"The War in Iraq Advanced the Cause of Democracy in the Middle East"

Not yet. The U.S.-led war in Iraq removed from power one of the most heinous, repressive dictators in the region and opened up the possibility that Iraq will one day have a pluralistic political system held together by consensus rather than violence. The actual achievement of democracy in Iraq, however, remains distant and uncertain. The Path to that goal will be measured in years rather than months.

The war's political effects in the rest of the region—especially the way it exposed the hollowness of Saddam Hussein's regime—has contributed to increased calls for political reform in many Arab countries. Real progress toward democracy, however, is minimal. In addition, the war provoked some Arab governments, such as Egypt, to limit the already constrained political space they allow as a defensive gesture against public protests and as an excuse for prosecuting opponents.

Regrettably, President George W. Bush's repeated justification of the war as a democratizing mission has discredited some Western-oriented Arab democrats in the eyes of their fellow citizens. Many Arabs have come to view democracy itself as a code word for U.S. regional domination. The unpopularity of the war and the abuses against Iraqis at Abu Ghraib prison have further tarnished the reputation of the United States and fueled Islamist extremism.

Proponents of democratic contagion argue that if Iraq holds successful elections in early 2005, this example will resound loudly in the Arab world. But much of the Arab world will likely view such elections, even if they come off well, as highly flawed. Some parts of the predominantly Sunni areas of Iraq are not expected to participate in the elections, and many Arabs will inevitably accuse the United States of manipulation, because the elections will be held under U.S. occupation. Few Arabs will be dazzled into holding a new view of democracy on the basis of one election. Many countries in the region already hold elections of varying degrees of seriousness and importance, including one in Algeria earlier this year, which a Western observer described as "one of the best conducted elections, not just in Algeria, but in Africa and much of the Arab world."

Promoting democracy throughout the Middle East will require doing away with fantasies of a sudden U.S.-led transformation of the region and taking seriously the challenge of building credibility with Arab societies. Moreover, if the United States is to play a constructive supporting role, it must seriously revise its cozy relations with autocratic regimes, show a sustained ability to apply nuanced diplomatic pressure for political change at key junctures, and back up this pressure with well-crafted and well-funded assistance. Washington must prepare to accept emboldened political forces, and eventually new governments, that are uninterested in doing the United States' bidding. Embracing Middle East democracy in principle is easy; truly supporting it remains an enormous challenge.

"Islamists Are the Main Obstacle to Arab Democracy"

Think again. The standard fear is the "one person, one vote, one time" scenario: Islamists would only participate in elections to win power and put an end to democracy immediately. Hence, the argument goes, they should not be allowed to participate.

True, the commitment to democracy of even moderate Islamists is uncertain and hedged by the caveat that democratic governments must accept Islamic law. However, the chances of an overwhelming electoral victory that would allow Islamists to abrogate all freedoms at once is remote in the Arab world. During the last decade, Islamist parties and candidates have participated in elections in eight Arab countries (Algeria, Bahrain, Egypt, Jordan, Kuwait, Lebanon, Morocco, and Yemen), always with modest results. (These elections suffered from various degrees of government interference, but there is no indication that the Islamists would have won in a more open environment.) And Turkey, a country where an Islamist party took power with a large majority, is becoming an encouraging example of democratic success.

Although the prediction that Islamist electoral victories would lead to democracy's demise in the Middle East have so far proved unfounded, the possibility cannot be ruled out. Fear of such takeovers remains in many Arab countries and the United States. Many Arab regimes use this fear to justify meddling in elections and placing restrictions on political participation. The presence of Islamist parties thus complicates the process of democratization.

But Islamist parties are also integral to democratization because they are the only nongovernmental parties with large constituencies. Without their participation, democracy is impossible in the Middle East. The future of democracy in the region depends on whether a sufficient number of such parties moderate their political views and become actors in a democratic process, rather than spoilers in the present autocratic states, and whether incumbent governments stop hiding behind the Islamist threat and accept that all their citizens have a right to participate.

Arab Countries Have a Historic Propensity Toward Authoritarianism"

Yes. But so what? Most societies have lived under authoritarian rule for some time, often for a long time. Democracy is a relatively recent historical phenomenon. Even in the United States and Europe it was only consolidated through universal suffrage in the last century.

Arab rulers have been highly authoritarian, but no more so than European or Asian rulers for most of history. Arabs developed a political system based on Islam through the caliph, an individual who served as supreme leader of all Muslims. Europeans clung to the concept of the Holy Roman Empire for centuries after it ceased to exist in practice, fought ferocious religious wars for hundreds of years, and adopted the concept of separation of

church and state rather late and incompletely. The Arab world, for most of its history, was quite similar to the rest of the world.

Even in the 1960s and 1970s, much of the Arab world was highly representative of the major political trends of the day. Most Arab countries outside the Gulf displayed the combination of nationalism and socialism that constituted typical Third World ideology at the time. Gamal Abdel Nasser in Egypt, alongside Jawaharlal Nehru in India and Marshal Tito in Yugoslavia, was a major champion of this ideology, which waned in the 1980s with the end of the Cold War and the rise of globally connected economies.

To ascribe the lingering Arab absence of democracy to some unique historic affinity for authoritarianism, stemming from Arab culture, Islam, or anything else is thus factually incorrect. It is also politically defeatist, attributing a quality of inevitability that belies the experience of political change in other parts of the world.

"Promoting Women's Rights Is Crucial for Democratic Change"

False. This myth, a favorite of women's organizations and Western governments, reflects the combination of correct observation and false logic. No country can be considered fully democratic if a part of its population (in some cases, the majority) is discriminated against and denied equal rights. But efforts to change the status quo by promoting women's rights are premature. The main problem at present is that Arab presidents and kings have too much power, which they refuse to share with citizens and outside institutions. This stranglehold on power must be broken to make progress toward democracy. Greater equality for women does nothing to diminish the power of overly strong, authoritarian governments.

Arab leaders know this truth all too well. Many autocrats implement policies to improve women's rights precisely to give themselves reformist credentials and score points with Western governments, media outlets, and nongovernmental organizations. These efforts, however, often amount to a trick of smoke and mirrors designed to disguise the governments' refusal to cede any real power. In the last few years, several Arab states have appointed women to high positions and hurriedly implemented or proposed reforms concerning marriage, divorce, inheritance, and other personal status issues. These are welcome steps, but they do not address the core issue of promoting democracy: breaking the authoritarian pattern of Arab politics.

"Arab Democrats Are the Key to Reform"

Paradoxically, no. All Arab countries boast a small number of Westernized liberals who advocate respect for human rights, freedom of thought and speech, and democratic change. But democratic transformation requires more than the ideological commitment of a few individuals. In Western societies, a small democratic cadre sufficed in the distant past, when political participation was the preserve of public-minded intellectual elites and wealthy property owners. But the Arab world of today is not the United States or Europe of the 18th century. The political elite faces a growing challenge by Islamist movements, which are developing a popular support base. As a result, democratic transformation also requires broad-based political parties and movements capable of transforming abstract democratic ideals into concrete programs that resonate with a public whose main concern is survival.

Arab democrats have so far shown little capacity—and less inclination—to translate abstract ideas into programs with mass appeal. Because they talk to Western organizations and each other more than to their fellow citizens, opposition political parties with a liberal agenda find themselves unable to build broad constituencies. This failure leaves the field open to government parties, which can build a following on the basis of patronage, and to Islamist parties, which build their following in the best tradition of mass parties, with a mixture of ideological fervor and grassroots social services.

Government repression and, at times, co-optation have also undermined Arab democrats' effectiveness. Some regimes—notably Saudi Arabia's—move quickly to clamp down on any nascent liberal debate. Others are more tolerant, giving liberals some intellectual space to write and discuss issues openly, as long as their talk is not followed by action. Arab democrats in countries such as Egypt are not a persecuted group. Rather, they tend to be professionals comfortably ensconced in the upper-middle class. Therefore, they are hesitant to demand genuine reforms that might lead to a hard-line takeover and content to advocate democratization from the top.

Under such conditions, it would be a serious mistake for U.S. and European democracy advocates to focus on Arab democrats as the key to political change. These individuals will play a role if democracy becomes a reality. But during this period of transition, they have neither the inclination to push for reform nor the political clout to do so successfully.

"Middle East Democracy Is the Cure for Islamist Terrorism"

No. This view is rooted in a simplistic assumption: Stagnant, repressive Arab regimes create positive conditions for the growth of radical Islamist groups, which turn their sights on the United

States because it embodies the liberal sociopolitical values that radical Islamists oppose. More democracy, therefore, equals less extremism.

History tells a different story. Modern militant Islam developed with the founding of the Muslim Brotherhood in Egypt in the 1920s, during the most democratic period in that country's history. Radical political Islam gains followers not only among repressed Saudis but also among some Muslims in Western democracies, especially in Europe. The emergence of radical Islamist groups determined to wreak violence on the United States is thus not only the consequence of Arab autocracy. It is a complex phenomenon with diverse roots, which include U.S. sponsorship of the mujahideen in Afghanistan in the 1980s (which only empowered Islamist militants); the Saudi government's promotion of radical Islamic educational programs worldwide; and anger at various U.S. policies, such as the country's stance on the Arab-Israeli conflict and the basing of military forces in the region.

Moreover, democracy is not a cure-all for terrorism. Like it or not, the most successful efforts to control radical Islamist political groups have been antidemocratic, repressive campaigns, such as those waged in Tunisia, Egypt, and Algeria in the 1990s. The notion that Arab governments would necessarily be more effective in fighting extremists is wishful thinking, no matter how valuable democratization might be for other reasons.

The experience of countries in different regions makes clear that terrorist groups can operate for sustained periods even in successful democracies, whether it is the Irish Republican Army in Britain or the ETA (Basque separatists) in Spain. The ETA gained strength during the first two decades of Spain's democratization process, flourishing more than it had under the dictatorship of Gen. Francisco Franco. In fragile democratic states—as new Arab democracies would likely be for years—radical groups committed to violence can do even more harm, often for long periods, as evidenced by the Tamil Tigers in Sri Lanka, Abu Sayyaf in the Philippines, or the Maoist rebels in Nepal.

Marina Ottaway and Thomas Carothers are senior associate and director, respectively, at the Democracy and Rule of Law Project of the Carnegie Endowment for International Peace. They are coeditors of Uncharted Journey: Democracy Promotion in the Middle East *(Washington: Carnegie Endowment, 2005).*

From *Foreign Policy*, November–December 2004, pp. 22-24, 26-28. © 2004 by the Carnegie Endowment for International Peace. **www.foreignpolicy.com** Permission conveyed through Copyright Clearance Center, Inc.

Plenty of seeds, but still a long way to fruition

Arab democracy in 2006

Xan Smiley

Democracy is not about to break out all over the Middle East. Monarchs and republican dynasts, however benevolent, will not be handing over power to the people. A Berlin-style wall in the desert, protecting rulers from the ballot box, is not about to crumble. But George Bush's determination to spread the notion of democracy as a hoped-for antidote to Islamist terrorism has changed the mood of the region—and will continue to do so.

The biggest steps towards democracy will take place in two of the most problematic and volatile places: Palestine and Iraq.

2006

Al-Jazeera, a Qatar-based Arabic news network, launches an English-language channel to compete with CNN and the BBC. Meanwhile, the BBC prepares to launch an Arabic television service in 2007.

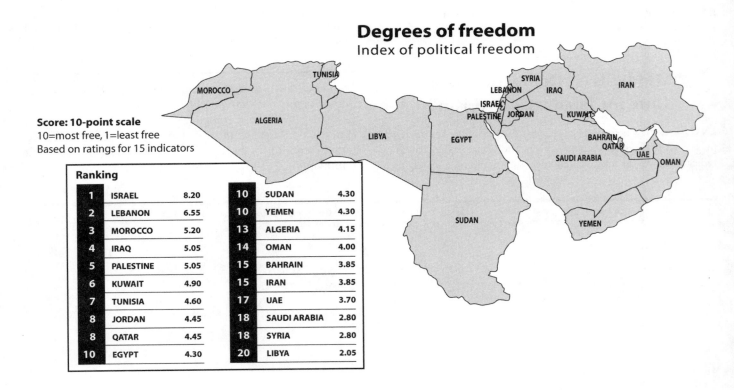

Degrees of freedom
Index of political freedom

Score: 10-point scale
10=most free, 1=least free
Based on ratings for 15 indicators

Ranking

#	Country	Score		#	Country	Score
1	ISRAEL	8.20		10	SUDAN	4.30
2	LEBANON	6.55		10	YEMEN	4.30
3	MOROCCO	5.20		13	ALGERIA	4.15
4	IRAQ	5.05		14	OMAN	4.00
5	PALESTINE	5.05		15	BAHRAIN	3.85
6	KUWAIT	4.90		15	IRAN	3.85
7	TUNISIA	4.60		17	UAE	3.70
8	JORDAN	4.45		18	SAUDI ARABIA	2.80
8	QATAR	4.45		18	SYRIA	2.80
10	EGYPT	4.30		20	LIBYA	2.05

Suez for beginners

1956 and all that

A heads-up: 2006 marks the 50th anniversary of the Suez crisis—the botched invasion of Egypt by Britain, France and Israel following Egypt's nationalization of the Suez canal. Now, anyone reading about the events of 1956 for the first time is likely to get a bit muddled. Words like "Europe" and "America" seem to be used the wrong way round and the key players seem weirdly interchangeable with present-day figures. So *The World in 2006* has compiled the following factsheet for Suez novices.

Anthony Eden. British prime minister, 1955-57. Not to be confused with George Bush (or indeed Tony Blair). Eden took the nationalization of the Suez Canal Company, in which Britain and France held a big stake, as clear evidence that Egypt was out to cause trouble in the region, perhaps by forming an Arab alliance that would cut off oil supplies to Europe. Britain and its allies, he argued, were justified in invading Egypt in order to "protect the security" of the canal. The Suez crisis presented what he took to be a fine opportunity to boost his popularity at home by bloodying the nose of a brutal Arab dictator, Nasser.

Dwight D. Eisenhower. American president, 1953-61. Not to be confused in Kofi Annan. Eisenhower was horrified by Eden's hawkishness and insisted there should be "no thought of military action" until the UN had done what it could be remedy the situation. Eden responded that, in the face of the odious Nasser, treaties were "history". The most destabilizing influence in the region, Eisenhower reckoned, was not Nasser but Eden, whose jingoism and saber-rattling succeeded only in rallying support for Nasser across the Middle East.

Gamal Abdel Nasser. Egyptian president, 1954-70. Not to be confused with Saddam Hussein or Osama bin Laden. Though Nasser did not threaten oil supplies or ships on the canal, Eden cast him as a cartoonish Arab villain and called him the "greatest hazard facing the Free World...active wherever Muslims can be found".

What lessons, if any, may be learnt from Suez—which ruined Eden's career and left the canal closed for 20 years—our unmuddled readers can decide for themselves.

In January the Palestinians will vote for a new parliament. For the first time, the Islamic Resistance Front, better known as Hamas, will probably take part, despite Israeli misgivings. It will do well, perhaps nearly matching the incumbent party, the late Yasser Arafat's Fatah, at the polls. The Palestinians' election is likely to be the freest and fairest in the Arab world. If Fatah does hold on to power under the leadership of Mahmoud Abbas, its fresh legitimacy will with luck enable it to engage with Israel's government in an effort to persuade it to give back nearly all of the territory conquered in the war of 1967.

Democracy in Iraq will be much more fraught—but it will advance. Despite the hostility of Iraq's Sunni Arabs to the new constitution, passed (just) in the autumn of 2005, they will start participating more fully in Iraq's democracy, even though many will continue to help the insurgents. And they will be much better represented in the new parliament. More of them will turn against the extreme end of the insurgency, where the likes of Abu Musab al-Zarqawi, who claims to be al-Qaeda's local representative and who detests the apparently godless notion of democracy, will become increasingly unpopular, even among Sunnis who want the Americans and their allies to quit.

Democracy in Iraq will be much more fraught—but it will advance

So the bomb will compete against the ballot box, the prevalence of violence making it harder for democracy to take hold. But many Iraqis, especially the Shia Arabs and Kurds, who together make up 80% of the people, are determined that it

should. The germ of democracy will spread in a number of less violent Arab countries. Lebanon, in particular, will continue to shed Syrian influence and will re-emerge as the most sophisticated and liberal Arab state in the region. And the Americans will promote a trio of more or less benevolent monarchies—Morocco, Jordan and Bahrain—as exemplars of their democracy campaign.

By most criteria, setting aside the odd cases of Palestine, Iraq and Lebanon, Morocco is the group leader among the rest of the Arab League's 22 countries. It will allow real political parties to compete. Its Equity and Reconciliation Commission will air and investigate past human-rights abuses, though rather more selectively than the South Africans did. Its family code should let women enjoy more rights.

Jordan and Bahrain, both quite open by Arab standards, are not as go-ahead. The only serious political party in Jordan's parliament is the opposition Islamic Action Front; King Abdullah will continue to call the shots. In Bahrain, the majority Shias will remain under-represented and politically surly.

More to the point, in all three of these front-runners towards democracy, the monarch has ultimate power. No one expects them to become real constitutional monarchs any time soon, though they all claim to be gently heading that way. But they will tiptoe ahead.

Islamists in moderation

The big question, for all Arab countries moving slowly towards greater political choice, is how much leeway to give Islamist groups, such as the Muslim Brotherhood, which has a wide following across the region. Sensing a chance to get back into the mainstream, moderate Islamists will make headway by persuading governments that it is wiser to have them working inside the system than undermining it from outside. Even so, the secular regimes that dominate the Arab world will remain nervous that Islamists, however well repackaged as moderates, will achieve too much influence through the ballot box—with no intention of retaining multi-party democracy should they ever achieve power. Yet continuing to suppress them is even more certain to stoke up dangerous discontent.

How to accommodate apparently moderate Islam, in order to spike the likes of al-Qaeda? Egypt is the litmus test here. It may

2006

In between hosting the Asian games and proceeding with giant gas projects, Qatar plans to hold its first parliamentary election. All Qataris over 18, male and female, can vote.

feel obliged to give the Muslim Brotherhood more space; but will not risk giving it a real chance of power.

Bin Laden, the Arab "Street," and the Middle East's Democracy Deficit

"Bin Laden speaks in the vivid language of popular Islamic preachers, and builds on a deep and widespread resentment against the West and local ruling elites identified with it. The lack of formal outlets to express opinion on public concerns has created [a] democracy deficit in much of the Arab world, and this makes it easier for terrorists such as bin Laden, asserting that they act in the name of religion, to hijack the Arab street."

DALE F. EICKELMAN

In the years ahead, the role of public diplomacy and open communications will play an increasingly significant role in countering the image that the Al Qaeda terrorist network and Osama bin Laden assert for themselves as guardians of Islamic values. In the fight against terrorism for which bin Laden is the photogenic icon, the first step is to recognize that he is as thoroughly a part of the modern world as was Cambodia's French-educated Pol Pot. Bin Laden's videotaped presentation of self intends to convey a traditional Islamic warrior brought up-to-date, but this sense of the past is a completely invented one. The language and content of his videotaped appeals convey more of his participation in the modern world than his camouflage jacket, Kalashnikov, and Timex watch.

Take the two-hour Al Qaeda recruitment videotape in Arabic that has made its way to many Middle Eastern video shops and Western news media.[1] It is a skillful production, as fast paced and gripping as any Hindu fundamentalist video justifying the destruction in 1992 of the Ayodhya mosque in India, or the political attack videos so heavily used in American presidential campaigning. The 1988 "Willie Horton" campaign video of Republican presidential candidate George H. W. Bush—in which an off-screen announcer portrayed Democratic presidential candidate Michael Dukakis as "soft" on crime while showing a mug shot of a convicted African-American rapist who had committed a second rape during a weekend furlough from a Massachusetts prison—was a propaganda masterpiece that combined an explicit although conventional message with a menacing, underlying one intended to motivate undecided voters. The Al Qaeda video, directed at a different audience—presumably alienated Arab youth, unemployed and often living in desperate conditions—shows an equal mastery of modern propaganda.

The Al Qaeda producers could have graduated from one of the best film schools in the United States or Europe. The fast-moving recruitment video begins with the bombing of the USS *Cole* in Yemen, but then shows a montage implying a seemingly coordinated worldwide aggression against Muslims in Palestine, Jerusalem, Lebanon, Chechnya, Kashmir, and Indonesia (but not Muslim violence against Christians and Chinese in the last). It also shows United States generals received by Saudi princes, intimating the collusion of local regimes with the West and challenging the legitimacy of many regimes, including Saudi Arabia. The sufferings of the Iraqi people are attributed to American brutality against Muslims, but Saddam Hussein is assimilated to the category of infidel ruler.

Osama bin Laden... is thoroughly imbued with the values of the modern world, even if only to reject them.

Many of the images are taken from the daily staple of Western video news—the BBC and CNN logos add to the videos' authenticity, just as Qatar's al-Jazeera satellite television logo rebroadcast by CNN and the BBC has added authenticity to Western coverage of Osama bin Laden.

Alternating with these scenes of devastation and oppression of Muslims are images of Osama bin Laden: posing in front of bookshelves or seated on the ground like a religious scholar, holding the Koran in his hand. Bin Laden radiates charismatic authority and control as he narrates the Prophet Mohammed's flight from Mecca to Medina, when the early Islamic movement was threatened by the idolaters, but returning to conquer them. Bin Laden also stresses the need for jihad, or struggle for the cause of Islam, against the "crusaders" and "Zionists." Later images show military training in Afghanistan (including target practice at a poster of Bill Clinton), and a final sequence—the word "solution" flashes across the screen—captures an Israeli soldier in full riot gear retreating from a Palestinian boy throwing stones, and a reading of the Koran.

THE THOROUGHLY MODERN ISLAMIST

Osama bin Laden, like many of his associates, is imbued with the values of the modern world, even if only to reject them. A 1971 photograph shows him on family holiday in Oxford at the age of 14, posing with two of his half-brothers and Spanish girls their own age. English was their common language of communication. Bin Laden studied English at a private school in Jidda, and English was also useful for his civil engineering courses at Jidda's King Abdul Aziz University. Unlike many of his estranged half-brothers, educated in Saudi Arabia, Europe, and the United States, Osama's education was only in Saudi Arabia, but he was also familiar with Arab and European society.

The organizational skills he learned in Saudi Arabia came in to play when he joined the mujahideen (guerrilla) struggle against the 1979 Soviet invasion of Afghanistan. He may not have directly met United States intelligence officers in the field, but they, like their Saudi and Pakistani counterparts, were delighted to have him participate in their fight against Soviet troops and recruit willing Arab fighters. Likewise, his many business enterprises flourished under highly adverse conditions. Bin Laden skillfully sustained a flexible multinational organization in the face of enemies, especially state authorities, moving cash, people, and supplies almost undetected across international frontiers.

The organizational skills of bin Laden and his associates were never underestimated. Neither should be their skills in conveying a message that appeals to some Muslims. Bin Laden lacks the credentials of an established Islamic scholar, but this does not diminish his appeal. As Sudan's Sorbonne-educated Hasan al-Turabi, the leader of his country's Muslim Brotherhood and its former attorney general and speaker of parliament, explained two decades ago, "Because all knowledge is divine and religious, a chemist, an engineer, an economist, or a jurist" are all men of learning.[2] Civil engineer bin Laden exemplifies Turabi's point. His audience judges him not by his ability to cite authoritative texts, but by his apparent skill in applying generally accepted religious tenets to current political and social issues.

THE MESSAGE ON THE ARAB "STREET"

Bin Laden's lectures circulate in book form in the Arab world, but video is the main vehicle of communication. The use of CNN-like "zippers"—the ribbons of words that stream beneath the images in many newscasts and documentaries—shows that Al Qaeda takes the Arab world's rising levels of education for granted. Increasingly, this audience is also saturated with both conventional media and new media, such as the Internet.[3] The Middle East has entered an era of mass education and this also implies an Arabic lingua franca. In Morocco in the early 1970s, rural people sometimes asked me to "translate" newscasts from the standard transnational Arabic of the state radio into colloquial Arabic. Today this is no longer required. Mass education and new communications technologies enable large numbers of Arabs to hear—and see—Al Qaeda's message directly.

Bin Laden's message does not depend on religious themes alone. Like the Ayatollah Ruhollah Khomeini, his message contains many secular elements. Khomeini often alluded to the "wretched of the earth." At least for a time, his language appealed equally to Iran's religiously minded and to the secular left. For bin Laden, the equivalent themes are the oppression and corruption of many Arab governments, and he lays the blame for the violence and oppression in Palestine, Kashmir, Chechnya, and elsewhere at the door of the West. One need not be religious to rally to some of these themes. A poll taken in Morocco in late September 2001 showed that a majority of Moroccans condemned the September 11 bombings, but 41 percent sympathized with bin Laden's message. A British poll taken at about the same time showed similar results.

Osama bin Laden and the Al Qaeda terrorist movement are thus reaching at least part of the Arab "street." Earlier this year, before the September terrorist attacks, United States policymakers considered this "street" a "new phenomenon of public accountability, which we have seldom had to factor into our projections of Arab behavior in the past. The information revolution, and particularly the daily dose of uncensored television coming out of local TV stations like al-Jazeera and international coverage by CNN and others, is shaping public opinion, which, in turn, is pushing Arab governments to respond. We don't know, and the leaders themselves don't know, how that pressure will impact on Arab policy in the future."[4]

Director of Central Intelligence George J. Tenet was even more cautionary on the nature of the "Arab street." In testimony before the Senate Select Committee on Intelligence in February 2001, he explained that the "right catalyst—such as the outbreak of Israeli-Palestinian violence—can move people to act. Through access to the Internet and other means of communication, a restive public is increasingly capable of taking action without any identifiable leadership or organizational structure."

Because many governments in the Middle East are deeply suspicious of an open press, nongovernmental organizations, and open expression, it is no surprise that the "restive" public, increasingly educated and influenced by hard-to-censor new media, can take action "without any identifiable leadership or organized structure." The Middle East in general has a democracy deficit, in which "unauthorized" leaders or critics, such as Egyptian academic Saad Eddin Ibrahim—founder and director of the Ibn Khaldun Center for Development Studies, a nongovernmental organization that promotes democracy in Egypt—suffer harassment or prison terms.

One consequence of this democracy deficit is to magnify the power of the street in the Arab world. Bin Laden speaks in the vivid language of popular Islamic preachers, and builds on a deep and widespread resentment against the West and local ruling elites identified with it. The lack of formal outlets to express opinion on public concerns has created the democracy deficit in much of the Arab world, and this makes it easier for terrorists such as bin Ladin, asserting that they act in the name of religion, to hijack the Arab street.

The immediate response is to learn to speak directly to this street. This task has already begun. Obscure to all except specialists until September 11, Qatar's al-Jazeera satellite television is a premier source in the Arab world for uncensored news and opinion. It is more, however, than the Arab equivalent of CNN. Uncensored news and opinions increasingly shape "public opinion"—a term without the pejorative overtones of "the street"—even in places like Damascus and Algiers. This public opinion in turn pushes Arab governments to be more responsive to their citizens, or at least to say that they are.

Rather than seek to censor al-Jazeera or limit Al Qaeda's access to the Western media—an unfortunate first response of the United States government after the September terror attacks—we should avoid censorship. Al Qaeda statements should be treated with the same caution as any other news source. Replacing Sinn Fein leader Gerry Adams' voice and image in the British media in the 1980s with an Irish-accented actor appearing in silhouette only highlighted what he had to say, and it is unlikely that the British public would tolerate the same restrictions on the media today.

Ironically, at almost the same time that national security adviser Condoleezza Rice asked the American television networks not to air Al Qaeda videos unedited, a former senior CIA officer, Graham Fuller, was explaining in Arabic on al-Jazeera how United States policymaking works. His appearance on al-Jazeera made a significant impact, as did Secretary of State Colin Powell's presence on a later al-Jazeera program and former United States Ambassador Christopher Ross, who speaks fluent Arabic. Likewise, the timing and content of British Prime Minister Tony Blair's response to an earlier bin Laden tape suggests how to take the emerging Arab public seriously. The day after al-Jazeera broadcast the bin Laden tape, Blair asked for and received an opportunity to respond. In his reply, Blair—in a first for a Western leader—directly addressed the Arab public through the Arab media, explaining coalition goals in attacking Al Qaeda and the Taliban and challenging bin Laden's claim to speak in the name of Islam.

PUTTING PUBLIC DIPLOMACY TO WORK

Such appearances enhance the West's ability to communicate a primary message: that the war against terrorism is not that of one civilization against another, but against terrorism and fanaticism in all societies. Western policies and actions are subject to public scrutiny and will often be misunderstood. Public diplomacy can significantly diminish this misapprehension. It may, however, involve some uncomfortable policy decisions. For instance, America may be forced to exert more diplomatic pressure on Israel to alter its methods of dealing with Palestinians.

Western public diplomacy in the Middle East also involves uncharted waters. As Oxford University social linguist Clive Holes has noted, the linguistic genius who thought up the first name for the campaign to oust the Taliban, "Operation Infinite Justice," did a major disservice to the Western goal. The expression was literally and accurately translated into Arabic as *adala ghayr mutanahiya,* implying that an earthly power arrogated to itself the task of divine retribution. Likewise, President George W. Bush's inadvertent and unscripted use of the word "crusade" gave Al Qaeda spokesmen an opportunity to attack Bush and Western intentions.

Mistakes will be made, but information and arguments that reach the Arab street, including on al-Jazeera, will eventually have an impact. Some Westerners might condemn al-Jazeera as biased, and it may well be in terms of making assumptions about its audience. However, it has broken a taboo by regularly inviting official Israeli spokespersons to comment live on current issues. Muslim religious scholars, both in the Middle East and in the West, have already spoken out against Al Qaeda's claim to act in the name of Islam. Other courageous voices, such as Egyptian playwright Ali Salem, have even employed humor for the same purpose.[5]

We must recognize that the best way to mitigate the continuing threat of terrorism is to encourage Middle Eastern states to be more responsive to participatory demands, and to aid local nongovernmental organizations working toward this goal. As with the case of Egypt's Saad Eddin Ibrahim, some countries may see such activities as subversive. Whether Arab states like it or not, increasing levels of education, greater ease of travel, and the rise of new communications media are turning the Arab street into a public sphere in which greater numbers of people, and not just a political and economic elite, will have a say in governance and public issues.

NOTES

1. It is now available on-line with explanatory notes in English. See <http://www.ciaonet.org/cbr/cbr00/video/excerpts_index.html>.

2. Hasan al-Turabi, "The Islamic State," in *Voices of Resurgent Islam,* John L. Esposito, ed. (New York: Oxford University Press, 1983), p. 245.

3. On the importance of rising levels of education and the new media, see Dale F. Eickelman, "The Coming Transformation in the Muslim World," *Current History,* January 2000.

4. Edward S. Walker, "The New US Administration's Middle East Policy Speech," *Middle East Economic Survey,* vol. 44, no. 26 (June 25, 2001). Available at <http://www.mees.com/news/a44n26d01.htm>.

5. See his article in Arabic, "I Want to Start a Kindergarten for Extremism," *Al-Hayat* (London), November 5, 2001. This is translated into English by the Middle East Media Research Institute as Special Dispatch no. 298, Jihad and Terrorism Studies, November 8, 2001, at <http://www.memri.org>.

DALE F. EICKELMAN *is Ralph and Richard Lazarus Professor of Anthropology and Human Relations at Dartmouth College. His most recent book is* The Middle East and Central Asia: An Anthropological Approach, *4th ed. (Englewood Cliffs, N. J.: Prentice Hall, 2002). An earlier version of this article appeared as "The West Should Speak to the Arab in the Street,"* Daily Telegraph *(London), October 27, 2001.*

Reprinted from *Current History,* January 2002, pp. 36–39. © 2002 by Current History, Inc. Reprinted by permission.

UNIT 5

Comparative Politics: Some Major Trends, Issues, and Prospects

Unit Selections

Key Points to Consider

- What is meant by the first, second, and third waves of democratization? Discuss the reversals that followed the first two. Where are most of the countries affected by the third wave located? What factors appear to have contributed to their democratization? What are the signs that the third wave may be over?

- What are some main problems and dilemmas of old and new democracies, as discussed by Thomas Carothers?

- In what ways can market capitalism and liberal democracy be said to be mutually supportive, according to Gabriel Almond?

- How do Martin Wolf and David Held differ in their approach to free market economics? What is the implication of the argument that in economics, one model or "size" is unlikely to "fit all"?

- What does Benjamin Barber mean when he warns that democracy is threatened by globalism and tribalism?

Student Website

www.mhcls.com/online

Internet References

Further information regarding these websites may be found in this book's preface or online.

Commission on Global Governance
http://www.sovereignty.net/p/gov/gganalysis.htm

IISDnet
http://www.iisd.org/default.asp

ISN International Relations and Security Network
http://www.isn.ethz.ch

United Nations Environment Program
http://www.unep.ch/

The articles in this unit deal with three major political trends or patterns of development that can be observed in much of the contemporary world. It is important at the outset to stress that, with the possible exception of Benjamin Barber, none of the authors predict some form of global convergence in which all political systems would become alike in major respects. On closer examination, even Barber turns out to argue that a strong tendency toward global homogenization is offset by a concurrent tendency toward intensified group differentiation and fragmentation.

Thus the trends or patterns discussed may be seen as widespread but they are neither unidirectional nor universal. They are situationally defined and may turn out to be temporary or partly reversible. Each has resulted in what could be called a countervailing trend. Moreover, the three trends (with countertrends) do not always reinforce one another. Their different forms of development are the very stuff of comparative politics.

After these cautionary preliminaries, we can proceed to identify three recent developments that singly and together have had a very important role in changing the political world in which we live. One is the process of **democratization,** which has been sweeping much of the world. This refers to a widespread trend toward some form of popularly chosen, accessible, and accountable government. In the last quarter of the twentieth century, it often took the form of a search for representative, pluralist democracy in countries that were previously ruled by some kind of authoritarian oligarchy or dictatorship.

A second trend is the even more widespread **shift toward some form of market economy.** It includes a greater reliance on private enterprise and the profit motive and involves a concurrent move away from strong regulation, central planning, and state ownership. The "social market economy," found in much of Western Europe, remains a form of capitalism, but one which includes a major role for the state in providing public goods and services, redistributing income, and setting overall societal goals. In some of the Asian Communist-ruled countries, above all China, we have become used to seeing self-proclaimed revolutionary socialists introduce and encourage what amounts to forms of capitalist practice in their formerly planned economies. Ironically, capitalism seems to have come to China by courtesy of leaders who used to be its most fervent ideological opponents.

The third major trend could be called **the revival of ethnic or cultural politics.** This refers to a growing emphasis on some form of an exclusive group identity as the primary basis for political expression. In modern times, it has been common for a group to identify itself by its special ethnic, religious, linguistic, or other cultural traits and to make this identity the basis for a claim to special recognition and, sometimes, to rule by and for itself.

The article that makes up the first section covers democratization as the first of these trends, that is, the spread of representative forms of government in recent years. Even if this development is often fragile and likely to be reversed in some countries, we need to remember how remarkable it was in the first place. Using very different criteria and data, skeptics on both right and left for a long time doubted whether representative government was sufficiently effective, attractive, or legitimate to spread or even survive in the modern world.

Samuel Huntington's widely discussed thesis concerning a recent wave of democratization underlies the article by Thomas Carothers. Huntington is one of the best-known observers of this trend. He is also someone who some years earlier had been skeptical of democracy's future prospects. Indeed, he had emphasized the existence of cultural, social, economic, and political obstacles to the spread of representative government in most of the world. But in the 1980s, before the collapse of the communist regimes in Europe, he had begun to identify a broad pattern of democratization. He traced its origins to the mid-1970s, when the three remaining dictatorships in Western Europe came to an almost simultaneous end (in Greece, Portugal, and Spain). In the following decade, democratization spread to most of Latin America. The countries of the Soviet bloc in Central and Eastern Europe then followed. The trend also reached some states in East and South Asia like Taiwan or South Korea as well as some parts of Africa, above all South Africa and now, more precariously, Nigeria. Mexico's presidential election of 2000, with its transfer of political power after more than seven decades of one-party hegemony, can also be seen in this context.

In a widely adopted phrase, Huntington identified this widespread trend as the "third" in a series of **successive "waves" of democratization** in modern history. The **"first wave"** had been slow to develop but long in its reach. It began in the 1820s and lasted about one century, until the 1920s. During this period the United States and subsequently 28 other countries established governments based on a broad franchise that eventually came to include women as well as men. Democratization was not only a drawn-out process in these countries, it was also a highly flawed and imperfect one. Thus it has been pointed out that not a single system of government at the beginning of the twentieth century (with the possible exception of New Zealand) would have met today's stricter minimum standards of what constitutes a democracy. Soon after the end of the war "to make the world safe for democracy," its spread came to a halt. In the first half of the 1920s, Mussolini's capture and consolidation of power in Italy began a period of severe democratic setbacks—a **first "reverse wave,"** as it has been called—that lasted until the mid-1940s. During those two decades, the number of democracies in the world plunged from 29 by more than half, as many became victims of indigenous dictatorial takeovers or subsequent military conquests. In the middle of World War II, there were only four full-fledged democratic states left in Europe, Britain and the three neutrals, Ireland, Sweden, and Switzerland.

A **"second wave"** of democratization started with the Allied victory in World War II and continued during the early postwar years. It lasted until the early 1960s and included the liberated countries in Western Europe that immediately restored their democratic institutions and practices—countries like the Netherlands, Belgium, Luxembourg, Denmark, Norway, and France. In addition, the major defeated powers, Western Germany and Japan, were steered to democratic politics by the occupying powers. There were democratic stirrings in several Latin American countries. Finally, in the process of decolonization, the newly independent countries often started out with a formal democratic framework—one that frequently proved to be fragile and sometimes of very short duration. These new states along with some countries in Latin America were the main settings for a series of authoritarian comebacks—the relatively short **second "reverse wave."** Although it only lasted a little over a decade, until the mid-1970s, some of the new authoritarian regimes held on quite a few years longer. During this period of setbacks, the total number of democracies fell from 36 to 30 and the number of non-democracies rose from 75 to 95, as various former colonies or newly minted democracies fell under authoritarian or dictatorial rule.

Then, in the mid-1970s, the important **"third wave" of democratization** got its start. It turned out to be more sweeping and universal than its predecessors. Already by beginning of the 1990s, Huntington counted about 60 democracies in the world. Larry Diamond, another authority on the subject, reported in 2000 that 120 states out of a world total of 192 independent states (63 percent) met at least the minimum requirements for being classified as **electoral democracies.** The number was reduced to 71 (or 37 percent) when he applied the stricter standards of **liberal democracy**—basic civil rights and liberties, rule of law, political independence and neutrality of the judiciary, an open, pluralist society, and civilian control of the military. That is still an impressive change, when one considers Robert Dahl's finding that only 22 countries can be identified as **"older democracies,"** in the sense of having a continuous political history as democracies since at least 1950. Both Huntington and Diamond's findings lend support to the conclusion that democracy's advance has been at best a "two steps forward, one step back" kind of process.

Writing in 2004, Thomas Carothers finds that the "third wave" has come to a standstill. The expectations associated with the coming of democracy were in some countries so high that disappointments were bound to follow. Already some earlier "third wave" democratic advances in countries like the Sudan, Algeria, and Peru have been followed by authoritarian reversals. Haiti (like Nigeria) has gone through its own double wave. The prospects for democracy on that poverty-stricken Caribbean island do not seem bright. There are ominous signs of authoritarian revivals elsewhere in the world.

What are the general conditions that inhibit or encourage the spread and stabilization of democracy? Huntington and Diamond are among the scholars who have identified specific historical factors that contributed to the third wave. One important factor was the loss of legitimacy by both right- and left-wing authoritarian regimes, as they have become discredited by failures. Another factor was the expansion in some developing countries of an urban middle class, with a strong interest in representative government and the rule of law. In Latin America, especially, the influence of a recently more liberal Catholic Church was important. There have also been various forms of external influence by the United States and the European Community, as they have tried, however tentatively, to promote a human rights agenda. Particularly noteworthy was the EU's use of "soft power" to encourage a democratic development in Greece, Portugal, and Spain. This strategy was repeated by the EU some years later, during the 1990s, in several East and Central European countries. There it followed a different but crucial instance of external influence, namely Mikhail Gorbachev's shift toward nonintervention by the Soviet Union in the late 1980s, when he abandoned the Brezhnev Doctrine's commitment to defend established communist regimes against "counterrevolution." Finally, there is the "snowballing" or demonstration effect with the successful early transitions to democracy in countries like Spain or Poland, which served as models for other countries in similar circumstances.

Huntington's rule of thumb is that a democratic form of government can be considered to have become stable when a country has had at least two successive peaceful turnovers of power. Such a development may take a generation or longer to complete, even under fortunate circumstances. Many of the new democracies have little historical experience with a democratic way of life. Where there has been such an experience, it may have been spotty and not very positive. There may be important cultural or socioeconomic obstacles to democratization, according to Huntington. Like most other observers, he sees extreme poverty as a principal obstacle to successful democratization. The stunted growth of democratization in Muslim societies has drawn a lot of attention, but there are exceptions as Marina Ottaway and Thomas Carothers point out in their article, "Middle East Democracy," in unit four.

Germany provides an often examined case study for testing some of these interpretations of democracy. After World War I, antidemocratic forces in Germany identified its democratic Weimar Republic with national disaster, socioeconomic ruin, and political weakness and instability. In the wake of the Great Depression, they supported Adolf Hitler's Nazi movement that came to power in January 1933 and abolished the fledgling constitutional democracy. After World War II, by contrast, the Federal Republic of Germany became increasingly credited with stability and growing prosperity. At first accepted passively, the West German democratic system soon generated an increasing measure of pragmatic support from its citizenry, based primarily on its widely perceived effectiveness. In time, the new republic also appeared to gain a deeper affection from much of the population. Careful observers, like David Conradt, detected a transformation of German values in a liberal democratic direction already in the early 1970s. The Federal Republic faced another test after Germany's unification with its wrenching changes and inevitable disappointments for many people in Eastern Germany. For many of them, national unification had been linked to unrealistic expectations of almost immediate socioeconomic alignment with the prosperous West. When the new order failed to deliver quite as promptly or bountifully as they had expected, some East Germans used their new freedom to protest. In dealing with this challenge, the Federal Republic is fortunate to have a stable set of institutions, a well-developed democratic tradition, and a solid economic structure.

The second section of this unit covers the trend toward capitalism or some form of **modern market-oriented economy**. Here Gabriel Almond explores the complex and ambiguous connections between capitalism and democracy in an article that draws upon both theory and empirical studies. His systematic discussion shows that there are ways in which capitalism and democracy support each other, and ways in which they tend to undermine each other. Is it possible to have the best of both? Almond answers at length that there is a non-utopian manner in which capitalism and democracy can be reconciled, namely in **democratic welfare capitalism.**

Almond's discussion can be linked to a theme emphasized by some contemporary political economists. They point out that the economic competition between capitalism and socialism, at least in socialism's traditional meaning of state ownership and centralized planning, has become a largely closed chapter in contemporary history. The central question now is which form of capitalism or market economy will be more successful and acceptable. A similar argument has been made by the French theorist, Michel Albert, who distinguished between the **British-American** or "Anglo-Saxon" and the continental **"Rhineland" models of capitalism.** The former is more individualistic, opposed to governmental intervention, and characterized by such traits as high employee turnovers and short-term profit-maximizing. It differs considerably from what the Germans themselves like to call their "social market economy." The latter is more team-oriented, emphasizes cooperation between management and organized labor, and leaves a considerable role for government in the setting of general economic strategy, the training of an educated labor force, and the provision of social welfare services.

These different conceptions of capitalism can be linked to different histories. Both Britain and the United States experienced a head start in their industrial revolutions and felt no great need for deliberate government efforts to encourage growth. By contrast, Germany and Japan both played the role of latecomers, who looked to government protection in their attempts to catch up. To be sure, governments were also swayed by military considerations to promote German and Japanese industrialization. But the emergence of a kind of "social capitalism" in other continental countries of Europe suggests that cultural and institutional factors played a major role in this development. We should continue to expect very differently mixed market economies, because one economic model or size is unlikely ever to fit all.

A crucial question is whether the relative prosperity and social security associated with this kind of mixed economy can be maintained in a time of technological breakthroughs and global competition. Those who expected a practical answer to come from the "new middle" policies and strategies adopted by the "red-green" government in Germany were at first disappointed. Then in 1999, Gerhard Schröder issued a joint statement with Tony Blair, in which the two European leaders reaffirmed their commitment to a "third way" and made a key distinction between **"a market economy"** and **"a market society."** Their outspoken support for the former was based on its demonstrated economic superiority, while their reservations about the latter were rooted in their conviction that a society should not be governed by the market's economic criteria alone.

In supporting this distinction, Blair enjoyed the advantage of having inherited Thatcher's economic reforms as consolidated by John Major's government. He could thus concentrate on the second part of the agenda, where there was more emphasis on the **social goal of equity** rather than the **economic goal of efficiency.** In Germany, there had been no equivalent of the Thatcher revolution. Instead, Schröder inherited from Helmut Kohl's chancellorship a socially generous system that could not be maintained without a major economic-minded reform. Yet Schröder appeared to hesitate more than five years after his assumption of office before he introduced a comprehensive reform project, Agenda 2010. It is aimed at major changes in social, economic, fiscal and labor market policies that are designed to shake up the German model and make it more competitive. Mainstream economists greeted it as a step in the right direction, although some wondered whether it had come "too slow, too little, too late." Many veteran supporters of the German Social Democrats reacted as though there had been no reform necessary at all or else that it had been "too quick, too much, too soon."

The third section deals with the revival of the ethnic and cultural dimension in politics. Until recently, relatively few observers foresaw that this element would play such a divisive role in the contemporary world. There were forewarnings, such as the ethno-nationalist stirrings in the late 1960s and early 1970s, sometimes in peripheral areas of such countries as Britain, Canada, or Spain. It also lay behind many of the conflicts in the newly independent countries of the developing world. But most Western observers seem to have been poorly prepared for the task of anticipating or understanding the resurgence of politicized religious, ethnic, or other cultural forces. Many non-Westerners were taken by surprise as well. Mikhail Gorbachev, for example, grossly underestimated the centrifugal force of the nationality question in his own country.

The politicization of religion in many parts of the world falls into this development of a "politics of identity." In recent years, religious groups in parts of Latin America, Asia, the Middle East, sub-Saharan Africa, Asia, and Southern Europe have set out on the political road in the name of their faith. As Max Weber warned in a classic lecture shortly before his death, it can be dangerous to seek "the salvation of souls" along the path of politics. The coexistence of people of divergent faiths is possible only because religious conviction need not fully determine or direct a person's or a group's politics. Where absolute and fervent convictions take over, they make it difficult to compromise pragmatically and live harmoniously with people who believe differently. Pluralist democracy requires an element of tolerance, which for many takes the form of a casual "live and let live" attitude.

There is an important debate among political scientists concerning the sources and scope of politics based on ethnic, religious, and cultural differences. Samuel Huntington has come to the conclusion that the most important and dangerous future conflicts will be based on clashes of civilizations, above all those of the Christian and Muslim worlds. In his view, they will be far more difficult to resolve than those rooted in socioeconomic or even ideological differences. His critics, including the German political observer Josef Joffe, argue that Huntington distorts the differences *among* civilizations and trivializes the differences *within* civilizations as sources of political conflict. Chandra Muzaffar, a Malaysian commentator, goes further by contending that Huntington's thesis provides a rationalization for a Western goal of dominating the developing world. Others have pointed out that ethnic conflicts are in fact often the result of political choices made by elites. This can turn out to be a hopeful thesis because it would logically follow that such conflicts are avoidable if other political choices were made. In her article, Amy Chua reminds us that markets have short-run impacts that can have devastating consequences in multi-ethnic societies. This is the case whenever ethnic minorities turn out to be "market-dominant" and become viewed as outside exploiters, as has happened to Chinese minorities in South East Asia on a number of occasions. The result has been very bitter ethnic conflict in a number of countries.

In a widely discussed article, Benjamin Barber brings a broad perspective to the discussion of identity politics in the contemporary world. He sees two major tendencies that threaten democracy. One is the force of globalism, brought about by modern technology, communications, and commerce. Its logical end station is what he calls a "McWorld," in which human diversity, individuality, and meaningful identity are erased. The second tendency works in the opposite direction. It is the force of tribalism, which drives human beings to exacerbate their group differences and engage in holy wars or "jihads" against each other. Barber argues that globalism is at best indifferent to liberal democracy, while militant tribalism is deeply antithetical to it. He argues in favor of seeking a confederal solution, based on democratic civil societies, which could provide human beings with a nonmilitant, parochial communitarianism as well as a framework that suits the global market economy fairly well.

DEMOCRACY'S SOBERING STATE

"Democracy still occupies the high ground in the world.... Yet, just a few years into the new century, the grand hope that it will prove the age of democracy's global triumph appears far more tenuous than it seemed just 10 or 15 years ago."

THOMAS CAROTHERS

What Samuel Huntington called the "third wave" of democracy—the multitude of democratic openings that began in southern Europe in the mid-1970s and then spread during the next two decades throughout Latin America, Asia, the former Soviet bloc, and sub-Saharan Africa—has come to a standstill. According to Freedom House, an organization that tracks democratization around the world, there were 118 electoral democracies in 1996. Today, eight years later, there are 117. The relative proportions of countries that Freedom House rates as free, partly free, or not free have been largely static since the end of the 1990s.

POLITICS
The World, 2005

Of course, good news about democracy around the globe can still be found. Indonesians, for example, are making impressive strides in building democracy in the world's most populous Muslim country and have just inaugurated their first democratically elected president. A year ago Georgians threw off the decaying rule of President Eduard Shevardnadze and embarked on a bold effort to breathe new life into their country's shaky democratic experiment. South Africans recently celebrated the tenth anniversary of their postapartheid democracy, a democracy that is holding together despite myriad challenges. Tens of millions of Central and Eastern Europeans are now citizens of both democratic states and the European Union. And millions of Afghans took part in successful presidential elections in Afghanistan in October. More generally, key prodemocratic values, like government accountability and citizen empowerment, continue to spark interest and activism on every continent. And the community of people, organizations, and governments committed to advancing democracy's fortunes worldwide continues to grow.

Still, the grand hopes that energized some of democracy's most ardent optimists in the heady peak years of the third wave have not been realized. The former Soviet Union has gone from democratic frontier to democratic wasteland in just over a decade. South America is facing a crisis of democracy marked by political instability, rising conflict, and declining public belief in democratic institutions. Significant parts of East Asia, including China, North Korea,

Vietnam, Burma, Laos, and Singapore, remain under authoritarian rule, with little sign of change in sight. Dozens of African countries have seen once-promising democratic openings deliver only weak pluralism at best, or destructive civil conflict at worst. And, the US occupation of Iraq notwithstanding, the Arab world remains a democracy-free zone—despite increased international pressure for reform and some mild efforts by Arab rulers to move a few steps away from long-established patterns of autocracy.

Behind these signs of trouble in different regions lies a diverse set of factors that are coalescing in the first decade of this century to blunt democracy's global advance. No one of the factors is determinative in and of itself, but when combined they present a daunting new context. Understanding this context is vital to shaping an effective response.

THE AUTHORITARIAN REBOUND

The first factor inhibiting democratization is the persistence and even rejuvenation of authoritarian forces and structures in many countries that appeared, at least for a short time, to be experiencing democratic openings. Authoritarian forces were able to lie low or become dormant during the initial period of political change, even as dictatorial regimes fell. The apparent democratic transitions often turned out to be relatively shallow, despite their grand early moments and the high hopes they spawned. Dramatic first-time elections were held, new constitutions written, civil society unleashed, and government reforms announced. But the process of change in many cases did not penetrate the resilient, adaptable institutions behind the day-to-day screen of pluralistic politics—institutions that often harbored authoritarian mindsets, legacies, and actors such as domestic security services, militaries, and crony-dominated, state-owned businesses. In an unfortunately large number of cases, nondemocratic forces have been able to reassert themselves, taking advantage of the often fractious or feckless character of fledgling democratic governments. The rising economic and personal insecurity that many nascent democracies have produced for average citizens has eased the task of resurgent authoritarians since these conditions render citizens susceptible to the argument that a strong hand can set daily life back on track.

> *There is a significant gap between the soaring rhetoric about freedom in the Middle East and actual Western policy in most of the region.*

This phenomenon has been vividly present in the former Soviet Union as well as in parts of sub-Saharan Africa. Post-Soviet authoritarians have gained a grip throughout a region that in the early 1990s seemed to be opening itself to genuine political change. Pluralism is hanging on in a few former Soviet republics, such as Ukraine, Georgia, Kyrgyzstan, and Moldova. But most have become mired again in authoritarian or semi-authoritarian rule.

Russia's authoritarian slide under President Vladimir Putin has been especially damaging and dispiriting. Putin has methodically hollowed out or co-opted every major institution—including the national broadcast media, the Russian Duma, political parties, and regional governorships—that had achieved any real degree of independence. The systematic disassembling of his country's nascent democratic system has been a textbook case of dedemocratization that will be studied, unfortunately, by both political scientists and would-be autocrats for years to come. With Russia's democratic experiment at least alive, albeit troubled, throughout the 1990s, the overall political direction of the region appeared to be still up for grabs, despite bad news out of Central Asia and the Caucasus. But Russia's recent turn, although not necessarily permanent, throws the weight of regional political life firmly in the wrong corner, where it is likely to stay for years.

Adding to the disappointment of the post-Soviet political record is the fact that neither the United States nor Europe really has done much to try to slow or reverse the backsliding. Western governments are comfortable doing business with strongmen leaders as long as access to oil and gas continues uninterrupted, and because these leaders remain helpful on Western counterterrorism concerns.

Although sub-Saharan Africa generally has made substantial progress toward greater political pluralism and openness in the past 15 years, a discouraging number of countries continue to suffer persistent authoritarian rule, especially in francophone Africa, but in other parts of the region as well, including Sudan, Zimbabwe, Eritrea, and Equatorial Guinea. In some cases, such as Ivory Coast and Zimbabwe, authoritarian rule has returned after what looked like an encouraging political opening. In most of the others, authoritarian leaders or parties that may have learned to say a few of the right things about democracy in the early 1990s have reverted fully to type.

THE PERFORMANCE PROBLEM

Although a troubling number of countries that were initially counted as part of the third wave have experienced a reassertion of authoritarian forces, quite a few others have managed to go from initial democratic openings to the establishment of reasonably open pluralistic systems. Many of these countries, however, are facing a different challenge to the consolidation of democracy: they are not succeeding in providing better lives for their citizens socially or economically. The economic reform measures that many new democracies adopt, though helping to reduce government deficits and stabilize currencies, have often produced only tepid growth. Citizens of these countries face higher prices for basic goods, an increased threat of unemployment, and stagnant incomes. Moreover, they are often beset with heightened social problems, especially rising crime and a breakdown of the traditional social safety net.

This overall problem, which has come to be known as the problem of democratic performance, can be debilitating to struggling democracies. It may not be fair in some philosophical sense for people to judge democracy on the basis of the socioeconomic performance of a given weak democratic regime. Democracy is in a strict sense about political values, choices, and processes; it does not per se provide answers to economic and social problems. Yet, fair or not, this is what citizens of new democracies (and for that matter, established ones as well) do. And when the performance is poor over time, the effects can be negative. In many new democracies, citizens are seriously disenchanted with their governments. This disenchantment is turning into a larger loss of belief in democracy itself and, in some more aggravated cases, into instability and political conflict.

> *The war on terrorism has hurt America's status as a model of democracy and weakened America's credibility as a prodemocratic actor.*

South America has been sharply afflicted with this problem, although the challenge of democratic performance has also dogged various countries in Central America, southeastern Europe, South Asia, and Southeast Asia as well. In South America, unlike in the former Soviet Union and some other regions, authoritarians were largely overcome or at least sent back to the barracks after democratic openings occurred. Almost all South American countries achieved flawed but real democratic systems, with most of the main institutional and procedural forms of democracy. Yet, in the past three or four years, the region has experienced what many South Americans and external observers increasingly view as a crisis of democracy. Argentina hit a frightening bump in its political road in 2001 when an economic crisis (itself partly caused by deficiencies in the political system, above all low levels of elite accountability) produced a period of vertiginous political instability; during one three-week spell the country went through five presidents. Venezuela has been suffering serious political polarization and conflict since the 1998 election of Hugo Chávez, a populist strongman with dubious fidelity to democratic norms who survived a recall referendum this year. Peru is undergoing a period of deep political malaise, marked by a hollow party system and the collapse of support for President Alejandro Toledo, whose election in 2001 was heralded as a rebirth of Peruvian democracy after the authoritarian reign of Alberto Fujimori. Bolivia and Ecuador have both experienced the ouster of presidents and the rise of serious new political fissures and tensions. Alongside these punishing developments are two longstanding political problems: the deeply corrupted dominant-power rule by the Colorado Party in Paraguay and the continuing civil war in Colombia.

South America's democratic woes derive from many causes and vary in nature from place to place. They are discouraging precisely because they highlight that democracy can corrode in so many different ways. But the problem of democratic performance—rooted in weak state institutions, entrenched, corrupted political elites, and poor systems of political representation and accountability—plays a role in much of the region. Fifteen to twenty years after the return of democracy, many South Americans do not feel that greater political freedom and choice have improved their lives very much, or at all, especially in terms of economic well-being and personal security. Given the high expectations that many people in the region had for what the end of dictatorship would bring, frustration over poor democratic performance turns easily into bitterness. The result has been a rising tide of cynicism, anger, and hostile actions against political parties, legislatures, governments, and even democracy itself.

DOING WELL UNDER DICTATORS

A third factor contributing to a newly challenging environment for global democracy is the sense that quite a few authoritarian countries have been doing well economically in recent years, giving new life to the old idea that dictatorship is better than democracy at producing socioeconomic development. This idea was popular in the 1960s and 1970s, both in the West and in developing countries. In the West it was an article of faith among economists worried about populist-oriented policy making and a convenient excuse by diplomats for supporting friendly tyrants who were useful on security issues. In developing countries, ruling elites found it a handy justification for their repressive grip on power. The idea lost some steam in the 1980s, weakened by the accumulated socioeconomic failures of dictatorial regimes in many developing countries, especially in sub-Saharan Africa. Across the 1990s the opposite idea gained considerable ground in international development circles—that democracy and economic development go hand in hand—or even more strongly, that democracy, with its presumably better systems of representation and accountable governance, actually facilitates economic development. The experience in the 1990s of much of the postcommunist world—where for a time progress on political reform and economic growth correlated strongly—added weight to the new view.

China's extraordinary economic success has presented a serious problem for those arguing that democracy is necessary for development or that dictatorial regimes cannot produce sustained economic development. In the current context, in which citizens of many developing countries are dissatisfied with the socioeconomic performance of their new democratic regimes, China's continued very rapid growth and its increasing economic muscle on the world stage have made it an increasingly powerful example. Talk of the "China model" has become much more common around the developing world than 10 years ago, both among ruling elites and average citizens. Magnifying this effect in the past several years are other authoritarian or semi-authoritarian countries, including Russia, Ukraine, Kazakhstan, and Vietnam, that have also been turning in high growth rates. Indeed, of the ten fastest-growing economies in the developing world between 1999 and 2002, only one—Albania—was led by a (somewhat) democratic government. This trend can be explained in part by the high price of oil, which has buoyed the economies of a number of oil-rich autocracies. Nevertheless, the trend fuels the belief in the developing world that a strong hand is best for development. And it undercuts the efforts of the international development community to make the case for a democracy-development link.

THE WAR ON TERRORISM

A fourth complicating element for democracy in today's international context is the US war on terrorism. The ouster of the Taliban regime in Afghanistan and of Saddam Hussein in Iraq have opened the possibility, still far from being realized, of establishing stable, peaceful, democratic rule in these countries. President George W. Bush has also made a declared push for democratic transformation of the Middle East a part of his antiterrorism campaign, although this has been problematic in implementation. Other elements of the war on terrorism, however, have hurt democracy's cause. The US government's strongly felt need for closer counterterrorism cooperation with governments in many parts of the world has led it to warm relations with various autocratic regimes, such as those in Pakistan and Uzbekistan, and to go easy on the democratic backsliding of others, such as Russia.

In addition, the war on terrorism has hurt America's status as a model of democracy and weakened America's credibility as a prodemocratic actor. The world has watched closely, and often with disappointment, America's troubled effort to balance heightened law enforcement concerns with domestic political and civil rights, above all for Muslim citizens or residents of the United States. And the abusive treatment of detainees in US-run prisons or detention facilities in Iraq, Afghanistan, and Guantánamo has badly tarnished America's standing as a defender of human rights. Americans may have largely moved on past the stories and images that emerged from the Abu Ghraib prison outside Baghdad, but in many other parts of the world the negative emotions produced by those events are still strongly felt. A further negative consequence of the war on terrorism for global democracy has been the tendency of governments in the Middle East and many parts of Asia to use the antiterrorism banner as an excuse to crack down on political opponents, a tendency the United States has protested too little.

AND NOW FOR THE HARD PART

The most pressing as well as complex and difficult issue concerning the advance of democracy over the next decade and beyond is the question of whether the Middle East can make any significant democratic progress. Policy makers in Washington and other Western capitals advance the idea that the arrival of democracy in the Middle East is necessary to eliminate the roots of radical Islamist terrorism. Although this proposition is badly oversimplified and potentially misleading as a policy credo, it has raised to an unprecedented degree the level of international attention paid to the Arab world's democratic deficit.

The Bush administration's push for democracy in the Middle East has consisted of both a massive military-led effort to reconstruct Iraqi politics on a democratic template and an interrelated series of much less intrusive measures in the rest of the region, including new aid programs, multilevel diplomatic steps like the Broader Middle East and North Africa Initiative, and some high-level jawboning of Arab leaders by top US officials. The region's skeptical and recalcitrant response to the new push has demonstrated how hard a prodemocratic policy toward the Middle East will be in practice. The political reconstruction of Iraq has been much more difficult and costly (in financial, human, and diplomatic terms) than those in charge of the intervention ever thought it would be. Certainly, many of the political forces in post-Saddam Iraq support some kind of pluralistic outcome, yet the road to achieving it remains littered with daunting obstacles. And although Iraq is less repressive today than it was under Saddam, it has not yet proved a positive model for the region. Arabs largely view Iraq as a violent, chaotic, frightening place, one where thousands of Arabs have died as a direct or indirect result of a foreign invasion and occupation and whose political life is still controlled, deep down, by the United States.

The new international attention to the absence of democracy in the Arab world, including the various US and European initiatives to encourage or stimulate positive movement, has helped engender more discussion in Arab countries about the need for political reform and democracy. A few governments, most notably perhaps that of Morocco, have continued along paths of reform that have led to some real pluralism, albeit still within a monarchical framework. And some of the more authoritarian Arab governments, such as those in Egypt and Saudi Arabia, have announced minor new reform steps, both to respond to these internal debates and to win some international favor.

But in general the region remains stuck in deeply entrenched patterns of autocratic rule. Arab states are willing to engage in limited off-again, on-again political reforms, but more as a liberalizing strategy to avoid democracy rather than to achieve it. Arab ruling elites do not share the new Western view that democratic change is necessary to combat Islamist extremism. In fact, they hold the opposite view: that democracy would likely unleash radical forces that could be harmful to both the region and the West. Pressure from below for democratic change is weak at best throughout the region, despite the steppedup activities of some civic groups and others speaking out on behalf of reform. Those who advocate for democracy (usually secular Western-oriented intellectuals) lack organized constituencies behind them. And the groups that do have mass-based constituencies—Islamist organizations—often do not frame their political objectives in terms of democracy and are placed under strict limits by regimes nervous about any mass-based processes of political change.

It is by no means impossible that the Arab world will over time make progress toward democracy. But the process is likely to be much slower than the current fervor for reform in Washington and other Western capitals might imply, not to mention more conflictive and unsettling to Western interests than the new policy credo suggests. Despite the rhetoric coming from the White House, in practice US and other Western policy makers are not at all sure that opening up Arab political systems to popular choice would actually serve Western economic and security interests overall. In some cases, dangerous instability or even civil conflict might result. Other Arab societies might choose Islamist leaders who are not inclined to be helpful on the Israeli-Palestinian conflict or other important issues. There is a significant gap between the soaring rhetoric about freedom in the Middle East and actual Western policy in most of the region. Policies more cautious in deeds than in words are likely to persist.

GETTING SERIOUS

The state of democracy in the world is sobering. Democracy still occupies the high ground across the world both as the only political ideology to command widespread legitimacy and as the political system of most of the world's wealthy or powerful countries. Yet, only a few years into the new century, the grand hope that it will prove the age of democracy's global triumph appears far more tenuous than it seemed just 10 or 15 years ago.

American policy makers determined to make democracy promotion a major element of US foreign policy will have to do better than rely on attractive but superficial slogans like "freedom is on the march." It is necessary to move away from the mindset that a democratic trend is advancing in the world and that US policy should aim to support it. The challenges now are more fundamental: how to stimulate democracy in regions where authoritarianism has bested the democratic trend, and how to support democracy where it is under siege because of poor performance. Responding to these challenges will require a greater willingness to pressure authoritarian leaders who offer short-term economic and security benefits to the United States but spell long-term trouble, especially in the former Soviet Union and the Middle East. And it will require the United States to construct more effective partnerships with South America and other regions where democracy is under siege. Democracy promotion is a convenient, even easy rhetorical framework for a global policy, especially in the context of the war on terrorism. Making it work in practice is neither convenient nor easy, and the state of democracy in the world is only getting more complex and demanding with each passing year.

THOMAS CAROTHERS is director of the Democracy and Rule of Law Project at the Carnegie Endowment for International Peace. He is coeditor with Marina Ottaway of *Uncharted Journey: Democracy Promotion in the Middle East* (Carnegie Endowment, forthcoming January 2005).

Capitalism and Democracy*

Gabriel A. Almond

Joseph Schumpeter, a great economist and social scientist of the last generation, whose career was almost equally divided between Central European and American universities, and who lived close to the crises of the 1930s and '40s, published a book in 1942 under the title, *Capitalism, Socialism, and Democracy*. The book has had great influence, and can be read today with profit. It was written in the aftergloom of the great depression, during the early triumphs of Fascism and Nazism in 1940 and 1941, when the future of capitalism, socialism, and democracy all were in doubt. Schumpeter projected a future of declining capitalism, and rising socialism. He thought that democracy under socialism might be no more impaired and problematic than it was under capitalism.

He wrote a concluding chapter in the second edition which appeared in 1946, and which took into account the political-economic situation at the end of the war, with the Soviet Union then astride a devastated Europe. In this last chapter he argues that we should not identify the future of socialism with that of the Soviet Union, that what we had observed and were observing in the first three decades of Soviet existence was not a necessary expression of socialism. There was a lot of Czarist Russia in the mix. If Schumpeter were writing today, I don't believe he would argue that socialism has a brighter future than capitalism. The relationship between the two has turned out to be a good deal more complex and intertwined than Schumpeter anticipated. But I am sure that he would still urge us to separate the future of socialism from

that of Soviet and Eastern European Communism.

Unlike Schumpeter I do not include Socialism in my title, since its future as a distinct ideology and program of action is unclear at best. Western Marxism and the moderate socialist movements seem to have settled for social democratic solutions, for adaptations of both capitalism and democracy producing acceptable mixes of market competition, political pluralism, participation, and welfare. I deal with these modifications of capitalism, as a consequence of the impact of democracy on capitalism in the last half century.

At the time that Adam Smith wrote *The Wealth of Nations*, the world of government, politics and the state that he knew—pre-Reform Act England, the French government of Louis XV and XVI—was riddled with special privileges, monopolies, interferences with trade. With my tongue only half way in my check I believe the discipline of economics may have been traumatized by this condition of political life at its birth. Typically, economists speak of the state and government instrumentally, as a kind of secondary service mechanism.

I do not believe that politics can be treated in this purely instrumental and reductive way without losing our analytic grip on the social and historical process. The economy and the polity are the main problem solving mechanisms of human society. They each have their distinctive means, and they each have their "goods" or ends. They necessarily interact with each other, and transform each other in the process. Democracy in particular generates goals and programs. You cannot give people the suffrage,

and let them form organizations, run for office, and the like, without their developing all kinds of ideas as to how to improve things. And sometimes some of these ideas are adopted, implemented and are productive, and improve our lives, although many economists are reluctant to concede this much to the state.

My lecture deals with this interaction of politics and economics in the Western World in the course of the last couple of centuries, in the era during which capitalism and democracy emerged as the dominant problem solving institutions of modern civilization. I am going to discuss some of the theoretical and empirical literature dealing with the themes of the positive and negative interaction between capitalism and democracy. There are those who say that capitalism supports democracy, and those who say that capitalism subverts democracy. And there are those who say that democracy subverts capitalism, and those who say that it supports it.

The relation between capitalism and democracy dominates the political theory of the last two centuries. All the logically possible points of view are represented in a rich literature. It is this ambivalence and dialectic, this tension between the two major problem solving sectors of modern society—the political and the economic —that is the topic of my lecture.

Capitalism Supports Democracy

Let me begin with the argument that capitalism is positively linked with democracy, shares its values and culture, and facilitates its development. This case has been made in historical, logical, and statistical terms.

Albert Hirschman in his *Rival Views of Market Society* (1986) examines the values, manners and morals of capitalism, and their effects on the larger society and culture as these have been described by the philosophers of the 17th, 18th, and 19th centuries. He shows how the interpretation of the impact of capitalism has changed from the enlightenment view of Montesquieu, Condorcet, Adam Smith and others, who stressed the *douceur* of commerce, its "gentling," civilizing effect on behavior and interpersonal relations, to that of the 19th and 20th century conservative and radical writers who described the culture of capitalism as crassly materialistic, destructively competitive, corrosive of morality, and hence self-destructive. This sharp almost 180-degree shift in point of view among political theorists is partly explained by the transformation from the commerce and small-scale industry of early capitalism, to the smoke blackened industrial districts, the demonic and exploitive entrepreneurs, and exploited laboring classes of the second half of the nineteenth century. Unfortunately for our purposes, Hirschman doesn't deal explicitly with the capitalism–democracy connection, but rather with culture and with manners. His argument, however, implies an early positive connection and a later negative one.

Joseph Schumpeter in *Capitalism, Socialism, and Democracy* (1942) states flatly, "History clearly confirms... [that]... modern democracy rose along with capitalism, and in causal connection with it... modern democracy is a product of the capitalist process." He has a whole chapter entitled "The Civilization of Capitalism," democracy being a part of that civilization. Schumpeter also makes the point that democracy was historically supportive of capitalism. He states, "... the bourgeoisie reshaped, and from its own point of view rationalized, the social and political structure that preceded its ascendancy..." (that is to say, feudalism). "The democratic method

was the political tool of that reconstruction." According to Schumpeter capitalism and democracy were mutually causal historically, mutually supportive parts of a rising modern civilization, although as we shall show below, he also recognized their antagonisms.

Barrington Moore's historical investigation (1966) with its long title, *The Social Origins of Dictatorship and Democracy; Lord and Peasant in the Making of the Modern World*, argues that there have been three historical routes to industrial modernization. The first of these followed by Britain, France, and the United States, involved the subordination and transformation of the agricultural sector by the rising commercial bourgeoisie, producing the democratic capitalism of the 19th and 20th centuries. The second route followed by Germany and Japan, where the landed aristocracy was able to contain and dominate the rising commercial classes, produced an authoritarian and fascist version of industrial modernization, a system of capitalism encased in a feudal authoritarian framework, dominated by a military aristocracy, and an authoritarian monarchy. The third route, followed in Russia where the commercial bourgeoisie was too weak to give content and direction to the modernizing process, took the form of a revolutionary process drawing on the frustration and resources of the peasantry, and created a mobilized authoritarian Communist regime along with a state-controlled industrialized economy. Successful capitalism dominating and transforming the rural agricultural sector, according to Barrington Moore, is the creator and sustainer of the emerging democracies of the nineteenth century.

Robert A. Dahl, the leading American democratic theorist, in the new edition of his book (1990) *After the Revolution? Authority in a Good Society*, has included a new chapter entitled "Democracy and Markets." In the opening paragraph of that chapter, he says:

It is an historical fact that modern democratic institutions... have existed only in countries with predominantly privately owned, market-oriented economies, or

capitalism if you prefer that name. It is also a fact that all "socialist" countries with predominantly state-owned centrally directed economic orders—command economies—have not enjoyed democratic governments, but have in fact been ruled by authoritarian dictatorships. It is also an historical fact that some "capitalist" countries have also been, and are, ruled by authoritarian dictatorships.

To put it more formally, it looks to be the case that market-oriented economies are necessary (in the logical sense) to democratic institutions, though they are certainly not sufficient. And it looks to be the case that state-owned centrally directed economic orders are strictly associated with authoritarian regimes, though authoritarianism definitely does not require them. We have something very much like an historical experiment, so it would appear, that leaves these conclusions in no great doubt. (Dahl 1990)

Peter Berger in his book *The Capitalist Revolution* (1986) presents four propositions on the relation between capitalism and democracy:

Capitalism is a necessary but not sufficient condition of democracy under modern conditions.

If a capitalist economy is subjected to increasing degrees of state control, a point (not precisely specifiable at this time) will be reached at which democratic governance becomes impossible.

If a socialist economy is opened up to increasing degrees of market forces, a point (not precisely specifiable at this time) will be reached at which democratic governance becomes a possibility.

If capitalist development is successful in generating economic growth from which a sizable proportion of the population benefits, pressures toward democracy are likely to appear.

This positive relationship between capitalism and democracy has also been sustained by statistical studies. The "Social Mobilization" theorists of the 1950s and 1960s which included

Daniel Lerner (1958), Karl Deutsch (1961), S. M. Lipset (1959) among others, demonstrated a strong statistical association between GNP per capita and democratic political institutions. This is more than simple statistical association. There is a logic in the relation between level of economic development and democratic institutions. Level of economic development has been shown to be associated with education and literacy, exposure to mass media, and democratic psychological propensities such as subjective efficacy, participatory aspirations and skills. In a major investigation of the social psychology of industrialization and modernization, a research team led by the sociologist Alex Inkeles (1974) interviewed several thousand workers in the modern industrial and the traditional economic sectors of six countries of differing culture. Inkeles found empathetic, efficacious, participatory and activist propensities much more frequently among the modern industrial workers, and to a much lesser extent in the traditional sector in each one of these countries regardless of cultural differences.

The historical, the logical, and the statistical evidence for this positive relation between capitalism and democracy is quite persuasive.

Capitalism Subverts Democracy

But the opposite case is also made, that capitalism subverts or undermines democracy. Already in John Stuart Mill (1848) we encounter a view of existing systems of private property as unjust, and of the free market as destructively competitive—aesthetically and morally repugnant. The case he was making was a normative rather than a political one. He wanted a less competitive society, ultimately socialist, which would still respect individuality. He advocated limitations on the inheritance of property and the improvement of the property system so that everyone shared in its benefits, the limitation of population growth, and the improvement of the quality of the labor force through the provision of high quality education for all by the state. On the eve of the emergence of the modern democratic capi-

talist order John Staurt Mill wanted to control the excesses of both the market economy and the majoritarian polity, by the education of consumers and producers, citizens and politicians, in the interest of producing morally improved free market and democratic orders. But in contrast to Marx, he did not thoroughly discount the possibilities of improving the capitalist and democratic order.

Marx argued that as long as capitalism and private property existed there could be no genuine democracy, that democracy under capitalism was bourgeois democracy, which is to say not democracy at all. While it would be in the interest of the working classes to enter a coalition with the bourgeoisie in supporting this form of democracy in order to eliminate feudalism, this would be a tactical maneuver. Capitalist democracy could only result in the increasing exploitation of the working classes. Only the elimination of capitalism and private property could result in the emancipation of the working classes and the attainment of true democracy. Once socialism was attained the basic political problems of humanity would have been solved through the elimination of classes. Under socialism there would be no distinctive democratic organization, no need for institutions to resolve conflicts, since there would be no conflicts. There is not much democratic or political theory to be found in Marx's writings. The basic reality is the mode of economic production and the consequent class structure from which other institutions follow.

For the followers of Marx up to the present day there continues to be a negative tension between capitalism, however reformed, and democracy. But the integral Marxist and Leninist rejection of the possibility of an autonomous, bourgeois democratic state has been left behind for most Western Marxists. In the thinking of Poulantzas, Offe, Bobbio, Habermas and others, the bourgeois democratic state is now viewed as a class struggle state, rather than an unambiguously bourgeois state. The working class has access to it; it can struggle for its interests, and can attain partial benefits from it. The state is now viewed as autonomous, or as relatively autonomous, and it can be re-

formed in a progressive direction by working class and other popular movements. The bourgeois democratic state can be moved in the direction of a socialist state by political action short of violence and institutional destruction.

Schumpeter (1942) appreciated the tension between capitalism and democracy. While he saw a causal connection between competition in the economic and the political order, he points out "... that there are some deviations from the principle of democracy which link up with the presence of organized capitalist interests.... [T]he statement is true both from the standpoint of the classical and from the standpoint of our own theory of democracy. From the first standpoint, the result reads that the means at the disposal of private interests are often used in order to thwart the will of the people. From the second standpoint, the result reads that those private means are often used in order to interfere with the working of the mechanism of competitive leadership." He refers to some countries and situations in which "... political life all but resolved itself into a struggle of pressure groups and in many cases practices that failed to conform to the spirit of the democratic method." But he rejects the notion that there cannot be political democracy in a capitalist society. For Schumpeter full democracy in the sense of the informed participation of all adults in the selection of political leaders and consequently the making of public policy, was an impossibility because of the number and complexity of the issues confronting modern electorates. The democracy which was realistically possible was one in which people could choose among competing leaders, and consequently exercise some direction over political decisions. This kind of democracy was possible in a capitalist society, though some of its propensities impaired its performance. Writing in the early years of World War II, when the future of democracy and of capitalism were uncertain, he leaves unresolved the questions of "... Whether or not democracy is one of those products of capitalism which are to die out with it..." or "... how well or ill capitalist society qualifies for the task of working the demo-cratic method it evolved."

Non-Marxist political theorists have contributed to this questioning of the reconcilability of capitalism and democracy. Robert A. Dahl, who makes the point that capitalism his-torically has been a necessary pre-condition of democracy, views contemporary democracy in the United States as seriously compro-mised, impaired by the inequality in resources among the citizens. But Dahl stresses the variety in distribu-tive patterns, and in politico-eco-nomic relations among contemporary democracies. "The category of capi-talist democracies" he writes, "in-cludes an extraordinary variety... from nineteenth century, laissez faire, early industrial systems to twentieth century, highly regulated, social welfare, late or postindustrial systems. Even late twentieth century 'welfare state' orders vary all the way from the Scandinavian systems, which are redistributive, heavily taxed, comprehensive in their social security, and neocorporatist in their collective bargaining arrangements to the faintly redistributive, moder-ately taxed, limited social security, weak collective bargaining systems of the United States and Japan" (1989).

In *Democracy and Its Critics* (1989) Dahl argues that the norma-tive growth of democracy to what he calls its "third transformation" (the first being the direct city-state de-mocracy of classic times, and the second, the indirect, representative inegalitarian democracy of the con-temporary world) will require de-mocratization of the economic order. In other words, modern cor-porate capitalism needs to be trans-formed. Since government control and/or ownership of the economy would be destructive of the plural-ism which is an essential require-ment of democracy, his preferred solution to the problem of the mega-corporation is employee con-trol of corporate industry. An econ-omy so organized, according to Dahl, would improve the distribu-tion of political resources without at the same time destroying the plu-ralism which democratic competi-tion requires. To those who question the realism of Dahl's solution to the

problem of inequality, he replies that history is full of surprises.

Charles E. Lindblom in his book, *Politics and Markets* (1977), con-cludes his comparative analysis of the political economy of modern cap-italism and socialism, with an essen-tially pessimistic conclusion about contemporary market-oriented de-mocracy. He says

We therefore come back to the cor-poration. It is possible that the rise of the corporation has offset or more than offset the decline of class as an instrument of indoctri-nation.... That it creates a new core of wealth and power for a newly constructed upper class, as well as an overpowering loud voice, is also reasonably clear. The execu-tive of the large corporation is, on many counts, the contemporary counterpart to the landed gentry of an earlier era, his voice amplified by the technology of mass commu-nication.... [T]he major institu-tional barrier to fuller democracy may therefore be the autonomy of the private corporation.

Lindblom concludes, "The large private corporation fits oddly into democratic theory and vision. Indeed it does not fit.

There is then a widely shared agreement, from the Marxists and neo-Marxists, to Schumpeter, Dahl, Lindblom, and other liberal political theorists, that modern capitalism with the dominance of the large cor-poration, produces a defective or an impaired form of democracy.

Democracy Subverts Capitalism

If we change our perspective now and look at the way democracy is said to affect capitalism, one of the dominant traditions of economics from Adam Smith until the present day stresses the importance for pro-ductivity and welfare of an economy that is relatively free of intervention by the state. In this doctrine of mini-mal government there is still a place for a framework of rules and services essential to the productive and effi-cient performance of the economy. In part the government has to protect the market from itself. Left to their

own devices, according to Smith, businessmen were prone to corner the market in order to exact the high-est possible price. And according to Smith businessmen were prone to bribe public officials in order to gain special privileges, and legal monopo-lies. For Smith good capitalism was competitive capitalism, and good government provided just those goods and services which the market needed to flourish, could not itself provide, or would not provide. A good government according to Adam Smith was a minimal government, providing for the national defense, and domestic order. Particularly im-portant for the economy were the rules pertaining to commercial life such as the regulation of weights and measures, setting and enforcing building standards, providing for the protection of persons and property, and the like.

For Milton Friedman (1961, 1981), the leading contemporary ad-vocate of the free market and free government, and of the interdepen-dence of the two, the principal threat to the survival of capitalism and de-mocracy is the assumption of the re-sponsibility for welfare on the part of the modern democratic state. He lays down a set of functions appropriate to government in the positive inter-play between economy and polity, and then enumerates many of the ways in which the modern welfare, regulatory state has deviated from these criteria.

A good Friedmanesque, demo-cratic government would be one "... which maintained law and order, defended property rights, served as a means whereby we could modify property rights and other rules of the economic game, adjudicated disputes about the interpretation of the rules, enforced contracts, promoted compe-tition, provided a monetary frame-work, engaged in activities to counter technical monopolies and to overcome neighborhood effects widely regarded as sufficiently im-portant to justify government inter-vention, and which supplemented private charity and the private fam-ily in protecting the irresponsible, whether madman or child ...." Against this list of proper activities for a free government, Friedman pin-pointed more than a dozen activities of contemporary democratic governments which might better be performed through the private sector, or not at all. These included setting and maintaining price supports, tariffs, import and export quotas and controls, rents, interest rates, wage rates, and the like, regulating industries and banking, radio and television, licensing professions and occupations, providing social security and medical care programs, providing public housing, national parks, guaranteeing mortgages, and much else.

Friedman concludes that this steady encroachment on the private sector has been slowly but surely converting our free government and market system into a collective monster, compromising both freedom and productivity in the outcome. The tax and expenditure revolts and regulatory rebellions of the 1980s have temporarily stemmed this trend, but the threat continues. "It is the internal threat coming from men of good intentions and good will who wish to reform us. Impatient with the slowness of persuasion and example to achieve the great social changes they envision, they are anxious to use the power of the state to achieve their ends, and confident of their own ability to do so." The threat to political and economic freedom, according to Milton Friedman and others who argue the same position, arises out of democratic politics. It may only be defeated by political action.

In the last decades a school, or rather several schools, of economists and political scientists have turned the theoretical models of economics to use in analyzing political processes. Variously called public choice theorists, rational choice theorists, or positive political theorists, and employing such models as market exchange and bargaining, rational self interest, game theory, and the like, these theorists have produced a substantial literature throwing new and often controversial light on democratic political phenomena such as elections, decisions of political party leaders, interest group behavior, legislative and committee decisions, bureaucratic, and judicial behavior, lobbying activity, and substantive public policy areas such as constitutional arrangements, health and en-

vironment policy, regulatory policy, national security and foreign policy, and the like. Hardly a field of politics and public policy has been left untouched by this inventive and productive group of scholars.

The institutions and names with which this movement is associated in the United States include Virginia State University, the University of Virginia, the George Mason University, the University of Rochester, the University of Chicago, the California Institute of Technology, the Carnegie Mellon University, among others. And the most prominent names are those of the leaders of the two principal schools: James Buchanan, the Nobel Laureate leader of the Virginia "Public Choice" school, and William Riker, the leader of the Rochester "Positive Theory" school. Other prominent scholars associated with this work are Gary Becker of the University of Chicago, Kenneth Shepsle and Morris Fiorina of Harvard, John Ferejohn of Stanford, Charles Plott of the California Institute of Technology, and many others.

One writer summarizing the ideological bent of much of this work, but by no means all of it (William Mitchell of the University of Washington), describes it as fiscally conservative, sharing a conviction that the "... private economy is far more robust, efficient, and perhaps equitable than other economies, and much more successful than political processes in efficiently allocating resources...." Much of what has been produced "... by James Buchanan and the leaders of this school can best be described as contributions to a theory of the failure of political processes." These failures of political performance are said to be inherent properties of the democratic political process. "Inequity, inefficiency, and coercion are the most general results of democratic policy formation." In a democracy the demand for publicly provided services seems to be insatiable. It ultimately turns into a special interest, "rent seeking" society. Their remedies take the form of proposed constitutional limits on spending power and checks and balances to limit legislative majorities.

One of the most visible products of this pessimistic economic analysis of democratic politics is the book by

Mancur Olson, *The Rise and Decline of Nations* (1982). He makes a strong argument for the negative democracy–capitalism connection. His thesis is that the behavior of individuals and firms in stable societies inevitably leads to the formation of dense networks of collusive, cartelistic, and lobbying organizations that make economies less efficient and dynamic and polities less governable. "The longer a society goes without an upheaval, the more powerful such organizations become and the more they slow down economic expansion. Societies in which these narrow interest groups have been destroyed, by war or revolution, for example, enjoy the greatest gains in growth." His prize cases are Britain on the one hand and Germany and Japan on the other.

The logic of the argument implies that countries that have had democratic freedom of organization without upheaval or invasion the longest will suffer the most from growth-repressing organizations and combinations. This helps explain why Great Britain, the major nation with the longest immunity from dictatorship, invasion, and revolution, has had in this century a lower rate of growth than other large, developed democracies. Britain has precisely the powerful network of special interest organization that the argument developed here would lead us to expect in a country with its record of military security and democratic stability. The number and power of its trade unions need no description. The venerability and power of its professional associations is also striking.... In short, with age British society has acquired so many strong organizations and collusions that it suffers from an institutional sclerosis that slows its adaptation to changing circumstances and technologies. (Olson 1982)

By contrast, post-World War II Germany and Japan started organizationally from scratch. The organizations that led them to defeat were all dissolved, and under the occupation inclusive organizations like the general trade union movement and general organizations of the industrial and commercial community were first formed. These inclusive organizations had more regard for the general national interest and exercised some discipline on the narrower interest organizations. And both countries in the post-war decades experienced "miracles" of economic growth under democratic conditions.

The Olson theory of the subversion of capitalism through the propensities of democratic societies to foster special interest groups has not gone without challenge. There can be little question that there is logic in his argument. But empirical research testing this pressure group hypothesis thus far has produced mixed findings. Olson has hopes that a public educated to the harmful consequences of special interests to economic growth, full employment, coherent government, equal opportunity, and social mobility will resist special interest behavior, and enact legislation imposing anti-trust, and anti-monopoly controls to mitigate and contain these threats. It is somewhat of an irony that the solution to this special interest disease of democracy, according to Olson, is a democratic state with sufficient regulatory authority to control the growth of special interest organizations.

Democracy Fosters Capitalism

My fourth theme, democracy as fostering and sustaining capitalism, is not as straightforward as the first three. Historically there can be little doubt that as the suffrage was extended in the last century, and as mass political parties developed, democratic development impinged significantly on capitalist institutions and practices. Since successful capitalism requires risk-taking entrepreneurs with access to investment capital, the democratic propensity for redistributive and regulative policy tends to reduce the incentives and the resources available for risk-taking and creativity. Thus it can be argued that propensities inevitably resulting from democratic politics, as Friedman, Olson and many

others argue, tend to reduce productivity, and hence welfare.

But precisely the opposite argument can be made on the basis of the historical experience of literally all of the advanced capitalist democracies in existence. All of them without exception are now welfare states with some form and degree of social insurance, health and welfare nets, and regulatory frameworks designed to mitigate the harmful impacts and shortfalls of capitalism. Indeed, the welfare state is accepted all across the political spectrum. Controversy takes place around the edges. One might make the argument that had capitalism not been modified in this welfare direction, it is doubtful that it would have survived.

This history of the interplay between democracy and capitalism is clearly laid out in a major study involving European and American scholars, entitled *The Development of Welfare States in Western Europe and America* (Flora and Heidenheimer 1981). The book lays out the relationship between the development and spread of capitalist industry, democratization in the sense of an expanding suffrage and the emergence of trade unions and left-wing political parties, and the gradual introduction of the institutions and practices of the welfare state. The early adoption of the institutions of the welfare state in Bismarck Germany, Sweden, and Great Britain were all associated with the rise of trade unions and socialist parties in those countries. The decisions made by the upper and middle class leaders and political movements to introduce welfare measures such as accident, old age, and unemployment insurance, were strategic decisions. They were increasingly confronted by trade union movements with the capacity of bringing industrial production to a halt, and by political parties with growing parliamentary representation favoring fundamental modifications in, or the abolition of capitalism. As the calculations of the upper and middle class leaders led them to conclude that the costs of suppression exceeded the costs of concession, the various parts of the welfare state began to be put in place—accident, sickness, unemployment insurance, old age insurance,

and the like. The problem of maintaining the loyalty of the working classes through two world wars resulted in additional concessions to working class demands: the filling out of the social security system, free public education to higher levels, family allowances, housing benefits, and the like.

Social conditions, historical factors, political processes and decisions produced different versions of the welfare state. In the United States, manhood suffrage came quite early, the later bargaining process emphasized free land and free education to the secondary level, an equality of opportunity version of the welfare state. The Disraeli bargain in Britain resulted in relatively early manhood suffrage and the full attainment of parliamentary government, while the Lloyd George bargain on the eve of World War I brought the beginnings of a welfare system to Britain. The Bismarck bargain in Germany produced an early welfare state, a postponement of electoral equality and parliamentary government. While there were all of these differences in historical encounters with democratization and "welfarization," the important outcome was that little more than a century after the process began all of the advanced capitalist democracies had similar versions of the welfare state, smaller in scale in the case of the United States and Japan, more substantial in Britain and the continental European countries.

We can consequently make out a strong case for the argument that democracy has been supportive of capitalism in this strategic sense. Without this welfare adaptation it is doubtful that capitalism would have survived, or rather, its survival, "unwelfarized," would have required a substantial repressive apparatus. The choice then would seem to have been between democratic welfare capitalism, and repressive undemocratic capitalism. I am inclined to believe that capitalism as such thrives more with the democratic welfare adaptation than with the repressive one. It is in that sense that we can argue that there is a clear positive impact of democracy on capitalism.

We have to recognize, in conclusion, that democracy and capitalism are both positively and negatively related, that they both support and subvert each other. My colleague, Moses Abramovitz, described this dialectic more surely than most in his presidential address to the American Economic Association in 1980, on the eve of the "Reagan Revolution." Noting the decline in productivity in the American economy during the latter 1960s and '70s, and recognizing that this decline might in part be attributable to the "tax, transfer, and regulatory" tendencies of the welfare state, he observes,

> The rationale supporting the development of our mixed economy sees it as a pragmatic compromise between the competing virtues and defects of decentralized market capitalism and encompassing socialism. Its goal is to obtain a measure of distributive justice, security, and social guidance of economic life without losing too much of the allocative efficiency and dynamism of private enterprise and market organization. And it is a pragmatic compromise in another sense. It seeks to retain for most people that measure of personal protection from the state which private property and a private job market confer, while obtaining for the disadvantaged minority of people through the state that measure of support without which their lack of property or personal endowment would amount to a denial of individual freedom and capacity to function as full members of the community. (Abramovitz 1981)

Democratic welfare capitalism produces that reconciliation of opposing and complementary elements which makes possible the survival, even enhancement of both of these sets of institutions. It is not a static accommodation, but rather one which fluctuates over time, with capitalism being compromised by the tax-transfer-regulatory action of the state at one point, and then correcting in the direction of the reduction of the intervention of the state at another point, and with a learning process over time that may reduce the amplitude of the curves.

The case for this resolution of the capitalism-democracy quandary is made quite movingly by Jacob Viner who is quoted in the concluding paragraph of Abramovitz's paper, "... If... I nevertheless conclude that I believe that the welfare state, like old Siwash, is really worth fighting for and even dying for as compared to any rival system, it is because, despite its imperfection in theory and practice, in the aggregate it provides more promise of preserving and enlarging human freedoms, temporal prosperity, the extinction of mass misery, and the dignity of man and his moral improvement than any other social system which has previously prevailed, which prevails elsewhere today or which outside Utopia, the mind of man has been able to provide a blueprint for" (Abramovitz 1981).

References

Abramovitz, Moses. 1981. "Welfare Quandaries and Productivity Concerns." *American Economic Review*, March.

Berger, Peter. 1986. *The Capitalist Revolution*. New York: Basic Books.

Dahl, Robert A. 1989. *Democracy and Its Critics*. New Haven: Yale University Press.

____. 1990. *After the Revolution: Authority in a Good Society*. New Haven: Yale University Press.

Deutsch, Karl. 1961. "Social Mobilization and Political Development." *American Political Science Review*, 55 (Sept.).

Flora, Peter, and Arnold Heidenheimer. 1981. *The Development of Welfare States in Western Europe and America*. New Brunswick, NJ: Transaction Press.

Friedman, Milton. 1981. *Capitalism and Freedom*. Chicago: University of Chicago Press.

Hirschman, Albert. 1986. *Rival Views of Market Society*. New York: Viking.

Inkeles, Alex, and David Smith. 1974. *Becoming Modern: Individual Change in Six Developing Countries*. Cambridge, MA: Harvard University Press.

Lerner, Daniel. 1958. *The Passing of Traditional Society*. New York: Free Press.

Lindblom, Charles E. 1977. *Politics and Markets*. New York: Basic Books.

Lipset, Seymour M. 1959. "Some Social Requisites of Democracy." *American Political Science Review*, 53 (September).

Mill, John Stuart. 1848, 1965. *Principles of Political Economy*, 2 vols. Toronto: University of Toronto Press.

Mitchell, William. 1988. "Virginia, Rochester, and Bloomington: Twenty-Five Years of Public Choice and Political Science." *Public Choice*, 56: 101–119.

Moore, Barrington. 1966. *The Social Origins of Dictatorship and Democracy*. New York: Beacon Press.

Olson, Mancur. 1982. *The Rise and Decline of Nations*. New Haven: Yale University Press.

Schumpeter, Joseph. 1946. *Capitalism, Socialism, and Democracy*. New York: Harper.

*Lecture presented at Seminar on the Market, sponsored by the Ford Foundation and the Research Institute on International Change of Columbia University, Moscow, October 29—November 2.

Gabriel A. Almond, professor of political science emeritus at Stanford University, is a former president of the American Political Science Association.

CULTURAL EXPLANATIONS

The man in the Baghdad café

Which "civilisation" you belong to matters less than you might think

GOERING, it was said, growled that every time he heard the word culture he reached for his revolver. His hand would ache today. Since the end of the cold war, "culture" has been everywhere—not the opera-house or gallery kind, but the sort that claims to be the basic driving force behind human behaviour. All over the world, scholars and politicians seek to explain economics, politics and diplomacy in terms of "culture-areas" rather than, say, policies or ideas, economic interests, personalities or plain cock-ups.

Perhaps the best-known example is the notion that "Asian values" explain the success of the tiger economies of South-East Asia. Other accounts have it that international conflict is—or will be—caused by a clash of civilisations; or that different sorts of business organisation can be explained by how much people in different countries trust one [an]other. These four pages review the varying types of cultural explanation. They conclude that culture is so imprecise and changeable a phenomenon that it explains less than most people realise.

To see how complex the issue is, begin by considering the telling image with which Bernard Lewis opens his history of the Middle East. A man sits at a table in a coffee house in some Middle Eastern city, "drinking a cup of coffee or tea, perhaps smoking a cigarette, reading a newspaper, playing a board game, and listening with half an ear to whatever is coming out of the radio or the television installed in the corner." Undoubtedly Arab, almost certainly

Muslim, the man would clearly identify himself as a member of these cultural groups. He would also, if asked, be likely to say that "western culture" was alien, even hostile to them.

Look closer, though, and the cultural contrasts blur. This coffee-house man probably wears western-style clothes—sneakers, jeans, a T-shirt. The chair and table at which he sits, the coffee he drinks, the tobacco he smokes, the newspaper he reads, all are western imports. The radio and television are western inventions. If our relaxing friend is a member of his nation's army, he probably operates western or Soviet weapons and trains according to western standards; if he belongs to the government, both his bureaucratic surroundings and the constitutional trappings of his regime may owe their origins to western influence.

The upshot, for Mr Lewis, is clear enough. "In modern times," he writes, "the dominating factor in the consciousness of most Middle Easterners has been the impact of Europe, later of the West more generally, and the transformation—some would say dislocation—which it has brought." Mr Lewis has put his finger on the most important and least studied aspect of cultural identity: how it changes. It would be wise to keep that in mind during the upsurge of debate about culture that is likely to follow the publication of Samuel Huntington's new book, "The Clash of Civilisations and the Remaking of World Order".

The clash of civilisations

A professor of international politics at Harvard and the chairman of Harvard's Institute for Strategic Planning, Mr Huntington published in 1993, in *Foreign Affairs*, an essay which that quarterly's editors said generated more discussion than any since George Kennan's article (under the by-line "x") which argued in July 1947 for the need to contain the Soviet threat. Henry Kissinger, a former secretary of state, called Mr Huntington's book-length version of the article "one of the most important books... since the end of the cold war."

The article, "The Clash of Civilisation?", belied the question-mark in its title by predicting wars of culture. "It is my hypothesis", Mr Huntington wrote, "that the fundamental source of conflict in this new world will not be primarily ideological or primarily economic. The great division among humankind and the dominating source of conflict will be cultural."

After the cold war, ideology seemed less important as an organising principle of foreign policy. Culture seemed a plausible candidate to fill the gap. So future wars, Mr Huntington claimed, would occur "between nations and groups of different civilisations"—western, Confucian, Japanese, Islamic, Hindu, Orthodox and Latin American, perhaps African and Buddhist. Their disputes would "dominate global politics" and the battle-lines of the future would follow the fault-lines between these cultures.

No mincing words there, and equally few in his new book:

Culture and cultural identities… are shaping the patterns of cohesion, disintegration and conflict in the post-cold war world… Global politics is being reconfigured along cultural lines.

Mr Huntington is only one of an increasing number of writers placing stress on the importance of cultural values and institutions in the confusion left in the wake of the cold war. He looked at the influence of culture on international conflict. Three other schools of thought find cultural influences at work in different ways.

• **Culture and the economy**. Perhaps the oldest school holds that cultural values and norms equip people—and, by extension, countries—either poorly or well for economic success. The archetypal modern pronouncement of this view was Max Weber's investigation of the Protestant work ethic. This, he claimed, was the reason why the Protestant parts of Germany and Switzerland were more successful economically than the Catholic areas. In the recent upsurge of interest in issues cultural, a handful of writers have returned to the theme.

It is "values and attitudes—culture", claims Lawrence Harrison, that are "mainly responsible for such phenomena as Latin America's persistent instability and inequity, Taiwan's and Korea's economic 'miracles', and the achievements of the Japanese." Thomas Sowell offers other examples in "Race and Culture: A World View". "A disdain for commerce and industry", he argues, "has… been common for centuries among the Hispanic elite, both in Spain and in Latin America." Academics, though, have played a relatively small part in this debate: the best-known exponent of the thesis that "Asian values"—a kind of Confucian work ethic— aid economic development has been Singapore's former prime minister, Lee Kuan Yew.

• **Culture as social blueprint**. A second group of analysts has looked at the connections between cultural factors and political systems. Robert Putnam, another Harvard professor, traced Italy's social and political institutions to its "civic culture", or lack thereof. He claimed that, even today, the parts of Italy where democratic institutions are most fully developed are similar to the areas which first began to generate these institutions in the 14th century. His conclusion is that democracy is not something

that can be put on like a coat; it is part of a country's social fabric and takes decades, even centuries, to develop.

Francis Fukuyama, of George Mason University, takes a slightly different approach. In a recent book which is not about the end of history, he focuses on one particular social trait, "trust". "A nation's well-being, as well as its ability to compete, is conditioned by a single, pervasive cultural characteristic: the level of trust inherent in the society," he says. Mr Fukuyama argues that "low-trust" societies such as China, France and Italy—where close relations between people do not extend much beyond the family—are poor at generating large, complex social institutions like multinational corporations; so they are at a competitive disadvantage compared with "high-trust" nations such as Germany, Japan and the United States.

• **Culture and decision-making**. The final group of scholars has looked at the way in which cultural assumptions act like blinkers. Politicians from different countries see the same issue in different ways because of their differing cultural backgrounds. Their electorates or nations do, too. As a result, they claim, culture acts as an international barrier. As Ole Elgstrom puts it: "When a Japanese prime minister says that he will 'do his best' to implement a certain policy," Americans applaud a victory but "what the prime minister really meant was 'no'." There are dozens of examples of misperception in international relations, ranging from Japanese-American trade disputes to the misreading of Saddam Hussein's intentions in the weeks before he attacked Kuwait.

What are they talking about?

All of this is intriguing, and much of it is provocative. It has certainly provoked a host of arguments. For example, is Mr Huntington right to lump together all European countries into one culture, though they speak different languages, while separating Spain and Mexico, which speak the same one? Is the Catholic Philippines western or Asian? Or: if it is true (as Mr Fukuyama claims) that the ability to produce multinational firms is vital to economic success, why has "low-trust" China, which has few such companies, grown so fast? And why has yet-more successful "low-trust" South Korea been able to create big firms?

This is nit-picking, of course. But such questions of detail matter because behind

them lurks the first of two fundamental doubts that plague all these cultural explanations: how do you define what a culture is?

In their attempts to define what cultures are (and hence what they are talking about), most "culture" writers rely partly on self definition: cultures are what people think of themselves as part of. In Mr Huntington's words, civilisation "is the broadest level of identification with which [a person] intensely identifies."

The trouble is that relatively few people identify "intensely" with broad cultural groups. They tend to identify with something narrower: nations or ethnic groups. Europe is a case in point. A poll done last year for the European Commission found that half the people of Britain, Portugal and Greece thought of themselves in purely national terms; so did a third of the Germans, Spaniards and Dutch. And this was in a part of the world where there is an institution—the EU itself—explicitly devoted to the encouragement of "Europeanness".

The same poll found that in every EU country, 70% or more thought of themselves either purely in national terms, or primarily as part of a nation and only secondly as Europeans. Clearly, national loyalty can coexist with wider cultural identification. But, even then, the narrower loyalty can blunt the wider one because national characteristics often are—or at least are often thought to be—peculiar or unique. Seymour Martin Lipset, a sociologist who recently published a book about national characteristics in the United States, called it "American Exceptionalism". David Willetts, a British Conservative member of Parliament, recently claimed that the policies espoused by the opposition Labour Party would go against the grain of "English exceptionalism". And these are the two components of western culture supposedly most like one another.

In Islamic countries, the balance between cultural and national identification may be tilted towards the culture. But even here the sense of, say, Egyptian or Iraqi or Palestinian nationhood remains strong. (Consider the competing national feelings unleashed during the Iran-Iraq war.) In other cultures, national loyalty seems preeminent: in Mr Huntington's classification, Thailand, Tibet and Mongolia all count as "Buddhist". It is hard to imagine that a Thai, a Tibetan and a Mongolian really have that much in common.

So the test of subjective identification is hard to apply. That apart, the writers define

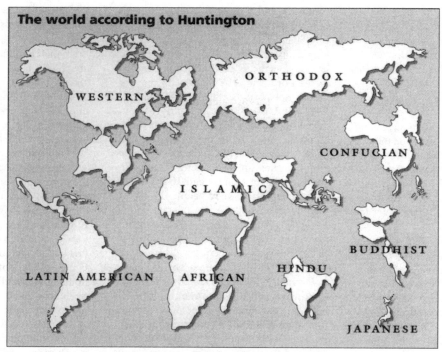

The world according to Huntington

Source: Adapted by The Economist from "The Clash of Civilisations and the Remaking of World Order" by Samuel Huntington

a culture in the usual terms: language, religion, history, customs and institutions and so on. Such multiple definitions ring true. As Bernard Lewis's man in the Levantine café suggests, cultures are not singular things: they are bundles of characteristics.

The trouble is that such characteristics are highly ambiguous. Some push one way, some another.

Culture as muddle

Islamic values, for instance, are routinely assumed to be the antithesis of modernising western ones. In Islam, tradition is good; departure from tradition is presumed to be bad until proven otherwise. Yet, at the same time, Islam is also a monotheistic religion which encourages rationalism and science. Some historians have plausibly argued that it was the Islamic universities of medieval Spain that kept science and rationalism alive during Europe's Dark Ages, and that Islam was a vital medieval link between the ancient world of Greece and Rome and the Renaissance. The scientific-rationalist aspect of Islam could well come to the fore again.

If you doubt it, consider the case of China and the "Confucian tradition" (a sort of proxy for Asian values). China has been

at various times the world's most prosperous country and also one of its poorest. It has had periods of great scientific innovation and times of technological backwardness and isolation. Accounts of the Confucian tradition have tracked this path. Nowadays, what seems important about the tradition is its encouragement of hard work, savings and investment for the future, plus its emphasis on co-operation towards a single end. All these features have been adduced to explain why the tradition has helped Asian growth.

To Max Weber, however, the same tradition seemed entirely different. He argued that the Confucian insistence on obedience to parental authority discouraged competition and innovation and hence inhibited economic success. And China is not the only country to have been systematically misdiagnosed in this way. In countries as varied as Japan, India, Ghana and South Korea, notions of cultural determination of economic performance have been proved routinely wrong (in 1945, India and Ghana were expected to do best of the four—partly because of their supposed cultural inheritance).

If you take an extreme position, you could argue from this that cultures are so complicated that they can never be used to explain behaviour accurately. Even if you

do not go that far, the lesson must be that the same culture embraces such conflicting features that it can produce wholly different effects at different times.

That is hard enough for the schools of culture to get to grips with. But there is worse to come. For cultures never operate in isolation. When affecting how people behave, they are always part of a wider mix. That mix includes government policies, personal leadership, technological or economic change and so on. For any one effect, there are always multiple causes. Which raises the second fundamental doubt about cultural explanations: how do you know whether it is culture—and not something else—that has caused some effect? You cannot. The problem of causation seems insoluble. The best you can do is work out whether, within the mix, culture is becoming more or less important.

Culture as passenger

Of the many alternative explanations for events, three stand out: the influence of ideas, of government and what might be called the "knowledge era" (shorthand for globalisation, the growth of service-based industries and so forth). Of these, the influence of ideas as a giant organising principle is clearly not what it was when the cold war divided the world between communists and capitalists. We are all capitalists now. To that extent, it is fair to say that the ideological part of the mix has become somewhat less important—though not, as a few people have suggested, insignificant.

As for the government, it is a central thesis of the cultural writers that its influence is falling while that of culture is rising: cultures are in some ways replacing states. To quote Mr Huntington again "peoples and countries with similar cultures are coming together. Peoples and countries with different cultures are coming apart."

In several respects, that is counter-intuitive. Governments still control what is usually the single most powerful force in any country, the army. And, in all but the poorest places, governments tax and spend a large chunk of GDP—indeed, a larger chunk, in most places, than 50 years ago.

Hardly surprising, then, that governments influence cultures as much as the other way around. To take a couple of examples. Why does South Korea (a low-trust culture, remember) have so many internationally competitive large firms? The answer is that the government decided that it should. Or another case: since 1945 German politicians of every stripe have been insisting that they want to "save Germany from itself"—an attempt to assert political control over cultural identity.

South Korea and Germany are examples of governments acting positively to create something new. But governments can act upon cultures negatively: ie, they can destroy a culture when they collapse. Robert Kaplan, of an American magazine *Atlantic Monthly*, begins his book, "The Ends of the Earth", in Sierra Leone: "I had assumed that the random crime and social chaos of West Africa were the result of an already-fragile cultural base." Yet by the time he reaches Cambodia at the end of what he calls "a journey at the dawn of the 21st century" he is forced to reconsider that assumption:

Here I was… in a land where the written script was one thousand two hundred years old, and every surrounding country was in some stage of impressive economic growth. Yet Cambodia was eerily similar to Sierra Leone: with random crime, mosquito-borne disease, a government army that was more like a mob and a countryside that was ungovernable.

His conclusion is that "The effect of culture was more a mystery to me near the end of my planetary journey than at its beginning." He might have gone further: the collapse of governments causes cultural turbulence just as much as cultural turbulence causes the collapse of governments.

Culture as processed data

Then there is the "knowledge era". Here is a powerful and growing phenomenon. The culture writers do not claim anything different. Like the Industrial Revolution before it, the knowledge era—in which the creation, storage and use of knowledge becomes the basic economic activity—is generating huge change. Emphasising as it does rapid, even chaotic, transformation, it is anti-traditional and anti-authoritarian.

Yet the cultural exponents still claim that, even in the knowledge era, culture remains a primary engine of change. They do so for two quite different reasons. Some claim that the new era has the makings of a world culture. There is a universal language, English. There are the beginnings of an international professional class that cuts across cultural and national boundaries: increasingly, bankers, computer programmers, executives, even military officers are said to have as much in common with their opposite numbers in other countries as with their next-door neighbors. As Mr Fukuyama wrote in his more famous book: the "unfolding of modern natural science… guarantees an increasing homogenisation of all human societies." Others doubt that technology and the rest of it are producing a genuinely new world order. To them, all this is just modern western culture.

Either way, the notion that modernity is set on a collision course with culture lies near the heart of several of the culture writers' books. Summing them up is the title of Benjamin Barber's "Jihad versus McWorld". In other words, he argues that the main conflicts now and in future will be between tribal, local "cultural" values (Jihad) and a McWorld of technology and democracy.

It would be pointless to deny that globalisation is causing large changes in every society. It is also clear that such influences act on different cultures differently, enforcing a kind of natural selection between those cultures which rise to the challenge and those which do not.

But it is more doubtful that these powerful forces are primarily cultural or even western. Of course, they have a cultural component: the artefacts of American culture are usually the first things to come along in the wake of a new road, or new television networks. But the disruptive force itself is primarily economic and has been adopted as enthusiastically in Japan, Singapore and China as in America. The world market is not a cultural concept.

Moreover, to suggest that trade, globalisation and the rest of it tend to cause conflict, and then leave the argument there, is not enough. When you boil the argument down, much of its seems to be saying that the more countries trade with each other, the more likely they are to go to war. That seems implausible. Trade—indeed, any sort of link—is just as likely to reduce the potential for violent conflict as to increase it. The same goes for the spread of democracy, another feature which is supposed to encourage civilisations to clash with each other. This might well cause ructions within countries. It might well provoke complaints from dictators about "outside interference". But serious international conflict is a different matter. And if democracy really did spread round the world, it might tend to reduce violence; wealthy democracies, at any rate, are usually reluctant to go to war (though poor or angrily nationalist ones may, as history has shown, be much less reluctant).

In short, the "knowledge era" is spreading economic ideas. And these ideas have three cultural effects, not one. They make cultures rub against each other, causing international friction. They also tie different cultures closer together, which offsets the first effect. And they may well increase tensions within a culture-area as some groups accommodate themselves to the new world while others turn their back on it. And all this can be true at the same time because cultures are so varied and ambiguous that they are capable of virtually any transformation.

The conclusion must be that while culture will continue to exercise an important influence on both countries and individuals, it has not suddenly become more important than, say, governments or impersonal economic forces. Nor does it play the all-embracing defining role that ideology played during the cold war. Much of its influence is secondary, ie, it comes about partly as a reaction to the "knowledge era". And within the overall mix of what influences people's behaviour, culture's role may well be declining, rather than rising, squeezed between the greedy expansion of the government on one side, and globalisation on the other.

The books mentioned in this article are:

Benjamin Barber. Jihad versus McWorld (Random House; 1995; 400 pages; $12.95).

Francis Fukuyama. The End of History and the Last Man (Free Press; 1992; 419 pages; $24.95. Hamish Hamilton; £20.) and Trust: The Social Virtues and the Creation of Prosperity (Free Press; 1995; 480 pages; $25. Hamish Hamilton; £25).

Lawrence E. Harrison. Who Prospers? How Cultural Values Shape Economic and Political Success (Basic Books; 1992; 288 pages; $14).

Samuel Huntington. The Clash of Civilisations? *Foreign Affairs* Vol. 72 (Summer 1993) and The Clash of Civilisations and the Remaking of World Order (Simon & Schuster; 1996; 367 pages; $26).

Robert Kaplan. The Ends of the Earth (Random House; 1996; 475 pages; $27.50. Papermac; £10).

Bernard Lewis. The Middle East (Wiedenfeld & Nicolson; 1995; 433 pages; £20. Simon & Schuster; $29.50).

Seymour Martin Lipset. American Exceptionalism (Norton; 1996; 352 pages; $27.50 and £19.95).

Robert Putnam. Making Democracy Work: Civic Traditions in Modern Italy (Princeton; 1993; 288 pages; $24.95 and £18.95).

Thomas Sowell. Race and Culture: A World View (Basic Books; 1994; 331 pages; $14).

Globalization Is About Blending, Not Homogenizing

Historical proof that globalization does not necessarily mean homogenization can be seen in Japan, a country that deliberately isolated itself from an earlier wave of globalization carried by 17th-century European seafarers. In the mid-19th century, it became the first Asian country to embrace globalization and to borrow successfully from the world without losing its uniqueness.

Joseph S. Nye Jr.

When anti-globalization protesters took to the streets of Washington at the end of September, they blamed globalization for everything from hunger to the destruction of indigenous cultures. And globalization meant the United States. The critics call it Coca-Colonization, and French sheep farmer Jose Bove has become a cult figure since destroying a McDonald's restaurant in 1999. Contrary to conventional wisdom, however, globalization is neither homogenizing nor Americanizing the cultures of the world.

To understand why not, we have to step back and put the current period in a larger historical perspective. Although they are related, the long-term historical trends of globalization and modernization are not the same. While modernization has produced some common traits, such as large cities, factories and mass communications, local cultures have by no means been erased. The appearance of similar institutions in response to similar problems is not surprising, but it does not lead to homogeneity. In the first half of the 20th century, for example, there were some similarities among the industrial societies of Britain, Germany, America and Japan, but there were even more important differences. When China, India and Brazil complete their current processes of industrialization and modernization, we should not expect them to be replicas of Japan, Germany or the United States.

Take the current information revolution. The United States is at the forefront of this great movement of change, so the uniform social and cultural habits produced by television viewing or Internet use, for instance, are often attributed to Americanization. But correlation is not causation. Imagine if another country had introduced computers and communications at a rapid rate in a world in which the United States did not exist. Major social and cultural changes still would have followed. Of course, since the United States does exist and is at the leading edge of the information revolution, there is a degree of Americanization at present, but it is likely to diminish over the course of the 21st century as technology spreads and local cultures modernize in their own ways.

Historical proof that globalization does not necessarily mean homogenization can be seen in the case of Japan, a country that deliberately isolated itself from an earlier wave of globalization carried by 17th-century European seafarers. In the mid-19th century, it became the first Asian country to embrace globalization and to borrow successfully from the world without losing its uniqueness. Following the Meiji Restoration of 1868, which marked the end of the feudal Tokugawa shogunate, Japan searched broadly for tools and innovations that would allow it to become a major power rather than a victim of Western imperialism. It sent young people to the West for education. Its delegations scoured the world for new ideas in science, technology and industry. In the political realm, Meiji reformers were well aware of Anglo-American ideas and institutions, but deliberately turned to German models because they were deemed more suitable to a country with an emperor.

The lesson that Japan has to teach the rest of the world is that even a century and a half of openness to global trends does not necessarily assure destruction of a country's separate cultural identity. Of course, there are American influences in contemporary Japan (and Japanese influences such as Sony and Pokemon in the United States). Thousands of Japanese youths are co-opting the music, dress and style of urban black America. But some of the groups they listen to dress up like samurai warriors on stage. As one singer explains, "We're trying to make a whole new culture and mix the music." One can applaud or deplore or simply be amused by such cultural transfers, but one should not doubt the persistence of Japan's cultural uniqueness.

THE PROTESTERS' IMAGE OF AMER-ICA homogenizing the world also reflects a mistakenly static view of culture. Efforts to portray cultures as unchanging more often reflect reactionary political strategies than descriptions of reality. The Peruvian writer Mario Vargas Llosa put it well when he said that arguments in favor of cultural identity and against globalization "betray a stagnant attitude toward culture that is not borne out by historical fact. Do we know of any cultures that have remained unchanged through time? To find any of them one has to travel to the small, primitive, magico-religious communities made up of people … who, due to their primitive condition, become progressively more vulnerable to exploitation and extermination."

Vibrant cultures are constantly changing and borrowing from other cultures. And the borrowing is not always from the United States. For example, many more countries turned to Canada than to the United States as a model for constitution building in the aftermath of the Cold War. Canadian views of how to deal with hate crimes were more congenial to countries such as South Africa and the post-Communist states of Eastern Europe than America's First Amendment practices.

Globalization is also a two-edged sword. In some areas, there has been not only a backlash against American cultural imports, but also an effort to change American culture itself. American policies on capital punishment may have majority support inside the United States, but they are regarded as egregious violations of human rights in much of Europe and have been the focus of transnational human rights campaigns. American attitudes toward climate change or genetic modification of food draw similar criticism. More

subtly, the openness of the United States to the world's diasporas both enriches and changes American culture.

Finally, there is some evidence that globalization and the information revolution may actually reinforce rather than reduce cultural diversity. Some French commentators have worried that in a world of Internet global marketing, there will no longer be room for a culture that cherishes some 250 different types of cheese.

But the opposite is true: The Internet allows dispersed customers, to come together in a way that encourages niche markets, including hundreds of sites dedicated only to cheese. The Internet also allows people to establish a more diverse set of political communities. The use of the Welsh language in Britain and Gaelic in Ireland is greater today than it was 50 years ago. Britain, Belgium and Spain, among others in Europe, have devolved more power to local regions.

Transnational corporations are changing poor countries but not homogenizing them. In the early stages of investment, a multinational company with access to the global resources of finance, technology and markets holds the high cards and often gets the best of the bargain with the poor country. But over time, as the poor country develops a skilled workforce, learns new technologies and opens its own channels to global finance and markets, it is often able to renegotiate the bargain and capture more of the benefits.

When the multinational oil companies first went into the Persian Gulf, they claimed the lion's share of the oil profits; today, the local governments do. Of course, there has been some change in Saudi Arabia as its engineers and financiers have trained abroad, incomes have risen and a degree of urbanization has oc-

curred. Yet after 60 years of investment from abroad, Saudi culture certainly does not look American.

SKEPTICS MIGHT ARGUE that transnational corporations will escape the fate of the giant oil companies because many are virtual companies that design and market products but farm out their manufacture to dozens of suppliers in poor countries. The big companies play small suppliers against each other, seeking ever lower labor costs. But as the technology of cheap communications allows nongovernmental organizations to conduct campaigns of "naming and shaming" that threaten the multinationals' market brands in rich countries, such corporations become vulnerable as well.

As technical capabilities spread and more and more people hook up to global communications systems, the United States' economic and cultural preponderance may diminish. This in turn has mixed implications for American "soft" power, our ability to get others to do what we want by attraction rather than coercion. A little less dominance may mean a little less anxiety about Americanization, fewer complaints about American arrogance and a little less intensity in the anti-American backlash. We may have less control in the future, but we may find ourselves living in a world somewhat more congenial to our basic values of democracy, free markets and human rights.

Joseph Nye is dean of Harvard's Kennedy School of Government and author of "The Paradox of American Power: Why the World's Only Superpower Can't Go It Alone" (Oxford University Press).

An explosive combination

Capitalism, democracy don't always go together as planned

By AMY CHUA

In May 1998, Indonesian mobs swarmed the streets of Jakarta, looting and torching more than 5,000 ethnic Chinese shops and homes. One hundred and fifty Chinese women were gang-raped, and more than 2,000 people died.

In the months that followed, anti-Chinese hate-mongering and violence spread throughout Indonesia's cities. The explosion of rage can be traced to an unlikely source: the rapid combination of democracy and free markets— the very prescription wealthy democracies have promoted for healing the ills of underdevelopment.

How did things go so wrong?

During the 1980s and 1990s, Indonesia's aggressive shift to unrestrained free-market policies allow the country's Chinese minority, just 3 percent of the population, to take control of 70 percent of the private economy.

When Indonesians ousted President General Suharto in 1998, the country's poor majority rose up in a violent backlash against the Chinese minority and against markets. The democratic elections that abruptly followed 30 years of autocratic rule, while free and fair, were rife with ethnic scapegoating by indigenous politicians and calls for confiscation of Chinese wealth and a "People's Economy."

Today, the Indonesian government sits on $58 billion worth of nationalized assets, almost all formerly owned by Chinese tycoons. These once-productive assets now lie stagnant, while unemployment and poverty deepen.

What occurred in Indonesia is part of a pattern. It is the rule of unintended—but reasonably predicted—consequences. It is also a lesson for U.S. policy-makers in running postwar Iraq.

The reality is that given the conditions that actually exist now in many post colonial countries—conditions created by history, colonialism, divide-and-conquer policies, corruption, autocracy—the combination of laissez-faire capitalism and unrestrained majority rule may well have catastrophic consequences.

Roots of resentment

The notion that market democracy promotes peaceful prosperity has not always held sway. In the 18th and 19th centuries, most leading political philosophers and economists believed that market capitalism and democracy could only coexist in fundamental tension with each other. It is one of history's great surprises that Western nations succeeded so spectacularly in integrating markets and democracy.

Conditions in today's developing world, however, make the combination of markets and democracy much more volatile than was the case when Western nations embarked on their own paths to market democracy.

One reason has to do with scale: The poor are vastly more numerous, and poverty far more entrenched, in the developing world today.

Another has to do with process: Universal suffrage in developing countries is often implemented wholesale and abruptly—a destabilizing approach that is quite removed from the gradual enfranchisement seen during Western democratization.

But the most formidable problem the developing world faces is structural—and it's one that the West has little experience with.

It's the phenomenon of the market-dominant minority, ethnic minorities who tend under market conditions to dominate economically, often to an astounding extent, the impoverished "indigenous" majorities around them.

They're the Chinese in Southeast Asia, Indians in East Africa and the West Indies, Lebanese in West Africa, Kikuyu in Kenya, Ibo in Nigeria, Jews in post-Communist Russia, and whites in Zimbabwe, South Africa, and Bolivia, to name just a few.

It is crucial to recognize that groups can be market-dominant for widely different reasons, ranging from superior entrepreneurialism to a history of apartheid or colonial oppression. If, for example, as with whites in South Africa, a minority uses force to relegate the indigenous majority to inferior education and inhumane conditions for over a century, then that minority is likely to be market-dominant, for reasons that have nothing to do with culture.

In countries with a market-dominant minority, the rich are not just rich but belong to a resented "outsider" ethnic group.

In free-market environments, these minorities, together with foreign investors (who are often their business partners), tend to accumulate starkly disproportionate wealth, fueling ethnic envy and resentment among the poor majorities.

When democratic reforms give voice to this previously silenced majority, opportunistic demagogues can swiftly marshal majoritarian animosity into powerful ethnonationalist movements that can subvert both markets and democracy.

That's what happened in Indonesia and is happening around the world. The same dynamic—in which markets and democracy pit a poor, frustrated majority against a rich "outsider" minority—has produced retaliation, violence, and even mass slaughter of market-dominant minorities, from Croats in the former Yugoslavia to Tutsi in Rwanda.

A stake in the game

How can Western nations advance capitalism and democracy in the developing world without encouraging conflagration and bloodshed? They must stop promoting unrestrained, bare-knuckled capitalism (a form of markets that the West, itself, has repudiated) and unrestrained, overnight majority rule (a form of democracy Western nations have also repudiated).

Instead of encouraging a caricature of free-market democracy, they should follow their own successful model and sponsor the gradual introduction of democratic reforms, tailored to local circumstances.

They also should cultivate stabilizing institutions and programs such as social safety nets, tax-and-transfer programs, antitrust laws, philanthropy, constitutionalism and property protections. Most crucially, they must find ways to give the poor majorities of the world an ownership stake in their countries' corporations and capital markets.

In the United States, a solid majority of Americans, even members of the lower middle classes, own shares in major U.S. companies, often through pension funds, and thus have a stake in the U.S. market economy.

This is not the case in the developing world, where corporations are typically owned by single families belonging to a market-dominant minority. In South Africa as of June 2002, for example, blacks, although making up 77 percent of the population, controlled only 2 percent of the Johannesburg Stock Exchange's total capitalization.

Continued global democratization seems inevitable. But in this climate, international businesses, Western investors and market-dominant minorities should heed the lessons from Jakarta. It is an act of enlightened self-interest to launch highly visible local corporate responsibility initiatives and innovative profit-sharing programs.

Consider these models:
- In East Africa, powerful families of Indian descent include Africans in top management positions in their companies and provide education, training, and wealth-sharing schemes for their African employees
- In Russia, where anti-Semitism is rampant, the Jewish billionaire Roman Abramovich was recently elected governor of Chukotka after spending tens of millions of dollars of his personal fortune to airlift food, medicine, computers and textbooks into the poverty-stricken region.
- In Central America, a few Western companies have started to contribute to local infrastructure development and to offer stock options to local employees.

In these ways, foreign investors and market-dominant minorities can give local populations a stake in their local economy and businesses. This is perhaps the best way to defuse tensions that, history tells us, can sabotage both markets and democracy, the very structures businesses need to thrive.

The Bush administration might consider these lessons as it decides how to rebuild Iraq.

Perhaps because of beliefs in the "melting pot" and America's own relatively successful-though halting and incomplete-history of ethnic assimilation, Americans don't always understand the significance of ethnicity, both in the United States and especially in other countries. Interestingly, British colonial governments were fastidiously conscious of ethnic divisions.

Of course, their ethnic policies are a dangerous model. When it was the British Empire's turn to deal with nation-building and ethnicity, the British engaged in divide-and-conquer policies, not only protecting but favoring ethnic minorities, and simultaneously aggravating ethnic resentments.

Laissez-faire markets and overnight democracy in Iraq could well favor different ethnic or religious groups in the short run, creating enormous instability.

As a result, when the British decamped, the time bombs often exploded, from Africa to India to Southeast Asia. This contrast can be seen in how the United States and Britain looked at the situation in postwar Iraq.

At least before the war, the U.S. government's ethnic policy for Iraq was essentially to have no ethnic policy. Instead, U.S. officials seemed strangely confident that Iraq's ethnic, religious, and tribal divisions would dissipate in the face of democracy and market-generated wealth.

But in countries as deeply divided as Iraq, every-thing—even freedom and wealth—has ethnic and sectar-ian ramifications. Who will comprise the police? Who has experience in engineering and oil or the skills to run a stock exchange? Given Saddam Hussein's sadistically un-fair and repressive regime, some groups—namely, the Sunni minority, particularly the Ba'athists—will almost certainly have a head start in terms of education, capital, and economic and managerial experience.

Consequently, as is true in so many other non-Western countries, laissez-faire markets and overnight democracy in Iraq could well favor different ethnic or religious groups in the short run, creating enormous instability.

At the same time, because by analogy at the global level, the United States has come to be seen as a kind of global market-dominant minority—wielding wildly dis-proportionate power relative to our size and numbers—every move we make with respect to Iraq is being closely—and perhaps even unfairly—scrutinized.

Despite Hussein's barbarous gulags, gross human-rights violations and repeated refusals to comply with U.N. requirements, international public opinion was overwhelmingly against the United States going to war with Iraq.

It is important to see that this opposition to U.S. poli-cies was closely bound up with deep feelings of resent-ment and fear of U.S. power and cynicism about American motives.

Deep ethnic and religious divisions remain in Iraq, but ironically one theme unifying the Iraqi people at the mo-ment is their intensifying opposition to American and British occupation.

Many Americans are bewildered—outraged—at the depth and pervasiveness of anti-Americanism in the world today. "Why do so many people want to come here if we're so terrible?" frustrated Americans demand. "What would France be doing if it were the world's su-perpower?" "Why do they hate us?" These are reasonable points.

But the fact of the matter is that because the United States is the world's sole superpower, we are going to be held to a higher standard than everyone else—market-dominant minorities always are.

For this reason, it is in the United States' own interest to avoid taking actions that suggest hypocrisy, look glar-ingly exploitative, or display lack of concern for the rest of the world, including of course the people of Iraq.

It is easy to criticize the United States, just as it is easy to hide behind facile calls for "free-market democracy." With the international community watching, I prefer to view this moment as a critical opportunity for the United States to surprise a skeptical world.

One thing, however, is clear:

The United States cannot simply call for elections and universal suffrage and at the same time support an eco-nomic system that is seen as benefiting only a tiny, privi-leged minority—whether an ethnic or religious minority or U.S. and British companies.

To do so would be a recipe for disaster.

Amy Chua is a professor of law at Yale University In New Haven, Conn., and the author of World on Fire: How Exporting Free Market Democracy Breeds Ethnic Hatred and Global Instability (Doubleday, 2003). Portions of this article previously appeared in the Harvard Business Review.

Jihad vs. McWorld

The two axial principles of our age—tribalism and globalism—clash at every point except one: they may both be threatening to democracy

Benjamin R. Barber

Just beyond the horizon of current events lie two possible political figures—both bleak, neither democratic. The first is a retribalization of large swaths of humankind by war and bloodshed: a threatened Lebanonization of national states in which culture is pitted against culture, people against people, tribe against tribe—a Jihad in the name of a hundred narrowly conceived faiths against every kind of interdependence, every kind of artificial social cooperation and civic mutuality. The second is being borne in on us by the onrush of economic and ecological forces that demand integration and uniformity and that mesmerize the world with fast music, fast computers, and fast food—with MTV, Macintosh, and McDonald's, pressing nations into one commercially homogenous global network: one McWorld tied together by technology, ecology, communications, and commerce. The planet is falling precipitantly apart and coming reluctantly together at the very same moment.

These two tendencies are sometimes visible in the same countries at the same instant: thus Yugoslavia, clamoring just recently to join the New Europe, is exploding into fragments; India is trying to live up to its reputation as the world's largest integral democracy while powerful new fundamentalist parties like the Hindu nationalist Bharatiya Janta Party, along with nationalist assassins, are imperiling its hard-won unity. States are breaking up or joining up: the Soviet Union has disap-

peared almost overnight, its parts forming new unions with one another or with like-minded nationalities in neighboring states. The old interwar national state based on territory and political sovereignty looks to be a mere transitional development.

The tendencies of what I am here calling the forces of Jihad and the forces of McWorld operate with equal strength in opposite directions, the one driven by parochial hatreds, the other by universalizing markets, the one re-creating ancient subnational and ethnic borders from within, the other making national borders porous from without. They have one thing in common: neither offers much hope to citizens looking for practical ways to govern themselves democratically. If the global future is to pit Jihad's centrifugal whirlwind against McWorld's centripetal black hole, the outcome is unlikely to be democratic—or so I will argue.

McWORLD, OR THE GLOBALIZATION OF POLITICS

Four imperatives make up the dynamic of McWorld: a market imperative, a resource imperative, an information-technology imperative, and an ecological imperative. By shrinking the world and diminishing the salience of national borders, these imperatives have in combination achieved a considerable victory over factiousness and

particularism, and not least of all over their most virulent traditional form—nationalism. It is the realists who are now Europeans, the utopians who dream nostalgically of a resurgent England or Germany, perhaps even a resurgent Wales or Saxony. Yesterday's wishful cry for one world has yielded to the reality of McWorld.

The market imperative. Marxist and Leninist theories of imperialism assumed that the quest for ever-expanding markets would in time compel nation-based capitalist economies to push against national boundaries in search of an international economic imperium. Whatever else has happened to the scientist predictions of Marxism, in this domain they have proved farsighted. All national economies are now vulnerable to the inroads of larger, transnational markets within which trade is free, currencies are convertible, access to banking is open, and contracts are enforceable under law. In Europe, Asia, Africa, the South Pacific, and the Americas such markets are eroding national sovereignty and giving rise to entities—international banks, trade associations, transnational lobbies like OPEC and Greenpeace, world news services like CNN and the BBC, and multinational corporations that increasingly lack a meaningful national identity—that neither reflect nor respect nationhood as an organizing or regulative principle.

The market imperative has also reinforced the quest for international peace and stability, requisites of an efficient international economy. Markets are enemies of parochialism, isolation, fractiousness, war. Market psychology attenuates the psychology of ideological and religious cleavages and assumes a concord among producers and consumers—categories that ill fit narrowly conceived national or religious cultures. Shopping has little tolerance for blue laws, whether dictated by pub-closing British paternalism, Sabbath-observing Jewish Orthodox fundamentalism, or no-Sunday-liquor-sales Massachusetts puritanism. In the context of common markets, international law ceases to be a vision of justice and becomes a workaday framework for getting things done—enforcing contracts, ensuring that governments abide by deals, regulating trade and currency relations, and so forth.

Common markets demand a common language, as well as a common currency, and they produce common behaviors of the kind bred by cosmopolitan city life everywhere. Commercial pilots, computer programmers, international bankers, media specialists, oil riggers, entertainment celebrities, ecology experts, demographers, accountants, professors, athletes—these compose a new breed of men and women for whom religion, culture, and nationality can seem only marginal elements in a working identity. Although sociologists of everyday life will no doubt continue to distinguish a Japanese from an American mode, shopping has a common signature throughout the world. Cynics might even say that some of the recent revolutions in Eastern Europe have had as their true goal not liberty and the right to vote but well-paying jobs and the right to shop (although the vote is proving easier to acquire than consumer goods). The market imperative is, then, plenty powerful; but, notwithstanding some of the claims made for "democratic capitalism," it is not identical with the democratic imperative.

The resource imperative. Democrats once dreamed of societies whose political autonomy rested firmly on economic independence. The Athenians idealized what they called autarky, and tried for a while to create a way of life simple and austere enough to make the polis genuinely self-sufficient. To be free meant to be independent of any other community or polis. Not even the Athenians were able to achieve autarky, however: human nature, it turns out, is dependency. By the time of Pericles, Athenian politics was inextricably bound up with a flowering empire held together by naval power and commerce—an empire that, even as it appeared to enhance Athenian might, ate away at Athenian independence and autarky. Master and slave, it turned out, were bound together by mutual insufficiency.

The dream of autarky briefly engrossed nineteenth-century America as well, for the underpopulated, endlessly bountiful land, the cornucopia of natural resources, and the natural barriers of a continent walled in by two great seas led many to believe that America could be a world unto itself. Given this past, it has been harder for Americans than for most to accept the inevitability of interdependence. But the rapid depletion of resources even in a country like ours, where they once seemed inexhaustible, and the maldistribution of arable soil and mineral resources on the planet, leave even the wealthiest societies ever more resource-dependent and many other nations in permanently desperate straits.

Every nation, it turns out, needs something another nation has; some nations have almost nothing they need.

The information-technology imperative. Enlightenment science and the technologies derived from it are inherently universalizing. They entail a quest for descriptive principles of general application, a search for universal solutions to particular problems, and an unswerving embrace of objectivity and impartiality.

Scientific progress embodies and depends on open communication, a common discourse rooted in rationality, collaboration, and an easy and regular flow and exchange of information. Such ideals can be hypocritical covers for power-mongering by elites, and they may be shown to be wanting in many other ways, but they are entailed by the very idea of science and they make science and globalization practical allies.

Business, banking, and commerce all depend on information flow and are facilitated by new communication technologies. The hardware of these technologies tends to be systemic and integrated—computer, television, cable, satellite, laser, fiber-optic, and microchip technologies combining to create a vast interactive communications and information network that can potentially give every person on earth access to every other person, and make every datum, every byte, available to every set of eyes. If the automobile was, as George Ball once said (when he gave his blessing to a Fiat factory in the Soviet Union during the Cold War), "an ideology on four wheels," then electronic telecommunication and information systems are an ideology at 186,000 miles per second—which makes for a very small planet in a very big hurry. Individual cultures speak particular languages; commerce and science increasingly speak English; the whole world speaks logarithms and binary mathematics.

Moreover, the pursuit of science and technology asks for, even compels, open societies. Satellite footprints do not respect national borders; telephone wires penetrate the most closed societies. With photocopying and then fax machines having infiltrated Soviet universities and *samizdat* literary circles in the eighties, and computer modems having multiplied like rabbits in communism's bureaucratic warrens thereafter, *glasnost* could not be far behind. In their social requisites, secrecy and science are enemies.

The new technology's software is perhaps even more globalizing than its hardware. The information arm of international commerce's sprawling body reaches out and touches distinct nations and parochial cultures, and gives them a common face chiseled in Hollywood, on Madison Avenue, and in Silicon Valley. Throughout the 1980s one of the most-watched television programs in South Africa was *The Cosby Show*. The demise of apartheid was already in production. Exhibitors at the 1991 Cannes film festival expressed growing anxiety over the "homogenization" and "Americanization" of the global film industry when, for the third year running, American films dominated the awards ceremonies. America has dominated the world's popular culture for much longer, and much more decisively. In November of 1991 Switzerland's once insular culture boasted best-seller lists featuring *Terminator 2* as the No. 1 movie, *Scarlett* as the No. 1 book, and Prince's *Diamonds and Pearls* as the No. 1 record album. No wonder the Japanese are buying Hollywood film studios even faster than Americans are buying Japanese television sets. This kind of software supremacy may in the long term be far more important than hardware superiority, because culture has become more potent than armaments. What is the power of the Pentagon compared with Disneyland? Can the Sixth Fleet keep up with CNN? McDonald's in Moscow and Coke in China will do more to create a global culture than military colonization ever could. It is less the goods than the brand names that do the work, for they convey lifestyle images that alter perception and challenge behavior. They make up the seductive software of McWorld's common (at times much too common) soul.

Yet in all this high-tech commercial world there is nothing that looks particularly democratic. It lends itself to surveillance as well as liberty, to new forms of manipulation and covert control as well as new kinds of participation, to skewed, unjust market outcomes as well as greater productivity. The consumer society and the open society are not quite synonymous. Capitalism and democracy have a relationship, but it is something less than a marriage. An efficient free market after all requires that consumers be free to vote their dollars on competing goods, not that citizens be free to vote their values and beliefs on competing political candidates and programs. The free market flourished in junta-run Chile, in military-governed Taiwan and Korea, and, earlier, in a variety of autocratic European empires as well as their colonial possessions.

The *ecological imperative*. The impact of globalization on ecology is a cliché even to world leaders who ignore it. We know well enough that the German forests can be destroyed by Swiss and Italians driving gas-guzzlers fueled by leaded gas. We also know that the planet can be asphyxiated by greenhouse gases because Brazilian farmers want to be part of the twentieth century and are burning down tropical rain forests to clear a little land to plough, and because Indonesians make a living out of converting their lush jungle into toothpicks for fastidious Japanese diners, upsetting the delicate oxygen balance and in effect puncturing our global lungs. Yet this ecological consciousness has meant not only greater awareness but also greater inequality, as modernized nations try to slam the door behind them, saying to developing nations, "The world cannot afford your modernization; ours has wrung it dry!"

Each of the four imperatives just cited is transnational, transideological, and transcultural. Each applies impartially to Catholics, Jews, Muslims, Hindus, and Buddhists; to democrats and totalitarians; to capitalists and socialists. The Enlightenment dream of a universal rational society has to a remarkable degree been realized—but in a form that is commercialized, homogenized, depoliticized, bureaucratized, and, of course, radically incomplete, for the movement toward McWorld is in competition with forces of global breakdown, national dissolution, and centrifugal corruption. These forces, working in the opposite direction, are the essence of what I call Jihad.

JIHAD, OR THE LEBANONIZATION OF THE WORLD

OPEC, the World Bank, the United Nations, the International Red Cross, the multinational corporation... there are scores of institutions that reflect globalization. But they often appear as ineffective reactors to the world's real actors: national states and, to an ever greater degree, subnational factions in permanent rebellion against uniformity and integration—even the kind represented by universal law and justice. The headlines feature these players regularly: they are cultures, not countries; parts, not wholes; sects, not religions; rebellious factions and dissenting minorities at war not just with globalism but with the traditional nation-state. Kurds, Basques, Puerto Ricans, Ossetians, East Timoreans, Quebecois, the Catholics of Northern Ireland, Abkhasians, Kurile Islander Japanese, the Zulus of Inkatha, Catalonians, Tamils, and, of course, Palestinians—people without countries, inhabiting nations not their own, seeking smaller worlds within borders that will seal them off from modernity.

A powerful irony is at work here. Nationalism was once a force of integration and unification, a movement aimed at bringing together disparate clans, tribes, and cultural fragments under new, assimilationist flags. But as Ortega y Gasset noted more than sixty years ago, having won its victories, nationalism changed its strategy. In the 1920s, and again today, it is more often a reactionary and divisive force, pulverizing the very nations it once helped cement together. The force that creates nations is "inclusive," Ortega wrote in *The Revolt of the Masses*. "In periods of consolidation, nationalism has a positive value, and is a lofty standard. But in Europe everything is more than consolidated, and nationalism is nothing but a mania...."

This mania has left the post-Cold War world smothering with hot wars; the international scene is little more unified than it was at the end of the Great War, in Ortega's own time. There were more than thirty wars in progress last year, most of them ethnic, racial, tribal, or religious in character, and the list of unsafe regions doesn't seem to be getting any shorter. Some new world order!

The aim of many of these small-scale wars is to redraw boundaries, to implode states and resecure parochial identities: to escape McWorld's dully insistent impera-

tives. The mood is that of Jihad: war not as an instrument of policy but as an emblem of identity, an expression of community, an end in itself. Even where there is no shooting war, there is fractiousness, secession, and the quest for ever smaller communities. Add to the list of dangerous countries those at risk: In Switzerland and Spain, Jurassian and Basque separatists still argue the virtues of ancient identities, sometimes in the language of bombs. Hyperdisintegration in the former Soviet Union may well continue unabated—not just a Ukraine independent from the Soviet Union but a Bessarabian Ukraine independent from the Ukrainian republic; not just Russia severed from the defunct union but Tatarstan severed from Russia. Yugoslavia makes even the disunited, ex-Soviet, nonsocialist republics that were once the Soviet Union look integrated, its sectarian fatherlands springing up within factional motherlands like weeds within weeds within weeds. Kurdish independence would threaten the territorial integrity of four Middle Eastern nations. Well before the current cataclysm Soviet Georgia made a claim for autonomy from the Soviet Union, only to be faced with its Ossetians (164,000 in a republic of 5.5 million) demanding their own self-determination within Georgia. The Abkhasian minority in Georgia has followed suit. Even the good will established by Canada's once promising Meech Lake protocols is in danger, with Francophone Quebec again threatening the dissolution of the federation. In South Africa the emergence from apartheid was hardly achieved when friction between Inkatha's Zulus and the African National Congress's tribally identified members threatened to replace Europeans' racism with an indigenous tribal war. After thirty years of attempted integration using the colonial language (English) as a unifier, Nigeria is now playing with the idea of linguistic multiculturalism—which could mean the cultural breakup of the nation into hundreds of tribal fragments. Even Saddam Hussein has benefited from the threat of internal Jihad, having used renewed tribal and religious warfare to turn last season's mortal enemies into reluctant allies of an Iraqi nationhood that he nearly destroyed.

The passing of communism has torn away the thin veneer of internationalism (workers of the world unite!) to reveal ethnic prejudices that are not only ugly and deep-seated but increasingly murderous. Europe's old scourge, anti-Semitism, is back with a vengeance, but it is only one of many antagonisms. It appears all too easy to throw the historical gears into reverse and pass from a Communist dictatorship back into a tribal state.

Among the tribes, religion is also a battlefield. ("Jihad" is a rich world whose generic meaning is "struggle"—usually the struggle of the soul to avert evil. Strictly applied to religious war, it is used only in reference to battles where the faith is under assault, or battles against a government that denies the practice of Islam. My use here is rhetorical, but does follow both journalistic practice and history.) Remember the Thirty Years War? Whatever forms of Enlightenment universalism might once have come to grace such historically related forms of monotheism as Judaism, Christianity, and Islam, in many of their modern incarnations they are parochial rather than cosmopolitan, angry rather than loving, proselytizing rather than ecumenical, zealous rather than rationalist, sectarian rather than deistic, ethnocentric rather than universalizing. As a result, like the new forms of hypernationalism, the new expressions of religious fundamentalism are fractious and pulverizing, never integrating. This is religion as the Crusaders knew it: a battle to the death for souls that if not saved will be forever lost.

The atmospherics of Jihad have resulted in a breakdown of civility in the name of identity, of comity in the name of community. International relations have sometimes taken on the aspect of gang war—cultural turf battles featuring tribal factions that were supposed to be sublimated as integral parts of large national, economic, postcolonial, and constitutional entities.

THE DARKENING FUTURE OF DEMOCRACY

These rather melodramatic tableaux vivants do not tell the whole story, however. For all their defects, Jihad and McWorld have their attractions. Yet, to repeat and insist, the attractions are unrelated to democracy. Neither McWorld nor Jihad is remotely democratic in impulse. Neither needs democracy; neither promotes democracy.

McWorld does manage to look pretty seductive in a world obsessed with Jihad. It delivers peace, prosperity, and relative unity—if at the cost of independence, community, and identity (which is generally based on difference). The primary political values required by the global market are

order and tranquility, and freedom—as in the phrases "free trade," "free press," and "free love." Human rights are needed to a degree, but not citizenship or participation—and no more social justice and equality than are necessary to promote efficient economic production and consumption. Multinational corporations sometimes seem to prefer doing business with local oligarchs, inasmuch as they can take confidence from dealing with the boss on all crucial matters. Despots who slaughter their own populations are no problem, so long as they leave markets in place and refrain from making war on their neighbors (Saddam Hussein's fatal mistake). In trading partners, predictability is of more value than justice.

The Eastern European revolutions that seemed to arise out of concern for global democratic values quickly deteriorated into a stampede in the general direction of free markets and their ubiquitous, television-promoted shopping malls. East Germany's Neues Forum, that courageous gathering of intellectuals, students, and workers which overturned the Stalinist regime in Berlin in 1989, lasted only six months in Germany's mini-version of McWorld. Then it gave way to money and markets and monopolies from the West. By the time of the first all-German elections, it could scarcely manage to secure three percent of the vote. Elsewhere there is growing evidence that *glasnost* will go and *perestroika*—defined as privatization and an opening of markets to Western bidders—will stay. So understandably anxious are the new rulers of Eastern Europe and whatever entities are forged from the residues of the Soviet Union to gain access to credit and markets and technology—McWorld's flourishing new currencies—that they have shown themselves willing to trade away democratic prospects in pursuit of them: not just old totalitarian ideologies and command-economy production models but some possible indigenous experiments with a third way between capitalism and socialism, such as economic cooperatives and employee stock-ownership plans, both of which have their ardent supporters in the East.

Jihad delivers a different set of virtues: a vibrant local identity, a sense of community, solidarity among kinsmen, neighbors, and countrymen, narrowly conceived. But it also guarantees parochialism and is grounded in exclusion. Solidarity is secured through war against outsiders. And solidarity often means obedience to a hierarchy in governance, fanaticism in beliefs,

and the obliteration of individual selves in the name of the group. Deference to leaders and intolerance toward outsiders (and toward "enemies within") are hallmarks of tribalism—hardly the attitudes required for the cultivation of new democratic women and men capable of governing themselves. Where new democratic experiments have been conducted in retribalizing societies, in both Europe and the Third World, the result has often been anarchy, repression, persecution, and the coming of new, non-communist forms of very old kinds of despotism. During the past year, Havel's velvet revolution in Czechoslovakia was imperiled by partisans of "Czechland" and of Slovakia as independent entities. India seemed little less rent by Sikh, Hindu, Muslim, and Tamil infighting than it was immediately after the British pulled out, more than forty years ago.

To the extent that either McWorld or Jihad has a *natural* politics, it has turned out to be more of an antipolitics. For McWorld, it is the antipolitics of globalism: bureaucratic, technocratic, and meritocratic, focused (as Marx predicted it would be) on the administration of things—with people, however, among the chief things to be administered. In its politico-economic imperatives McWorld has been guided by laissez-faire market principles that privilege efficiency, productivity, and beneficence at the expense of civic liberty and self-government.

For Jihad, the antipolitics of tribalization has been explicitly antidemocratic: one-party dictatorship, government by military junta, theocratic fundamentalism—often associated with a version of the *Führerprinzip* that empowers an individual to rule on behalf of a people. Even the government of India, struggling for decades to model democracy for a people who will soon number a billion, longs for great leaders; and for every Mahatma Gandhi, Indira Gandhi, or Rajiv Gandhi taken from them by zealous assassins, the Indians appear to seek a replacement who will deliver them from the lengthy travail of their freedom.

THE CONFEDERAL OPTION

How can democracy be secured and spread in a world whose primary tendencies are at best indifferent to it (McWorld) and at worst deeply antithetical to it (Jihad)? My guess is that globalization will eventually vanquish retribalization. The ethos of material "civilization" has not yet encountered an obstacle it has been unable to thrust aside. Ortega may have grasped in the 1920s a clue to our own future in the coming millennium.

Everyone sees the need of a new principle of life. But as always happens in similar crises—some people attempt to save the situation by an artificial intensification of the very principle which has led to decay. This is the meaning of the "nationalist" outburst of recent years… things have always gone that way. The last flare, the longest; the last sigh, the deepest. On the very eve of their disappearance there is an intensification of frontiers—military and economic.

Jihad may be a last deep sigh before the eternal yawn of McWorld. On the other hand, Ortega was not exactly prescient; his prophecy of peace and internationalism came just before blitzkrieg, world war, and the Holocaust tore the old order to bits. Yet democracy is how we remonstrate with reality, the rebuke our aspirations offer to history. And if retribalization is inhospitable to democracy, there is nonetheless a form of democratic government that can accommodate parochialism and communitarianism, one that can even save them from their defects and make them more tolerant and participatory: decentralized participatory democracy. And if McWorld is indifferent to democracy, there is nonetheless a form of democratic government that suits global markets passably well—representative government in its federal or, better still, confederal variation.

With its concern for accountability, the protection of minorities, and the universal rule of law, a confederalized representative system would serve the political needs of McWorld as well as oligarchic bureaucratism or meritocratic elitism is currently doing. As we are already beginning to see, many nations may survive in the long term only as confederations that afford local regions smaller than "nations" extensive jurisdiction. Recommended reading for democrats of the twenty-first century is not the U.S. Constitution or the French Declaration of Rights of Man and Citizen but the Articles of Confederation, that suddenly pertinent document that stitched together the thirteen American colonies into what then seemed a too loose confederation of independent states but now appears a new form of political realism, as veterans of

Yeltsin's new Russia and the new Europe created at Maastricht will attest.

By the same token, the participatory and direct form of democracy that engages citizens in civic activity and civic judgment and goes well beyond just voting and accountability—the system I have called "strong democracy"—suits the political needs of decentralized communities as well as theocratic and nationalist party dictatorships have done. Local neighborhoods need not be democratic, but they can be. Real democracy has flourished in diminutive settings: the spirit of liberty, Tocqueville said, is local. Participatory democracy, if not naturally apposite to tribalism, has an undeniable attractiveness under conditions of parochialism.

Democracy in any of these variations will, however, continue to be obstructed by the undemocratic and antidemocratic trends toward uniformitarian globalism and intolerant retribalization which I have portrayed here. For democracy to persist in our brave new McWorld, we will have to commit acts of conscious political will—a possibility, but hardly a probability, under these conditions. Political will requires much more than the quick fix of the transfer of institutions. Like technology transfer, institution transfer rests on foolish assumptions about a uniform world of the kind that once fired the imagination of colonial administrators. Spread English justice to the colonies by exporting wigs. Let an East Indian trading company act as the vanguard to Britain's free parliamentary institutions. Today's well-intentioned quick-fixers in the National Endowment for Democracy and the Kennedy School of Government, in the unions and foundations and universities zealously nurturing contacts in Eastern Europe and the Third World, are hoping to democratize by long distance. Post Bulgaria a parliament by first-class mail. Fed Ex the Bill of Rights to Sri Lanka. Cable Cambodia some common law.

Yet Eastern Europe has already demonstrated that importing free political parties, parliaments, and presses cannot establish a democratic civil society; imposing a free market may even have the opposite effect. Democracy grows from the bottom up and cannot be imposed from the top down. Civil society has to be built from the inside out. The institutional superstructure comes last. Poland may become democratic, but

then again it may heed the Pope, and prefer to found its politics on its Catholicism, with uncertain consequences for democracy. Bulgaria may become democratic, but it may prefer tribal war. The former Soviet Union may become a democratic confederation, or it may just grow into an anarchic and weak conglomeration of markets for other nations' goods and services.

Democrats need to seek out indigenous democratic impulses. There is always a desire for self-government, always some expression of participation, accountability, consent, and representation, even in traditional hierarchical societies. These need to be identified, tapped, modified, and incorporated into new democratic practices with an indigenous flavor. The tortoises among the democratizers may ultimately outlive or outpace the hares, for they will have the time and patience to explore conditions along the way, and to adapt their gait to changing circumstances. Tragically, democracy in a hurry often looks something like France in 1794 or China in 1989.

It certainly seems possible that the most attractive democratic ideal in the face of the brutal realities of Jihad and the dull realities of McWorld will be a confederal union of semi-autonomous communities smaller than nation-states, tied together into regional economic associations and markets larger than nation-states—participatory and self-determining in local matters at the bottom, representative and accountable at the top. The nation-state would play a diminished role, and sovereignty would lose some of its political potency. The Green movement adage "Think globally, act locally" would actually come to describe the conduct of politics.

This vision reflects only an ideal, however—one that is not terribly likely to be realized. Freedom, Jean-Jacques Rousseau once wrote, is a food easy to eat but hard to digest. Still, democracy has always played itself out against the odds. And democracy remains both a form of coherence as binding as McWorld and a secular faith potentially as inspiring as Jihad.

Benjamin R. Barber is the Whitman Professor of Political Science at Rutgers University. Barber's most recent books are Strong Democracy *(1984),* The Conquest of Politics *(1988), and* An Aristocracy of Everyone.

Published originally in *The Atlantic Monthly*, March 1992, pp. 53–55, 58–63, as an introduction to the book, *Jihad vs. McWorld* (Ballantine, 1996), a volume that discusses and extends the themes of the original article. Copyright © 1992 by Benjamin R. Barber. Reprinted by permission of the author.

Index

Index

Test Your Knowledge Form

We encourage you to photocopy and use this page as a tool to assess how the articles in *Annual Editions* expand on the information in your textbook. By reflecting on the articles you will gain enhanced text information. You can also access this useful form on a product's book support Web site at *http://www.mhcls.com/online/*.

NAME: _____   DATE: _____

TITLE AND NUMBER OF ARTICLE: _____

BRIEFLY STATE THE MAIN IDEA OF THIS ARTICLE:

_____

LIST THREE IMPORTANT FACTS THAT THE AUTHOR USES TO SUPPORT THE MAIN IDEA:

_____

WHAT INFORMATION OR IDEAS DISCUSSED IN THIS ARTICLE ARE ALSO DISCUSSED IN YOUR TEXTBOOK OR OTHER READINGS THAT YOU HAVE DONE? LIST THE TEXTBOOK CHAPTERS AND PAGE NUMBERS:

_____

LIST ANY EXAMPLES OF BIAS OR FAULTY REASONING THAT YOU FOUND IN THE ARTICLE:

_____

LIST ANY NEW TERMS/CONCEPTS THAT WERE DISCUSSED IN THE ARTICLE, AND WRITE A SHORT DEFINITION:

We Want Your Advice

ANNUAL EDITIONS revisions depend on two major opinion sources: one is our Advisory Board, listed in the front of this volume, which works with us in scanning the thousands of articles published in the public press each year; the other is you—the person actually using the book. Please help us and the users of the next edition by completing the prepaid article rating form on this page and returning it to us. Thank you for your help!

ANNUAL EDITIONS: Comparative Politics 06/07

ARTICLE RATING FORM

Here is an opportunity for you to have direct input into the next revision of this volume.
We would like you to rate each of the articles listed below, using the following scale:

1. **Excellent: should definitely be retained**
2. **Above average: should probably be retained**
3. **Below average: should probably be deleted**
4. **Poor: should definitely be deleted**

Your ratings will play a vital part in the next revision.
Please mail this prepaid form to us as soon as possible.
Thanks for your help!

RATING	ARTICLE	RATING	ARTICLE
	1. A Constitutional Revolution in Britain?		32. What Does Putin Want?
	2. Weighing the Votes: Why the Electoral System Favours Labour		33. Fox's Mexico: Democracy Paralyzed
	3. The British General Election of 2005		34. Latin America Looks Leftward Again
	4. The Strange Tale of Tony Blair		35. Return to Lundazi
	5. A Divided Self: A Survey of France		36. Nigeria: Chronicle of a Dying State
	6. Next French Revolution: A Less Colorblind Society		37. China: The Quiet Revolution
	7. French Inch Toward Social Reform		38. China's Leader, Ex-Rival at Side, Solidifies Power
	8. A System in Crisis, a Country Adrift		39. Sonia: And Yet So Far
	9. Angela Merkel: Politician Who Can Show a Flash of Steel		40. India's Democracy Provides Lessons
	10. Only Marginal Reforms Are Expected in Germany		41. Middle East Democracy
	11. Immigration Law Hailed as a Vital Turning Point in Germany's Attitude to a Multiracial Society		42. Plenty of Seeds, But Still a Long Way to Fruition
	12. Japanese Spirit, Western Things		43. Bin Laden, the Arab "Street," and the Middle East's Democracy Deficit
	13. Koizumi's Party, Backing Reforms, Wins by Landslide		44. Democracy's Sobering State
	14. Public Opinion: Is There a Crisis?		45. Capitalism and Democracy
	15. Political Parties: Empty Vessels?		46. Cultural Explanations: The Man in the Baghdad Café
	16. Interest Groups: Ex Uno, Plures		47. Globalization Is About Blending, Not Homogenizing
	17. Advanced Democracies and the New Politics		48. An Explosive Combination
	18. Women in National Parliaments		49. Jihad vs. McWorld
	19. The True Clash of Civilizations		
	20. Europe Crawls Ahead. …		
	21. What Political Institutions Does Large-Scale Democracy Require?		
	22. What Democracy Is. … and Is Not		
	23. Judicial Review: The Gavel and the Robe		
	24. Referendums: The People's Voice		
	25. The Great Divide		
	26. Living With a Superpower		
	27. The Case for a Multi-Party U.S. Parliament? American Politics in Comparative Perspective		
	28. Now That We Are All Bundled Inside, Let's Shut the Door		
	29. A Too Perfect Union? Why Europe Said "No"		
	30. After the Votes: Europe's Leaders Confront the Consequences of "The Wrong Answer"		
	31. Putin Gambles on Raw Power		

(Continued on next page)

BUSINESS REPLY MAIL
FIRST CLASS MAIL PERMIT NO. 551 DUBUQUE IA

POSTAGE WILL BE PAID BY ADDRESEE

McGraw-Hill Contemporary Learning Series
2460 KERPER BLVD
DUBUQUE, IA 52001-9902

ABOUT YOU

Name   Date

_____

Are you a teacher? ☐ A student? ☐
Your school's name

_____

Department

_____

Address   City   State   Zip

_____

School telephone #

_____

YOUR COMMENTS ARE IMPORTANT TO US!

Please fill in the following information:
For which course did you use this book?

_____

Did you use a text with this ANNUAL EDITION? ☐ yes ☐ no
What was the title of the text?

_____

What are your general reactions to the *Annual Editions* concept?

_____

Have you read any pertinent articles recently that you think should be included in the next edition? Explain.

_____

Are there any articles that you feel should be replaced in the next edition? Why?

_____

Are there any World Wide Web sites that you feel should be included in the next edition? Please annotate.

_____

May we contact you for editorial input? ☐ yes ☐ no
May we quote your comments? ☐ yes ☐ no